Lecture Notes in Computer Science　6340

Commenced Publication in 1973
Founding and Former Series Editors:
Gerhard Goos, Juris Hartmanis, and Jan van Leeuwen

Editorial Board

Marina L. Gavrilova   C.J. Kenneth Tan
Edward David Moreno (Eds.)

Transactions on Computational Science X

Special Issue on Security in Computing, Part I

Springer

Editors-in-Chief

Marina L. Gavrilova
University of Calgary, Department of Computer Science
2500 University Drive N.W., Calgary, AB, T2N 1N4, Canada
E-mail: mgavrilo@ucalgary.ca

C.J. Kenneth Tan
Exascala Ltd.
Unit 9, 97 Rickman Drive, Birmingham B15 2AL, UK
E-mail: cjtan@exascala.com

Guest Editor

Edward David Moreno
DCOMP/UFS - Federal University of Sergipe
Aracaju/SE, Brazil
E-mail: edwdavid@gmail.com

Library of Congress Control Number: 2010939851

CR Subject Classification (1998): C.2, D.2, K.6.5, D.4.6, H.4, E.3

ISSN   0302-9743 (Lecture Notes in Computer Science)
ISSN   1866-4733 (Transaction on Computational Science)
ISBN-10   3-642-17498-1 Springer Berlin Heidelberg New York
ISBN-13   978-3-642-17498-8 Springer Berlin Heidelberg New York

Typesetting: Camera-ready by author, data conversion by Scientific Publishing Services, Chennai, India
Printed on acid-free paper   06/3180

LNCS Transactions on Computational Science

Computational science, an emerging and increasingly vital field, is now widely recognized as an integral part of scientific and technical investigations, affecting researchers and practitioners in areas ranging from aerospace and automotive research to biochemistry, electronics, geosciences, mathematics, and physics. Computer systems research and the exploitation of applied research naturally complement each other. The increased complexity of many challenges in computational science demands the use of supercomputing, parallel processing, sophisticated algorithms, and advanced system software and architecture. It is therefore invaluable to have input by systems research experts in applied computational science research.

Transactions on Computational Science focuses on original high-quality research in the realm of computational science in parallel and distributed environments, also encompassing the underlying theoretical foundations and the applications of large-scale computation. The journal offers practitioners and researchers the opportunity to share computational techniques and solutions in this area, to identify new issues, and to shape future directions for research, and it enables industrial users to apply leading-edge, large-scale, high-performance computational methods.

In addition to addressing various research and application issues, the journal aims to present material that is validated – crucial to the application and advancement of the research conducted in academic and industrial settings. In this spirit, the journal focuses on publications that present results and computational techniques that are verifiable.

Scope

The scope of the journal includes, but is not limited to, the following computational methods and applications:

- Aeronautics and Aerospace
- Astrophysics
- Bioinformatics
- Climate and Weather Modeling
- Communication and Data Networks
- Compilers and Operating Systems
- Computer Graphics
- Computational Biology
- Computational Chemistry
- Computational Finance and Econometrics
- Computational Fluid Dynamics
- Computational Geometry

- Computational Number Theory
- Computational Physics
- Data Storage and Information Retrieval
- Data Mining and Data Warehousing
- Grid Computing
- Hardware/Software Co-design
- High-Energy Physics
- High-Performance Computing
- Numerical and Scientific Computing
- Parallel and Distributed Computing
- Reconfigurable Hardware
- Scientific Visualization
- Supercomputing
- System-on-Chip Design and Engineering

Editorial

The Transactions on Computational Science journal is part of the Springer series *Lecture Notes in Computer Science*, and is devoted to the gamut of computational science issues, from theoretical aspects to application-dependent studies and the validation of emerging technologies.

The journal focuses on original high-quality research in the realm of computational science in parallel and distributed environments, encompassing the facilitating theoretical foundations and the applications of large-scale computations and massive data processing. Practitioners and researchers share computational techniques and solutions in the area, identify new issues, and shape future directions for research, as well as enable industrial users to apply the techniques presented.

The current volume is devoted to Security in Computing (Part 1) and is edited by Edward David Moreno. It is comprised of 14 selected papers that represent the diverse applications and designs being addressed today by the security and cryptographic research community. This special issue is devoted to state-of-the-art research on security in computing and includes a broad spectrum of applications such as new architectures, novel hardware implementations, cryptographic algorithms, and security protocols.

We would like to extend our sincere appreciation to Special Issue Guest Editor Edward David Moreno for his dedication and insights in preparing this high-quality special issue. We also would like to thank all authors for submitting their papers to the special issue, and to all associate editors and referees for their valuable work. We would like to express our gratitude to the LNCS editorial staff of Springer, in particular Alfred Hofmann, Ursula Barth, and Anna Kramer, who supported us at every stage of the project.

It is our hope that the fine collection of papers presented in this special issue will be a valuable resource for Transactions on Computational Science readers and will stimulate further research into the vibrant area of computational science applications.

September 2010

Marina L. Gavrilova
C.J. Kenneth Tan

Security in Computing:
Research and Perspectives, Part I
Special Issue Guest Editor's Preface

In an increasingly connected world, security has become an essential component of modern information systems. Our ever-increasing dependence on information implies that the importance of information security is growing. Several examples of security applications are present in everyday life such as mobile phone communication, internet banking, secure e-mail, data encryption, etc.

The thrust of embedded computing has both diversified and intensified in recent years as the focus on mobile computing, ubiquitous computing, and traditional embedded applications has begun to converge. A side effect of this intensity is the desire to support sophisticated applications such as speech recognition, visual feature recognition, and secure wireless networking in a mobile, battery-powered platform. Unfortunately these applications are currently intractable for the embedded space.

Another consideration is related to mobile computing, and, especially, security in these environments. The first step in developing new architectures and systems that can adequately support these applications is to obtain a precise understanding of the techniques and methods that come close to meeting the needs of security, performance, and energy requirements; with an emphasis on security aspects.

This special issue brings together high-quality and state-of-the-art contributions on security in computing. The papers included in this issue deal with some hot topics in the security research sphere: new architectures, novel hardware implementations, cryptographic algorithms and security protocols, and new tools and applications. Concretely, the special issue contains 14 selected papers that represent the diverse applications and designs being addressed today by the security and cryptographic research community.

As a whole, this special issue provides a vision on research and new perspectives in security research. With authors from around the world, these articles bring us an international sample of significant work.

The title of the first paper is "A Dynamic Security Framework for Ambient Intelligent Systems: Design Implementation of a Smart-Home-Based eHealth Application" by Luca Compagna, Paul El Khoury, Fabio Massacci, and Ayda Saidane. This paper presents a flexible and generic security and dependability framework for the dynamic provision of security and dependability (S&D) solutions at runtime. The aim of the framework is to support security in AmI environments and in particular the automated integration, monitoring, and adaptation of security and dependability mechanisms for such ecosystems. Finally, the authors show the effectiveness and feasibility of their approach in a reference eHealth case study. In this eHealth scenario, patients are continuously monitored by ambient sensors of a smart home and by wearable health sensors.

In the second contribution, which is entitled "Ntru-like Public Key Cryptosystems beyond Dedekind Domain up to Alternative Algebra", Ehsan Malekian and Ali Zakerolhosseini introduce two practical cryptosystems similar to NTRU, and they illustrate that the algebraic structure of NTRU is not limited to Euclidean or Dedekind domains and can be extended to an algebra which is not necessarily commutative or associative. The first cryptosystem, QTRU, works based on quaternions and the second one, OTRU, is constructed based on the octonions algebra, which is a non-associative but alternative algebra. They have analyzed, the security of the proposed non-associative public key cryptosystem against lattice attack and they believe that the OTRU could be more secure than NTRU, because its lattice structure does not completely fit into the category of convolutional modular lattices.

In the third contribution, which is entitled "Identity-Based Key Exchange Protocols without Pairings", Dario Fiore and Rosario Gennaro propose a new identity-based key agreement protocol. The authors prove that it that can be implemented over any cyclic group in which the Diffie-Hellman problem is supposed to be hard. Another relevant point is that it is more efficient than any KA protocols in the public key model, and its performance is competitive with respect to the MQV protocol.

In the fourth contribution, which is entitled "Building a Side Channel Based Disassembler", Thomas Eisenbarth, Christof Paar, and Björn Weghenkel exploit side channel information to recover large parts of the program executed on an embedded processor. The authors show that a program running on a microcontroller can be reconstructed by passively monitoring the power consumption or other electromagnetic emanations only. For this purpose, they apply methods from side channel analysis that are known to be optimal for extracting information to reconstruct executed instruction sequences, and their employed recognition methods achieve a high average instruction recognition rate of up to 70% for tests with a PIC microcontroller.

In the fifth contribution, which is entitled "A Versatile Framework for Implementation Attacks on Cryptographic and Embedded Devices", by Timo Kasper, David Oswald, and Christof Paar, researchers specialized in embedded security present a versatile and unified framework that allows the implementation of different attacks on virtually all types of cryptographic devices (such as RFIDs, smartcards, microcontrollers, ASICs, FPGAs, and mobile computing devices). They demonstrate the effectiveness of the system by profiling a contactless smartcard and identifying the appropriate leakage model. On this basis, they perform and report successful full key-recovery of a commercial cryptographic RFID employing Triple-DES by means of DEMA. Another aspect is that the authors prove the feasibility of multiple successive fault injections on a widespread PIC microcontroller using power glitches. Finally, they show that most implementation attacks, including the injection of multiple faults, can be conducted with a low-cost, public domain LAB.

In the sixth paper, "An Adaptive Robust Watermarking Algorithm for Audio Signal Using SVD" by Malay Kishore Dutta, Vinay K. Pathak, and Phalguni Gupta, a synchronization code is embedded in the audio signal with reference to the high energy peaks. This synchronization code is used for countering the positive false alarm generated due to data modification as a result of watermark embedding. The watermarking is done in the SVD (Singular Value Decomposition) domain, which makes the process perceptually transparent. The results obtained from robustness tests against signal processing attacks conclude that the proposed method is quite robust to attacks.

In the seventh paper, which is entitled "Trust-Based Security Level Evaluation Using Bayesian Belief Networks", Siv Hilde Houmb, Indrakshi Ray, Indrajit Ray, and Sudip Chakraborty propose an approach for evaluating the security level of a system using information collected from a number of different sources, including subjective judgments such as those of evaluators and the like. It is well known that the trustworthiness of an information source depends on two factors, namely, its knowledge level and expertise level; and they show how to evaluate these two factors and quantify the trustworthiness of sources and from that derive a security level prediction. The approach is quantitative and implemented as a Bayesian Belief Network (BBN) topology, and for this reason scalable. The authors conclude that their approach can also be used in the context of security solution trade-off analysis.

In the eighth paper, which is entitled "Implementation of QoSS (Quality of Security Service) for NoC Protection", Johanna Sepúlveda, Ricardo Pires, Marius Strum, and Wang Jiang present the implementation of QoSS to overcome present SoC (System-on-Chip) vulnerabilities. For this study, the authors developed power models for the main components in the NoC (Network-on-Chip) architecture and integrated these models into a NoC simulator, taking the architectural and technological-parameters into account. In terms of security, the authors propose the implementation of two security services: access control and authentication; and they show that the inclusion of security issues in an NoC implies a tradeoff between trustworthiness and performance, and the designer can select the more suited among different security levels in order to satisfy both (security and performance) requirements.

In the ninth paper, "Signcryption with Non-interactive Non-repudiation without Random Oracles", by Jia Fan, Yuliang Zheng, and Xiaohu Tang, a model for signcryption with NINR (non-interactive non-repudiation) that can be proved secure without random oracles is presented. The new signcryption scheme is based on the signature scheme of Boneh et al. The authors show that adding two more security requirements, their scheme is very compact when compared with the underling signature scheme.

The paper "Block-Level Added Redundancy Explicit Authentication for Parallelized Encryption and Integrity Checking of Processor-Memory Transactions", authored by Reouven Elbaz, Lionel Torres, Gilles Sassatelli, Pierre Guillemin, Michel Bardouillet, and Albert Martinez, focuses on physical non-invasive attacks (i.e., such attacks do not necessitate any modifications of the processor chip) called board level attacks. These attacks are conducted on buses between the SoC and off-chip volatile memory or directly in the RAM memory. According to the authors, hardware mechanisms must ensure the confidentiality and the integrity of the off-chip memory content while considering the constraints relative to the processor context – particularly random access of variable data size – to optimize hardware resources, memory access latencies, and the memory bandwidth at runtime. Then, the authors propose, describe and evaluate an engine, PE-ICE (Parallelized Encryption and Integrity Checking Engine), based on the concept of BLAREA, to highlight its relevance and efficiency in ensuring data integrity in addition to data confidentiality in the context of processor-memory transaction. PE-ICE provides integrity checking in addition to encryption for a low hardware overhead and for a low run-time performance hit (less than 4%).

The paper "A Weakest Precondition Approach to Robustness", by Musard Balliu and Isabella Mastroeni, shows that in the presence of active attackers, the weakest precondition semantics computation can be exploited for characterizing the information disclosed, and therefore for revealing program vulnerabilities. The authors also propose using the weakest precondition-based analysis in order to certify the robustness of programs. Then, they introduce the notion of relative robustness which is a relaxation of robustness dealing with a restricted class of attacks. Finally, the authors conclude with two real applications: the analysis of the API for PIN verification and the analysis of code vulnerable to XSS attacks.

The paper "PET SNAKE: A Special Purpose Architecture to Implement an Algebraic Attack in Hardware", by Willi Geiselmann, Kenneth Matheis, and Rainer Steinwandt, proposes a dedicated hardware design to implement an algebraic attack against block ciphers, specifically MRHS (Multiple Right Hand Sides) to handle polynomial systems of equations over F2, which according to their analysis enables significant performance gains compared with an MRHS implementation in software.

The paper "Green Secure Processors: Towards Power-Efficient Secure Processors", authored by Siddhartha Chhabra and Yan Solihin, studied the power implications of using secure processor architectures. The authors evaluated the sources of power in currently proposed secure processor mechanisms and analyzed the power overheads of various hardware security mechanisms for general purpose as well as embedded systems. Finally, they outlined the design of a hybrid cryptographic engine that has been designed with the primary goal of minimizing power overheads, but at the same time ensuring an insignificant loss in performance.

The last paper in this special issue, "A New Peer-to-Peer Micropayment Protocol Based on Transferable Tokens" by Sung-Ming Yen, Kuo-Zhe Chiou, Je Zhang, and Po-Han Lee, shows that PPay and OFPPay schemes, which are two representative P2P (peer-to-peer) micropayment protocols, are vulnerable to double spending by presenting a replay attack and a collusion attack against them, respectively. Then, they propose a new P2P micropayment scheme by exploiting the idea of a transferable debt token. Finally, the authors use security analysis and show that their new scheme is secure against double spending, and when performance analysis is applied, the proposed scheme is superior to the PPay scheme and the OFPPay scheme.

Finally, we sincerely hope that this special issue stimulates your interest in the many subjects surrounding the area of security. The topics covered in the papers are timely and important, and the authors have done an excellent job of presenting their different approaches and their promptness. Regarding the reviewing process, our referees (integrated by recognized researchers from the international community) made a great effort to evaluate the papers. We would like to acknowledge their effort in providing us the excellent feedback at the right time. So, we wish to thank all the authors and reviewers. To conclude, we would also like to express our gratitude to the Editor-in-Chief of TCS, Dr. Marina L. Gavrilova, for her advice, vision, and support.

September 2010   Edward David Moreno

LNCS Transactions on
Computational Science –
Editorial Board

Table of Contents – Part I

Table of Contents – Part II

A Dynamic Security Framework for Ambient Intelligent Systems: A Smart-Home Based eHealth Application

Luca Compagna[2], Paul El Khoury[2,3], Fabio Massacci[1], and Ayda Saidane[1]

[1] University of Trento, Italy
name.surname@unitn.it
[2] SAP Research, France
name.surname@sap.com
[3] LIRIS, University of Lyon 1, France
paul.el-khoury@liris.cnrs.fr

Abstract. Providing context-dependent security services is an important challenge for ambient intelligent systems. The complexity and the unbounded nature of such systems make it difficult even for the most experienced and knowledgeable security engineers, to foresee all possible situations and interactions when developing the system. In order to solve this problem context based self- diagnosis and reconfiguration at runtime should be provided.

We present in this paper a generic security and dependability framework for the dynamic provision of Security and Dependability (S&D) solutions at runtime[1]. Through out the paper, we use a smart items based e-health scenario to illustrate our approach. The eHealth prototype has been implemented and demonstrated in many scientific and industrial events[2,3].

1   Introduction

Future Ambient Intelligence (AmI) environments will contain a large number of heterogeneous computing and communication infrastructures hosted by devices providing new functionalities, enhancing productivity, and facilitating everyday tasks. In the new AmI scenarios, not only systems but also applications will have to make effective use of the resources that are available on-the-fly, and adapt to different hardware, software and even firmware configurations. The combination of heterogeneity, mobility, dynamism and just the sheer number of devices will make the provisioning of security solutions more challenging.

Let's make a simple example based on the AmI scenario that we will use throughout the paper: a doctor wishing to remotely monitor the conditions of a patient. Clearly we would like some authentication from the doctor (so that, e.g., a passer-by cannot take the

---

[1] This work has been done in the context of the SERENITY project
www.serenity-project.org

[2] http://ec.europa.eu/information_society/events/cf/ict2008/
item-display.cfm?id=171

[3] http://www.strategiestm.com/serenity/serenity_day.htm

M.L. Gavrilova et al. (Eds.): Trans. on Comput. Sci. X, LNCS 6340, pp. 1–24, 2010.

pulse of our old father) but also from the device (e.g., we do not want the same passer-by to send false alarms to the doctor). If actors are confined (e.g., a domotic home or a hospital) the problem is well understood: we specify the communication facilities and sensors in use and look in the vast literature of security protocols and sensors networks [35] to find the right solutions. No need of an autonomous system.

The challenge is that actors do move and by moving they change the context and the part of the ambient in charge of security. For instance, patients might exit to meet their relatives, or doctors might be on call from a public place. A designer might have identified a good security protocol which no longer works (e.g., the PDA of the doctor might not be able to support strong cryptography) or is no longer appropriate (e.g., sensors transmit authentic data as if everything is still, while our patient is dead and the doctor went out for a beer).

We need an autonomous system that can detect changes of the environment by the mobile agents and can provide new security solutions that fit the new environment and the new facilities and capabilities of the actors in these new surroundings.

Unfortunately, while a large number of old and new security infrastructures exist they do not deal with the dynamic provision of security solutions (such as a different authentication protocol suitable for the new context), but rather with the dynamic access of different users to distributed servers. The general idea of Akenti [38], PERMIS [11], Secure Mediator [5], SPKI [17] projects and many others [41,22,8,43,6,21], is that the information needed for an access decision, such as identity, authorization, and attributes is stored and conveyed in certificates, which are widely dispersed over the Internet (e.g., LDAP (Lightweight Directory Access Protocol) directories, Web servers). The authorization engine has to gather and verify the certificates needed for the user's request and then evaluate them to compute an access decision (see Figure 1 taken from [11]).

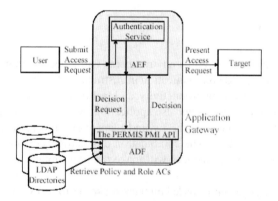

Fig. 1. Sample Interactions - PERMIS Architecture

In this paper we present a flexible and generic framework for the provision of security and dependability solutions at runtime. The aim of the framework is to support security in AmI environments and in particular the automated integration, monitoring and adaptation of security and dependability mechanisms for such ecosystems.

We also demonstrate the effectiveness and feasibility of our approach on a reference eHealth case study, that integrates the AmI aspect in its security and privacy sensitive nature. We describe the development process of the eHealth prototype in detail: requirements, security analysis and mitigation through runtime monitoring and security patterns. In the scope of our research, this approach has been validated with three additional case studies, i.e. eBusiness, Air Trafic Management and eGovernment [37], that opens security and dependability challenges. The main purpose for adopting a smart items prototype[4] is to capture, in a sample, the essense of the security challenges in an AmI environment.

In the next section we describe our case study that will be the running example throughout the paper. Section 3 presents the general features of AmI environments that an autonomic system must consider. Section 4 details the outcome of the security analysis aiming at identifying the potential threats. Section 5 describes our approach and its application to the case study while the description of the prototype is described in Section 6. Section 7 presents an overview of the main security architectures proposed in the literature with a comparison with our approach. Finally we conclude the paper.

2 Case Study: Smart Items Based eHealth Application

The objective of remote healthcare systems is to remotely monitor the patient health status and provide the necessary assistance. To reach this objective, healthcare systems should support the interaction and collaboration between doctors, pharmacists, patients, social workers and emergency medical teams especially during emergency situations.

The case study is an eHealth scenario: patients are continuously monitored by ambient sensors of a smart home and by wearable health sensors.

Example 1. Bob, a cardiopatic patient, wears a *Smart T-Shirt* that regularly measures his heart rate, blood pressure and some other critical data. The Smart T-Shirt is linked to an *eHealth mobile terminal* (e.g., a standard PDA phone available in the market) that provides, in addition to the usual mobile services, an advanced eHealth application ranging from reminding Bob to take his daily medicines to promptly communicating Bob's medical data to his doctor. Bob's *smart home* has been enhanced with sensors to monitor and adjust room's temperature, lamp status, people's movement, etc.

Since houses, t-shirts, PDAs, etc. cannot do diagnoses (and even if they could [4] the final opinion of a human will always be sought) the process requires interaction and collaboration with several human and organizational actors.

Example 2. The *Monitoring and Emergency Response Centre* (MERC) reacts to the different situations and orchestrates other actors in order to deliver effective medical care for the patients. Doctors, Pharmacists, Social workers and Emergency Medical teams can act as rescuers assisting Bob in his medical treatment while abiding to the European Health Care regulations.

---

[4] Demonstrated in different scientific and industrial events, e.g. http://ec.europa.eu/information_society/events/cf/ict2008/item-display.cfm?id=171 and http://www.strategiestm.com/serenity/serenity_day.htm

This eHealth scenario constitutes a complex social-technical system with strong security, safety and privacy requirements. In this paper, we limit the discussion to the security analysis of the system considering the emergency use case depicted in Figure 2.

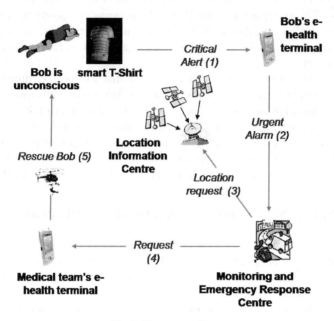

Fig. 2. Emergency Scene

Example 3. The health sensors of Bob's Smart T-Shirt report a decrease in Bob's blood pressure and body temperature. Bob's PDA analyses the critical situation and sends immediately an alert to the MERC (2). The MERC receives the request and analyzes it. *Low* priority alert comprises medical situations where a doctor's remote diagnosis (e.g., to prescribe to Bob a new medecine) usually is sufficient. *High* priority emergency situations require an urgent on-site intervention by rescue teams (4 and 5). In the latter case the MERC must determine Bob's location (3).

Table 1 summarizes the main features to be considered when building such system with regards to the aspects cited previously.

At this stage one may ask: this is all nice and good, but where is the autonomous aspect of the scenario? After-all we just said that we want have humans in the loop. The key observation is that the humans in our scenario have no network security expertise whatsoever.

So we do not expect the doctor, the nurse or the operator at the MERC to know the appropriate security protocol to authenticate the doctor or the appropriate cryptographic mechanism to protect the confidentiality of the patient's data. *The system should rely on*

Table 1. Major features of the case study

Autonomy & Ambient Intelligence	The patient may not be in the position to act, but still the system should be able to carry-out the work without any intervention from him. Moreover, the system should be able to adapt and react to the behavior of the patient and to the context change. The main AmI aspect of the case study corresponds to the deployment of a set of diversified passive unattended sensors dispersed over the environment that collect, transmit, and authenticate local data. Those sensors might not implement all these functionalities at once.
Genericity & Heterogeneity	The system-to-be is not designed to be used by Bob only. Therefore, it is mandatory to envisage at design time inter-operability of wide range of processes, communication protocols, sensors and devices.
Mobility	It reflects the changing context of the system. In fact, the patients are mobile. Essentially we consider two locations: 1) Home (prevalent) location and 2) Mobile locations. We borrowed this terminology from the mobile IP standard [7]. So in a different context the "Home location" might not be at home.
Dynamism	It is related to the need for adaptability and context-awareness. In fact, in order to ensure permanently the critical services for the patient different *AmI entities* should be available in the different locations.
Security, Privacy and Dependability	The scenario presents strong requirements on integrity and confidentiality of exchanged data and reliability of the infrastructure that allows the acquisition and transmission of relevent information about patient rescue. Moreover, the sentivity of the processed data implies requirements on the compliance with privacy regulations (i.e: EU Data Protection Directive, 95/46/EC2 and EU Directive on Privacy in Electronic Communications).

humans to make medical decision, but should be autonomous in making decisions on security solutions and in their deployment.

3   Abstract Components of an AmI Environment

In order to produce a general architecture that can be deployed in a variety of scenarios we must elicit the characteristics of our AmI environment. Our baseline is a generic ubiquitous application for monitoring a *mobile subject* with strong requirements on security and privacy for data sharing between the different entities and safety of the monitored subject.

As an intellectual exercise, one could ask oneself what would change if Bob was not an elderly patient but rather a bear and our objective avoiding its prowls on domestic cattle[5]. The system could be easily adapted to the monitoring of these animals by replacing the Smart T-Shirt by a collar that could be used to detect the position of the animal. The clever cave would replace the smart home, the clever collar would take the place of the Smart T-Shirt and so on.

In order to function, each component may play one or more of the above roles:

Sensors/Actuators. They collect data from the environment and/or execute actions on the environment.

Hot Spots. Communication end points that are used to connect remote entities to one another.

Servents. They are responsible for computing i.e., decision making. We use the P2P term servent as it might both act as a client and as server depending on the context.

A system component can play one or a combination of the above classes.

In this way we separate functionalities that are blurred in traditional wireless sensor networks literature. Indeed, as noted in [25], proper sensors do not network: the traditional configuration of sensors network [2] is in reality the combination of two different conceptual components:

- a sink is just a hot-spot which is close to the sensor just because of power limitation of the communication link, but conceptually it can be located anywhere;
- a sensor node in a wireless sensor network is a combination of a proper unattended sensor and an hot-spot.

An orthogonal classification identifies their ability to move with the subjects:

Localized entities offer or request services that are available locally. Different services can be offered or requested in different locations.

Carry-on entities move jointly with the mobile subject. They might be always tied on to the subject or may be dropped off.

In the sequel we will use the wording *servent* for the combination of the hot-spot with the processor.

Example 4. The Smart T-Shirt of Bob is an example of a carry-on entity with sensors. The PDA of the doctor is an example of a carry-on entity which combines a servent, a hot-spot and a sensor (to read the Smart T-Shirt local data). If it could read sensors directly (e.g., with an RFID reader), it would incorporate sensors capabilities as well. The smart home is an example of a localized entity combining the three functionalities.

As we show in Figure 3 certain components group together all three functionalities: the Smart T-Shirt combined with Bob's eHealth terminal is a carry-on servent with sensors.

---

[5] Bears are being re-introduced in the Alps with significant fuss on the German and Italian sides. In particular, a wild bear was roaming the German countryside where it was eventually killed.

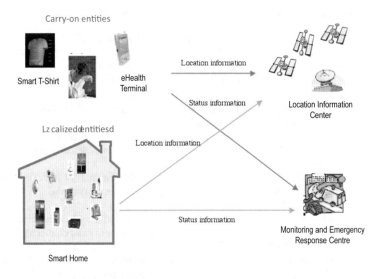

Carry-on entities

Smart T-Shirt

eHealth Terminal

Location information

Status information

Lz calizeddentitiesd

Location information

Status information

Smart Home

Location Information Center

Monitoring and Emergency Response Centre

Fig. 3. Carry-on and Localized entities in the eHealth Scenario

Some of the services offered by servents might be functional services or might be non-functional services such as security services:

Example 5. It is required to have some kind of identification (e.g., facial recognition, RFID tags or bluetooth authentication) for the patient in order to ensure that the services are provided to the right subject. However the information provided for identification might be sensitive (e.g., biometrics) and therefore has to be protected to meet the privacy requirements.

For our case study, the interactions between the sensors, hot-spots, and servents, whether localized or carry-on, must be subject to a threat analysis to identify risks and mitigation mechanisms suitable to address the security requirements.

A change in the context, for instance due to the mobility of the agents, might require a change in the security solution. A mechanism for autonomous decisions is thus needed. The autonomous aspect could be refined into different functionalities to be implemented in the system-to-be:

– *Runtime monitoring.* We are targeting safety-critical systems with strong requirements on reliability of the provided services. Thus runtime monitoring allows prompt failures detection and reaction. Here, we monitor both the environment and the internal system status together with the S&D solutions.
– *Self-diagnosis.* The information provided by the runtime monitoring should be automatically processed in order to identify the causes of the detected errors/failures.
– *Self-reconfiguration.* Once the corrupted components are identified, a reconfiguration step is required in order to bring the system back in a safe state.

Table 2. Some sample security, safety, and privacy requirements for the Emergency scene

Req 1 If the patient (i) loses consciousness, (ii) requests assistance, or (iii) feels guidy, then the patient eHealth terminal shall receive enough data from the patient Smart T-Shirt to promptly identify the dangerous status and send an urgent alert to the MERC.
Req 2 If the emergency procedure has started, then the MERC shall discover a medical team or a doctor able and available to go to rescue/assist the patient.
Req 3 The doctor discovery process shall successfully terminate (i.e., one and only one doctor shall proceed in assisting the patient) in due time.
Req 4 The system shall guarantee that the commitment of actors (e.g., doctors, rescue teams) to actions cannot be later repudiated and that such commitment is actually followed by the corresponding actions.
Req 5 Each communication between the MERC and the eHealth terminals of the selected doctor and of the medical team shall guarantee integrity and confidentiality of the data exchanged, and mutual authentication.
Req 6 Similarly, each communication between the eHealth terminal of the selected doctor, the medical team and the patient eHealth terminal shall guarantee integrity and confidentiality of the data exchanged, and mutual authentication.
Req 7 The selected doctor and the medical team using the eHealth terminal shall remotely be identified and granted access to the patient eHealth terminal to retrieve patient health status.

4 Security Analysis

Performing a systematic threat analysis consists in identifying all possible attack scenarios exploiting the vulnerabilities of the system and the capabilities of attackers needed to succeed (see e.g. the OCTAVE Methodology[6]). Thus, while analyzing different contexts, we come out with different threat models that require different security solutions to be deployed in order to mitigate them [10]. In this study, we base the security analysis on the exploration of failures scenarios affecting the security requirements cited in Table 2. We may decide that certain attacks scenarios are not worth to be considered as the probability of their occurrence is very low.

It is not difficult to lift the requirements in Table 2 to our abstract components: carry-on sensors identify a pre-defined alarm situation, a carry-on servent with sensors capabilities reads the alert and uses an hot-spot to connect to a localized servent. Localized servents communicate mutually to orchestrate a result. Along the whole process they need to use security solutions to identify the players and to protect their privacy. A security solution may require the intervention of different localized and Carry-on entities.

Let us analyze the threat models corresponding to the emergency scene. Considering the security requirements in Table 2, we are going to identify the different security threats obstructing their fulfillment. Table 3 presents the dependencies between the security requirements and the system components.

At this level we provide some intuition and constraints on possible solutions. More details are given in the implementation section later on.

Req 1. This requirement emphasizes on the reliability of the Smart T-Shirt. Any failure due to both malicious (i.e., someone intentionally changes the configuration,

---

[6] http://www.cert.org/octave/

Table 3. Dependencies between the identified security requirements and system's components

Component	Req 1	Req 2	Req 3	Req 4	Req 5	Req 6	Req 7
MERC's server	-	X	X	X	X	X	-
MERC's Database	-	-	-	X	-	-	-
Bob's PDA	X	-	-	-	-	X	-
GPS	-	X	-	-	-	-	-
EHR	-	-	-	-	-	-	X
Doctor's PDA	-	X	-	X	X	X	X
Directory service	-	X	-	-	-	-	-
Doctor's registry	-	X	-	-	-	-	-
Smart T-Shirt	X	-	-	-	-	-	-

buffer over flow on the diagnosis software via interaction with Bob's PDA, etc.) or accidental (i.e., software bug, Smart T-Shirt not correctly installed, etc.) would compromise Bob's safety. It is necessary to provide monitoring services that ensure that the software and hardware infrastructure are functioning correctly.

Req 2,3. It is critical for the patient's safety to securely and reliably identify Bob's location (and a close doctor). The sensors communicate on demand information about Bob's location to the MERC. After processing of this information, MERC requests complementary information to the GPS server. The main threats to reliably identify Bob's location concern: 1) failure of MERC's server, 2) corrupted information stored on Doctor's repository, 3) wrong information provided by GPS, and 4) failure on Doctor's PDA. Any of these threats would make it impossible the safe termination of the doctor's search.

When a critical information needs to be reliably retrieved from the Carry-on entities, some fault tolerance techniques should be deployed to ensure the information collection, storage and communication. These techniques should decrease risk level related to the identified threats since they increase the resiliency capabilities of the system.

Req 4. This is a composite requirement combining both non repudiation of commitment by the doctor and proof of fulfilment of the emergency call.

In order to meet the first element of the requirement, a PKI based authentication can with a signed confirmation message sent by the selected doctor to the MERC. This only provides a non-repudiation of committment. It would not be enough to fulfill the whole requirement because it doesn't prove that the doctor actually went to visit Bob. We need to add another proximity-based authentication between Bob's Smart T-Shirt (or his health terminal) and the doctor's PDA that would satisfy the proof on fulfilment of the rescue. Any corruption of Doctor's PDA would allow the intruder to falsify confirmation messages, or reject rescue requests when available, etc.

Req 5. There are three security properties that should be ensured during the communications between MERC and Doctor's PDA: Integrity, Confidentiality and mutual authentication. An encryption based solution could be used, namely PKI infrastructure. Some of the identified threats for the PDA are equivalent to those related to Req 4.

Additional flexibility would be required to cope with diversified mobile devices that may be used by doctors [20]. For example, a failure may occur on the doctor's device after confirmation sent and he may use a less performant or resource restricted device for further interaction with MERC, in this case different context-aware authentication schemas should be allowed.

Req 6. Integrity, confidentiality and mutual authentication are required for interactions between Bob's and doctor's devices. This case is similar to the previous one.

Req 7. An authorization solution managing Bob's medical data could be deployed. The enforcement point (where requests are intercepted for access control) and the decision points (where evaluation between requests and access control policies are determined) could be implemented on the same component or separated according to the latter computational capabilities, in other word we can place a decision point where a trusted servent is located.

Example 6. In our scenario, we may deploy a simple XACML based authorization solution where the MERC integrates both the enforcement and decision points as it represents the provider for the services and data requested by doctors and rescuers through their PDAs. Moreover, due to the privacy requirements on the patient data, only the minimal required data are sent on demand to the patient's PDA. The access to these data is granted according to the credential provided by the doctor's eHealth terminal with a lightweight authentication mechanism. In this way any successful Bob's device would not allow a complete access to Bob's data.

5   An Autonomic Framework for Dynamic Security Provisioning

Before presenting our autonomic framework, it is necessary to introduce some basic notions:

Context. It is the set of elements that are recorded and tracked by the Framework in order to evaluate the state of the system as a whole and assist in choosing the appropriate patterns or undertaking pre-active or pro-active actions.

Pattern. It is a self-contained description of a security solution including context in which it can be applied and a set of functions defining a public interface to be used by our security framework compliant applications.

Implementation. It represents the actual working solution. These solutions are made accessible to applications thanks to our autonomic framework.

The basic idea behind our autonomic framework is that as the context changes we should be able to deliver to the interested parties a new security solution.

If we consider a security requirement related to the confidentiality of some data. According to the application context, we may need an SSL (Secure Socket Layer) connection or a one time password or combination of both solution. This implies that all these security solutions provide the same security property and should be put in the same class within the S&D patterns' library. In fact, not only each S&D requirement can have different solutions, but also each solution may have different implementations. As a mere example, SSL or TLS describe a protocol that has different implementations depending on the provider (e.g., OpenSSL from BSD and JSSE from Java are just two of the most popular implementations of SSL). Depending on the facilities available one or the other implementations might be selected.

For each available implementation, a different implementation document is included in the library, describing: the specific system requirements, the necessary interface to use when calling the implementation, and the location of the Executable Component. So that once a solution is selected by the framework, a pointer to that implementation is made available for the application connected to the framework. As a concrete solution can be implemented not only via a programming language, but also via hardware elements such as a TPM (Trusted Platform Module) or a SmartCard, an implementation might also refer to a programming module, but to a physical (perhaps human) element.

The *Autonomic Security Framework (ASF)* has been designed to allow different security requirements to be fulfilled through a number of available patterns and implementations. The ASF architecture developed within the SERENITY project is shown in Figure 4. It is composed by the following components:

- **S&D Library:** it is a collection of patterns and implementations as defined previously. At runtime, the S&D library includes a limited set of appropriate solutions that are specific to the actual platform and applications that may be used on the device.
- **Query System:** it is responsible for contacting the Library and retrieving either patterns or implementations and forwarding them to the component that requested them. The query is like a translator used by the ASF Manager to get a specific implementation of the ASF Library.
- **Pattern Manager:** it implements the logic of patterns by combining application requirements, available patterns and current system context in order to choose the appropriate implementation that needs to be activated. The Manager is the component responsible for activating and deactivating pattern implementations and will also be accountable for taking necessary actions (based on the monitoring rules) when informed by the Monitor Service of a violation.
- **Event Manager:** it is responsible for collecting events from the Event Collector, updating the context based on these events and forwarding them to the Monitor Service for processing.
- **Console:** it is the main interface through which the ASF Manager will interact with end users (e.g., pop-up windows providing awareness about the current security solution in place).
- **Context Manager:** it is in charge of the context, as previously defined for the ASF environment. It gives the system a vision of the environment. The ASF Context Manager is responsible for updating it and responding to requests for specific elements.
- **Monitoring Service:** it is in charge of analyzing events and mapping them onto the monitoring rules, in order to identify any violations and consequently inform the ASF Manager. The monitor service can be located internally or externally to the ASF.

The application will be able to request either general requirements in the form of patterns or even explicitly request for a pattern implementation. Due to the dynamic nature

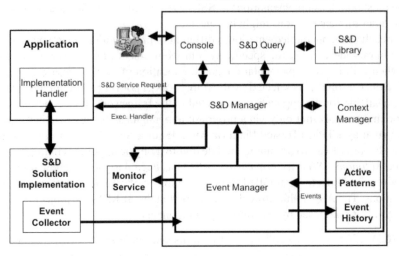

Fig. 4. Autonomic Security Framework

of the framework, the application must be able to interchange pattern implementations at run-time. As such the application should be designed in such a way as to refer to specific interfaces and not explicit run-time code. In practice, it must have an execution implementation handler that is programmed in such a way as to use at runtime different pattern implementations (using technologies such as jini or web services).

Hereafter we describe the objectives associated to each of the ASF components and show possible links to active research work in the research community. In general, the objectives tackled with the ASF can be achieved by an engineering approach, that requires no more than integrating concepts from different research topics varying from semantic querying, explanation, design by contract and different others.

The role of Event Manager in this framework is to capture events to be used as triggers for obligations on the selection of S&D patterns at the S&D Manager level. These obligations are in principal actions halting the execution of specific S&D patterns and/or swapping between S&D patterns. In some sense, we figure out similarities between these goals and ones in distributed systems. In particular, we highlight "events"" definition in the Ponder project. The events in Ponder trigger policies in the rationale of initiating negotiation between different ones [13]. For sure it is convenient to define events separately, and re-use them in multiple obligation policies, which is the approach followed by Ponder. With this perspective, we imagine events at the Event Manager level and policies at the S&D Manager level. By definition a policy in Ponder is a rule that can be used to change the behavior of a system. According our initial specification/expectation from ⟨Event Manager, S&D Manager⟩, obviously this brick from Ponder serves well our study. To protect the client and servers resources in distributed systems, [14] proposes a policy-based approach. These policies represent a semantic annotation of the constraints and capabilities required to initiate a negotiation between clients and servers. During negotiation, these annotations are used to reason about and communicate the need to reveal requested credentials from the other participant (client or server). The advantages in adding a negotiation framework in the S&D Manager of the ASF enables reasoning on the candidate S&D patterns.

We should adapt our framework to the use of contrasting requirements from software developers and security experts. Software developers are common users for our framework, with no technical training in computer security, nevertheless should be able to formulate their own queries to our S&D library. In [9] the authors arguments the need for high level specification and query languages requirement to satisfy such goals. Later, in [32], they propose their declarative rule-based language to specify policies in order to enable reasoning (such the one required above). Their proposal focuses on explanation mechanism for answering why, why-not, how-to, and what-if queries on rule-based policies. Similar objective is tackled in [26] from Stanford University for the explanation for (Semantic) Web based systems. Both of those approaches can be largely re-used in our work.

In the S&D library we will describe our security patterns in two different components. The first component comprises the executable code, while the second one provides the necessary information to reason on it. The actual code should be described in a plug-and-play form. The component required by the ASF for reasoning is actually described in the "design by contract" approach [29,27,28]: we will have to adjust the contract describing the relevant security behavior and the constraints for applicability. We complement this design approach by moving preconditions, invariants, post-conditions from just internal annotations in the code to be publicly exposed in the library. Therefore the previously described techniques for trust negotiation and semantic web matching using security policies [14,9,32] can be applied for selecting patterns. Actually, the mentioned reasoning and negotiation tools such as Ponder or Protune can be used to find out a consistent selection of various S&D patterns.

6 The eHealth Scenario Prototype

This section describes how we implement the case study presented in Section 2 and demonstrates how the security needs of the case study can be answered through the integration with the ASF.

Figure 5 depicts the communication architecture underlying our eHealth prototype. The overall logistics required for the development of the described prototype and depicted in Figure 5 is provided in Table 4. Patients' remote assistance is accomplished by means of a set of workflows properly defined, stored, and maintained by the MERC. These workflows define the tasks to be performed to accomplish the medical request and how these tasks should be orchestrated among the different actors. Tasks are realized by means of web services and human intervention. For instance, to cope with an emergency request (cf., Figure 2), the MERC activates and executes the workflow of Figure 6: a web service `AlertMERC_WS` running at the MERC interprets the alert request sent by the patient's Smart T-shirt through the patient's PDA and depending on the alert level (either `low` or `high`), it proceeds either calling for a doctor's diagnostic via the `FindAndSelectDoctor_WS` web service or asking for rescuers' intervention by means of the `Rescue_WS` web service.

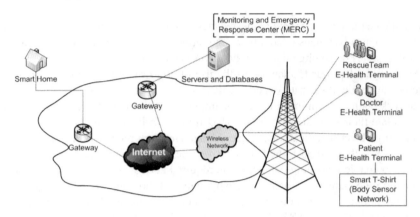

Fig. 5. Smart Items Architecture

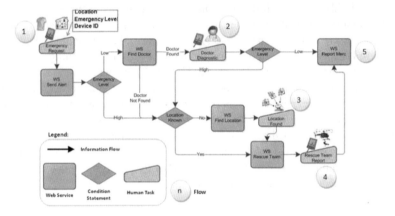

Fig. 6. Emergency alert handling process

To implement all these features, the MERC mounts activeBPEL as workflow engine to orchestrate remote medical tasks [1], an Apache Tomcat server configured with Axis2 to provide several remote medical web services using Apache and HSQLDB as relational database management system to store and maintain medical data of patients, doctors, etc. Table 4 summarizes the implementation choices made for the components of our eHealth prototype. In more details, the Smart T-Shirt is simulated as a JavaServer Page (JSP) invoking a web service to signal a medical alert.[7] As patient's Smart Home we have recently integrated in our case study the AmI infrastructure developed at the DOMUS laboratory[8]. It relies on RFIDs, sensors, effectors and other advanced communication technologies to provide eHealth monitoring capabilities [33]. The eHealth terminals used by patients, doctors and rescue teams will be PDA phones running a proper eHealth client application. For simulation and testing purposes, we emulate that application as a JSP running on a standard computer.

---

[7] Smart T-shirts to monitor patient's vital health parameters is a promising business area. Few prototypes are available in the research community.

[8] http://domus.usherbrooke.ca/

Table 4. Prototype implementation

Component	Implementation	AmI Class Type
Smart T-Shirt	Simulated as a GUI — JSP hosted on an Apache Tomcat server	carry-on — sensor
Smart Home	DOMUS AmI infrastructure — Power-Line equipment, sensitive mats, RFIDs, Programmable Logic Controller, Server and Ethernet infrastructure, Video over IP, Crestron software, etc	localized — sensor, servent, hot spot
eHealth terminals (for patients, doctors, etc)	PDA phones simulated as a GUI — JSP hosted on an Apache Tomcat server	carry-on — servent, hot spot
MERC	Workflow management system, web services, and DB management system — activeBPEL, Apache Tomcat server, Axis2, HSQLDB	localized — servent, hot spot

The eHealth prototype so far described addresses the remote assistance capabilities required for patients monitoring, but it does not answer to any of the security requirements identified in Section 4. For instance, (SOAP) messages exchanged between the doctor's PDA and the MERC are sent in plain text and without any digital signature by exposing patient's sensible data (e.g., Electronic Health Records, Emergency Records) to the public and by missing any guarantee on the sender's identity (see Req. 5). Specific built-in security mechanisms could be put in place to answer to this and other security requirements, but they would likely be not adaptable.

Decoupling the system from its security functionalities would allow for adapting the security mechanisms at runtime. Through its enhanced notion of patterns and monitoring features, the ASF tries to answer to these needs. For this smart items scenario we find convenient to adopt a centralized deployment of the ASF under the control of the MERC.

The basic idea is to enforce security by means of security patterns referring to plug-and-play software code. The execution of these pieces of software integrates the security functionalities into the prototype. Of course, entry points for these pieces of software need to be considered already during the design phase of the prototype.

At the current stage, the ASF library comprises several security patterns and a few plug-and-play implementations. Some examples are presented in our previous work [12,34]. Out of this library we select four security patterns to demonstrate the integration of the ASF into our eHealth prototype:

- **Dependable Alert Communication.** Is a classical dependability pattern that is achieved through replicated and independent communication lines;
- **Direct authentication.** Is a peer-to-peer authentication pattern based on shared keys providing confidentiality and proof of origin of the requester;

- **Brokered authentication.** Is an authentication pattern working in different configuration than Direct authentication since it requires a trusted third party to authenticate the requesters. It tackles the same security requirement (i.e., proof of origin);
- **Authorization using a PMI**[9]. Provides context-aware access control to resources.

In order to achieve the dependability requirements for the communication link used
for receiving the alert, we designed our prototype with a classical redundancy pattern:
the on-line selection of three publicly available infrastructures (namely the Internet,
the GSM, and the GPRS communication networks) results in a hybrid communication
architecture that meets the reliability needs of our eHealth case study.

A more sophisticated example shows how our eHealth prototype can take advantage
of the ASF.

Example 7. The eHealth prototype developer queries the ASF for security patterns applicable in the context of the eHealth prototype and providing authentication in the
communication between the doctor's PDA and the MERC. The direct authentication
pattern is proposed by the ASF. The applicability conditions of the pattern implementation match the technology underlying the prototype. The prototype developer invokes
the pattern auto-deployment function, with the parameters properly instantiated, and
the pattern is thus deployed on both the client (the doctor's PDA) and the server (the
MERC). SOAP messages sent by the doctor's PDA to the MERC are then digitally
signed to guarantee the proof-of-origin requirement.

Behind the scenes, the pattern's auto-deployment function acts on both the client and
the server workspaces to properly enable the Rampart module (see[10]) for encryption and
signature of the SOAP messages. This is totally transparent to the prototype developer.

The direct authentication pattern is a suited solution for proof-of-origin as long as
the two communication parties trust each other. On the contrary, in an distrustful environment where two endpoints need to exchanging data with lack in trust, a trusted third
party should authenticate the service requester to the service provider.

Example 8. If a doctor receives suspect emails requesting for his services, a stronger
authentication mechanism than direct authentication is recommended to restore trustworthiness in the eHealth infrastructure.

The ASF monitoring capability recognizes the need to replace the direct authentication mechanism with a more suited one, based on a trusted third party. Thus, the ASF
looks up for such an authentication pattern and the brokered authentication pattern is
retrieved.

All this happens during the execution of the system and therefore the deployment
of the brokered authentication pattern cannot take advantage of the knowledge of the
prototype developer. The ASF has to deal with this deployment by its own, involving the
prototype's security and IT administrators anytime that decisions and/or actions cannot
be made automatically: pattern deployment at runtime might require for re-starting the
eHealth prototype system.

---

[9] PMI stands for Privilege Management Infrastructure.

[10] http://ws.apache.org/axis2/modules/rampart/1_2/security − module.html

```
1- Resource = WebServiceAddress
2- XACMLPolicy = policyaddress
3- enforcementPoint = PEPaddress
...
4- myEC = New ExecutableComponent AP(
5-                  myASF,
6-          "P: Authorization.SAP",
7-                    Parameters
8-          );
9- myAnswer =myEC.callOperation("authorization",
10-                 parameters);
   ...
11- If (myAnswer == DENY)
    ... //business logic
12- Elseif (myAnswer == PERMIT)
    .../business logic
```

Fig. 7. Deployment of Authorization using XACML Executable Component

During deployment, the monitoring events signals a re-deployment of the authentication mechanism. Hence, ASF checks the compatibility of the new authentication mechanism with the already available authorization mechanism. PERMIS authorization already installed in the prototype fails to be integrated with the new authentication pattern, referred to as (P2). The tokens sent by P2 and the one required by PERMIS are incompatible. Again, the ASF will have to query for an adequate authorization mechanism. The pattern Authorization using XACML referred to as (P3) provides similar granularity for PERMIS authorization.

In the attempt to exchange the authorization using PERMIS with P3 while keeping transparency, ASF checks for the availability of an adapter able to extract the RBAC policies of PERMIS and feed them to P3 as XACML policies.

This runtime illustration of ASF is illustrative rather than prescriptive and thus we could have a much wider spectrum of combinations.

6.1 *Access Control* Executable Component Artefact

The EC we have developed is based on the reference implementation of SUN XACML. XACML (eXtensible Access Control Markup Language), the newest standard for access control for web services, makes possible a simple, flexible way to express and enforce access control policies in a variety of environments, using a single language [31].

In order to correctly integrate this Security Pattern within the library, we (playing the role of security experts) defined at this step the EC and its Executable Component Description. To create the EC, we implemented the function calls for the XACML solution, we anticipated dependency errors through exceptions and then we overwrote required interfaces. The description is packaged into the security patterns library as an EC for the access control security pattern provided earlier.

When the access control security pattern and its correspondent authorization using XACML description are populated in the security patterns library, software developers will have to query for them and then deploy the EC in their application. In Figure 7 we

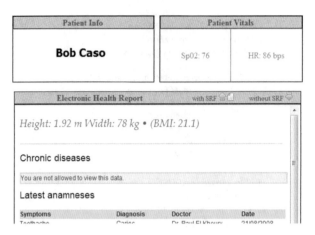

Fig. 8. Snapshot from the Prototype Showing the Enforcement of the XACML based EC of the Access Control Pattern

Table 5. Effective Deployment of Sample S& D Patterns

S& D Patterns	Implemenation	Fully autonomic
Alert Communication	yes	yes
Central authentication	standard tech.	yes
E-to-E authentication	yes	yes
Brokered authentication	yes	yes
Context-aware Auth. XACML	yes	yes
PeRMIS Auth. XACML	yes	current application may require wrapper to become plug and play
Localization services	yes	yes

provide the information required from the software developer to use this authorization solution. Specifically, the **P:** presented at *line* 6 corresponds to the Security Pattern artifact. At *line* 9 **"authorization"** corresponds to the operation exposed by the interface for this Security Pattern.

Executable Component Usage in the Case Study. In the lines of Figure 7 the software developer needs to add the address of the *resource to be secured*, the address of the access control policies annotated as *configuration* for the security pattern and finally creates the enforcement point and link it to the environment where it needs to be deployed. Similarly, as in the same scenes of the pattern, the case study will use the Executable Component based on XACML prior to any access to the earlier specified resources. The deployment of the EC in the case study and the interaction with the Autonomic Security Framework are depicted in Figures 8 and Figure 9 respectively.

Table 5 shows the status of the patterns that we have just described in the eHealth-prototype.

Though preliminary, our experiments with the running eHealth prototype indicate that the approach is feasible and promising. At design time the integration of security functionalities through the enhanced concept of security patterns operates smoothly and simplifies significantly the work of system developers for what concerns provision of security in the system. Not surprisingly, the ASF runtime support is more challenging and subtle as deployment of patterns during the system execution might requires the intervention of system's administrators and/or the re-booting of the system itself. Nevertheless the approach is innovative and significantly advances the state-of-the-art in the monitoring and adaptation of security at runtime.

7 Related Works

The majority of proposals for security architectures (Akenti, PERMIS, etc.) focus on a particular aspect of security like providing authentication or access control whereas our run-time framework is a generic security provisioning framework. For example, the PERMIS PMI architecture [11] consists of a privilege allocation subsystem and a privilege verification subsystem. The privilege allocation subsystem allocates privileges to the users by generating X.509 role assignment attribute certificates that are stored in an LDAP directory. Authentication is performed in an application-specific manner, but authorization is performed in an application-independent manner according to the PERMIS RBAC authorization policy. All these authentication solutions are considered in our framework as different security patterns which implementation, configuration and applicability condition are stored in the S&D library. The selection of the appropriate pattern is driven by context change.

Other systems focused on providing autonomous operations based on monitoring and reconfiguration. Even if implementations and experiments have been done in order to prove the generality and adaptability of the frameworks they lack the mechanism of patterns. For example, Abendroth et al. [3] propose a Unified Security Framework for Networked Applications based on active software capabilities. It is able to support most of the existing access control models. The proposed framework consists of four layers: 1) Security model; 2) Security Policy; 3) Security mechanism; and 4) Security Protocol. Each abstraction layer provides requirements and constraints on the following layer but such notions are soldered into the application.

The Willow survivability architecture [23] is a secure, automated framework for a wide spectrum of both proactive and reactive reconfigurations of distributed systems. It is based on the notion that survivability of a network requires reconfiguration at both the system and the application levels. The Willow notion of reconfiguration is very general, and the architecture provides reconfiguration mechanisms for both automatic and manual network control. Once again, the individual schemes for dealing with different reconfiguration scenarios might be different, but conceptually they are instances of a common control paradigm that pervades the architecture.

PASIS (Perpetually Available and Secure Information Storage) [16] is a survivable storage system. It provides intrusion tolerance on both server and client sides. To do so, on the server side, it uses a strategy of decentralization so that any M-out-of-N storage nodes can collectively provide valid information. On the client side, it enables intrusion diagnosis and recovery. Covington et al [15] propose another context-aware security architecture for emerging applications. Their architecture focuses on authentication and access control.

Execution flow

Time	End-to-end	Operation
1	user -> proxy	getPhysicalCharacteristics()
2	proxy -> Autonomic Security Framework	authorization
3	Autonomic Security Framework-> proxy	PERMIT
4	proxy -> EHR web service	getPhysicalCharacteristics()
5	EHR web service -> proxy	The physical characteristics
6	proxy -> user	The physical characteristics

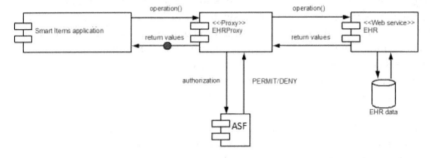

Fig. 9. Snapshot from the Prototype Showing the Execution Flow Between eHealth Application, the ASF and the authorization using XACML based Executable Component for the request getPhysicalCharacteristics() from the web service exposing the EHR

Moloney et al [30] propose a context-aware Trust-based security framework. The proposed framework allow the system to take appropriate security decisions according the current context where it is evolving. The architecture consists of four main components: Entity recognition (ER) , Trust/Risk engines, Evidence Manager (EM) and Decision-making component. The ER collects context information, that will be evaluated by the trust and risk engines according to the information stored by the EM. The decision is taken according to the outcome of the trust and risk analysis. There is no monitoring service to make sure that the required security level is maintained during the execution of the system.

What makes the ASF more flexible than the above proposals is the use of patterns [36]. This makes it possible to provide automated support in the development of secure systems. A well-known work on the field of security patterns is the one presented by IBM in 2003 [40] as result of a set of interviews with institutions in financial services, government, manufacturing, health, transportation, retail and other sectors. The patterns focus is on implementation of efficient and effective security as an integral part of a business delivering value to its customers by measuring risk. Business security patterns

Table 6. Adequacy of the prototype

Autonomy & Ambient Intelligence	The ASF ensures autonomy of the system. In fact, the security manger is designed to take all decisions at runtime without external intervention.
Genericity & Heterogeneity	The system can be adapted to other scenarios where runtime monitoring and reaction are required for passive subjects.
Mobility	We have demonstrated the feasibility of the solution by checking that services will be available both inside and outside the smart home.
Dynamism	The system dynamic aspects are based on the ASF.
Security and Dependability	The security patterns provided by the ASF allow a continuous fulfillment of the S&D requirements.

such as Web Presence, Business-to-Consumer or Operational Security are presented as valuable guidelines for a Chief Security Officer. Still, those patterns are only available at business level and lack a formal semantics.

In general, most security patterns are expressed in textual form, as informal indications on how to solve some security problem [24,42,36]. Some of them do use more precise representations based on UML diagrams, but even these patterns do not include sufficient semantic descriptions in order to automate their processing and to extend their use [18].

Wassermann and Cheng [39] revised most patterns from [42,19] and categorized them according their abstraction level (i.e. Application, Host or Network). The proposal conveys additional information such as behavior (UML State diagrams), structure (UML Class diagrams), constraints and related security principles.

The critical innovation in our work is that patterns are actually deployed at runtime, rather than being selected by designers during system development. They must of course be specified in a way that is suitable for automatic replacement.

8   Conclusions

The key innovation of our Autonomic Security Framework is the computer aided runtime proactive and reactive support for identification of potential threats and attacks of implemented security solutions, the adaptation of attacked applications, and the amendment of patterns to address weaknesses identified during their deployment through appropriate evolution mechanisms.

We are now in the position to evaluate qualitatively the adequacy of the implementation with regards to the functional and non-functional requirements expressed previously. Table 6 summarizes the outcomes of the analysis and explains how we have addressed the challenges previously identified. A full fledged experimentation of the system-as-a-whole is our next step. We are currently doing the integration of the full run-time ASF. The ability of the system to adapt itself when the monitored subject is moving from trusted environments to hostile ones would be one of the main challenges.

At runtime the ASF, monitoring the application, needs to perform several reasoning activities in order to fetch and deploy appropriate security solutions suitable for correcting the available vulnerabilities in the application. These interactions between the

ASF and application are driven by priorities set by the threat models and the available resources. The balance between availability of resources and their protection could be the final benchmark.

References

1. ActiveBPEL, LLC, ActiveBPEL, the Open Source BPEL Engine, No longer supported by the company as Open Source since 2010, http://www.activebpel.org
2. Prediction-based strategies for energy saving in object tracking sensor networks (2004)
3. Abendroth, J., Jensen, C.D.: A unified security framework for networked applications. In: Proc. of the 2003 ACM Symp. on Applied Comp., pp. 351–357. ACM Press, New York (2003)
4. Acampora, G., Gaeta, M., Loia, V., Vasilakos, A.V.: Interoperable and adaptive fuzzy services for ambient intelligence applications. ACM Trans. Auton. Adapt. Syst. (2010)
5. Altenschmidt, C., Biskup, J., Flegel, U., Karabulut, Y.: Secure mediation: Requirements, design, and architecture. JCS 11(3), 365–398 (2003)
6. Au, R., Looi, M., Ashley, P.: Cross-domain one-shot authorization using smart cards. In: Proc. of CCS 2000, pp. 220–227. ACM Press, New York (2000)
7. Aura, T., Roe, M.: Designing the mobile ipv6 security protocol. Annales des Télécommunications 61(3-4), 332–356 (2006)
8. Beznosov, K., Deng, Y., Blakley, B., Burt, C., Barkley, J.: A resource access decision service for CORBA-based distributed systems. In: Proc. of ACSAC 1999, pp. 310–319. IEEE Press, Los Alamitos (1999)
9. Bonatti, P.A.: Rule languages for security and privacy in cooperative systems. COMPSAC (1), 268–269 (2005)
10. Butler, S.A.: Security attribute evaluation method: a cost-benefit approach. In: ICSE, pp. 232–240. ACM, New York (2002)
11. Chadwick, D.W., Otenko, A.: The permis x.509 role based privilege management infrastructure. In: Proc. of SACMAT 2002, pp. 135–140. ACM Press, New York (2002)
12. Compagna, L., Khoury, P.E., Massacci, F., Thomas, R., Zannone, N.: How to capture, model, and verify the knowledge of legal, security, and privacy experts: a pattern-based approach. In: ICAIL 2007: Proceedings of the 11th International Conference on Artificial Intelligence and Law, pp. 149–153. ACM Press, New York (2007)
13. Constandache, I., Olmedilla, D., Siebenlist, F.: Policy-driven negotiation for authorization in the grid, pp. 211–220. IEEE Press, Los Alamitos (2007)
14. Constandache, I., Olmedilla, D., Siebenlist, F.: Policy-driven negotiation for authorization in the grid. In: IEEE International Policies for Distributed Systems and Networks (POLICY 2007). IEEE Computer Society Press, Los Alamitos (2007)
15. Covingtony, M.J., Fogla, P., Mustaque Ahamad, Z.Z.: A context-aware security architecture for emerging applications. In: ACSAC 2002 (2002)
16. Cukier, M., Courtney, T., Lyons, J., Ramasamy, H.V., Sanders, W.H., Seri, M., Atighetchi, M., Rubel, P., Jones, C., Webber, F., Watro, P.P.R., Gossett, J.: Providing intrusion tolerance with itua. In: Supplement of the 2002 Int. Conf. on Dependable Systems and Networks. IEEE Press, Los Alamitos (2002)
17. Ellison, C., Frantz, B., Lampson, B., Rivest, R., Thomas, B.M., Ylonen, T.: SPKI Certificate Theory, IETF RFC 2693 (September 1999)
18. Fernandez, E.: Metadata and authorization patterns. Technical report, Florida Atlantic University (2000)
19. Fernandez, E., Pan, R.: A pattern language for security models. In: Proc. of the 8th Conf. on Pattern Languages of Programs (2001)

20. Gomez, L., Thomas, I.: Towards user authentication flexibility. In: Proc. of the ACM International Conference of Security and Cryptography. ACM Press, New York (2007)
21. Hine, J.A., Yao, W., Bacon, J., Moody, K.: An architecture for distributed OASIS services. In: Coulson, G., Sventek, J. (eds.) Middleware 2000. LNCS, vol. 1795, pp. 104–120. Springer, Heidelberg (2000)
22. Johnston, W., Mudumbai, S., Thompson, M.: Authorization and attribute certificates for widely distributed access control. In: Proc. of the 7th IEEE Int. Work. on Enabling Technologies: Infrastructure for Collaborative Enterprises (WET ICE 1998), pp. 340–345. IEEE Press, Los Alamitos (1998)
23. Knight, C., Heimbigner, D., Wolf, A.L., Carzaniga, A., Hill, J.C., Devanbu, P., Gertz, M.: The willow survivability architecture. In: Proc. of the 4th Information Survivability Workshop (2001)
24. Konrad, S., Cheng, B.H.C., Campbell, L.A., Wassermann, R.: Using security patterns to model and analyze security requirements. In: Proceedings of the Requirements for High Assurance Systems Workshop (RHAS 2003), Monterey Bay CA, USA. IEEE Computer Society, Los Alamitos (September 2003)
25. Ma, D., Tsudik, G.: Extended abstract: Forward-secure sequential aggregate authentication. In: SP 2007: Proceedings of the 2007 IEEE Symposium on Security and Privacy, Washington, DC, USA. IEEE Computer Society, Los Alamitos (2007)
26. McGuinness, D.L., da Silva, P.P.: Explaining answers from the semantic web: The inference web approach. Journal of Web Semantics 1(4), 397–413 (2004)
27. Meyer, B.: Design by contract. In: Mandrioli, D., Meyer, B. (eds.) Advances in Object-Oriented Software Engineering, pp. 1–50. Prentice-Hall, Englewood Cliffs (1991)
28. Meyer, B.: Applying "design by contract". Computer 25(10), 40–51 (1992)
29. Meyer, B.: The grand challenge of trusted components. In: ICSE 2003: Proceedings of the 25th International Conference on Software Engineering, Washington, DC, USA, pp. 660–667. IEEE Computer Society, Los Alamitos (2003)
30. Moloney, M., Weber, S.: A context-aware trust-based security system for ad hoc networks. In: Proc. of the Security and Privacy for Emerging Areas in Communication Networks Workshop, pp. 153–160. IEEP (2005)
31. Moses, T.: extensible access control markup language tc v2.0 (xacml) (February 2005)
32. Piero, J.P., Bonatti, A., Olmedilla, D.: Advanced policy explanations on the web. In: ECAI 2006, pp. 200–204 (2006)
33. Pigot, H., Mayers, A., Giroux, S.: The intelligent habitat and everyday life activity support. In: Proc. of the 5th Int. Conf. on Simulations in Biomedicine, pp. 507–516 (2003)
34. Sanchez-Cid, F., Munoz, A., Khoury, P.E., Compagna, L.: Xacml as a security and dependability pattern for access control in ami environments. In: Proc. of the Ambient Intelligence Developments Conf. (AmI.d 2007). Springer, Heidelberg (2007)
35. Sang, Y., Shen, H., Inoguchi, Y., Tan, Y., Xiong, N.: Secure data aggregation in wireless sensor networks: A survey. In: International Conference on Parallel and Distributed Computing Applications and Technologies, pp. 315–320 (2006)
36. Schumacher, M., Roedig, U.: Security Engineering with Patterns. In: Proceedings of the 8th Conference on Pattern Languages of Programs (PLoP 2001). ACM Press, New York (2001)
37. Spanoudakis, G., Gomez, A.M., Kokolakis, S. (eds.): Security and Dependability for Ambient Intelligence. Advances in Information Security, vol. 45. Springer, Heidelberg (2009) ISBN: 978-0-387-88774-6
38. Thompson, M., Johnston, W., Mudumbai, S., Hoo, G., Jackson, K., Essiari, A.: Certificate-based access control for widely distributed resources. In: Proc. of 8th USENIX Security Symposium, pp. 215–228 (August 1999)

39. Wassermann, R., Cheng, B.: Security patterns. Technical Report MSU-CSE-03-23, Comp. Sci. and Eng., Michigan State Univ. (2003)
40. Wimmel, G., Wisspeintner, A.: Extended description techniques for security engineering. In: Proc. of the 16th Int. Conf. on Information Security (2001)
41. Woo, T., Lam, S.: Authorization in distributed systems: a formal approach. In: Proceedings of the IEEE Symposium on Security and Privacy, pp. 529–536. IEEE Press, Los Alamitos (1992)
42. Yoder, J., Barcalow, J.: Architectural patterns for enabling application security. In: Conference on Pattern Languages of Programs (PLoP 1997). ACM, New York (1997)
43. Zurko, M., Simon, R., Sanfilippo, T.: A user-centered, modular authorization service built on an RBAC foundation. In: Proc. of Symp. on Sec. and Privacy, pp. 57–71. IEEE Press, Los Alamitos (1999)

NTRU-Like Public Key Cryptosystems beyond Dedekind Domain up to Alternative Algebra

Ehsan Malekian and Ali Zakerolhosseini

Faculty of Electrical and Computer Engineering
Shahid Beheshti University, Evin, Tehran, Iran
{e_malekian,a-zaker}@sbu.ac.ir

Abstract. The main purpose of this paper is to illustrate the fundamental concepts behind the NTRU public key cryptosystem can be extended to a broader algebra than Dedekind domains and the NTRU underlying ring may be replaced by a non-commutative or even non-associative algebra.

To cross the border of Dedekind or Euclidean domains, we prove that it is possible to extend NTRU to the algebra of polynomials with coefficients in the non-commutative ring of quaternions as well as the non-associative octonions algebra (a power-associative and alternative algebra of dimension eight over a principal ideal domain).

We also demonstrate that the security of the proposed non-associative cryptosystem relies on the intractability of shortest vector problem in a certain type of lattice. The least advantage of the non-associativity of the underlying algebra is that the resulting lattice is not fully classified under Convolutional Modular Lattice (CML). To the best of our knowledge, no non-associative public key cryptosystem based on non-associative algebra has been proposed in the literature.

Keywords: Public Key Cryptography, Lattice-based Cryptosystems, NTRU Extension, Non-associative Cryptosystems.

1 Introduction

The NTRU public key cryptosystem which was officially introduced in 1998 [10], is the only practical lattice-based cryptosystem that finally managed to win public trust after numerous modifications and optimizations [12] and it has now been fully standardized within IEEE P1363.1 NTRUEncrypt [14]. Compared to other well-known cryptosystems such as RSA, ECC or ElGamal, the greatest advantage of NTRU is that the basic operations take place in the ring of convolution polynomials of rank N over $\mathbb{Z}$ with the worst-case running time $\mathcal{O}(N^2)$. Computational efficiency along with low cost of implementation have turned NTRU into a very suitable choice for a large number of applications such as embedded systems, mobile phones, RFID tags, portable devices and resource constrained devices [3,15].

Most sophisticated attacks against NTRU are based on lattice reduction techniques [6,19]. Although it has been shown that the Closest Vector Problem

M.L. Gavrilova et al. (Eds.): Trans. on Comput. Sci. X, LNCS 6340, pp. 25–41, 2010.

(CVP) is $\mathcal{NP}$-hard and the Shortest Vector Problem (SVP) is also $\mathcal{NP}$-hard under randomized reduction [1,20,21], however, the NTRU lattice is classified as a Cyclic Modular Lattice (CML) and it is not determined, yet, whether or not the cyclic structure and Hermite normal form of CML is going to help reducing the complexity of CVP or SVP [9].

After recognition of NTRU as a secure and safe scheme, several researches were conducted on generalization of the NTRU algebraic structure to different Euclidean rings beyond $\mathbb{Z}$, including the non-commutative ring of $k \times k$ matrices of polynomials in $\mathbb{Z}[x]/(x^N - 1)$ (MaTRU) [4], $GF(2^k)[x]$ (CTRU) [7] and generally Dedekind domains such as $\mathbb{Z}[i]$ [17], $\mathbb{Z}[\sqrt{-2}]$, $\mathbb{Z}[\zeta_3]$ and $\mathbb{Z}[\zeta_5]$ (ETRU) [16,23]. Although generalization of NTRU to $GF(2^k)[x]$ in [7] never had a desirable result and was broken soon after [17], however, it resulted in a better understanding of the NTRU cryptosystem and suggested the idea of replacing NTRU algebraic structure with other rings, free modules and algebras.

NTRU relies on two fundamental concepts: According to the first concept, this cryptosystem has acquired its inherent security from intractability of the Shortest Vector Problem (SVP) in a certain type of lattice which is assumed to be $\mathcal{NP}$-hard. From this aspect, NTRU is different from all known number-theoretic cryptosystems like RSA or ECC. According to the second concept that has not been considered in the sense of algebraic generalization, is the possibility of decryption failure, which may lead to the concept of *provable security* based on worst-case intractability assumptions (though this feature has not been proven yet). In NTRU, decryption failure arises from the fact that there is no well-defined and non-trivial homomorphism between two rings $\mathbb{Z}_p$ and $\mathbb{Z}_q$ as well as the polynomial rings $\mathbb{Z}_p[x]$ and $\mathbb{Z}_q[x]$ (assuming $gcd(p,q) = 1$). Despite this fact, one may impose some restrictions on the coset representatives and switch over $\mathbb{Z}_p[x]$ and $\mathbb{Z}_q[x]$.

In this paper, by introducing two practical cryptosystems similar to NTRU, we illustrate that the algebraic structure of NTRU is not limited to Euclidean or Dedekind domains and can be extended to an algebra which is not necessarily commutative or associative. Those two examples are public key cryptosystems with non-associative and non-commutative algebraic structure which can be implemented in software or hardware in addition to crossing borders of Dedekind domain. We also show that similar to NTRU, the security of the proposed non-associative cryptosystem relies on the intractability of shortest vector problem in a non-circular lattice.

This paper is organized as follows: Section 2 summarizes the NTRU cryptosystem over any arbitrary Dedekind domain including $\mathbb{Z}$. In section 3, we provide a sketch of the theory on which the proposed cryptosystems are based. In section 4, we describe two NTRU-like public key cryptosystems that are constructed based on polynomial algebra with coefficient in the non-commutative ring of quaternions and non-associative octonions, respectively. Section 5 is dedicated to the security analysis of the proposed non-associative public key cryptosystem.

2   NTRU Cryptosystem over a Dedekind Domain

This section briefly introduces the NTRU cryptosystem over a Dedekind domain including $\mathbb{Z}$. It is presumed that the reader is familiar with precise details of this cryptosystem as well as concepts of abstract algebra. Otherwise, references [11] and [25] are recommended for comprehensive introduction to NTRU and abstract algebra concepts, respectively.

Suppose $\mathcal{D}$ is a Dedekind domain and consider the convolution polynomial ring $\mathcal{R} = \mathcal{D}[x]/(x^N - 1)$ with multiplication denoted by the symbol $\star$, where N is a fixed prime number. The convolution product $h := f \star g$ can be explicitly defined as follows

$$f(x) := \sum_{i=0}^{N-1} f_i x^i = [f_0, f_1, \ldots, f_{N-1}]_{1 \times N}, \quad f_i \in \mathcal{D}$$

$$g(x) := \sum_{i=0}^{N-1} g_i x^i = [g_0, g_1, \ldots, g_{N-1}]_{1 \times N}, \quad g_i \in \mathcal{D}$$

$$h(x) := \sum_{i=0}^{N-1} h_i x^i = [h_0, h_1, \ldots, h_{N-1}]_{1 \times N}, \quad h_i \in \mathcal{D} \tag{1}$$

$$h_k := \sum_{i=0}^{k} f_i \cdot g_{k-i} + \sum_{i=k+1}^{N-1} f_i \cdot g_{N+k-i} = \sum_{i+j \overset{N}{\equiv} k} f_i \cdot g_i.$$

Let a be an arbitrary element in $\mathcal{D}$ and $\langle a \rangle$ be the ideal generated by a. Let $\mathcal{R}_a$ denote $(\mathcal{D}/\langle a \rangle)[x]/(x^N - 1)$ which is evidently isomorphic to $\mathcal{R}/\langle a \rangle$. Let p and q be two elements in $\mathcal{D}$ such that $\langle p \rangle \cap \langle q \rangle = \{1\}$. Also let $\mathcal{L}_f$, $\mathcal{L}_g$, $\mathcal{L}_m$ and $\mathcal{L}_\phi$, be *suitable* subsets of $\mathcal{R}$. By *suitable* we mean a subset of relatively sparse polynomials with coefficients of small norm. Note that the process of key generation, encryption and decryption are exactly the same as NTRUEncrypt but with two differences: (i) $\mathbb{Z}$ has been replaced with an arbitrary Dedekind domain $\mathcal{D}$, (ii) Modular arithmetic is generalized to its abstract equivalent, i.e., modular arithmetic modulo an ideal generated by $a \in \mathcal{D}$. Having set the above notations, the NTRU cryptosystem over a Dedekind domain can now be described as follows.

Public Parameters. The following parameters in (Generalized) NTRU are assumed to be fixed and public and must be agreed upon by both the sender and the receiver: N is a prime number which determines the structure of the ring $\mathcal{D}[x]/(x^N - 1)$ and p and q are two elements in $\mathcal{D}$ such that $\langle p \rangle \cap \langle q \rangle = \{1\}$ and $\|q\|$ is much greater than $\|p\|$, where $\|.\|$ denotes Euclidean function (when $\mathcal{D}$ is also Euclidean Domain) or a function that admit unique remainder for a specific subset of $\mathcal{D}$ with respect to the ring operations. d_f, d_g, d_m, and d_ϕ are constant integers less than N which determine the distribution of the coefficients of the polynomials in the subsets $\mathcal{L}_f$, $\mathcal{L}_g$, $\mathcal{L}_m$ and $\mathcal{L}_\phi$.

Key Generation. In the key generation process, two *small* polynomials f and g are randomly chosen from $\mathcal{L}_f$ and $\mathcal{L}_g$, respectively. The polynomial f must be invertible in $\mathcal{R}_p$ and $\mathcal{R}_q$ ($\mathcal{R}_a = (\mathcal{D}/\langle a \rangle)[x]/(x^N - 1)$). Upon suitable selection of public parameters, when f is randomly selected from the subset $\mathcal{L}_f$, the probability for this polynomial to be invertible in $\mathcal{R}_p$ and $\mathcal{R}_q$ is very high. However, in rare event that f is not invertible, a new polynomial f can be easily generated. The inverse of f over $\mathcal{R}_p$ and $\mathcal{R}_q$ are computed using the generalized extended Euclid algorithm. As is pointed out in [16,23], when p and q are prime elements (or power of a prime) in a Dedekind domain $\mathcal{D}$, there exist a polynomial time algorithm for computing the inverse of a unit element in $\mathcal{R}_p$ and $\mathcal{R}_q$. We call those two inverses f_p^{-1} and f_q^{-1}, respectively. Hence, we have $f_p^{-1} \star f \equiv 1 \,(\bmod\ p)$ and $f_q^{-1} \star f \equiv 1 \,(\bmod\ q)$. While f, g, f_p^{-1}, and f_q^{-1} are kept private, the public key h is computed as follows

$$h = f_q^{-1} \star g \,(\bmod\ q).$$

Encryption. The cryptosystem generates a random polynomial $\phi \in \mathcal{L}_\phi$, called the blinding polynomial (or ephemeral key), and converts the input message to a polynomial $m \in \mathcal{L}_m$. The ciphertext is computed as follows

$$e = p.(h \star \phi) + m \,(\bmod\ q).$$

Reduction modulo the ideal $\langle q \rangle$ is performed based on a predefined mapping which assigns a member of $\mathcal{D}$ as a representative to each equivalence class $\mathcal{D}/\langle q \rangle$. Let denote the set of all representatives for each equivalence class modulo the ideal $\langle q \rangle$ as $\mathcal{S}$.

Decryption. The first step of decryption process starts by multiplying (convolving) the received polynomial e by the private key f

$$\begin{aligned} a := f \star e \,(\bmod\ q) &= f \star (p.h \star \phi + m) \quad (\bmod\ q) \\ &= p.f \star f_q^{-1} \star g \star \phi + f \star m \quad (\bmod\ q) \\ &= p.g \star \phi + f \star m \quad (\bmod\ q). \end{aligned}$$

In the second step, the coefficients of $a \in \mathcal{R}_q$ are identified with the equivalent representatives in $\mathcal{S}$. Assuming that the public parameters have been chosen properly, the resulting polynomial is exactly equal to $p.g \star \phi + f \star m$ in $\mathcal{R}$. With this assumption, when we reduce the coefficients of a modulo p, the term $p.g \star \phi$ vanishes and $f \star m \,(\bmod\ p)$ remains. In order to extract the message m, it is enough to multiply $f \star m \,(\bmod\ p)$ by f_p^{-1}.

Successful Decryption. In order to ensure that the decryption process never fails or has a very high probability of succeeding, we have to impose some constraints on the cryptosystem constants and derive conditions under which the coefficients of $p.g \star \phi + f \star m$ in $\mathcal{R}$ lie in $\mathcal{S}$ almost always. For example, in standard NTRU if the public parameters (N, p, q, d) are chosen to satisfy $q > (6d + 1).p$ (where

$d := d_f = d_g = d_\phi$ as defined above) then decryption process will never fail. However, to have a better performance and also to reduce the size of the public key, smaller value of q may be chosen for q such that the probability of decryption failure be very small of order 2^{-80} [11, p. 395].

Security of Generalized NTRU over Dedekind Domains. When one selects an arbitrary Dedekind or Euclidean domain as $\mathcal{D}$, an efficient and functional cryptosystem will emerge, but the security and efficiency of the cryptosystem have no connection to its abstract definition and must be studied precisely and independently. In [17,16], it has been proven that besides $\mathbb{Z}$, if we choose $\mathcal{D}$ to be one of the Dedekind domains: $\mathbb{Z}[i]$, $\mathbb{Z}[\sqrt{-2}]$, $\mathbb{Z}[\zeta_3]$ and $\mathbb{Z}[\zeta_5]$, a NTRU-like cryptosystem will emerge that works well and enjoys high security. On the other hand, in CTRU where the ring of integers is replaced by the finite field $GF(2^k)$, the emerged cryptosystem is totally insecure [17].

3   A Sketch of the Underlying Algebra in the Proposed Cryptosystems

In this section we fix some definitions and notations and review a few basic properties of the algebras which will be used in the sequel. By *algebra* it means a vector space V over a field $\mathbb{F}$ (or generally a R-module over any ring $\mathcal{R}$ denoted by $\mathcal{R}$-algebra) that is equipped with a bilinear map.

Real quaternions and octonions, denoted respectively by $\mathbb{H} := \{\alpha + \beta.i + \gamma.j + \delta.k \mid \alpha, \beta, \gamma, \delta \in \mathbb{R}\}$ and $\mathbb{O} := \left\{x_0 + \sum_{i=1}^{7} x_i.e_i \mid x_0, \cdots, x_7 \in \mathbb{R}\right\}$, are the second and third normed division algebra in the sense of Cayley-Dickson doubling method. As a vector space, addition and scalar multiplication in $\mathbb{H}$ and $\mathbb{O}$ are defined by ordinary element-wise vector addition and scalar multiplication. However, multiplication of two quaternions in $\mathbb{H}$ (which is not commutative) is defined according to the rules:

$$i^2 = j^2 = k^2 = -1 \text{ and } ij = -ji = k. \tag{2}$$

For non-associative octonions with the basis $\{\, 1, e_1, e_2, e_3, e_4, e_5, e_6, e_7 \,\}$, multiplication is given by the following rules

$$\begin{cases} \mathbf{1} \text{ is the multiplicative identity, } e_i^2 = -1, \quad e_i.e_j = -e_j.e_i, \quad i \neq j, \\ e_i.e_j = e_k \rightarrow e_{i+1}.e_{j+1} = e_{k+1}, \quad e_i.e_j = e_k \rightarrow e_{2i}.e_{2j} = e_{2k}, \ i \neq j \end{cases} \tag{3}$$

where the indices greater than 7 should be reduced mod 7.

The octonion algebra is alternative, i.e., a non-associative algebra in which the subalgebra generated by any two elements is associative. [26, p. 17] In a non-associative but alternative algebra, the following three identities which are known as the *Moufang Identities* hold

$$\forall\, a, x, y \in \mathbb{O} \rightarrow \begin{cases} a(x(ay)) = (axa)y, \\ ((xa)y)a = x(aya), \\ (ax)(ya) = a(xy)a \end{cases} \tag{4}$$

The set of all integral quaternions $\mathbb{L}$, i.e., quaternions whose components are all in $\mathbb{Z}$, is known as Lipschitz integers and indeed forms a subring of the real quaternions $\mathbb{H}$. Similarly, the set of all integral octonions $\mathbb{G}$, which is sometimes called Gravesian or Cayley integers, is regarded as a normed division algebra of signature (8,0) that form a lattice inside $\mathbb{O}$. Lipschitz and Gravesian integers may be considered as two lattices in $\mathbb{R}^4$ and $\mathbb{R}^8$ which are not *densely well-packed* in the sense of Conway-Smith [5]. Consequently, the unique prime factorization property in $\mathbb{L}$ and $\mathbb{G}$ will fail [5].

The concepts of the homomorphism, kernel of a homomorphism and coset representatives, do not involve associativity of multiplication and have the same definitions for algebras in general. Let $\mathbb{A}$ and $\mathbb{A}'$ be two quaternionic or octonionic algebras over the commutative rings $\mathcal{R}$ and $\mathcal{R}'$ respectively, and let $\circ : \mathbb{A} \times \mathbb{A} \to \mathbb{A}$ denote corresponding bilinear multiplication. Assume there exists a homomorphism ρ from the ring $\mathcal{R}$ into $\mathcal{R}'$. Evidently, there exists a homomorphism ϕ between two algebras $\mathbb{A}$ and $\mathbb{A}'$ defined as follows

$$\phi : \mathbb{A} \to \mathbb{A}'$$

$$\forall \underset{\sim}{x} \in \mathbb{A}, \quad \underset{\sim}{x} := \sum_{i=1}^{n} x_i \mathbf{b}_i, \quad \phi(\underset{\sim}{x}) = \sum_{i=1}^{n} \rho(x_i) \mathbf{b}_i$$

where $\mathbf{b}_i$'s are the basis of the corresponding algebra (i.e., $\langle 1, i, j, k \rangle$ for $\mathbb{H}$ or $\langle 1, e_1, \cdots, e_7 \rangle$ for $\mathbb{O}$) and x_i's are scalars in $\mathcal{R}$. When $\mathbb{A}$ is one of the known quaternion or octonion algebra, the multiplication in $\mathbb{A}$ can be determined by the rules (2) or (3), but in general, for an arbitrary algebra $\mathbb{A}$, the bilinear multiplication can be completely determined by mean of *structure coefficients* via the following rule

$$\mathbf{b}_i \mathbf{b}_j = \sum_{k=1}^{n} c_{i,j,k} \mathbf{b}_k \tag{5}$$

where $c_{i,j,k}$ are scalars in $\mathcal{R}$ (called structure coefficients or multiplication constants) and must be specified such that the resulting multiplication satisfies the algebra laws. (For more comprehensive details see [26].)

Now let us turn our attention to the NTRU underlying algebra. Dedekind domains has been chosen as NTRU base ring in order to guarantee that there exist an efficient algorithm for finding the inverse of an invertible polynomial in $\mathcal{R}_a = (\mathcal{D}/\langle a \rangle)[x]/(x^N - 1)$ [16]. Since every prime ideal in a Dedekind domain is maximal, it would allow us to use the polynomial time extended Euclidean algorithm to find the inverse of a scalar in $\mathcal{R}$. By choosing $\mathbb{A}$ to be one of the quaternions or octonions algebra defined over a Dedekind domain $\mathcal{R}$, the algebra $\mathbb{A}$ satisfies the following properties:

- Finding the inverse of an element depends on finding the inverse of its *norm* over the ground ring/field on which the algebra is defined. Thus, $\mathbb{A}$ has an explicit rule for finding the inverse of a unit element in polynomial time. For quaternions ($\mathbb{H}$) or octonions ($\mathbb{O}$), the inverse of a unit element $\underset{\sim}{x}$ is computed by the explicit rule $\underset{\sim}{x}^{-1} = N(\underset{\sim}{x})^{-1}.\underset{\sim}{x}^*$, provided that it has a nonzero norm, i.e., $N(\underset{\sim}{x}) \neq 0$. The symbol $*$ denotes conjugate of $\underset{\sim}{x}$ and $N(.) : \mathbb{A} \to \mathcal{R}$ is a multiplicative norm function that assigns to every elements in $\mathbb{A}$ a scalar in the ground ring $\mathcal{R}$.

- Let $\mathcal{R}$ be the base ring on which the quaternionic or octonionic algebra $\mathbb{A}$ is defined. Assume that there exist two nontrivial homomorphisms ρ_1 and ρ_2 from $\mathcal{R}$ into the rings $\mathcal{R}_1$ and $\mathcal{R}_2$, respectively. It can be verified that $\phi_1(\underset{\sim}{x}) = \sum_{i=1}^{n} \rho_1(x_i)\mathbf{b}_i$ and $\phi_2(\underset{\sim}{x}) = \sum_{i=1}^{n} \rho_2(x_i)\mathbf{b}_i$ are two nontrivial algebra homomorphisms.

- Assume that there exist a surjective homomorphism from quaternionic or octonionic algebra $\mathbb{A}$ into finite split algebras $\mathbb{A}_1$ and $\mathbb{A}_2$ respectively. Obviously, every element in the finite split algebras $\mathbb{A}_1$ and $\mathbb{A}_2$ can be represented by a coset representative in $\mathbb{A}$.

4 Description of Two Cryptosystems Based on $\mathcal{R}$-Algebra beyond Dedekind Domain

In this section, we show that the ring of convolution polynomials of rank N over $\mathbb{Z}$ (i.e., $\mathbb{Z}[x]/(x^N - 1)$) in the NTRU scheme can be replaced by the algebra of polynomials with coefficients in the non-commutative ring of quaternions $\mathbb{H}$ or non-associative octonions $\mathbb{O}$. If we replace the underlying ring of NTRU by the quaternions or octonions algebra, then a new multi-dimensional public key cryptosystem will be emerged that is at least as secure against lattice attack as NTRU and also provides more capability for protocol design. The main difference between the proposed cryptosystems and those proposed in [23,17,4] is that the underlying algebra can be even non-associative. In this paper we focus on the quaternions and octonions algebras but we conjecture that the proposed extension may also be adapted to some other type of algebras.

4.1 A NTRU-Like Cryptosystem Based on Quaternions Algebra

In this cryptosystem, the underlying ring in the NTRU scheme is assumed to be quaternions non-commutative algebra. Let us call the proposed cryptosystem QTRU. Detailed and analytical description of the proposed cryptosystem are beyond the scope of this paper; see our report [18] for further details. Similar to NTRU we fix an integer prime N and two co-prime moduli[1] and we define the polynomial algebras $\mathbb{A}$, $\mathbb{A}_p$ and $\mathbb{A}_q$ as follows

$$\mathbb{A} := \{f_0(x) + f_1(x).i + f_2(x).j + f_3(x).k \mid f_0, f_1, f_2, f_3 \in \mathbb{Z}[x]/(x^N - 1)\}.$$
$$\mathbb{A}_p := \{f_0(x) + f_1(x).i + f_2(x).j + f_3(x).k \mid f_0, f_1, f_2, f_3 \in \mathbb{Z}_p[x]/(x^N - 1)\}.$$
$$\mathbb{A}_q := \{f_0(x) + f_1(x).i + f_2(x).j + f_3(x).k \mid f_0, f_1, f_2, f_3 \in \mathbb{Z}_q[x]/(x^N - 1)\}.$$

---

[1] Assuming $p = 3$, the best choice for q would be a prime number of the form $2^s \pm 1$.

One can easily conclude that $\mathbb{A}$, $\mathbb{A}_0$ and $\mathbb{A}_1$ are split algebras. In other words, $\mathbb{A}$, $\mathbb{A}_0$ and $\mathbb{A}_1$ algebras possess all characteristics of quaternion algebra, except that there are some nonzero elements whose norm is zero and naturally such elements do not have a multiplicative inverse. (See references [5] and [27] for an introduction to quaternion algebra.)

Note that for the sake of simplicity, from here on the arguments (x) have been dropped, i.e., we denote $\underset{\sim}{F} \in \mathbb{A}$ by $f_0 + f_1.i + f_2.j + f_3.k$ instead of $f_0(x) + f_1(x).i + f_2(x).j + f_3(x).k$. The symbol $\circ$ denotes the quaternionic multiplication and can be computed as follows

$$\underset{\sim}{F} \circ \underset{\sim}{G} = (f_0 + f_1.i + f_2.j + f_3.k) \circ (g_0 + g_1.i + g_2.j + g_3.k)$$

$$= (f_0 \star g_0 - f_1 \star g_1 - f_3 \star g_3 - f_2 \star g_2) + (f_0 \star g_1 + f_1 \star g_0 - f_3 \star g_2 + f_2 \star g_3).i \qquad (6)$$

$$+ (f_3 \star g_1 + f_2 \star g_0 + f_0 \star g_2 - f_1 \star g_3).j + (f_1 \star g_2 + f_0 \star g_3 - f_2 \star g_1 + f_3 \star g_0).k$$

where $\star$ denotes the convolution product. We denote the conjugate of a quaternion $\underset{\sim}{F} = (f_0 + f_1.i + f_2.j + f_3.k)$ by $\underset{\sim}{F}^* = (f_0 - f_1.i - f_2.j - f_3.k)$. Let the subsets $\mathcal{L}_f$, $\mathcal{L}_g$, $\mathcal{L}_m$ and $\mathcal{L}_\phi$ have the same definitions as defined in NTRU (i.e. the subsets of binary or ternary polynomials with some degree of sparseness determined by the public constant d). The QTRU cryptosystem can now be described as follows.

Key Generation. In order to generate a pair of public and private keys, two small quaternions $\underset{\sim}{F}$ and $\underset{\sim}{G}$ (i.e., quaternions with small norm) are randomly generated.

$$\underset{\sim}{F} = f_0 + f_1.i + f_2.j + f_3.k, \quad \text{such that} \quad f_0, f_1, f_2, f_3 \in \mathcal{L}_f \subset \mathbb{A},$$

$$\underset{\sim}{G} = g_0 + g_1.i + g_2.j + g_3.k, \quad \text{such that} \quad g_0, g_1, g_2, g_3 \in \mathcal{L}_g \subset \mathbb{A}.$$

The quaternion $\underset{\sim}{F}$ must be invertible in $\mathbb{A}_p$ and $\mathbb{A}_q$. The necessary and sufficient condition for $\underset{\sim}{F}$ to be invertible in $\mathbb{A}_p$ and $\mathbb{A}_q$ is that the polynomial $\left\| \underset{\sim}{F} \right\| = (f_0^2 + f_1^2 + f_2^2 + f_3^2)$ is invertible over the rings $\mathbb{Z}_p[x]/(x^N - 1)$ and $\mathbb{Z}_q[x]/(x^N - 1)$. The inverses (denoted by $\underset{\sim}{F}_p$ and $\underset{\sim}{F}_q$) will be computed as follows.

$$\underset{\sim}{F}_p := (f_0^2 + f_1^2 + f_2^2 + f_3^2)^{-1} \cdot \underset{\sim}{F}^* \triangleq \mu_0 + \mu_1.i + \mu_2.j + \mu_3.k,$$

$$\underset{\sim}{F}_q := (f_0^2 + f_1^2 + f_2^2 + f_3^2)^{-1} \cdot \underset{\sim}{F}^* \triangleq \eta_0 + \eta_1.i + \eta_2.j + \eta_3.k$$

Now, the public key, which is a quaternion, is computed as follows

$$\underset{\sim}{H} = \underset{\sim}{F}_q \circ \underset{\sim}{G} = (\eta_0 \star g_0 - \eta_1 \star g_1 - \eta_3 \star g_3 - \eta_2 \star g_2) + (\eta_0 \star g_1 + \eta_1 \star g_0 - \eta_3 \star g_2 + \eta_2 \star g_3).i +$$

$$(\eta_3 \star g_1 + \eta_2 \star g_0 + \eta_0 \star g_2 - \eta_1 \star g_3).j + (\eta_1 \star g_2 + \eta_0 \star g_3 - \eta_2 \star g_1 + \eta_3 \star g_0).k. \qquad (7)$$

The quaternions $\underset{\sim}{F}$, $\underset{\sim}{F}_p$ and $\underset{\sim}{F}_q$ will be kept secret in order to be used in the decryption phase.

Encryption. In the encryption process, the cryptosystem first generates a random quaternion $\underset{\sim}{\Phi}$. The plaintext must be converted into a quaternion $\underset{\sim}{M} \in \mathcal{L}_m$ including four small polynomials. The messages could be generated from the same or four different sources but transformed into one quaternion based on a simple and pre-determined encoding scheme. The ciphertext will be computed as follows

$$\underset{\sim}{E} = p.\underset{\sim}{H} \circ \underset{\sim}{\Phi} + \underset{\sim}{M} \in \mathbb{A}_q.$$

Decryption. In the first step, the received ciphertext $\underset{\sim}{E}$ is first multiplied by the private key $\underset{\sim}{F}$ on the left

$$\underset{\sim}{B} := \underset{\sim}{F} \circ \underset{\sim}{E} = \underset{\sim}{F} \circ (p.\underset{\sim}{H} \circ \underset{\sim}{\Phi} + \underset{\sim}{M}) \mod q$$

$$= (p.\underset{\sim}{F} \circ \underset{\sim}{F}_q \circ \underset{\sim}{G} \circ \underset{\sim}{\Phi} + \underset{\sim}{F} \circ \underset{\sim}{M}) \mod q$$

$$= (p.\underset{\sim}{G} \circ \underset{\sim}{\Phi} + \underset{\sim}{F} \circ \underset{\sim}{M}) \in \mathbb{Z}_q[x]/(x^N - 1).$$

The components of the resulting quaternions (including $4.N$ coefficients from the ground ring) must be reduced mod q into the interval $(-q/2, +q/2]$, i.e., $\Omega = \{-q/2 + 1, \cdots, +q/2\}$ is regarded as the set of representatives. Assuming that $\underset{\sim}{B} \in \mathbb{Z}_q[x]/(x^N - 1)$ is exactly equal to $p.\underset{\sim}{G} \circ \underset{\sim}{\Phi} + \underset{\sim}{F} \circ \underset{\sim}{M}$ in $\mathbb{A}$, when $\underset{\sim}{B}$ is reduced mod p, the term $p.\underset{\sim}{G} \circ \underset{\sim}{\Phi}$ vanishes and $\underset{\sim}{F} \circ \underset{\sim}{M}$ (mod p) remains. In order to extract the original message $\underset{\sim}{M}$, it will suffice to multiply $\underset{\sim}{F} \circ \underset{\sim}{M}$ (mod p) by $\underset{\sim}{F}_p$ on the left and adjust the resulting coefficients within the interval $\Lambda = [-p/2, +p/2]$.

In [18] using some simple calculations we have shown that in QTRU, the variance of the coefficients $p.\underset{\sim}{G} \circ \underset{\sim}{\Phi} + \underset{\sim}{F} \circ \underset{\sim}{M}$ increases by a factor of 4 (since 4 coefficients with the same distribution must be added in every quaternionic multiplication) and, hence, the probability for decryption failure increases. In return, constant parameters of the cryptosystem, including d_ϕ, d_g, d_f, q, and N, can be chosen in such a way that the decryption failure rate in QTRU remains equal to that of NTRU.

Although in totally equal circumstances (i.e., choosing the same parameters for both NTRU and QTRU cryptosystems), QTRU seems to be about four times slower than NTRU, one can partially compensate for the speed by reducing N and still obtain the same level of security. In addition, it can be optimized for efficiency based on the various methods proposed in [12].

In [18] we have shown that lattice attack on QTRU may be applied using two methods *Partial Lattice Attack* and *Full Quaternionic Lattice Attack* and both of the methods will not succeed in finding a short quaternion for full or partial recovery of the plaintext. Since the quaternions algebra may be regarded as an associative subalgebra of the octonions algebra, thus, QTRU may be regarded as a sub-cryptosystem of the OTRU that will be described in the following subsection. Thus, the lattice of QTRU may be considered as a sub-lattice of the OTRU lattice, analyzed in Section 5.

4.2   A NTRU-Like Cryptosystem Based on Non-associative Octonions Algebra

In this cryptosystem, called OTRU, the underlying ring in the NTRU scheme has been replaced by octonions non-associative algebra. Although this cryptosystem resembles to QTRU and NTRU with regard to key generation and encryption algorithm, however, the non-associativity of the cryptosystem algebraic structure improves the security.

We begin by assuming that the reader is fully familiar with the theoretical background of non-associative algebra and octonions. (See [2,5] for comprehensive introduction to the octonions.) Consider three public parameters (N, p, q) as well as four subsets $\mathcal{L}_f$, $\mathcal{L}_g$, $\mathcal{L}_m$ and $\mathcal{L}_\phi$ with definitions similar to QTRU or NTRU. Let us define the required polynomial algebras $\mathbb{A}$, $\mathbb{A}_p$ and $\mathbb{A}_q$ as follows.

$$\mathbb{A} := \{f_0(x) + \sum_{i=1}^{7} f_i(x).e_i \mid f_0(x), \cdots, f_7(x) \in \mathbb{Z}[x]/(x^N - 1)\}$$

$$\mathbb{A}_p := \{f_0(x) + \sum_{i=1}^{7} f_i(x).e_i \mid f_0(x), \cdots, f_7(x) \in \mathbb{Z}_p[x]/(x^N - 1)\} \quad (8)$$

$$\mathbb{A}_q := \{f_0(x) + \sum_{i=1}^{7} f_i(x).e_i \mid f_0(x), \cdots, f_7(x) \in \mathbb{Z}_q[x]/(x^N - 1)\}$$

Let $\underset{\sim}{F} := f_0(x)+f_1(x)e_1+f_2(x)e_2+f_3(x)e_3+f_4(x)e_4+f_5(x)e_5+f_6(x)e_6+f_7(x)e_7$ and $\underset{\sim}{G} := g_0(x) + g_1(x)e_1 + g_2(x)e_2 + g_3(x)e_3 + g_4(x)e_4 + g_5(x)e_5 + g_6(x)e_6 + g_7(x)e_7$ be two octonions in $\mathbb{A}$. The multiplication operation is defined in the following way (here again, for ease of notation, we omit the argument (x) when no ambiguity arises)

$$\begin{aligned}
\underset{\sim}{F} \circ \underset{\sim}{G} = &(f_0.g_0 - f_1.g_1 - f_2.g_2 - f_3.g_3 - f_4.g_4 - f_5.g_5 - f_6.g_6 - f_7.g_7) \\
&+ (f_0.g_1 + f_1.g_0 + f_2.g_4 + f_3.g_7 - f_4.g_2 + f_5.g_6 - f_6.g_5 - f_7.g_3).e_1 \\
&+ (f_0.g_2 - f_1.g_4 + f_2.g_0 + f_3.g_5 + f_4.g_1 - f_5.g_3 + f_6.g_7 - f_7.g_6).e_2 \\
&+ (f_0.g_3 - f_1.g_7 - f_2.g_5 + f_3.g_0 + f_4.g_6 + f_5.g_2 - f_6.g_4 + f_7.g_1).e_3 \\
&+ (f_0.g_4 + f_1.g_2 - f_2.g_1 - f_3.g_6 + f_4.g_0 + f_5.g_7 + f_6.g_3 - f_7.g_5).e_4 \\
&+ (f_0.g_5 - f_1.g_6 + f_2.g_3 - f_3.g_2 - f_4.g_7 + f_5.g_0 + f_6.g_1 + f_7.g_4).e_5 \\
&+ (f_0.g_6 + f_1.g_5 - f_2.g_7 + f_3.g_4 - f_4.g_3 - f_5.g_1 + f_6.g_0 + f_7.g_2).e_6 \\
&+ (f_0.g_7 + f_1.g_3 + f_2.g_6 - f_3.g_1 + f_4.g_5 - f_5.g_4 - f_6.g_2 + f_7.g_0).e_7
\end{aligned} \quad (9)$$

Note that in the algebras $\mathbb{A}$, $\mathbb{A}_p$ and $\mathbb{A}_q$, scalars are polynomials in the convolution polynomial rings $\mathbb{Z}[x]/(x^N - 1)$, $\mathbb{Z}_p[x]/(x^N - 1)$ and $\mathbb{Z}_q[x]/(x^N - 1)$ respectively, and the operations of addition, subtraction and multiplication will be performed over the underlying ring. Let denote the conjugate and inverse of an octonion $\underset{\sim}{F} = f_0 + \sum_{i=1}^{7} f_i(x).e_i$ by $\underset{\sim}{F}^* = f_0 - \sum_{i=1}^{7} f_i(x).e_i$ and $\underset{\sim}{F}^{-1} =$

$(\sum_{i=0}^{7} f_i^2(x))^{-1}.\underset{\sim}{F}^*$, respectively. Let us fix a set Ω of coset representatives in a way that every elements in $\mathbb{A}_q$ could be identified with a unique coset representative in $\mathbb{A}$. Also, let Λ be the set of representatives for every elements of $\mathbb{A}_p$ in $\mathbb{A}$. OTRU operates as described below.

Key Generation. Similar to QTRU, two small octonions $\underset{\sim}{F}$ and $\underset{\sim}{G}$ are randomly generated.

$$\underset{\sim}{F} := f_0 + f_1.e_1 + \cdots + f_7.e_7 \in \mathbb{A}, \qquad f_0, \cdots, f_7 \in \mathcal{L}_f \subset \mathbb{A}$$

$$\underset{\sim}{G} := g_0 + g_1.e_1 + \cdots + g_7.e_7 \in \mathbb{A}, \qquad g_0, \cdots, g_7 \in \mathcal{L}_g \subset \mathbb{A}$$

The octonion $\underset{\sim}{F}$ must be invertible over $\mathbb{A}_p$ and $\mathbb{A}_q$. If such an inverse does not exist (i.e., when $\sum_{i=0}^{7} f_i^2(x)$ is not a unit element in $\mathbb{Z}_p[x]/(x^N-1)$ or $\mathbb{Z}_q[x]/(x^N-1)$), a new octonion $\underset{\sim}{F}$ will be generated. The inverses of $\underset{\sim}{F}$ over the algebras $\mathbb{A}_p$ and $\mathbb{A}_q$ are denoted by $\underset{\sim}{F}_p^{-1}$ and $\underset{\sim}{F}_q^{-1}$. The public key, which is an octonion, is computed as follows

$$\underset{\sim}{H} = \underset{\sim}{F}_q^{-1} \circ \underset{\sim}{G} \in \mathbb{A}_q.$$

Encryption. Initially, a random octonion $\underset{\sim}{\Phi}$ is generated. The incoming data must be converted into an octonion including eight polynomial in $\mathcal{L}_\phi$. This can be performed according to a simple and predetermined convention. The ciphertext $\underset{\sim}{E}$ is then calculated as follows

$$\underset{\sim}{E} = p.\underset{\sim}{H} \circ \underset{\sim}{\Phi} + \underset{\sim}{M} \in \mathbb{A}_q.$$

Decryption. Since the octonions algebra is non-associative, not only the terms of $(\underset{\sim}{F}_q^{-1} \circ \underset{\sim}{G}) \circ \underset{\sim}{\Phi}$ do not commute, but also the parentheses order can not be changed, and this will reveal some problem during decryption, because one cannot simply remove the term $\underset{\sim}{F}_q^{-1}$ from $((\underset{\sim}{F}_q^{-1} \circ \underset{\sim}{G}) \circ \underset{\sim}{\Phi})$ by multiplying $\underset{\sim}{F}$ on the left. Thus, in order to decrypt, first of all, the received octonion $\underset{\sim}{E}$ is multiplied on the left by the private key $\underset{\sim}{F}$ and then on the right as follows

$$\underset{\sim}{B} := (\underset{\sim}{F} \circ \underset{\sim}{E}) \circ \underset{\sim}{F} \in \mathbb{A}_q$$

$$= (p.\underset{\sim}{F} \circ (\underset{\sim}{H} \circ \underset{\sim}{\Phi} + \underset{\sim}{M})) \circ \underset{\sim}{F} \in \mathbb{A}_q$$

$$= p.(\underset{\sim}{F} \circ (\underset{\sim}{H} \circ \underset{\sim}{\Phi})) \circ \underset{\sim}{F} + (\underset{\sim}{F} \circ \underset{\sim}{M}) \circ \underset{\sim}{F} \in \mathbb{A}_q$$

Based on the Moufang Identity (4) we can rearrange the parentheses as follows

$$= p.(\underset{\sim}{F} \circ \underset{\sim}{H}) \circ (\underset{\sim}{\Phi} \circ \underset{\sim}{F}) + (\underset{\sim}{F} \circ \underset{\sim}{M}) \circ \underset{\sim}{F} \in \mathbb{A}_q$$

$$= p.(\underset{\sim}{F} \circ (\underset{\sim}{F}_q^{-1} \circ \underset{\sim}{G})) \circ (\underset{\sim}{\Phi} \circ \underset{\sim}{F}) + (\underset{\sim}{F} \circ \underset{\sim}{M}) \circ \underset{\sim}{F} \in \mathbb{A}_q$$

$$= p.\underset{\sim}{G} \circ (\underset{\sim}{\Phi} \circ \underset{\sim}{F}) + (\underset{\sim}{F} \circ \underset{\sim}{M}) \circ \underset{\sim}{F} \in \mathbb{A}_q.$$

In the second step, $\underset{\sim}{B} \in \mathbb{A}_q$ should be identified with its equivalent representative in Ω and then, all the coefficients in the polynomials should be reduced mod p. Thus we have $(\underset{\sim}{B} \bmod p) = (\underset{\sim}{F} \circ \underset{\sim}{M}) \circ \underset{\sim}{F} \in \mathbb{A}_p$. In order to extract message $\underset{\sim}{M}$, simply multiply $\underset{\sim}{B}$ on the right by $\underset{\sim}{F}_p^{-1}$ and then repeat the same operation on the left and adjust the resulting coefficients in $[-p/2, +p/2]$.

The cost of encryption and decryption in OTRU. Let us assume that NTRU and OTRU work with public parameters $(N, q, p = 3, d = N/3)$(where $d := d_f = d_g = d_\phi$) and $(N', q', p' = 3, d' \approx N'/3)$, respectively. Thus, the public key size in NTRU is $\lceil N.\log_2 q \rceil$ bits and the key size in OTRU is $\lceil 8N'.\log_2 q' \rceil$. Also, in each encryption (decryption) round, NTRU encrypts (decrypts) $N.\log_2 p$ bits of plaintext, whereas in OTRU $8.N'.\log_2 p$ bits of data are encrypted (decrypted) in every round.

A single block encryption in NTRU takes approximately $2N^2/3$ steps (see [11][p. 396]) while in each ecryption round, OTRU needs to convolve 64 polynomials of length N' and consequently, the same operation in the proposed scheme takes about $64(2N'^2/3)$ steps (see Eqn. 9). Similarly, the decryption algorithm in (standard) NTRU takes $2(2N^2/3)$ steps while in OTRU it needs $256(2N'^2/3)$ steps (2 octonionic multiplication including 64 polynomial convolutions in the first and second phase of decryption).

The encryption process in OTRU compared with NTRU (with an equal dimension) is almost eight times slower than NTRU (since in OTRU, 8 data vectors are encrypted simultaneously) and its decryption process runs almost 16 times slower. On the other hand, considering that the complexity of the convolution multiplication is $\mathcal{O}(N^2)$, the reduction of N with the power of two affects the speed of the calculations. Therefore, the NTRU cryptosystem with a dimension of $8.N$ is almost 64 times slower than NTRU with a dimension of N. Hence, we claim that with the reduction of N within a reasonable range (see Section 5), one can compensate for the decrease of the speed of OTRU in such a way that a higher security is achieved. In addition, there are multiple parallelism levels in OTRU that can be exploited to improve encryption and decryption speed.

Now, let us turn our attention to the security of OTRU against lattice attack.

5 Security Analysis of the Proposed Non-associative Cryptosystem against Lattice Attack

In this section in order to have a more rigorous security analysis, we show that the security of the OTRU cryptosystems relies on the intractability of shortest vector problem (SVP) in a certain type of lattice. The octonions do not have a matrix isomorphic representation and consequently, for finding a small norm octonion satisfying $\underset{\sim}{F} \circ \underset{\sim}{H} = \underset{\sim}{G}$ (mod q), one cannot form an octonionic lattice by building a matrix with octonionic entries and use a lattice reduction algorithm to find an octonions with any desired norm. Since the public key in the proposed scheme is in the form $\underset{\sim}{H} = \underset{\sim}{F}_q^{-1} \circ \underset{\sim}{G} \in \mathbb{A}_q$, the only way which remains for attacking this special scheme and finding a suitable key for decryption is to expand $\underset{\sim}{F} \circ \underset{\sim}{H} = \underset{\sim}{G}$ (mod q) as a system of linear equations and form a lattice of dimension $16.N$. In the following proposition we prove that the security of the proposed scheme relies on the intractability of the SVP in a certain type of lattice.

Proposition 1. *Given the octonion $\underset{\sim}{H} \in \mathbb{A}_q$ and assuming that the octonionic equation $\underset{\sim}{F} \circ \underset{\sim}{H} = \underset{\sim}{G}$ has at least a pair of solutions $\langle \underset{\sim}{F}, \underset{\sim}{G} \rangle$ in $\mathbb{A}_q$, then*

(a) the set of all pairs of solutions (which are not all distinct), forms the integer lattice $\mathcal{L}_{\mathcal{H}} :=$ Row Span $\begin{bmatrix} I_{8N \times 8N} & \mathcal{H}(\underset{\sim}{H}) \\ & 8N \times 8N \\ 0 & q.I_{8N \times 8N} \\ 8N \times 8N & \end{bmatrix}$ of determinant $q^{8.N}$

and dimension $16.N$ in $\mathbb{Z}^{16N}$.

(b) Let $\left\| \underset{\sim}{F} \right\|_2 \leqslant \lambda$ and $\left\| \underset{\sim}{G} \right\|_2 \leqslant \lambda$. If $\lambda < \sqrt{\frac{8N.q}{\pi e}}$, then with a probability greater than $1 - \frac{\lambda}{2\sqrt{\frac{N.q}{\pi e}}}$, finding $\langle \underset{\sim}{F}, \underset{\sim}{G} \rangle$ will be transformed into an SVP in the lattice $\mathcal{L}_{\mathcal{H}}$.

Proof. (a) Let $\underset{\sim}{F} := \langle f_0(x), \cdots, f_7(x) \rangle \in \mathbb{A}_q$ and $\underset{\sim}{G} := \langle g_0(x), \cdots, g_7(x) \rangle \in \mathbb{A}_q$ be a pair of solutions for the octonionic equation $\underset{\sim}{F} \circ \underset{\sim}{H} = \underset{\sim}{G}$. Let expand $\underset{\sim}{F} \circ \underset{\sim}{H} = \underset{\sim}{G}$ as a system of linear equations as follows

$$\begin{cases} \sum_{s+t \overset{N}{\equiv} k} f_{0,s}.h_{0,t} - \sum_{s+t \overset{N}{\equiv} k} f_{1,s}.h_{1,t} - \ldots - \sum_{s+t \overset{N}{\equiv} k} f_{7,s}.h_{7,t} = g_{0,k} + qk_{0,k} \\ \sum_{s+t \overset{N}{\equiv} k} f_{0,s}.h_{1,t} + \sum_{s+t \overset{N}{\equiv} k} f_{1,s}.h_{0,t} + \ldots - \sum_{s+t \overset{N}{\equiv} k} f_{7,s}.h_{3,t} = g_{1,k} + qk_{1,k} \\ \vdots \\ \sum_{s+t \overset{N}{\equiv} k} f_{0,s}.h_{7,t} + \sum_{s+t \overset{N}{\equiv} k} f_{1,s}.h_{3,t} + \ldots + \sum_{s+t \overset{N}{\equiv} k} f_{7,s}.h_{0,t} = g_{7,k} + qk_{7,k} \end{cases} \quad (10)$$

Let represent the polynomials $h_0, h_1, \ldots, h_7 \in \mathbb{Z}[x]/(x^N - 1)$ in their circulant matrix isomorphic representation as follows

$$(\mathcal{H}_i)_{N \times N} \overset{\triangle}{=} \begin{bmatrix} h_{i,0} & h_{i,1} & h_{i,2} & \cdots & h_{i,N-1} \\ h_{i,N-1} & h_{i,0} & h_{i,1} & & h_{i,N-2} \\ h_{i,N-2} & h_{i,N-1} & h_{i,0} & & h_{i,N-3} \\ \vdots & & & \ddots & \vdots \\ h_{i,2} & h_{i,3} & & & \\ h_{i,1} & h_{i,2} & & \cdots & h_{i,0} \end{bmatrix}, \quad i = 0, 1, \cdots, 7. \quad (11)$$

where $h_i(x) = \sum_{j=0}^{N-1} h_{i,j}.x^i \overset{\triangle}{=} [h_{i,0}, h_{i,1}, \ldots, h_{i,N-1}]$.

Based upon the above notations, we can form the lattice $\mathcal{L}_{\mathcal{H}}$ of dimension $16.N$ spanned by the rows of the following matrix

$$
\mathcal{M}_{\mathcal{H}} := \left[
\begin{array}{cccc|cccccccc}
1\,0 & \cdots & & 0 & +\mathcal{H}_0 & +\mathcal{H}_1 & +\mathcal{H}_2 & +\mathcal{H}_3 & +\mathcal{H}_4 & +\mathcal{H}_5 & +\mathcal{H}_6 & +\mathcal{H}_7 \\
0\,1 & & & \cdot & -\mathcal{H}_1 & +\mathcal{H}_0 & -\mathcal{H}_4 & -\mathcal{H}_7 & +\mathcal{H}_2 & -\mathcal{H}_6 & +\mathcal{H}_5 & +\mathcal{H}_3 \\
\cdot\, & & & \cdot & -\mathcal{H}_2 & +\mathcal{H}_4 & +\mathcal{H}_0 & -\mathcal{H}_5 & -\mathcal{H}_1 & +\mathcal{H}_3 & -\mathcal{H}_7 & +\mathcal{H}_6 \\
\cdot\, & & & \cdot & -\mathcal{H}_3 & +\mathcal{H}_7 & +\mathcal{H}_5 & +\mathcal{H}_0 & -\mathcal{H}_6 & -\mathcal{H}_2 & +\mathcal{H}_4 & -\mathcal{H}_1 \\
\cdot\, & & & \cdot & -\mathcal{H}_4 & -\mathcal{H}_2 & +\mathcal{H}_1 & +\mathcal{H}_6 & +\mathcal{H}_0 & -\mathcal{H}_7 & -\mathcal{H}_3 & +\mathcal{H}_5 \\
\cdot\, & & \cdot & & -\mathcal{H}_5 & +\mathcal{H}_6 & -\mathcal{H}_3 & +\mathcal{H}_2 & +\mathcal{H}_7 & +\mathcal{H}_0 & -\mathcal{H}_1 & -\mathcal{H}_4 \\
\cdot\, & & 1\,0 & & -\mathcal{H}_6 & -\mathcal{H}_5 & +\mathcal{H}_7 & -\mathcal{H}_4 & +\mathcal{H}_3 & +\mathcal{H}_1 & +\mathcal{H}_0 & -\mathcal{H}_2 \\
0 & \cdots & 0\,0\,1 & & -\mathcal{H}_7 & -\mathcal{H}_3 & -\mathcal{H}_6 & +\mathcal{H}_1 & -\mathcal{H}_5 & +\mathcal{H}_4 & +\mathcal{H}_2 & +\mathcal{H}_0 \\
\hline
0\,0 & \cdots & & 0 & q & 0 & \cdot & \cdot & \cdot & \cdot & & 0 \\
0\,0 & & \cdot & & 0 & q & & & & & & \cdot \\
\cdot\, & & \cdot & & & & q & & & & & \\
\cdot\, & & \cdot & & & & & \ddots & & & & \\
\cdot\, & & \cdot & & & & & & & & & \\
\cdot\, & 0 & \cdot & & \cdot & & & & & q & 0 \\
0 & \cdots & & 0 & 0 & & \cdot & \cdot & \cdot & \cdot & 0 & q
\end{array}
\right]
\tag{12}
$$

As we can see from the system of linear equations (10) and the matrix $\mathcal{M}_{\mathcal{H}}$, it is clear that the vector $\langle f_0, f_1, \cdots, f_7, g_0, g_1, \cdots, g_7 \rangle_{1 \times 16.N}$ is in the lattice $\mathcal{L}_{\mathcal{H}}$, because we can get this vector as a $\mathbb{Z}$-linear combination of the rows of $\mathcal{M}_{\mathcal{H}}$ as follows

$$
\underbrace{\langle f_{0,0}, f_{0,1}, \dots, f_{0,N-1}}_{\langle f_0 \rangle}, \dots, \underbrace{f_{7,0}, f_{7,1}, \dots, f_{7,N-1}}_{\langle f_7 \rangle}, \underbrace{-k_{0,0}, \dots, -k_{0,N-1}}_{\langle k_0 \rangle}, \dots, \underbrace{-k_{7,0}, \dots, -k_{7,N-1}}_{\langle k_7 \rangle} \rangle_{1 \times 16.N} \cdot \mathcal{M}_h =
$$

$$
\underbrace{\langle f_{0,0}, f_{0,1}, \dots, f_{0,N-1}}_{\langle f_0 \rangle}, \dots, \underbrace{f_{7,0}, f_{7,1}, \dots, f_{7,N-1}}_{\langle f_7 \rangle}, \underbrace{g_{0,0}, g_{0,1}, \dots, g_{0,N-1}}_{\langle g_0 \rangle}, \dots, \underbrace{g_{7,0}, g_{7,1}, \dots, g_{7,N-1}}_{\langle g_7 \rangle} \rangle_{1 \times 16.N}
$$

Thus we have $\langle f_0, f_1, \cdots, f_7, g_0, g_1, \cdots, g_7 \rangle_{1 \times 16.N} \in \mathcal{L}_{\mathcal{H}}$.

(b) Since $\left\| \underset{\sim}{F} \right\|_2, \left\| \underset{\sim}{G} \right\|_2 \leqslant \lambda$, it is clear that $\| \langle f_0, f_1, \dots, f_7, g_0, g_1, \dots, g_7 \rangle \|_2 \leqslant \sqrt{2}\lambda$. Based on the Gaussian heuristic, the average length of the shortest nonzero vector in $\mathcal{L}_{\mathcal{H}}$ is

$$
\mathrm{E}\{\|v_{\text{Shortest}}\|\} = \sqrt{\frac{n}{2\pi e}} \cdot \det(\mathcal{L}_{\mathcal{H}})^{\frac{1}{n}} = \sqrt{\frac{16N}{2\pi e}} \cdot (q^{8N})^{\frac{1}{16N}} = \sqrt{\frac{8N.q}{\pi e}}. \tag{13}
$$

Hence, if we have $\| \langle f_0, f_1, \dots, f_7, g_0, g_1, \dots, g_7 \rangle \|_2 \ll \sqrt{\frac{8N.q}{\pi e}}$, then based on the Markov inequality (which states that $\Pr\{Y > \alpha E[Y]\} < \frac{1}{\alpha}$) the vector $\langle f_0, f_1, \cdots, f_7, g_0, g_1, \cdots, g_7 \rangle_{1 \times 16.N}$ will be one of the shortest vector in $\mathcal{L}_{\mathcal{H}}$ with a probability greater than $1 - \frac{\sqrt{2}\lambda}{\sqrt{\frac{8N.q}{\pi e}}} = 1 - \frac{\lambda}{2\sqrt{\frac{N.q}{\pi e}}}$. Consequently, finding a solution to the octonionic equation $\underset{\sim}{F} \circ \underset{\sim}{H} = \underset{\sim}{G}$ such that $\left\| \underset{\sim}{F} \right\|_2, \left\| \underset{\sim}{G} \right\|_2 \leqslant \sqrt{\frac{8N.q}{\pi e}}$, is transformed into an SVP in the lattice $\mathcal{L}_{\mathcal{H}}$ of dimension $16.N$ and determinant $Det(\mathcal{L}_{\mathcal{H}}) = q^{8.N}$. $\qquad\square$

It is clear that the pair of private keys $\langle f_0, f_1, \cdots, f_7, g_0, g_1, \cdots, g_7 \rangle_{1 \times 16.N}$ is in $\mathcal{L}_{\mathcal{H}}$ and finding a short vector in this lattice may be used as the decryption key. As in NTRU, assuming that $d \approx N/3$, we can estimate that the length of the decryption key is about $\lambda = \|\langle f_0, f_1, \cdots, f_7 \rangle\| = \|\langle g_0, g_1, \cdots, g_7 \rangle\| \approx \sqrt{16.d} \approx 2.3\sqrt{N}$. Thus, based on the above proposition, the target vectors in $\mathcal{L}_{\mathcal{H}}$ are about $\mathcal{O}(\sqrt{q})$ shorter than the Gaussian expected shortest length and with a probability greater than $1 - \frac{2.3\sqrt{N}}{2\sqrt{\frac{N.q}{\pi e}}} \approx 1 - \frac{3.36}{\sqrt{q}}$, the problem of finding a decryption (spurious) key for the proposed scheme is equal to solving SVP to within a factor of approximately $\sqrt{q}$, which is believed to be intractable for a lattice of dimension greater than 334 (2×167) [13,28].

Let us sum up this section with the following argument: Assuming the average Hermite factor $(1.01)^n$ for the best lattice reduction algorithm [9,24,22] and given the octonion $\underset{\sim}{H} \in \mathbb{A}_q$, solving the octonionic equation $\underset{\sim}{F} \circ \underset{\sim}{H} = \underset{\sim}{G}$ over the algebra $\mathbb{A}$ and finding a spurious key for OTRU, is intractable for $N > 21$ ($16N > 334$). We argue that because the OTRU lattice is not completely convolutional, the open problems and doubts which exist with respect to the exceptional structure of the NTRU lattice [8] are not there in the case and we believe that the Hermite factor $(1.01)^n$ could not be achieved with the existing lattice reduction algorithms.

6 Conclusion

In this paper we have focused on the fact that the underlying algebra of the NTRU public key cryptosystem is not limited to Dedekind domains and can be extended to the non-commutative quaternions algebra as well as non-associative octonions algebra. For this purpose, by introducing two cryptosystems (which have been simulated and implemented by the authors) we have shown that using non-commutativity and non-associativity in a lattice-based cryptosystem is not only possible but also if we design a non-associative public key cryptosystem exactly identical to the NTRU scheme, it will remain both secure and efficient.

The first cryptosystem, QTRU, works based on quaternions and the second one, OTRU, is constructed based on the octonions algebra which is a non-associative but alternative algebra. The proposed cryptosystems may be regarded as multi-dimensional probabilistic public key cryptosystems over $\mathbb{Z}$ which encrypts four/eight data vectors in parallel.

We have analyzed the security of the proposed non-associative public key cryptosystem against lattice attack. We believe that the proposed cryptosystems (specially OTRU) could be more secure than NTRU, because its lattice structure does not completely fit into the category of Convolutional Modular Lattices. We claim that the proposed cryptosystem is the first functional cryptosystem with a non-associative algebra that its security relies on the intractability of the shortest vector problem (SVP) in a special type of lattice.

7   Future Works

We would like to emphasize that in order to take full advantage of the non-associativity in the octonions algebra, it is not necessary to follow the encryption/decryption scheme used in OTRU. We are working on a different non-linear scheme for a public key cryptosystem based on non-associative algebra which is different from the NTRU scheme. If we use a different non-linear scheme other than proposed for NTRU or OTRU, a public key cryptosystem will emerged which will be hard to break using lattice attack techniques; an idea which may result in more fruitful research in secure public key cryptosystem studies.

Acknowledgment

The authors would like to thank the Iran Telecommunications Research Center for its support of this project. Furthermore, we are sincerely grateful for the generous guidance of Professor Hossein Hajiabolhassan, Faculty of Mathematics at Shahid Beheshti University. We also thank the anonymous reviewers for their detailed and helpful comments.

References

1. Ajtai, M.: The shortest vector problem in L2 is NP-hard for randomized reductions. In: Proceedings of the Thirtieth Annual ACM Symposium on Theory of Computing, STOC 1998, pp. 10–19. ACM, New York (1998)
2. Baez, J.C.: The octonions. Bulletin of the American Mathematical Society 39, 145 (2002)
3. Bailey, D.V., Coffin, D., Elbirt, A., Silverman, J.H., Woodbury, A.D.: NTRU in constrained devices. In: Koç, Ç.K., Naccache, D., Paar, C. (eds.) CHES 2001. LNCS, vol. 2162, pp. 262–272. Springer, Heidelberg (2001)
4. Coglianese, M., Goi, B.M.: MaTRU: A new NTRU-based cryptosystem. In: Maitra, S., Veni Madhavan, C.E., Venkatesan, R. (eds.) INDOCRYPT 2005. LNCS, vol. 3797, pp. 232–243. Springer, Heidelberg (2005)
5. Conway, J.H., Smith, D.A.: On Quaternions and Octonions: Their Geometry, Arithmetic, and Symmetry. A. K. Peters, Ltd., Wellesley (2003)
6. Coppersmith, D., Shamir, A.: Lattice attacks on NTRU. In: Fumy, W. (ed.) EUROCRYPT 1997. LNCS, vol. 1233, pp. 52–61. Springer, Heidelberg (1997)
7. Gaborit, P., Ohler, J., Solé, P.: CTRU, a polynomial analogue of NTRU. Tech. rep., INRIA (2002),
   ftp://ftp.inria.fr/INRIA/publication/publi-pdf/RR/RR-4621.pdf
8. Gama, N., Howgrave-Graham, N., Nguyen, P.Q.: Symplectic lattice reduction and ntru. In: Vaudenay, S. (ed.) EUROCRYPT 2006. LNCS, vol. 4004, pp. 233–253. Springer, Heidelberg (2006)
9. Gama, N., Nguyen, P.Q.: Predicting lattice reduction. In: Smart, N.P. (ed.) EUROCRYPT 2008. LNCS, vol. 4965, pp. 31–51. Springer, Heidelberg (2008)
10. Hoffstein, J., Pipher, J., Silverman, J.H.: NTRU: A ring-based public key cryptosystem. In: Buhler, J.P. (ed.) ANTS 1998. LNCS, vol. 1423, pp. 267–288. Springer, Heidelberg (1998)

11. Hoffstein, J., Pipher, J., Silverman, J.H.: An Introduction to Mathematical Cryptography. Springer, Heidelberg (2008)
12. Hoffstein, J., Silverman, J.: Optimizations for NTRU. In: Public Key Cryptography and Computational Number Theory, pp. 11–15 (2000)
13. Hoffstein, J., Silverman, J.H., Whyte, W.: On estimating the lattice security of NTRU (2005)
14. IEEE P1363: Standard Specifications for Public-Key Cryptographic Techniques Based on Hard Problems over Lattices (December 2008), http://grouper.ieee.org/groups/1363/
15. Kaps, J.P.: Cryptography for Ultra-Low Power Devices. Ph.d. dissertation, ECE Department, Worcester Polytechnic Institute, Worcester, Massachusetts, USA (May 2006)
16. Karimianpour, C.: Lattice-Based Cryptosystems. Master's thesis, Ottawa, Canada (2007)
17. Kouzmenko, R.: Generalizations of the NTRU Cryptosystem. Master's thesis, Polytechnique, Montreal, Canada (2006)
18. Malekian, E., Zakerolhosseini, A., Mashatan, A.: QTRU: A lattice attack resistant version of NTRU PKCS. Cryptology ePrint Archive, Report 2009/330, submitted for publication (2009), http://eprint.iacr.org/
19. May, A.: Cryptanalysis of NTRU (1999) (unpublished paper)
20. Micciancio, D.: The shortest vector problem is NP-hard to approximate to within some constant. SIAM Journal on Computing 30(6), 2008–2035 (2001); preliminary version in FOCS 1998
21. Micciancio, D., Goldwasser, S.: Complexity of Lattice Problems: a cryptographic perspective. The Kluwer International Series in Engineering and Computer Science, vol. 671. Kluwer Academic Publishers, Boston (2002)
22. Schneider, M., Johannes Buchmann, R.L.: Probabilistic analysis of LLL reduced bases. In: Algorithms and Number Theory. Dagstuhl Seminar Proceedings (2009)
23. Nevins, M., Karimianpour, C., Miri, A.: NTRU over rings beyond Z. Accepted to Designs, Codes and Cryptography (May 2009)
24. Nguyen, P.Q., Stehlé, D.: LLL on the average. In: Hess, F., Pauli, S., Pohst, M. (eds.) ANTS 2006. LNCS, vol. 4076, pp. 238–256. Springer, Heidelberg (2006)
25. Rotman, J.J.: Advanced Modern Algebra. Prentice Hall, Englewood Cliffs (2002)
26. Schafer, R.D.: An introduction to non-associative algebras. Dover Publications Inc., New York (1996); corrected reprint of the 1966 original
27. Sham, Z.Y.: Quaternion Algebras and Quadratic Forms. Master's thesis, Waterloo, Ontario, Canada (2008)
28. Silverman, J.H.: Dimension-reduced lattices, zero-forced lattices, and the NTRU public key cryptosystem (1999)

Identity-Based Key Exchange Protocols without Pairings[*]

Dario Fiore[1],[**] and Rosario Gennaro[2]

[1] École Normale Supérieure, CNRS - INRIA, Paris
dario.fiore@ens.fr
[2] IBM T.J. Watson Research Center – Hawthorne, New York 10532
rosario@us.ibm.com

Abstract. This paper presents a new identity based key agreement protocol. In id-based cryptography (introduced by Adi Shamir in [34]) each party uses its own identity as public key and receives his secret key from a master Key Generation Center, whose public parameters are publicly known.

The novelty of our protocol is that it can be implemented over any cyclic group of prime order, where the Diffie-Hellman problem is supposed to be hard. It does not require the computation of expensive bilinear maps, or additional assumptions such as factoring or RSA.

The protocol is extremely efficient, requiring only twice the amount of bandwidth and computation of the *unauthenticated* basic Diffie-Hellman protocol. The design of our protocol was inspired by MQV (the most efficient authenticated Diffie-Hellman based protocol in the public-key model) and indeed its performance is competitive with respect to MQV (especially when one includes the transmission and verification of certificates in the MQV protocol, which are not required in an id-based scheme). Our protocol requires a single round of communication in which each party sends only 2 group elements: a very short message, especially when the protocol is implemented over elliptic curves.

We provide a full proof of security in the Canetti-Krawczyk security model for key exchange, including a proof that our protocol satisfies additional security properties such as forward secrecy, and resistance to reflection and key-compromise impersonation attacks.

1 Introduction

Identity-based cryptography was introduced in 1984 by Adi Shamir [34]. The goal was to simplify the management of public keys and in particular the association of a public key to the identity of its holder. Usually such binding of a public key to an identity is achieved by means of *certificates* which are signed statements by trusted third parties that a given public key belongs to a user. This requires users

---

[*] An extended abstract of this paper appears in the proceedings of CT-RSA 2010 [18].
[**] Part of this work have been done while student at University of Catania and visiting NYU and IBM Research.

M.L. Gavrilova et al. (Eds.): Trans. on Comput. Sci. X, LNCS 6340, pp. 42–77, 2010.

to obtain and verify certificates whenever they want to use a specific public key, and the management of public key certificates remains a technically challenging problem.

Shamir's idea was to allow parties to use their identities as public keys. An id-based scheme works as follows. A trusted *Key Generation Center* (KGC) generates a master public/secret key pair, which is known to all the users. A user with identity ID receives from the KGC a secret key S_{ID} which is a function of the string ID and the KGC's secret key (one can think of S_{ID} as a signature by the KGC on the string ID). Using S_{ID} the user can then perform cryptographic tasks. For example in the case of *id-based encryption* any party can send an encrypted message to the user with identity ID using the string ID as a public key and the user (and only the user and the KGC) will be able to decrypt it using S_{ID}. Note that the sender can do this even if the recipient has not obtained yet his secret key from the KGC. All the sender needs to know is the recipient's identity and the public parameters of the KGC. This is the major advantage of id-based encryption.

ID-BASED KEY AGREEMENT AND ITS MOTIVATIONS. This paper is concerned with the task of *id-based key agreement*. Here two parties Alice and Bob, with identities A, B and secret keys S_A, S_B respectively, want to agree on a common shared key, in an *authenticated* manner (i.e. Alice must be sure that once the key is established, only Bob knows it – and viceversa). Since key agreement is inherently an interactive protocol (both parties are "live" and ready to establish a session) there is a smaller gain in using an id-based solution: indeed certificates and public keys can be easily sent as part of the protocol communication.

Yet the ability to avoid sending and verifying public key certificates is a significant practical advantage (see e.g. [37]). Indeed known shortcomings of the public key setting are the requirement of centralized certification authorities, the need for parties to cross-certify each other (via possibly long certificate chains), and the management of some form of large-scale coordination and communication (possibly on-line) to propagate certificate revocation information. Identity-based schemes significantly simplify identity management by bypassing the certification issues. All a party needs to know in order to generate a shared key is its own secret key, the public information of the KGC, and the identity of the communication peer (clearly, the need to know the peer's identity exists in any scheme including a certificate-based one).

Another advantage of identity-based systems is the versatility with which identities may be chosen. Since identities can be arbitrary string, they can be selected according to the function and attributes of the parties (rather than its actual "name"). For example in vehicular networks a party may be identified by its location ("the checkpoint at the intersection of a and b") or in military applications a party can be identified by its role ("platoon x commander"). This allows parties to communicate securely with the intended recipient even without knowing its "true" identity but simply by the definition of its function in the network.

Finally, identities can also include additional attributes which are temporal in nature: in particular an "expiration date" for an identity makes revocation of the corresponding secret key much easier to achieve.

For the reasons described above, id-based KA protocols are very useful in many systems where bandwidth and computation are at a premium (e.g. sensor networks), and also in ad-hoc networks where large scale coordination is undesirable, if not outright impossible. Therefore it is an important question to come up with very efficient and secure id-based KA protocols.

PREVIOUS WORK ON ID-BASED KEY AGREEMENT. Following Shamir's proposal of the concept of id-based cryptography, some early proposals for id-based key agreement appeared in the literature: we refer in particular to the works of Okamoto [29] (later improved in [30]) and Gunther [22]. A new impetus to this research area came with the breakthrough discovery of bilinear maps and their application to id-based encryption in [5]: starting with the work of Sakai et al. [33] a large number of id-based KA protocols were designed that use pairings as tool. We refer the readers to [6] and [12] for surveys of these pairing-based protocols.

The main problem with the current state of the art is that many of these protocols lack a proof of security, and some have even been broken. Indeed only a few (e.g., [8, 38]) have been proven according to a formal definition of security.

OUR CONTRIBUTION. By looking at prior work we see that provably secure id-based KAs require either groups that admit bilinear maps [8, 38], or to work over a composite RSA modulus [30].

This motivated us to ask the following question: can we find an efficient and provably secure id-based KA protocol such that:

1. it that can be implemented over *any* cyclic group in which the Diffie-Hellman problem is supposed to be hard. The advantages of such a KA protocol would be several, in particular: (i) it would avoid the use of computationally expensive pairing computations; (ii) it could be implemented over much smaller groups (since we could use 'regular' elliptic curves, rather than the ones that admit efficient pairings computations for high security levels, or the group Z_N^* for a composite N needed for Okamoto-Tanaka).

2. it is more efficient than any KA protocols in the public key model (such as MQV [27]), when one includes the transmission and verification of certificates which are not required in an id-based scheme. This is a very important point since, as we pointed out earlier in this Section, id-based KA protocols are only relevant if they outperform PKI based ones in efficiency.

Our new protocol presented in this paper (whose description appears in Figure 1), achieves all these features.

It can be implemented over any cyclic group over which the Diffie-Hellman problem is assumed to be hard. In addition it requires an amount of bandwidth and computation similar to the *unauthenticated* basic Diffie-Hellman protocol. Indeed our new protocol requires a single round of communication in which each party sends just two group elements (as opposed to one in the Diffie-Hellman

---

The IB-KA Protocol

Setting: A Key Generation Center (KGC) chooses a group $\mathbb{G}$ of prime order q together with a random generator $g \in \mathbb{G}$ and an exponent $x \xleftarrow{\$} \mathbb{Z}_q$. KGC publishes $\mathbb{G}, q, g, y = g^x$ and two hash functions H_1, H_2.

Key Derivation: A user with identity U receives its private key (r_U, s_U) from the KGC computed as the Schnorr's signature of the string U under public key y. That is $r_U = g^{k_U}$ for $k_U \xleftarrow{\$} \mathbb{Z}_q$ and $s_U = k_U + xH_1(U, r_U) \bmod q$.

Key agreement: A and B choose ephemeral private exponents t_A and t_B, respectively.

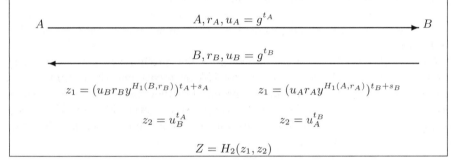

Fig. 1. A and B share session key Z. See Section 3 for more specific details.

protocol). Each party must compute four exponentiations to compute the session key (as opposed to two in the Diffie-Hellman protocol).

A similar favorable comparison holds with the Okamoto-Tanaka protocol in [30]. While that protocol requires only two exponentiations, it does works over Z_N^* therefore requiring the use of a larger group size, which almost totally absorbs the computational advantage, and immediately implies a much larger bandwidth requirement. Detailed efficiency comparisons to other protocols in the literature are discussed in Section 6.

We present a full proof of security of our protocol in the Canetti-Krawczyk security model. Our results hold in the random oracle model, under the Strong Diffie-Hellman Assumption. We also present some variations of our protocol that can be proven secure under the basic Computational Diffie-Hellman Assumption. Our protocol can be proven to satisfy additional desirable security properties such as perfect forward secrecy[1], and resistance to reflection and key-compromise impersonation attacks.

---

[1] We can prove PFS only in the case the adversary was passive in the session that he is attacking – though he can be active in other sessions. As proven by Krawczyk in [26], this is the best that can be achieved for 1-round protocols with *implicit* authentication, such as ours.

OUR APPROACH. The first direction we took in our approach was to attempt to analyze the id-based KA protocols by Gunther [22] and Saeednia [32]. They also work over any cyclic group where the Diffie-Hellman problem is assumed to be hard, but their protocols lack a formal proof of security. While the original protocols cannot be shown to be secure, we were able to prove the security of modified versions of them. Nevertheless these two protocols were not very satisfactory solutions for the problem we had set out to solve, particularly for reasons of efficiency since they required a large number of exponentiations, which made them less efficient than say MQV with certificates.

Our protocol improves over these two protocols by using Schnorr's signatures [35], rather than ElGamal, to issue secret keys to the users. The simpler structure of Schnorr's signatures permits a much more efficient computation of the session key, resulting in less exponentiations and a single round protocol. Our approach was inspired by the way the MQV protocol [27] achieves *implicit authentication* of the session key. Indeed our protocol can be seen as an id-based version of the MQV protocol.

ORGANIZATION. In Section 2 we recall a few preliminary notions, such as the Canetti-Krawczyk security model for KA protocols, and the computational assumptions that we will use in our proofs. Our new protocol is described in Section 3, and its proof in Section 4. Comparison to other id-based KA protocols is in Section 6. The modifications and proofs of the Gunther and Saeednia protocols are in Section 7.

2   Preliminaries

In this section we present some standard definitions needed in the rest of the paper.

Let $\mathbb{N}$ the set of natural numbers. We will denote with $\ell \in \mathbb{N}$ the security parameter. The participants to our protocols are modeled as probabilistic Turing machines whose running time is bounded by some polynomial in ℓ. If S is a set, we denote with $s \xleftarrow{\$} S$ the process of selecting an element uniformly at random from S.

Definition 1 (Negligible function). *A function $\epsilon(\ell)$ is said to be negligible if for every polynomial $p(\ell)$ there exists a positive integer $c \in \mathbb{N}$ such that $\forall \ell > c$ we have $\epsilon(\ell) < 1/p(\ell)$.*

In the following assume $\mathbb{G}$ to be a cyclic multiplicative group of order q where q is a ℓ-bit long prime. We assume that there are efficient algorithms to perform multiplication and membership test in $\mathbb{G}$. Finally we denote with g a generator of $\mathbb{G}$.

Assumption 1 (Computational Diffie-Hellman [16]). *We say that the Computational Diffie-Hellman (CDH) Assumption (for $\mathbb{G}$ and g) holds if for any probabilistic polynomial time adversary $\mathcal{A}$ the probability that $\mathcal{A}$ on input $(\mathbb{G}, g, g^u, g^v)$ outputs W such that $W = g^{uv}$ is negligible in ℓ. The probability of* *success of $\mathcal{A}$ is taken over the uniform random choice of $u, v \in \mathbb{Z}_q$ and the coin tosses of $\mathcal{A}$.*

The CDH Assumption has a *Decisional* version in which no adversary can actually *recognize* the value g^{uv} when given g^u, g^v. In the proof of our basic protocol we are going to need the ability to perform such decisions when one of the two elements is fixed, while still assuming that the CDH holds. The assumption below basically says that the CDH Assumption still holds in the presence of an oracle $\mathsf{DH}(U, \cdot, \cdot)$ that solves the decisional problem[2] for a fixed U.

Assumption 2 (Strong-DH Assumption [1]). *We say that the Strong-DH (SDH) Assumption holds (for $\mathbb{G}$ and g) if the CDH Assumption holds even in the presence of an oracle $\mathsf{DH}(U, \cdot, \cdot)$ that on input two elements $\hat{V}, \hat{W}$ in the group generated by g, output "yes" if and only if $\hat{W}$ is the Diffie-Hellman of U and $\hat{V}$.*

Finally we recall the Gap-DH assumption that is stronger than the Strong-DH in that the oracle can be queried on an arbitrary triple (U, V, W).

Assumption 3 (Gap-DH Assumption). *We say that the Gap-DH Assumption holds (for $\mathbb{G}$ and g) if the CDH Assumption holds even in the presence of an oracle $\mathsf{DH}(\cdot, \cdot, \cdot)$ that on input three elements $U = g^u, V = g^v, W = g^w$ in the group generated by g, output "yes" if and only if $W = g^{uv}$.*

The oracle DH for the Decisional DH problem exists for some groups $\mathbb{G}$, e.g. the ones that admit a bilinear map. We stress, however that we need the oracle *only for the proof of security, and it is not needed in the execution of the protocol by the real-life parties.* This means that we can efficiently implement our protocol over any cyclic group $\mathbb{G}$.

The question, then, is the real-life meaning of a proof under the Strong-DH assumption when the protocol is implemented over a group $\mathbb{G}$ that does not admit such oracle DH. If we prove the security of our protocol under the SDH assumption, then if a successful adversary can be constructed one of two things must be true:

1. either the CDH Assumption is false
2. or we have a proof that the hardness of the Decisional problem is implied by the CDH Assumption (in other words the CDH and DDH Assumptions are equivalent). Indeed in this case the CDH holds, and the protocol is insecure, this means that the oracle DH cannot exists (if it existed, given that the CDH holds, the protocol should be secure).

In other words, while proofs under the Strong-DH assumption do not necessarily offer a constructive cryptanalysis of a conjectured hard problem in case of a successful attack, they do offer the "dual" ability to prove the equivalence of the CDH Assumption (with any other additional assumption required by the proof) with the DDH Assumption over the underlying group.

---

[2] We remark that in recent papers the name strong Diffie-Hellman assumption was used to denote a different conjecture defined over bilinear groups [4]. In this paper, we refer to the original terminology from [1].

2.1   Definitions for Identity-Based Key Agreement

The security of our protocols is analyzed in a version of the Canetti-Krawczyk (CK) [9, 10] model for key agreement, adapted to the identity-based setting. We present an informal summary of the model and we refer the reader to [9, 10] for details.

An identity-based key-agreement protocol is runned by parties interacting in a network where each party is identified by a unique identity which is publicly known to all the other parties (e.g. Alice's identity is a string ID_A). In addition there exists a trusted entity called *Key Generation Center* (KGC) that generates the public parameters of the system and also issues secret keys to users associated with their public identities, e.g. the KGC generates a secret key SK_A associated to ID_A.

An instance of the protocol is called a *session*. The two parties participating in the session are called its *peers*. Each peer maintains a *session state* which contains incoming and outgoing messages and its random coins. If the session is *completed* then each party outputs a *session key* and erases its session state. A session may also be *aborted*. In this case no session key is generated.

Each party assigns an unique identifier to a session he is participating in. For simplicity, we assume it to be the quadruple $(Alice, Bob, m_{Out}, m_{In})$ where Alice is the identity of the party, Bob its peer, m_{Out} and m_{In} are the outgoing and incoming messages, respectively, for Alice. If Alice holds a session $(Alice, Bob, m_{Out}, m_{In})$ and Bob holds a session $(Bob, Alice, m_{In}, m_{Out})$ then the two sessions are *matching*.

The adversary. The CK definition models a very realistic adversary which basically controls all communication in the network. In particular it can intercept and modify messages exchanged by parties, delay or block their delivery, inject its own messages, schedule sessions etc. The adversary is allowed to choose the identities of the parties, and obtain private keys from the KGC for identities of its choice.

Finally we allow the adversary to access some of the parties' secret information, via the following attacks: *party corruption, state-reveal queries* and *session-key queries*. When an adversary *corrupts* a party, it learns its private information (the private key and all session states and session keys currently stored), and it later controls its actions. In a *state-reveal query* to a party running a session, the adversary learns the session state for that session (since we assume that session states are erased at the end of the session, such query makes sense only against sessions that are still incomplete). Finally a *session-key query* allows the adversary to learn the session key of a complete session. A session is called *exposed* if it or its matching session (if existing) is compromised by one of the attacks above.

Security Definition. Let $\mathcal{A}$ be a probabilistic polynomial time adversary modeled as described above. Then consider the following experiment running $\mathcal{A}$.

At the beginning of the game the adversary receives as input the public parameters of the system (generated by the KGC) and then can perform all the actions described in the section before.

At some point, $\mathcal{A}$ chooses a *test session* among all the completed and unexposed sessions. We toss a random bit $b \xleftarrow{\$} \{0,1\}$. If $b = 0$ we give $\mathcal{A}$ the session key K_0 of the test session. Otherwise we take a random session key K_1 and provide $\mathcal{A}$ with K_1.

After having received K_b, the adversary can continue to perform its actions against the protocol with the exception that it cannot expose the test session. At the end of the game $\mathcal{A}$ outputs a bit b' as its guess for b.

Definition 2. *An identity-based key-agreement protocol is said to be secure if for any PPT adversary $\mathcal{A}$ the following holds:*

1. *if two uncorrupted parties complete matching sessions then they output the same session key with overwhelming probability;*
2. *the probability that $\mathcal{A}$ guesses the correct b in the above experiment is at most $1/2$ plus a negligible fraction of the security parameter.*

We define the advantage of $\mathcal{A}$ as $\mathbf{Adv}_{\mathcal{A}}^{IB-KA} = |\Pr[b = b'] - 1/2|$.

Additional security properties. In addition to the notion of session key security presented above, an identity-based key-agreement protocol should satisfy other important properties: resistance to *reflection attacks*, *forward secrecy* and resistance to *key-compromise impersonation* attacks.

A *reflection attack* occurs when an adversary can compromise a session in which the two parties have the same identity (and the same private key). Though, at first glance, this seems to be only of theoretical interest, there are real-life situations in which this scenario occurs. For example consider the case when Alice is at her office and wants to establish a secure connection with her PC at home, therefore running a session between two computers with the same identity and private key.

We would also like to achieve resistance to *key compromise impersonation* (KCI) attacks. Suppose that the adversary learns Alice's private key. Then, it is trivial to see that this knowledge enables the adversary to impersonate Alice to other parties. A KCI attack can be carried out when the knowledge of Alice's private key allows the adversary to impersonate another party to Alice.

Finally, *Forward secrecy* is probably the most important additional security property we would like to achieve. We say that a KA protocol has forward secrecy, if after a session is completed and its session key erased, the adversary cannot learn it *even if* it corrupts the parties involved in that session. In other words, learning the private keys of parties should not jeopardize the security of past completed sessions.

A relaxed notion of forward secrecy (which we call *weak*) assumes that only past sessions in which the adversary was passive (i.e. did not choose the messages) are not jeopardized.

3   The New Protocol IB-KA

Protocol setup. The Key Generation Center (KGC) chooses a group $\mathbb{G}$ of prime order q (where q is ℓ-bits long), a random generator $g \in \mathbb{G}$ and two hash functions $H_1 : \{0,1\}^* \to \mathbb{Z}_q$ and $H_2 : \mathbb{Z}_q \times \mathbb{Z}_q \to \{0,1\}^\ell$. Then it picks a random $x \xleftarrow{\$} \mathbb{Z}_q$ and sets $y = g^x$. Finally the KGC outputs the public parameters $MPK = (\mathbb{G}, g, y, H_1, H_2)$ and keeps the master secret key $MSK = x$ for itself.

Key Derivation. A user with identity ID receives, as its secret key, a Schnorr's signature [35] of the message $m = ID$ under public key y. More specifically, the KGC after verifying the user's identity, creates the associated secret key as follows. First it picks a random $k \xleftarrow{\$} \mathbb{Z}_q$ and sets $r_{ID} = g^k$. Then it uses the master secret key x to compute $s_{ID} = k + H_1(ID, r_{ID})x$. (r_{ID}, s_{ID}) is the secret key returned to the user. The user can verify the correctness of its secret key by using the public key y and checking the equation $g^{s_{ID}} \overset{?}{=} r_{ID} \cdot y^{H_1(ID, r_{ID})}$.

A protocol session. Let's assume that Alice wants to establish a session key with Bob. Alice owns secret key (r_A, s_A) and identity A while Bob has secret key (r_B, s_B) and identity B.

Alice selects a random $t_A \xleftarrow{\$} \mathbb{Z}_q$, computes $u_A = g^{t_A}$ and sends the message $\langle A, r_A, u_A \rangle$ to Bob. Analogously Bob picks a random $t_B \xleftarrow{\$} \mathbb{Z}_q$, computes $u_B = g^{t_B}$ and sends $\langle B, r_B, u_B \rangle$ to Alice. After the parties have exchanged these two messages, they are able to compute the same session key $Z = H_2(z_1, z_2)$. In particular Alice computes

$$z_1 = (u_B r_B y^{H_1(B, r_B)})^{t_A + s_A} \quad \text{and} \quad z_2 = u_B^{t_A}.$$

On the other hand Bob computes

$$z_1 = (u_A r_A y^{H_1(A, r_A)})^{t_B + s_B} \quad \text{and} \quad z_2 = u_A^{t_B}.$$

It is easy to see that both the parties are computing the same values $z_1 = g^{(t_A + s_A)(t_B + s_B)}$ and $z_2 = g^{t_A t_B}$. The state of a user ID during a protocol session contains only the fresh random exponent t_{ID}. We assume that after a session is completed, the parties erase their state and keep only the session key.

Remark: In the next section we show that protocol IB-KA is secure under the Strong Diffie-Hellman Assumption. However, in Section 5 we show how to modify IB-KA to obtain security under the basic CDH Assumption, at the cost of a slight degradation in efficiency.

4   Security Proof

We prove the security of the protocol by a usual reduction argument. More precisely we show how to reduce the existence of an adversary breaking the protocol into an algorithm that is able to break the SDH Assumption with non-negligible probability. The adversary is modeled as a CK attacker: (see Section 2.1 for details): in particular it will choose a test session among the complete and un-exposed sessions and will try to distinguish between its real session key and a random one.

In our reduction we will make use of the General Forking Lemma, stated by Bellare and Neven in [2]. It follows the original forking lemma of Pointcheval and Stern [31], but, unlike that, it makes no mention of signature schemes and random oracles. In this sense it is more general and it can be used to prove the security of our protocol. We briefly recall it in the following.

Lemma 1 (General Forking Lemma [2]). *Fix an integer $Q \geq 1$ and a set H of size $|H| \geq 2$. Let $\mathcal{B}$ be a randomized algorithm that on input $x, h_1, \ldots, h_Q$ returns a pair (J, σ) where $J \in \{0, \ldots, Q\}$ and σ is referred as* side output. *Let IG be a randomized algorithm called the input generator. Let $acc_{\mathcal{B}} = \Pr[J \geq 1 : x \xleftarrow{\$} IG, h_1, \ldots, h_Q \xleftarrow{\$} H; (J, \sigma) \xleftarrow{\$} \mathcal{B}(x, h_1, \ldots, h_Q)]$ be the accepting probability of $\mathcal{B}$.*

The forking algorithm $F_{\mathcal{B}}$ associated to $\mathcal{B}$ is the randomized algorithm that takes as input x and proceeds as follows:

> *Algorithm $F_{\mathcal{B}}(x)$*
>   *Pick random coins ρ for $\mathcal{B}$*
> $h_1, \ldots, h_Q \xleftarrow{\$} H$
> $(J, \sigma) \xleftarrow{\$} \mathcal{B}(x, h_1, \ldots, h_Q; \rho)$
>   *If $J = 0$ then return $(0, \perp, \perp)$*
> $h'_1, \ldots, h'_Q \xleftarrow{\$} H$
> $(J', \sigma') \xleftarrow{\$} \mathcal{B}(x, h_1, \ldots, h_{J-1}, h'_J, \ldots, h'_Q; \rho)$
>   *If $(J = J'$ and $h_J \neq h'_J)$ then return $(1, \sigma, \sigma')$*
>   *Else return $(0, \perp, \perp)$.*

Let $frk = \Pr[b = 1 : x \xleftarrow{\$} IG; (b, \sigma, \sigma') \xleftarrow{\$} F_{\mathcal{B}}(x)]$. Then $frk \geq acc_{\mathcal{B}}\left(\frac{acc_{\mathcal{B}}}{Q} - \frac{1}{|H|}\right)$.

Roughly speaking the lemma says that if an algorithm $\mathcal{B}$ accepts with some non-negligible probability, then a "rewind" of $\mathcal{B}$ is likely to accept with a polynomially related probability (more specifically squared). If we look at the details of this lemma, the intuitions are that: (1) $h_1, \ldots, h_Q$ can be seen as the set of replies to random oracle queries made by the original adversary and (2) the forking algorithm implements the rewinding. Moreover it is important that in $F_{\mathcal{B}}$ the two executions of $\mathcal{B}$ are run with the same random coins ρ. We defer to [2] for the proof of the lemma.

Theorem 4. *Under the Strong-DH Assumption, if we model H_1 and H_2 as random oracles, then protocol IB-KA is a secure identity-based key agreement protocol.*

Proof. For sake of contradiction let us suppose there exists a PPT adversary $\mathcal{A}$ that has non-negligible advantage ϵ into breaking the protocol IB-KA , then we show how to build a solver algorithm S for the CDH problem.

In our reduction we will proceed into two steps. First, we describe an intermediate algorithm $\mathcal{B}$ (i.e. the simulator) that interacts with the IB-KA adversary $\mathcal{A}$ and returns a side output σ. Second, we will show how to build an algorithm S that exploits $F_{\mathcal{B}}$, the forking algorithm associated with $\mathcal{B}$, to solve the CDH problem under the Strong-DH Assumption.

$\mathcal{B}$ receives as input a tuple $(\mathbb{G}, g, U, V)$, where $U = g^u, V = g^v$ and u, v are random exponents in $\mathbb{Z}_q$, and a set of random elements $h_1, \ldots, h_Q \in \mathbb{Z}_q$. The simulator is also given access to a DH oracle $\mathsf{DH}(U, \cdot, \cdot)$ that on input $(\hat{V}, \hat{W})$ answers "yes" if $(U, \hat{V}, \hat{W})$ is a valid DDH tuple . The side output of $\mathcal{B}$ is $\sigma \in \mathbb{G} \times \mathbb{Z}_q$ or $\perp$. Let n be an upper bound to the number of sessions of the protocol run by the adversary $\mathcal{A}$ and Q_1 and Q_2 be the number of queries made by $\mathcal{A}$ to the random oracles H_1, H_2 respectively. Moreover, let Q_c be the number of users corrupted by $\mathcal{A}$ and $Q = Q_1 + Q_c + 1$.

Algorithm $\mathcal{B}^{\mathsf{DH}(U, \cdot, \cdot)}(\mathbb{G}, g, U, V, h_1, \ldots, h_Q)$
    Initialize $ctr \leftarrow 0; bad \leftarrow false$; empty tables $\overline{H_1}, \overline{H_2}$;
    Run $\mathcal{A}$ on input $(\mathbb{G}, g, y = U)$ as the public parameters of the protocol and simulates the protocol's environment for $\mathcal{A}$ as follows:
        Guess the test session by choosing at random the user (let us call him Bob) and the order number of the test session. If n is an upper bound to the number of all the sessions initiated by $\mathcal{A}$ then the guess is right with probability at least $1/n$.
    H_2 **queries:** On input a pair (z_1, z_2):
        If $\overline{H_2}[z_1, z_2] = \perp$: choose a random string $Z \in \{0, 1\}^{\ell}$ and store $\overline{H_2}[z_1, z_2] = Z$
        Return $\overline{H_2}[z_1, z_2]$ to $\mathcal{A}$
    H_1 **queries:** On input (ID, r):
        If $\overline{H_1}[ID, r] = \perp$, then $ctr \leftarrow ctr + 1; \overline{H_1}[ID, r] = h_{ctr}$
        Return $\overline{H_1}[ID, r]$ to $\mathcal{A}$
    Party Corruption: When $\mathcal{A}$ asks to corrupt party $ID \neq B$, then:
        $ctr \leftarrow ctr + 1; s \xleftarrow{\$} \mathbb{Z}_q; r = g^s y^{-h_{ctr}}$
        If $\overline{H_1}[ID, r] \neq \perp$ then $bad \leftarrow true$
        Store $\overline{H_1}[ID, r] = h_{ctr}$ and return (r, s) as ID's private key.
        For the case of Bob, the simulator simply chooses the r_B component of Bob's private key by picking a random $k_B \xleftarrow{\$} \mathbb{Z}_q$ and setting $r_B = g^{k_B}$. We observe that in this case $\mathcal{B}$ is not able to compute the corresponding s_B. However, since Bob is the user guessed for the test session, we can assume that the adversary will not ask for his secret key.
    Simulating sessions: First we describe how to simulate sessions different from the test session. Here the main point is that the adversary is allowed to ask session-key queries and thus the simulator must be able to produce the correct session key for each of these sessions. The simulator has full information about all the users' secret keys except Bob. Therefore $\mathcal{B}$ can easily simulate all the protocol sessions that do not include Bob, and answer any of the attacker's queries about

these sessions. Hence we concentrate on describing how $\mathcal{B}$ simulates interactions with Bob.

Assume that Bob has a session with Charlie (whose identity is the string C). If Charlie is an uncorrupted party this means that $\mathcal{B}$ will generate the messages on his behalf. In this case $\mathcal{B}$ knows Charlie's secret key and also has chosen his ephemeral exponent t_C. Thus it is trivial to see that $\mathcal{B}$ has enough information to compute the correct session key. The case when the adversary presents a message $\langle C, r_C, u_C \rangle$ to Bob as coming from Charlie is more complicated. Here is where $\mathcal{B}$ makes use of the oracle $\mathsf{DH}(y, \cdot, \cdot)$ to answer a session-key query about this session. The simulator replies with a message $\langle B, r_B, u_B = g^{t_B} \rangle$ where t_B is chosen by $\mathcal{B}$. Recall that the session key is $H_2(z_1, z_2)$ with $z_1 = g^{(s_C+t_C)(s_B+t_B)}$ and $z_2 = u_C^{t_B}$. So z_1 is the Diffie-Hellman result of the values $u_C g^{s_C}$ and $u_B g^{s_B}$, where $g^{s_C} = r_C y^{H_1(C, r_C)}$ and $g^{s_B} = r_B y^{H_1(B, r_B)}$ can be computed by the simulator. Notice also that the simulator knows t_B and k_B (the discrete log of r_B in base g). Therefore it checks if $\overline{H_2}[z_1, z_2] = Z$ where $z_2 = u_C^{t_B}$ and $\mathsf{DH}(y, u_C g^{s_C}, \bar{z}_1) = \text{``yes''}$ where $\bar{z}_1 = \frac{z_1}{(u_C g^{s_C})^{(k_B+t_B)H_1(B, r_B)^{-1}}}$. If $\mathcal{B}$ finds a match then it outputs the corresponding Z as session key for Bob. Otherwise it generates a random $\zeta \xleftarrow{\$} \{0,1\}^{\ell}$ and gives it as response to the adversary. Later, for each query (z_1, z_2) to H_2, if (z_1, z_2) satisfies the equation above it sets $\overline{H_2}[z_1, z_2] = \zeta$ and answers with ζ. This makes the oracle's answers consistent.

In addition observe that the simulator can easily answer any state reveal queries as it chooses the fresh exponents on its own.

Simulating the test session: Let $\langle B, \rho_B, u_B = g^{t_B} \rangle$ be the message from Bob to Alice sent in the test session. We notice that such message may be sent by the adversary who is trying to impersonate Bob. In this case $\mathcal{A}$ may use a value $\rho_B = g^{\lambda_B}$ of its choice as the public component of Bob's private key (i.e. different than $r_B = g^{k_B}$ which $\mathcal{B}$ simulated and for which it knows k_B). $\mathcal{B}$ responds with the message $\langle A, r_A, u_A = V \rangle$ as coming from Alice. Finally $\mathcal{B}$ provides $\mathcal{A}$ with a random session key.

Run until $\mathcal{A}$ halts and outputs its decision bit

If $\overline{H_1}[B, \rho_B] = \perp$ then set $ctr \leftarrow ctr + 1$ and $\overline{H_1}[B, \rho_B] = h_{ctr}$

If $bad = true$ then return $(0, \perp)$

Let $i \in \{1, \ldots, Q\}$ such that $H_1(B, \rho_B) = h_i$

Let $Z = H_2(z_1, z_2)$ be the correct session key for the test session where $z_1 = (u_A r_A y^{H_1(A, r_A)})^{(t_B + \lambda_B + x h_i)}$ and $z_2 = u_A^{t_B}$.

If $\mathcal{A}$ has success into distinguishing Z from a random value it must necessarily query the correct pair (z_1, z_2) to the random oracle H_2. This means that $\mathcal{B}$ can efficiently find the pair (z_1, z_2) in the table $\overline{H_2}$ using the Strong-DH oracle.

Compute $\tau = \frac{z_1}{z_2(u_B \rho_B y^{h_i})^{s_A}} = \rho_B^v W^{h_i}$

Return $(i, (\tau, h_i))$

Let IG be the algorithm that generates a random Diffie-Hellman tuple $(\mathbb{G}, g, U, V)$ and acc_B be the accepting probability of $\mathcal{B}$.[3] Then we have that:

$$acc_B \geq \frac{\epsilon}{n} - \Pr[bad = true].$$

The probability that $bad = true$ is the probability that the adversary has guessed the "right" r for a corrupted party ID before corrupting it, in one of the H_1 oracle queries beforehand. Since r is uniformly distributed the probability of guessing it is $1/q$, and since the adversary makes at most Q queries to H_1 and corrupts at most Q_c parties (and $q > 2^\ell$) we have that

$$acc_B \geq \frac{\epsilon}{n} - \frac{Q_c(Q)}{2^\ell}.$$

which is still non-negligible, since ϵ is non-negligible.

Once we have described the algorithm $\mathcal{B}$ we can now show how to build a solver algorithm S that can exploit $F_\mathcal{B}$, the forking algorithm associated with the above $\mathcal{B}$.

The algorithm S plays the role of a CDH solver under the Strong-DH Assumption. It receives as input a CDH tuple $(\mathbb{G}, g, U, V)$ where $U = g^u, V = g^v$ and u, v are random exponents in $\mathbb{Z}_q$. S is also given access to a decision oracle $\mathsf{DH}(U, \cdot, \cdot)$ that on input $(\hat{V}, \hat{W})$ answers "yes" if $(U, \hat{V}, \hat{W})$ is a valid DH tuple .

Algorithm $S^{\mathsf{DH}(U, \cdot, \cdot)}(\mathbb{G}, g, U, V)$

  $(b, \tau, \tau') \xleftarrow{\$} F_\mathcal{B}^{\mathsf{DH}(U, \cdot, \cdot)}(\mathbb{G}, g, U, V)$

  If $b = 0$ then return 0 and halt

  Parse σ as (τ, h) and σ' as (τ', h')

  Return $W = (\tau/\tau')^{(h-h')^{-1}}$

If the forking algorithm $F_\mathcal{B}$ has success, this means that there exist random coins ρ, an index $J \geq 1$ and $h_1, \ldots, h_Q, h'_J, \ldots, h'_Q \in \mathbb{Z}_q$ with $h = h_J \neq h'_J = h'$ such that: the first execution of $\mathcal{B}(\mathbb{G}, g, U, V, h_1, \ldots, h_Q; \rho)$ outputs $\tau = \rho_B^v W^h$ where $\overline{H_1}[B, \rho_B] = h$; the second execution of $\mathcal{B}(\mathbb{G}, g, U, V, h_1, \ldots, h_{J-1}, h'_J, \ldots, h'_Q; \rho)$ outputs $\tau' = (\rho'_{B'})^v W^{h'}$ where $\overline{H_1}[B', \rho'_{B'}] = h'$. Since the two executions of $\mathcal{B}$ are the same until the response to the J-th query to H_1, then we must have $B = B'$ and $\rho_B = \rho'_{B'}$. Thus it is easy to see that S achieves its goal by computing $W = (\tau/\tau')^{\frac{1}{h-h'}} = g^{uv}$.

Finally, by the General Forking Lemma, we have that if $\mathcal{A}$ has non-negligible advantage into breaking the security of IB-KA , then S's success probability is also non-negligible.

---

[3] We say that $\mathcal{B}$ accepts if it outputs (J, σ) such that $J \geq 1$.

4.1   Additional Security Properties of IB-KA

Below we describe the additional security properties enjoyed by IB-KA .

Forward secrecy. The following theorem shows that the protocol IB-KA satisfies *weak forward secrecy* as described in Section 2.1.

Theorem 5. *Let $\mathcal{A}$ be a PPT adversary that is able to break the weak forward secrecy of the IB-KA protocol with advantage ϵ. Let n be the an upper bound to the number of sessions of the protocol run by $\mathcal{A}$ and Q_1 and Q_2 be the number of queries made by the adversary to the random oracles H_1, H_2 respectively. Then we can solve the CDH problem with probability at least $\epsilon/(nQ_2)$.*

Proof. For sake of contradiction let us suppose there exists a PPT adversary $\mathcal{A}$ that is able to break the weak forward secrecy of the protocol IB-KA with non-negligible advantage ϵ. Then we show how to build a simulator S that uses $\mathcal{A}$ to solve the CDH problem with probability at least ϵ/nQ_2. S receives as input a tuple $(\mathbb{G}, g, U, V)$ where $U = g^u, V = g^v$ and u, v are random exponents in $\mathbb{Z}_q$. The simulator plays the role of the CDH solver and its goal it to compute the value $W = g^{uv}$.

SETUP. S sets up a simulated execution of the protocol, with simulated KGC, users and sessions. First of all S defines the public parameters of the protocol simulating the KGC. So it chooses a random $x \xleftarrow{\$} \mathbb{Z}_q$ and sets $y = g^x$. Then it provides the adversary with input $(\mathbb{G}, g, y)$ and oracle access to H_1 and H_2. Since H_1 and H_2 are modeled as random oracles, S can program their output. For each input (ID, r_{ID}) S chooses a random $e_{ID} \xleftarrow{\$} \mathbb{Z}_q$ and sets $H_1(ID, r_{ID}) = e_{ID}$.

Since S knows the master secret key x, it can simulate the KGC in full, and give secret keys to all the parties in the network, including answering private key queries from the adversary.

At the beginning of the game S guesses the test session and its peers Alice and Bob.

SIMULATING PROTOCOL SESSIONS. Sessions different from the test session are easily simulated since S knows all the information needed to compute the session keys and answer any query (including **session key** and **state reveal** queries) from the adversary.

SIMULATING THE TEST SESSION. We now show how to simulate the test session in order to extract $W = g^{uv}$ from the adversary. Since in this game the adversary is assumed to be passive during the test session, the parties (i.e. the simulator in this case) choose the messages exchanged in this session.

Let $(A, r_A, s_A), (B, r_B, s_B)$ be the identity information and the secret keys of Alice and Bob respectively (S knows these values). The simulator sets Alice's message as $(A, r_A, u_A = U)$ while the one from Bob is $(B, r_B, u_B = V)$. S is implicitly setting $t_A = u, t_B = v$. In this case the correct session key is $Z = H_2(g^{(s_A+u)(s_B+v)}, g^{uv})$. Since H_2 is modeled as a random oracle, if $\mathcal{A}$ has success into distinguishing Z from a random value, it must have queried H_2 on the correct input $(z_1 = g^{(s_A+u)(s_B+v)}, z_2 = g^{uv})$. Thus S can choose a random value among all the queries that it received from the adversary. Since the number of queries Q_2 is polynomially bounded, S can find the correct $z_2 = W$ with non-negligible probability ϵ/nQ_2. This completes the proof of this case[4].

Resistance to reflection attacks. A *reflection attack* occurs when an adversary can compromise a session in which the two parties have the same identity (and the same private key). Though, at first glance, this seems to be only of theoretical interest, there are real-life situations in which this scenario occurs. For example consider the case when Alice is at her office and wants to establish a secure connection with her PC at home, therefore running a session between two computers with the same identity and private key.

Here we extend the proof of security given in Section 4 to support reflection attacks. We observe that in the case when the test session has a matching session the proof remains valid even if the test session is between Bob and himself. On the other hand, when there is no matching session we have to show a little modification of the proof. In fact the current proof actually does not work when the adversary sends a message with the same value r_B provided by the KGC (for which the simulator knows the discrete logarithm k_B, but cannot compute the corresponding s_B). The issue is that the knowledge of s_B would be needed to extract the solution of the CDH problem.

We point out that a reflection attack using a value $\rho_B \neq r_B$ is captured by the current proof. Moreover it is reasonable to assume that a honest party refuses connections from itself that use a "wrong" key. However it is possible to adapt the proof in this specific case. In particular we can show that a successful run of the adversary enables the simulator to compute g^{u^2} instead of g^{uv}. As showed in [28] by Maurer and Wolf, such an algorithm can be easily turned into a solver for CDH.

In this section we show how to adapt the proof in this specific case. In particular, we show that a successful run of the adversary enables the simulator to compute g^{u^2} instead of g^{uv}. As showed in [28] by Maurer and Wolf, such an algorithm can be easily turned into a solver for CDH.

Let us consider the following modification of the proof given in Section 4. If in the test session the adversary sends a message from Bob to Bob of type $\langle B, r_B, u_B = g^{t_B} \rangle$ then the simulator picks a random $e \xleftarrow{\$} \mathbb{Z}_q$ and replies with message $\langle B, r_B, u'_B = U^e \rangle$. Let h^* be the random oracle response to $H_1(B, r_B)$. We observe that in this case the correct session key is the hash $Z = H_2(z_1, z_2)$ where $z_1 = g^{(k_B+uh^*+ue)(k_B+uh^*+t_B)}$ and $z_2 = g^{uet_B}$. If the adversary has success into distinguishing Z from a random value it must necessarily query the correct pair (z_1, z_2) to the random oracle H_2. This means that S can efficiently find the

---

[4] We could give the simulator access to the Strong-DH oracle DH, and then S could use it to "test" all queries to H_2 to find the correct W. The reduction would be tighter (removing the factor of Q_2^{-1} from the success probability) but would require the Strong-DH Assumption also in this case.

pair (z_1, z_2) in the table $\overline{H_2}$ using the Strong-DH oracle. Once it has recovered these values, it can compute:

$$g^{u^2} = \left(\frac{z_1}{g^{k_B^2} U^{2k_B h^*} U^{ek_B} u_B^{k_B} z_2 z_2^{h^*/e}} \right)^{\frac{1}{h^*(h^*+e)}} .$$

Resistance to Key Compromise Impersonation. Suppose that the adversary learns Alice's private key. Then, it is trivial to see that this knowledge enables the adversary to impersonate Alice to other parties. A *key compromise impersonation* (KCI) attack can be carried out when the knowledge of Alice's private key allows the adversary to impersonate another party to Alice.

To see that the protocol IB-KA is resistant to KCI attacks it suffices to observe that in the proof of security, when the adversary tries to impersonate Bob to Alice, we are able to output Alice's private key whenever it is asked by the adversary. This means that the proof continues to be valid even in this case.

Ephemeral Key Compromise Impersonation. A recent paper by Cheng and Ma [14] shows that our protocol is susceptible to an ephemeral key compromise attack. Roughly speaking this attack considers the case when the adversary can make state-reveal queries (in order to learn the ephemeral key of a user) even in the test session. Though the paper is correct, we point out that this kind of attack is not part of the standard Canetti-Krawczyk security model that is considered in this paper.

5   A Protocol Secure under CDH

The protocol IB-KA given in section Section 3 is proven secure under the Strong-DH Assumption. In this section we show how to modify that protocol so that its security can be based directly on CDH. The cost is a few more exchanged elements and a few more exponentiations. We call this modified protocol 2IB − KA.

The basic idea is to use the *Twin Diffie-Hellman* (2DH) Assumption introduced by Cash *et al.* in [11]. Informally 2DH states that an adversary which is given in input random $U_1, U_2, V \in \mathbb{G}$, should not be able to compute a pair (W_1, W_2) such that W_1 and W_2 are the DH of U_1, V and U_2, V respectively. It is easy to see that this assumption is equivalent to the well known CDH. The valuable contribution of [11] was to show that its "strong" version is equivalent to CDH too.

Informally the Strong-2DH assumption says that 2DH holds even in the presence of an oracle $2DH(U_1, U_2, \cdot, \cdot, \cdot)$ that solves its decisional version for fixed U_1, U_2.

Therefore we modify the IB-KA protocol in such a way it can be proven secure under the Strong-2DH Assumption. Then, since Cash *et al.* proved in [11] that Strong-2DH and CDH are equivalent, we obtain a protocol secure under CDH.

In order to modify the protocol we apply the idea of "twinning" some elements so that the construction can be proven under the Strong-2DH assumption. The new protocol is almost the same as IB-KA except for the following:

- the master public key consists of two group elements y_1, y_2. This means that each user ID owns a secret key $(r_{ID}^1, s_{ID}^1, r_{ID}^2, s_{ID}^2)$ which are two Schnorr's signatures of its identity corresponding to public keys y_1, y_2 respectively.
- each user ID generates two elements $u_{ID}^1 = g^{t_{ID}^1}, u_{ID}^2 = g^{t_{ID}^2}$ and sends $\langle r_{ID}^1, r_{ID}^2, u_{ID}^1, u_{ID}^2 \rangle$.
- the session key of a session between users with identities A and B is

$$K = H(z_{11}, z_{12}, z_{21}, z_{22}, \omega_{11}, \omega_{12}, \omega_{21}, \omega_{22})$$

where $z_{11} = g^{(s_A^1 + t_A^1)(s_B^1 + t_B^1)}$, $z_{12} = g^{(s_A^1 + t_A^1)(s_B^2 + t_B^2)}$, $z_{21} = g^{(s_A^2 + t_A^2)(s_B^1 + t_B^1)}$, $z_{22} = g^{(s_A^2 + t_A^2)(s_B^2 + t_B^2)}$, $\omega_{11} = g^{t_A^1 t_B^1}$, $\omega_{12} = g^{t_A^1 t_B^2}$, $\omega_{21} = g^{t_A^2 t_B^1}$ and $\omega_{22} = g^{t_A^2 t_B^2}$.

It is also possible to instantiate a simpler version of this protocol in which the public key is only y as in IB-KA . This is slightly more efficient since a user has to send one less element. This variant can also be proven secure under the CDH provided that the adversary is not allowed to issue state-reveal queries.

The following theorem prove the security of the above protocol.

Theorem 6. *Under the CDH Assumption, if we model H_1 and H_2 as random oracles, then protocol 2IB-KA is a secure identity-based key agreement protocol.*

Proof. For sake of contradiction let us suppose there exists a PPT adversary $\mathcal{A}$ that has non-negligible advantage ϵ into breaking the protocol 2IB-KA , then we show how to build a solver algorithm S for the CDH problem under Strong-2DH.

In our reduction we will proceed into two steps. First, we describe an intermediate algorithm $\mathcal{B}$ (i.e. the simulator) that interacts with the IB-KA adversary $\mathcal{A}$ and returns a side output σ. Second, we will show how to build an algorithm S that exploits $F_{\mathcal{B}}$, the forking algorithm associated with $\mathcal{B}$, to solve the CDH problem under the Strong-2DH Assumption.

$\mathcal{B}$ receives as input a set of random elements $h_1, \ldots, h_{2Q} \in \mathbb{Z}_q$ and a tuple $(q, \mathbb{G}, g, U_1, U_2, V)$, where $U_1 = g^{u_1}, U_2 = g^{u_2}, V = g^v$ and u_1, u_2, v are random exponents in $\mathbb{Z}_q$. The simulator is also given access to a 2DH oracle $2DH(U_1, U_2, \cdot, \cdot, \cdot)$ that on input $(\hat{V}, \hat{W}_1, \hat{W}_2)$ answers "yes" if $(U_1, \hat{V}, \hat{W}_1)$ and $(U_2, \hat{V}, \hat{W}_2)$ are valid DDH tuples. The side output of $\mathcal{B}$ is $\sigma \in \mathbb{G}^2 \times \mathbb{Z}_q^2$ or $\perp$. Let n be an upper bound to the number of sessions of the protocol run by the adversary $\mathcal{A}$ and Q_1 and Q_2 be the number of queries made by $\mathcal{A}$ to the random oracles H_1, H_2 respectively. Moreover, let Q_c be the number of users corrupted by $\mathcal{A}$ and $Q = Q_1 + Q_c + 1$.

Algorithm $\mathcal{B}^{2DH(U_1, U_2, \cdot, \cdot, \cdot)}(q, \mathbb{G}, g, U_1, U_2, V, h_1, \ldots, h_{2Q})$
    Initialize $ctr \leftarrow 0; bad \leftarrow false$; empty tables $\overline{H_1}, \overline{H_2}$;
    Run $\mathcal{A}$ on input $(q, \mathbb{G}, g, y_1 = U_1, y_2 = U_2)$ as the public parameters of the
    protocol and simulates the protocol's environment for $\mathcal{A}$ as follows:

Guess the test session by choosing at random the user (let us call him Bob) and the order number of the test session. If n is an upper bound to the number of all the sessions initiated by $\mathcal{A}$ then the guess is right with probability at least $1/n$.

H_2 **queries:** On input a tuple $z = (z_{11}, z_{12}, z_{21}, z_{22}, \omega_{11}, \omega_{12}, \omega_{21}, \omega_{22})$:
   If $\overline{H_2}[z] = \perp$: choose a random string $Z \in \{0,1\}^\ell$ and store $\overline{H_2}[z] = Z$
   Return $\overline{H_2}[z]$ to $\mathcal{A}$

H_1 **queries:** On input (ID, r):
   If $\overline{H_1}[ID, r] = \perp$, then $ctr \leftarrow ctr + 1; \overline{H_1}[ID, r] = h_{ctr}$
   Return $\overline{H_1}[ID, r]$ to $\mathcal{A}$

Party Corruption: When $\mathcal{A}$ asks to corrupt party $ID \neq B$, then:
   $ctr \leftarrow ctr + 1; s_{ID}^1 \xleftarrow{\$} \mathbb{Z}_q; r_{ID}^1 = g^{s_{ID}^1} y^{-h_{ctr}};$ Store $\overline{H_1}[ID, r_{ID}^1] = h_{ctr}$
   $ctr \leftarrow ctr + 1; s_{ID}^2 \xleftarrow{\$} \mathbb{Z}_q; r_{ID}^2 = g^{s_{ID}^2} y^{-h_{ctr}}$ Store $\overline{H_1}[ID, r_{ID}^2] = h_{ctr}$
   If $\overline{H_1}[ID, r_{ID}^1] \neq \perp$ or $\overline{H_1}[ID, r_{ID}^2] \neq \perp$ then $bad \leftarrow true$
   Return $(r_{ID}^1, s_{ID}^1, r_{ID}^2, s_{ID}^2)$ as ID's private key.
   For the case of Bob, the simulator simply chooses the "r components" of Bob's private key by picking random $k_B^1, k_B^2 \xleftarrow{\$} \mathbb{Z}_q$ and setting $r_B^1 = g^{k_B^1}, r_B^2 = g^{k_B^2}$. We observe that in this case $\mathcal{B}$ is not able to compute the corresponding s_B^1, s_B^2. However, since Bob is the user guessed for the test session, we can assume that the adversary will not ask for his secret key. Moreover the simulator sets $ctr \leftarrow ctr + 2$ and store $\overline{H_1}[B, r_B^1] = h_{ctr-1}, \overline{H_1}[B, r_B^2] = h_{ctr}$.

Simulating sessions: First we describe how to simulate sessions different from the test session. Here the main point is that the adversary is allowed to ask **session-key** queries and thus the simulator must be able to produce the correct session key for each of these sessions. The simulator has full information about all the users' secret keys except Bob. Therefore $\mathcal{B}$ can easily simulate all the protocol sessions that do not include Bob, and answer any of the attacker's queries about these sessions. Hence we concentrate on describing how $\mathcal{B}$ simulates interactions with Bob.

   Assume that Bob has a session with Charlie (whose identity is the string C). If Charlie is an uncorrupted party this means that $\mathcal{B}$ will generate the messages on behalf of him. In this case $\mathcal{B}$ knows Charlie's secret key and also has chosen his ephemeral exponents. Thus it is trivial to see that $\mathcal{B}$ has enough information to compute the correct session key. The case when the adversary presents a message $\langle C, r_C^1, r_C^2, u_C^1, u_C^2 \rangle$ to Bob as coming from Charlie is more complicated. Here is where $\mathcal{B}$ makes use of the oracle $2\mathsf{DH}(y_1, y_2, \cdot, \cdot, \cdot)$ to answer a **session-key query** about this session. The simulator replies with a message $\langle B, r_B^1, r_B^2, u_B^1 = g^{t_B^1}, u_B^2 = g^{t_B^2} \rangle$ where t_B^1 and t_B^2 are chosen by $\mathcal{B}$. Recall that the session key is

$$K = H(z_{11}, z_{12}, z_{21}, z_{22}, \omega_{11}, \omega_{12}, \omega_{21}, \omega_{22}).$$

Since the simulator knows t_B^1, t_B^2, k_B^1 and k_B^2 it can check if

$$\overline{H_2}[z_{11}, z_{12}, z_{21}, z_{22}, \omega_{11}, \omega_{12}, \omega_{21}, \omega_{22}] = Z$$

such that all the ω_{ij} have the right form (notice that $\mathcal{B}$ can compute them since it knows t_B^1 and t_B^2) and $2\mathsf{DH}(y_1, y_2, u_C^1 g^{s_C}, \overline{z_{11}}, \overline{z_{12}}) =$ "yes" and $2\mathsf{DH}(y_1, y_2, u_C^2 g^{s_C}, \overline{z_{21}}, \overline{z_{22}}) =$ "yes" where $\overline{z_{ij}}$'s are computed as follows:

$$\overline{z_{11}} = \frac{z_{11}}{(u_C^1 g^{s_C})^{(k_B^1 + t_B^1) H_1(B, r_B^1)^{-1}}} = g^{(s_C^1 + t_C^1) x_1},$$

$$\overline{z_{12}} = \frac{z_{12}}{(u_C^1 g^{s_C})^{(k_B^1 + t_B^2) H_1(B, r_B^2)^{-1}}} = g^{(s_C^1 + t_C^1) x_2},$$

$$\overline{z_{21}} = \frac{z_{21}}{(u_C^2 g^{s_C})^{(k_B^1 + t_B^1) H_1(B, r_B^1)^{-1}}} = g^{(s_C^2 + t_C^2) x_1},$$

and $\overline{z_{22}} = \frac{z_{12}}{(u_C^2 g^{s_C})^{(k_B^2 + t_B^2) H_1(B, r_B^2)^{-1}}} = g^{(s_C^2 + t_C^2) x_2}.$

If $\mathcal{B}$ finds a match then it outputs the corresponding Z as session key for Bob. Otherwise it generates a random $\zeta \xleftarrow{\$} \{0,1\}^\ell$ and gives it as response to the adversary. Later, for each query to H_2, if the queried tuple z satisfies the equation above it sets $\overline{H_2}[z] = \zeta$ and answers with ζ. This makes oracle's answers consistent.

In addition observe that the simulator can easily answer to state reveal queries as it chooses the fresh exponents on its own.

Simulating the test session: Let $\langle B, \rho_B^1, \rho_B^2, u_B^1 = g^{t_B^1}, u_B^2 = g^{t_B^2} \rangle$ be the message from Bob to Alice sent in the test session. We notice that such message may be sent by the adversary who is trying to impersonate Bob. $\mathcal{B}$ responds with the message $\langle A, r_A^1, r_A^2, u_A^1 = V, u_A^2 = V^e, \rangle$ (where $e \xleftarrow{\$} \mathbb{Z}_q$) as coming from Alice. Finally $\mathcal{B}$ provides $\mathcal{A}$ with a random session key.

Run until $\mathcal{A}$ halts and outputs its decision bit

If $\overline{H_1}[B, \rho_B^1] = \bot$ and $\overline{H_1}[B, \rho_B^2] = \bot$ then set $ctr \leftarrow ctr+2$ and $\overline{H_1}[B, \rho_B^1] = h_{ctr-1}, \overline{H_1}[B, \rho_B^2] = h_{ctr}$

If $bad = true$ then return $(0, \bot)$

Let $i \in \{1, \ldots, 2Q\}$ such that $H_1(B, \rho_B^1) = h_i$ and $H_1(B, \rho_B^2) = h_{i+1}$

Let $Z = H_2(z_{11}, z_{12}, z_{21}, z_{22}, \omega_{11}, \omega_{12}, \omega_{21}, \omega_{22})$ be the correct session key for the test session.

If $\mathcal{A}$ has success into distinguishing Z from a random value it must necessarily query the correct tuple to the random oracle H_2. This means that $\mathcal{B}$ can efficiently find such tuple in the table $\overline{H_2}$ using the Strong-DH oracle.

Compute $\tau_1 = \frac{z_{11}}{\omega_{11}(u_B^1 \rho_B^1 y_1^{h_i})^{s_A^1}} = (\rho_B^1)^v W_1^{h_i}$ and $\tau_2 = \frac{z_{12}}{\omega_{12}(u_B^2 \rho_B^2 y_2^{h_{i+1}})^{s_A^1}} = (\rho_B^2)^v W_2^{h_{i+1}}$

Return $(i, (\tau_1, \tau_2, h_i, h_{i+1}))$

Let IG be the algorithm that generates a random Diffie-Hellman tuple $(q, \mathbb{G}, g, U_1, U_2, V)$ and $acc_{\mathcal{B}}$ be the accepting probability of $\mathcal{B}$. Then we have that:

$$acc_{\mathcal{B}} \geq \frac{\epsilon}{n} - \Pr[bad = true].$$

The probability that $bad = true$ is the probability that the adversary has guessed the "right" r's for a corrupted party ID before corrupting it, in one of the H_1 oracle queries beforehand. Since r is uniformly distributed the probability of guessing it is $1/q$, and since the adversary makes at most $2Q$ queries to H_1 and corrupts at most Q_c parties (and $q > 2^\ell$) we have that

$$acc_{\mathcal{B}} \geq \frac{\epsilon}{n} - \frac{Q_c(2Q)}{2^\ell}.$$

which is still non-negligible, since ϵ is non-negligible.

Once we have described the algorithm $\mathcal{B}$ we can now show how to build a solver algorithm S that can exploit $F_{\mathcal{B}}$, the forking algorithm associated with the above $\mathcal{B}$.

The algorithm S plays the role of a CDH solver under the Strong-2DH Assumption. It receives as input a CDH tuple $(q, \mathbb{G}, g, U_1, U_2, V)$ where $U_1 = g^{u_1}, U_2 = g^{u_2}, V = g^v$ and u_1, u_2, v are random exponents in $\mathbb{Z}_q$. S is also given access to a decision oracle $\text{2DH}(U_1, U_2, \cdot, \cdot, \cdot)$ that on input $(\hat{V}, \hat{W}_1, \hat{W}_2)$ answers "yes" if $(U_1, \hat{V}, \hat{W}_1)$ and $(U_2, \hat{V}, \hat{W}_2)$ are a valid DH tuples .

Algorithm $S^{\text{2DH}(U_1, U_2, \cdot, \cdot, \cdot)}(q, \mathbb{G}, g, U_1, U_2, V)$
  $(b, \sigma, \sigma') \xleftarrow{\$} F_{\mathcal{B}}^{\text{2DH}(U_1, U_2, \cdot, \cdot, \cdot)}(q, \mathbb{G}, g, U_1, U_2, V)$
  If $b = 0$ then return 0 and halt
  Parse σ as $(\tau_1, \tau_2, h_1, h_2)$ and σ' as $(\tau_1', \tau_2', h_1', h_2')$
  Return $W_1 = (\tau_1/\tau_1')^{(h_1 - h_1')^{-1}}, W_2 = (\tau_2/\tau_2')^{(h_2 - h_2')^{-1}}$

If the forking algorithm $F_{\mathcal{B}}$ has success, this means that there exist random coins γ, an index $J \geq 1$ and $h_1, \ldots, h_{2Q}, h_J', \ldots, h_{2Q}' \in \mathbb{Z}_q$ with $h_1 = h_J \neq h_J' = h_1'$ and $h_2 = h_{J+1} \neq h_{J+1}' = h_2'$ such that: the first execution of $\mathcal{B}(q, \mathbb{G}, g, U_1, V, h_1, \ldots, h_{2Q}; \gamma)$ outputs $\tau_1 = (\rho_B^1)^v W_1^{h_1}$ and $\tau_2 = (\rho_B^2)^v W_2^{h_2}$ where $\overline{H_1}[B, \rho_B^1] = h_1$ and $\overline{H_1}[B, \rho_B^2] = h_2$; the second execution of $\mathcal{B}(q, \mathbb{G}, g, U_1, U_2, V, h_1, \ldots, h_{J-1}, h_J', \ldots, h_{2Q}'; \rho)$ outputs $\tau_1' = (\rho_{B'}^1)^v W_1^{h_1'}$ and $\tau_2' = (\rho_{B'}^2)^v W_2^{h_2'}$ where $\overline{H_1}[B', \rho_{B'}^1] = h_1'$ and $\overline{H_1}[B', \rho_{B'}^2] = h_2'$. Since the two executions of $\mathcal{B}$ are the same until the response to the J-th query to H_1, then we must have $B = B'$, $\rho_B^1 = \rho_{B'}^1$ and $\rho_B^2 = \rho_{B'}^2$. It is worth noting that responses to $H_1(B, r_B^1)$ and $H_1(B, r_B^2)$ are always answered with consecutive values h_{ctr} and h_{ctr+1} respectively. Thus it is easy to see that S achieves its goal by computing $W_1 = (\tau_1/\tau_1')^{\frac{1}{h_1 - h_1'}} = g^{u_1 v}$ and $W_2 = (\tau_2/\tau_2')^{\frac{1}{h_2 - h_2'}} = g^{u_2 v}$.

Finally, by the General Forking Lemma, we have that if $\mathcal{A}$ has non-negligible advantage into breaking the security of 2IB-KA , then S's success probability is also non-negligible.

5.1 Forward Secrecy

The id-based key agreement protocol 2IB-KA described in the previous section satisfies weak forward secrecy as proven in the following theorem.

Theorem 7. *Under the 2DH Assumption, if we model H_1 and H_2 as random oracles then the protocol* 2IB-KA *has weak forward secrecy.*

Proof. For sake of contradiction let us suppose there exists a PPT adversary $\mathcal{A}$ that is able to break the weak forward secrecy of the protocol 2IB-KA with non-negligible advantage ϵ. Let n be an upper bound to the number of sessions of the protocol run by $\mathcal{A}$ and Q_1 and Q_2 be the number of queries made by the adversary to the random oracles H_1, H_2 respectively. Then we show how to build a simulator S that uses $\mathcal{A}$ to solve the 2DH problem with probability at least ϵ/nQ_2. S receives as input a tuple $(q, \mathbb{G}, g, U_1, U_2, V)$ where $U_1 = g^{u_1}, U_2 = g^{u_2}, V = g^v$ and u_1, u_2, v are random exponents in $\mathbb{Z}_q$. The simulator plays the role of the CDH solver and its goal it to compute the values $W_1 = g^{u_1 v}$ and $W_2 = g^{u_2 v}$.

SETUP. S sets up a simulated execution of the protocol, with simulated KGC, users and sessions. First of all S defines the public parameters of the protocol simulating the KGC. So it chooses random $x_1, x_2 \xleftarrow{\$} \mathbb{Z}_q$ and sets $y_1 = g^{x_1}, y_2 = g^{x_2}$. Then it provides the adversary with input $(q, \mathbb{G}, g, y_1, y_2)$ and oracle access to H_1 and H_2. Since H_1 and H_2 are modeled as random oracles, S can program their output. For each input (ID, r) S chooses a random $e_{ID} \xleftarrow{\$} \mathbb{Z}_q$ and sets $H_1(ID, r) = e_{ID}$. Similar work is done for H_2.

Since S knows the master secret key (x_1, x_2), it can simulate the KGC in full, and give secret keys to all the parties in the network, including answering private key queries from the adversary. At the beginning of the game S guesses the test session and its peers Alice and Bob.

SIMULATING PROTOCOL SESSIONS. Sessions different from the test session are easily simulated since S knows all the information needed to compute the session keys and answer any query (including session key and state reveal queries) from the adversary.

SIMULATING THE TEST SESSION. We now show how to simulate the test session in order to extract W_1, W_2 from the adversary. Since in this game the adversary is assumed to be passive during the test session, the parties (i.e. the simulator in this case) choose the messages exchanged in this session.

Let $(A, r_A^1, r_A^2, s_A^1, s_A^2), (B, r_B^1, r_B^2, s_B^1, s_B^2)$ be the identity information and the secret keys of Alice and Bob respectively (S knows these values). The simulator sets Alice's message as $\langle A, r_A^1, r_A^2, u_A^1 = U_1, u_A^2 = U_2 \rangle$ while the one from Bob is $\langle B, r_B^1, r_B^2, u_B^1 = V, u_B^2 = V^d \rangle$ (for random $d \xleftarrow{\$} \mathbb{Z}_q$). S is implicitly setting $t_A^1 = u_1, t_A^2 = u_2, t_B^1 = v, t_B^2 = vd$. In this case the correct session key contains $\omega_{11} = g^{u_1 v}, \omega_{21} = g^{u_2 v}$. Since H_2 is modeled as a random oracle, if $\mathcal{A}$ has success into distinguishing Z from a random value, it must have queried H_2 on the correct input. Thus S can choose a random value among all the queries that it received from the adversary. Since the number of queries Q_2 is polynomially bounded, S can find the correct $\omega_{11} = W_1, \omega_{21} = W_2$ with non-negligible probability ϵ/nQ_2. This completes the proof of this case[5].

6   Comparisons with Other IB-KA Protocols

In this section we compare IB-KA with other id-based KA protocols from the literature. In particular, we consider the protocol by Chen and Kudla [13] (SCK-2) (which is a modification of Smart's [36]) and two protocols proposed very recently by Boyd et al. [7] (BCNP1, BCNP2).

For our efficiency comparisons we consider a security parameter of 128 and implementations of SCK-2, BCNP1 and BCNP2 with Type 3 pairings[6], which are the most efficient pairings for this kind of security level (higher than 80). Our protocol is assumed to be implemented in an elliptic curves group $\mathbb{G}$ with the same security parameter. In this scenario elements of $\mathbb{G}$ and $\mathbb{G}_1$ need 256 bit to be represented, while 512 bits are needed for $\mathbb{G}_2$ elements and 3072 bits for an element of $\mathbb{G}_T$.

We estimate the computational cost of all the protocols using the costs per operation for Type 3 pairings given by Chen et al. in [12]. The bandwidth cost is expressed as the amount of data in bits sent by each party to complete a session of the protocol[7].

According to the work of Chen et al. [12] SCK-2 is the most efficient protocol with a proof of security in the CK model for all types of pairings. It is proved secure using random oracles under the Bilinear Diffie-Hellman Assumption and requires one round of communication with only one group element sent by each party. To be precise, we point out that the protocol of Boyd et al. (BMP) [8] would appear computationally more efficient than SCK-2, but unfortunately it works only in type 1 and type 4 pairings and is proven secure only in symmetric pairings. BCNP1 and BCNP2 are generic constructions based on any CCA-secure IB-KEM. When implemented (as suggested by the authors of [7]) using one of the IB-KEMs by Kiltz [24], Kiltz-Galindo [25] or Gentry [21] they lead to a two-pass single-round protocol with (CK) security in the standard model. BCNP2 provides weak FS and resistance to KCI attacks, while BCNP1 satisfies only the former property.

The results are summarized in Table 1 assuming protocols BCNP1 and BCNP2 to be implemented with Kiltz's IB-KEM (the most efficient for this application according to the work of Boyd et al. [7]). We defer to the original papers of SCK-2 [13] and BCNP1, BCNP2 [7] for more details about these costs. As described

---

[5] We could give the simulator access to the Strong-2DH oracle 2DH, and then S could use it to "test" all queries to H_2 to find the correct W_1, W_2. The reduction would be tighter (removing the factor of Q_2^{-1} from the success probability) but would require the Strong-2DH Assumption also in this case.

[6] This classification of pairing groups into several types is provided by Galbraith et al. in [19].

[7] We do not consider the identity string sent with the messages as it can be implicit and, in any way, appears in all the protocols.

Table 1. Comparisons between IB-KA protocols

	weak FS	KCI	Standard model	Efficiency	
				Bandwidth	Cost per party
BCNP1	✗	✓	✓	768	56
BCNP2	✓	✓	✓	1024	59
SCK-2	✓	✓	✗	256	43
IB-KA	✓	✓	✗	512	6

in the table, our protocol has a reasonable bandwidth requirement and achieves the best computational efficiency among the other id-based KA protocols.

COMPARISON WITH PKI-BASED PROTOCOLS. We also compare our protocol to MQV [27], and its provably secure version HMQV [26], which is the most efficient protocol in the public-key setting. When comparing our protocol to a PKI-based scheme, like MQV, we must also consider the additional cost of sending and verifying certificates.

We measure the computation costs of the protocols in terms of the number of exponentiations in the underlying group needed to compute the session key. If the exponentiations is done with an exponent that is half the length of the group size, then obviously we count it as $1/2$ exponentiation. Also if an exponentiation is done over a fixed basis, we apply precomputation schemes to speed up the computation, e.g. [20].

Our protocol requires each party to send a single message consisting of two group elements. To compute the session key, the parties perform 2 full exponentiations over variable basis, and one half exponentiation over a fixed basis[8]. For our security parameter, following [20], the latter half exponentiation can be computed with less than 20 group multiplications, with a precomputation table of moderate size.

In MQV, each party sends a single message consisiting of one group element, and performs 1.5 exponentiations to compute the session key. Moreover, in HMQV certificates are sent and verified. Here we distinguish two cases: the certificate is based either on an RSA signature, or on a discrete-log signature, e.g. Schnorr's.

In the RSA case, a short exponent e.g. $e = 2^{16} + 1$, is typically used, and the verification cost is basically equivalent to the cost of the half exponentiation with precomputation in our protocol above. Therefore in this case, MQV is faster, but by a mere half exponentiation. The price to pay however is a massive increase in bandwidth to send the RSA signature (i.e. 3072 bits), and the introduction of the RSA Assumption in order to prove security of the entire scheme.

If we use a Schnorr signature for the certificate, then MQV require sending two more group elements, and therefore its bandwidth requirement is already worse than our protocol (by one group element). The parties then must compute one

---

[8] Indeed since the input to the hash function H_1 is randomized, we can set its output length to be half of the length of the group size.

full and one half exponentiation, both with fixed basis[9] to verify the certificate. This extra computational cost can be compared to an additional half exponentiation, making the computation requirement of MQV with Schnorr certificates equivalent to that of our protocol.

In conclusion, when comparing our protocol with MQV with certificates we find that our protocol: (i) has comparable computational cost; (ii) has better bandwidth (by far in the case of RSA certificates) and (iii) simplifies protocol implementation by removing entirely the need to manage certificates and to interact with a PKI[10].

7   Security Analysis of Related Protocols

As an additional contribution of the paper, in this section we present a formal security analysis of two id-based KA protocols that use techniques that inspired our work: the first by Gunther [22] and the second by Saeednia [32] (which is is an improvement of the previous one). In particular we show variants of these protocols that allow to prove their security in the CK model while only an intuition of security was stated in the original works [22, 32].

7.1   Gunther's Protocol

We present a slightly different variant of Gunther's protocol [22] which we prove secure under the Gap-DH and KEA assumptions.

The Knowledge of Exponent Assumption (KEA) was first stated by Damgård in [15] and later discussed in [3, 23]. Let $\mathbb{G}$ be a group of prime order q with generator g. Then we say that KEA holds over $\mathbb{G}$ if: for any efficient algorithm $\mathcal{A}$ that on input (g, g^a) outputs a pair (B, C) such that $C = B^a$ there exists an efficient "extractor" algorithm $\mathcal{A}'$ that given the same input of $\mathcal{A}$ outputs (B, C, b) such that $C = B^a$ and $B = g^b$.

The modified protocol is summarized in Figure 2. We recall that the session key in the original protocol was just $z_1 z_2 z_3$ and the key generation process computed the hash only on the identity string $H(ID)$. So what we change is: to hash the session key and include the value r_{ID} when hashing the identity. Since the key derivation process is essentially an El Gamal signature on the identity string, the latter modification follows what Pointcheval and Stern proposed in [31] to prove the security of the El Gamal signature scheme.

The following theorem proves the security of the protocol.

Theorem 8. *If H_1 and H_2 are modeled as random oracles and the Gap-DH and KEA assumptions hold, then Gunther's protocol is a secure identity-based key agreement protocol.*

---

[9] Though different basis, which means that in order to apply precomputation techniques, the parties need to maintain two tables.

[10] In the above, we did not account for the cost of verifying group membership for the elements sent by the parties, which is necessary both in the case of MQV and our protocol, and is the same in both protocols.

Gunther's protocol

Setting: A Key Generation Center (KGC) chooses a group $\mathbb{G}$ of prime order q together with a random generator $g \in \mathbb{G}$ and an exponent $x \xleftarrow{\$} \mathbb{Z}_q$. KGC publishes $\mathbb{G}, q, g, y = g^x$ and two hash functions H_1, H_2. It distributes to each user with identity U a private key (r_U, s_U) computed as follows: $r_U = g^k, s_U = k^{-1}(H_1(U, r_U) - xr_U) \bmod q$ for random $k \xleftarrow{\$} \mathbb{Z}_q$.

Key agreement: A and B choose ephemeral private exponents t_A, w_A and t_B, w_B, respectively.

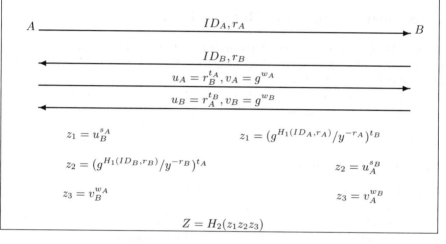

$$Z = H_2(z_1 z_2 z_3)$$

Fig. 2. A and B share session key Z

Proof. For sake of contradiction let us suppose there exists a PPT adversary $\mathcal{A}$ that has non-negligible advantage ϵ into breaking Gunther's protocol, then we show how to build a solver algorithm S for the CDH problem.

In our reduction we will proceed into two steps. First, we describe an intermediate algorithm $\mathcal{B}$ (i.e. the simulator) that interacts with the protocol adversary $\mathcal{A}$ and returns a side output σ. Second, we will show how to build an algorithm S that exploits $F_\mathcal{B}$, the forking algorithm associated with $\mathcal{B}$, to solve the CDH problem under the Gap-DH Assumption.

$\mathcal{B}$ receives as input a tuple $(\mathbb{G}, g, U, V)$, where $U = g^u, V = g^v$ and u, v are random exponents in $\mathbb{Z}_q$, and a set of random elements $h_1, \ldots, h_Q \in \mathbb{Z}_q$. The simulator is also given access to a DH oracle $\mathsf{DH}(\cdot, \cdot, \cdot)$ that on input (U, V, W) answers "yes" if (U, V, W) is a valid DDH tuple . The side output of $\mathcal{B}$ is $\sigma \in \mathbb{G}^2 \times \mathbb{Z}_q$ or $\bot$. Let n be an upper bound to the number of sessions of the protocol run by the adversary $\mathcal{A}$ and Q_1 and Q_2 be the number of queries made by $\mathcal{A}$ to the random oracles H_1, H_2 respectively. Moreover, let Q_c be the number of users corrupted by $\mathcal{A}$ and $Q = Q_1 + Q_c + 1$.

Algorithm $\mathcal{B}^{\mathsf{DH}(U,\cdot,\cdot)}(\mathbb{G}, g, U, V, h_1, \dots, h_Q)$

  Initialize $ctr \leftarrow 0; bad \leftarrow false$; empty tables $\overline{H_1}, \overline{H_2}$;

  Run $\mathcal{A}$ on input $(\mathbb{G}, g, y = U)$ as the public parameters of the protocol and
  simulates the protocol's environment for $\mathcal{A}$ as follows:

   Guess the test session by choosing at random the user (let us call him
   Bob) and the order number of the test session. If n is an upper bound
   to the number of all the sessions initiated by $\mathcal{A}$ then the guess is right
   with probability at least $1/n$.

  H_2 **queries:** On input a value z:
   If $\overline{H_2}[z] = \perp$: choose a random string $Z \in \{0,1\}^{\ell}$ and store $\overline{H_2}[z] = Z$
   Return $\overline{H_2}[z]$ to $\mathcal{A}$

  H_1 **queries:** On input (ID, r):
   If $\overline{H_1}[ID, r] = \perp$, then $ctr \leftarrow ctr + 1; \overline{H_1}[ID, r] = h_{ctr}$
   Return $\overline{H_1}[ID, r]$ to $\mathcal{A}$

  Party Corruption: When $\mathcal{A}$ asks to corrupt party $ID \neq B$, then:
   $ctr \leftarrow ctr + 1; d \xleftarrow{\$} \mathbb{Z}_q; r = g^{h_{ctr}} y^d; s = -rd^{-1}$
   If $\overline{H_1}[ID, r] \neq \perp$ then $bad \leftarrow true$
   Store $\overline{H_1}[ID, r] = h_{ctr}s$ and return (r, s) as ID's private key.

   For the case of Bob, the simulator simply chooses the r_B compo-
   nent of Bob's private key by picking a random $k_B \xleftarrow{\$} \mathbb{Z}_q$ and setting
   $r_B = g^{k_B}$ and $\overline{H_1}[B, r_B] = h_{ctr}$. We observe that in this case $\mathcal{B}$ is
   not able to compute the corresponding s_B. However, since Bob is the
   user guessed for the test session, we can assume that the adversary
   will not ask for his secret key.

  Simulating sessions: First we describe how to simulate sessions different from the test session. Here the main point is that the adversary
   is allowed to ask **session-key** queries and thus the simulator must be
   able to produce the correct session key for each of these sessions. The
   simulator has full information about all the users' secret keys except
   Bob. Therefore $\mathcal{B}$ can easily simulate all the protocol sessions that
   do not include Bob, and answer any of the attacker's queries about
   these sessions. Hence we concentrate on describing how $\mathcal{B}$ simulates
   interactions with Bob.

   Assume that Bob has a session with Charlie (whose identity is
   the string C). If Charlie is an uncorrupted party this means that $\mathcal{B}$
   will generate the messages on behalf of him. In this case $\mathcal{B}$ knows
   Charlie's secret key and also has chosen his ephemeral exponents
   t_C, w_C. Thus it is trivial to see that $\mathcal{B}$ has enough information
   to compute the correct session key. The case when the adversary
   presents messages $\langle C, r_C \rangle, \langle u_C, v_C \rangle$ to Bob as coming from Charlie is more complicated. Here is where $\mathcal{B}$ makes use of the oracle
   $\mathsf{DH}(\cdot, \cdot, \cdot)$ to answer a **session-key query** about this session. The simulator replies with messages $\langle B, r_B \rangle, \langle u_B = g^{t_B}, v_B = g^{w_B} \rangle$ where t_B
   and w_B are chosen by $\mathcal{B}$. Recall that the session key is $H_2(z_1 z_2 z_3)$
   with $z_1 = u_B^{s_C}$, $z_2 = u_C^{s_B}$ and $z_3 = g^{w_B w_C}$. Notice that z_2 is the
   Diffie-Hellman result of the values $u_C = r_B^{t_C}$ and $r_B^{s_B}$. Since the

simulator can compute $r_B^{s_B} = g^{H_1(B,r_B)-x r_B}$, it can check if $\overline{H_2}[z] = Z$ where $\mathsf{DH}(r_B^{s_B}, u_C, \bar{z}) = \text{"yes"}$ and $\bar{z} = z/z_1 z_3$. If $\mathcal{B}$ finds a match then it outputs the corresponding Z as session key for Bob. Otherwise it generates a random $\zeta \xleftarrow{\$} \{0,1\}^\ell$ and gives it as response to the adversary. Later, for each query z to H_2, if z satisfies the equation above it sets $\overline{H_2}[z] = \zeta$ and answers with ζ. This makes oracle's answers consistent.

In addition observe that the simulator can easily answer to state reveal queries as it chooses the fresh exponents on its own.

Simulating the test session: Let $\langle B, \rho_B \rangle, \langle u_B = r_A^{t_B}, v_B = g^{w_B} \rangle$ be the messages from Bob to Alice sent in the test session. We notice that such message may be sent by the adversary who is trying to impersonate Bob. In this case $\mathcal{A}$ may use a value $\rho_B = g^{\lambda_B}$ of its choice as the public component of Bob's private key (i.e. different than $r_B = g^{k_B}$ which $\mathcal{B}$ simulated and for which it knows k_B). $\mathcal{B}$ responds with the messages $\langle A, r_A \rangle, \langle u_A = V, v_A = g^{w_A} \rangle$ as coming from Alice. Finally $\mathcal{B}$ provides $\mathcal{A}$ with a random session key.

Run until $\mathcal{A}$ halts and outputs its decision bit
If $\overline{H_1}[B, \rho_B] = \bot$ then set $ctr \leftarrow ctr + 1$ and $\overline{H_1}[B, \rho_B] = h_{ctr}$
If $bad = true$ then return $(0, \bot)$
Let $i \in \{1, \ldots, Q\}$ such that $H_1(B, \rho_B) = h_i$
Let $Z = H_2(z_1 z_2 z_3)$ be the correct session key for the test session where
$$z_1 = u_B^{s_A}, z_2 = \rho_B^{(h_i - x \rho_B) t_A} \text{ and } z_3 = v_B^{w_A}.$$
If $\mathcal{A}$ has success into distinguishing Z from a random value it must necessarily query the correct value $z = z_1 z_2 z_3$ to the random oracle H_2. This means that $\mathcal{B}$ can efficiently find z in the table $\overline{H_2}$ using the Gap-DH oracle.
Compute $\tau = \frac{z}{z_1 z_3} = V^{h_i/\lambda_B} W^{-\rho_B/\lambda_B}$
Return $(i, (\tau, h_i, \rho_B))$

Let IG be the algorithm that generates a random Diffie-Hellman tuple $(\mathbb{G}, g, U, V)$ and $acc_\mathcal{B}$ be the accepting probability of $\mathcal{B}$. Then we have that:

$$acc_\mathcal{B} \geq \frac{\epsilon}{n} - \Pr[bad = true].$$

For the same argument given in Section 4 we have that

$$acc_\mathcal{B} \geq \frac{\epsilon}{n} - \frac{Q_c(Q)}{2^\ell}.$$

which is still non-negligible, since ϵ is non-negligible.

Once we have described the algorithm $\mathcal{B}$ we show how to build an algorithm S' that exploits $F_\mathcal{B}$, the forking algorithm associated with the above $\mathcal{B}$. Then we will show another algorithm S that solves CDH under the Gap-DH Assumption.

Algorithm $S'^{\mathsf{DH}(\cdot,\cdot,\cdot)}(\mathbb{G}, g, U, V)$
$\quad (b, \sigma, \sigma') \xleftarrow{\$} F_\mathcal{B}^{\mathsf{DH}(U,\cdot,\cdot)}(\mathbb{G}, g, U, V)$

If $b = 0$ then return 0 and halt

Parse σ as (τ, h, ρ) and σ' as (τ', h', ρ')

Compute $V' = V^{\lambda_B^{-1}} = (\tau/\tau')^{(h-h')^{-1}}$ and output (V', ρ, τ, h).

If the forking algorithm $F_{\mathcal{B}}$ has success, this means that there exist random coins γ, an index $J \geq 1$ and $h_1, \ldots, h_Q, h'_J, \ldots, h'_Q \in \mathbb{Z}_q$ with $h = h_J \neq h'_J = h'$ such that: the first execution of $\mathcal{B}(\mathbb{G}, g, U, V, h_1, \ldots, h_Q; \gamma)$ outputs $\tau = g^{vh/\lambda} W^{-\rho/\lambda}$ where $\overline{H_1}[B, \rho] = h$; the second execution of $\mathcal{B}(\mathbb{G}, g, U, V, h_1, \ldots, h_{J-1}, h'_J, \ldots, h'_Q; \gamma)$ outputs $\tau' = g^{vh'/\lambda'} W^{-\rho'/\lambda'}$ such that $\overline{H_1}[B', \rho'] = h'$. Since the two executions of $\mathcal{B}$ are the same until the response to the J-th query to H_1, then we must have $B = B'$ and $\rho = \rho'$ (and $\lambda = \lambda'$). In other words we have an algorithm that given in input a pair (g, g^v) is returning in output $(V', \rho = g^\lambda)$ such that $V' = g^{v/\lambda}$. If the KEA assumption holds then there exists an extractor algorithm that given the same input (g, g^v) outputs (V', ρ, λ). Therefore we can run such algorithm to get λ. We can define S as the algorithm that runs the corresponding extractor algorithm of S' on its same input and gets $(V', \rho, \lambda, \tau, h)$. Finally S can compute

$$W = \left(\frac{\tau}{V^{\lambda/h}}\right)^{-\rho^{-1}} = g^{uv}.$$

By the General Forking Lemma, we have that if $\mathcal{A}$ has non-negligible advantage into breaking the security of Gunther's protocol, then the probability that S has success is also non-negligible.

Vulnerability to reflection attack. In this section we show that Gunther's protocol is vulnerable to the reflection attack. We recall that this attack occurs when an adversary tries to impersonate a party, e.g. Bob to Bob himself. In the case of Gunther's protocol we can restrict this attack to the case when an adversary presents to Bob the first message containing Bob's identity B and the key r_B. In particular, we do not consider the case in which the adversary uses a value $r'_B \neq r_B$ because one can imagine that the honest Bob (who knows his secret key r_B) refuses the connections from himself with $r'_B \neq r_B$.

In this scenario, when (the honest) Bob generates $u_B = g^{t_B}, v_B = g^{w_B}$ and the adversary sends $u'_B = g^{t'_B}, v'_B = g^{w'_B}$ the session key will be $(r_B^{s_B})^{t_B + t'_B} g^{w_B w'_B}$. Thus an adversary, after seeing the message from Bob, can set $u'_B = g^t/u_B$ and $v'_B = g^{w'_B}$ and then is able to compute the session key $H(\bar{z})$ where $\bar{z} = (r_B^{s_B})^t \cdot v_B^{w'_B} = (g^{H(B, r_B)} y^{-r_B})^t \cdot v_B^{w'_B}$.

Other security properties of Gunther's protocol. Following an argument similar to that used for protocol IB-KA in Section 4.1, it is possible to show that Gunther's protocol is resistant to KCI attacks. Moreover we prove the following theorem to show that it satisfies weak forward secrecy.

Theorem 9. *Let $\mathcal{A}$ be a PPT adversary that is able to break the weak forward secrecy of Gunther's protocol with advantage ϵ. Let n be the an upper bound to the number of sessions of the protocol run by $\mathcal{A}$ and Q_1 and Q_2 be the number of* queries made by the adversary to the random oracles H_1, H_2 respectively. Then we can solve the CDH problem with probability at least $\epsilon/(nQ_2)$.

In the following we show how to build an efficient algorithm S that can solve the CDH problem.

S receives as input a tuple $(\mathbb{G}, q, g, U = g^u, V = g^v)$ and wants to compute $W = g^{uv}$. First S simulates the KGC setting up the public parameters of the protocol. It chooses a random $x \xleftarrow{\$} \mathbb{Z}_q$ and sets $y = g^x$. Then it provides the adversary with input $(\mathbb{G}, q, g, y)$ and oracle access to H_1 and H_2. Since H_1 and H_2 are modeled as random oracles, S can program their output. For each input (ID, r_{ID}) S chooses a random $e_{ID} \xleftarrow{\$} \mathbb{Z}_q$ and sets $H_1(ID, r_{ID}) = e_{ID}$. Similar work is done for H_2.

The adversary is allowed to ask the KGC for the secret keys of users of its choice and thus S must be able to simulate the key derivation process. As one can notice, when the adversary asks for the secret key of a user, the simulator is always able to respond, since it has chosen the master secret key x by itself.

At the beginning of the game S guesses the test session and its holder (let us call him Bob). Also let Alice be the other party of the session. If n is an upper bound to the number of all the sessions initiated by $\mathcal{A}$ then the guess is right with probability at least $1/n$.

Without loss of generality we assume that the test session is at Bob (thus the corresponding matching session is at Alice). Since we are in the case when the adversary is passive during the execution of the protocol, the simulator chooses the messages exchanged in the test session.

Let $(A, r_A, s_A), (B, r_B, s_B)$ be the identity informations and the secret keys of Alice and Bob respectively. The simulator uses these values to create the first two messages between the parties. To generate the other ones S chooses random $t_A, t_B \xleftarrow{\$} \mathbb{Z}_q$ and sets $\langle u_A = r_B^{t_A}, v_A = U \rangle$ and $\langle u_B = r_A^{t_B}, v_B = V \rangle$. Thus S is implicitly setting $w_A = u, w_B = v$. Since H_2 is modeled as a random oracle, if the adversary has success into distinguishing the real session key from a random value, it must have queried H_2 on the correct input $\bar{z} = u_B^{s_A} u_A^{s_B} g^{uv}$. Thus S can choose a random value among all the queries that it received from the adversary and then extract $W = \bar{z}/(u_B^{s_A} u_A^{s_B})$ from it. In conclusion S can find W with non-negligible probability ϵ/nQ_2. This completes the proof of this case.

Remark 1. If we would assume the simulator having access to a Gap-DH oracle, S might use the oracle to test, for all queries z made by the adversary, if $DH(U, V, z_3) = \text{"yes"}$ (where z_3 is computed as $z/z_1 z_2$) and then output z_3 for which the test is satisfied. In this case the security of Gunther's protocol would reduce to the Gap-DH Assumption instead of CDH, but we would not have the Q_2 loss factor.

7.2 Saeednia's Protocol

Saeednia proposed in [32] a variant of Gunther's protocol that allows to reduce to 2 the number of messages exchanged by the parties. The idea of Saeednia was basically to use a different equation for computing the El Gamal signature to generate users' keys. Here we propose a variant of Saeednia's protocol that can be proved secure in the CK model under the Gap-DH assumption. The modified protocol is summarized in Figure 3.

Saeednia's protocol

Setting: A Key Generation Center (KGC) chooses a group $\mathbb{G}$ of prime order q together with a random generator $g \in \mathbb{G}$ and an exponent $x \xleftarrow{\$} \mathbb{Z}_q$. KGC publishes $\mathbb{G}, q, g, y = g^x$ and two hash functions H_1, H_2. It distributes to each user with identity U a private key (r_U, s_U) computed as follows:
$r_U = g^k, s_U = kH_1(U, r_U) + xr_U \bmod q$ for random $k \xleftarrow{\$} \mathbb{Z}_q$.

Key agreement: A and B choose ephemeral private exponents t_A and t_B, respectively.

$$A \xrightarrow{\hspace{3cm} ID_A, r_A, u_A = g^{t_A} \hspace{3cm}} B$$

$$\xleftarrow{\hspace{3cm} ID_B, r_B, u_B = g^{t_B} \hspace{3cm}}$$

$$z_1 = u_B^{s_A} \qquad\qquad\qquad z_1 = (r_A^{H_1(ID_A, r_A)} y^{r_A})^{t_B}$$

$$z_2 = (r_B^{H_1(ID_B, r_B)} y^{r_B})^{t_A} \qquad\qquad\qquad z_2 = u_A^{s_B}$$

$$z_3 = u_B^{t_A} \qquad\qquad\qquad\qquad z_3 = u_A^{t_B}$$

$$Z = H_2(z_1 z_2, z_3)$$

Fig. 3. A and B share session key Z

We did almost the same modifications proposed for Gunther's protocol in Section 7.1, namely adding the value r when hashing the identity and hashing the session key. We recall that the session key in the original version of the protocol is the value $z_1 z_2 z_3$ where z_3 is needed to obtain (weak) FS. In our variant we include z_3 in the hash of the session key as $H_2(z_1 z_2, z_3)$.

The following theorem proves the security of the modified Saeednia's protocol.

Theorem 10. *If H_1 and H_2 are modeled as random oracles and the Gap-DH assumption holds, then Saeednia's protocol is a secure identity-based key agreement protocol.*

Proof. For sake of contradiction let us suppose there exists a PPT adversary $\mathcal{A}$ that has non-negligible advantage ϵ into breaking Saeednia's protocol, then we show how to build a solver algorithm S for the CDH problem.

In our reduction we will proceed into two steps. First, we describe an intermediate algorithm $\mathcal{B}$ (i.e. the simulator) that interacts with the protocol adversary

$\mathcal{A}$ and returns a side output σ. Second, we will show how to build an algorithm S that exploits $F_\mathcal{B}$, the forking algorithm associated with $\mathcal{B}$, to solve the CDH problem under the Gap-DH Assumption.

$\mathcal{B}$ receives as input a tuple $(\mathbb{G}, g, U, V)$, where $U = g^u, V = g^v$ and u, v are random exponents in $\mathbb{Z}_q$, and a set of random elements $h_1, \ldots, h_Q \in \mathbb{Z}_q$. The simulator is also given access to a DH oracle $\mathsf{DH}(\cdot, \cdot, \cdot)$ that on input (U, V, W) answers "yes" if (U, V, W) is a valid DDH tuple . The side output of $\mathcal{B}$ is $\sigma \in \mathbb{G}^2 \times \mathbb{Z}_q$ or $\bot$. Let n be an upper bound to the number of sessions of the protocol run by the adversary $\mathcal{A}$ and Q_1 and Q_2 be the number of queries made by $\mathcal{A}$ to the random oracles H_1, H_2 respectively. Moreover, let Q_c be the number of users corrupted by $\mathcal{A}$ and $Q = Q_1 + Q_c + 1$.

Algorithm $\mathcal{B}^{\mathsf{DH}(U, \cdot, \cdot)}(\mathbb{G}, g, U, V, h_1, \ldots, h_Q)$

    Initialize $ctr \leftarrow 0; bad \leftarrow false$; empty tables $\overline{H_1}, \overline{H_2}$;

    Run $\mathcal{A}$ on input $(\mathbb{G}, g, y = U)$ as the public parameters of the protocol and simulates the protocol's environment for $\mathcal{A}$ as follows:

        Guess the test session by choosing at random the user (let us call him Bob) and the order number of the test session. If n is an upper bound to the number of all the sessions initiated by $\mathcal{A}$ then the guess is right with probability at least $1/n$.

        H_2 **queries:** On input a pair (z, z_3):

            If $\overline{H_2}[z, z_3] = \bot$: choose a random string $Z \in \{0,1\}^\ell$ and store $\overline{H_2}[z, z_3] = Z$

            Return $\overline{H_2}[z, z_3]$ to $\mathcal{A}$

        H_1 **queries:** On input (ID, r):

            If $\overline{H_1}[ID, r] = \bot$, then $ctr \leftarrow ctr + 1; \overline{H_1}[ID, r] = h_{ctr}$

            Return $\overline{H_1}[ID, r]$ to $\mathcal{A}$

        Party Corruption: When $\mathcal{A}$ asks to corrupt party $ID \neq B$, then:

            $ctr \leftarrow ctr + 1; e \xleftarrow{\$} \mathbb{Z}_q; r = g^e y^{h_{ctr}}; s = -erd^{-1}$

            If $\overline{H_1}[ID, r] \neq \bot$ then $bad \leftarrow true$

            Store $\overline{H_1}[ID, r] = -rh_{ctr}^{-1}$ and return (r, s) as ID's private key.

            For the case of Bob, the simulator simply chooses the r_B component of Bob's private key by picking a random $k_B \xleftarrow{\$} \mathbb{Z}_q$ and setting $r_B = g^{k_B}$. Moreover it sets $\overline{H_1}[B, r_B] = h_{ctr}$. We observe that in this case $\mathcal{B}$ is not able to compute the corresponding s_B. However, since Bob is the user guessed for the test session, we can assume that the adversary will not ask for his secret key.

        Simulating sessions: First we describe how to simulate sessions different from the test session. Here the main point is that the adversary is allowed to ask **session-key** queries and thus the simulator must be able to produce the correct session key for each of these sessions. The simulator has full information about all the users' secret keys except Bob. Therefore $\mathcal{B}$ can easily simulate all the protocol sessions that do not include Bob, and answer any of the attacker's queries about these sessions. Hence we concentrate on describing how $\mathcal{B}$ simulates interactions with Bob.

Assume that Bob has a session with Charlie (whose identity is the string C). If Charlie is an uncorrupted party this means that $\mathcal{B}$ will generate the messages on behalf of him. In this case $\mathcal{B}$ knows Charlie's secret key and also has chosen his ephemeral exponent t_C. Thus it is trivial to see that $\mathcal{B}$ has enough information to compute the correct session key. The case when the adversary present a message $\langle C, r_C, u_C \rangle$ to Bob as coming from Charlie is more complicated. Here is where $\mathcal{B}$ makes use of the oracle $\mathsf{DH}(\cdot, \cdot, \cdot)$ to answer a session-key query about this session. The simulator replies with the message $\langle B, r_B, u_B = g^{t_B} \rangle$ where t_B is chosen by $\mathcal{B}$. Recall that the session key is $H_2(z_1 z_2, z_3)$ with $z_1 = u_B^{s_C}$, $z_2 = u_C^{s_B}$ and $z_3 = g^{u_B u_C}$. Notice that z_2 is the Diffie-Hellman result of the values u_C and g^{s_B}, where $g^{s_B} = r_B^{H_1(B, r_B)} y^{r_B}$. Since the simulator can compute z_1 and $z_3 = u_C^{t_B}$, it can check if $\overline{H_2}[z, z_3] = Z$ where $\mathsf{DH}(g^{s_B}, u_C, \bar{z}) = \text{"yes"}$ and $\bar{z} = z/z_1$. If $\mathcal{B}$ finds a match then it outputs the corresponding Z as session key for Bob. Otherwise it generates a random $\zeta \xleftarrow{\$} \{0,1\}^\ell$ and gives it as response to the adversary. Later, for each query (z, z_3) to H_2, if z satisfies the equation above it sets $\overline{H_2}[z, z_3] = \zeta$ and answers with ζ. This makes oracle's answers consistent.

In addition observe that the simulator can easily answer to state reveal queries as it chooses the fresh exponents on its own.

Simulating the test session: Let $\langle B, \rho_B, u_B = g^{t_B} \rangle$ be the message from Bob to Alice sent in the test session. We notice that such message may be sent by the adversary who is trying to impersonate Bob. In this case $\mathcal{A}$ may use a value $\rho_B = g^{\lambda_B}$ of its choice as the public component of Bob's private key (i.e. different than $r_B = g^{k_B}$ which $\mathcal{B}$ simulated and for which it knows k_B). $\mathcal{B}$ responds with the message $\langle A, r_A, u_A = V \rangle$ as coming from Alice. Finally $\mathcal{B}$ provides $\mathcal{A}$ with a random session key.

Run until $\mathcal{A}$ halts and outputs its decision bit
If $\overline{H_1}[B, \rho_B] = \perp$ then set $ctr \leftarrow ctr + 1$ and $\overline{H_1}[B, \rho_B] = h_{ctr}$
If $bad = true$ then return $(0, \perp)$
Let $i \in \{1, \ldots, Q\}$ such that $H_1(B, \rho_B) = h_i$
Let $Z = H_2(z_1 z_2, z_3)$ be the correct session key for the test session where $z_1 = u_B^{s_A}$, $z_2 = g^{(\lambda_B h_i + x \rho_B) t_A}$ and $z_3 = u_B^{t_A}$.
If $\mathcal{A}$ has success into distinguishing Z from a random value it must necessarily query the correct value $(z_1 z_2, z_3)$ to the random oracle H_2. This means that $\mathcal{B}$ can efficiently find such a pair in the table $\overline{H_2}$ using the Gap-DH oracle.
Compute $\tau = \frac{z}{z_1} = V^{\lambda_B h_i} W^{\rho_B}$
Return $(i, (\tau, h_i, \rho_B))$

Let IG be the algorithm that generates a random Diffie-Hellman tuple $(\mathbb{G}, g, U, V)$ and $acc_\mathcal{B}$ be the accepting probability of $\mathcal{B}$. Then we have that:

$$acc_\mathcal{B} \geq \frac{\epsilon}{n} - \Pr[bad = true].$$

For the same argument of Section 4 we have that

$$acc_{\mathcal{B}} \geq \frac{\epsilon}{n} - \frac{Q_c(Q)}{2^\ell}$$

which is still non-negligible, since ϵ is non-negligible.

Once we have described the algorithm $\mathcal{B}$ we can now show how to build a solver algorithm S that can exploit $F_{\mathcal{B}}$, the forking algorithm associated with the above $\mathcal{B}$.

The algorithm S plays the role of a CDH solver under the Gap-DH Assumption. It receives in input a CDH tuple $(\mathbb{G}, g, U, V)$ where $U = g^u$, $V = g^v$ and u, v are random exponents in $\mathbb{Z}_q$. S is also given access to a decision oracle $\mathsf{DH}(\cdot, \cdot, \cdot)$ that on input (U, V, W) answers "yes" if (U, V, W) is a valid DH tuple .

Algorithm $S^{\mathsf{DH}(\cdot,\cdot,\cdot)}(q, \mathbb{G}, g, U, V)$
    $(b, \sigma, \sigma') \xleftarrow{\$} F_{\mathcal{B}}^{\mathsf{DH}(U,\cdot,\cdot)}(\mathbb{G}, g, U, V)$
    If $b = 0$ then return 0 and halt
    Parse σ as (τ, h, ρ) and σ' as (τ', h', ρ')
    Compute $\omega = (\tau/\tau')^{(h-h')^{-1}}$ and output $W = (\frac{\tau}{\omega^h})^{\rho^{-1}}$.

If the forking algorithm $F_{\mathcal{B}}$ has success, this means that there exist random coins γ, an index $J \geq 1$ and $h_1, \ldots, h_Q, h'_J, \ldots, h'_Q \in \mathbb{Z}_q$ with $h = h_J \neq h'_J = h'$ such that: the first execution of $\mathcal{B}(\mathbb{G}, g, U, V, h_1, \ldots, h_Q; \gamma)$ outputs $\tau = V^{h\lambda}W^\rho$ where $\overline{H_1}[B, \rho] = h$; the second execution of $\mathcal{B}(\mathbb{G}, g, U, V, h_1, \ldots, h_{J-1}, h'_J, \ldots, h'_Q; \gamma)$ outputs $\tau' = V^{h'\lambda'}W^{\rho'}$ where $\overline{H_1}[B', \rho'] = h'$. Since the two executions of $\mathcal{B}$ are the same until the response to the J-th query to H_1, then we must have $B = B'$ and $\rho = \rho'$ (and $\lambda = \lambda'$). Therefore it is easy to see that S compute $W = g^{uv}$.

By the General Forking Lemma, we have that if $\mathcal{A}$ has non-negligible advantage into breaking the security of Saeednia's protocol, then the probability that S has success is also non-negligible.

Other security properties of Saeednia's protocol. Saeednia's protocol with the modifications presented above satisfies resistance to KCI and reflection attacks. To see this, it is possible to observe that the same arguments given in Section 4.1 for the IB-KA protocol apply to this case. In particular, resistance to reflection attacks can be proven under the Square-DH assumption as well, namely we can build an algorithm that computes g^{u^2} when given in input g, g^u.

Moreover we can prove the following theorem to show that the protocol has weak forward secrecy.

Theorem 11. *Let $\mathcal{A}$ be a PPT adversary that is able to break the weak forward secrecy of Saeednia's protocol with advantage ϵ. Let n be the an upper bound to the number of sessions of the protocol run by $\mathcal{A}$ and Q_1 and Q_2 be the number of queries made by the adversary to the random oracles H_1, H_2 respectively. Then we can solve the CDH problem with probability at least $\epsilon/(nQ_2)$.*

In the following we show how to build an efficient algorithm S that can solve the CDH problem.

S receives as input a tuple $(\mathbb{G}, q, g, U = g^u, V = g^v)$ and wants to compute $W = g^{uv}$. First S simulates the KGC setting up the public parameters of the protocol. It chooses a random $x \xleftarrow{\$} \mathbb{Z}_q$ and sets $y = g^x$. Then it provides the adversary with input $(\mathbb{G}, q, g, y)$ and oracle access to H_1 and H_2. Since H_1 and H_2 are modeled as random oracles, S can program their output. For each input (ID, r_{ID}) S chooses a random $e_{ID} \xleftarrow{\$} \mathbb{Z}_q$ and sets $H_1(ID, r_{ID}) = e_{ID}$. Similar work is done for H_2.

The adversary is allowed to ask the KGC for the secret keys of users of its choice and thus S must be able to simulate the key derivation process. As one can notice, when the adversary asks for the secret key of a user, the simulator is always able to respond, since it has chosen the master secret key x by itself.

At the beginning of the game S guesses the test session and its holder (let us call him Bob). Also let Alice be the other party of the session. Sessions different from the test session are easily simulated since S knows all the informations needed to compute the session keys and answer to session key queries.

Without loss of generality we assume that the test session is at Bob (and thus the corresponding matching session is at Alice). Since we are in the case when the adversary is passive during the execution of the protocol, the simulator chooses the messages of the test session.

Let $(A, r_A, s_A), (B, r_B, s_B)$ be the identity informations and the secret keys of Alice and Bob respectively. The simulator sets Alice's message as $(A, r_A, u_A = U)$ while the one from Bob is $(B, r_B, u_B = V)$. S is implicitly setting $t_A = u, t_B = v$. Since H_2 is modeled as a random oracle, if the adversary has success into distinguishing the real session key from a random value, it must have queried H_2 on the correct input $(z = u_B^{s_A} u_A^{s_B}, z_3 = g^{uv})$. Thus S chooses a random value among all the queries that it received from the adversary. Since the number of queries Q_2 is polynomially bounded, the simulator can find $z_3 = W$ with non-negligible probability ϵ/nQ_2. This completes the proof of this case.

Remark 2. If we would assume the simulator having access to a Gap-DH oracle, S might use the oracle to test, for all queries (z, z_3) made by the adversary, if $DH(U, V, z_3) = ``yes"$ and then output z_3 for which the test is true. In this case the security of Saeednia's protocol would reduce to the Gap-DH Assumption instead of CDH, but we would not have the Q_2 loss factor.

Acknowledgements

The authors would like to thank Gregory Neven for suggesting the use of the General Forking Lemma.

References

1. Abdalla, M., Bellare, M., Rogaway, P.: The oracle Diffie-Hellman assumptions and an analysis of DHIES. In: Naccache, D. (ed.) CT-RSA 2001. LNCS, vol. 2020, pp. 143–158. Springer, Heidelberg (2001)

2. Bellare, M., Neven, G.: New Multi-Signature Schemes and a General Forking Lemma. In: Proceedings of the 13th Conference on Computer and Communications Security – ACM CCS 2006. ACM Press, New York (2006)
3. Bellare, M., Palacio, A.: The Knowledge-of-Exponent Assumptions and 3-round Zero-Knowledge Protocols. In: Franklin, M. (ed.) CRYPTO 2004. LNCS, vol. 3152, pp. 273–289. Springer, Heidelberg (2004)
4. Boneh, D., Boyen, X.: Short Signatures without Random Oracles. In: Cachin, C., Camenisch, J.L. (eds.) EUROCRYPT 2004. LNCS, vol. 3027, pp. 56–73. Springer, Heidelberg (2004)
5. Boneh, D., Franklin, M.K.: Identity-Based Encryption from the Weil Pairing. SIAM J. Comput. 32(3), 586–615 (2003) (Also in CRYPTO 2001)
6. Boyd, C., Choo, K.-K.R.: Security of Two-Party Identity-Based Key Agreement. In: Dawson, E., Vaudenay, S. (eds.) Mycrypt 2005. LNCS, vol. 3715, pp. 229–243. Springer, Heidelberg (2005)
7. Boyd, C., Cliff, Y., Nieto, J.G., Paterson, K.G.: Efficient One-Round Key Exchange in the Standard Model. In: Mu, Y., Susilo, W., Seberry, J. (eds.) ACISP 2008. LNCS, vol. 5107, pp. 69–83. Springer, Heidelberg (2008)
8. Boyd, C., Mao, W., Paterson, K.G.: Key Agreement Using Statically Keyed Authenticators. In: Jakobsson, M., Yung, M., Zhou, J. (eds.) ACNS 2004. LNCS, vol. 3089, pp. 248–262. Springer, Heidelberg (2004)
9. Canetti, R., Krawczyk, H.: Universally Composable Notions of Key Exchange and Secure Channels. In: Knudsen, L.R. (ed.) EUROCRYPT 2002. LNCS, vol. 2332, pp. 337–351. Springer, Heidelberg (2002)
10. Canetti, R., Krawczyk, H.: Analysis of Key-Exchange Protocols and Their Use for Building Secure Channels. In: Pfitzmann, B. (ed.) EUROCRYPT 2001. LNCS, vol. 2045, pp. 453–474. Springer, Heidelberg (2001)
11. Cash, D., Kiltz, E., Shoup, V.: The Twin Diffie-Hellman Problem and Applications. In: Smart, N.P. (ed.) EUROCRYPT 2008. LNCS, vol. 4965, pp. 127–145. Springer, Heidelberg (2008)
12. Chen, L., Cheng, Z., Smart, N.P.: Identity-based key agreement protocols from pairings. Int. J. Inf. Sec. 6(4), 213–241 (2007)
13. Chen, L., Kudla, C.: Identity Based Authenticated Key Agreement Protocols from Pairings. In: 16th IEEE Computer Security Foundations Workshop - CSFW 2003, pp. 219–233. IEEE Computer Society Press, Los Alamitos (2003)
14. Cheng, Q., Ma, C.: Ephemeral Key Compromise Attack on the IB-KA protocol. Cryptology Eprint Archive, Report 2009/568, http://eprint.iacr.org/2009/568
15. Damgård, I.: Towards Practical Public Key Systems Secure Against Chosen Ciphertext Attacks. In: Feigenbaum, J. (ed.) CRYPTO 1991. LNCS, vol. 576, pp. 445–456. Springer, Heidelberg (1992)
16. Diffie, W., Hellman, M.: New Directions in Cryptography. IEEE Transactions on Information Theory 22(6), 644–654 (1976)
17. Fiat, A., Shamir, A.: How to Prove Yourself: Practical Solutions of Identification and Signature Problems. In: Odlyzko, A.M. (ed.) CRYPTO 1986. LNCS, vol. 263, pp. 186–194. Springer, Heidelberg (1987)
18. Fiore, D., Gennaro, R.: Making the diffie-hellman protocol identity-based. In: Pieprzyk, J. (ed.) CT-RSA 2010. LNCS, vol. 5985, pp. 165–178. Springer, Heidelberg (2010), http://eprint.iacr.org/2009/174
19. Galbraith, S.D., Paterson, K.G., Smart, N.P.: Pairings for Cryptographers. Cryptology ePrint Archive, Report 2006/165 (2006), http://eprint.iacr.org

20. Lim, C.H., Lee, P.J.: More Flexible Exponentiation with Precomputation. In: Desmedt, Y.G. (ed.) CRYPTO 1994. LNCS, vol. 839, pp. 95–107. Springer, Heidelberg (1994)
21. Gentry, C.: Practical Identity-Based Encryption Without Random Oracles. In: Vaudenay, S. (ed.) EUROCRYPT 2006. LNCS, vol. 4004, pp. 445–464. Springer, Heidelberg (2006)
22. Gunther, C.G.: An Identity-Based Key-Exchange Protocol. In: Quisquater, J.-J., Vandewalle, J. (eds.) EUROCRYPT 1989. LNCS, vol. 434, pp. 29–37. Springer, Heidelberg (1990)
23. Hada, S., Tanaka, T.: On the Existence of 3-round Zero-Knowledge Protocols. In: Krawczyk, H. (ed.) CRYPTO 1998. LNCS, vol. 1462, p. 408. Springer, Heidelberg (1998)
24. Kiltz, E.: Direct Chosen-Ciphertext Secure Identity-Based Encryption in the Standard Model with short Ciphertexts. Cryptology Eprint Archive, Report 2006/122, http://eprint.iacr.org/2006/122
25. Kiltz, E., Galindo, D.: Direct Chosen-Ciphertext Secure Identity-Based Key Encapsulation Without Random Oracles. Cryptology Eprint Archive, Report 2006/034, http://eprint.iacr.org/2006/034
26. Krawczyk, H.: HMQV: A High-Performance Secure Diffie-Hellman Protocol. In: Shoup, V. (ed.) CRYPTO 2005. LNCS, vol. 3621, pp. 546–566. Springer, Heidelberg (2005)
27. Law, L., Menezes, A., Qu, M., Solinas, J., Vanstone, S.: An efficient Protocol for Authenticated Key Agreement. Designs, Codes and Cryptography 28, 119–134 (2003)
28. Maurer, U., Wolf, S.: Diffie-Hellman oracles. In: Koblitz, N. (ed.) CRYPTO 1996. LNCS, vol. 1109, pp. 268–282. Springer, Heidelberg (1996)
29. Okamoto, E.: Key Distribution Systems Based on Identification Information. In: Pomerance, C. (ed.) CRYPTO 1987. LNCS, vol. 293, pp. 194–202. Springer, Heidelberg (1988)
30. Okamoto, E., Tanaka, K.: Key Distribution System Based on Identification. Information. IEEE Journal on Selected Areas in Communications 7(4), 481–485 (1989)
31. Pointcheval, D., Stern, J.: Security Arguments for Digital Signatures and Blind Signatures. Journal of Cryptology 13(3), 361–396 (2000)
32. Saeednia, S.: Improvement of Gunther's identity-based key exchange protocol. Electonics Letters 36(18), 1535–1536 (2000)
33. Sakai, R., Ohgishi, K., Kasahara, M.: Cryptosystems based on pairing. In: Symposium on Cryptography and Information Security, Okinawa, Japan (2000)
34. Shamir, A.: Identity-Based Cryptosystems and Signature Schemes. In: Blakely, G.R., Chaum, D. (eds.) CRYPTO 1984. LNCS, vol. 196, pp. 47–53. Springer, Heidelberg (1985)
35. Schnorr, C.P.: Efficient identification and signatures for smart cards. In: Brassard, G. (ed.) CRYPTO 1989. LNCS, vol. 435, pp. 239–252. Springer, Heidelberg (1990)
36. Smart, N.P.: An identity-based authenticated key-agreement protocol based on the Weil pairing. Electronics Letters 38, 630–632 (2002)
37. Smetters, D.K., Durfee, G.: Domain-based Administration of Identity-Based Cryptosystems for Secure E-Mail and IPSEC. In: Proceedings of the 12th Conference on USENIX Security Symposium, SSYM 2003, p. 15. USENIX Association (2003)
38. Wang, Y.: Efficient Identity-Based and Authenticated Key Agreement Protocol. Cryptology ePrint Archive, Report 2005/108 (2005), http://eprint.iacr.org/2005/108/

Building a Side Channel Based Disassembler

Thomas Eisenbarth[1], Christof Paar[2], and Björn Weghenkel[2]

[1] Department of Mathematical Sciences
Florida Atlantic University, Boca Raton, FL 33431, USA
teisenba@fau.edu
[2] Horst Görtz Institute for IT Security
Ruhr University Bochum, 44780 Bochum, Germany
{christof.paar,bjoern.weghenkel}@rub.de

Abstract. For the last ten years, side channel research has focused on extracting data leakage with the goal of recovering secret keys of embedded cryptographic implementations. For about the same time it has been known that side channel leakage contains information about many other internal processes of a computing device.

In this work we exploit side channel information to recover large parts of the program executed on an embedded processor. We present the first complete methodology to recover the program code of a microcontroller by evaluating its power consumption only. Besides well-studied methods from side channel analysis, we apply Hidden Markov Models to exploit prior knowledge about the program code. In addition to quantifying the potential of the created side channel based disassembler, we highlight its diverse and unique application scenarios.

1 Motivation

Reverse engineering code of embedded devices is often difficult, as the code is stored in secure on-chip memory. Many companies rely on the privacy of their code to secure their intellectual property (IP) and to prevent product counterfeiting. Yet, in some cases reverse engineering is necessary for various reasons. A company might rely on a discontinued product it does not get any information about from its previous vendor. Or no information is available to ensure flawless interoperability of a component. Often, companies are interested in the details of a competitors new product. Finally, companies may want to identify possible copyright or patent infringements by competitors. In most of these cases that are quite common in embedded product design a disassembler for reconstructing an embedded program is necessary or at least helpful. On most embedded processors, access to code sections can be restricted via so-called lock bits. While it has been shown that for many processors the read protection of the on-chip memory can be circumvented with advanced methods [20], we show in this work that code can be reconstructed with strictly passive methods by analyzing side channel information such as the power consumption of the CPU during code execution.

M.L. Gavrilova et al. (Eds.): Trans. on Comput. Sci. X, LNCS 6340, pp. 78–99, 2010.
© Springer-Verlag Berlin Heidelberg 2010

Side channel analysis has changed the way of implementing security critical embedded applications in the last ten years. Many methods for physical crypt-analysis have been proposed, such as differential power/EM analysis, fault attacks and timing analysis [9,1,10]. Since then, methods in side channel analysis as well as countermeasures have been greatly improved by a broad research effort in the cryptographic community. Up to now, most efforts in power and EM analysis have been put into reconstructing data dependencies in the side channel. Yet, all activity within a device leaves a 'fingerprint' in the power trace. When Kocher *et al.* [10] published power based side channel attacks in 1999, they already mentioned the feasibility of reverse engineering code using side channel analysis. Despite this, virtually all previous work in the are of side channel analysis focus on breaking cryptographic implementations.

We want to show that a program running on a microcontroller can be reconstructed by passively monitoring the power consumption or other electromagnetic emanations only.

1.1 Related Work

Although Kocher *et al.* [10] already mentioned the feasibility of reverse engineering algorithms using side channel analysis, only little work following this idea has been performed. Novak [14] presents a method to recover substitution tables of the secret A3/A8 algorithm. For Novak's attack, one of the two substitution tables and the secret key must be known. Clavier [4] improves reverse engineering of A3/A8 by proposing an attack retrieving the values of both permutation tables and the key without any prior knowledge. Yet, both works concentrate on one specific look-up table and do not consider other parts of the algorithm. In [24], Vermoen shows how to acquire information about bytecodes executed on a Java smart card. The method used in his work is based on averaging traces of certain bytecodes in order to correlate them to an averaged trace of an unknown sequence of bytecodes. Further, Quisquater *et al.* [16] present a method that recognizes executed instructions in single traces by means of self-organizing maps, which is a special form of neural network. Both works restate the general feasibility without quantifying success rates.

1.2 Our Approach

Our final goal is the reconstruction of the program flow and program code. In other words, we want to reconstruct the executed instructions and their execution order of the device under test, the microcontroller, from a passive physical measurement (*i.e.*, an EM measurement or a power trace).

The approach we follow is different from the previous ones, since it is the intention to retrieve information of a program running on a microcontroller by means of single measurements. Under this premise, averaging like in Vermoens approach is not (at least not in the general case) practicable. Although [16] states the general feasibility of a side channel based disassembler, no quantified results are presented. Furthermore, the use of self-organizing maps seems to be inadequate since the possibilities to readjust this approach in case of insufficient results is highly limited.

We apply methods from side channel analysis that are known to be optimal for extracting information to reconstruct executed instruction sequences. We further explore methods to utilize prior information we have about the executed instructions, which is a new approach in side channel analysis. Many publications in side channel analysis borrow methods from other disciplines to enhance side channel cryptanalysis. We want to reverse this trend by showing that methods from side channel analysis can be applied to interesting problems outside of the context of cryptology.

The remaining work is structured as follows: In Section 2 we present methods that recover as much information from the physical channel as possible. Here we apply the most advanced models from side channel analysis research. In Section 3 we apply a hidden Markov model to our problem and introduce methods that increase the performance of our disassembler. All methods are applied to a sample microcontroller platform in Section 4. We also describe and compare the performances of all previously introduced methods. Section 5 discusses possible applications of the proposed methods and Section 6 concludes our work.

2   Extracting Information from Side Channel Leakage

Monitoring side channels for gaining information about a non-accessible or not easily-accessible system is a classical engineering problem, e.g., in control engineering. But especially in cryptography, a lot of effort has been put into methods for retrieving information from emanations of a microcontroller. Hence, we explore the state-of-the-art in side channel information extraction in cryptography to find optimal methods for our purposes. Yet, our goal is different as we extract information about the instruction rather than data.

But how does information about an instruction leak via the side channel? For data in processors, we assume that the leakage originates from the buses which move the data, as well as the ALU processing the data and registers storing the data. The physical representation of an instruction in a microcontroller is more subtle. A unique feature of each instruction is the opcode stored in program memory and moved to the instruction decoder before execution. Besides this, an instruction is characterized by a certain behavior of the ALU, the buses, etc., and possibly other components.

When trying to determine which instruction has been executed, we have in a worst case scenario only one observation of the instruction. Even if we are able to repeat the measurement, the behavior of the instruction will remain the same. Hence we are not able to follow a DPA approach, but rather have to do simple power analysis. In order to succeed, we assume that when trying to recover a program from a microcontroller, we have access to an identical microcontroller which we can analyze and profile. We can use this profiling step to train a Bayesian classifier, as is typically done in template attacks [3]. A Bayesian classifier is a better choice than, e.g., stochastic models [19] when the underlying leakage function is not known [22].

Template Construction. The first step of template classification is the construction of a template for every class [3]. Classes are in our case equivalent to individual microcontroller instructions. Each template is constructed by estimating the instructions' distribution of the power consumption from the sample data. Later, during the attack phase, the template recognition is then performed by assigning each new observation of power consumption to the most probable class.

As sample data we consider N D-dimensional observations of the processor's power consumption $\{x_n\}$, where $x_n \in \mathbb{R}^D$, $n = 1, \ldots, N$. Each observation belongs to exactly one of K classes $\mathcal{C}_k$, representing the instructions modeled by a finite set of instruction states q_k, $k = 1, \ldots, K$. Each class $\mathcal{C}_k$ contains $N_k = |\mathcal{C}_k|$ elements. We assume that for each class our samples are drawn from a multivariate normal distribution

$$\mathcal{N}(x|\mu_k, \mathbf{S}_k) = \frac{1}{(2\pi)^{D/2} |\mathbf{S}_k|^{1/2}} \exp\left(-\frac{1}{2}(x - \mu_k)^T \mathbf{S}_k^{-1}(x - \mu_k)\right). \quad (1)$$

Given the sample data $\{x_n\}$, the maximum-likelihood estimations for the class mean μ_k and the class covariance $\mathbf{S}_k$ are given by

$$\mu_k = \frac{1}{N_k} \sum_{x_n \in \mathcal{C}_k} x_n \quad (2)$$

and

$$\mathbf{S}_k = \frac{1}{N_k} \sum_{x_n \in \mathcal{C}_k} (x_n - \mu_k)(x_n - \mu_k)^T. \quad (3)$$

Thus, the template for each class is defined by $(\mu_k, \mathbf{S}_k)$.

Template Classification. During the classification phase, a new observation of power consumption x is assigned to one of the possible instruction states q_k. This is done by evaluating every template and determining the class state $\tilde{q}$ with the highest posterior probability. Considering the Bayes rule, we get:

$$\tilde{q} = \arg\max_{q_k} p(q_k|x) = \arg\max_{q_k} p(x|q_k) \Pr(q_k), \quad (4)$$

where $p(x|q_k) = \mathcal{N}(x|\mu_k, \mathbf{S}_k)$ and $\Pr(q_k)$ is the prior probability of instruction state q_k.

In practice, the observations x_n available for training a template are too high dimensional and too closely correlated to generate a well-conditioned covariance matrix $\mathbf{S}_k$, making its inversion impossible [18]. Building the templates in a suitable subspace can solve these problems. In the subspace, less observations x_n are necessary to create a regular covariance matrix and the estimated class distributions become more reliable.

Several methods for the reduction of the size of the observations x_n have been proposed in the context of side channel analysis [18,21]. Even more are available in the standard literature [2]. We tried Principal Component Analysis and Fisher's Linear Discriminant Analysis.

Principal Component Analysis. Principal Component Analysis (PCA) is a technique to reduce the dimensionality of our data while keeping as much of its variance as possible. This is achieved by orthogonally projecting the data onto a lower dimensional subspace.

Consider again the N observations of power consumption $\{x_n\}$, $n = 1, \ldots, N$, and their global covariance matrix $\mathbf{S}$ which is built in analogy to (3). A one-dimensional subspace in this Euclidean space can be defined by a D-dimensional unit vector $\mathbf{u}_1$. The projection of each data point x_n onto that subspace is given by $\mathbf{u}_1^T x_n$. It can be shown that the direction that maximizes the projected variance $\mathbf{u}_1^T \mathbf{S} \mathbf{u}_1$ with respect to $\mathbf{u}_1$ corresponds to the eigenvector of $\mathbf{S}$ with the largest eigenvalue λ_1 [2]. Analogous, an M-dimensional subspace, $M < D$, that maximizes the projected variance is given by the M eigenvectors $\mathbf{u}_1, \ldots, \mathbf{u}_M$ of $\mathbf{S}$ corresponding to the M largest eigenvalues $\lambda_1, \ldots, \lambda_M$.

Since our goal is the reliable distinction of many different instructions it seems reasonable not only to maximize the overall variance of the data but alternatively to maximize the variance of the different class means $\boldsymbol{\mu}_k$. If moving the class means away from each other also results in less overlapping, the classification will be easier. We apply PCA in both ways, *i.e.*, for the whole data and for class means.

Fisher's Linear Discriminant Analysis. Similar to PCA, with Fisher's Linear Discriminant Analysis (or Fisher LDA) we have another method for dimensionality reduction. But instead of just maximizing the variance of the projected data, information about the different classes and their covariances is taken into consideration.

Again, we have our N observations $\{x_n\}$ in a D-dimensional Euclidean space. Each observation belongs to one of K different classes $\mathcal{C}_k$, $k = 1, \ldots, K$, of size $N_k = |\mathcal{C}_k|$.

Then, the within-class covariance $\mathbf{S}_W$ for all classes is given by

$$\mathbf{S}_W = \sum_{k=1}^{K} N_k \mathbf{S}_k \tag{5}$$

and the covariance of the class means, the between-class covariance $\mathbf{S}_B$, given by

$$\mathbf{S}_B = \sum_{k=1}^{K} N_k (\boldsymbol{\mu}_k - \boldsymbol{\mu})(\boldsymbol{\mu}_k - \boldsymbol{\mu})^T, \tag{6}$$

where $\boldsymbol{\mu}$ is the mean of the total data set and $\boldsymbol{\mu}_k$ and $\mathbf{S}_k$ are the individual class mean and covariance as defined in (2) and (3).

Now consider again a D-dimensional unit vector $\mathbf{u}_1$ defining a one-dimensional subspace onto which the data is projected. This time, the objective used to be maximized in the subspace is the ratio of the projected between-class variance to the projected within-class variance:

$$J(\mathbf{u}_1) = (\mathbf{u}_1^T \mathbf{S}_W \mathbf{u}_1)^{-1}(\mathbf{u}_1^T \mathbf{S}_B \mathbf{u}_1). \tag{7}$$

As for PCA it can be shown that this objective is maximized when $\mathbf{u}_1$ corresponds to the eigenvector of $\mathbf{S}_W^{-1}\mathbf{S}_B$ with the largest eigenvalue λ_1, leading to a one-dimensional subspace in which the class means are wide-spread and the average class variance will be small [2]. Again, the M-dimensional subspace, $M \leq K - 1$, created by the first M orthogonal directions that maximize the objective J are given by the M eigenvectors $\mathbf{u}_1, \ldots, \mathbf{u}_M$ of $\mathbf{S}_W^{-1}\mathbf{S}_B$ with the largest eigenvalues $\lambda_1, \ldots, \lambda_M$.

The PCA approach of maximizing the variance will not always lead to good separability of the classes. In these cases Fisher LDA can be clearly superior. On the other hand it is more prone to overfitting since more model parameters have to be estimated.

In addition to the described template recognition we also tried different multiclass Support Vector Machines implemented in the Shark machine learning library [8]. Unfortunately, with 41 classes and 2000 training examples per class (cf. Section 4) the computational costs were too high for a thorough search for parameters. Furthermore, the first results we received were not very promising. Therefore we did not further pursue this approach.

3   How to Include Code Properties

In this section we extend the model of a microcontroller's power consumption by a second level. In the previous section we modeled the power consumption of single instruction states. We expand our approach by additionally exploiting general knowledge about microcontroller code.

Up to now we did not consider *a priori* knowledge we have about the code we want to reverse engineer. Even in a scenario where we do not know anything specific about the target code, we have prior knowledge about source code in general. For instance, some instructions occur more often than others. As an example we can focus on the PIC microcontroller we analyze in Section 4.2. Since one of the operands of two-operand instructions must be stored in the accumulator, move commands to and from the accu are frequent. Other instructions such as NOP (no operation) are quite rare in most programs. By performing an instruction frequency analysis we can provide meaningful prior probabilities to the instruction distinguisher from Section 2. In particular, the performance of the template recognition can be boosted by including the prior probabilities in Equation (4).

For many microprocessor architectures instruction frequency analyses have been performed, mainly for optimizing instruction sets. Unfortunately, for microcontrollers and especially the PIC, no major previous work has been performed. The analysis we performed is described in Section 4.2.

Besides a simple instruction frequency analysis, additional information can be gained by looking at tuples of instructions that usually are executed subsequently. One example are the few two-cycle instructions such as CALL and GOTO, which are always followed by their second instruction part. But it is also true for conditional commands such as BTFSS (bit test a register, skip next instruction if zero), which is commonly used to build a conditional branch, hence followed by a GOTO (when branching) or by a virtual NOP (when skipping the GOTO). The Microchip Assembler itself supports 13 built-in macros which virtually extend the instruction set and are replaced by more than one physical instruction at compile time [13]. Their use will consequently influence the occurrence probability of the corresponding tuples. Similar effects occur if a compiler like a certain C compiler has been used for code generation. Tuple frequency analysis is also a classical method for doing cryptanalysis of historic ciphers.

Other information about the code can also be helpful. A crypto implementation uses different instructions than a communication application or a control algorithm. Additional information can be gained by exact knowledge about certain compiler behavior if the code was compiled, e.g., from C source code. Different compilers can generate assembly code with different properties. Hence, prior knowledge about the application or the compiler can be exploited to improve recognition results.

Hidden Markov Model. The microprocessor can be considered as a state machine, for which we want to reconstruct the sequence of taken states. Each state corresponds to an instruction, or, more precisely, to a part of an instruction if the instruction needs several cycles to be executed. We cannot directly observe the state. Instead, the only information we have is the side channel information provided by the power measurement of a full instruction cycle. Yet, we assume that the physical information depends on the state, $i.e.$, the executed instruction of the microcontroller.

We define our system to be described by a hidden Markov model (HMM). At each discrete time instance i we make one observation $\boldsymbol{x}_i$, resulting in a sequence of observations $\hat{\boldsymbol{x}}$. These observations are generated by a hidden Markov chain passing through a state sequence $\boldsymbol{\pi}$, with $\pi_i = q_k$ being the state the model is in at time instance i. Each state q_k is followed by a new state q_l with a probability of $a_{kl} = \Pr(\pi_i = q_l | \pi_{i-1} = q_k)$. We implicitly assume that the probability of the new state q_l depends only on the preceding state q_k, but not on any earlier states. The Markov process cannot directly be observed, instead we observe certain emissions of that process. We expect to see an observation $\boldsymbol{x}_i$ with a certain probability $e_k(\boldsymbol{x}_i) = p(\boldsymbol{x}_i | \pi_i = q_k)$, depending on the actual state q_k of the processor.

A simple Markov model with three states A, B and C is given in Figure 1. Unlike for classical HMMs, for which the observations are drawn from a discrete set of symbols, our observations $\boldsymbol{x}_i$ are continuous distributions over $\mathbb{R}^D$ and our emission probabilities are consequently described by the continuous probability density functions $e_k(\boldsymbol{x}_i) = p(\boldsymbol{x}_i | \pi_i = q_k)$.

Our system can completely be described as a hidden Markov model (HMM) consisting of the state transition probability distribution $\boldsymbol{A} = \{a_{kl}\}$, the emission probability distribution $\boldsymbol{E} = e_k(\boldsymbol{x}_i)$, and an initial state distribution $\boldsymbol{\kappa} = \{\kappa_k | \kappa_k = \Pr(q_k)\}$. We will use tuple analysis of executed instruction sequences to derive the transition probabilities $\boldsymbol{A}$ of the hidden Markov chain. The instruction probabilities derived from the frequency analysis can also serve as an initial state

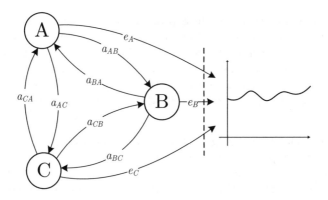

Fig. 1. HMM with three hidden states A, B and C. Only the output on the right of the dashed line is observable.

distribution κ for the HMM. Finally, the emission probability distribution E is provided by the templates described in Section 2. The process of the actual parameter derivation for our model (A,E,κ) is described in Section 4. Having the model and a set of observations x, several methods for optimal reconstruction of the state sequence π exist.

3.1 Optimal Instruction Reconstruction

Assuming that we have reconstructed all parameters of our HMM, namely A, E and κ, we assume a sequence of observations x for which we want to reconstruct the state sequence π of the hidden Markov process, namely the instructions executed on the microprocessor. Given our model (A,E,κ), we are able to reconstruct either

- the state sequence that was executed most likely, or
- the most probable state executed at a certain time instance, given the set of observations.

Though similar, the solutions are not always the same and are derived using two different algorithms. We evaluate both algorithms, the Viterbi algorithm and the Forward-Backward algorithm.

Viterbi Algorithm. The Viterbi algorithm determines the most probable state path $\pi = \{\pi_i\}$ that might have caused the observations $\hat{x} = \{x_i\}$ [17,6]. The path with the highest probability is given by

$$\pi^* = \operatorname{argmax}_{\pi} p(\pi|\hat{x}) = \operatorname{argmax}_{\pi} \frac{p(\hat{x}, \pi)}{p(\hat{x})} = \operatorname{argmax}_{\pi} p(\hat{x}, \pi)$$

and can be determined recursively by $v_l(i+1) = e_l(x_{i+1})\max_k(v_k(i)a_{kl})$ and $v_k(1) = \kappa_k e_k(x_1)$, where $v_k(i)$ is the probability of the most probable path ending in state q_k. Hence we drop all transition probabilities leading to state q_k, except for the one with the highest probability. Usually for every $v_l(i+1)$ a pointer to the preceding state probability $v_k(i)$ is stored together with the probability itself. After reaching the last observation, the path yielding the optimal state sequence is computed by simple back tracking from the final winning state.

When viewing the states as nodes and the transitions as edges of a trellis, as is typically done in (de-) coding theory, the algorithm becomes more ostensive [11].

The Forward-Backward Algorithm. The forward-backward algorithm maximizes the posterior probability that an observation x_i came from state q_k, given the full observed sequence $\hat{x}$, i.e., the algorithm optimizes $p(\pi_i = q_k|\hat{x})$ for every i [17,6]. In contrast to the Viterbi algorithm, it includes the probabilities of all transitions leading to one state, and browses all transitions twice, once in the forward direction like the Viterbi, and once in the backward direction.

For the *forward* direction we define $\alpha_k(i) = p(x_1 x_2 \dots x_i, \pi_i = q_k)$, α being the probability of the observed sequence up to x_t, and $\pi_i = q_k$. The forward algorithm is performed recursively by evaluating all $\alpha_k(i)$. The *backward* algorithm is performed in the same way, just backwards, i.e., $\beta_k(i) = p(x_{i+1} x_{i+2} \dots x_L | \pi_i = q_k)$. The computation of $\beta_k(i)$ and $\alpha_k(i)$ is performed recursively by evaluating

$$\alpha_l(i+1) = e_l(x_{i+1}) \sum_k \alpha_k(i) a_{kl} \text{ and}$$

$$\beta_k(i) = \sum_l \beta_l(i+1) a_{kl} e_l(x_{i+1}).$$

The initial values for the recursions are $\alpha_k(1) = \kappa_k e_k(x_1)$ and $\beta_k(T) = 1$, respectively. By simply multiplying $\alpha_k(i)$ and $\beta_k(i)$ we gain the production probability of the observed sequence with the ith symbol being produced by state q_k:

$$p(x, \pi_i = k) = \alpha_k(i)\beta_k(i) = p(x_1 x_2 \dots x_i, \pi_i = k)p(x_{i+1} x_{i+2} \dots x_L | \pi_i = k)$$

We can now easily derive the posterior probability $\gamma_k(i) = p(\pi_i = k|\hat{x})$ by simply dividing $p(\hat{x}, \pi_i = k)$ by $p(\hat{x})$:

$$\gamma_k(i) = \frac{\alpha_k(i)\beta_k(i)}{p(\hat{x})} = \frac{\alpha_k(i)\beta_k(i)}{\sum_k \alpha_k(i)\beta_k(i)}$$

The forward-backward algorithm consequently calculates the maximum a-posteriori probability for each observation, hence minimizes the number of state errors. This can sometimes cause problems as the resulting state sequence might not be an executable one. The forward-backward algorithm is also known as 'MAP algorithm', or 'BCJR algorithm'.

For a complete description of both algorithms, refer to [17,5,11]. The Viterbi algorithm used to be more popular for decoding of convolutional codes (at least until the advent of Turbo codes) due to its lower computational complexity and almost equally good results. It is also easier to take care of numerical difficulties that often occur for both algorithms.

4   Reconstructing a Program from Side Channel Leakage

This section presents the practical results of the code reconstruction from actual power measurements. The methods and models we introduced in the previous two sections are applied to a PIC microcontroller. The PIC microcontroller makes a good choice for a proof-of-concept implementation of the side-channel disassembler, since it features a comparably small instruction set, a short pipeline and is a well-understood target for side-channel attacks [21]. We present the results of every step taken and compare alternative methods where available.

All measurements were done on a PIC16F687 microcontroller mounted on a printed circuit board. The board enables easy measurement of the power consumption of the running microcontroller. The power consumption is measured via the voltage drop over a shunt resistor connecting the PIC's ground pin to the ground of the power supply. The PIC is clocked at 1 MHz using its internal clock generator. Measurements are performed using an Agilent Infiniium 54832D digital sampling oscilloscope featuring a maximum sampling rate of 4 GS/s at 1 GHz bandwidth. All measurements have been sampled at 1 GS/s. The same measurement setup is used for the generation of sample measurements for template generation, template verification, and the measurement of sample programs we used to verify our final choice of methods.

The analyzed PIC16F687 microcontroller features an instruction set of 35 different instructions. We excluded instructions like SLEEP that will not occur in the program flow. Most of the instructions are one-cycle instructions. Yet some instructions, especially branching instructions, can last two instruction cycles. In those cases we created two different templates for each instruction cycle, resulting in a set of 41 different templates or instruction classes, respectively.

Each instruction cycle of the PIC lasts four clock cycles. The power consumption of each peak depends on different properties, of which we can only assume a limited number to be known or predictable. Two typical power traces of the PIC are shown in Figure 2. Each trace depicts the power consumption during the execution of three instructions. Every instruction lasts four clock cycles, each clock cycle being indicated by a peak in the power trace. The first instruction, executed during the first four clock cycles Q1 through Q4, is the same in both cases, *i.e.*, a NOP instruction. The second executed instruction is either an ADDLW or a MOVWF, as indicated. As can be easily seen, the power consumption of two different instructions differs even before the execution cycle of the instruction itself. The PIC features a pipeline of one instruction, hence an instruction is prefetched while the previous instruction is being executed. The different Hamming weights (for ADDLW and MOVWF the difference is 6 of 14 bit) of the prefetched opcodes account in part for the differences in Q1 through Q3. In Q5, at the first execution clock cycle of the monitored instruction, the data is mapped to the ALU, e.g., via the data bus. Hence, the replacement of values on the data bus affects the power consumption in Q5. In Q6, the ALU actually reads the applied data, before processing it and putting the result on the bus in Q7. In Q8, the result is stored at the target register. Of course, these are only some of the effects that show up in the power trace.

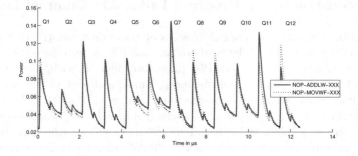

Fig. 2. Power trace showing three examples for the execution of NOP and ADDLW versus the execution of NOP and MOVWF

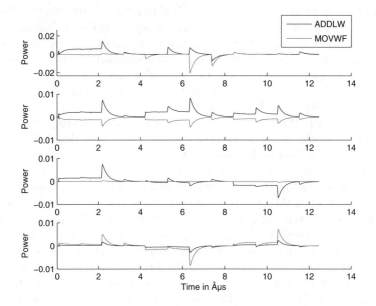

Fig. 3. Sum of the PCA components (top figure) and the three first components of the PCA of the both instructions of Figure 2

Again, we saw that data values, especially those written to the bus, have a significant influence on the variation of the power consumption.

Unfortunately, the data dependencies do not help identifying the instruction. They rather obfuscate smaller changes caused by the control logic, the ALU and other instruction-dependent power consumers. Hence, for effective instruction reconstruction, we apply the methods introduced in Section 2 to extract the maximum amount of information from the observed power trace x.

4.1   Template Construction

The first step for building templates is the profiling step. To build templates for the instructions, we need several different power measurements of the same instruction. For this purpose we executed specifically generated training code on the training device described above. Since the template must be independent of other factors except the instruction itself, we varied all other variables influencing the power consumption. We generated several code snippets containing the target instruction while varying the processed data, memory location, as well as the instructions before and after the target instruction. The new code is programmed into the microcontroller and executed while the oscilloscope samples the power consumption. The post-processing is explained after the explanation of the training code snippets for the profiling.

To generate a training code set for the profiling of a chosen instruction, this instruction is executed several times. For each execution the data processed by the instruction is initialized to a random value. If the instruction operates on a register, one of the general purpose registers is chosen at random and is initialized with random data prior to being accessed. The accu is always initialized with a random value for every instruction, even if it is not accessed. This is due to the observation in [7] that the Hamming weight of the working registers content has a noticeable effect on the PICs power consumption even while executing a NOP instruction.

Due to the pipeline, we also have to vary the pre-instruction and the post-instruction surrounding the target instruction we want to profile. We also made the pre-instructions and post-instructions operate on random data. Since we included the measurement of the pre- and the post-instruction into the templates, the post-instruction was also followed by another random instruction working on random data. By this we are able to minimize the bias that the surrounding instructions can have on our observations. Finally, we also varied the position of the instructions in program memory, just in case this could influence the power consumption as well.

Target instructions taking two instruction cycles to execute are treated as two consecutive instructions, hence two templates are generated for these instructions. Of course, only the post-instruction or the pre-instruction can be varied in this case. For each of the 41 instruction classes we generated 2500 observations with randomly varying data and surrounding instructions. The raw power traces including pre- and the post-instruction are then aligned to an arbitrary reference instruction to neutralize small variations in the length of clock cycles.

PCA. When performing a template attack in a principal subspace, the dimensionality M of the subspace has to be chosen carefully. On one hand, if M is too low, too much of the variance of the original data gets lost and with it, most likely, important information about the class distribution. If M gets too large, on the other hand, the templates get less reliable again. One reason for this could be the bad conditioning of a large covariance matrix. Another reason is the risk of overfitting model parameters to distributions which we kept random in the template creation process, such as surrounding instructions and processed data.

As the plots of the power consumption profile shows (cf. Figure 2), there are twelve large peaks and another twelve small peaks for three instruction cycles. Thus, we can assume an upper bound of 24 for the number of components containing information. Indeed, as shown in Figure 4, our experiments for PCA show no significant improvements in performance after $M = 16$ dimensions, leading to an average recognition rate of 65.6%.

To find a good subspace, the performance for a given number of dimensions is determined using 5-fold cross validation: 2000 examples per class are split into five parts and, successively, one part is kept as test data, one as training data for the PCA and the remaining three parts as training data for the templates. The PCA is applied to the test data, which is then evaluated using the generated templates. The final result of the cross validation run is the average recognition rate on all five unseen (*i.e.*, not included in any manner in the template building process) test data sets.

After deciding that $M = 16$ is a good choice for the subspace, the 2000 examples per class were taken to compute a new model (750 examples for PCA, 1250 for the templates) which was validated on 41×500 yet unseen examples, resulting again in a recognition rate of 65.2%.

We also tried to normalize the data to $[0 \ldots 1]$ and to zero mean and standard deviation $\sigma = 1$, respectively. The normalization steps did not result in better recognition rates.

Following another approach, we used PCA to create a subspace that maximizes the variance between the different class means instead of maximizing the overall variance [21]. This variation of PCA resulted in an improved average recognition rate of 66.5% for $M = 20$. Again, we used 5-fold cross validation to determine the success rate and additional normalization lead to worse results.

Figure 3 shows the sum of all PCA components (upper plot) and the first three PCA components separately (three lower plots) of the PCA-based template means of the ADDLW and MOVWF instructions. The plots show that the four instruction cycles of the post-instruction contain no information for the instruction recognition. Parts of the pre-instructions, however, contain useful information, due to the instruction prefetch.

Fisher LDA. Since the Fisher-LDA, like our second PCA approach, not only takes into consideration the variance of the class means, but also the variance of the different classes, we expect a subspace with less overlaps of the classes and thus better classification results. In accordance to the cross-validation steps above, we reached a recognition rate of 70.1% with $M = 17$ on unseen data. However, for subspaces with $M < 15$ the performance has been significantly higher than for PCA, as shown in Figure 4. Hence, LDA needs less dimensions resulting in smaller templates to achieve comparable results.

A comparison of the recognition rates for the different instructions reveals large differences between instructions. Table 1 shows a part of the recognition rates for selected instructions. The recognition rates vary from 30% for DECF

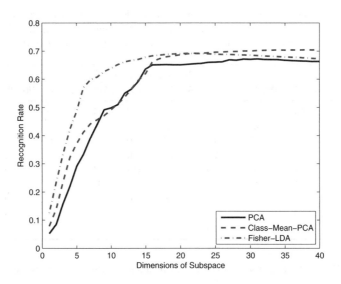

Fig. 4. Results of 5-fold cross validation on generated training data

instruction to 100% for CALL. Furthermore, one observes *similarities* between certain instructions. For instance, there are many false positives amongst instructions working on file registers, e.g., ADDWF, ANDWF, DECF. Some instructions, like BTFSC and BTFSS, seem especially hard to distinguish while others, like RETURN, show very few false positives or false negatives.

Similar to BTFSC and BTFSS or the file register instructions, there seem to be several *families* of instructions with a template distribution very close to each other, resulting in a huge cross-error. Therefore we also tried an hierarchical LDA which performs the recognition in a layered manner, first identifying a family of instructions and then, applying a second set of templates, identifying the actual instruction within the family. However, this approach did not result in an increased recognition rate and was hence not further explored.

Until approximately 16 dimensions, LDA clearly outperforms the two PCA approaches. The class mean PCA shows a better performance to the classical PCA and should hence be preferred. All three sets of templates make a decent choice for the generation of the emission probabilities E for our HMM, as they all achieve a similar recognition rate of almost 65% for a choice of 16 or more dimensions.

4.2 Source Code Analysis

For the instruction frequency analysis and tuple frequency analysis we analyzed the source code of several programs. We built up a code base by using publicly available source code from various web sites, e.g., the microchip PIC sample source code [23,15,25]. We also included several implementations of own source code, cryptographic as well as general purpose code.

Table 1. Percentage of true positives (bold) and false positives during recognition of selected instructions with 17 dimensional Fisher-LDA on unseen test data. The columns indicate the recognized instructions while the line indicates the executed instruction.

Instruction	Recognized as [%]								
	ADDWF	ANDWF	BTFSC	BTFSS	CALL	DECF	MOVLW	MOVWF	RETURN
ADDWF	**41**	8	1	5	0	5	0	1	0
ANDWF	4	**38**	3	1	0	11	0	2	0
BTFSC	2	5	**45**	19	0	1	0	0	0
BTFSS	1	2	23	**54**	0	0	0	0	0
CALL	0	0	0	0	**100**	0	0	0	0
DECF	3	9	0	0	0	**30**	0	3	0
MOVLW	0	0	0	0	0	0	**79**	0	0
MOVWF	1	1	0	0	0	3	0	**56**	0
RETURN	0	0	0	0	0	0	0	0	**99**

Table 2. Results for instruction frequency from code analysis

Instruction	Freq. [%]	Instruction	Freq. [%]
MOVWF	10.72	BSF	6.95
BCF	9.68	MOVF	6.14
MOVLW	8.22	BTFSS	3.69
GOTO	8.12	BTFSC	3.67
CALL	8.06	RETURN	3.48

Due to loops and branches, the instruction frequency of source code is not equal to the instruction frequency of actually executed code. In absence of a reliable simulator platform which is needed to perform an analysis of the executed code, we decided to further process the disassembly listings of the code base. We extracted function calls and loops and unrolled them into the code, just as they would be executed. Also lookup-tables, which are implemented as a list of RETLW (assign literal to accu and return) were reduced to a single RETLW, as would be executed by a program.

Still, actually executed code can deviate from the assessed probabilities for various reasons. One should keep in mind that microcontroller code is often very special-purpose and can deviate strongly from one application to another. We included different kinds of programs in the code frequency and tuple analysis. Classical controller applications such as reading A/D converter info or driving displays and other outputs involves a lot of 'bit-banging', *i.e.*, instructions like BCF or BSF (clear/set bit of register). Other applications that involve more complex data processing such as crypto applications, include more arithmetic.

The result of the instruction frequency analysis is shown in Table 2. Move instructions are the most frequent ones. The PIC increases their general commonness on most microprocessor platforms further by limiting arithmetic to always include the accu and one other register. Table 3 shows the 12 most common

Table 3. Frequency of 12 most frequent instruction tuples

| Instruction Pair | | Freq. | Instruction Pair | | Freq. |
first	second	[%]	first	second	[%]
MOVLW	MOVWF	3.40	MOVWF	BCF	2.09
BCF	BSF	2.36	ANDLW	MOVWF	1.83
MOVLW	CALL	2.35	BSF	BSF	1.78
BTFSS	GOTO	2.31	MOVWF	MOVLW	1.75
MOVWF	MOVF	2.25	CALL	MOVLW	1.70
BTFSC	GOTO	2.11	MOVF	MOVWF	1.65

instruction tuples. The MOVLW-MOVWF combination is typical for loading values from the code to registers. Also quite common is a conditional skip (BTFSC or BTFSS) followed by a GOTO, hence the emulation of a branch instruction. If, as shown here, some tuples are much more common than others (the expected tuple frequency for a uniform distribution of the tuples is 0.08%), the post processing step based on HMM presented in Section 3 will further increase the detection rate considerably.

With the instruction frequency and tuples analyzed, we can now build the HMM of the microprocessor. As mentioned in Section 3, the instruction frequency and tuple frequency are used to construct the initial state distribution κ and the state transition probabilities A, respectively. We constructed the HMM transition matrix A by performing the following steps:

For non-jumping instructions the post-instructions are directly taken from the tuple analysis. Instructions always lasting two cycles, *i.e.*, CALL and GOTO, consist of two states. While CALL1 (or GOTO1) is always succeeded by CALL2 (GOTO2), the latter is assumed to be succeeded by their target address instruction (due to the jump). For the transition probabilities of conditionally branching instructions, like BTFSC, we analyzed the first succeeding instruction as well as the second succeeding instruction. The second succeeding instruction were counted as post-instruction for the second part, e.g., BTFSC2, while the first successors became the weighted post-instructions for the first part of the instruction. The weight is necessary, because in a certain number of cases the first part of the instruction will be succeeded by its second part rather than the following instruction. In lack of better information we chose the weight to be 50%. Hence, in half the cases the instruction was considered jumping and its second part was counted as post-instruction (e.g., BTFSC-BTFSC2). Finally the resulting transition matrix is normalized row-wise to represent a proper probability distribution and averaged with uniformly distributed transition probabilities. For the latter step, all impossible transitions are excluded, e.g., ADDLW-CALL2.

The initial state distribution κ is simply directly set to the derived instruction frequency. Here we only have to take care of assigning probabilities to the non-included second parts of the two-cycle instructions which are equal or half the occurrence number of the first part instruction, depending on whether the execution is conditional or static.

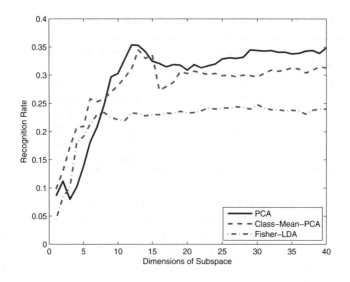

Fig. 5. Recognition rate on 1000 examples of random code. Each time, 750 training examples were used to calculate the subspace and 1750 others for the templates.

Together with the emission probabilities given by the templates, we now have the full HMM specified and can apply it to the measurements of real programs.

4.3   Analyzing Programs

During the generation of test data we paid special attention to randomization of everything that could bias the distribution of the target instruction. It is unlikely, however, that the same distribution will hold for real code. Indeed we are, as shown in Section 4.2, far away from uniformly distributed instructions or tuples of instructions. The same holds for data: for instance, in real code we can expect to find far more data words like 0x00 or 0xFF than in uniformly distributed data. As a consequence, the recognition rate of our template attack will drop as soon as the distribution of data values changes. The data dependency can be shown through executing random (in this case non-jumping) instructions without taking care of the content of file registers and the working register. Thus, the main difference to the known distribution is the data the instructions work on. As Figure 5 shows that in this case the best recognition rate reached by our templates is only 35% while, for a similar set of instructions from the test set, we expect a recognition rate of 47%.

As an example for real code we picked an implementation of the KeeLoq crypto algorithm and measured the execution of the first 500 instructions. Now, the highest recognition rate achieved was 40.7% with $M = 19$ and Fisher-LDA, while about 60% could have been expected on similar instructions from the test set. For the template evaluation (cf. Equation (4)) the prior probabilities from the code analysis have been taken into account.

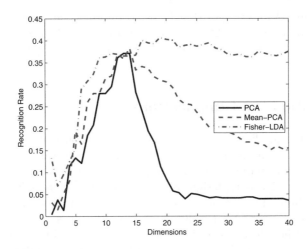

Fig. 6. Recognition rate on the first 500 instructions of the KeeLoq crypto algorithm. Each time, 750 training examples were used to calculate the subspace and 1750 others for the templates.

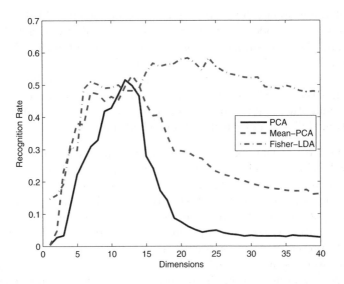

Fig. 7. Recognition rate for the first 500 examples of the Keeloq algorithm in different subspaces after applying the Viterbi algorithm to determine the most probable path

After having modeled the complete Hidden Markov Model with the results from the source code analysis we are now able to apply the Viterbi algorithm and the Forward-Backward-Algorithm to the results from Section 4.1 to calculate the most probable sequence of instruction states as well as the instructions with the highest a posteriori probability. Given the above code example of the KeeLoq crypto algorithm, Viterbi algorithm helps to improve the recognition rate by another 17% points to up to 58% as shown in Figure 7. With recognition rates of up to 52% the Forward-Backward-Algorithm performed slightly worse on this code example.

5   Applications and Implications

The most obvious application of the side channel disassembler is reverse engineering of embedded programs. Reverse engineering of software is an established method not only for product counterfeiting, but also for many legal applications. A common application is re-design, where an existing functionality is analyzed and possibly rebuilt. The reasons for this can be manifold, e.g., lost documentation, lost source code, or product discontinuation. But often, reverse engineering does not go that far. Reversing of interfaces is often applied to ensure interoperability with other systems. Debugging is another important application scenario of reverse engineering. It can also be performed for learning purposes, to understand how a code works. Then reverse engineering is very important for security auditing, where a user has to ensure code properties such as the absence of malware.

Many of these applications are highly relevant for embedded applications where access to the code is usually even more difficult than in PC software cases. Usually the program memory is read protected. Often the whole system is proprietary and supplied as-is by a single manufacturer. Many times the user has almost no access to any internal information of the underlying device. In such scenarios the side channel disassembler can be an effective tool for reverse engineering and other applications. Compared to other reverse engineering tools, the side channel disassembler features several advantages:

- it is a low-cost method, as it does not require special equipment, except for a digital sampling oscilloscope which nowadays is available for as little as 1500 $ or can be found in almost every electronics lab.
- it is a non-invasive procedure. Either the power is measured on one of the power supply pins of the target device or, even easier, only the electromagnetic emanation is used for reversing the code. In both cases only limited access to the microprocessor is needed.
- contrary to classical disassembler designs, the side channel disassembler directly gives information on the program flow, as the executed code rather than the code in program memory is analyzed.

Especially the last advantage makes the side channel disassembler unique and hence a useful and innovative addition to other existing reverse engineering methods. Out of the many possible scenarios for usage, we have extracted three application scenarios that highlight the advantages of the side channel disassembler.

Code Recognition. One scenario where the side channel disassembler is useful is in cases where known code needs to be recognized. The presented methods can be used to locate certain code segments, e.g. to detect where an error occurred or even to detect a firmware version executed on an embedded system. In a similar application a company might suspect a copyright breach or a potential patent infringement by a similar product. It can then use the side channel disassembler to identify such an infringement or breach by showing that an own known code is executed on the suspicious device, even if the program memory is read-protected.

In general, the disassembler can be operated on a portable device equipped with an antenna. Ideally, holding an antenna close to the processor might be sufficient to track the program flow executed on the target device[1]. The disassembler is then used to locate the relevant code parts.

Code Flow Analysis. A related problem in embedded software analysis is tracking which parts of a code are executed at a certain time. This case occurs when the code is known, but the functionality is not, a typical scenario in reverse engineering. Using the methodology described in this paper allows mapping known code to a certain functionality. The user might also just be interested in learning which parts of the code are used most often, e.g., for evaluating possible beneficiary targets for performance optimization.

Code Reverse Engineering. The side channel disassembler can be used to reconstruct unknown executed code. Ideally, if well trained, it can directly reconstruct the program code, identify functions etc. Furthermore, it might be able to identify higher language properties, the used compiler (if the code was generated from a higher language) etc. The latter points can be achieved in combination with other available code reverse engineering tools.

Reverse engineering can also be very interesting for analyzing embedded crypto applications. Especially in cases where the applied cipher is unknown, the disassembler is a great tool to reconstruct unknown routines. It can also be used to align code as a preparatory step for DPA attacks on code with a varying execution time or the shuffling countermeasure.

It might not always be desirable by the implementer that his code can be reverse engineered by a power disassembler. Since the methods of the side channel disassembler are borrowed from side channel research, we can do the same for the countermeasures. One should keep in mind that we are not targeting data, hence masking or shuffling of data will not increase resistance. Instead, the additional variation of data might be used to get better results through repeated measurements. Hence, countermeasures in hardware show better properties to prevent side channel disassembly. Hardware countermeasures have been proposed on different design levels and can be found on smart card processors and also on other secure microcontrollers [12]. All of them are very strong against SPA approaches such as the side channel disassembler. Keep in mind that the countermeasures need only be as good as the protection of the program code itself. So if the code can be easily extracted, simple countermeasures against power analysis suffice.

---

[1] Standaert et al. [21] showed in a setup similar to ours that the EM side channel can be expected to contain more information than the power side channel.

6 Conclusion

In this work we have presented a methodology for recovering the instruction flow of microcontrollers based on side channel information only. We proved the chosen methods by applying them to a PIC microcontroller. We have shown that subspace based template recognition makes an excellent choice for classifying power leakage of a processor. The employed recognition methods achieve a high average instruction recognition rate of up to 70%. To exploit prior general knowledge about microcontroller code we proposed Markov modeling of the processor to further increase the recognition rate of the template process. Depending on the chosen algorithm, the recognition rate was increased by up to 17% points.

The recognition performance is strongly influenced by the assumed distribution of data, resulting in a decreased recognition rate of up to 58% for real programs. Though the recognition rates on real code are leaving space for further improvements, they are more than an order of magnitude higher than the lower boundary given by simply guessing the instructions.

Hence, we can positively assure that side channel based code reverse engineering is more than just a theoretic possibility. Applying the presented methodology allows for building a side channel disassembler that will be a helpful tool in many areas of reverse engineering for embedded systems.

References

1. Biham, E., Shamir, A.: Differential Fault Analysis of Secret Key Cryptosystems. In: Kaliski Jr., B.S. (ed.) CRYPTO 1997. LNCS, vol. 1294, pp. 513–525. Springer, Heidelberg (1997)
2. Bishop, C.M.: Pattern Recognition and Machine Learning (Information Science and Statistics). Springer, Heidelberg (August 2006)
3. Chari, S., Rao, J.R., Rohatgi, P.: Template Attacks. In: Kaliski Jr., B.S., Koç, Ç.K., Paar, C. (eds.) CHES 2002. LNCS, vol. 2523, pp. 13–28. Springer, Heidelberg (2003)
4. Clavier, C.: Side Channel Analysis for Reverse Engineering (Scare) - an Improved Attack Against a Secret a3/a8 gsm Algorithm. Cryptology ePrint Archive, Report 2004/049 (2004), http://eprint.iacr.org/
5. Durbin, R., Eddy, S., Krogh, A., Mitchison, G.: Biological Sequence Analysis: Probabilistic Models of Proteins and Nucleic Acids. Cambridge University Press, Cambridge (1998)
6. Fink, G.A.: Markov Models for Pattern Recognition. Springer, Heidelberg (2008)
7. Goldack, M.: Side-Channel Based Reverse Engineering for Microcontrollers. Master's thesis, Ruhr-Universität Bochum, Germany (2008)
8. Igel, C., Glasmachers, T., Heidrich-Meisner, V.: Shark. Journal of Machine Learning Research 9, 993–996 (2008)
9. Kocher, P.C.: Timing Attacks on Implementations of Diffie-Hellman, RSA, DSS, and other Systems. In: Koblitz, N.I. (ed.) CRYPTO 1996. LNCS, vol. 1109, pp. 104–113. Springer, Heidelberg (1996)
10. Kocher, P.C., Jaffe, J., Jun, B.: Differential Power Analysis. In: Wiener, M. (ed.) CRYPTO 1999. LNCS, vol. 1666, pp. 388–397. Springer, Heidelberg (1999)

11. MacKay, D.: Information Theory, Inference and Learning Algorithms. Cambridge University Press, Cambridge (2003)
12. Mangard, S., Oswald, E., Popp, T.: Power Analysis Attacks. Springer, Heidelberg (2007)
13. Microchip Technology Inc. MPASM Assembler, MPLINK Object Linker, MPLIB Object Librarian User's Guide (2005),
    http://ww1.microchip.com/downloads/en/DeviceDoc/33014J.pdf
14. Novak, R.: Side-Channel Attack on Substitution Blocks. In: Zhou, J., Yung, M., Han, Y. (eds.) ACNS 2003. LNCS, vol. 2846, pp. 307–318. Springer, Heidelberg (2003)
15. Permadi, E.: The Hardware Side of Cryptography. Personal Blog,
    http://edipermadi.wordpress.com/
16. Quisquater, J.-J., Samyde, D.: Automatic Code Recognition for Smart Cards using a Kohonen Neural Network. In: Proceedings of the 5th Smart Card Research and Advanced Application Conference, CARDIS 2002. USENIX Association, Berkeley (2002)
17. Rabiner, L.R.: A Tutorial on Hidden Markov Models and Selected Applications in Speech Recognition. Proceedings of the IEEE 77(2), 257–286 (1989)
18. Rechberger, C., Oswald, E.: Practical Template Attacks. In: Lim, C.H., Yung, M. (eds.) WISA 2004. LNCS, vol. 3325, pp. 440–456. Springer, Heidelberg (2005)
19. Schindler, W., Lemke, K., Paar, C.: A Stochastic Model for Differential Side Channel Cryptanalysis. In: Rao, J.R., Sunar, B. (eds.) CHES 2005. LNCS, vol. 3659, pp. 30–46. Springer, Heidelberg (2005)
20. Skorobogatov, S.P.: Semi-Invasive Attacks – A New Approach to Hardware Security Analysis. PhD thesis, University of Cambridge (April 2005),
    http://www.cl.cam.ac.uk/techreports/UCAM-CL-TR-630.pdf
21. Standaert, F.-X., Archambeau, C.: Using Subspace-Based Template Attacks to Compare and Combine Power and Electromagnetic Information Leakages. In: Oswald, E., Rohatgi, P. (eds.) CHES 2008. LNCS, vol. 5154, pp. 411–425. Springer, Heidelberg (2008)
22. Standaert, F.-X., Koeune, F., Schindler, W.: How to Compare Profiled Side-Channel Attacks. In: Abdalla, M., Pointcheval, D., Fouque, P.-A., Vergnaud, D. (eds.) ACNS 2009. LNCS, vol. 5536, pp. 485–498. Springer, Heidelberg (2009)
23. Tolmie, S.: PIC Sample Code in C, http://www.microchipc.com/
24. Vermoen, D.: Reverse Engineering of Java Card Applets using Power Analysis. Master's thesis, TU Delft (2006),
    http://ce.et.tudelft.nl/publicationfiles/1162_634_thesis_Dennis.pdf
25. Web site. Program Code for Keeloq Decryption,
    http://www.pic16.com/bbs/dispbbs.asp?boardID=27&ID=19437

A Versatile Framework
for Implementation Attacks on
Cryptographic RFIDs and Embedded Devices

Timo Kasper, David Oswald, and Christof Paar

Horst Görtz Institute for IT Security, Ruhr-University Bochum, Germany
{Timo.Kasper,David.Oswald,Christof.Paar}@rub.de

Abstract. We present a unified framework for advanced implementation attacks that allows for conducting automated side-channel analysis and fault injection targeting all kinds of embedded cryptographic devices including RFIDs. Our proposed low-cost setup consists of modular functional units that can be interchanged, depending on the demands of a concrete attack scenario. We give details of customized modules for the communication with many types of embedded devices and other modules that allow to inject various types of faults. An FPGA-based approach enables very accurate timing and flexible adaption to any extension module. The corresponding data acquisition system for side-channel attacks makes precise power and EM analyses possible. Our setup facilitates the promising combination of active and passive techniques, which is known to render many established security countermeasures ineffective. We introduce several methods for the automatic profiling of cryptographic devices and model their behaviour both with respect to side-channel analysis and fault injection. To demonstrate the capabilities of our framework, we perform the first practical full key-recovery on a cryptographic contactless smartcard employing Triple-DES reported in the literature and inject multiple faults in a widespread microcontroller. We thereby disprove the common belief that highly sophisticated and expensive equipment is required to conduct such attacks. Rather, we illustrate a cost-effective setup that can be tailored to any desired type of security evaluation or penetration test.

Keywords: Side-channel, fault injection, security evaluation, models, RFID, mobile and embedded computing.

1 Introduction

There exist solutions for both symmetric and asymmetric cryptography that are highly secure from the mathematical point of view. It is well-known that, when these cryptographic mechanisms are realised in practice, unprotected implementations are vulnerable to *passive attacks*, i.e., power analysis (Differential Power Analysis (DPA), Simple Power Analysis (SPA), template attacks), and *active attacks*, i.e., fault injection or microprobing. This especially matters in the case

M.L. Gavrilova et al. (Eds.): Trans. on Comput. Sci. X, LNCS 6340, pp. 100–130, 2010.
© Springer-Verlag Berlin Heidelberg 2010

of embedded devices, such as Radio Frequency Identification Devices (RFIDs), smartcards, remote controls and mobile computing devices, which potential attackers can obtain in large numbers.

Countermeasures exist for both types of attacks, however, it is not clear how susceptible the secured devices are to a combination of power analysis with various fault-injection techniques. Furthermore, many manufacturers do not seem to care or are not aware of the attacks, hence many unprotected (or badly protected) cryptographic devices are currently used in security-sensitive applications in the field.

There is a lack of realistic, practically verified models of the adversary, especially in the case of fault injections. Each cryptographic device can show a significantly different behaviour, that is, an RFID device is vulnerable to different types of attacks than the microcontroller of a smartcard or an Application Specific Integrated Circuit (ASIC). Hence it is necessary to investigate the susceptibility of each new target, e.g., which types of faults can be injected with which success rate or whether multiple fault injections are realistic. For each device, an in-depth profiling is necessary, which accordingly has to be automated. We focus on those attacks that are realistic for an adversary with a limited budget (typical university lab equipment) and that rely on public domain or publicly available, self-made solutions for the equipment, where possible.

The general structure of our versatile framework enabling active and passive implementation attacks, as well as their combination, is presented in Sect. 2. One part of our setup are modules as detailed in Sect. 3 that provide the means to communicate with any device, including wireless interfaces. Extensions allowing for the injection of various types of faults are covered in Sect. 4, while Sect. 5 is dedicated to the acquisition of information leakage emanated by the device under test. In Sect. 6 we exemplify the comprehensive capabilities of our framework by practically analysing the security of two widespread commercial products, i.e., a cryptographic contactless smartcard and a microcontroller. We demonstrate a full key-recovery of the secret key of the Triple-DES hardware employed in the former RFID device by means of side-channel analysis, and an automatic profiling with respect to faults of the latter, revealing the parameters for a subsequent, practically verified injection of multiple faults with a success rate of almost 100%. We aim to show that penetration tests, tampering with cryptographic devices and complex side-channel analyses do not require costly tools and equipment as used in the labs of the industry, but can rather be performed with inexpensive or self-built equipment.

1.1 Classification of Implementation Attacks

Implementation attacks are well documented in the literature [30,28,27], hence we do not give a detailed compendium of the possible implementation attacks here, but rather classify the attacks and specify the scope of our framework. Figure 1 highlights the focus of this article, i.e., DPA, SPA, fault injection and their combination. We do not cover invasive attacks here which rely on directly tampering with the silicon wafer, e.g., probing attacks [16] or reverse engineering

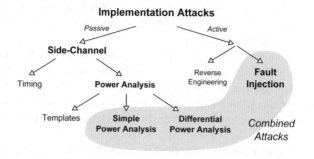

Fig. 1. Classification of implementation attacks

by taking microscopic photos of all layers of a chip [33]. For state-of-the-art implementations of cryptographic algorithms, these attacks generally demand for highly sophisticated equipment and require a very strong and well-funded adversary, while we are considering an ordinary attacker and low-cost equipment.

2   System Overview

The here proposed system is designed on a flexible modular basis such that it can be adapted to test the security of any cryptographic device. The different functional units are categorised in modules for the communication with the DUT, modules for side-channel analysis, and modules for fault injection. These modules may in turn consist of a set of smaller sub-modules that are detailed in the following subsections, and that allow for arbitrary extensions of the framework according to the requirements of the evaluator. Note that their tasks may partially overlap, e.g., parallel and serial communication can be carried out directly from the controlling Personal Computer (PC), from a microcontroller of any sub-module, or by means of the Field Programmable Gate Array (FPGA) mainly used for fault injection. Likewise, processing of the data and digital filtering is not restricted to software inside the PC but can also be realised in hardware on the FPGA.

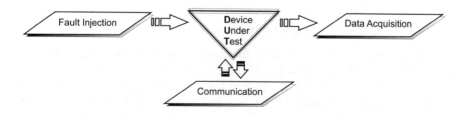

Fig. 2. Modules for side-channel analysis of a cryptographic device

As a Device Under Test (DUT) we take into account any microcontroller, FPGA, ASIC, or other embedded system including contactless devices and RFIDs. In case of specialities, e.g., concerning communication via Radio Frequency (RF), or if special faults are desired, it is straightforward to incorporate additional modules to the ones described in this article. Figure 2 illustrates the structure of the functional units as detailed in the following.

For carrying out side-channel attacks, generally an adversary must have access to the plain- or ciphertext that is processed by the DUT, in order to evaluate measurements or determine whether a fault was successful. This information is in most cases delivered by the communication modules described in Sect. 3.

For passive side-channel attacks, the behaviour of the DUT with respect to timing, power consumption, Electro-Magnetic (EM) emanation, etc. has to be accurately monitored. The corresponding data acquisition module described in Sect. 5 serves for this purpose, while the recorded data is often post-processed and evaluated by a controlling PC.

The fault injection module detailed in Sect. 4 takes care of the active aspects of side-channel analysis. Due to the variety of faults that can be injected to the DUT, this FPGA-based functional group is designed most versatile, such that it can be extended to induce literally any type of fault.

3   Communication Modules

Though it is possible to carry out most side-channel attacks using commercially available equipment, customised hardware for communicating with the DUT is highly advantageous. Commercial readers often rely on proprietary Integrated Circuits (ICs) that carry out certain tasks automatically, e.g., a built-in Random Number Generator (RNG) will generate the nonces for a challenge-response-protocol, compute the correct parity bits and checksums, data will be encrypted, encoded, and sent, and this all happens without that an adversary can directly influence the process. Thus, in the following we present customised readers for the relevant standards that are tailored to the requirements of implementation attacks, in order to gain complete control over the communication, i.e., send arbitrary bits, send repeatedly the same chosen plaintext, intentionally compute wrong checksums and — most important in the context of side-channel attacks — have complete control over the timing and generate reliable trigger signals. Note that it is often sufficient to implement only some part of the protocol, until the DUT performs the targeted cryptographic operation, e.g., encryption, which happens often at the beginning of the communication.

For many practical attacks, additionally a device is required that can serve as a replacement for the original DUT, e.g., an emulated smartcard that can be fully controlled by the adversary. For each form of communication covered in this article, we describe such an emulation extension that is compatible with the corresponding reader. Accordingly, in combination with the self-built reader devices, communication data can be monitored and unknown protocols can be automatically reverse-engineered.

3.1 Communication with RFIDs

A minimum RFID system consists of two main components, namely a reader generating a sinusoidal magnetic field which supplies the second component of the system often called tag, transponder or contactless smartcard, with energy and often a clock. Both components are equipped with a coupling element, e.g., a coil, that allows for data transfer in both directions. In the literature, a reader is sometimes named Proximity Coupling Device (PCD), and a contactless smartcard called Proximity Integrated Circuit Card (PICC). In the context of wireless devices, attacks based on measuring the EM field, e.g., a Differential Electro-Magnetic Analysis (DEMA) [9,23], are obviously most convenient, since the whole circuitry is packaged, e.g., in plastic cards, and hence neither a contact interface nor the chip itself is accessible to an attacker in a non-invasive attack scenario. Previous results [2,15,36] suggest that this approach is suitable for a wide range of RFID devices.

The following section we detail communication modules for contactless smartcards according to the ISO 14443 standard [20], operating at a frequency of $f_c = 13.56$ MHz, that are widely deployed in various security sensitive applications such as the electronic passport to store biometric data, RFID-enabled credit cards, and access control systems. Contactless smartcards have sufficient energy to perform complex computations and are hence capable of using both symmetric and asymmetric state-of-the-art cryptography, e.g., an Elliptic Curve Cryptography (ECC) engine in the electronic passport (ePass) is used to verify signatures, and 3DES or AES is often used to encrypt the current balance in the context of contactless payment systems.

A similar module has been developed for communicating with RFIDs operating on 125 kHz (as presented in Sect. 3.1), which are mainly used for car immobilizers and access control. Compared to contactless smartcards, these devices possess less computational power, thus often simple (and often insecure) proprietary ciphers are used here, if cryptography is used at all.

Contactless Smartcards. For the communication with contactless smartcards, we employ a self-built embedded system [22] consisting of a multi-purpose reader that is based on a freely programmable Atmel ATMega32 [6] microcontroller, an ISO 14443 compliant RF interface and some components for signal processing. Various types of antennas and amplifiers can be connected, e.g., for increasing the activation- or eavesdropping range. A second device that cooperates with the reader is designed to appear like an authentic tag to an RFID reader, i.e., can emulate any contactless smartcard, and furthermore can acquire the information contained in the field. Both devices allow for a comprehensive control of the communication on the physical layer, i.e., every single bit sent and received as well as the RF field is completely controlled by the adversary with an accurate timing of ≈ 75 ns. Communication with a controlling PC takes place via an USB interface, and reliable trigger signals can be issued at any instant during the protocol. Further details as well as all schematics and layouts to build the here employed devices for contactless smartcards at a cost of less than 40 $ are fully made public in [21].

While for side-channel analysis of RFIDs as practically detailed in Sect. 6.1 mainly the reader functionality is used, it is also possible to practically perform other attacks, e.g., a simple replay attack or a relay attack in the field [22]. The software running on the microcontroller has been vastly improved, such that active relay attacks can be carried out, i.e., the information transmitted can be modified in real-time. This is amongst others useful to falsify the Unique Identifier (UID) of an RFID tag, that is usually fixed in the hardware, or to enforce communication at a lower data rate than the original one.

We have fully implemented the authentication protocols for several contactless smartcards employing 3DES, AES and proprietary ciphers. The precise timing control of the RF field has amongst others been advantageous in the context of spoofing the random number generator built into Mifare Classic cards [34]. By exactly fixing the timing when the RF field is switched on and when the commands are sent during the authentication, the attacked Mifare card will always generate the same fixed value instead of random numbers, which extremely facilitates key-recovery attacks and allows to reveal a full 48 Bit key of a Mifare Classic card — much more efficiently than all previously reported attacks — in seconds [24].

125 kHz RFID Tags. The module for communicating with RFID tags operating in the range of 100 kHz to 150 kHz is designed similar to the ISO 14443 module. Again, it is controlled by an ATMega32 microcontroller, while an Atmel U2270B IC (price: approx. 1 $), which is capable of all relevant modulation schemes and a typical data rate of 5 kBaud, takes care of the handling of the RF communication. Due to the small data rate we opted for a standard RS232C serial communication with the controlling PC, instead of an USB port. The schematic is similar to the one given in Application 3 in the datasheet [7].

3.2   Communication with Contact-Based Smartcards

For the side-channel analysis of contact-based smartcards according to ISO 7816 [1] we have built an adaptor with the appropriate dimensions and the specified contact interface on the one side, which fits into any commercial smartcard reader. On the other side of the adaptor, a socket for smartcards allows any ISO 7816 card to be plugged in. The device allows for relay attacks with contact-based smartcards, and facilitates implementation attacks on smartcards. The data and power wires are tapped and rewired, such that the bitstreams can be relayed from and to a standard reader, e.g., for the analysis of communication protocols. The power lines allow to connect an external stable power supply (or our module detailed in Sect. 4.6 for inducing power faults), while a variable resistor is inserted in series with the ground pin of the smartcard for performing power analyses. Similar to the tools for contactless cards and RFIDs a smartcard can be emulated, a relay attack can be conducted or only the pure reader functionality can be used, while simultaneously faults can be injected or measurements for side-channel analysis can be recorded. We have successfully tested the adaptor in combination with our measurement setup by performing a power-analysis of an 8-Bit smartcard by Atmel containing an AES implementation in software: The correct 128-Bit key was revealed in minutes from approx. 100 measurements.

3.3   Arbitrary Parallel/Serial Communication

Embedded systems and cryptographic devices that do not feature an RFID- or ISO 7816-based interface usually employ a serial or parallel protocol to communicate with their environment. In the context of implementation attacks, example targets may be FPGAs that are configured with an encrypted bitstream or cryptographically protected USB dongles. Therefore, we support a variety of corresponding protocols, either by the controlling PC if the timing is not crucial (e.g., USB, RS-232, or parallel port) or by means of the fault injection FPGA platform, if precise timing is required (e.g., Serial Peripheral Interface (SPI) and general purpose I/O pins). If necessary in future applications, further methods can easily be added thanks to the modular nature of our setup.

4   Fault Injection Modules

Many different approaches can be utilised to inject faults in ICs. In order to unify the application of this methods, we propose an FPGA-based control board which is extended with *fault modules* that realise the actual physical effect. The FPGA provides an RS-232 interface to the controlling PC, supervises the injection of faults with precisely adjustable parameters (e.g., position in time, duration etc.) and is able to communicate with the DUT if required.

4.1   Modelling Fault Injection

Before detailing the diverse methods to inject faults in ICs, we identify general properties of faults in order to provide a model that helps to characterise the requirements for concrete attacks.

Permanence: If a fault injection permanently alters the DUT, for instance, destroys a hardware part or overwrites the firmware, it is said to be *permanent*. Otherwise, if the fault only affects the outcome of a limited number of computations, it is *non-permanent* or *transient*.

Precision of Time Position: Subsequent attacks may require the fault to occur either at a *random* (indeterminate) position, within some *region* or at a *precisely determined* point in time.

Number of Affected Bits: A fault is called *single-bit* fault if it alters exactly one bit, or *multi-bit*, if it changes ≥ 2 bit, e.g., the state of a complete register.

Effect: The induced modification can manifest itself in a *bit flip*, i.e., logic values are inverted, a *fixed state*, i.e., logic values are tied to 0 or 1, or *inconsistent behaviour* of the DUT. In the latter case, the fault injection causes inconsistencies in the state of a device by affecting a distinct part of its control logic. A common example of this effect is the skipping of instructions on a microcontroller, e.g., due to the instruction pointer being incremented but the current instruction not being executed.

Despite the need for theoretical models, we would like to stress here that in practice it is often difficult, even in case of a successful fault injection, to exactly determine which part of the device is malfunctioning due to the fault, i.e., what exactly happened in the internal circuits of the attacked cryptographic device when it shows a certain behaviour. This applies particularly for black box analyses, where an attacker knows nothing about the implementation.

4.2   Types of Physical Faults in Integrated Circuits

There is a variety of ways to trigger faulty behaviour of ICs, differing (amongst others) in complexity, cost, effectiveness and the possible effects caused by the fault. In the following, we give a brief survey of methods that have been proposed in the literature.

Microprobing. One of the most direct yet complicated fault injection methods is to de-package the silicon die and contact a specific circuit path using *microprobes*. As detailed in [26], the attacker is able to exactly monitor the waveforms present on the tapped wire, or can actively modify the value, for instance by short-circuiting it to ground. Due to the immediate access to the DUT, virtually all types of faults can be injected. Moreover, the method allows for reverse engineering of the circuit. However, the needed equipment is expensive (in [26], the authors estimate a cost of 10 000 - 100 000 $) and requires considerable skill and experience to be handled efficiently. Additionally, the invasive nature of the attack makes it unusable in scenarios where permanent, obvious physical modification of the DUT is not desired. For these reasons, we do not consider microprobing attacks in this article.

Temperature Variation. Since the characteristics of circuit elements vary with temperature, ICs only work correctly within the temperature range specified by the vendor. Thus, cooling or heating the DUT and operating it outside of its maximum specifications can lead to faulty behaviour. High or low temperature especially affects memory cells and can cause random modification of Static Random Access Memory (SRAM) cells or disable read/write operations of Non-volatile Memory (NVM), i.e., Electrically Erasable Programmable Read-Only Memory (EEPROM) or Flash [14]. Generally, exact timing of the fault is complicated due to the limited thermal conductivity of the IC package and the die itself. Besides, most of the fault parameters mentioned in Sect. 4.1 are hard to control with this approach, limiting the possible application scenarios. In the current version of our setup, temperature variations can only be applied manually, i.e., using coolant spray or heating devices.

Optical Effects. By exposing the circuit to white or laser light, electron-hole pairs are created that can cause current flow at p-n junctions [38,14] of semiconductors, resulting in changes of logic levels in the affected region of the IC, e.g., switch a transistor. By applying a mask to focus a small area, optical faults allow for precise targeting of certain parts of a circuit, down to the single-transistor level [42], with fine control over the fault effect. Note that inducing optical faults is a semi-invasive attack, as the plastic packaging of the chip has to be opened mechanically or by etching, which is straightforward for standard IC packages, e.g., Dual Inline Package (DIP) or Small-Outline Integrated Circuit (SOIC), but can become infeasible for an adversary in the case of sophisticated smartcards.

Variation of Power Supply. Temporarily increasing (*positive glitch*) or reducing (*negative glitch*) the supply voltage of an IC to a certain level is a well-established method to inject faults [13,12], particularly with regard to the skipping or misinterpretation of processor instructions. As the power is supplied via an external pin (for the case of most embedded device) or the surrounding EM field (for contactless (RFID) devices), the fault injection path is easily accessible, allowing for non-invasive attacks. However, at the same time, this single entry point can also be disadvantegous from an attacker's point of view: Countermeasures such as monitoring or filtering the supply voltage before it enters the core of the circuit are relatively inexpensive, because they only need to be implemented for one isolated section of the IC.

Electro-Magnetic Pulses. Transients of the EM field cause induction of currents in conductors and can thereby change logic levels present on an IC. In contrast to power glitches, the fault injection is not performed over a single wire. Rather, the fault can affect any part of the DUT, making it harder to prevent and detect than variations of the supply voltage. This approach is especially suited for RFIDs [17], for which direct access to the power supply would require an invasive manipulation of the antenna connection.

Variation of an External Clock. For devices with external oscillators, i.e., for which manipulations of the clock signal are feasible, slightly modifying the clock period for one or few (half-)cycles may lead to data corruption [26]. Due to different delays of distinct circuit paths, values that take longer to propagate (e.g., because they are transported over the *critical path*[1]) may not be handled correctly in the following clock cycle.

4.3   FPGA-Based Platform for Fault Injection

The use of an FPGA has certain advantages compared to a microcontroller-based solution, particularly with regard to precise timing of control signals at high clock frequencies. To minimize the design time, we use the commercial Xilinx

---

[1] The critical path is the register-to-register path with the largest delay and thus limits the maximum clock frequency.

Spartan-3 board [44] as a basis. The system clock frequency is set to 100 MHz, so that the FPGA runs significantly faster than most of the considered embedded systems, which are usually clocked at between ≈ 32 kHz and 20 MHz [11], thus enabling the injection of faults at multiple instants during one clock cycle of the DUT. Note that at higher frequencies, it becomes increasingly difficult to select and apply the involved analogue (and digital) components appropriately. To simplify the implementation of complex control logic, our design is built around a general 8-bit microcontroller softcore (Xilinx PicoBlaze, cf. [45], available as VHDL source file for Xilinx FPGAs) which is internally connected to several application-specific modules, as depicted in Fig. 3.

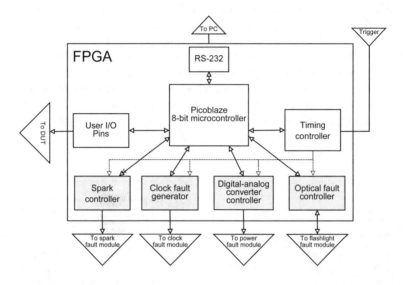

Fig. 3. Internal structure of the control FPGA for fault injection

The PicoBlaze softcore is a Reduced Instruction Set Computing (RISC) microcontroller programmable using a simple assembler language [43]. It has low resource requirements (96 slices + 1 block Random Access Memory (RAM) on a Spartan 3 FPGA) and is well suited for implementing non timing-critical control and interface logic.

All timing-critical operations that have to respond to external inputs instantly, and require guaranteed timing behaviour, are moved into the application specific blocks. The central module in this respect is the *timing controller*, which is responsible for starting previously configured faults with precise timing parameters. The purpose of the microcontroller is to provide a unified and extensible interface for the controlling PC to setup the timing controller and the fault injection modules. Currently, we support fault injection by means of optical methods, EM pulses, power glitches and variations of the clock signal.

4.4 Optical Fault Injection

A modified electronic flash of a photo-camera serves as the basis for a low-cost module for optical fault injections as described, e.g., in [38]. A small Printed Circuit Board (PCB) that is connected to the flash of the camera could be re-used for our purposes with only small modifications. It mainly consists of a High Voltage Generator (HVG) that produces up to 400 V DC out of the 3 V battery supply of the camera, and a 220 pF capacitor C_1 that is charged with electrons by the HVG. Figure 4 illustrates the principle of the module.

A pin of the PCB ('Ready') that was used to drive a green Light Emitting Diode (LED) to indicate when C_1 is fully charged, i.e., a flash is ready to be triggered, is connected to an input pin of an FPGA. The switch S_1 that had been mechanically switched when pressing the button of the camera, more precisely, when the lens opens to take a picture, was replaced by a transistor and can now also be controlled by the FPGA. Turning it on instantly discharges C_1 into the flash and thereby releases an optical fault. The FPGA is programmed such that it busy-waits until the flash is ready, then starts the interaction with the DUT, and finally triggers an optical fault at the desired instant.

If a coil is connected instead of the flash, it is reported [10] that the resulting strong magnetic field can inject permanent faults into RFIDs such as electronic passports, i.e., the device can be forever deactivated.

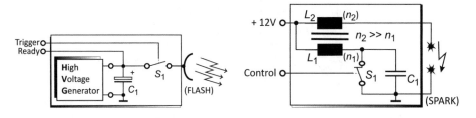

Fig. 4. Optical fault injection module   **Fig. 5.** Injecting faults with sparks

4.5 Electro-Magnetic Fault Injection with Sparks

It is well-known in electronics that a sudden change in electric current gener-ates an EM field (cf. Sect. 4.2) – the higher the amplitude and the faster the alteration, the stronger will the resulting EM field be. Thus, in the following we describe our module for the injection of faults by generating sparks, as illustrated in Fig. 5. The idea for this module is borrowed from an ignition system for petrol engines and allows for triggering a spark by means of an ignition coil, a switch S_1 realised by a high voltage Insulated Gate Bipolar Transistor (IGBT) [41], and a common spark plug for cars.

The ignition coil consists of two inductances L_1 and L_2 with different numbers of turns n_1 and n_2, that are coupled to form an electric transformer. The voltages V_1 and V_2 over the coils L_1 and L_2 follow the equation $\frac{V_1}{V_2} = \frac{n_1}{n_2}$. The turn ratio is such that $n_2 \gg n_1$, hence any voltage occurring on the side of L_1 will be amplified orders of magnitude higher on the side of L_2. To ignite an arc, a large over-voltage pulse is required: 250 V to 300 V on the side of L_1, corresponding to approx. 20 kV on the side of L_2, are sufficient to generate a spark [31]. An STP10NK50Z IGBT employed as the switch S_1 withstands high voltages up to 500 V and can be turned on with a gate voltage of approx. 3 V. This allows for diretly switching the 'Control' signal and thereby triggering the switch S_1 in Fig. 5 by means of the controlling FPGA.

The generation of a spark consists of two phases, controlled by the time during which S_1 is switched on: During the first phase, the coil needs to be charged for a minimum amount of time. Then, in the second phase, the spark is released by opening the switch. While the switch S_1 is turned on, a DC current flows through the coil L_1, and hence charges L_1 with energy, until S_1 opens the connection: The sudden interruption of the electric current flow through L_1 implies that the magnetic field collapses rapidly, inducing a high voltage on the side of L_1, whose amplitude depends on how much energy has been stored during the charging phase. The much higher voltage transformed to L_2 instantly ignites the desired spark at the spark plug, while the capacitor C_1 limits the voltage overshooting to protect the switch from getting damaged.

The strength of the induced fault can be steered by varying the amount of time during which the ignition coil can store energy. During our tests, a charge phase of 5 ms was sufficient to produce reliable, strong sparks. As a power source we are using a 12 V car battery, as it supplies very large currents. If a standard power supply is used, it is recommended to connect a very large capacitor ($> 10\,000\,\mu F$) in parallel to the power source, to provide a sufficient amount of current. Optionally, a coil could be connected instead of the spark plug to generate a purely magnetic field.

Note that extra caution has to be taken when conducting this type of fault injection in order to prevent destruction of the DUT or other nearby equipment[2]. Hence for every unknown device tests should be carried out starting with a big distance between the arc and the DUT. Note that, in the near field the field strength falls as a function of the distance r to the DUT, i.e., proportional to $\frac{1}{r^3}$, hence small changes in r have a strong effect on the outcome of the faults.

4.6   Power Fault Injection

As described in Sect. 4.2, power faults can be both triggered by positive (i.e., increase of the supply voltage) and negative (i.e., reduction of the supply voltage) glitches. For maximum flexibility in this respect and for fine control over the actual waveform, we have chosen a Digital-Analogue Converter (DAC) based approach, as depicted in Fig. 6.

The voltage V_{DAC} at the DAC output pin can be controlled via an 8 bit bus, passing a binary-encoded number $D_{DAC} \in \{0, \ldots, 255\}$. V_{DAC} is then given

---

[2] In most countries it is illegal to use the here described module, because the EM emanation can cause radio waves that disturb other electronic equipment, and the device is thus not compatible to FCC rules. It is recommended to perform tests with EM faults in a shielded environment (aluminum foil is usually sufficient).

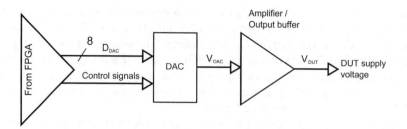

Fig. 6. Principle of the module for generating power faults

as $V_{DAC} = \frac{D_{DAC}}{255} \cdot V_{DAC,max}$ where $V_{DAC,max}$ denotes the maximum output voltage. Because the DAC generates a voltage of max. ≈ 1 V and its output current is limited to 20 mA, an additional output amplifier is required to provide higher voltages and greater driver strength.

Implementation Details. A PCB has been designed with the structure introduced above. The used DAC is the AD9708 manufactured by Analog Devices [5], capable of running at max. 125 MSamples/s. The signal from the DAC is amplified up to a maximum of ≈ 5.5 V, using the AD8058 Operational amplifier (OP) by Analog Devices [4], providing a theoretical bandwidth of 325 MHz at a gain of $+1$ and a slew rate[3] of 1000 V/μs.

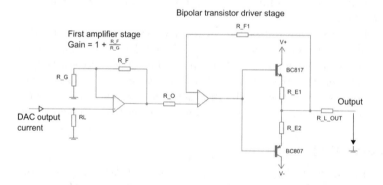

Fig. 7. Output stage of the power fault module

The OP is applied in a non-inverting configuration with the gain set to ≈ 4.7. Additionally, a bipolar transistor-based output stage according to [29] has been implemented, which enables output currents of max. 150 mA at a supply voltage of 7.5 V. By selecting different transistors, this value could be further improved if required. The schematic of the output stage is shown in Fig. 7.

---

[3] The slew rate indicates the maximum rate of change of the output voltage.

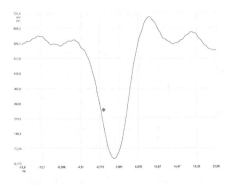 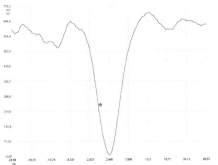

Fig. 8. Full-scale 10 ns negative voltage glitch at amplifier output, ×10 probe

Fig. 9. Full-scale 10 ns negative voltage glitch after transistor output stage, ×10 probe

As an example for the output waveform, Fig. 8 and 9 depict a 10 ns full-scale pulse generated with the proposed power fault module, recorded after the amplifier and the transistor output stage, respectively. All depicted signals have been recorded using a probe set to ×10 attenuation to minimize the influence of the probe capacitance on the rise and fall times.

4.7   Fault Injection with Clock Variations

Clock faults are small, temporary variations of the fraction of time the clock signal is high in one period which is commonly referred to as the *duty cycle*. For maximum flexibility, a module for this type of fault has to provide

- a wide range of output frequencies, especially covering the range of embedded systems, and
- precise control over the duty cylce of the clock signal.

Our approach makes use of the Digital Clock Manager (DCM) of the Xilinx FPGA which is able to generate a clock signal with very fine control over its phase shift. By outputting both an unshifted and a shifted clock and combining these signals logically with external circuitry, several useful waveforms can be created. The module provides the signals $o_1 = clk \wedge clk_s$ and $o_2 = clk \vee clk_s$ for both shortened and stretched clock cycles. These are illustrated in Fig. 10 and Fig. 11, in which clk denotes a clock signal, clk_s this signal shifted by Δt, $\wedge$ a logical AND and $\vee$ a logical OR.

Implementation Details. The generation of the shifted clock signals clk_s is performed by the FPGA using a combination of a fine phase shift, followed by clock (down-)scaling and a coarse phase shift. The phase shift function of the Xilinx DCM is used to shift the clock by $\frac{1}{256}$th of its period. The input to the

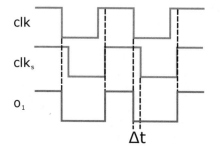

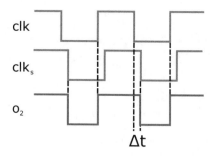

Fig. 10. Clock signal $o_1 = clk \wedge clk_s$ width shortened clock cycles

Fig. 11. Clock signal $o_2 = clk \vee clk_s$ witch stretched clock cycles

DCM is the global system clock clk_{sys} and the output is termed $clk_{sys,\,s}$ (shifted by Δ_{fine}) and both are running at 100 MHz.

clk_{sys} and $clk_{sys,\,s}$ are then passed to a prescaler (and coarse phase shifter), which toggles the output clock when an internal counter reaches half of the configured prescaling factor. The coarse phase shift by Δ_{coarse} is accomplished by pre-loading the internal counter on startup. This way, clk_s can be shifted in multiples of the system clock period, i.e., in steps of 10 ns, with respect to clk. The downscaled clocks clk and clk_s are routed via the output pins of the FPGA to the actual fault module PCB. Figure 12 summarises the complete process.

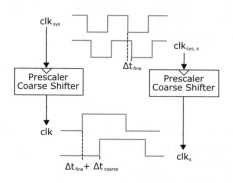

Fig. 12. Clock signal shifting and prescaling on FPGA

On the external board, the logical operations proposed above are performed by discrete, high speed Complementary Metal Oxide Semiconductor (CMOS) ICs. According to the datasheets [37], these ICs can be operated at frequencies above 1 GHz, enabling precise adjustment of the signal timing. An example output signal for o_1 (i.e., a slightly shortened clock cycle) is depicted in Fig. 13, with the prescaler set such that the output clock frequency is 16.67 MHz.

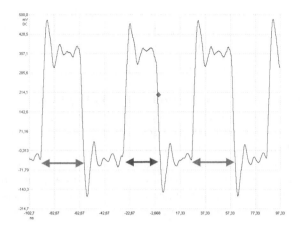

Fig. 13. Fault on 16.67 MHz clock signal, x10 probe, 20 ns/time division

5   Data Acquisition

A controlling PC and a USB oscilloscope form the basis for the data acquisition system. The acquired data can be side-channel information (e.g., current, voltage, EM emanation or timing information), or communication data such as bitstreams in any format which then later can be evaluated by a PC. The software framework follows our modular approach and allows for straightforward substitution of its parts, e.g., when switching to a new oscilloscope or analysing a DUT that has different requirements with regard to the data necessary for mounting an attack.

In the context of combined active and passive attacks, the configuration of the fault injection device and the recording of the side-channel information can both be performed by the controlling PC, simplifying the synchronisation of the respective processes. Additionally, the PC can process the data directly after recording, so that adaptive attacks are possible, in which, e.g., a challenge is selected based on the outcome of prior steps, such as a successful fault injection.

6   Practical Attacks

In this section, we present results of attacks on real-world devices. By the example of a commercial RFID smartcard, we show the capabilities of out framework with respect to side-channel analysis. Aside, we describe an active fault injection on a widespread microcontroller.

6.1   Power-Analysing a 3DES Cryptographic Contactless Smartcard

Before detailing the analysis of an RFID smartcard employing Triple-DES, we briefly outline the applied techniques used to attack the device and propose appropriate leakage models. For the analysis, we use the well-established method of Correlation Power Analysis (CPA) [8]. As mentioned in Sect. 3.1, for RFIDs it is the natural choice to mount a non-invasive attack by measuring the EM emanation, i.e., perform a DEMA.

Modelling the Power Consumption of RFID Devices. For a simple model of the frequencies where we would expect the EM leakage to occur, consider a band-limited power consumption $p(t)$ that directly affects the amplitude of the $\omega_0 = 2\pi \cdot 13.56\,\text{MHz}$ frequency of the reader, i.e., the amplitude of the field will be slightly smaller in an instant when the chip requires more energy than in an instant when no energy is consumed. This results in possibly detectable frequency components in the side bands of the carrier, as depicted in Fig. 14. Equation 1 describes this model more precisely, where $\circ\!\!-\!\!\bullet$ denotes the Fourier transform[4].

$$p(t)\cos(\omega_0 t) \circ\!\!-\!\!\bullet X(j\omega) = \frac{1}{2}\left(P(j\omega - j\omega_0) + P(j\omega + j\omega_0)\right) \tag{1}$$

We refer to this approach as *Remote Power Analysis* according to Oren and Shamir [35], because the fluctuations in the power consumption of the device are modulated onto the strong carrier signal of the PCD.

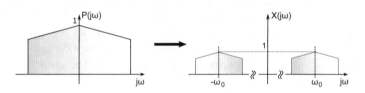

Fig. 14. Frequency spectrum of the carrier signal at ω_0 and the assumed information leakage for remote power analysis

Another model assumes that the internal switching of transistors on gate-level can be detected by means of near-field probes, such that the bits of a secret key might be extracted from signals in frequency bands that are independent of the carrier of the PCD. The signal model in Equation 2 for this case is additive, so that the best possible suppression of all other components - in particular the carrier frequency - is desirable. As illustrated in Fig. 15, now $P(j\omega)$ is assumed to be band-limited with a center frequency ω_s that is independent of the carrier frequency ω_0.

$$p(t) + \cos(\omega_0 t) \circ\!\!-\!\!\bullet X(j\omega) = P(j\omega) + \frac{1}{2}\left(\delta(j\omega - j\omega_0) + \delta(j\omega + j\omega_0)\right) \tag{2}$$

---

[4] The Fourier transform is commonly used to transform signals from the time domain into the frequency domain.

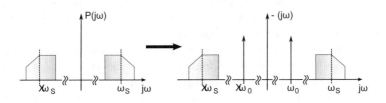

Fig. 15. Frequency spectrum of the carrier signal at ω_0 and the assumed information leakage for the additive model

Difference-of-Means Test. To determine the quality of the traces acquired with a particular measurement setup and to find out if and in which instants the traces contain data-dependent information, a Difference-of-Means (DOM) test can be conducted as a preparation for the key-recovery. The idea is to send two (or more) challenges alternately that cause a different electromagnetic emanation according to the assumed power model, acquire the corresponding traces $\boldsymbol{t}^{(1)}$ and $\boldsymbol{t}^{(2)}$ of length K, and then form four equally sized sets S_i with $|S_i| = N$ the number of traces per set.

Let $S_1 = \left\{ \boldsymbol{t}_0^{(1)}, \ldots, \boldsymbol{t}_{N-1}^{(1)} \right\}$ contain the traces of the first challenge and $S_2 = \left\{ \boldsymbol{t}_0^{(2)}, \ldots, \boldsymbol{t}_{N-1}^{(2)} \right\}$ those for the second challenge. The average traces $\bar{t}^{(1)}$ (k), $\bar{t}^{(2)}(k)$ and their DOM timeseries $\delta^{(1-2)}(k)$, where $0 \leq k < K$ denotes the current sampling point, are given as:

$$\bar{t}^{(1)}(k) = \frac{1}{N} \sum_{n=0}^{N-1} \boldsymbol{t}_n^{(1)}(k)$$

$$\bar{t}^{(2)}(k) = \frac{1}{N} \sum_{n=0}^{N-1} \boldsymbol{t}_n^{(2)}(k)$$

$$\delta^{(1-2)}(k) = \bar{t}^{(1)}(k) \ - \ \bar{t}^{(2)}(k)$$

In order to estimate the amount of noise, let two sets S_3 and S_4 contain uniformly distributed traces belonging to *either* challenge, i.e., assign all traces randomly to the two sets, and define accordingly:

$$\bar{t}^{(3)}(k) = \frac{1}{N} \sum_{n=0}^{N-1} \boldsymbol{t}_n^{(3)}(k)$$

$$\bar{t}^{(4)}(k) = \frac{1}{N} \sum_{n=0}^{N-1} \boldsymbol{t}_n^{(4)}(k)$$

$$\delta^{(3-4)}(k) = \bar{t}^{(3)}(k) \ - \ \bar{t}^{(4)}(k)$$

The DOM $\delta^{(3-4)}(k)$ would ideally vanish, if the measurements contained no noise. Accordingly, maxima of $\delta^{(1-2)}$ correspond to the points in time where a data-dependent behaviour occurs — the higher the ratio between the amplitude of the peaks and the noise level, the more information is contained in the measurements, hence for more traces, a higher signal-to-noise ratio is expected. In contrast, the maxima of $\delta^{(3-4)}$, indicating the amount of noise in the traces, should all have a similar amplitude that becomes smaller with more traces acquired and would become zero for an infinite amount of traces.

Contactless Smartcard Attack. In this section, we turn towards a more complex scenario and analyse a commercially available contactless smartcard. This time, we are facing a *black-box situation*, i.e., we do not know anything about the implementation of the cipher, existent countermeasures etc., so extensive profiling is necessary in preparation for a key-recovery attack. The following results base on the analysis performed in [23], which we summarise before presenting our new achievements.

The DUT is an ISO 14443-compliant RFID device (cf. [18,19]), operating at 13.56 MHz. It features a challenge-response authentication protocol which relies on a 3DES using the two 56 bit halves of $k_C = k_1 || k_2$ as the symmetric key in Encrypt-Decrypt-Encrypt (EDE) mode. The process of performing the analysis can be split up into the following steps, which we will cover in this section:

1. Align the traces in time.
2. Profile the device and locate the 3DES encryption.
3. Optimise the position of the EM probe.
4. Perform the EM analysis of the 3DES encryption.

Challenge-Response Authentication Protocol. Using the RFID reader detailed in Sect. 3.1 we reverse-engineered and implemented the whole authentication protocol, but focus on the step relevant for our analyses as depicted in Fig. 16, where $3DES_{k_C}(\cdot) = DES_{k_1}\left(DES_{k_2}^{-1}\left(DES_{k_1}(\cdot)\right)\right)$ denotes a 3DES encryption involving the key $k_C = k_1 || k_2$. The values B_1 and B_2 are encrypted by the PICC during the mutual authentication. B_2 originates from a random number previously generated by the PICC and is always encrypted by the PICC in order to check the authenticity of the PCD. The protocol will abort after the encryption of B_2, in case its verification is not successful. B_1, a random value chosen by the PCD that serves for authenticating the PICC to the PCD, is mentioned here for completeness only and is not required in the context of our analyses.

We observe that the card unconditionally encrypts any value B_2 sent to it, hence we can freely choose the plaintext. For the CPA described in the following, we will send random, uniformly distributed plaintexts for B_2 and attack the first DES round.

Trace Preprocessing and Alignment. The raw traces recorded between the last bit of the command sent by the reader and the first bit of the answer of the card do not expose any distinctive pattern, hence, digital preprocessing is applied in

PCD   PICC

$$\text{Choose } B_1, B_2 \xrightarrow{\quad B_1, B_2 \quad} 3DES_{k_C}(B_2)$$

Fig. 16. Excerpt of the authentication protocol relevant for a DEMA attack

order to identify interesting patterns useful for a precise alignment of the traces. On the basis of the remote power model introduced in Sect. 6.1, we assume that the power consumption of the smartcard modulates the amplitude of the carrier wave at frequencies much lower than the 13.56 MHz carrier frequency, which is justified by a preliminary spectral analysis and the well-known fact that the on-chip components (such as capacitances, resistors, inductances) typically imply a strong low-pass filter characteristic.

In order to obtain the relevant side-channel information, we record raw (not demodulated) traces and perform the demodulation digitally on a standard PC, using a straightforward incoherent demodulation approach (Fig. 17, following [40]). The raw trace is first rectified, then low-pass filtered using an appropriate digital filter. An additional high-pass filter removes the constant amplitude offset resulting from the demodulation principle and low-frequency noise. Good values for the filter cutoff frequencies $f_{lowpass}$ and $f_{highpass}$ were determined experimentally and are given in this section.

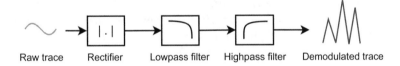

Raw trace   Rectifier   Lowpass filter   Highpass filter   Demodulated trace

Fig. 17. Block diagram of incoherent digital amplitude demodulator

For precise alignment during the digital processing, we select a short reference pattern in a demodulated *reference trace*. This pattern is then located in all subsequent traces by finding the shift that minimises the squared difference between the reference and the trace to align, i.e., we apply a least-squares approach. In our experiments we found that the analysed smartcard performs the operations in an asynchronous manner, i.e., the alignment may be wrong in portions not belonging to the region the reference pattern is taken from. A re-alignment has thus to be performed with respect to the part of the trace we aim to examine by means of CPA.

Probe Positioning. The DOM test turns out to be an appropriate utility for finding the optimal position of the near-field probe used to capture the EM emanation. For that purpose, we implement a *Live DOM* application on the controlling PC that sends the alternating challenges to the card, records and digitally preprocesses the EM trace. After the automatic detection of the alignment pattern[5], all subsequent traces are aligned accordingly and passed to the DOM algorithm. The DOM results are displayed instantly and are continously updated while the probe can be moved. Figure 18 depicts a screenshot of the utility, where the upper window displays the processed and aligned traces with the alignment pattern highlighted, while the lower shows the squared DOM of S_1 and S_2, i.e., $\left(\delta^{(1-2)}(k)\right)^2$.

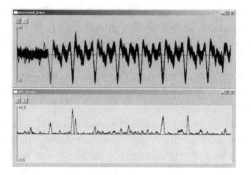

Fig. 18. Screenshot of Live DOM test utility

By iteratively adjusting the probe position to maximise the DOM, we discovered that the results are optimal if the probe is placed directly above the IC and in parallel to the long side of the card, at a vertical angle of $\approx 35\,°$ (with respect to the card plane), as shown in Fig. 19. It furthermore turned out that placing the smartcard at a vertical distance of ≈ 5 mm to the antenna considerably improves the amount of side-channel leakage.

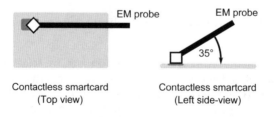

Fig. 19. Optimal positioning of EM probe

Device Profiling. As the plaintext for the targeted 3DES operation is known and the ciphertext can be computed in a known-key scenario, we are able to isolate the location of the 3DES encryption by correlating on these values. From the profiling phase with a known key it turns out that the smartcard uses an

---

[5] The pattern detection is accomplished by finding the first peak whose amplitude exceeds a fixed threshold.

8 bit data bus to transfer plain- and ciphertexts. The corresponding values can be clearly identified from 2000 - 5000 traces using a Hamming weight model. Figure 20 was compiled from these profiling observations, with the shape of the 3DES operation marked. The first 3DES encryption (labeled 3DES 1) results from a prior protocol step, the correlation with the correct ciphertext appears after the execution of the second 3DES (labeled 3DES 2).

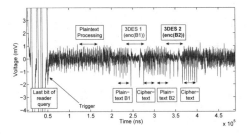

Fig. 20. Overview of operations in amplitude-demodulated trace

3DES Engine. Figure 21 shows the targeted 3DES operation identified during the profiling phase, filtered with $f_{lowpass} = 8\,\text{MHz}$ and $f_{highpass} = 50\,\text{kHz}$. The short duration of the encryption suggests that the 3DES is implemented in a special, separate hardware module, hence we assume a Hamming distance model. We also considered a Hamming weight model, but did not reach conclusive results with it.

The three marked peaks seemingly appear at the end of one complete Single-DES and are thus promising candidates as alignment patterns. We conduct a CPA on demodulated traces aligned to each of these peaks, where we consider

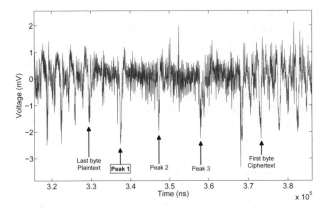

Fig. 21. Part of a trace with 3DES encryption, filtered with $f_{lowpass} = 8\,\text{MHz}$, $f_{highpass} = 50\,\text{kHz}$

the Hamming distance between the DES registers (L_0, R_0) and (L_1, R_1), i.e, the state before and after the first round of the first Single-DES. When performing a standard CPA with 1 000 000 traces, correlation peaks with maximum amplitude occur for the correct subkey candidate of each S-Box, at a position which we consider as the start point of the first DES. The results are given in Fig. 22.

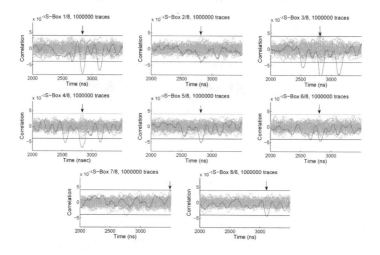

Fig. 22. Correlation coefficients for CPA after 1 000 000 traces, $f_{lowpass} = 8\,\text{MHz}$, $f_{highpass} = 50\,\text{kHz}$

We observe that 1. the correlation for the output of some S-Boxes is significantly stronger than for others (e.g., for S-Box 1 and 3, for which the correct subkey can already be identified after 150 000 traces), 2. several peaks appear at different points in time for one S-Box and 3. the point of maximum correlation varies depending on the S-Box.

As the attack works (albeit after a large number of traces), we suppose that no masking scheme [30] is used to protect the hardware engine. Rather, we conjecture that hiding in the time dimension is used, i.e., dummy cycles with no computation or similar measures, to prevent correct alignment of the traces. This assumption is justified by the above observation that more than one peak occurs in the correlation curve and further strengthened by the fact that even when repeatedly sending the same plaintext B_2 to the smartcard, the shape of the DES operation and the position of the peaks depicted in Fig. 21 vary[6].

Note that with our measurement setup, recording one million traces takes approx. two days, i.e., we achieve a rate of approx. 700 measurements per minute. Having extensively profiled the DUT, we are able to focus on the relevant region of the EM trace and thus achieve substantial savings both with regard to disk space and processing time. Therefore, our attack is still feasible in a practical scenario, despite the considerable amount of traces.

---

[6] This misalignment also hinders improving the SNR by means of averaging.

6.2   Fault Injection Attacks

After demonstrating the capabilities of the developed framework with regard to passive side-channel analysis, we address active fault injection and accordingly carry out an attack against a widespread 8-bit microcontroller, the PIC16F687 [32]. Note that the main focus in the following is on the demonstration of the fault injection capabilities, not on the implementation of actual attacks against cryptographical algorithms.

Single Faults. Consequently, we start with defining a simple test scenario, attempting to skip one instruction executed by the microcontroller. The microcontroller executes a simple program to detect that a fault has been successfully injected. After the initialization, a status pin `PIN_STATUS` (connected to an FPGA input) is constantly set to high in a first infinite loop. In a subsequent infinite loop, the same pin is pulled low and additionally, another status pin `PIN_STATUS_2` is repeatedly toggled, thereby indicating whether the microcontroller is still alive.

Our attack targets the `goto` instruction at the end of the first loop. Without external influence, the DUT never exits this loop. The aim of the fault attack is to jump over this instruction, so that the second loop gets executed. This condition can be detected by checking for `PIN_STATUS = 0`, indicating a successful fault injection. To provide a second indicator that the DUT is definitely executing the second loop, the toggling of `PIN_STATUS_2` can be tested.

We investigate the effect of a negative voltage glitch, as this method has been reported to be successful for other microcontrollers [25,39]. In our framework, the following parameters (cf. Fig. 23) can be varied:

- The glitch offset t_{offset} with respect to the trigger rising edge,
- the glitch width t_{width}, and
- the glitch voltage level V_{low}, i.e., the value to which the supply voltage is temporarily reduced to.

In order to systematically determine the settings that lead to the desired effect, we implemented an application with a "sweep mode" that consecutively tests all combinations in a certain range for each of the values. This way, the device is fully

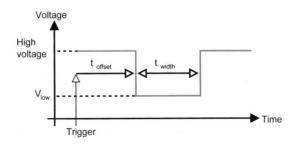

Fig. 23. Parameters characterising a single negative power glitch

profiled for all possible parameters without human interaction. To demonstrate the integration of fault injection with the measurement framework and to be able to analyse the fault effect afterwards, the application also records oscilloscope traces of the voltage glitch on the supply rail and the state of the status pins.

Results. Using the data gathered by the parameter sweep, three effects can be identified:

1. Injection not successful, i.e., `PIN_STATUS` remains set and the first loop is not left, see Fig. 25.
2. The device is reset, resulting in `PIN_STATUS` to be set low for a short time (during the initialization instructions) and then high again when the first loop is entered, see Fig. 24.
3. The desired fault is injected, i.e., `PIN_STATUS` stays low permanently, indicating that the microcontroller executes the second loop, see Fig. 26.

Figures 25, 24 and 26 display example oscilloscope traces for each outcome. For case 3, Fig. 27 additionally shows the toggling waveform on `PIN_STATUS_2` in `loop2` after a successful instruction skip fault.

Based on these experiments, we conclude that power glitch attacks to skip instructions on the PIC16F687 are possible, provided that the voltage is reduced to a value within a region from 1.65 V to 1.73 V and the fault occurs at the correct

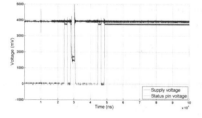

Fig. 24. Waveform of reset after fault injection on PIC16F687

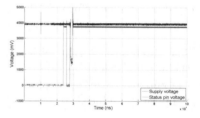

Fig. 25. Waveform of unsuccessful fault injection on PIC16F687

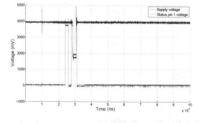

Fig. 26. Waveform of successful fault injection on PIC16F687, displaying `PIN_STATUS`

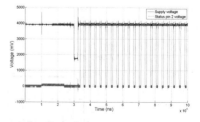

Fig. 27. Waveform of successful fault injection on PIC16F687, displaying `PIN_STATUS_2`

point in time, where a rather large set of timing parameters turned out to work for the scenario of leaving an endless loop.

Multiple Faults. On the basis of the results of the previous section, the scenario is now extended to multiple fault injection. The test code has been modified: The first loop remains unchanged, while in the second loop the toggling of PIN_STATUS_2 has been removed. The third loop catches the successful exit from loop1 and loop2, indicating this condition by setting PIN_STATUS_3 and toggling PIN_STATUS_2 as additional criterion for loop3.

Thus, if the first two loops can be skipped using two successive faults, this condition is detected by checking for PIN_STATUS = 0 and PIN_STATUS_3 = 1, which can again be accomplished automatically using the FPGA user I/O pins. For illustration, we recorded the waveform on PIN_STATUS_2, as the toggling provides visual evidence that the microcontroller is indeed executing loop3. The two successive negative voltage glitches are now characterised by 6 parameters, summarised in Fig. 28:

- The first glitch offset $t_{offset,1}$ with respect to the trigger rising edge,
- the first glitch width $t_{width,1}$,
- the first glitch voltage level $V_{low,1}$,
- the second glitch offset $t_{offset,2}$ with respect to the end of the first glitch,
- the second glitch width $t_{width,2}$, and
- the second glitch voltage level $V_{low,2}$.

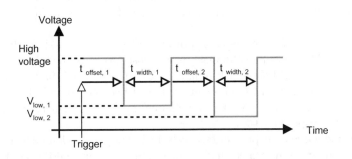

Fig. 28. Parameters characterising a negative double power glitch

To reduce the overhead for the search through all parameter combinations, the first glitch is fixed based on a setting that led to a successful fault in the single fault scenario. Moreover, the low voltage level is set equal for both glitches.

Results. By conducting a parameter sweep with the first pulse fixed, we were able to skip both loop1 and afterwards loop2, resulting in the waveform in Fig. 29. Having profiled the device, we could repeat the experiments with identical parameters and reliably perform the fault injection, thereby achieving a success rate close to 100 %.

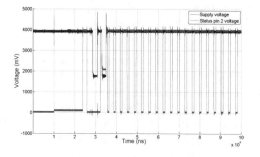

Fig. 29. Waveform of successful multiple fault injections on a PIC16F687, displaying PIN_STATUS_2

Implications. Depending on the cryptographic primitive and its actual implementation (and on the adversary's knowledge about the implementation), the injection of power faults as practically demonstrated above can have various dramatic effects on the security. Some examples are listed below, while the list could be vastly extended.

- In the case of a block cipher, e.g., AES, that is normally executed for several rounds to produce a cryptographically secure output, it is conceivable to skip the appropriate jump instruction that will execute the next round of the cipher: Having the plaintext and the output after one round, it is straightforward to mathematically conclude to the secret key used for the encryption.
- If a device is protected against power analysis with masking, the injection of a fault [3], e.g, while the mask is initialised, may allow to circumvent the countermeasure. If the mask remains set to zeroes it will have no protecting effect and a subsequent power analysis will become possible by this combination of active and passive side-channel analysis, which is easily possible with our proposed setup.
- Since inducing multiple faults is relatively simple, as demonstrated above, even common countermeasures against fault injection could be circumvented: Often two computations of, for example, the same exponentiation are carried out and the results are compared. If they are equal, the device assumes that no fault has occurred. To spoof the protection mechanism, hence one fault needs to be induced during the computation, and a second fault during the comparison.
- An induced fault could also allow for reverse-engineering of a (secret) program code that is executed by the microcontroller: Many devices feature a read-out protection, i.e., if a protection bit is set to one in the internal circuit of the microcontroller, the program code cannot be read out. A fault injected at the right moment in time, whilst trying to read out the device, could make this bit read zero, disabling the code protection mechanism.

Since all tests can be carried out automatically with varying parameters, and the success of the fault injection is automatically detected (the feedback via the data acquisition module even allows to determine, whether a reset of the DUT needs to be triggered), no human interaction is required. Thus, it is conceivable to perform a thorough profiling and find the correct points in time for inducing faults even in a black-box scenario.

7   Conclusion

In this article, we present a versatile framework, allowing for implementation attacks on virtually all types of cryptographic devices. Our setup provides functions for the automatic profiling and security evaluation of a cryptographic (or non-cryptographic) device, both with respect to side-channel analysis, i.e., the evaluation of EM or power measurements, and for fault injection, including the determination of parameters required to actively attack a black-box device.

The introduced functional units cover amongst others the analysis of (contactless) smartcards, RFIDs, microcontrollers, ASICs, FPGAs and mobile computing devices. After discussing models and possible effects of inducing faults, we describe our customised self-built hardware modules for generating faults based on power glitches, clock variations, as well as optical and EM fault injections. To our knowledge, we propose the first circuit for automatically inducing faults based on sparks in cryptographic devices published in the literature. The modules allow for automatically profiling the parameters and the strength of faults required for a particular device, as a function of the data processed and by using the data acquisition module as a feedback channel. The data acquisition module itself is based on a USB oscilloscope and enables inter alia for side-channel analysis based on the EM field, current consumption, and timing of the DUT.

We exemplarily demonstrate the effectiveness of the system by profiling a contactless smartcard and identify the appropriate leakage model. On this basis, we perform the first reported successful full key-recovery of a commercial cryptographic RFID employing Triple-DES by means of DEMA. As a second practical result, we prove the feasibility of multiple successive fault injections on a widespread PIC microcontroller using power glitches. This has severe implications with respect to the effectiveness of many countermeasures that often — due to overrating the efforts required for such an attack — protect only against one single fault during a computation. As all parts of our framework may operate independently of each other, powerful combined active and passive attacks are enabled. These attacks, e.g., circumventing countermeasures against power analysis by injecting faults, have been theoretically proposed in the literature, but so far there has been a lack of practical results regarding their feasibility.

We conclude that most implementation attacks, including the injection of multiple faults, can be conducted with a low-cost, public domain lab setup as described in this article. The common belief that highly sophisticated and expensive equipment is required is proven to be wrong: State-of-the-art implementation cryptanalysis can be performed by anyone who has a sufficient know-how about the attacks.

References

1. ISO 7816 Identification Cards - Integrated Circuit Cards with Contacts (2004)
2. Agrawal, D., Archambeault, B., Rao, J., Rohatgi, P.: The EM Side-Channel(s). In: Kaliski Jr., B.S., Koç, Ç.K., Paar, C. (eds.) CHES 2002. LNCS, vol. 2523, pp. 29–45. Springer, Heidelberg (2003)
3. Amiel, F., Villegas, K., Feix, B., Marcel, L.: Passive and active combined attacks: Combining fault attacks and side channel analysis. In: Proceedings of the Workshop on Fault Diagnosis and Tolerance in Cryptography, FDTC 2007, Washington, DC, USA, pp. 92–102. IEEE Computer Society, Los Alamitos (2007)
4. Analog Devices, Inc. AD8058 Dual, High Performance Voltage Feedback, 325 MHz Amplifier Datasheet (2003)
5. Analog Devices, Inc. AD9708 8-Bit, 100 MSPS+ TxDAC D/A Converter Datasheet (2009)
6. Atmel. ATMega32 Data Sheet, http://www.atmel.com
7. Atmel. Datasheet of Read/Write Base Station U2270B (2008), http://www.atmel.com
8. Brier, E., Clavier, C., Olivier, F.: Correlation Power Analysis with a Leakage Model. In: Joye, M., Quisquater, J.-J. (eds.) CHES 2004. LNCS, vol. 3156, pp. 16–29. Springer, Heidelberg (2004)
9. Carluccio, D., Lemke, K., Paar, C.: Electromagnetic Side Channel Analysis of a Contactless Smart Card: First Results. In: RFIDSec 2005 Workshop on RFID and Lightweight Crypto (July 2005), http://events.iaik.tugraz.at/RFIDandLightweightCrypto05/ RFID-SlidesandProceedings/Carluccio-EMSideChannel.pdf
10. Club, C.C.: RFID Zapper (2005)
11. Corson, D.: Comparing 8-bit Microcontrollers for Ultra-low-power Applications, 3 p., table 1 (October 2005)
12. Fournier, J.J.A., Moore, S., Li, H., Mullins, R., Taylor, G.: Security Evaluation of Asynchronous Circuits, pp. 137–151 (2003)
13. Giraud, C., Thiebeauld, H.: A Survey on Fault Attacks. In: Quisquater, J.-J., Paradinas, P., Deswarte, Y., Kalam, A.A.E. (eds.) CARDIS, pp. 159–176. Kluwer, Dordrecht (2004)
14. Hamid, H.B.-E., Choukri, H., Tunstall, D.N.M., Whelan, C.: The Sorcerer's Apprentice Guide to Fault Attacks (2004)
15. Handschuh, H.: Contactless Technology Security Issues. Information Security Bulletin 9 (2004), http://www.chi-publishing.com/samples/ISB0903HH.pdf
16. Handschuh, H., Paillier, P., Stern, J.: Probing Attacks on Tamper-Resistant Devices. In: Koç, Ç.K., Paar, C. (eds.) CHES 1999. LNCS, vol. 1717, pp. 303–315. Springer, Heidelberg (1999)
17. Hutter, M., Schmidt, J.-M., Plos, T.: RFID and Its Vulnerability to Faults. In: Oswald, E., Rohatgi, P. (eds.) CHES 2008. LNCS, vol. 5154, pp. 363–379. Springer, Heidelberg (2008)
18. International Organization for Standardization. ISO/IEC 14443-3: Identification Cards - Contactless Integrated Circuit(s) Cards - Proximity Cards - Part 3: Initialization and Anticollision, 1st edition (February 2001)
19. International Organization for Standardization. ISO/IEC 14443-4: Identification cards - Contactless Integrated Circuit(s) Cards - Proximity Cards - Part 4: Transmission Protocol, 1st edition (February 2001)

20. ISO/IEC 14443. Identification cards - Contactless integrated circuit(s) cards - Proximity cards - Part 1-4 (2001), http://www.iso.ch
21. Kasper, T.: Embedded Security Analysis of RFID Devices. Master's thesis, Ruhr Universität Bochum (2006)
22. Kasper, T., Carluccio, D., Paar, C.: An Embedded System for Practical Security Analysis of Contactless Smartcards. In: Sauveron, D., Markantonakis, K., Bilas, A., Quisquater, J.-J. (eds.) WISTP 2007. LNCS, vol. 4462, pp. 150–160. Springer, Heidelberg (2007)
23. Kasper, T., Oswald, D., Paar, C.: EM Side-Channel Attacks on Commercial Contactless Smartcards using Low-Cost Equipment. In: Youm, H.Y., Yung, M. (eds.) WISA 2009. LNCS, vol. 5932, pp. 79–93. Springer, Heidelberg (2009)
24. Kasper, T., Silbermann, M., Paar, C.: All You Can Eat or Breaking a Real-World Contactless Payment System. In: Sion, R. (ed.) FC 2010. LNCS, vol. 6052, pp. 343–350. Springer, Heidelberg (2010)
25. Kim, C.H., Quisquater, J.-J.: Fault Attacks for CRT Based RSA: New Attacks, New Results, and New Countermeasures. In: Sauveron, D., Markantonakis, K., Bilas, A., Quisquater, J.-J. (eds.) WISTP 2007. LNCS, vol. 4462, pp. 215–228. Springer, Heidelberg (2007)
26. Kömmerling, O., Kuhn, M.G.: Design Principles for Tamper-Resistant Smartcard Processors, pp. 9–20 (1999)
27. Kocher, P.: Timing Attacks on Implementations of Diffie-Hellman, RSA, DSS, and Other Systems. In: Koblitz, N. (ed.) CRYPTO 1996. LNCS, vol. 1109, pp. 104–113. Springer, Heidelberg (1996)
28. Kocher, P., Jaffe, J., Jun, B.: Differential Power Analysis. In: Wiener, M.J. (ed.) CRYPTO 1999. LNCS, vol. 1666, pp. 388–397. Springer, Heidelberg (1999)
29. Kugelstadt, T.: Op Amps for Everyone. In: Interfacing D/A Converters to Loads, ch. 14, 2nd edn., p. 239. Texas Instruments (2003)
30. Mangard, S., Oswald, E., Popp, T.: Power Analysis Attacks: Revealing the Secrets of Smart Cards. Springer, Secaucus (2007)
31. Melito, M.: Application Note 484/1293, Car Ignition with IGBTs (1999)
32. Microchip Technology Inc. PIC16F631/677/685/687/689/690 Data Sheet 20-Pin Flash-Based, 8-Bit CMOS Microcontrollers with nanoWatt Technology(2008)
33. Nohl, K., Evans, D., Starbug, Plötz, H.: Reverse-Engineering a Cryptographic RFID Tag. In: van Oorschot, P.C. (ed.) USENIX Security Symposium, pp. 185–194 (2008)
34. NXP. Data Sheet of Mifare Classic 4k chip MF1ICS70 (2008)
35. Oren, Y., Shamir, A.: Power Analysis of RFID Tags, http://www.wisdom.weizmann.ac.il/~yossio/rfid/
36. Plos, T.: Susceptibility of UHF RFID Tags to Electromagnetic Analysis. In: Malkin, T. (ed.) CT-RSA 2008. LNCS, vol. 4964, pp. 288–300. Springer, Heidelberg (2008)
37. Potato Semiconductor Corporation. PO74G08A Quadruple 2-input positive AND gate (2009)
38. Schmidt, J.-M.: Differential Fault Analysis - Final Report. Technical report, TU Graz (June 2008)
39. Schmidt, J.-M., Herbst, C.: A Practical Fault Attack on Square and Multiply. In: Proc. 5th Workshop on Fault Diagnosis and Tolerance in Cryptography, FDTC 2008, pp. 53–58 (August 10, 2008)
40. Shanmugam, K.S.: Digital & Analog Communication Systems, ch. 8.3.2. Wiley-India (2006)
41. ST Microelectronics. Data Sheet for STP10NK50Z, N-Channel Zener-Protected MOSFET (2005)

42. Waddle, J., Wagner, D.: Fault Attacks on Dual-Rail Encoded Systems. In: Computer Security Applications Conference, Annual, pp. 483–494 (2005)
43. Xilinx Inc. PicoBlaze 8-bit Embedded Microcontroller User Guide, v. 1.1.2 edition (June 2008)
44. Xilinx Inc. Spartan-3 FPGA Starter Kit Board User Guide, v 1.2 edition (June 2008)
45. Xilinx Inc. PicoBlaze User Resources. Web resource (2009)

An Adaptive Robust Watermarking Algorithm for Audio Signals Using SVD

Malay Kishore Dutta[1], Vinay K. Pathak[2], and Phalguni Gupta[3]

[1] Department of Electronics and Communication Engineering,
Galgotias College of Engineering and Technology, Greater NOIDA, India
[2] Department of Computer Science and Engineering, HBTI – Kanpur, India
[3] Department of Computer Science and Engineering, IIT -Kanpur, India
malay_kishore@rediffmail.com, vinaypathak.hbti@gmail.com,
pg@cse.iitk.ac.in

Abstract. This paper proposes an efficient watermarking algorithm which embeds watermark data adaptively in the audio signal. The algorithm embeds the watermark in the host audio signal in such a way that the degree of embedding (DOE) is adaptive in nature and is chosen in a justified manner according to the localized content of the audio. The watermark embedding regions are selectively chosen in the high energy regions of the audio signal which make the embedding process robust to synchronization attacks. Synchronization codes are added along with the watermark in the wavelet domain and hence the embedded data can be subjected to self synchronization and the synchronization code can be used as a check to combat false alarm that results from data modification due to watermark embedding. The watermark is embedded by quantization of the singular value decompositions in the wavelet domain which makes the process perceptually transparent. The experimental results suggest that the proposed algorithm maintains a good perceptual quality of the audio signal and maintains good robustness against signal processing attacks. Comparative analysis indicates that the proposed algorithm of adaptive DOE has superior performance in comparison to existing uniform DOE.

Keywords: Watermarking, Digital right management, Singular value decomposition, Robustness, Audio Signals.

1 Introduction

Illegal reproduction and unauthorized distribution of digital audio has become a high alarming problem in protecting the copyright of digital media [1]. Digital watermarking is one of the possible solutions for copyright protection and digital right management. A watermark is designed for residing permanently in the original audio data even after repeated reproduction and distribution. Since human auditory system (HAS) is more sensitive than human visual system (HVS) embedding watermark to the audio signal is more difficult than embedding in an image. According to IFPI (International Federation of the phonographic Industry) [2], a good audio watermarking algorithm should meet requirements of imperceptibility, robustness and security.

M.L. Gavrilova et al. (Eds.): Trans. on Comput. Sci. X, LNCS 6340, pp. 131–153, 2010.
© Springer-Verlag Berlin Heidelberg 2010

Imperceptibility means that embedded watermark should be imperceptible to human auditory system (HAS). The watermark should be robust so that it can survive intentional and unintentional signal processing attacks. The watermarking algorithm should be secure which means that the watermark can only be detected by the authorized person. These requirements are often contradictory with each other and there is a need to make a trade-off among them. There are some well known watermarking algorithms in time domain [3], [4] and in frequency domain [5], [6]. Some algorithms are proposed using quantization methods and cepstrum domain [7], [8]. It has been seen in the methods that synchronization attacks cause a severe problem in detection and recovery of watermark. In such an attack the watermark is actually present in the audio signal but cannot be detected because the synchronization is lost. Synchronization attacks such as cropping and TSM (time-scale modification) cause dislocation between embedding and detection in the time domain and hence although the watermark is present in the audio signal it is difficult to recover it. Some methods proposed to solve the problem of synchronization attacks are exhaustive search [9], peak point extraction with special shaping [10], content based localized watermarking [11], high energy reference points based watermarking [12] and self synchronization for audio watermarking [13]. In [21] a sound synthesized process in digital instruments is proposed as a real-time watermarking method. Both musical performance and the insertion of watermark can be actualized in real time. A method to enhance the security of vocal communication over an open network is proposed in [22]. The method divides speech data using the secret sharing scheme and transfers the shared data using the multipath routing technique to realize secure voice communication over the network. To solve the problems associated with de-synchronization attacks, an audio watermarking scheme is proposed in [23] based on support-vector-machine (SVM) theory by using audio statistics characteristics and a synchronization code technique. In [24] a Multiplicative Patchwork Method (MPM) for audio watermarking is presented. The watermark signal is embedded by selecting two subsets of the host signal features and modifying one subset multiplicatively regarding the watermark data, whereas another subset is left unchanged. In [25], the issue of audio source separation from a single channel is addressed, i.e., the estimation of several source signals from a single observation of their mixture. The presented results open up new perspectives in both underdetermined source separation and audio watermarking domains

The synchronization codes are used to locate the positions where the watermark is embedded in the audio. In time domain the embedding strength is limited to maintain perceptual transparency and hence not robust to signal processing attacks. If synchronization codes are embedded in frequency domain the robustness increases to a great extent, but in doing so the computational cost for searching the codes also increases. High energy points used as reference for watermark embedding regions are also used in watermarking [12]. These peak points after special shaping [10] serve as reference points for embedding and detection of the watermark. The performance of these peak point extraction methods is found to be moderate and there is a requirement for enhancing the performance of such methods.

This paper embeds a synchronization code in the audio signal with reference to the high energy peaks. In doing so the accuracy in detecting the watermark increases in comparison to normal high energy reference point method. This synchronization code is useful to combat false alarm which is generated by the modification of audio data on watermark embedding. Since the synchronization code is embedded only in selected high energy regions, the computation load in searching such codes decreases to a great extent. Hence in the proposed method the synchronization is maintained with higher accuracy and at lower computational cost in comparison to other existing methods.

Singular value decomposition (SVD) based watermarking methods [14], [15] have been proposed for image watermarking, but not enough research has been reported for SVD based audio watermarking. In this paper an adaptive SVD based audio watermarking method is proposed which is localized according to the content of the audio signal. The basis of the SVD based image watermarking method is that the singular values of the image remains unaltered even if some alterations are made in the image. Accordingly the inverse of this property where the singular values are modified without changing the perceptual property of the signal is used in watermarking the signals.

The paper is organized as follows; Section 2 gives an overview of singular value decomposition (SVD). The watermark generation from an image and enhancing its security are discussed in Section 3. The method for finding watermark embedding region and determining the degree of embedding for each region are described in Section 4. The synchronization code generation and its implementation are explained in Section 5. The Section 6 comprehensively describes the watermark embedding and detection in the SVD domain in the audio signals. Various parameters used to measure the performance of the proposed method have been discussed in Section 7. The experimental results are given in Section 8 and the last section concludes the paper.

2 Singular Value Decomposition

Singular value decomposition (SVD) is used to diagonalize matrices. It packs most of the signal energy into a few singular values. The SVD belongs to the group of orthogonal transformations, which decompose the input matrix into several matrices and one of which has only nonzero values in the main diagonal. SVD has been a successful method for image watermarking and in this paper it is proposed to use the SVD based method for watermarking of audio signals. An arbitrary matrix A of size $M \times N$ can be represented by its SVD as:

$$A = USV^{T}$$

where U and V are $M \times M$ and $N \times N$ matrices respectively. The columns of U and V are mutually orthogonal unit vectors. The $M \times N$ matrix S is a pseudo-diagonal matrix and its diagonal elements, which are arranged by descending gradation, are all nonnegative values. They are called SVs and the first value is far larger than others. While both U and V are not unique, the singular values are fully determined by A.

To apply the SVD in an audio signal each audio frames (coefficients in time domain or any other domain like DWT, DCT, FFT domain etc.) is converted into two dimensional matrix. Once the SVD operation is done, the matrix S which has diagonal elements in the descending order can be modified or quantized as per the watermark bit to be embedded. To explain the method let us consider the original audio frame as A and W is the watermark bits to be embedded.

$$A = USV^T$$

$$S_W = \text{Modified / Quantized value of S}$$
$$A_W = US_wV^T$$

where S_W is the modified singular values and A_W is the watermarked audio frame whose SVs are modified.

3   Watermark Generation

An image is used as the watermark. To ensure the security and to improve the robustness of the proposed method, the watermark should be pre-processed before embedded into the host signal. Due to the periodicity of the Arnold transform, the image can be recovered easily after permutation. So, the Arnold transform is applied to the original binary image watermark [16]. To use Arnold transform we make $M=N$. If the size of the image is $N \times N$, $(x, y)^T$ is the coordinate of the watermark image's pixel, $(x', y')^T$ is the coordinate after the transform. Arnold transform can be expressed as:

$$\begin{bmatrix} \overline{x} \\ \overline{y} \end{bmatrix} = \begin{bmatrix} 1 & 1 \\ 1 & 2 \end{bmatrix} \begin{bmatrix} x \\ y \end{bmatrix} (\mathrm{mod}\, N)^{\ddot{\imath}}$$

The steps in converting the image into a watermark for audio signals are given below:

1. Compute a global threshold that can be used to convert an intensity image to a binary image. The threshold has to be normalized intensity value that lies in the range [0, 1].
2. Using the above threshold convert the image into a BW image.
3. Resize the image into $M \times N$ as per the design requirement of the Watermarking model.
4. The resized image is scrambled by applying the Arnold transform.
5. Convert the scrambled image I into a vector W as:

$$for\ i = 1{:}M$$
$$for\ j = 1{:}N$$
$$W(k) = I(i, j)$$
$$k = k + 1;$$
$$end$$
$$end$$

6. Rescale the vector W as $\alpha \times W$ where α is the strength of the watermark.

The choice of α depends on the design requirements of the watermarking method. Proper values of α can optimize imperceptibility and robustness of the watermarking method. Lower values of α makes the watermark imperceptible while higher values of α makes the watermark robust against signal processing attacks.

4   Selection of Watermark Embedding Regions

Finding the watermark embedding region is one of the most challenging steps in audio watermarking. If the embedding regions are not properly selected, the detection and recovery of the watermark under signal processing attacks can be very difficult. This paper proposes a method of selecting such regions on the original audio waveform which is based on selecting high energy peaks as reference points.

Prominent instruments like drum, tabla (an Indian instrument), piano etc. form a sequence of high energy peaks. These peaks are so dominant that the other sounds are normally masked at that instant. Also considering the pre-masking and post masking of these peaks, the region around these peaks can be modified without affecting the quality of the audio for human auditory system. These peaks are normally 0.1 to 0.2 second in length, so under the sampling rate of 44100 KHz they spread over 4410 to 8820 samples. These sharp transients are less prone to synchronization attack. Thus these regions are ideal for watermark embedding. It is shown in [11] that after TSM (time scale modification) attack although the absolute time-domain positions of those local regions with high energy have some change after time scaling, these shapes do not change much. Fig. 1 shows an original signal and time scaled signal of a sample audio. It can be seen from the figure that although the positions of the high energy peak has changed but the surrounding localized region does not change much. Thus, by embedding the watermark in these areas, it is reasonable to believe that the watermark be safe under TSM attacks to some extent.

This proposed method chooses the high-energy peaks and these peaks act as reference points for region of watermark embedding. For selecting high-energy peaks a threshold is chosen above which all such peaks are considered as reference points. This threshold is taken as a fraction of the maximum value of the sample in the time domain signal. The number of regions for watermark embedding (ROE) depends on the selected threshold. So the threshold for deciding the number of regions for embedding of watermark data has to be properly chosen as per the characteristics and size of the watermark data.

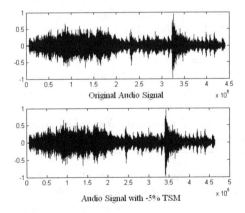

Fig. 1. Waveform of Original and -5 % TSM Audio Signal sample

It has been shown in [17] that in synchronization attacks like time scale modifications (TSM) are performed on the harmonic components and the residual components separately. The harmonic portion is changed in time scale by modulating each harmonic component to DC, interpolating and decimating the DC signal and then demodulating each component back to its original frequency. The residual portion, which can be further separated into high energy transients and noise in the wavelet transform domain. In doing so the edges and the relative distances between the edges are preserved and the noise component is time scaled. In contemporary music, there is use of percussion instruments like drum, tabla etc. The beats of these instruments are the high energy music edges which can be used as reference points. Also since these high energy edges maintain the rhythm of the music, cropping degrades the quality of the music to an annoying extent. Hence we can conclude that the time scale modification method changes the audio signal in the low energy regions (minimum transients) and tends to conserve the high energy transients. Hence it is clearly apparent that if the watermark is embedded in audio segments near the high energy peaks, the effect of synchronization attacks is minimum. On the other hand, if the watermark is embedded in the minimum transient regions synchronization attacks severely effect the detection and recovery of the watermark from the audio signal.

Based on the above discussion the watermark embedding regions are chosen in high energy transients. The amount of watermark information to be embedded in these regions is kept adaptive. It is intended to embed more information in the more sharp music edges and less information in less sharp music edges which makes the embedding process adaptive in nature. The reason for this adaptive embedding process is that more sharp edges are more resistant to synchronization attacks and hence more watermark information can be embedded in such regions. The number of watermark bits to be embedded in a high energy region is decided by some local characteristics of that particular region.

Algorithm 1

C is vector containing reference points and F is a zero vector equal to the size of C. n is the degree of embedding.

$\quad K = zeros\ [length(C), n]$

$\quad F[i] = C[i]/max(C)$

$\quad F[i]$ mapped to degree of embedding

$\quad for\ i = 1: length(C)$

$\quad\quad K\ [F\ (i) \times n]\ [i] = F[i]$

$\quad for\ i = 1: length(c)$ (there is one non-zero entry in every column)

$\quad\quad if\ K\ (i, j) > 0$ then

j is the number of watermark bits to be embedded for the ROEWM(i) corresponding to i^{th} element of vector C.

The number of watermark bits to be embedded in the *ROE* is called as degree of embedding *(DOE)* and depend on the sharpness of the music edge at that region. More watermark data is embedded in more sharp regions whereas less watermark data is embedded in less sharp regions. So the degree of embedding of watermark is made localized according to the sharpness of the music edge which acts as the reference point for the embedding region. In doing so the watermark can embedded in a justified manner and the watermark becomes robust to synchronization attacks. The point i (high energy peak) is excluded from *ROE* so that it is not modified in the process of watermark embedding and creates a possibility of not detecting it in the watermark detection process. This point i is used as a reference and not for embedding of watermark. A generic method of selecting *DOE* for the reference points is given in Algorithm 1. For example if ten levels of adaptive *DOE* are used then using Algorithm 1 *DOE* can be selected from a set of pre-decided ranges as shown in Table 1.

Table 1. Degree of Embedding for the Set of Reference Points using Algorithm 1 for Ten Level DOE

	Range of Reference point (i)	Degree of Embedding (j)
1	*[max(X(i))] > i ≥ 0.95* [max(X(i))]*	*10*
2	*0.95* [max(X(i))] > i ≥ 0.90* [max(X(i))]*	*9*
3	*0.90* [max(X(i))] > i ≥ 0.85 *[max(X(i))]*	*8*
4	*0.85* [max(X(i))] > i ≥ 0.80 *[max(X(i))]*	*7*
5	*0.80* [max(X(i))] > i ≥ 0.75 *[max(X(i))]*	*6*
6	*0.75* [max(X(i))] > i ≥ 0.70 *[max(X(i))]*	*5*
7	*0.70* [max(X(i))] > i ≥ 0.65 *[max(X(i))]*	*4*
8	*0.65* [max(X(i))] > i ≥ 0.60 *[max(X(i))]*	*3*
9	*0.60* [max(X(i))] > i ≥ 0.55 *[max(X(i))]*	*2*
10	*0.55* [max(X(i))] > i ≥ 0.50 *[max(X(i))]*	*1*

Once the reference points are determined and the *DOE* is selected the region of watermarking *ROE* has to be determined for the reference point. Further the *ROE* has to be divided for embedding the watermark data and a synchronization code (*syncode*) as *ROEWM* and *ROESYNC*. The synchronization code is used as a tool against false alarm due to data modification as a result of watermark embedding. The details of this synchronization code are explained in the next Section. The block diagram of the watermark embedding method is shown in Fig. 2.

Steps in selection of reference points and determination of ROE for watermark embedding are given in Algorithm 2.

Algorithm 2

1. *Let X be the Audio Signal.*
2. *Find the max value of the samples $X(i)_{max}$ in X.*
3. *Find all the peaks above $[(1-n\alpha)(X(i)_{max}]$ where α is a fraction. Store these values in a vector D.*
4. *A new vector C is created as*

   for n =1: |D|
   if D(i+1) – D(i) > |A|+|WM|
   then C(i) = D(i);
   where A = length (Audio signal) /length (watermark +p X syncode)
   where p is the length of the block used for quantization to embed one bit of the syncode.

Algorithm 2 (Contd.)

5. *Select DOE for each ROE corresponding to each element of Vector C using Algorithm 1.*

6. $\qquad$ *z=0*
    $\qquad$ *for i = 1:length(C)*
    $\qquad$ *if K(i,j)>0*
    $\qquad$ *z = z + j;*
    $\qquad$ *C is the required set of reference points*
    $\qquad$ *else*
    $\qquad$ *n=n+1*
    $\qquad$ *go to step 3*

The region of watermark and synchronization code embedding (ROE) is given as:
$\qquad$ *$ROE_i = [C (i) - |A| /2 – p \times length (syncode): C (i) + |A| /2]$*
$\qquad$ *(Excluding the point i)*

The embedding region ROE_i is sub divided into two parts as region of embedding sync code ROESYNC and region of embedding watermark ROEWM as:
$\qquad$ *$ROESYNC (i) = ROE_i(1:length (p \times syncode))$*
$\qquad$ *$ROEWM (i) = ROE_i(length\ p \times (syncode) +1: length (R_i))$*

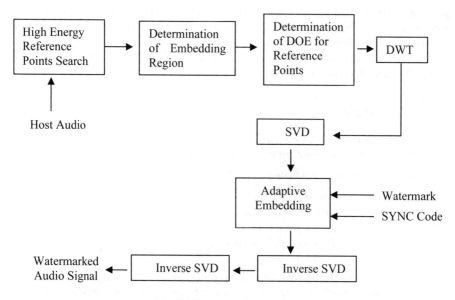

Fig. 2. Watermark Embedding

5 SYNC Code Generation and Embedding

Under the de-synchronization attacks like cropping and time scale modifications the watermarked audio is prone to suffer dislocations of the watermark embedded regions. The synchronization codes embedded into the original audio serves as a method to locate correctly the watermarked embedded regions after the signal has suffered de-synchronization attacks.

The embedding of watermark data in the audio signal causes slight modifications in the audio signal. Although the changes are made in a strategic way so that they are imperceptible to human auditory system (HAS) but there may be other problems that may arise as a result of these modifications. In this proposed method the reference points and the degree of embedding are based on the magnitude of the high energy points considered above a certain threshold. It may happen that as a result of watermark embedding, a certain point which was below the threshold goes above it and a false alarm is generated. The reverse of this problem i.e. a point above threshold going below is not applicable in this method as the reference point is excluded from the *ROE*. To counter this kind of false alarm the synchronization code is embedded in the *ROE* which serves as a check for finding an authentic *ROE* in the detection and recovery process. It can be noted that this self-synchronization check for authentic detection of *ROE* involves less computational load in comparison to existing conventional synchronization check methods. In this proposed method synchronization code is searched only in specific regions and not in all parts of the audio file. Hence the computation load is reduced to a great extent which is a good feature of the proposed method of watermarking. Use of such localized synchronization codes eliminates false alarm generated due to data modification on watermark embedding.

In the proposed method PN sequences based on chaotic maps have been used as a synchronization code. If $\{a_i\}$ is an original synchronization code and $\{b_i\}$ is an unknown sequence both having the same length. If the number of different bits between $\{a_i\}$ and $\{b_i\}$, when compared bit-by-bit, is less than or equal to a predefined threshold τ, the $\{b_i\}$ is determined as the synchronization code.

In order to generate the synchronization code chaotic maps are used. Chaotic systems are deterministic systems that are governed by non-linear dynamics. These systems show deterministic behavior which is very sensitive to initial conditions, in a way that the results are uncorrelated and seem to be random in nature. To increase the security of the sync code, a random chaotic sequence generated by the hybrid chaotic dynamical system is used [18]. The synchronization code (sync code) is generated by thresholding the chaotic map. The initial point of the chaotic sequence generator is a secret key. By using generators of a strongly chaotic nature we can ensure that the system is cryptographically secure, i.e., the sequence generation mechanism cannot be inversely engineered even if an attacker can manage to obtain a part of the sequence. For example a chaotic dynamic is given below:

$$\text{Chaotic } (x) = \begin{cases} 1 - 2x^2, & -1 \leq x < -0.5 \\ 1 - \tfrac{1}{2}(-2x)^{1.2}, & -0.5 \leq x < 0 \\ 1 - 2x, & 0 \leq x < 0.5 \\ -(2x-1)^{0.7}, & 0.5 < x \leq 1 \end{cases} \tag{1}$$

The above chaotic map (1) can produce almost uncountable random sequences that are extremely sensitive to the initial secret key. Steps in generating the chaos based watermark are as follows:

Step 1: Generate a chaotic sequence S with an initial key (within the given limit) using any of the chaotic equation given in (1) of length M. (M depends on the design choice)

Step 2: Use zero as threshold for the chaotic sequence S. All elements greater than zero are made equal to 1 otherwise -1.

Step 3: Repeat the Step 1 and Step 2 for different values of initial keys to generate different sequences that can be used in different audio samples.

After the Synchronization points $C(i)$ and the embedding segments $R(i)$ are determined, the sync code is embedded in the audio signal. The embedding segment should be large enough to have room for the sync code and some watermark bits. In the proposed method we choose quantization index modulation (QIM) for embedding the sync code because of its good robust nature. Also by using QIM method the search for sync is blind in nature, which means the original audio is not needed in sync code extraction.

The quantization parameter is made adaptive in nature by using the mean of each *ROESYNC* segment in the QIM process. The quantization parameter is made localized depending on the nature of the signal. The steps used for embedding the sync code in the audio signal is given in Algorithm 3.

Algorithm 3

1. Divide the coefficients of 3rd level DWT using Haar filter of *ROESYNC(i)* into p sub-segments where p is the length of the syncode.

2. The mean value of the coefficients of pth sub-segment of ith reference point is calculated as: $\overline{ROESYNC\ (i)\ (p)} = \sum ROESYNC\ (i)\ (p)\ /\ length(p^{th}\ sub\text{-}segment)$ where $\sum$ is the summation of all the DWT coefficients in the pth sub-segment of the ith *ROEWM*.

3. Embed each bit of the synchronization code in each sub-segment p as
   if syncode(p) = 1
   $ROESYNC\ '(i)\ (p) = ROESYNC\ (i)(p) + 2 * \overline{ROESYNC\ (i)(p)}$
   else
   $ROESYNC\ '(i)(p) = ROESYNC\ (i)(p) - 2 * \overline{ROESYNC\ (i)(p)}$

   where $ROESYNC(i)(p)$ and $ROESYNC'(i)(p)$ are the original and modified p^{th} sub-segment of the ith *ROESYNC* respectively.

4. Take IDWT of the *ROESYNC'(i)(p)* to convert back to the time domain

6 Watermark Embedding and Detection

Once the watermark embedding regions and the degree of embedding for every region are decided, the watermarking is done in a content based adaptive manner in the discrete wavelet domain (DWT). The choice of DWT for watermarking has several advantages such as it needs lower computation load in comparison to DCT and DFT and it has variable decomposition level.

6.1 Watermark Embedding

The high energy reference points are determined as discussed in Section 4. The indices of these points is stored in the vector C and the region of embedding for the ith point is determined as discussed in Section 4 and is given by:

$$ROE\ (i) = [C\ (i) - |A|\ /2 - p\ X\ length\ (syncode) : C\ (i) + |A|\ /2 - 1] \tag{2}$$

DWT is performed on this ROE segment. The syncode is embedded successively into the low frequency sub-band of segments. The length of this ROE segment depends on the amount of data that is to be embedded. It should be large enough to accommodate the synchronization code and some watermark bits. The number of watermark bits to be added in a ROE segment is decided by the degree of embedding of that segment as was discussed in Algorithm 1 which makes the watermark embedding adaptive in nature according to the content of the audio.

As discussed in Algorithm 1 for the matrix K, there is one non-zero element in every row corresponding to one high energy reference point. This non-zero element will indicates the degree of embedding. For mathematical simplicity this is restricted to a limited number of quantization levels and the value of this non-zero entry indicated the number of watermark bits to be embedded in that ROE. However a more complicated relation can be customized as per contents and nature of the host audio.

If K is and $i\ X\ j$ matrix, where i indicate the number of reference points and j indicates the degree of embedding. We need to search all the non-zero elements (every row has one) in K and then decide the degree of embedding. The watermarking technique used here is quantization index modulation (QIM) [19], [20] because of its robustness to signal processing attacks and since it is blind in nature (original signal not required for watermark extraction). The watermark embedding steps are given in Algorithm 4.

Algorithm 4

Step 1: Determine the region of embedding $ROE(i)$ using Equation 4.2.

Step 2: Obtain region of embedding the watermark $ROEWM$ as discussed in Section 4.4 is given as:
$ROEWM(i) = ROE(i)\ (length\ (syncode) + 1 : length\ (R(i))$

Step 3: Apply third level DWT to the audio segment using Haar wavelet.

Algorithm 4 (Contd.)

Step 4: Find the non-zero element in each row of matrix K. The index of this non zero element is the degree of embedding *(DOE)*. So for all the i rows of the matrix K, there is one *DOE(i)*.

Step 5: Divide the low frequency approximate wavelet components of each *ROEWM(i)* segment into j equal sub-segments where j is the degree of embedding *DOE(i)* for that corresponding *ROEWM(i)*

Step 6: Convert the sub-segments into blocks *ROEWM(i)(j)* of size $m \times m$ (blocks are converted into matrix to apply SVD, Zero padding may be done to achieve $m \times m$ size).

Step 7: Calculate SVD for each *ROEWM(i)(j)* as $ROEWM(i)(j) = USV^T$
Let $S_{ij} = (S_{11} \ S_{22} \ldots\ldots\ldots S_{mm})$ be the non zero diagonal elements of the matrix S for the jth sub- segment of the ith reference point.

Step 8: Embed the watermark using QIM. The embedding is done as follows:
$for \ i = 1: length(wm)$
$\quad if \ K[i][j] > 0$
$$S_{ij}' = \begin{array}{ll} \lfloor S_{ij}/\mu \rfloor . \mu + 3\mu/4 & if \ wm \ (i) = 1 \\ \lfloor S_{ij}/\mu \rfloor . \mu + \mu/4 & if \ wm \ (i) = 0 \end{array}$$
$\quad i = i + 1;$
$end \ for$

where $\lfloor \ \ \rfloor$ indicates the floor function and S_{ij} and S_{ij}' are the SVD of DWT coefficients of the low frequency sub-segment of the original and watermarked audio data respectively. By increasing the value of μ one increases the robustness but decreases imperceptibility. This value of μ has to be maximized in such a way that the watermark maintains perceptual transparency.

Step 9: Obtain the watermarked sub-segment *ROEWM(i)(j)* by applying inverse SVD to the modified singular values.

Step10: Convert the modified audio segment from all the modified sub-segments. The inverse DWT is performed to get the watermarked signal.

6.2 Watermark Extraction

The watermark extraction is the reverse process of the watermark embedding process. The first step in this process is to identify the embedding regions *(ROE)*. Once the embedding regions are identified then the watermark detection and recovery can be performed. The synchronization points are to be determined first and then *ROE* is to be estimated. As discussed in the Section 5 there is a synchronization code that is embedded in the *ROE*. This synchronization code can now be a check in determining the *ROE* for all the high energy reference points. The steps for detection and recovery of the watermark are given in Algorithm 5.

Algorithm 5

Step 1:   Determine vector *C* containing the index (*i* elements) of all the high energy reference points as discussed in Section 4.4 using the same value of threshold that is used in the embedding process.

Step 2:   Determine the *ROESYNC(i)* for all reference points *i*, as discussed in Section 4. Divide the *ROESYNC(i)* into *p* sub-segments as discussed in the embedding process, where *p* is the length of the SYNCODE.

Step 3:   Calculate the mean value of each sub-segment *ROESYNC(i)(j)*. If the mean value is greater than or equal to zero, a bit "1" is detected otherwise bit "0" is detected.

Step 4:   Use the normalized correlation (NC) to find the similarity between the extracted syncode and the original syncode as follows:

$$NC \ (sync, sync^*) = \frac{\sum_{i=1}^{M} sync(i)\, sync^*(i)}{\sqrt{\sum_{i=1}^{M} sync(i)^2}\ \sqrt{\sum_{i=1}^{M} sync^*(i)^2}}$$

where *sync* and *sync** are the original and extracted syncode, respectively and *M* is the length of the sub-segment. If the NC between sync and sync* is greater than or equal to a pre-defined threshold σ then *sync** is accepted as a synchronization code and then go to Step 7. Otherwise go to Step 5 and Step 6 in an alternate repetitive way, i.e. go to step 5 and in next turn go to step 6 and repeat this till it goes to Step 7.

Step 5: Shift the *ROESYNC* by 1 sample to the left, i.e. *ROESYNCL(i)* =*ROESYNC (i- 1)* and repeat Step2 to Step 4.

Step 6: Shift the *ROESYNC* by 1 sample to the right, i.e *ROESYNCR(i)* = *ROESYNC(i+1)*and repeat Step 2 to Step 4.

Step 7: Once a NC above the pre-determined value is determined it indicates the identification of a *ROESYNC(i)*. The updated value of *i* is used to determine the *ROE(i)*. From this updated value of *i*, calculate the degree of embedding *j*.

Step 8: Calculate the *ROEWM(i)* from the *ROE(i)* calculated in step 7. Take DWT of this segment. This DWT segment *ROEWM(i)* is divided into *j* equal sub- segments. The sub-segments are converted into blocks *ROEWM(i)(j)* of size *m* X *m* (blocks are

---

Algorithm 5 (Contd.)

converted into matrix to apply SVD, Zero padding may be done to achieve $m \times m$ size).

Step 9: Calculate SVD for each *ROEWM(i)(j)* as
$$ROEWM(i)(j) = USV^T$$
Let $S_{ij} = (S_{11}\ S_{22} \ldots\ldots\ldots S_{mm})$ be the non zero diagonal elements of the matrix S for the jth sub-segment of the ith reference point.

Step 10: Extract the watermark *wm'* as follows:
$$wm'\ (k) = 1\quad if\ S_{ij}* - \lfloor\_ S_{ij}*/S\_\rfloor \cdot S \geq S/2$$
$$wm'\ (k) = 0\quad if\ S_{ij}* - \lfloor\_ S_{ij}*/S\_\rfloor \cdot S < S/2$$
$k = 1$: *length(wm)*. The extracted watermark is de-scrambled using inverse Arnold transform to obtain the original watermark image.

It is clear from the above that for extracting the watermark we need to search bit by bit the synchronization code for every reference points. After the synchronization codes are found the embedding regions of the watermark *ROEWM* is determined. In case no synchronization codes are found the search window is shifted and searched again alternately in both directions till the code is found. It can be seen that the original SVD coefficients are not required in the extraction process and thus the algorithm is blind in nature.

7   Performance Evaluation Parameters

The performance of the proposed method of audio watermarking is evaluated by some performance coefficients as discussed below:

a.   Signal to noise ratio (SNR)

The SNR is the objective quality measure to evaluate the perceptual transparency of the watermarked signal. It can be defined as:

$$SNR = 10 \log_{10} \frac{\sum_{i=1}^{L} X^2(i)}{\sum_{i=1}^{L} \left[X^2(i) - \bar{X}(i)^2\right]}\ dB$$

where X and X' are the original and watermarked audio signals and M is the length of the audio signal.

b.   Normalized Correlation (NC)

It is used to evaluate the similarity measurement of extracted binary watermark, which can be defined as:

$$NC\left(W,\bar{W}\right) = \frac{\sum_{i=1}^{M} W(i)\ \bar{W}(i)}{\sqrt{\sum_{i=1}^{M} W(i)^2}\ \sqrt{\sum_{i=1}^{M} \bar{W}(i)^2}}$$

where W and $W*$ are original and extracted watermark respectively, i is the index of the watermark and M is the length of the watermark.

c. Bit Error Rate (BER)

The bit error rate (BER) is used to find the percentage of error bits between original watermark and extracted watermark. The BER is given by:

$$BER = \frac{1}{M} \sum_{i=1}^{1 \le i \le M} W(i) \oplus \bar{W}(i)$$

where W and $\bar{W}$ are the original and the extracted watermark respectively, $\oplus$ is exclusive OR (XOR) operator and M is the length of the watermark.

c. Subjective Listening Test

To evaluate the audio quality, subjective listening tests can be performed to find the mean opinion score (MOS). These MOS is one of the most widely used subjective methods for watermarked audio signal quality evaluation. Ten listeners of different age groups are provided with the original and the watermarked audio signal and they are asked to classify the difference in terms the MOS grades. The MOS grades are defined in Table 2.

Table 2. MOS Grades

Effect of Watermark	Quality of Audio	Score
Imperceptible	Excellent	0
Perceptible but not annoying	Good	-1
Slightly annoying	Fair	-2
Annoying	Poor	-3
Very Annoying	Very Poor	-4

8   Experimental Results

Experiments have been performed with different types of audio files. As discussed in Section 4 the degree of embedding is dependent on the localized audio characteristics which make a justified method of embedding data in the audio. In case of non-adaptive data embedding more number of ROE may be required which can be achieved by decreasing the threshold (which is a fraction of the maximum value of the audio signal, as shown in Table 1). In doing so, data will be embedded in less sharp music edges which is more prone to synchronization attacks. In addition to that for embedding watermark data in the less sharp music edges, the threshold for determining ROE has to be decreased. This in turn may cause false alarm due to data modification on watermark embedding.

It is found that on watermark embedding the audio signal undergoes modification and the SNR for the watermarked signal is shown in Table 3. Although there is a modification in the audio signal, but it remains imperceptible to human auditory system because the masking effects. The length of the SYNC code used in the experiments is 64 and the size of the watermark image is 32*32 =1024. Since the audio samples are sampled at 44100 KHz and the high energy peaks are 0.1 sec length, these peaks spreads over 4410 samples. (Some peaks like that of drum last for 0.2 sec and hence spreads over 8820 samples). So it is clearly seen that these high energy peaks and the pre and post-masking associated with them provides enough room for embedding watermark in these regions that remain imperceptible to human auditory system.

Table 3. The SNR of the Watermarked Audio Signal and the Mean Opinion Score (MOS) from Subjective Listening Test

No.	Watermarked Audio Sample	SNR (dB)	MOS	No.	Watermarked Audio Sample	SNR (dB)	MOS
1	Classical 1	36.1	0	14	Piano	31.1	0
2	Classical2	33.2	0	15	Flute	26.2	0
3	Classical 3	34.2	0	16	Guitar1	32.1	-1
4	Country 1	36.1	0	17	Guitar 2	33.4	0
5	Country 2	39.0	0	18	Vocal1	27.1	-1
6	Country 3	32.1	0	19	Vocal2	23.1	-2
7	Pop1	33.0	0	20	Vocal3	28.3	-1
8	Pop2	32.9	0	21	Sitar 1	28.9	0
9	Pop 3	32.7	-1	22	Sitar 2	23.1	0
10	Blues	31.3	0	23	Violin 1	28.1	0
11	Folk 1	36.1	0	24	Violin2	26.1	0
12	Folk 2	29.5	0	25	Tabla	38.1	0
13	Folk 3	23.3	0				

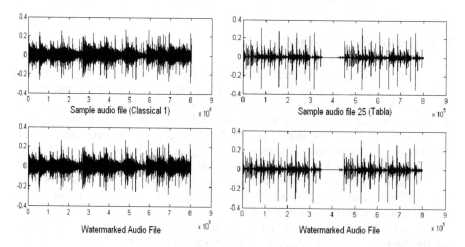

Fig. 3. Original and Watermarked Audio Signals

The scores MOS of the subjective listening tests are presented in Table 3. It can be en from Table 3 that the watermark embedded in the audio signal is imperceptible to human auditory system and also the SNR computed for watermarked signals is above 20dB which is considered good according to IFPI (International Federation of the phonographic Industry)

In order to test the robustness of the proposed method, different types of signal processing attacks are performed on the watermarked audio signal as described below:

a) Filtering: Low pass filtering with a cut off frequency of 8 KHz. The filter used is a second order Butterworth filter.

b) Resampling: The watermarked signal originally was sampled at 44.1 KHz, re sampled at 22 KHz and restored by sampling again at 44.1KHz.

c) AWGN: White Gaussian noise is added to the signal so that the resulting signal has a SNR more than 20 dB.

d) Time scale modification: TSM processing is done in the watermarked audio signal to change the time scale to an extent of +10% and -10%.

e) MP3 Compression: The MPEG -1 layer 3 compression with 32 kbps is applied.

f) Cropping: Segments of 500 samples are removed randomly from the watermarked signal.

In the watermark recovery process the first step is the detection of correct regions of embedding. To evaluate the performance of the method a parameter called ratio of correctly detected regions (ROCDR) is defined. It is the ratio of the number of correct embedded regions detected to the total embedding regions detected. It gives an indication of the false alarm that is generated in the detection process.

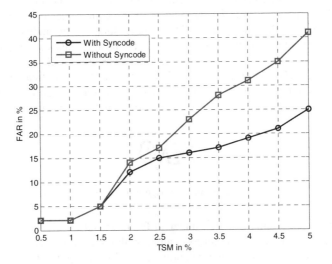

Fig. 4. (a) Positive FAR under different values of TSM foe audio sample Classical 1 with and without Syncode

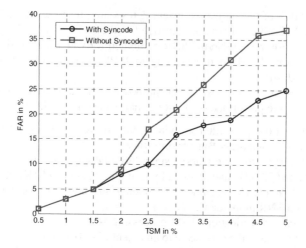

Fig. 4. (b) Positive FAR under different values of TSM foe audio sample Tabla with and without Syncode

The ROCDR for the proposed method for various samples under different signal processing attacks are shown in Table 4. To make a comparison with existing methods comparative results are also shown in Table 4 which reveals that the proposed method is better in comparison to the other two methods. The integration of the synchronization code makes the proposed scheme perform better since the positive false alarm is countered by it. Negative FAR condition does not apply since the peak reference point has not been used for data embedding. Fig. 4(a) and Fig. 4(b) shows the positive false alarm rate with and without the sync code under different degrees of TSM. It can be seen that the positive FAR is reduced specially under high degree of time scale modification attacks. A comparison of robustness tests against signal processing attacks for the proposed adaptive method (variable DOE) with non-adaptive method (uniform DOE) is given in Table 5. It can be seen clearly that performance of the proposed adaptive method is better than the non-adaptive uniform method. An image used as a watermark as discussed in Section 2 is shown in Fig. 5.

MKD

Fig. 5. Binary image watermark

The recovered watermark image under different signal processing attacks is presented in Fig 6. For comparison purpose, along with the performance of the proposed method the performance of the non-adaptive method is also presented. It can be seen the watermark recovered under serious synchronization attacks is of decent quality. The proposed method has good performance against low pass filtering, addition of white Gaussian noise, MP3 compression, cropping, re-sampling and time scale modification up to ± 5%.

Table 4. RCDR of Audio Samples under Audio Signal Processing

Attack	Audio Sample	ROCDR		
		Scheme [10]	Scheme [12]	Proposed Scheme
Cropping	Classical 1	91%	88%	91%
	Piano	92%	86%	94%
	Multiple Instruments	91%	88%	94%
	Pop 1	94%	91%	95%
	Vocal1	92%	91%	94%
	Tabla	88%	85%	89%
Re sampling	Classical 1	83%	80%	91.1%
	Piano	94%	88%	97.2%
	Multiple Instruments	75%	70%	93.1%
	Pop 1	73%	71%	89%
	Vocal1	91%	82%	97%
	Tabla	93%	91%	99%
AWGN	Classical 1	77%	72%	87%
	Piano	73%	55%	81%
	Multiple Instruments	88%	79%	86%
	Pop 1	69%	71%	79%
	Vocal1	71%	67%	86%
	Tabla	92%	87%	97%
Low pass filtering	Classical 1	64%	56%	79%
	Piano	85%	67%	88%
	Multiple Instruments	70%	66%	85%
	Pop 1	76%	71%	87%
	Vocal1	85%	70%	92%
	Tabla	84%	80%	88%
MP3 compressi on	Classical 1	70%	45%	71%
	Piano	56%	53%	77%
	Multiple Instruments	68%	56%	71%
	Pop 1	78%	69%	81%
	Vocal1	61%	56%	69%
	Tabla	79%	71%	89%
TSM -1%	Classical 1	81%	91%%	97%
	Piano	60%	56%	61%
	Multiple Instruments	66%	59%	62%
	Pop 1	70%	66%	72%
	Vocal1	61%	57%	64%
	Tabla	82%	81%	97%
TSM -2%	Classical 1	81%	83%	88%
	Piano	62%	51%	67%
	Multiple Instruments	39%	50%	59%
	Pop 1	47%	57%	64%
	Vocal1	28%	49%	57%
	Tabla	79%	78%	91%
TSM +1%	Classical 1	82%	91%%	93%
	Piano	42%	51%	57%
	Multiple Instruments	39%	50%	59%
	Pop 1	47%	57%	64%
	Vocal1	28%	49%	57%
	Tabla	81%	86%	97%
TSM +2%	Classical 1	79%	78%	91%
	Piano	42%	51%	57%
	Multiple Instruments	39%	50%	59%
	Pop 1	47%	57%	64%
	Vocal1	28%	49%	57%
	Tabla	41%	51%	51%

Table 5. Comparison of performance of the proposed adaptive method against signal processing attacks to non-adaptive method

Non-adaptive method (Uniform DOE)

Audio Sample	No. of ROE used for water-marking	Threshold value required	+5% TSM		-5% TSM		Low pass filtering		MP3 compression	
			BER	NC	BER	NC	BER	NC	BER	NC
Tabla	4096	0.65	49%	0.52	48%	0.52	14%	0.91	17%	0.89
Classical 1	4096	0.58	46%	0.53	47%	0.52	15%	0.90	21%	0.86
Classical 2	4096	0.53	42%	0.57	36%	0.63	21%	0.77	25%	0.73
Instruments	4096	0.49	24%	0.82	24%	0.83	11%	0.93	19%	0.88
Country 1	4096	0.51	27%	0.80	29%	0.78	12%	0.92	21%	0.86
Country 2	4096	0.57	31%	0.68	34%	0.66	19%	0.88	25%	0.79
Pop 1	4096	0.56	32%	0.68	34%	0.66	18%	0.88	27%	0.80
Pop 2	4096	0.58	31%	0.66	33%	0.68	20%	0.82	26%	0.81
Blues	4096	0.54	22%	0.89	31%	0.72	13%	0.9	22%	0.75
Folk1	4096	0.49	43%	0.57	36%	0.63	21%	0.78	24%	0.73
Folk2	4096	0.51	31%	0.65	34%	0.67	19%	0.88	28%	0.81
Piano	4096	0.56	26%	0.76	29%	0.69	18%	0.88	27%	0.80
Flute	4096	0.44	28%	0.71	31%	0.67	21%	0.80	26%	0.72
Guitar1	4096	0.53	31%	0.67	34%	0.67	20%	0.81	22%	0.80
Guitar2	4096	0.57	30%	0.66	34%	0.66	19%	0.80	22%	0.78
Vocal 1	4096	0.48	23%	0.82	24%	0.77	12%	0.93	20%	0.81
Vocal 2	4096	0.43	22%	0.79	28%	0.73	26%	0.73	22%	0.79
Sitar 1	4096	0.57	21%	0.80	26%	0.71	22%	0.81	19%	0.82
Sitar 2	4096	0.56	31%	0.67	34%	0.67	19%	0.81	22%	0.78
Violin 1	4096	0.42	36%	0.62	33%	0.67	24%	0.73	26%	0.73

Proposed adaptive method (DOE based on localized property)

Audio Sample	No. of ROE used	Threshold value	+5% TSM		-5% TSM		Low pass filtering		MP3 compression	
			BER	NC	BER	NC	BER	NC	BER	NC
Tabla	887	0.78	41%	0.61	40%	0.62	8%	0.97	11%	0.93
Classical 1	1022	0.69	41%	0.58	40%	0.59	6%	0.96	12%	0.92
Classical 2	1019	0.68	33%	0.66	22%	0.75	9%	0.96	15%	0.90
Instruments	918	0.72	16%	0.90	15%	0.90	8%	0.97	11%	0.93
Country 1	987	0.77	15%	0.90	16%	0.90	7%	0.96	10%	0.94
Country 2	991	0.71	20%	0.79	19%	0.79	14%	0.89	14%	0.81
Pop 1	894	0.76	13%	0.91	14%	0.91	11%	0.94	15%	0.90
Pop 2	892	0.79	12%	0.90	12%	0.93	15%	0.92	16%	0.91
Blues	966	0.76	11%	0.92	23%	0.81	9%	0.93	15%	0.86
Folk1	1012	0.69	23%	0.68	22%	0.74	9%	0.96	14%	0.91
Folk2	899	0.78	13%	0.90	17%	0.91	12%	0.91	17%	0.88
Piano	981	0.73	17%	0.84	21%	0.80	11%	0.88	16%	0.86
Flute	1028	0.68	18%	81%	20%	0.81	0.12	0.88	18%	0.83
Guitar1	881	0.77	13%	0.92	14%	0.95	11%	0.93	11%	0.91
Guitar2	902	0.74	17%	0.84	13%	0.93	14%	0.95	13%	0.88
Vocal 1	919	0.71	15%	0.87	15%	0.92	8%	0.93	11%	0.90
Vocal 2	1031	0.61	19%	0.81	22%	0.77	19%	0.81	15%	0.86
Sitar 1	921	0.77	16%	0.82	19%	0.79	12%	0.89	12%	0.89
Sitar 2	913	0.73	16%	0.83	13%	0.94	14%	0.96	13%	0.87
Violin 1	1011	0.61	22%	0.77	25%	0.74	17%	0.82	17%	0.84

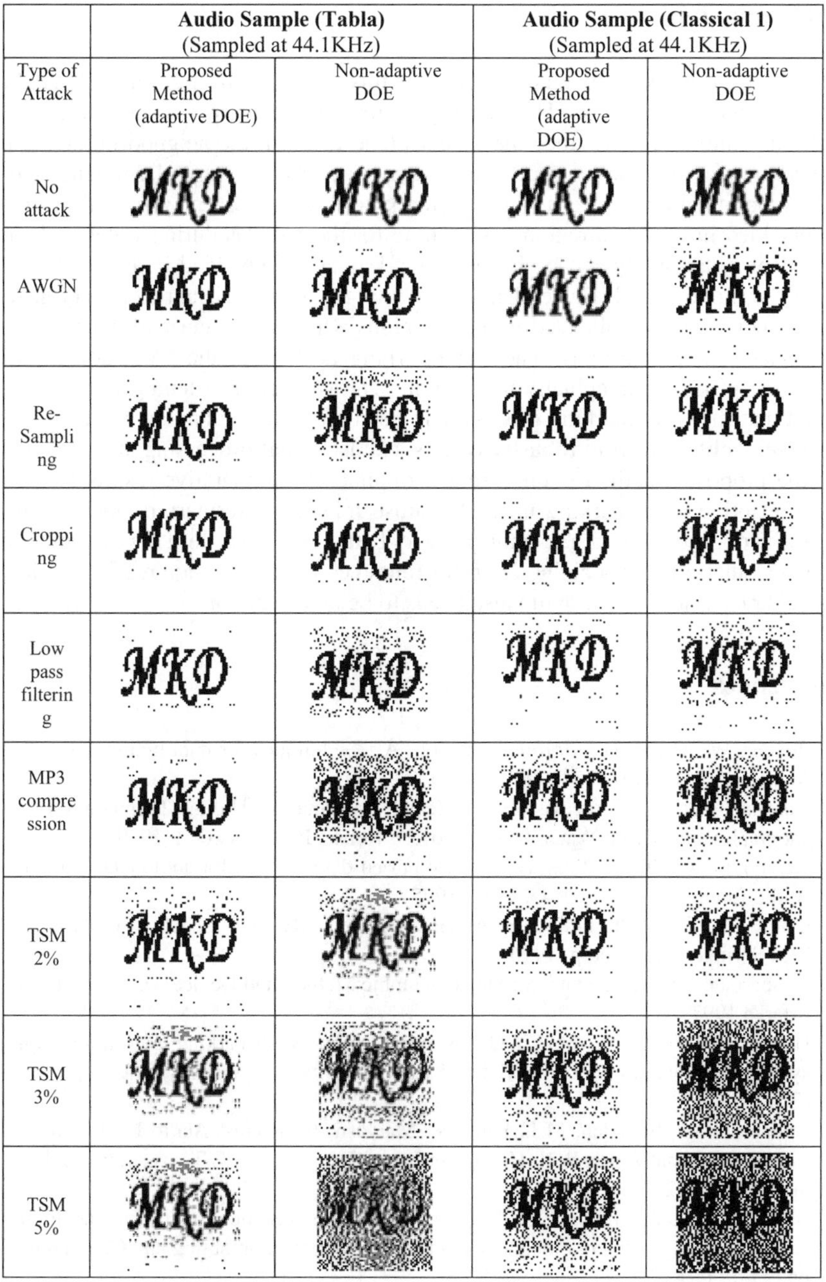

Type of Attack	Audio Sample (Tabla) (Sampled at 44.1KHz)		Audio Sample (Classical 1) (Sampled at 44.1KHz)	
	Proposed Method (adaptive DOE)	Non-adaptive DOE	Proposed Method (adaptive DOE)	Non-adaptive DOE
No attack	MKD	MKD	MKD	MKD
AWGN	MKD	MKD	MKD	MKD
Re-Sampling	MKD	MKD	MKD	MKD
Cropping	MKD	MKD	MKD	MKD
Low pass filtering	MKD	MKD	MKD	MKD
MP3 compression	MKD	MKD	MKD	MKD
TSM 2%	MKD	MKD	MKD	MKD
TSM 3%	MKD	MKD	MKD	MKD
TSM 5%	MKD	MKD	MKD	MKD

Fig. 6. Recovery of Binary Watermark under Signal Processing Attacks

9   Conclusion

An audio watermarking method presented in this paper is robust to seriously challenging synchronization attacks. High energy regions in the audio are selected for watermark embedding regions since these peaks tend to mask the neighboring audio data. A synchronization code is used for countering the positive false alarm generated due to data modification as a result of watermark embedding. Since synchronization code is embedded in localized regions, searching for these codes during watermark detection is computationally cheap. The watermark data is embedded in an adaptive manner in the audio signal. Since sharp transients are more resistant to synchronization attacks more data is embedded in these regions while less watermark data is embedded in less sharp transients. The watermarking is done in the SVD domain which makes the process perceptually transparent. The subjective listening tests have confirmed that the watermarking process is imperceptible to the human auditory system. The results obtained from robustness tests against signal processing attacks conclude that the proposed method is quite robust to attacks. Comparative results of the proposed adaptive watermarking method against uniform watermarking method reveals that the proposed method has comparatively better performance. However more optimized calculations for deciding *DOE* for reference points are required in which some other characteristics of the audio also needs to be taken care of.

References

1. Bender, W., Gruhl, D., Morimoto, N., Lu, A.: Techniques for data hiding. IBM Systems Journal 35(3-4), 313–336 (1996)
2. Katzenbeisser, S., Petitcolas, F.A.P. (eds.): Information Hiding Techniques for Steganography and Digital Watermarking. Artech House, Inc., Norwood (2000)
3. Gerzon, M.A., Graven, P.G.: A high-rate buried-data channel for audio CD. Journal of the Audio Engineering Society 43, 3–22 (1995)
4. Gruhl, D., et al.: Echo hiding. In: Anderson, R. (ed.) IH 1996. LNCS, vol. 1174, pp. 295–315. Springer, Heidelberg (1996)
5. Cooperman, M., Moskowitz, S.: Steganographic Method and Device, U.S. Patent 5613 004 (March 1997)
6. Huang, J., Wang, Y., Shi, Y.Q.: A blind audio watermarking algorithm with self-synchronization. In: Proc. IEEE Int. Symp. Circuits and Systems, vol. 3, pp. 627–630 (2002)
7. Akhaee, M.A., Saberian, M.J., Feizi, S., Marvasti, F.: Robust Audio Data Hiding Using Correlated Quantization With Histogram-Based Detector. IEEE Transactions on Multimedia, 834–842 (2009)
8. Bhat, V., Sengupta, I., Das, A.: Audio Watermarking Based on Mean Quantizationin Cepstrum Domain. In: International Conference on Advance Computing and Communications, pp. 73–77 (2008)
9. Arnold, M.: Audio watermarking: Features, applications, and algorithms. In: Proc. IEEE Int. Conf. Multimedia & Expo., vol. 2, pp. 1013–1016 (2000)
10. Wei, F.S., Feng, X., Mengyuan, L.: A Blind Audio Watermarking Scheme Using Peak Point Extraction. In: Proceedings of IEEE International Symposium on Circuits and Systems, vol. 5, pp. 4409–4412 (2005)

11. Li, W., Xue, X., Lu, P.: Localized Audio Watermarking Technique Robust Against Time-Scale Modification. IEEE Transactions on Multimedia 8, 60–69 (2006)
12. Dutta, M.K., Gupta, P., Pathak, V.K.: Biometric Based Audio Watermarking. In: Proceedings of International Conference on Multimedia Information Networking and Security, pp. 10–14 (2009)
13. Wu, S., Huang, J., Huang, D.: Efficiently Self-Synchronized Audio Watermarking for Assured Audio Data Transmission. IEEE Transactions on Broadcasting 51, 69–76 (2005)
14. Liu, Tan, T.: A SVD-Based Watermarking Scheme for Protecting Rightful Ownership. IEEE Transactions on Multimedia 4(1), 121–128 (2002)
15. Yavuz, E., Telatar, Z.: Improved SVD-DWT based digital image watermarking against watermark ambiguity. In: Proceedings of ACM Symposium on Applied Computing, pp. 1051–1055 (2007)
16. Voyatzis, G., Pitas, I.: Applications of toral automorphisms in image watermarking. In: Proceedings of International Conference on Image Procesing, vol. 1, pp. 273–240 (1996)
17. Duxbury, C., Davies, M.E., Sandier, M.B.: Separation of transient information in audio using multi-resolution analysis techniques. In: Proceedings of International Workshop on Digital Audio Effects, pp. 21–27 (December 2001)
18. Kennedy, M.P., Kolumban, G.: Digital communication using chaos. Elsevier Signal Processing 80, 1307–1320 (2000)
19. Liu, J.: The application of wavelet in image compression and digital watermarking. In: Doctoral dissertation, Zhejiang University, China (April 2001)
20. Chen, B., Wornell, G.W.: Quantization index modulation methods for digital watermarking and information embedding of multimedia. J. VLSI Signal Processing 27, 7–33 (2001)
21. Yamamoto, K., Iwakiri, M.: Real-Time Audio Watermarking Based on Characteristicsof PCM in Digital Instrument. Journal of Information Hiding and Multimedia Signal Processing 1(2), 59–71 (2010)
22. Nishimura, R., Abe, S.-i., Fujita, N., Suzuki, Y.: Reinforcement of VoIP Security with Multipath Routing and Secret Sharing Scheme. Journal of Information Hiding and Multimedia Signal Processing 1(3), 204–219 (2010)
23. Wang, X.-Y., Niu, P.-P., Yang, H.Y.: A Robust, Digital-Audio Watermarking Method" Multimedia. Multimedia 16(3), 60–69 (2009)
24. Kalantari, N.K., Akhaee, M.A., Ahadi, S.M., Amindavar, H.: Robust Multiplicative Patchwork Method for Audio Watermarking. IEEE Transactions on Audio, Speech, and Language Processing 17(6), 1133–1141 (2009)
25. Girin Parvaix, M., Brossier, L.: A Watermarking-Based Method for Informed Source Separation of Audio Signals With a Single Sensor. IEEE Transactions on Audio, Speech, and Language Processing 18(6), 1467–1475 (2010)

Trust-Based Security Level Evaluation Using Bayesian Belief Networks

Siv Hilde Houmb[1], Indrakshi Ray[2], Indrajit Ray[2], and Sudip Chakraborty[3]

[1] SecureNOK Ltd.
sivhoumb@securenok.com
[2] Colorado State University
{iray,indrajit}@cs.colostate.edu
[3] Valdosta State University
schakraborty@valdosta.edu

Abstract. Security is not merely about technical solutions and patching vulnerabilities. Security is about trade-offs and adhering to realistic security needs, employed to support core business processes. Also, modern systems are subject to
a highly competitive market, often demanding rapid development cycles, short
life-time, short time-to-market, and small budgets. Security evaluation standards,
such as ISO 14508 Common Criteria and ISO/IEC 27002, are not adequate for
evaluating the security of many modern systems for resource limitations, time-to-
market, and other constraints. Towards this end, we propose an alternative time
and cost effective approach for evaluating the security level of a security solution,
system or part thereof. Our approach relies on collecting information from different sources, who are trusted to varying degrees, and on using a trust measure
to aggregate available information when deriving security level. Our approach
is quantitative and implemented as a Bayesian Belief Network (BBN) topology,
allowing us to reason over uncertain information and seemingly aggregating disparate information. We illustrate our approach by deriving the security level of
two alternative Denial of Service (DoS) solutions. Our approach can also be used
in the context of security solution trade-off analysis.

Keywords: security evaluation, trust, bayesian belief networks, common criteria.

1 Introduction

Often times there is a need to build a security solution that has a rapid development
cycle, short time-to-market, and a short life-time. It is important to predict the security
of such a system before it can be deployed, due to a number of constraints put on the
system including cost, schedule and security. One approach for evaluating the security
level of security solutions is by using standards, such as ISO 14508 Common Criteria
for Information Technology Security Evaluation [1]).

However, predicting the security level using the Common Criteria has many drawbacks. First, the result of a Common Criteria evaluation is not given as a statement of
the security level of a system, but rather as the level of assurance that the evaluator has
in whether the set of security features present in the system in combination provide adequate security. This is hard for decision makers to relate to. Second, Common Criteria

M.L. Gavrilova et al. (Eds.): Trans. on Comput. Sci. X, LNCS 6340, pp. 154–186, 2010.

evaluations are time and resource demanding and may not always be worth in terms of effort and cost. In Norway, for example, where one of the authors work, a security evaluation according to Common Criteria for EAL 4/4+ has an estimated cost of 1.5 million NOK (about 250,000 USD). It also takes 2-3 working days to arrive at a trustworthy estimate about the security of even a small system. Third, the documentation and tests required by Common Criteria may not be suitable for a particular system or deployment environment.

The above mentioned difficulties in adopting a security evaluation standards like Common Criteria for predicting security level of a system, motivates us to develop an alternative approach. We propose an approach for evaluating the security level of a system using information collected from a number of different sources, including subjective judgments as those of evaluators and similar. A source can be an active agent or a domain expert. We need to consider the trustworthiness of the sources before aggregating the information provided by each of them. We propose a model of trust to formally capture the concept of trustworthiness of information sources. Trust, in our model, is a relationship between a truster and a trustee with respect to some given context. For instance, a truster A may trust a trustee B in the context of understanding network protocols but may not trust B in the context of understanding database security. Here, the entity trying to obtain information from the sources is the truster, the information source is the trustee, and the problem for which the information is requested is the trust context, also called security evaluation case. The trustworthiness of an information source depends on two factors, namely, its *knowledge level* and *expertise level*. Knowledge level captures the level of knowledge possessed by the information source with respect to the security evaluation case; the trust context. Expertise level captures the experience and qualifications of the information source.

We show how to evaluate these two factors and quantify the trustworthiness of sources and from that derive a security level prediction. The approach is implemented as a Bayesian Belief Network (BBN) topology, which allows us to reason over uncertain information and to aggregate disparate information in a step-wise and seamless manner. Our approach is semi-automatic in the sense that it does require some human intervention; however, it significantly eases the burden of deciding on appropriate security solutions in a structured and well-informed manner. We demonstrate our approach by showing how to evaluate five information sources and aggregate the information provided by these when evaluating the security level of two alternative Denial of Service (DoS) solutions. We chose this particular example because it relates closely to the type of security solutions that we are targeting with our approach.

The rest of the paper is organized as follows. Section 2 summarizes the related work to place our work into context. Section 3 discusses information sources of relevance for security evaluations. Section 4 presents the approach for deriving the security level of a given security solution, part of a system or a system. It shows how to evaluate the factors on which trust depends, provides a model for calculating trustworthiness, and describes how this can be used for aggregating the information obtained from various sources. Section 5 gives the details of the Bayesian Belief Network (BBN) implementation, and Section 6 illustrates our approach by showing an example of security level evaluation of two alternative DoS security solutions. In section 7 we discuss some of the issues related to using this approach for predicting security levels that the user needs to be aware of. Finally, Section 8 concludes the paper with pointers to future directions.

2   Related Work

The trust-based security level evaluation approach builds on techniques from three distinctive domains: security evaluation, expert judgment aggregation, and trust.

The literature on trust can be broadly classified into three distinct areas - (i) trust models, (ii) trust management and negotiation, and (iii) application of trust concepts. Here, trust models are of most relevance.

Jøsang [2,3] propose a model for trust based on a general model for expressing relatively uncertain beliefs about the truth of statements. Cohen et al. [4] describe an alternative, more differentiated concept of trust called Argument-based Probabilistic Trust model (APT). Yahalom et al. [5,6] outline a formal model for deriving new trust relationships from existing ones. Beth et al. [7] extend the ideas presented by Yahalom et al. to include relative trust. Xiong and Liu [8] present a coherent adaptive trust model for quantifying and comparing the trustworthiness of peers based on a transaction-based feedback system. Other works include logic-based formalisms of trust [9,10,11,12] that allow one to reason about trust relationships. While each of these models have their individual strengths and applicability, none of them discuss which parameters should be considered in evaluating the trustworthiness of users or systems.

Bacharach and Gambetta, on the other hand, [13] define trust as a particular belief, which arises in games with a certain payoff structure. The authors observe that in most games, the truster sees or observes a trustee before making any decision and, therefore, can use these observations as evidence for the trustee's having, or lacking, trustworthy-making qualities. Purser [14] presents a simple, graphical approach to model trust. In particular, the author emphasizes the relationship between trust and risk and argues that for every trust relationship, there exists a risk associated with a breach of the trust extended. Ray and Chakraborty [15] and Ray et al. [16] were among the first to describe the factors on which trust depends. They show how to quantify these factors, and from that how to obtain a quantitative value for trust. In addition, there is the work by Sun and Yang [17] on theoretical analysis and evaluation of trust models. Our approach borrow from these works. It builds on the trust decision making aspects discussed in Bacharach and Gambetta, the granulated trust evaluation model of Ray et al. [16] and the perspective of direct and indirect trust relationships discussed by Sun and Yang. In particular, our approach enables the granulated evaluation of the trustworthy-making qualities of a trustee based on observations, and also tangible aspects related to trustee knowledge and experience (such as education and number of years of professional experience and expertise domains). Different from most other work, our approach focuses on the evaluation of experts as information sources in the context of expert judgment aggregation.

In the domain of security evaluation there are mainly three categories of techniques - (i) operational and quantitative measurement of security, (ii) security management standards, and (iii) security evaluation and certification approaches, such as ISO 15408 the Common Criteria.

Littlewood et al. [18] was one of the earliest works on measuring operational security. The authors argue for the importance of extending the capabilities of current security evaluation approaches to include techniques for quantitative measure of the perceived level of security, as well as evaluating the operational security level. Subsequently, Ortalo et al. [19] proposed a quantitative model for evaluating Unix security vulnerabilities using a privilege graph. Madan et al. [20] discuss how to quantify security attributes of software systems using traditional reliability theory for modeling random processes, such as stochastic modeling and Markov analysis. Jonsson and Olovsson [21] look at the problem in a more practical way by analyzing attacker behavior through controlled experiments. Houmb et al. [22] and Houmb [23] build on these works emphasizing the importance of quantitative measures of security and the role of security trade-off analysis. The goal is to assist decision makers in choosing among alternative security solutions, based on security, cost, resources, time-to-market and other trade-off parameters, and to reduce time, cost and effort in security evaluations. The current work draws upon Houmb's earlier works [22,23].

Security management standards aid in the overall management of security in an organization. The most important standards in this area are the ISO/IEC 27002:2005 Information technology – Code of Practice for information security management [24], ISO/IEC TR 13335:2004 Information technology – Guidelines for management of IT Security [25], and AS/NZS ISO 31000:2009, Risk management - Principles and guidelines [26]. ISO/IEC 27002 provides recommendations for information security management and supports those that are responsible for initiating, implementing or maintaining security in their organization. ISO/IEC 13335 provides guidance on management aspects of IT security. This standard's main objectives are: to define and describe the concepts associated with the management of IT security, to identify the relationships between the management of IT security and management of IT in general, to present several models which can be used to explain IT security, and to provide general guidance on the management of IT security. AS/NZS ISO 31000:2009 is a widely recognized and used standard within the field of risk assessment and management. It is a general risk management standard that have been tailored for security critical systems in the CORAS framework. The standard includes a risk management process, a detailed activity description, a separate guideline companion standards, and general management advices.

Security evaluation standards includes TCSEC [27], ITSEC [28] and ISO 14508 Common Criteria [1]. TCSEC is the oldest known standard for evaluation and certification of information security in IT products. The standard was developed by the Department of Defense (DoD) in the US in the 1980ies. The standard evaluates systems according to six predefined classes: C1, C2, B1, B2, B3 and A1. These classes are hierarchically arranged, meaning that A1 is the strongest and C1 is the weakest. Each class contains both functional and assurance requirements. The functional requirements are divided into authentication, role based access control, obligatory access control, logging and reuse of objects. TCSEC is also known as the Orange Book and was tailored for military IT systems.

The International Organization for Standardization (ISO) harmonized TCSEC, ITSEC and other security evaluation/assurance standards and published the first version of ISO 14508, also know as the Common Criteria, in 1999. The idea behind the Common Criteria was to develop a world wide approach for evaluating security properties of IT products and systems. The standard incorporates experience from TCSEC, ITSEC and other related standards, and provides a common set of requirements for the security functions of IT products and systems. Among other things, the standard provides a common evaluation methodology such that results from independent evaluations can be compared and thereby aid decision makers in choosing between security solutions. Certification is done according to the seven predefined classes: EAL1, EAL2, EAL3, EAL4, EAL5, EAL6 and EAL7.

A common problem for most security evaluations, however, is the large amount of information involved. The result of such evaluations is also subject to bias as the evaluation is done by one or a few evaluators. Although evaluators must be certified to perform evaluations according to the Common Criteria, evaluations still include many tasks that only rely on subjective assessment (someone saying something about something as it cannot be directly observed). It is these problems that our trust-based security level evaluation approach is designed to aid. Rather than relying on single information sources, our approach combine multiple sources and aggregates information provided by these sources based on the trustworthiness of the source. However, this does not mean that the biases are completely removed. The level of bias has been reduced significantly. Also, these biases are not directly related to the information provided but to the ways in which we derive the knowledge and experience level of an information source.

Managing security is, in general, difficult and there is a lack of industry standard security metrics. The reason for this is that there is very little empirical data available for estimating the risks facing a system. Thus, one must often rely solely on the opinions of domain experts and risk analysts. This is particularly problematic for risk estimation (estimating the likelihood and impact of a potential threat). The trust-based information aggregation part of our approach (part 1 of the approach) can aid in the process of risk estimation by aggregating whatever information that is available. The same is the case for quantifying operational security level, where our approach evaluates the security level directly by the notion of trust rather than through stochastic modeling techniques. Stochastic modeling techniques, such as Markov models, are effective, but rather time consuming to create and suffer from the problem of state explosion. Our approach avoid this problem as it does not model the problem itself but rather the information available to assess the problem.

3   Information Sources for Security Level Evaluation

Evaluating the security of a system involves information, whether it is given as an expert judgment from a formally certified Common Criteria evaluator or from a log-file of some kind. Information always comes from a source and it is the trustworthiness of these sources that we evaluate in our approach, not the information itself. This is because an information source can be assessed in terms of observable properties, while this is rather difficult with information. These properties can also be used to calibrate various types of information and enables us to aggregate over all available information of relevance.

Definition 1. *An **information source** is an active or a passive entity which has obtained, either directly or indirectly, relevant information for evaluating the security level of a system.*

Active entities have the ability to observe events, interpret the observations, and generate additional information from these observations. A domain expert is considered an active entity. Software and agents operating using rule sets as well as all types of intelligent software are additional examples of active entities. Passive entities merely record or receive information but do not interpret or manipulate the information themselves. An example of a passive entity is a log file. Note that neither active nor passive entities can, by default, be completely trusted. For instance, domain experts can have their individual biases or can be influenced, software agents may contain Trojan horses, and configuration of a log file may be set up to disregard important information. We call active entities *indirectly observable sources* and passive entities *directly observable sources*.

Definition 2. *An **indirectly observable source** is an information source that has interpreted an observed phenomenon or event of relevance to the particular security evaluation case (including recommendations), and provides the information as its subjective opinion (judgment).*

Indirectly observable sources may be biased. When it comes to the use of indirectly observable information sources for evaluating the security level, two types are commonly used: subjective expert judgment and third-party interpreted information (recommendation). In subjective expert judgment, the experts have gained knowledge and experience of relevance to the security evaluation case that they use when providing information. Third party interpreted information refers to an expert interpreting events observed by another source, such as another expert or a directly observable source. This means that the expert interprets the information given by other sources before providing the information.

Definition 3. *A **directly observable source** is an information source that either has gathered empirical information or that has directly observed a phenomena or events relevant for the particular security evaluation case.*

Directly observable sources have not been biased by subjective influence. This means that the sources have gained knowledge and experience by observing actual events themselves. Commonly used directly observable information sources are real-time information sources, such as Intrusion Detection Systems (IDS), log-files from firewalls, Internet gateways (routers), honeypots, and scanners for virus, vulnerability, and spy-ware.

4 Model and Computational Engine for Evaluating Security Level

Our approach to security level evaluation comprises two main phases: (i) evaluate the trustworthiness of the information sources to determine their trust level scores, and (ii) derive the security level by combining the result of (i) with the information provided.

The first phase deals with assessing the trustworthiness of an information source. The trustworthiness of a source depends on two parameters: *knowledge level* and *expertise level* of an information source. *Knowledge level* of an information source is defined as a measure of awareness of the information source about the knowledge domains of relevance to the particular security evaluation case. It is represented in terms of a number called *knowledge score*. *Expertise level* of an information source is defined as a measure of degree of ability of the information source to assess the security level of a security solution. It is represented in terms of a number called *expertise score*. *Trustworthiness* of an information source is defined as a measure of the competence of the information source to act desirably and to provide information to the best of its abilities. It is represented in terms of a number called *trustworthiness score*. Trustworthiness score is then derived by combining the knowledge and expertise scores.

4.1 Evaluate Knowledge Score of an Information Source

The knowledge score of an information source gives a measure of how closely the knowledge of that information source is related to the desired knowledge for the security evaluation case (trust/problem context). The knowledge score is calculated from two scores – *reference knowledge domain score* and *information source knowledge domain score*. These two scores are derived using two models – *reference knowledge domain model* and *information source knowledge domain model*. The reference knowledge domain model provides the relative importance of different knowledge domains regarding the problem context. The information source knowledge domain model gives an assessment, by a third party, of the relative importance of knowledge level of an information source corresponding to the knowledge domains identified in the reference knowledge domain model.

Reference Knowledge Domain Model

Evaluating the security level of a security solution typically benefits from knowledge in several domains, not all of which are equally important. Knowledge level of an information source expresses his/her awareness about these knowledge domains. We develop a reference knowledge domain model that captures the domains that are of interest and their relative importance with respect to the security level evaluation case (problem context). The relative importance of a domain is measured in terms of *importance weight* which is defined to be the percentage of the whole reference knowledge domain covered by that particular knowledge domain. Figure 1 shows a reference knowledge domain model for a security solution consisting of four domains: domain A (network security) domain B (Internet Protocol), domain C (authentication) and domain D (access control). The four domains cover the security solution to various degrees. Thus the difference in the importance weights. Note that this is just an example reference knowledge domain model and does not refer to any specific security level evaluation case.

In the computation of reference knowledge domain weights, we first find out the knowledge domains that are of relevance to the particular security level evaluation case. A discussion on how the relevant knowledge domains are determined is beyond the scope of this paper. Once we determine the knowledge domains that are of interest, we

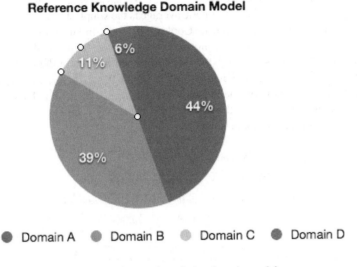

Fig. 1. Reference knowledge domain model

arrange the domains in some order and find their respective importance weight. Often, the process of determining the knowledge domains itself will provide clues about their relative importance. This order could also be arrived at following some specific guidelines of the evaluator. A vector, called *reference knowledge domain scores*, specifies the relative importance of all involved knowledge domains. Each element of the vector indicates the importance weight of the corresponding domain. This evaluation is shown next.

Calculating Reference Knowledge Domain Score

Each knowledge domain in the reference model has a particular importance weight associated with it. Note that multiple stakeholders are often involved in formalizing the problem context. Consequently, different stakeholders can assign different weights for importance. Suppose the stakeholders are denoted by the set X and the cardinality of the set is q. We use x to denote an individual stakeholder. Suppose m is the number of knowledge domains in the problem context. The importance of knowledge domains, from the point of view of a stakeholder x, is represented as an m-element vector. This vector is denoted by $W_{Kimp}(x)$ where $W_{Kimp}(x) = [w_{Kimp}(x(j))]_{j=1}^{m}$. This is shown by Equation 1. Here, $w_{Kimp}(x(j)) \in [0, 1] \; \forall j = 1, \ldots, m$ and $\sum_{j=1}^{m} w_{Kimp}(x(j)) = 1$. Note that, we obtain such vector for each of the q stakeholders in the set X. The importance of the m different domains given by q stakeholders is then represented in a $q \times m$ matrix denoted by $W_{allKimp}(X)$. Equation 2 gives the formula for $W_{allKimp}(X)$. The next step is to aggregate the information obtained from q stakeholders. The aggregation can be done using some aggregation technique. The idea is to apply an aggregation function, denoted by $f_{aggregation1}$, on the $q \times m$ matrix $W_{allKimp}(X)$ to merge the rows, resulting in a vector of size m. Equation 3 indicates the result of this aggregation. Here we do the aggregation by taking the arithmetic average for each m elements from all q number of vectors and put them into a single vector (for X), $W_{aggregatedKimp}(X)$, which is given by $[w_{aggregatedKimp}(X(j))]_{j=1}^{m}$. The arithmetic average is the simplest type of expert opinion aggregation. The reader is referred to Cooke [29] and similar sources for examples of other aggregation techniques. To normalize this vector, the normalization factor is obtained using Equation 4. Finally, the weight of each domain in the problem context is obtained by normalizing each element in the vector $W_{aggregatedKimp}(X)$ by the above normalization factor to obtain the vector $W_{refKnowledgeDomainScore}(X)$. This is shown in Equation 5. This vector derives the relative importance for each knowledge domain in the reference knowledge domain model.

$$W_{Kimp}(x) = [w_{Kimp}(x(j))]_{j=1}^{m} \tag{1}$$

$$W_{allKimp}(X) = [W_{Kimp}(x)]_{x=1}^{q} \tag{2}$$

$$W_{aggregatedKimp}(X) = f_{aggregation1}(W_{allKimp}(X))$$
$$= [w_{aggregatedKimp}(X(j))]_{j=1}^{m} \tag{3}$$

$$f_{refKnorm} = \frac{1}{\sum_{j=1}^{m} w_{aggregatedKimp}(X(j))} \tag{4}$$

$$W_{refKnowledgeDomainScore}(X) = f_{refKnorm} \times W_{aggregatedKimp}(X)$$
$$= [w_{refKnowledgeDomainScore}(X(j))]_{j=1}^{m} \tag{5}$$

Note, if simple average is used as an aggregation technique there is no need to normalize the vector $W_{aggregatedKimp}(X)$ as each element of the vector will be in $[0, 1]$ and sum of all elements will be 1. In that case, we can ignore Equation 4 and $W_{aggregatedKimp}(X) = W_{refKnowledgeDomainScore}(X)$.

Information Source Knowledge Domain Model

An information source may not have comprehension in all the knowledge domains represented in the reference domain model. The information source knowledge domain model is used to derive the relative importance of the knowledge level of the information source according to the knowledge domains in the reference knowledge domain model. This relative importance is assessed by a third party or an expert and not by the information source itself. This helps reduce the bias involved in self-assessment.

Consider the reference knowledge domain example shown in Figure 1. For an information source, say b, a third party assessor assesses the relative importance of knowledge level of b on the identified knowledge domains as (say) 30% on domain A, 30% on domain B, and 40% on domain D. Thus, the relative importance of b's knowledge level on the domains, as assessed by the third party, is $[0.3, 0.3, 0.0, 0.4]$.

Suppose we have n information sources, denoted by $b_1, b_2, \ldots, b_n$, in a security level evaluation. Assume Y is the set of third parties assessing the expertise of these n information sources. Let the cardinality of Y be z, and an individual third party in the set Y be denoted by y. Then, information source knowledge domain score is represented as an m-element vector where each element corresponds to some knowledge domain of the information source. Each element indicates the relative weight of that domain and has a weight between 0 and 1. Equations 6–10 show how to compute the information source knowledge domain score for a source b_i.

$$W_{Kis}(y(b_i)) = [w_{Kis}(y(b_i(j)))]_{j=1}^{m} \tag{6}$$

$$W_{allKis}(Y(b_i)) = [W_{Kis}(y(b_i))]_{y=1}^{z} \tag{7}$$

$$W_{aggregatedKis}(Y(b_i)) = f_{aggregation2}(W_{allKis}(Y(b_i)))$$
$$= [w_{aggregatedKis}(Y(b_i(j)))]_{j=1}^{m} \tag{8}$$

$$f_{isKnorm} = \frac{1}{\sum_{j=1}^{m} w_{aggregatedKis}(Y(b_i(j)))} \tag{9}$$

$$W_{isKnowledgeDomainScore}(Y(b_i)) = f_{isKnorm} \times W_{aggregatedKis}(Y(b_i))$$
$$= [w_{isKnowledgeDomainScore}(Y(b_i(j)))]_{j=1}^{m} \tag{10}$$

Each third party $y \in Y$ provides a vector, denoted by $W_{Kis}(y(b_i))$, of m-elements. Each element represents the assessed weight of knowledge level of the information source b_i corresponding to the domain represented by that element as shown in Equation 6. This step is repeated for each y in the set Y and results in z such vectors. To aggregate information from all y for the information source b_i, these z vectors are first combined in a $z \times m$ matrix in Equation 7 and then aggregated using some aggregation function in Equation 8. The aggregation function is denoted as $f_{aggregation2}$ in the equation. The aggregation technique used here is arithmetic average. We normalize this vector using the normalization factor obtained in Equation 9. Finally, the weight of each domain in the problem context is obtained by normalizing each element in the vector $W_{aggregatedKis}$ by the above normalization factor to obtain the vector $W_{isKnowledgeDomainScore}$. This is shown in Equation 10. The result gives one vector for the set Y holding the relative knowledge domain scores for the information source b_i. All these steps are then repeated n times (as we have n number of information sources).

Calculating Knowledge Score of Information Sources
The knowledge score of an information source b_i, denoted by $K_{score}(b_i)$, gives a measure of the source's knowledge level and is calculated using the reference knowledge domain score and the information source knowledge domain score of b_i. For an information source b_i, this score is calculated as follows.

$$K_{score}(b_i) = \sum_{j=1}^{m} \{w_{refKnowledgedomainScore}(X(j)) \times w_{isKnowledgeDomainScore}(Y(b_i(j)))\} \tag{11}$$

The result of the above equation is a real number derived by component-wise multiplication of the two vectors $W_{refKnowledgeDomainScore}(X)$ and $W_{isKnowledgeDomainScore}(Y(b_i))$ and then adding all the product values.

4.2 Evaluating Expertise Score of an Information Source

Expertise level of an information source with respect to evaluating the security level of a security solution is represented by the *expertise score*. We propose to evaluate the expertise score using questionnaires to reduce the bias of self-assessment. Each questionnaire consists of a set of *calibration variables* which are further divided into *categories*. Table 1 provides an example questionnaire.

Table 1. Example calibration variables for assessing expertise level of information sources

Variables	Categories
level of expertise	low, medium and high
age	under 20, [20-25), [25-30), [30-40), [40-50), over 50
years of relevant education	1 year, 2 years, Bsc, Msc, PhD, other
years of education others	1 year, 2 years, Bsc, Msc, PhD, other
years of experience from industry	[1-3) years, [3-5) years, [5-10) years, [10-15) years, over 15 years
years of experience from academia	[1-3) years, [3-5) years, [5-10) years, [10-15) years, over 15 years
role experience	database, network management, developer, designer, security management and decision maker

Each information source is assessed on each calibration variable according to the information source's category for that variable. However, not all calibration variables are of equal importance, neither all categories of a particular calibration variable have the same weight. The importance value for each calibration variable and the value associated with each category is determined by some external source, such as an expert[1]. To derive expertise score of an information source, we develop *calibration variable importance weight model* and *calibration variable category importance weight model*.

Calibration Variable Importance Weight Model
The relative importance of a calibration variable is assessed by external sources. Suppose the set of such external sources is denoted by X' and the cardinality of the set is u. Each calibration variable that is pertinent to the problem context is associated with an importance value. A member x' of the set X' assigns an importance value from the range $(0,1]$ to a calibration variable such that the sum of the importance value of all the calibration variables used is 1. Let there be p calibration variables denoted by $l_1, l_2, \ldots, l_p$ and $W_{l_1}, W_{l_2}, \ldots, W_{l_p}$ be their relative importance value assigned by the external source x'. This is represented by a vector $W_l(x') = [w_{l_j}(x')]_{j=1}^p$ and shown in Equation 12. All u members of X' will assign such values. For each calibration variable, the final importance value is derived by applying an aggregation function, $f_{aggregation3}$, on $W_l(X')$. This is shown in Equation 14. A possible choice for such an aggregation function is the arithmetic average. Since, $w_{l_j}(x') \in (0, 1]$ for all $j = 1, \ldots, p$ and for each $x' \in X'$, the aggregation function is so chosen that each element of $W_l(X')$ is in $(0, 1]$ and $\sum_{j=1}^p W_{l_j}(X') = 1$.

$$W_l(x') = [w_{l_j}(x')]_{j=1}^p \tag{12}$$

$$W_l(X') = [W_l(x')]_{x'=1}^u \tag{13}$$

$$W_{aggregatedCalwt}(X') = f_{aggregation3}(W_l(X')) \tag{14}$$

---

[1] Interested readers are referred to Cooke [29] and Goossens et al. [30] for an overview of challenges and benefits related to expert judgments.

Calibration Variable Category Importance Weight Model

Each category in a calibration variable is also associated with a value. This value denotes the importance weight of the category of that calibration variable. These values are assigned by the external sources in X'. Let the calibration variable l_j have s categories denoted by $l_{j_1}, l_{j_2}, \ldots, l_{j_s}$ where $l_{j_k} \in [0, 1]$ for all $k = 1, \ldots, s$. This is shown in Equation 15. All u members of X' assign weights and then an aggregation function is used to derive the category weights for calibration variable l_j (Equation 16 and Equation 17 respectively).

$$W_c(x'(l_j)) = [w_c(x'(l_j(i)))]_{i=1}^s \tag{15}$$

$$W_c(X'(l_j)) = [W_c(x'(l_j))]_{x'=1}^u \tag{16}$$

$$W_{aggregatedC}(X'(l_j)) = f_{aggregation4}(W_c(X'(l_j))) \tag{17}$$

Therefore, $W_{aggregatedC}(X'(l_j))$ holds the importance weight (as derived by all external sources in X') of each category of the calibration variable l_j. The above is done for all the calibration variables ($j = 1, \ldots, p$). Note that not every p calibration variables will have s categories.

Information Source Calibration Variable Category Score Model

An information source (b_i) receives scores for applicable categories within each calibration variable by a set Y' of external sources where cardinality of y' is v. This score is computed as follows. Each information source b_i is required to fill the questionnaire. Each member of Y' assesses the completed questionnaire and assigns relative scores to applicable categories within each calibration variable. This score value lies within $[0, 1]$. Equation 18 shows such scores, assigned by an $y' \in Y'$, for the calibration variable l_j. All v members of Y' assigns such scores and then an aggregation is used to reduce it to single set of values. Equations 19 and 20 show this. Hence, information source calibration variable category score model is designed as

$$W_{isCat}(y'(b_i(l_j))) = [w_{isCat}(y'(b_i(l_j(m))))]_{m=1}^s \tag{18}$$

$$W_{isCatAll}(Y'(b_i(l_j))) = [W_{isCat}(y'(b_i(l_j)))]_{y'=1}^v \tag{19}$$

$$W_{isCatAggregated}(Y'(b_i(l_j))) = f_{aggregation5}(W_{isCatAll}(Y'(b_i(l_j)))) \tag{20}$$

The above is normally done for all calibration variables, but one may choose to limit the number of calibration variables depending on the resources and time available for the security level evaluation case. Note that for some calibration variables the members of Y' may not need to assign any score. For example, for the calibration variable *level of expertise*, the importance weight of the applicable category (according to filled questionnaire) can work as the score. Hence, members of Y' can assign simply 1.0 to the category.

Calculating Expertise Score of Information Sources

The set X' of external experts assign importance weights of each category within each calibration variable. Also the information source b_i receives scores for applicable categories within each calibration variable by another set of experts Y'. These two are combined to derive the information source's score for each calibration variable. Equation 21 gives the value obtained by b_i for calibration variable l_j. The weighted sum of all these calibration variable scores, where the weight is the importance weight of the corresponding calibration variable, gives the expertise score of b_i, denoted by $E_{score}(b_i)$ as demonstrated by Equation 22.

$$W_{calScore}(b_i(l_j)) = \sum_{m=1}^{s} W_{aggregatedC}(X'(l_j(m))) \times W_{isCatAggregated}(Y'(b_i(l_j(m)))) \quad (21)$$

$$E_{score}(b_i) = \sum_{j=1}^{p} W_{aggregatedCalwt}(X'(j)) \times W_{calScore}(b_i(l_j)) \quad (22)$$

4.3   Computing Information Source Trustworthiness

The information sources involved in the security level prediction have varying degrees of trustworthiness, which depends on their knowledge levels and expertise levels. Therefore, the knowledge score and the expertise score must be combined to derive the trustworthiness of an information source. Here again, the problem context will determine the relative importance of each score. Let k and e be the relative importance of the knowledge and expertise score. The following relations hold: $0 \le k, e \le 1$ and $k + e = 1$. The values of k and e can be set by the evaluator (or, truster). The trustworthiness score for information source b_i, denoted by $T_{score}(b_i)$ is computed as follows.

$$T_{score}(b_i) = k \times K_{score}(b_i) + e \times E_{score}(b_i) \quad (23)$$

4.4   Computing Security Level of a Security Solution

The trustworthiness score of an information source is used to compare the security level of different security solutions. The information obtained from each source b_i (in the form of a number $\in [0, 1]$), denoted by $b_i(I)$, is multiplied by the trustworthiness score of that source. This is done for all sources. The results are then added and divided by n. This gives the initial security level for the security solution s_j as shown by Equation 24. This is done for all s_j in the set of security solutions S. Since the r security solutions are compared against each other, we must obtain a relative security level for each solution. The relative security level of s_j is computed using Equation 25.

$$F_{initialSL}(s_j) = \frac{\sum_{i=1}^{n} \{b_i(I) \times T_{score}(b_i)\}}{n} \quad (24)$$

$$F_{SL}(s_j) = \frac{F_{initialSL}(s_j)}{\sum_{j=1}^{r} F_{initialSL}(s_j)} \quad (25)$$

5   Trust-Based Security Level Evaluation BBN Topology

The trust-based security level evaluation is implemented as a Bayesian Belief Network (BBN) topology to enable a flexible and effective platform for reasoning under uncertainty. In the following we give some background of BBN and a short description of the BBN topology. The next section demonstrates the use of the various parts of the BBN topology in a step-by-step manner for evaluating the security level of two DoS solutions.

5.1 Bayesian Belief Network Overview

Bayesian Network (BN) or Bayesian Belief Network (BBN) is based on Bayes rule and designed for reasoning under uncertainty. Bayes rule calculates conditional probabilities of events and BBN can handle large scale conditional event expressions due to its formalism. The BBN formalism [31,32,33,34] offers, in addition to the mathematical formalism and computational engine, an intuitive and compact graphical model representation. The graphical model is formed as a connected and directed acyclic graph (DAG) that consists of a set of nodes or variables and directed arcs (or, links). Nodes correspond to events or concepts, and are defined as stochastic or decision variables. Possible outcomes of the nodes are specified using a set of states, and multiple variables may be used to determine the state of a node. Each state of each node is expressed using probability density functions (pdf). Probability density expresses ones confidence in the various outcomes of the set of variables connected to a node, and depends conditionally on the status of the parent nodes at the incoming edges. There are three type of nodes in BBN: 1) target node, which represents the target of the assessment (here, security level evaluation case), 2) intermediate node, which is a node that one have limited information or beliefs on (the intermediate level). The associated variables are hidden variables that represent aspects that may increase or decrease the belief in the target node, and 3) observable node, which represents information and evidence that can be directly observed or in other ways obtained. These three type of nodes are then connected in a topology and the status of the network is continuously updated as evidence are entered and propagated backward and forward along the edges in the network.

5.2 Structure of the BBN Topology

The trust-based security level evaluation approach involves a variety of information and information sources. These pieces of information are used as input to the different models described in Section 4. Figure 2 gives a schematic overview of the BBN topology structure, which is constructed such that it resembles the underlying process. The BBN topology has been implemented using the HUGIN software tool [35].

As shown in Figure 2, information and evidence are structured according to four levels. The first level contains the five models used to derive the *knowledge level* and *expertise level* of the information sources (*B*). This includes: 1) reference knowledge domain model, 2) information source knowledge domain model, 3) calibration variable importance weight model, 4) calibration variable category importance weight model, and 5) information source calibration variable category score model. Here, the first two are involved in *knowledge score model* and thus internally dependent. The other three belongs to the *expertise score model*, and are also internally dependent. There is, however, independence between these two score models. In level two, these models are combined into the *information source knowledge score model* and *information source expertise score model*. These two scores are further combined in the third level by the *information source trustworthiness score model*. Then, to determine the security level, the resulting trustworthiness scores are combined with the set of information provided for all information source. This results in an security level prediction in level four.

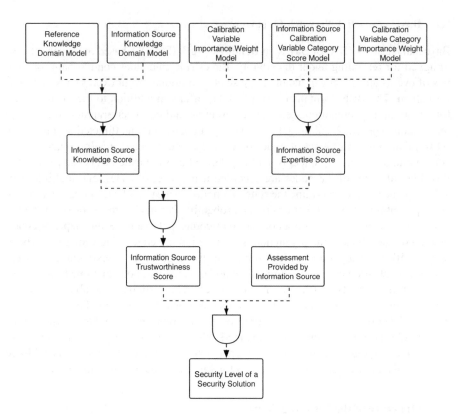

Fig. 2. Schematic overview of the trust-based security level evaluation BBN topology

Figure 3 shows the top-level network in the BBN topology. The notation consists of ovals, dotted ovals, diamonds and squares. The ovals represent observable nodes, which are nodes where evidence is directly inserted. The dotted ovals represent intermediate nodes, meaning nodes that have a underlying subnet and that gets information as input from one or more observable nodes in its underlying subnet. The diamonds are utility functions which combine evidence from observable and intermediate nodes and it is these nodes that implement the equation sets described in Section 4. All other nodes in the topology represent the discrete variables providing input to the utility functions. Utility functions specify the relations between their input nodes and differ from ordinary nodes in that the probability density functions can be expressions, or equation sets that specify how information are aggregated. The squares in the figure represent decision nodes, which define the different outcomes from an utility function and are used to make intermediate or target decisions. As can be seen, we have two subnets in our BBN topology: 1) knowledge level, and 2) expertise level. In the following we describe these subnets using an example. However, first we take a look at how the BBN topology was constructed and how it can be evolved as new information and insight is made available.

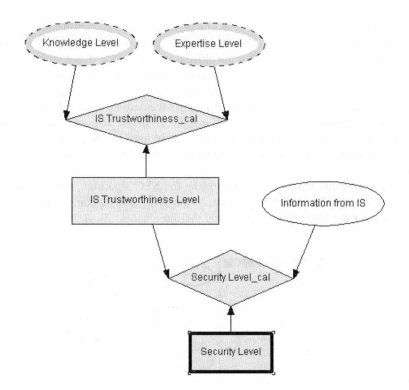

Fig. 3. Top-level network in the trust-based security level evaluation BBN topology

The BBN topology was constructed from available empirical data and the underlying process and structure are shown in Figure 2. It is important to note, however, that the structure of the topology is a critical factor of the BBN method, which consists of the following three steps: (1) construction of the BBN topology, (2) elicitation of probabilities to nodes and edges, and (3) making computations. We have used both a top-down and a bottom-up approach when deriving the BBN topology. The top-down approach is performed by manually modeling the associated nodes and their internal relations according to the information flows of Figure 2 and the models from Section 4. This resulted in a preliminary sets of DAGs together making up the BBN topology. The bottom-up approach was then performed by structural learning from available empirical data. This means that the bottom-up approach also represents an evaluation of the models in Section 4 and the resulting BBN topology from the top-down approach, as the bottom-up approach only uses the empirical data and is carried out independently of the models.

The HUGIN software tool was selected as the implementation tool because of its structural learning capabilities. Two algorithms are available for structural learning in the HUGIN software tool and these are the PC (Path Condition) algorithm and the NPC (Necessary Path Condition) algorithm. The Hugin PC algorithm is a variant of the original PC algorithm (for more information the reader is referred to [36]) and belongs to the class of constraint-based learning algorithms. The NPC algorithm is an extension of the PC algorithm that solves some of the problems of the constraint-based learning in the PC algorithm. However, both algorithms generate the skeleton of the DAG or topology by the use of statistical tests for conditional independence. Their main difference lies in that for the NPC algorithm one needs to provide additional information to indicate the direction of dependencies in the graph, which result in a more complete DAG when little empirical data is available. To simplify the demonstration of our bottom-up approach, we show the result of structural learning from one data set from the example in Section 6 using both the PC and the NPC algorithms with an informally reasoning about the relationship between the variables of the resulting DAGs. This is shown in the figure 4(a).

Figure 4(a) shows the resulting DAG using the NPC algorithm, while Figure 4(b) shows the same using the PC algorithm. When using the NPC algorithm we get a suggestion for the internal relation among the three nodes: $E_{score}(b_i)$, $K_{score}(b_i)$ and

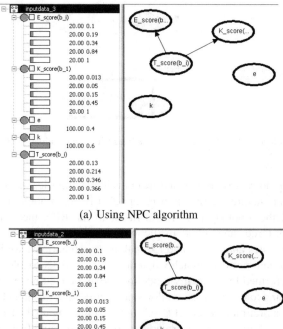

(a) Using NPC algorithm

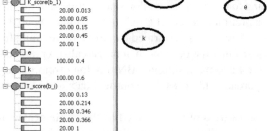

(b) Using PC algorithm

Fig. 4. DAG using structural learning algorithms in HUGIN

$T_{score}(b_i)$. For demonstrational purposes, we have used the data from the input file shown in Figure 5. This is part of the data set used for the demonstration given in Section 6, and covers the nodes 'Knowledge level', 'Expertise level', 'IS trustworthiness_cal' and 'IS trustworthiness Level' in figure 3.

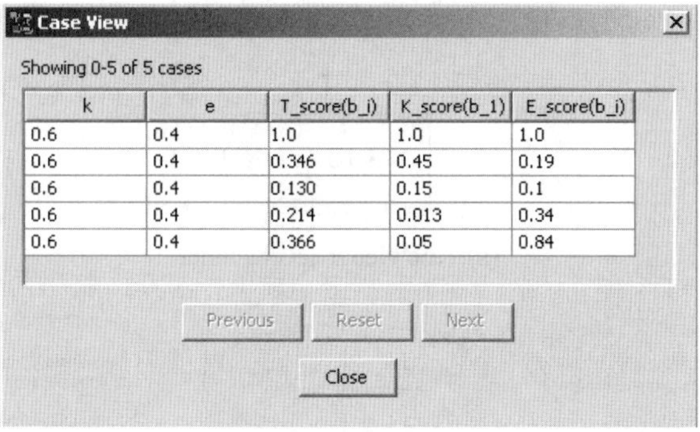

k	e	T_score(b_i)	K_score(b_1)	E_score(b_i)
0.6	0.4	1.0	1.0	1.0
0.6	0.4	0.346	0.45	0.19
0.6	0.4	0.130	0.15	0.1
0.6	0.4	0.214	0.013	0.34
0.6	0.4	0.366	0.05	0.84

Fig. 5. Data in input file

The resulting DAG using the NPC algorithm shows that there are relationships between the three nodes: $E_{score}(b_i)$, $K_{score}(b_i)$ and $T_{score}(b_i)$. However, as we use a limited data set in this example, it is not clear what the nature of this relationship is. The algorithm tells us that there is a direct relationship between the nodes $T_{score}(b_i)$ and $K_{score}(b_i)$, and that there is a direct relationship either between the nodes $T_{score}(b_i)$ and $E_{score}(b_i)$, or between the nodes $K_{score}(b_i)$ and $E_{score}(b_i)$. As described earlier, we assume independence between the knowledge and experience subnets and thus we choose to keep the direct relationship between the $T_{score}(b_i)$ and $E_{score}(b_i)$ nodes. When it comes to the direction of the relationships, it is used to specify parent-child relations between the nodes in the DAG. Informally reasoning over the result and the assumed independence leads to the conclusion that $T_{score}(b_i)$ is the parent node. This is also the result from structural learning from both the PC and the NPC algorithms. The same strategy was followed for the rest of the data sets from the example. Note that there are no utility or decision nodes in the resulting DAG from structural learning but that the resulting DAGs in the BBN topology presented in the following is built around utility and decision nodes. This is because the input data does not indicate any such constructs and so the utility and decision node constructs are introduced during the top-down approach.

Figures 6(a) and 6(b) show the resulting networks for the knowledge and expertise level subnets taking both the top-down and bottom-up approaches into consideration.

Subnets are connected based on the dependency they have on each other. Since we model calculations with some numbers and not with any state of any variable, we make some modification to the interpretation of the BBN nodes. Each observable node (represented with oval) represents an input variable from the models in Section 4 and are assigned values accordingly. The intermediate nodes are modeled as utility nodes, represented with diamonds in the figures, and are the formula evaluators. This means that

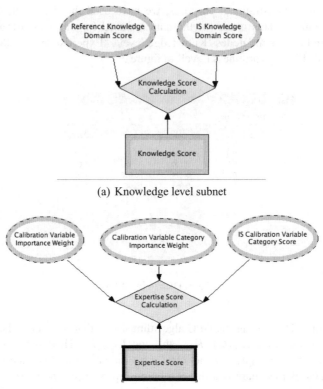

(a) Knowledge level subnet

(b) Expertise level subnet

Fig. 6. Knowledge level and expertise level subnets

each utility node uses the relevant equation from the models in Section 4 to express the relationship between its input nodes. Each target node, represented as a square in the figures, represents a variable whose value is to be computed by the intermediate node. This means the output variables of the respective models in Section 4.

6 Example: Evaluating the Security Level of Two DoS Solutions

We now describe how to use our approach to evaluate the security level of two solutions for protecting against Denial of Service (DoS) attacks that can be launched at the user authentication mechanism of ACTIVE, an e-Commerce platform that was developed by the EU EP-27046-ACTIVE project [37]. Here, we evaluate two such mechanisms – a cookie solution and a filtering mechanism. The cookie solution adds a patch to the network stack software that keeps track of sessions and their states. It begins by sending a cookie to the client. If the client does not respond within a short period of time, the cookie expires and the client must re-start the request for a connection. If the client responds in time, the SYN-ACK message is sent and the connection is set up.

Adding the cookie message makes it unlikely that an attacker can respond in time to continue setting up the connection. If the client address has been spoofed, the client will not respond in any event. The filtering mechanism works a bit differently. The filtering mechanism has an outbound and an inbound part, shown in Figures 7(a) and 7(b) respectively, that checks the source address (srcAddr) against a set of accepted source IP addresses stored in internalNetAddr. The filtering mechanism is implemented on the server side (usually on a firewall or an Internet router) and configured to block unauthorized connection attempts.

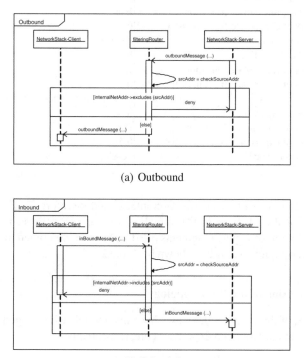

(a) Outbound

(b) Inbound

Fig. 7. Filter mechanism

A decision maker (truster) A needs help to choose between the two security solutions. For this purpose A seeks guidance from a number of information sources regarding anticipated number of DoS attacks for the two solutions. In our example, we have five information sources; one honeypot [38] and four domain experts from a pool of 18 domain experts. The four domain expert judgments included was drawn randomly from the expert pool and denoted as b_4, b_6, b_{15}, b_{18}, and the honeypot is denoted by $b_{honeypot}$. (Note that to simplify the demonstration we choose not to include all 18 domain experts that we had consulted). These five information sources provide information on the anticipated number of DoS attacks for the two involved solutions to A. The truster A has complete trust in the abilities of 'honeypot' to provide accurate and correct information

Table 2. The combined knowledge and expertise level questionnaire and the information provided on the four domain experts

Expert no.	Calibration variable	Information provided
4	level of expertise	medium
	years of relevant of education	Bsc
	years of experience from industry	0
	role experience	database, security management
6	level of expertise	low
	years of relevant of education	Bsc
	years of experience from industry	0
	role experience	database
15	level of expertise	high
	years of relevant of education	Bsc
	years of experience from industry	0
	role experience	designer, developer, security management
18	level of expertise	low
	years of relevant of education	Bsc
	years of experience from industry	0.5
	role experience	developer

on the potential number of successful DoS attacks and therefore $T_{score}(b_{honeypot}) = 1$. Thus, no additional evaluation of the knowledge and expertise level is necessary for honeypot. Elicitation of expert judgments are done using a combined knowledge level and expertise level questionnaire as shown by Table 2.

6.1   Demonstration of the BBN Topology

In the first level of the BBN topology, we have five models which together are used to derive the knowledge score and expertise score, respectively.

Implementation of reference knowledge domain model
The reference knowledge domain score is on level 1 in the information flow process shown in Figure 2. Recall that the BBN topology must reflect this structure to ensure accurate information aggregation and propagation. Because all models on level 1 are independent, they can be computed in any order, and hence all score models on level 1 are implemented as series of subnets on the lowest level in the topology.

Figures 8(a) and 8(b) show the implementation of equations 4 and 5 respectively. Note, in the example, we only use one external source x_1 in X. Importance weights for the knowledge domains in the reference knowledge domain model, as given by x_1, are denoted by the observable variables $wKimp(1), wKimp(2), \ldots$, respectively for knowledge domain 1, 2 etc. Since we only have one stakeholder (external source) x_1 in X, $W_{aggregatedKimp}(X) = W_{allKimp}(X) = W_{Kimp}(x_1)$. As the knowledge domains are already normalized with each other, we have: $W_{refKnowledgeDomainScore}(X) = W_{aggregatedKimp}(X) = W_{Kimp}(x_1)$ ($f_{refKnorm} = 1$ as can be seen from Figure 9).

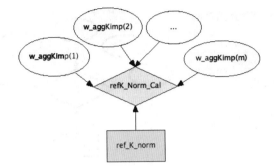

(a) Subnet evaluating normalization factor

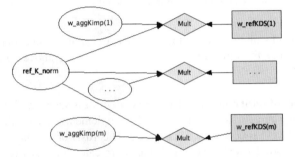

(b) Subnet evaluating reference knowledge domain scores

Fig. 8. Subnets in reference knowledge domain model

Implementation of information source knowledge domain model

Similar subnets as above are constructed for the information source knowledge domain model as defined by the equations 6 through 10. Figure 10 gives an overview of the resulting information source knowledge domain models and scores for the four domain experts.

Implementation of knowledge score model

The knowledge score is derived by combining the result from the reference knowledge domain score subnet and the information source knowledge domain score subnet. This is done by a component-wise multiplication of the reference knowledge domain score by information source knowledge domain score using equation 11 from Section 4.1, and populated for each information source b_i. Figure 11(a) shows the subnet that implements the above mentioned equation. Evaluation of knowledge score of the information source b_4 using the data in our example is shown in Figure 11(b). Note that the $Kscore(b4)\_1$ refers to knowledge domain number 1 (security management), etc.

Implementation of information source expertise level model

The 'expertise score' of an information source b_i is evaluated in a similar manner as 'knowledge score' of b_i. Values obtained by an information source b_i for each calibration variable l_j is implemented using a separate subnet. Then another subnet is used to

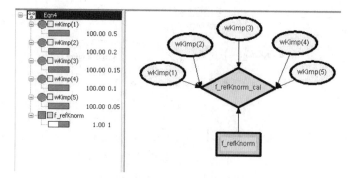

Fig. 9. Subnet calculating normalization factor with information inserted for the example

aggregate the results obtained from these subnets to evaluate the expertise score of b_i (equation 22). Since the illustrations are very similar to the above figures, we do not show them here.

Implementation of information source trustworthiness score model

The information source trustworthiness level is implemented as a utility and decision node in the top-level network shown in Figure 3. The trustworthiness score is dependent on knowledge score and expertise score which are calculated by two sets of subnets as described above. These subnets return the two scores through output nodes which, in turn, work as input nodes of the subnet implementing trustworthiness score. These two inputs, together with weight values k and e, derive the trustworthiness score. The corresponding subnet topology is shown in Figure 12(a), while Figure 12(b) shows the resulting trustworthiness score of information source b_4 (using equation 23) using the data from our example.

Deriving the security level

Recall from the example description that each of the five information sources provides information on the number of DoS attacks for the two DoS solutions, $s_1 = cookiesolution$ and $s_2 = filtermechanism$. Figure 12(b) shows the resulting trustworthiness score with information inserted and propagated for information source b_4 (expert number 4 in the example). We can then derive and interpret the information from b_4 using the utility function 'Security_Level_cal' and the decision node 'Security Level' in the top level BBN (Figure 3). The same is done for all information sources, which eventually results in the "final" security level prediction.

In our presentation of the implementation we have shown an example-driven version of the topology, as well as presented only parts of the implementation. This simplified version is not ready for population of large amount of evidence and for use of several external sources X and Y, as well as dynamic and unknown amount of knowledge domains, calibration variables, and calibration variable categories. The complete version of the BBN topology is an aggregation of the top-down and bottom-up approaches, as described earlier. This means that the BBN topology can even be changed dynamically by structural learning when new empirical data are made available or when new insights

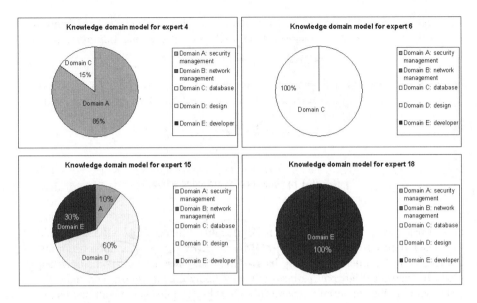

Fig. 10. Information source knowledge domain scores for b_4, b_6, b_{15}, and b_{18}

into the relationships between the involved variables are gained. This may, quite possibly, change the very foundation of our model over time. Thus, the learning capability is essential in that it makes our approach adaptable and dynamic. Evaluating security is challenging, and new insight will become available as more experience is gained. The benefit of our approach is that such eventuality can be countered for directly in the BBN implementation by feeding insights into the topology as empirical data, and using the structural learning capabilities to re-structure the topology whenever necessary.

6.2 Validation of Example Application Results

DoS attacks are becoming more sophisticated and hence increasingly difficult to detect and protect against. The attacks are often performed using legitimate protocols and services; the malicious activities differ from legitimate ones only by intent and not by content. Since it is hard to measure intent, many of the existing DoS solutions do not offer a proper defense. Many solutions are deployed on the network device level, such as the filtering mechanism described in this paper. However, filtering on the network device level has been demonstrated as being infeasible to deploy in an effective manner [39]. In fact, filtering against a defined legitimate or expect type of traffic may even contribute in completing the attacker's task by causing legitimate services to be denied [39].

In [40] Karig and Lee gives an overview of common DoS attacks and potential countermeasures for DoS attacks. In this context, the filtering mechanism is categorized as a network device level countermeasure while the cookie solution is categorized as an OS level countermeasure. A network device level DoS solution provides measures to protect against potential misuse of a communication protocol. Thus, the protection is often

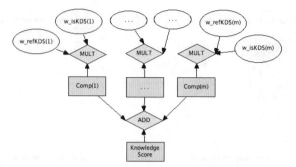

(a) Evaluation of knowledge score

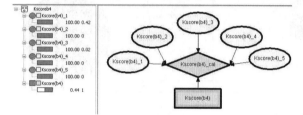

(b) Knowledge score of information source b_4

Fig. 11. Subnets involved in calculating K_{score}

on the IP or transport layer and hence there are possible ways around the mechanism, such as those discussed in [40]. The main shortage of filtering mechanisms are their inability to filter out spoofed packets [40]. There are, however, more efficient filtering mechanisms available, such as the one discussed in [41].

The other DoS solution discussed in this paper, the cookie solution, operates on the OS level. An OS level DoS solution integrates protection into the way a protocol is implemented in a particular operating system. Thus, the measure is deployed on the source (target) and refers to a host-based protection solution. Hence, the cookie solution represents a more defense-in-depth DoS solution than the filtering mechanism. Furthermore, the cookie solution discussed in this paper is a SYN cookie, which has been well tested and is well understood. SYN cookies have also been incorporated as a standard part of Linux and Free BSD and are recognized as one of the most effective DoS mechanisms [42].

In general, a DoS solution should be effective, transparent to existing Internet infrastructure, have low performance overhead, be invulnerable to attack aimed at the defense system, be incrementally deployable and have no impact on the legitimate traffic [39]. The filtering mechanism is somewhat effective in stopping attacks on the spot. It is not transparent to existing Internet infrastructure and results in some performance overhead. The filter mechanism can also be vulnerable to attacks due to its scanning of each packet and hence may have impact on legitimate traffic. However, the mechanism can be incrementally deployed. The cookie solution is documented to be effective against DoS attacks, but has been demonstrated to be somewhat unable to detect and prevent against zombie attacks. The mechanism is transparent to the network infrastructure, but

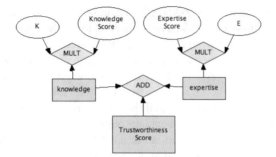

(a) Subnet evaluating trustworthiness score

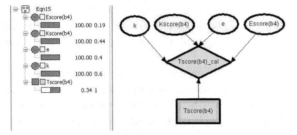

(b) Subnet for computing the trustworthiness score of information source b_4

Fig. 12. Subnets involved in calculating T_{score})

leads to some performance overhead, but in practice no impact on legitimate traffic. The cookie solution is already included in some operating systems and is easy to deploy. Thus, we can conclude that the cookie solution is a better choice than filtering mechanism for DoS attacks. Our trust-based information aggregation approach shows that the cookie solution is approximately 2.76 times better than the filtering mechanism.

7 Discussion

Evaluating the security level or security of a system can be done in many ways. Examples include qualitative risk assessment and security evaluation techniques using standards such as the Common Criteria, and ad-hoc security assessments or judgments. For the most part, these assessments are subjective since these are essentially opinions of experts. Risk assessment of a typical size system of medium complexity is, in general, estimated to involve approximately 200 hours of work. This number is not derived from scientific experiments; rather it is the opinion of one of the authors who has more than 15 years of experience providing risk assessment and security evaluation consultancy services to the industry. It is also based on anecdotal evidence and experience of colleagues of the authors. It is hard to get an exact cost and effort calculation for such activities, so one may question its soundness, as it is merely a best effort estimate based on experience from the industry. In Norway, for example, where one of the authors work, an evaluation according to the Common Criteria for EAL 4/4+ has an estimated cost of 1.5

million NOK (approximately 250,000 USD). Traditional security evaluation is also time consuming. For small systems, 2-3 days are needed to derive a good estimate/opinion. This limits the ability to carry out risk assessments and rules out the use of any formal security evaluation. This has been the primary motivation for our approach.

Two of the main challenges in the security evaluation process that contribute significantly to its cost and efficiency are (i) how to gather relevant information within a short time frame and make best use of it, and (ii) how to aggregate in a sound manner across both empirical data and expert judgments. In our opinion, the second challenge is the most critical and time consuming and hence has been the focus of this work. Instead of manually performing this aggregation, we have proposed an approach that is automated for the most part. Hence, it is more cost effective and efficient than traditional approaches. In addition, since it is the sources and not the information that are evaluated, such evaluations can be reused. This (reusability) makes our approach effective and enables it to scale as the complexity of the problem context and the number of information sources grows.

A related challenge is how to ensure that the information collected in true. This is a major challenge in risk assessment and security evaluations, as subjective evaluations are involved. It is hard to assess whether humans provide accurate information and it is hard to assess other sources as well, owing to false positives and the inability to calibrate the information provided. There is nothing firm (observed facts) to calibrate against. However, in our approach we calibrate information sources according to knowledge of relevance to the particular security level evaluation case and the expertise of information sources. We implement our model as a BBN topology, enabling the reasoning with uncertain information. BBN is based on the Bayesian or subjective interpretation of probability, where there does not exist a true value but only beliefs. The goal then is to assess whether the beliefs are reasonable and accurate. We do this by introducing the evaluation of the source providing the information and not the information itself. We use external sources or most often experts to do the evaluation of the knowledge level and expertise level of an information source. Furthermore, we use a structured way for performing this evaluations using standardized knowledge level and expertise level questionnaires. This makes the evaluations comparable and enables the decision maker or the analyst to reason about the goodness and accuracy of the evaluations given by the external sources.

One question that is relevant here is how the knowledge domains are determined. Establishing the reference knowledge domain model is a two-step process. First, knowledge domains of relevance are identified and then their relative importance is determined. When identifying knowledge domains, one analyses the security solution being considered. The structured way of performing this analysis is to use ISO 15408 (Common Criteria) part 2 [1] and go through all security functional components. Each of the ISO 15408 security functional components belongs to a functional family, which again belongs to a functional class. In our approach, the functional class is looked upon as a knowledge domain, as they describe distinctive security functionality. One can then aggregate over the number of relevant components in each class and normalize. This results in a coverage weight, where a functional class with more components of relevance receives a higher coverage weight. In the paper, we do not distinguish between coverage and importance weight. Thus, the coverage weight is incorporated into the importance weight. Note that other standards can be used in a similar way. This process does take more time than having experts provide their opinions about which knowledge domains are relevant and their relative weights. If such an approach is used we recommended using a pool of experts divided into two groups. One group acts solely as experts while the other group does not provide its opinions but judge the opinions of the experts. This reduces the biases of subjective judgements, but unfortunately does not remove them.

One of the pitfalls of using this approach is that if the recommender is not trustworthy, deriving trust based on the provided information has problems. This is a challenge for almost all recommendation/reputation systems including ours. While this problem cannot be completely eliminated, its effect can be considerably mitigated using one of two approaches. One approach is to calibrate or assess the external sources (third parties). The idea is to use an external source trust hierarchy, where other parties evaluate the external sources. The other approach that we have used in some of our other works is to evaluate the trust level of recommender and use that trust level to scale the recommendation score provided by her. Prior works by some of the authors have proposed the Vector Trust model [15,16] that allows evaluating and reasoning about trust over the three variables knowledge, experience and recommendation. Since trust is evaluated from multiple angles in this model, the bias of an untrustworthy recommender is considerably mitigated. Both the external source trust hierarchy approach as well as the Vector trust-model approach will increase the belief in the evaluation of the information sources. However, an extra evaluation of the external sources will no doubt add time and cost complexity to the evaluation. In practice, one can be pragmatic and use experts that one already has an established trust relationship with. This is a decision that must be taken in each case, depending on whether there are experts available that can act as external sources and the budget, time and resources available.

A second concern which is very typical in reputation systems is the possibility that if the attackers are familiar with the trust system or aggregation algorithm, then they may try to manipulate the final results in ways such as those discussed in [43,44]. However, ours is not an online user opinion scheme unlike other such systems. Thus, the manipulation of external sources in our approach Honeypots and IDSes cannot be automated in the manner discussed in [43,44]. In addition, assuming that these sources can be manipulated, the evaluation is not done on the information from these sources but rather on the sources themselves. Since the information is gathered by trained human beings and not by automatons such manipulations can be easily detected. It is critical that the human beings used to evaluate the Honeypots and IDS are in fact knowledgeable and have experience with IDS and can account for the problem of false alarms and false positives for the particular IDS. The information aggregation is done automatically by the BBN topology; however, this tool is not remotely accessible and hence cannot be manipulated.

8   Conclusion and Future Work

Security evaluation is inherently difficult. There have been several attempts over the past decade but still no wide-spread industry-adopted standards or best practises are at hand. This article addresses parts of the gap, in particular the challenges related to lack of resources, short time-to-market, limited budget, lack of empirical information, and variable quality of information. Our approach to security evaluation or security level evaluation is a BBN realization of a trust-based security level evaluation approach. The approach derives the security level of a security solution, system or parts thereof, resulting in quantifiable and comparable security level expressions. An earlier version of the approach was presented in [45]. Our approach is an alternative to traditional evaluation approaches, such as that of ISO 14508, the Common Criteria.

The approach is built on the principles of performance-based expert aggregation techniques and is an information source ability based aggregation technique where abilities are measured in terms of information source trustworthiness. Our approach allows the company performing the evaluation, to exercise additional control of the information provided. This is in contrast to current trends where the company hires consultants who provide information and input to the evaluation. Moreover, as it is the sources of information and not the information themselves that are evaluated, the company can reuse such evaluations.

The implementation of the model as a BBN topology makes our approach scalable. BBN has the ability to store experience and to update this experience simply by inserting the new or available information at the observable nodes in the BBN topology. The computation (evidence propagation) is handled by the computational engine in HUGIN. It splits the conditional probability graph into independent computational subtrees, computes these in parallel and then aggregates over the result. This makes it possible to work with multiple variables, multiple information sources, hierarchy of external sources, and complex probability relations. Furthermore, as the various models of our approach (described in Section 4) are deployed directly in the BBN topology, these are not computed manually but automatically by inserting information about expertise and knowledge of information sources into the relevant parts of the topology. In fact, it is possible to directly observe how specific information on expertise and knowledge affects the overall trustworthiness of an information source. As trustworthiness is computed separately from the evaluation of the security level, it is possible to directly observe the effect on the security level estimate from information of particular information sources. This also gives the analyst or decision maker the ability to identify missing information and understand how it affects the resulting security level estimate. In the absence of BBN implementation, we would have to manually insert information, and perform computation and what if analysis, thus reducing the scalability.

We have demonstrated the approach for evaluating two alternative DoS solutions. These two DoS solutions are well known and so are their advantages and weaknesses. This way we have been able to use empirical data and observations made on the two solutions, to argue about the outcome of the evaluation using our approach. (We have also used this example in earlier related publications [45,46]. Thus readers can easily see how the approach has evolved over time.) The example shows how to derive the trustworthiness scores of information sources and how to use these trustworthiness scores to derive the security level for each alternative solution. Our model determines the trustworthiness using two trust variables: (1) knowledge level and (2) expertise level, measured in terms of knowledge score and expertise score, respectively. The two scores are derived using associated score models, and then combined into a trustworthiness score.

However, the resulting security level prediction is highly sensitive to the models involved in deriving the information source trustworthiness scores (presented in Section 4), as the trustworthiness scores are the information aggregation constraint. It is therefore important to ensure accurate and representable trustworthiness scores. Our case studies show that the knowledge and expertise score models covers a significant range of relevant calibration variables to evaluate information source trustworthiness. There is, though, room for improvement and for extending the categories of information source calibration variables beyond knowledge and expertise, and to continuously evaluate and improve the representation of the relationship between these. This is the underlying reason for implementing the approach as an BBN topology and for using the HUGIN tool, as the HUGIN tool offers the ability of structural learning capability to construct the BBN topology, in addition to the ability of BBN to reason over uncertain and incomplete information. The structural learning capabilities enable us to evolve the approach as new experience is gained. This means that the implementation has evolved based on current experience and that it will continue to evolve by absorbing experience data as it becomes available.

Evaluation of the effectiveness of the approach is best done by applying it in a real world industrial security evaluation study. However, before this can be achieved the industry needs to be convinced that taking part in this study will benefit it. Towards this end, we have made a series of demonstration projects. The largest demonstration made has been on the evaluation of the security level of a machine-to-machine (M2M) platform. We have also deployed the approach in a security investment support prototype called SecInvest (see [47]). In SecInvest, the goal is to enable aggregation of disparate information in a trustworthy and efficient way. In practice, experts provide information and input to security level evaluations and companies often hire security consultancy services for such work. Our approach enables the company to do so, and at the same time allows the company to exercise additional control of the information provided. As it is the sources and not the information itself that is evaluated, such evaluations can be reused (which makes sense as companies tend to use the same consultancy company several times, sometimes even on a regular basis). This (reusability) makes our approach effective and enables it to scale as the complexity of the problem context and the number of information sources grows. It is the design choice of evaluating the sources that differentiates our approach from similar approaches developed in the safety domain (so far, no similar information aggregation approach exist in the security domain), making it more effective to use in practice.

Future work includes controlled experiments, and eventually a industrial-scale case study, to gain realistic experience with the current version of the trust-based security level evaluation approach and in particular to investigate the relation between the variables used to assess the knowledge and expertise level of an information source. The result of these will be used to evolve the BBN topology to even better reflect the factors involved when choosing between security solutions, which are not known at the current time but that can be observed over time. Furthermore, the approach is part of a larger trust-based information aggregation approach that takes more trust variables and trust relationships into account when combining information. This includes, among others, an information source trust hierarchy and external sources X and Y hierarchies.

Acknowledgment. This work was partially supported by the U.S. Air Force Office of Scientific Research under contract FA9550-07-0042 and by the National Science Foundation under contract CNS 0905232. The views and conclusions contained in this document are those of the authors and should not be interpreted as representing official policies, either expressed or implied, of the U.S. Air Force, the National Science Foundation or other federal government agencies.

References

1. International Organization for Standardization (ISO/IEC): ISO 15408:2007 Common Criteria for Information Technology Security Evaluation, Version 3.1, Revision 2, CCMB-2007-09-001, CCMB-2007-09-002 and CCMB-2007-09-003 (2007)
2. Jøsang, A.: A Subjective Metric of Authentication. In: Quisquater, J.-J., Deswarte, Y., Meadows, C., Gollmann, D. (eds.) ESORICS 1998. LNCS, vol. 1485, pp. 329–344. Springer, Heidelberg (1998)
3. Jøsang, A.: An Algebra for Assessing Trust in Certification Chains. In: Proceedings of the 1999 Network and Distributed Systems Security Symposium (1999)
4. Cohen, M.S., Parasuraman, R., Freeman, J.T.: Trust in Decision Aids: A Model and a Training Strategy. Technical Report USAATCOM TR 97-D-4, Cognitive Technologies Inc. (1997)
5. Yahalom, R., Klein, B., Beth, T.: Trust Relationship in Secure Systems: A Distributed Authentication Perspective. In: Proceedings of the IEEE Symposium on Security and Privacy, pp. 150–164 (1993)
6. Yahalom, R., Klein, B., Beth, T.: Trust-based Navigation in Distributed Systems. Computing Systems 7(1), 45–73 (1994)
7. Beth, T., Borcherding, M., Klein, B.: Valuation of Trust in Open Networks. In: Gollmann, D. (ed.) ESORICS 1994. LNCS, vol. 875, pp. 3–18. Springer, Heidelberg (1994)
8. Xiong, L., Liu, L.: A Reputation-Based Trust Model For Peer-To-Peer Ecommerce Communities. In: Proceedings of the IEEE Conference on E-Commerce, pp. 275–284 (2003)
9. Abdul-Rahman, A., Hailes, S.: Supporting Trust in Virtual Communities. In: Proceedings of the 33rd Annual Hawaii International Conference on System Sciences, pp. 4–7 (2000)
10. Burrows, M., Abadi, M., Needham, R.: A Logic of Authentication. ACM Transactions on Computer Systems 8(1), 18–36 (1990)
11. Jones, A.J.I., Firozabadi, B.S.: On the Characterization of a Trusting Agent – Aspects of a Formal Approach. In: Trust and Deception in Virtual Societies, pp. 157–168. Kluwer Academic Publishers, Dordrecht (2000)
12. Jajodia, S., Samarati, P., Subrahmanian, V.: A Logical Language for Expressing Authorizations. In: Proceedings of the IEEE Symposium on Security and Privacy, pp. 31–42 (1997)
13. Bacharach, M., Gambetta, D.: Trust as Type Identification. In: Trust and Deception in Virtual Societies, pp. 1–26. Kluwer Academic Publishers, Dordrecht (2000)
14. Purser, S.: A Simple Graphical Tool For Modelling Trust. Computers & Security 20(6), 479–484 (2001)
15. Ray, I., Chakraborty, S.: A Vector Model of Trust for Developing Trustworthy Systems. In: Samarati, P., Ryan, P.Y.A., Gollmann, D., Molva, R. (eds.) ESORICS 2004. LNCS, vol. 3193, pp. 260–275. Springer, Heidelberg (2004)

16. Ray, I., Ray, I., Chakraborty, S.: An Interoperable Context Sensitive Model of Trust. Journal of Intelligent Information Systems 32(1), 75–104 (2009)
17. Sun, Y.L., Yang, Y.: Trust Establishment in Distributed Networks: Analysis and Modeling. In: Proceedings of the IEEE International Conference on Communications (ICC 2007), pp. 1266–1273 (2007)
18. Littlewood, B., Brocklehurst, S., Fenton, N., Mellor, P., Page, S., Wright, D., Dobson, J., McDermid, J., Gollmann, D.: Towards Operational Measures of Computer Security. Journal of Computer Security 2, 211–229 (1993)
19. Ortalo, R., Deswarte, Y.: Experiments with Quantitative Evaluation Tools for Monitoring Operational Security. IEEE Transaction on Software Engineering 5(25), 633–650 (1999)
20. Madan, B.B., Popstojanova, K.G., Vaidyanathan, K., Trivedi, K.S.: Modeling and Quantification of Security Attributes of Software Systems. In: Proceedings of the International Conference on Dependable Systems and Networks, pp. 505–514 (2002)
21. Jonsson, E., Olovsson, T.: A Quantitative Model of the Security Intrusion Process based on Attacker Behavior. IEEE Transaction on Software Engineering 4(25), 235–246 (1997)
22. Houmb, S.H., Georg, G., France, R., Bieman, J., Jürjens, J.: Cost-Benefit Trade-Off Analysis using BBN for Aspect-Oriented Risk-Driven Development. In: Proceedings of 10th IEEE International Conference on Engineering of Complex Computer Systems, pp. 195–204 (2005)
23. Houmb, S.H.: Decision Support for Choice of Security Solution: The Aspect-Oriented Risk Driven Development (AORDD) Framework. PhD thesis, Norwegian University of Science and Technology, Trondheim (2007)
24. International Organization for Standardization (ISO/IEC): ISO/IEC 27002:2005 Information Technology – Security Techniques – Code of Practice for Information Security Management (2000)
25. International Organization for Standardization (ISO/IEC): ISO/IEC TR 13335:2004 Information Technology – Guidelines for Management of IT Security (2001)
26. Australian/New Zealand Standards and International Organization for Standardization: AS/NZS ISO 31000:2009, Risk management - Principles and guidelines (2004)
27. Department of Defence: Trusted Computer System Evaluation Criteria, DoD 5200.28-STD, Supersedes, CSC-STD-001-83, dtd 15 Aug 83, Library No. S225,711 (1985)
28. Department of Trade and Industry, London: Information Technology Security Evaluation Criteria (1991),
http://www.itsec.gov.uk/ or http://nsi.org/Library/Compsec/eurooran.txt
29. Cooke, R.M.: Experts in Uncertainty: Opinion and Subjective Probability in Science. Oxford University Press, Oxford (1991)
30. Goossens, L.H.J., Harper, F.T., Kraan, B.C.P., Meacutetivier, H.: Expert Judgement for a Probabilistic Accident Consequence Uncertainty Analysis. Radiation Protection and Dosimetry 90(3), 295–303 (2000)
31. Cowell, R.G., Dawid, A.P., Lauritzen, S.L., Spiegelhalter, D.J.: Probabilistic Networks and Expert Systems. Springer, Heidelberg (1999)
32. Jensen, F.V.: Bayesian Networks and Decision Graphs. Springer, Heidelberg (2001)
33. Neapolitan, R.E.: Learning Bayesian Networks. Prentice Hall, Englewood Cliffs (2004)
34. Pearl, J.: Probabilistic Reasoning in Intelligent Systems: Network for Plausible Inference. Morgan Kaufmann, San Francisco (1988)
35. Hugin Expert A/S, Alborg, Denmark: HUGIN Decision Support Tool (2004),
http://www.hugin.dk
36. Spirtes, P., Glymour, C., Scheines, R.: Causation, Prediction, and Search. MIT Press, Cambridge (2000)
37. EU Project EP-27046-ACTIVE: EP-27046-ACTIVE, Final Prototype and User Manual, D4.2.2, Ver. 2.0, 2001-02-22 (2001)

38. Østvang, M.E.: The Honeynet Project, Phase 1: Installing and Tuning Honeyd using LIDS, Project assignment, Norwegian University of Science and Technology (2003)
39. Lin, S., Chiueh, T.: A Survey on Solutions to Distributed Denial of Service Attacks. Technical report RPE TR-201, Department of Computer Science, Stony Brook University (2006)
40. Karig, D., Lee, R.: Remote Denial of Service Attacks and Countermeasures. Technical report CE-L2001-002, Department of Electrical Engineering, Princeton University (2001)
41. Barkley, A., Liu, S., Gia, Q., Dingfield, M., Gokhale, Y.: A Testbed for Study of Distributed Denial of Service Attacks (WA 2.4). In: Proceedings of the IEEE Workshop on Information Assurance and Security, pp. 218–223 (2000)
42. Bernstein, D.J.: SYN Cookies, http://cryptosyncookies.html (accessed November 2006)
43. Yang, Y., Feng, Q., Sun, Y.L., Dai, Y.: RepTrap: A Novel Attack on Feedback-based Reputation Systems. In: Proceedings of the 4th International Conference on Security and Privacy in Communication Networks (2008)
44. Feng, Q., Sun, Y.L., Liu, L., Dai, Y.: Voting Systems with Trust Mechanisms in Cyberspace: Vulnerabilities and Defenses. IEEE Transactions on Knowledge and Data Engineering (2010) (to appear)
45. Houmb, S.H., Ray, I., Ray, I.: Estimating the Relative Trustworthiness of Information Sources in Security Solution Evaluation. In: Stølen, K., Winsborough, W.H., Martinelli, F., Massacci, F. (eds.) iTrust 2006. LNCS, vol. 3986, pp. 135–149. Springer, Heidelberg (2006)
46. Houmb, S.H., Chakraborty, S., Ray, I., Ray, I.: Using Trust-Based Information Aggregation for Predicting Security Level of Systems. In: Foresti, S., Jajodia, S. (eds.) Data and Applications Security and Privacy XXIV. LNCS, vol. 6166, pp. 241–256. Springer, Heidelberg (2010)
47. Franqueira, V.N.L., Houmb, S.H., Daneva, M.: Using Real Option Thinking to Improve Decision Making in Security Investment. In: Proceedings of the 5th International Symposium on Information Security (2010) (to appear)

Implementation of QoSS (Quality-of-Security Service) for NoC-Based SoC Protection

Johanna Sepúlveda[1], Ricardo Pires[1,2], Marius Strum[1], and Wang Jiang Chau[1]

[1] Microelectronics Laboratory - EPUSP, University of São Paulo, Brazil
[2] Federal Institute of Education, Science and Technology - IFSP, Brazil
{jsepulveda,rpires,strum,jcwang}@lme.usp.br

Abstract. Many of the current electronic systems embedded in a SoC (System-on-Chip) are used to capture, store, manipulate and access critical data, as well as to perform other key functions. In such a scenario, security is considered as an important issue. The Network-on-chip (NoC), as the foreseen communication structure of next-generation SoC devices, can be used to efficiently incorporate security. Our work proposes the implementation of QoSS (Quality of Security Service) to overcome present SoC vulnerabilities. QoSS is a novel concept for data protection that introduces security as a dimension of QoS. In this paper, we present the implementation of two security services (access control and authentication), that may be configured to assume one from several possible levels, the implementation of a technique to avoid denial-of-service (DoS) attacks, evaluate their effectiveness and estimate their impact on NoC performance.

Keywords: Network-on-Chip, System-on-Chip, Quality-of-Security-Service, Security, Performance.

1 Introduction

Embedded electronics applications are characterized by a set of ever increasing requirements, demanding more functionality, efficiency, portability, flexibility and resource sharing [1]. Many of the current electronic systems embedded in a SoC (System-on-chip) are used to capture, store, manipulate and access sensitive data and perform several critical functions without security guarantee. The SoC is a computational system integrated into a single chip. The challenge is to provide SoC security features that result in a trustworthy system that meets the security and performance requirements.

SoC design is characterized by two design strategies: *meet-in-the-middle* that combines top-down and bottom-up design strategies and *orthogonality* that splits the SoC design into communication structure and computation structure design. The communication structure can be based on different physical structures: crossbar, bus or network-on-chip (NoC). The physical structure type selection is carried out depending upon to system requirements. This paper addresses the design of a NoC-based communication structure. As the number of IP (Intellectual Property) cores

M.L. Gavrilova et al. (Eds.): Trans. on Comput. Sci. X, LNCS 6340, pp. 187–201, 2010.
© Springer-Verlag Berlin Heidelberg 2010

integrated on a single system-on-chip (SoC) has been growing, NoCs are becoming prevalent as the on-chip communication structure. An NoC is an integrated network that uses routers to allow the communication among the computation structure components. As security requirements vary dramatically for different applications, different levels of security services are necessary. The ability of a distributed system to provide services such that application requirements for timeliness and performance quality are met is called QoS (Quality of service).

Current pervasive computing and flexibility in SoC design trends promote resource sharing and upgrading capabilities that integrates the SoC onto an aggressive world. SoCs can be subject of several kinds of attacks. One of the most obvious threat to SoC security during its normal operation occurs at its interface to external devices, frequently involving reconfigurable devices or wireless communication IPs embedded onto the SoC. It is possible that during SoC operation vulnerable IPs fall under control of an external attacker. Thus, these IPs may become malicious. Under the attacker control, they may try, for example, to obtain sensitive information, like passwords or FPGA (Field-Programmable Gate Array) bitstreams, stored inside the SoC and to send it to the external world. An interface IP may also become a door by which viruses enter the SoC. It is reported that previous attacks to SoCs have succeeded [2]. An IBM report [3] estimates an exorbitant increasing of computer attacks and foresee the embedded devices as the future targets of such attacks. Embedded attacks will cost billions of dollars [4].

Our work proposes the implementation of QoSS (Quality of security service) to overcome present SoC vulnerabilities. QoSS is a novel concept for data protection that introduces security as a dimension of QoS. In contrast with previous works, different security levels deployment allow a best trade off of system security and performance requirements. QoSS uses a Network-on-Chip (NoC) to provide predictable security levels of the system by adding functionality to the routers of the network and consequently changing some local configuration parameters or modifying the network interfaces. QoSS take advantage of the NoC wide system visibility and critical role in enabling system operation, exploiting the NoC to detect and prevent a wide range of attacks.

The goals of our work are: 1- to provide two security services (access control and authentication) that avoid modification and extraction attacks, 2- evaluate its effectiveness and 3 - estimate its impact on NoC performance. Each security service offers four security levels: level L0 (no security) to level L3 (maximum security). All of them were implemented in two alternative ways: at the NoC interface and within the routers. The access control service works as a firewall module. Flow control was modified to manage packet accesses using a table which contains the access rights of each SoC computation component. A higher security level has a larger table, allowing the verification of more packet characteristics (source, type of operation and master role). The authentication service verifies source integrity. Router architecture was modified in order to certify the information transfer through the addition of a code into the packets. We developed an algorithm that uses the routing technique information to determine the correct master-slave path and compares it with the route trace inserted into the packet by the routers. A higher security level also allows verification of a sequential counting of the number of transactions between a master-slave pair inserted into the packets. Experiments were performed using a SystemC-TLM (Transaction Level Model) timed simulation framework. It automatically carries out performance evaluations for a wide variety of traffic conditions (hot spot, transpose and uniform traffic patterns) for different NoC configurations.

The remaining text is organized as follows: Section 2 presents an overview of previous NoC security works. Section 3 presents the main concepts of NoC security. Section 4 presents the NoC architecture. TLM framework used to evaluate the NoC is described in Section 5. Section 6 shows our experimental results. Finally we present our conclusions in Section 7.

2 Previous Works

Security-aware design of communication architectures is becoming a necessity in the context of overall embedded SoC/device security. However, security integration at SoC communication structure remains, so far, mainly unexplored. Communication infrastructure such as NoC may contribute to the overall security of the system, providing the ideal mean for monitoring systems behavior and detecting specific attacks [5,6]. Security in systems adopting NoC paradigm has been only recently addressed by the community [7-10].

The work presented in [7] proposes a security interface. The NoC security mechanism is implemented at NoC interface in order to ensure the secrecy of exchanged information through the utilization of cyphering techniques. The proposed mechanism ensures that no unencrypted data leaves the NoC. A key-keeper secure core is responsible to key distribution on the NoC. New keys can be downloaded and stored in a key-keeper core through encryption techniques. The work presented in [8] proposes the first solution to secure a reconfigurable-based NoC. This system integrates secure network interfaces, for filtering possible denial-of-service attacks, and a secure network manager, in order to monitor the NoC behavior. [9] identifies denial-of-service (DoS), draining, extraction of secret information and modification as the most common NoC attacks. They propose the implementation of an Address Protection Unit (APU) at NoC interface that enforces access control rules. They specify how a component of the NoC can access the protected device. In [10] the principles of [9] are adopted to develop a Data Protection Unit (DPU) for MPSoCs.

These previous works [7-10] present two main limitations. 1) they implement a single NoC security level through the integration of a security manager core and the increase of the functionality of network interfaces. However, they do not take advantage of all the distributed property of the NoC structure. 2) they do not evaluate the effect of security mechanism upon NoC performance. The purpose of our work is to overcome these two limitations.

3 SoC Security Challenges

Current SoCs are used to perform several critical functions. They are pervading our lives. However, SoCs can be subject of several kinds of attacks. Pervasive computing and flexibility trends in SoC design promote resource sharing and upgrading capabilities. Such characteristics introduce the computational system encapsulated in a chip (SoC) onto an aggressive and dangerous world. Many SoCs interact with other electronic devices, in many cases wirelessly. By interacting with other digital devices, a SoC may receive viruses (or other similar malicious pieces of code). Among the motivations for someone to attack a SoC, we underline three examples: 1) Economical gain by obtaining confidential information (e.g. passwords, IP bitstreams) stored in a SoC; 2) Reputation: a hacker may attack a SoC by viewing this action as a personal challenge; and 3) Vandalism: the purpose is to cause loss or damage to an SoC. Viruses may be used for this purpose.

4 NoC-Based Security

4.1 NoC Architecture

An NoC is an integrated network that uses routers and links to provide communication among processing SoC units. It also has an interface that implements the communication protocol. The NoC design flow is composed of 3 phases [11-12]: 1) NoC specification, whose characteristics result from the SoC communication requirements (IP types and number, communication protocols, network interface); 2) NoC global (NoC topology, size and mapping) and local (link width, buffer allocation, flow control, routing technique, arbitration mechanism) parameters instantiation; and 3) NoC evaluation, checking if the NoC meets communication requirements. If the NoC instance does not meet the requirements, phases 2 to 3 have to be repeated. Security implementation is also introduced in phases 2 and 3 of NoC design (shaded regions in Figure 1). The NoC router defines the path that data must follow through the network from the source to the destination.

The communication structure has become the heart of the SoC [11]. It has a significant impact on overall SoC design. The wide system visibility turns NoC security implementation advantageous compared to security implementation at the computation structure [7,8]. NoCs could monitor data exchange, detect violations, block attacks and provide diagnostic information for triggering suitable response and recovery mechanisms. However, NoC-based systems can be subjected to attacks addressing their specific structure [8]. These attacks may succeed depending on vulnerabilities in NoC design, configuration and implementation. A NoC attack is defined by [9] as any unauthorized attempt to access or to use the network resources. According to the purpose of the attacks, they can be classified in three categories: 1) Extraction: unauthorized reading of critical data that is being exchanged through the network from/to a secure target; 2) Modification: unauthorized change of critical data. Includes writing actions, state modification, data creation or removal; and 3) Denial of Service, whose aim is to bring down the system performance. In order to prevent and to mitigate attacks to the NoC, security services can be implemented.

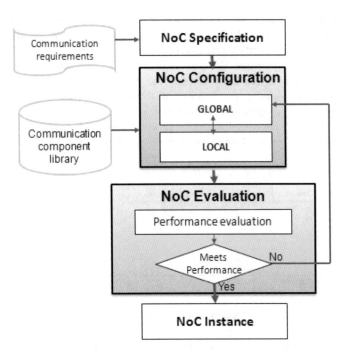

Fig. 1. NoC design Flow

The main function of security services is to protect network resources and data exchanged by means of communication management [9,10]. There are six security services [10]: 1) Confidentiality: ensures the data secrecy; 2) Integrity: assurance that data are identically maintained during any operation; 3) Authentication: validating the sender IP integrity; 4) Access Control: allowing or denying the use of a particular resource; 5) Availability: ensuring the use of the network resources; and 6) Non-repudiation: maintains evidence of NoC communication events. In this paper we do not address confidentiality and integrity security services. They can be handled with complementary cyphering techniques [13]. We address access control and authentication services in order to neutralize extraction and modification attacks. The implementation of security services increases the complexity of the NoC. Optimal NoC configuration demands a deep exploration of the wide NoC design space.

4.2 QoSS (Quality-of-Security-Service)

The traffic of a single embedded application may integrate several flows, each of which characterized by different security requirements. The QoSS concepts allow differentiated treatment to data exchange carried out through the NoC. The advantage of the use of QoSS is the adoption of different security levels. Each level represents a tradeoff between security and performance. The QoSS concept can be implemented by adding functionality to NoC routers and consequently changing some local configuration parameters or modifying network interfaces. Different security levels are implemented through security mechanisms.

In this work, we study two alternatives to implement security services: 1- At the NoC interface and 2- inside the routers of the NoC. Our work assumes a network interface compliant with the specifications of the OCP/IP (Open Core Protocol) interface. Messages coming from the computation structure component are translated by the interface into packets compliant to the protocol used within the NoC. The adopted OCP compliant NoC packet format (see Figure 2) is composed of 9 fields.

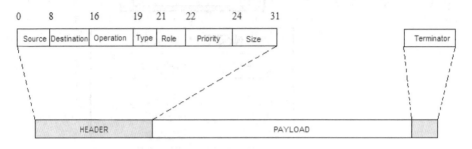

Fig. 2. NoC packet structure

- **Source:** Identifies the master component. It is the initiator of the communication.
- **Destination:** Identifies the slave component. It is the target of the communication.
- **Operation:** Codes the transaction type, i.e. a read, read-linked, read-exclusive, write, write-non-post, write-conditional, and broadcast.
- **Type:** Defines the information type that is being exchanged, i.e. data, instruction or signal types.
- **Role:** Represents the role of the initiator component. i.e. user, root. The roles are defined by the security policy of the system.
- **Priority:** allows traffic priority classification.
- **Size:** Defines the number of bytes contained in the payload of the packet.
- **Payload:** Embodies the information generated by the master.
- **Terminator:** Register the path of the packet through the NoC and the sequential number of this packet in the current transaction between this master-slave pair.

Our security mechanisms make use of information embodied within the packet to perform access control and authentication on the packet arriving at 1- the NoC interface or 2- the router. The description of the mechanisms and the results of their effectiveness and performance are presented at the next sections.

4.3 Access Control

Shared resources of the NoC can be targeted by intruders (unauthorized access) whose purpose is to modify the system status, compromising the correct execution of software, or reading confidential data. Such attacks can be carried out by means of writing or reading operations [9]. The access control service works as a firewall module. This service is implemented through a filter component. It regulates NoC traffic, allowing or denying data exchange between a master-slave pair based upon a set of rules. The control flow was modified to manage packet accesses by using a table which contains the access rights of each SoC computation component. Table 1 shows the different access control levels. A higher security level has a larger table, allowing the verification of more packet characteristics (source, type of operation and master role). The filter module can be easily modified to implement different security levels. This module specifies the way by which each master component can access a slave. The filter component checks the source, role, destination and operation fields of the packet and verifies them consulting the rules embodied into a table (see table 2). It allows the verification of the rights of master M (source, role) over the slave S (destination) and allows or blocks the requested transaction (operation). Additionally, our mechanism verifies the existence of the message destination and that the master and slave components have not identical NoC addresses. Such characteristic avoid possible DoS attacks through *livelock*, characterized by the insertion of a packet that cannot reach its destination, and draining attacks, which is characterized by the intentional wasting of NoC resources.

Access control at the interface: The access control service is implemented at the slave interface. It examines the information embodied at the packet and verifies if the incoming packet satisfies access rules specified for each slave. Unauthorized packets are discarded.

Table 1. Access control levels

Level	Source Verification	Operation Verification	Role Verification
L0			
L1	X		
L2	X	X	
L3	X	X	X

Table 2. Example of filter utilization

Master	Role	Slave 1	Slave 2	Slave 3
Master 1	User	Read	-	-
	Root	Write	Read	Read/Write
Master 2	User	-	Read/Write	-
	Root	Read	Write	Read

Access control at the router: The NoC uses a deterministic routing algorithm to route the packets. This implies that the path for each communication flow is predictable. At each router, it is specified the portion of the total NoC traffic that is allowed to communicate according to its destination field. The size of the table implemented by the filter component depends on router localization and the routing algorithm. This strategy is the first attempt to implement a distributed access control over the NoC. Its advantage is the elimination of unauthorized packets sooner inside the communication path, avoiding bandwidth wasting.

4.4 Authentication

After access control process is finished, the authentication security service verifies the integrity of the source of critical data. It does this by checking if the route taken by the packet is consistent with the source IP field contents. For this purpose, a routing trace is embodied at the terminator field of the packet. This field contents are altered by the routers along the communication path of each packet. In this process, when a packet traverses a router, the packet terminator receives this router signature. A simple strategy to do this, adopted in this work, is to use a trace field containing R bits, where R is the number of routers in the NoC. Our experiments have been carried out using a 4x4 NoC, having thus R=16 routers and using a trace field containing 16 bits. The routers are numbered from 0 to (R-1). To each router r corresponds the bit in the trace field whose position inside the field is also r. When a packet enters the NoC, all of the bits of its trace field are equal to 0. Each time the packet crosses a router, this router makes its corresponding bit in the trace field equal to 1. Then, at the end of the route, the packet terminator reveals the complete path that has been taken by the packet, indicating with 1 which routers have been crossed by the packet and with 0 which have not. By knowing the NoC topology, the slave can deduce what is the true packet sender and thus it can verify if the alleged source is in fact this sender. For this purpose, the slave NI has a table containing the expected value for the trace field coming from each possible master. In the case of a mismatch (i.e. the trace field does not correspond to the expected one) the packet is discarded. This strategy makes very difficult to a malicious master to successfully send a packet as it would be another master, because the contents of the trace field are determined by the routers after it is sent by the master, preventing that they remain under the master control. Table 3 shows the different authentication levels.

Table 3. Authentication levels

Level	Source Verification	Path Calculation	Master-Slave Verification
L0			
L1	X		
L2	X	X	
L3	X	X	X

Each master-slave pair may also keep track of the sequential number of its transactions. In this case, this sequential number is also included in the terminator. The slave then verifies if the transactions occur according to the expected numbering. To overcome this feature, an intruder would have to know the current expected sequential number of the transaction of the master-slave pair it intends to attack. A packet whose sequential number differs from the expected one is discarded.

5 NoC Evaluation

Experiments were performed using a SystemC-TLM (Transaction Level Model) timed simulation framework [14]. Our model automatically carries out performance evaluations for a wide variety of traffic conditions (hot spot, transpose and uniform traffic patterns) for different NoC configurations (see Figure 3).

5.1 Traffic Generators

Application specific traffic generators were used to emulate the behaviour of master IPs. During SoC operation, they have established different application dependent traffic conditions. In order to achieve a broad performance evaluation coverage we adopted two types of application independent traffic generators: 1) parametric and 2) pseudorandom.

In this process, in order to simulate attacks, each time a master had to initiate a transaction, a random number p uniformly distributed between 0 and 1 has been generated inside this master, to decide if it should act as a malicious one by faking its identity. In order to maintain the frequency of attacks at reasonable values (the major part of the communication events should not be attacks, but several attacks must occur to validate the adopted security schemes), the probability of a master have lied about its identity have been maintained below 5% ($0 < p < 0.05$). In order to verify the system reaction to denial of service attacks, during simulation masters have sent some packets to nonexistent slaves (to nonexistent addresses) or to themselves. By doing this, an attacker may expect that these packets will run indefinitely inside the NoC, consuming its resources, causing congestion and wasting energy. The traffic receptors emulate the behavior of slave IPs. They confirm the reception of the correct information.

5.2 Network-on-Chip

In order to perform NoC evaluation, a communication model has been developed. This model allowed us to analyze both the global as well as the inner behavior/performance of the NoC. Information flows through an NoC as packets. A packet is composed of headers, a payload of arbitrary size and a trail. A packet can be decomposed into smaller sized information called flits.

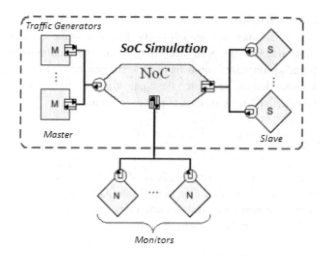

Fig. 3. TLM NoC evaluation framework

The exchange of information between any master-slave pair of IPs is carried out through data commutations (switch information at each router). In our work, each communication exchange is modeled as the set of events shown in Figure 4, in which communication exchange is composed of two commutations at routers r and r+1. Each line represents a packet commutation composed of the events: filtering (FIL), authentication process (ANA), store (STO), arbitration (ARB), switching (SWI), send header flit (HDR), sent the set of payload flits (PAY) and packet marking (MAR).

Router (r)	FIL	ANA	STO	ARB	SWI	HDR	PAY	MAR					
						Router (r+1)	FIL	ANA	STO	ARB	SWI	HDR	PAY	MAR

Fig. 4. NoC communication model

5.3 Monitor

Monitors annotate communication events. This information is employed to calculate a set of performance metrics. There are 2 global metrics: 1) NoC latency (cycles) defined as the average time required to complete the data exchange; 2) NoC power, composed of the links, interfaces and routers power. There are 3 inner metrics: 3) Average number of routers to complete a transaction (routers), defined as the number of routers required to commute a packet from its source router (RS) until its destination router (Rd); 4) Router/Interface utilization rate, that expresses the percentage of packet commutations performed by each router R/ interface I during simulation time;

and 5) Channel utilization rate, that expresses the percentage of the simulation time that each channel is keeping busy.

6 Results

Figures 5 to 10 show the average packet latency and NoC power results of a 4x4 mesh-based NoC by adding each service separately and when the two security services were implemented simultaneously. Each value of the Figures 5 to 10 corresponds to the average obtained after 50 simulations and 95% as confidence interval. The NoC uses a XY routing scheme, round-robin (RR) arbiter and FIFO memory organization.

The average packet latency corresponds to the average amount of cycles required to complete a transaction. The *NoC* Power (P_{NoC}) is the sum of links power (P_{Li}), interfaces power (P_{Int}) and routers power (P_{Ri}) due to transaction completion. P_{NoC} is given by equation (1) [16]. P_{Li} and P_{Ri} are proportional to the *channel utilization rate* and *router utilization rate* respectively.

$$P_{NoC} = P_{Li} + P_{Int} + P_{Ri} \tag{1}$$

For this study, we developed power models for the main components in the *NoC* architecture. We integrated these models into the simulator, taking the architectural and technological parameters into account. The characterization was made under the 0,25 μm process constraints, 2.5 volts as a power supply and a 25° temperature. Our power estimation strategy is based on identifying the activity of each *NoC* component. In order to fulfill this task, the monitor annotates the communication events on the *NoC*. At the end of the simulation, the number of activity occurrences is obtained for each NoC component. A power consumption cost is also evaluated for each activity. At the end of the simulation, the activity occurrences of each component are used to calculate the total power dissipation.

We evaluate both security implementation alternatives, at network interface (A1) and at the routers (A2). The performance evaluation was based on three traffic patterns: 1) Hot spot (each master has a preferential slave to communicate); 2) transpose (each (x,y) node communicates with its corresponding (y,x) node); and 3) pseudo-random (NoC nodes communicate according to the uniform distribution). These patterns were used as NoC benchmarks in previous works [15]. Each traffic pattern is composed five flit size packets of three types: real-time, write or read and signalling, characterized by a different generation rate (40.000, 160.000 and 20.000 packets per second respectively). The percentage of critical data varied from 30% to 70% of the total amount of NoC traffic.

We compared the performance of an NoC with QoSS and a best-effort NoC. Average latency penalties due to security implementation at the interface (16%) were greater than those obtained by implementation at routers (9%). It was observed that in simulations for the latter case, latency penalties were amortized along the communication path. The security functionality did not block the routers, so that, the temporary gap due to security functionality was used to commute other packets. Such behavior helped to reduce average NoC latency. As the percentage of critical packets increases, differences between the latency penalties of the security implementations at the interface and at the routers became gradually smaller. This is due to the fact that security actions taken at the routers cause less performance penalties because they take advantage from pipeline characteristics of NoC operation, but an increase in critical traffic increases packet queues waiting for security treatment at each router, attenuating pipeline advantages. Average power penalties for the interface and router security implementation are 13% and 5% respectively.

A master network interface links each master component to the NoC. When the NoC identifies a fake packet at a master network interface, the waste of NoC resources is avoided, by immediately discarding that packet. Such mechanism reduces NoC latency and NoC power consumption because no extra commutations at routers must be performed. The percentage of the latency and power savings depends on the relative location of the master and slave components on the NoC and on traffic pattern. The average percentages for these savings of latency for 3 traffic patterns (hot spot, transpose and pseudo-random) are 33%, 19% and 13% respectively. The savings for the hot spot case are the largest because in such traffic pattern most of the packets are competing for the same NoC resources. Early discarding the fake packets reduces NoC congestion. Inversely in the pseudo-random traffic pattern, the larger variety of alternative paths taken by packets through the NoC naturally reduces NoC congestion. Therefore, early discarding fake packets has less effect on NoC overall latency. The averages for NoC power savings are 21%, 16% and 14% respectively. In the case of hot spot traffic pattern, the savings are tightly determined by the proximity of the master that is producing the fake packet to the hot spot of the NoC. For sources close to the hot spot, we achieve saving up to 45% for latency and 27% for power. Results show that security implementation at the routers of the NoC is more efficient than the implementation at the interface. Access control and authentication services always increase NoC latency and NoC power consumption.

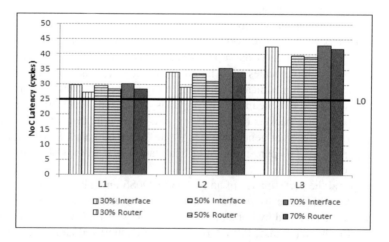

Fig. 5. NoC latency results for access control service

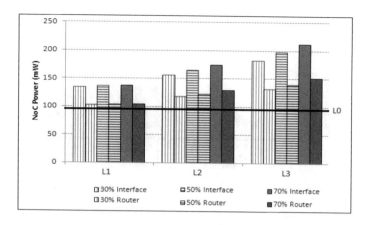

Fig. 6. NoC power results (access control)

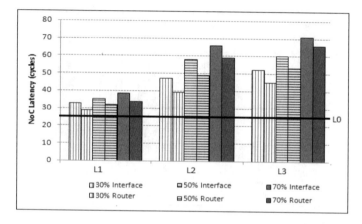

Fig. 7. NoC latency results (authentication)

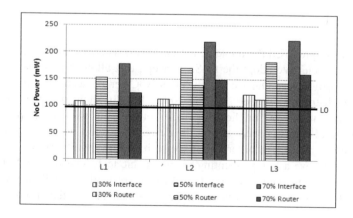

Fig. 8. NoC power results (authentication)

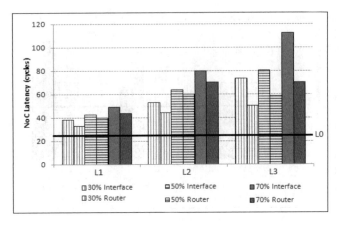

Fig. 9. NoC latency results (access control and authentication)

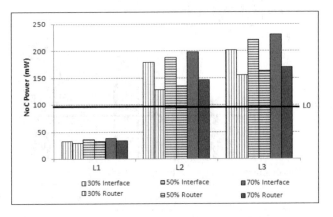

Fig. 10. NoC latency results (access control and authentication)

7 Conclusions

In this work we proposed the implementation of two security services: access control and authentication. We adopt the QoSS concept, that allows the implementation of different security levels. Our work shows that NoC-centric security may take advantage of the distributed property of the NoC. Results show that the inclusion of security issues in an NoC implies a tradeoff between trustworthy and performance. The inclusion of QoSS concept allows the designer to select the more suited among different security levels in order to satisfy both, security and performance requirements. Currently we are implementing cryptographic techniques to our NoC mechanism in order to guarantee its security. As a future work, we will study different techniques that allow an improvement in the implementation of the proposed security mechanisms.

Acknowledgments. This work was supported by the "Fundação de Amparo à pesquisa do Estado de São Paulo" FAPESP under Grant number 2007/55047-0.

References

1. ARM. Trustzone, `http://www.arm.com`
2. FSECURE, `http://www.f-secure.com/v-descs/cabir.shtml`
3. IBM, Global Business Security Index Report,
   `http://www-03.ibm.com/press/fr/fr/pressrelease/26379.wss`
4. Kocher, P., Lee, R., McGraw, G., Raghunathan, A., Ravi, S.: Security as a New Dimension in Embedded System Design. In: Design Automation Conference, DAC 2004 (2004)
5. Ogras, U., Hu, J., Marculescu, R.: Communication-centric SoC design for nanoscale domain. In: IEEE International Conference on Application-Specific Systems (2005)
6. Benini, L.: Application Specific NoC Design. In: Design, Automation and Test in Europe Conference and Exhibition (DATE 2006), vol. 1, pp. 1–5 (March 2006)
7. Gebotys, C., Zhang, Y.: Security wrappers and power analysis for SoC technologies. In: CODES 2003 (2003)
8. Evain, S., Diguet, J.: From NoC security analysis to design solutions. In: Design, Automation and Test in Europe Conference and Exhibition, DATE 2006 (2006)
9. Fiorin, L., Silvano, C., Sami, M.: Security Aspects in Networks-on-Chips: Overview and Proposals for Secure Implementations. In: Proc. 10th Euromicro Conference on Digital System Design Architectures, Methods and Tools (2007)
10. Fiorin, L., Lukovic, S., Palermo, G.: Implementation of a Reconfigurable Data Protection Module for NoC-based MPSoCs. In: Proc. IEEE Parallel and Distributed Processing (2008)
11. Benini, L., Bertozzi, D.: Network-on-Chip architectures and design methods. Comput. Digit. Tech. 152 (March 2005)
12. Goossens, K., Dielissen, J., Prakash, O., González, S., Rädulescu, A., Rijpkema, E.: A Design Flow for Application-Specific Networks on Chip with Guaranteed Performance to Accelerate SoC design and verification. In: Proc. Design, Automation and Test in Europe Conference and Exhibition, DATE 2005 (2005)
13. Kocher, P., Lee, R., McGraw, G., Raghunathan, A., Ravi, S.: Security as a new Dimension in Embedded System Design. In: Design Automation Conference, DAC 2004 (2004)
14. Sepulveda, J., Strum, M., Wang, J.C.: A TLM-Based Network-on-Chip Performance Evaluation Framework. In: Proc. 3rd Symposium on Circuits and Systems, Colombian Chapter, pp. 54–60 (2007)
15. Bolotin, E., Cidon, I., Ginosar, R., Kolodny, A.: QNoC: QoS architecture and design process for network on chip. Journal of System Architecture (2004)
16. Lee, H., Ogras, U., Marculescu, R., Chang, N.: Design Space Exploration and Prototyping for on-Chip Multimedia applications. In: Proceedings of DAC 2006, California, USA (2006)

Signcryption with Non-interactive Non-repudiation without Random Oracles

Jia Fan[1,2], Yuliang Zheng[1], and Xiaohu Tang[2]

[1] University of North Carolina at Charlotte, NC 28223, USA
[2] Southwest Jiaotong University, 610031, P.R. China
{jfan1,yzheng}@uncc.edu, xhutang@ieee.org

Abstract. Non-repudiation is a very important requirement of sign-cryption. It ensures that a sender cannot deny the fact that he has sign-crypted a message. Non-interactive non-repudiation enables a receiver to settle a repudiation dispute with the help of a judge without the need to engage in costly multi-round interactive communications with the judge. In this paper, we strengthen Malone-Lee's security model for signcryption with non-interactive non-repudiation by introducing two additional, more subtle and useful security requirements, one about the unforgeability and the other about the confidentiality of non-repudiation evidence. A further contribution of this paper is to design a concrete signcryption scheme that admits provable security without random oracles in our strengthened security model for signcryption.

Keywords: signcryption, non-repudiation, public key cryptography, non-interaction, random oracle, bilinear map.

1   Introduction

Asymmetric encryption and signature are two basic primitives in public-key cryptography. They provide us with confidentiality and authenticity independently. When both functions are required, traditionally one has to carefully sign and encrypt the data sequentially. In 1997, Zheng [26] proposed a new primitive called signcryption. It combines the functions of both primitives with a cost much less than the sign-then-encrypt (or encrypt-then-sign) method.

Let us consider a scenario where a sender signcrypts a message which is then forwarded to a receiver. Afterwards the sender denies the fact. We note that in the original signcryption, only the receiver can decrypt the signcryptext, that is, he is the only one who can check the validity of the message. The challenge the receiver faces is what he can do to ask a judge to help prove the fact, while without revealing to the judge more information than that is required. Non-repudiation is defined to guarantee that the sender cannot deny the fact that the message is signcrypted by her in the first place.

One technique suggested by Zheng [26] is to rely on a judge who can be totally trusted. In this case, a receiver simply gives his private key to the judge. The judge can decrypt the signcryptext and verify the validity of the message by

M.L. Gavrilova et al. (Eds.): Trans. on Comput. Sci. X, LNCS 6340, pp. 202–230, 2010.

making use of the receiver's private key. A second technique suggested by Zheng deals with a situation where the judge is not fully trusted. With the second method, the receiver engages an interactive zero-knowledge proof protocol with the judge. At the end of the execution of the protocol, the judge can make a decision as to whether the signcrytext is indeed from the sender. Clearly, the second method suggested by Zheng is not quite efficient in practice.

Bao and Deng [3] proposed a modified signcryption scheme, with the aim of offering non-repudiation in a non-interactive way. With their method, when there is a dispute on a message M and a signcryptext σ between a receiver R and a sender S, the receiver R computes some non-repudiation evidence d, and forwards (M, σ, d) together with the public keys (PK_S, PK_R) to a not necessarily trusted judge. The judge can verify whether S has signcrypted M into σ for the receiver R. However, it was later pointed out in [15] and [20] that the non-repudiation evidence d would destroy the confidentiality of the message.

To address problems with Bao and Deng's scheme, Malone-Lee [15] proposed a new security model specifically for signcryption with non-interactive non-repudiation (NINR). This model ensures that the exposure of evidence d does not ruin the security of both confidentiality and unforgeability.

Our model. Now a natural question to ask is whether a signcryption scheme in Malone-Lee's model can be assured to be provably secure. We will show that the answer to the question is unfortunately negative. The main reason for this is that Malone-Lee's model addresses only two basic security requirements, namely confidentiality and unforgeability, which turns out to be inadequate to properly define the model of signcryption with NINR. We now analyze it in greater detail.

First, it is required that a given piece of evidence d can help the judge make a correct decision, especially when a given M is not the unsigncryption result of a given σ. It turns out that Malone-Lee's model does not provide this guarantee. As an example we examine a signcryption scheme proposed by Chow et al [9]. Interestingly, although that scheme can be proved to be secure in Malone-Lee's model, a piece of not well-formed evidence d can lead a judge to incorrectly regard a wrong message M' as being the unsigncryption of a signcryptext σ. To rectify the above problem, we consider a new security requirement for signcryption with NINR, namely soundness of non-repudiation. Fulfilling this requirement will guarantee that a judge can always make a right decision.

Second, we observe that in some previous schemes, such as those proposed in [17] [18] [14] [24], non-repudiation evidence d can be generated not only by the receiver but also by the sender. That is to say, even if a judge is sure that a signcryptext σ is in fact signcrypted from some message M, he still can not be sure who generated this non-repudiation evidence d. This ambiguity can cause troubles in many practical uses. As an example, consider a patient who receives a signcrypted medical report from his doctor. If the patient is malicious, he can generate a piece of well-formed evidence d, and then deliberately expose the contents of the report to a third party. Latter, he claims that it is the doctor who exposes his report to the third party, and asks for compensation. A judge in this case will not be able to decide who, the patient or the doctor, is on the wrong side. Problems of similar nature may occur in many other situations, e.g. military scenarios, on-line business transactions etc. In order to clarify the above ambiguity, we consider an additional new security requirement, namely unforgeability of non-repudiation evidence, which guarantees that only the receiver can generate valid non-repudiation evidence d.

Our scheme. Since the concept of signcryption introduced by Zheng [26], a number of signcryption schemes with the property of non-interactive non-repudiation [15] [17] [18] [9] etc. have been designed and proved secure in the random oracle model [6] which assumes that certain functions, such as one-way hash functions, output truly random values. While the random oracle model has been a very useful tool in the field of provable security, no real hash function behaves like a random function. As a result, designing a signcryption scheme with NINR that does not rely on a random oracle for its security is both attractive in scholarly research and useful in practice. In the past few years, a number of research papers e.g.[22] [23] [14] have been published on the topic of signcryption without random oracles. However, according to the best of our knowledge, none of these schemes is provably secure for non-interactive non-repudiation.

In this paper, we design a signcryption scheme with NINR that can be proved secure without random oracles. Our signcryption scheme is based on the signature scheme of Boneh, Shen and Waters [8], and is very compact when compared with the underling signature scheme. We will provide a specific efficiency comparison in Section 5.1.

Organization. The rest of the paper is organized as follows: We introduce some preliminary facts in Section 2. In Section 3 we describe our model for signcryption with NINR by defining the syntax, analyzing Malone-Lee's model, defining four security requirements, together with in depth discussions on core aspects of the model. In Section 4, we construct a concrete signcryption scheme with NINR, and prove that it is secure without random oracles. In Section 5, we discuss how to improve the efficiency of the scheme together with its practical applications. Finally, we draw some conclusions in Section 6. As a side contribution, we note that our contruction can be turned into an even more efficient scheme when random oracles are allowed. We discuss this in the appendix.

2   Preliminaries

2.1   Bilinear Maps

Throughout this paper we use the following standard notations on bilinear maps.

Let $\mathbb{G}$ and $\mathbb{G}_T$ be two (multiplicative) cyclic groups of prime order p. Let g be a generator of $\mathbb{G}$. A symmetric bilinear map is a map $e : \mathbb{G} \times \mathbb{G} \to \mathbb{G}_T$ with the following properties:

1. Bilinear: for all $u, v \in \mathbb{G}$ and $a, b \in \mathbb{Z}_p$, we have $e(u^a, v^b) = e(u, v)^{ab}$.
2. Non-degenerate: all $u, v \in \mathbb{G}$ satisfy $e(u, v) \neq 1$.

2.2   Collision Resistant Hash Functions

Throughout this paper we use ϵ with an appropriate subscript to indicate a negligible function that vanishes at least as fast as the inverse of a polynomial in an appropriate security parameter.

A hash function H is said to be collision resistant if it is infeasible for an adversary to find two different inputs m_0 and m_1 such that $H(m_0) = H(m_1)$. A more formal definition follows.

Definition 1. *A hash function H is (t, ϵ_H)-collision-resistant if for any adversary $\mathcal{A}$ running in time t, it has possibility at most ϵ_H in finding two different inputs m_0 and m_1 such that $H(m_0) = H(m_1)$.*

We require two collision resistent functions with different ranges for their outputs. Specifically, let $\mathbb{G}$ and $\mathbb{G}_T$ be two groups of prime order p. The first collision resistent function H_1 maps input from $\mathbb{G}_T \times \mathbb{G} \times \mathbb{G}$ to an element in Z_p, and the second resistent function H_2 maps input from $\mathbb{G}$ to a string in $\{0,1\}^n$.

2.3   Discrete Logarithm Assumption

The discrete logarithm problem applies to mathematical structures called groups. Let $\mathbb{G}$ be a group of prime order p, and g be a generator for $\mathbb{G}$. We have the following definition for the discrete logarithm (D-Log) assumption.

Definition 2. *The (t, ϵ_{DLog}) D-Log assumption holds in $\mathbb{G}$, if for any adversary $\mathcal{A}$, given a random element $g_3 \in \mathbb{G}$, running in time t, $\mathcal{A}$ has possibility at most ϵ_{DLog} in finding an integer $x \in Z_p$ such that $g^x = g_3$.*

2.4   Decisional Bilinear Diffie-Hellman (DBDH) Assumption

Let $\mathbb{G}$, $\mathbb{G}_T$ be groups of a same prime order p, g be a generator of $\mathbb{G}$, and $e : \mathbb{G} \times \mathbb{G} \to \mathbb{G}_T$ be a bilinear map. Choose a, b, c, k from Z_p at random, and let

$$BDH = \{g, g^a, g^b, g^c, T \leftarrow e(g,g)^{abc}\},$$
$$Random = \{g, g^a, g^b, g^c, T \leftarrow e(g,g)^k\}.$$

The DBDH assumption claims that BDH and $Random$ are indistinguishable. For any adversary $\mathcal{A}$, consider two experiments. $\mathcal{A}$ is given BDH in experiment 0, and is given $Random$ in experiment 1. $\mathcal{A}$'s advantage for solving the DBDH assumption is

$$\epsilon_{dbdh} = |Pr[\mathcal{A} = 1 \ in \ experiment \ 0] - Pr[\mathcal{A} = 1 \ in \ experiment \ 1]|.$$

Definition 3. *The (t, ϵ_{dbdh})-DBDH assumption holds, if any adversary $\mathcal{A}$ running in time t has advantage at most ϵ_{dbdh} in solving the DBDH assumption.*

3   The Proposed Model of Signcryption with NINR

3.1   Syntax of Signcryption with NINR

A signcryption scheme with NINR is composed of six algorithms. The first four algorithms constitute a signcryption scheme, and the last two algorithms fulfill the requirements of NINR.

- SetupPub(1^η), run by a trusted party: Given a security parameter 1^η, a trusted party generates and outputs the system's public parameter Pub.
- KeyGen(Pub, ID_P), run by every user: User P takes the public parameter Pub as input, outputs a pair of private/public keys (SK_P, PK_P).
- Signcryption(SK_S, PK_R, M), run by a sender: To communicate a message $M \in \mathcal{M}$ ($\mathcal{M}$ is the message space) from a sender S to a receiver R, the algorithm produces a signcryptext σ on M by using S's private key SK_S and R's public key PK_R. The signcryptext σ is sent to R.
- Unsigncryption(SK_R, PK_S, σ), run by a receiver: Upon receiving a signcryptext σ from S, the algorithm first checks whether σ is valid. It returns a plaintext M if σ is valid, or a special symbol $\perp$ otherwise.
- NR-Evidence-Gen(SK_R, PK_S, σ), run by a receiver: If σ is a valid signcryptext, the algorithm computes and returns a piece of non-repudiation evidence d. Otherwise, the algorithm returns a symbol $\perp$.
- JG-Verification (σ, M, d, PK_S, PK_R), run by a judge: Upon receiving a signcryptext/message pair (σ, M), a piece of non-repudiation evidence d, a sender S' public key PK, and a receiver R's public key PK_R, the algorithm returns a special symbol $\top$ if it is S who has signcrypted the message M into σ for R, or a symbol $\perp$ otherwise.

For consistency, we require that for all $\sigma = Signcryption(SK_S, PK_R, M)$, we should have $M = Unsigncryption(SK_R, PK_S, \sigma)$.

For completeness, we require that for all signcryptext σ and all possible $d = NR\text{-}Evidence\text{-}Gen(SK_R, PK_S, \sigma)$, if $M = Unsigncryption(SK_R, PK_S, \sigma)$, then we should have $\top \leftarrow JG\text{-}Verification(\sigma, d, M, PK_S, PK_R)$.

Remark 1. *The public parameter Pub is not explicitly taken as input to the last four algorithms, since we assume that all the users in the system know Pub.*

3.2   Analysis of Malone-Lee's Model

We first review security models for regular signcryption. Baek *et al.* [8] proposed a formal security model for signcryption in 2001. Independently of this, An *et al.* [1] also came up with similar security models for signcryption. Both models consider two security definitions, namely confidentiality and unforgeability. And in the models of both papers, two factors are considered:

1. If there are only two users (a sender and a receiver) in the network, then it is called a two-user setting; otherwise if there are many (more than two) users in the network, then it is called a multi-user setting.

2. If the adversary is a sender (in the attack game of unforgeability) or a receiver (in the attack game of confidentiality) in the communication for challenge, then we call it an inside attacker setting. Otherwise, we call it an outside attacker setting.

Melone-Lee's model [15] is different from the widely used definitions proposed by Baek *et al.* [8] and An *et al.*[1] in the following two aspects:

1. In Molone-Lee's model, an adversary $\mathcal{A}$ is able to get the value of evidence d by asking for non-repudiation oracles. For each non-repudiation oracle, $\mathcal{A}$ makes queries with a signcryptext σ together with a sender and a receiver's public keys, and receives as a return from the oracle a piece of corresponding evidence d.

2. Malone-Lee's model is defined in a multi-user attacker setting, but the basic underling security definitions are different from the definitions proposed by Baek *et al.* [8] and An *et al.*[1]. For example, in the attack game (for either confidentiality or unforgeability) with a multi-user inside attacker setting in [1] and [8], the adversary is able to generate public keys for all users in the system except the one who is an attack target. In comparison, with the attack game (e.g. confidentiality) of Malone-Lee's model, the adversary is given public keys for all users in the system at the beginning. Afterwards, he chooses one of them as his attack target. An advantage of Malone-Lee's model is that the user (whom the adversary will attack against) can be arbitrarily chosen by the attacker. But the total number of all users in the system needs to be pre-decided, and the public keys of all users should be pre-computed by the simulator. When there are a large number of users in the system (which happens frequently in practise), security bounds provided by the proof become less tight.

3.3   Security Definitions in Our Model

In our model, we will consider four security requirements, namely confidentiality, unforgeability, soundness of non-repudiation, and unforgeability of non-repudiation evidence. If a signcryption scheme with NINR can be proved secure under the first three definitions, we say that it is *SCNINR secure*. If a signcryption scheme with NINR is SCNINR secure and can also be proved secure under the definition of unforgeability of non-repudiation evidence, we say that it is *strong SCNINR secure*.

Our definitions do not follow Malone-Lee's model directly. Instead we mainly refer to the basic definitions of [8] and [1] in a multi-user inside attacker setting, together with Malone-Lee's idea [15] of adding non-repudiation oracles in the attack game.

Confidentiality. The attack game for indistinguishability of signcryption under chosen ciphertext attack (IND-SCNINR-CCA) contains five steps as follows:

– *Setup system:* An adversary $\mathcal{A}$ is given the system's public parameter $Pub \leftarrow SetupPub(1^\eta)$, and a challenge user B's public key $PK_B \leftarrow KeyGen(Pub, ID_B)$.

- *Oracles before challenge:* $\mathcal{A}$ is able to ask for a number of signcryption, unsigncryption and non-repudiation oracle queries associated with the challenge user B.
  - For each signcryption oracle query, $\mathcal{A}$ generates a receiver's public key PK_R, a message $M \in \mathcal{M}$, and outputs (PK_S, PK_R, M) with $PK_S = PK_B$. This oracle returns to $\mathcal{A}$ with $\sigma \leftarrow Signcryption(SK_B, PK_R, M)$.
  - For each unsigncryption oracle query, $\mathcal{A}$ generates a sender's public key PK_S and a signcryptext σ, outputs (PK_S, PK_R, σ) with $PK_R = PK_B$. This oracle returns to $\mathcal{A}$ with the result of $Unsigncryption(PK_S, SK_B, \sigma)$.
  - For each non-repudiation oracle query, $\mathcal{A}$ generates a sender's public key PK_S, a signcryptext σ, and outputs (PK_S, PK_R, σ) with $PK_R = PK_B$. This oracle returns to $\mathcal{A}$ with the result of $NR\text{-}Evidence\text{-}Gen(PK_S, SK_B, \sigma)$.
- *Challenge:* $\mathcal{A}$ generates a sender's public key PK_{S^*}, and produces two equal length messages (M_0, M_1) in $\mathcal{M}$. $\mathcal{A}$ outputs $(PK_{S^*}, PK_{R^*}, M_0, M_1)$ with $PK_{R^*} = PK_B$, then is returned with $\sigma^* \leftarrow Signcryption(SK_{S^*}, PK_B, M_\gamma)$, where γ is randomly chosen from $\{0, 1\}$.
- *Oracles after challenge:* This step is the same as Oracles before challenge step, except that $\mathcal{A}$ is not allowed to ask for an unsigncrypiton oracle query or a non-repudiation oracle query on σ^* with sender/receiver public key $(PK_{S^*}, PK_{R^*} = PK_B)$.
- *Guess:* $\mathcal{A}$ outputs a guess bit γ' for γ.

If $\gamma' = \gamma$, then $\mathcal{A}$ wins the above attack game. We define the advantage for $\mathcal{A}$ to win this game is $\epsilon = |Pr[\gamma' = \gamma] - 1/2|$.

Definition 4. *The signcryption scheme with NINR is $(t, q_s, q_u, q_n, \epsilon)$ IND-SCNINR-CCA secure, if for running in time t, any adversary $\mathcal{A}$ who has asked for signcryption oracle queries q_s times, unsigncryption oracle queries q_u times and non-repudiation oracle queries q_n times, has advantage at most ϵ in winning the IND-SCNINR-CCA game.*

Unforgeability. The attack game for strong existential unforgeability of signcryption with NINR under chosen message attack (SEU-SCNINR-CMA) contains three steps as follows:

- *Setup system:* The same as the Setup system step in the IND-SCNINR-CCA game.
- *Oracles:* The same as the Oracles before the challenge step in the IND-SCNINR-CCA game.
- *Forge:* $\mathcal{A}$ generates a receiver's public key PK_{R^*}, and outputs a forged signcryptext σ^* on (PK_{S^*}, PK_{R^*}) with $PK_{S^*} = PK_B$.

If the following two conditions are both satisfied, then we say that $\mathcal{A}$ wins the SEU-SCNINR-CMA game:

1. $Unsigncryption(PK_B, SK_{R^*}, \sigma^*) \neq \bot$;

2. σ^* is not a result of any the signcryption oracle queries with sender/receiver public key $(PK_{S^*} = PK_B, PK_{R^*})$.

Definition 5. *The signcryption scheme with NINR is $(t, q_s, q_u, q_n, \epsilon)$ SEU-SCNINR-CMA secure, if for running in time t, any adversary $\mathcal{A}$, who has asked for signcryption oracle queries q_s times, unsigncryption oracle queries q_u times and non-repudiation oracle queries q_n times, has possibility at most ϵ in winning the SEU-SCNINR-CMA game.*

Soundness of Non-repudiation. As we have described in the introduction, soundness of non-repudiation should ensure a judge always make a right decision. That is, if a given M is not the unsigncryption result of a given σ, the judge should not let it pass the verification. We first give an intuition for the attack game:

To achieve this goal, our attack game described below for the soundness of non-repudiation assumes a very strong adversary $\mathcal{A}$, who can generate all users' public/private keys, including the challenge user B. Then in the challenge, $\mathcal{A}$ asks for one signcryption oracle. He outputs (M, PK_S), the signcryption oracle returns a signcryptext $\sigma = Signcryption(SK_S, PK_R = PK_B, M)$. Finally, if $\mathcal{A}$ outputs another message $M'(M' \neq M)$, and a piece of evidence d' such that $JG\text{-}Verification(\sigma, M', d', PK_S, PK_B) = \top$, then $\mathcal{A}$ wins.

In this attack game, we do not have oracle stages(as in pervious attack games), since $\mathcal{A}$ is stronger than the attackers (in confidentiality and unforgeability). $\mathcal{A}$ knows all users' public/private keys, therefore, he can compute all the algorithms in the scheme himself. Finally, if $\mathcal{A}$ wins, it implies the judge makes a wrong decision.

This definition is similar to the definition of proof soundness in the model of public-key encryption with non-interactive opening by Damgard *et al.* [11] and Galindo *et al.* [12].

The game for the soundness of non-repudiation of signcryption with NINR consists of three steps as follows:

- *Setup system:* First, the adversary $\mathcal{A}$ is given the system's public parameter Pub. Then he generates a challenge user B's public/private key pair (PK_B, SK_B), and forwards (PK_B, SK_B) to the system.
- *Challenge:* In this stage, $\mathcal{A}$ has access to a signcryption oracle query once. $\mathcal{A}$ generates a sender's public key PK_S and a message $M \in \mathcal{M}$, then outputs (PK_S, PK_R, M) with $PK_R = PK_B$ to the signcryption oracle. Finally, $\mathcal{A}$ is returned with $\sigma \leftarrow Signcryption(SK_S, PK_B, M)$.
- *Output:* $\mathcal{A}$ outputs a message M' together with some non-repudiation evidence d'.

If $JG\text{-}Verification(\sigma, M', d', PK_S, PK_B) = \top$ and $M' \neq M$, then $\mathcal{A}$ wins this game.

Definition 6. *A SCNINR scheme satisfies (t, ϵ) computational the soundness of non-repudiation, if any adversary running in time t has probability at most ϵ in winning the above game where ϵ is negligible. If $\epsilon = 0$, the SCNINR scheme satisfies the perfect soundness of non-repudiation.*

Unforgeability of Non-repudiation Evidence. The attack game is similar to the attack game of unforgeability in most stages, but is different in the forge stage. The adversary's object here is to forge a piece of valid non-repudiation evidence on a new signcryptext.

The game for existential unforgeability of non-repudiation evidence in signcryption with NINR under chosen message attack (EUF-NR-evidence-SCNINR-CMA) contains three steps as follows:

- *Setup system:* The same as the Setup system step in SEU-SCNINR-CMA game.
- *Oracles:* The same as the Oracles step in the SEU-SCNINR-CMA game.
- *Forge:* $\mathcal{A}$ generates the sender's public key PK_{S^*}, outputs a message M^*, a piece of non-repudiation evidence d^*, and a signcryptext σ^*.

$\mathcal{A}$ wins the game if $JG\text{-}Verification(\sigma^*, d^*, M^*, PK_{S^*}, PK_{R^*}) = \top$ with $PK_{R^*} = PK_B$ and $\mathcal{A}$ has never asked for a non-repudiation oracle query or an unsigncryption oracle query on σ^* with sender/receiver public key (PK_{S^*}, PK_B).

Definition 7. *The signcryption scheme with NINR is $(t, q_s, q_u, q_n, \epsilon)$ EUF-NR-evidence-SCNINR-CMA secure if for running in time t, $\mathcal{A}$ has asked for q_s signcryption oracle queries, q_u unsigncryption oracle queries, q_n non-repudiation oracle queries and has possibility at most ϵ in winning this game.*

3.4   Adapt Our Model to Existing Schemes

When we adapt our model to existing schemes, we find out that some schemes e.g. Malone-Lee's scheme in [15] and the second scheme of Chow *et al.* in [9] achieve the first three security requirements[1], but no schemes can fulfill the security requirement of unforgeability of non-repudiation evidence. The reason why none of the existing schemes (including [15] and [9]) meets the last security requirement is that, traditionally, the evidence d is secret information (normally the Diffie-Hellman key) embedded by the sender to prevent other users except for the receiver from verifying the regular signature of M. In this method, the sender is the one who directly generates d, and the receiver can regenerate the value of d indirectly. In other words, both the sender and the receiver hold d. In signcryption, this results in an attack on the security requirement of unforgeability of non-repudiation evidence (as the sender can be a successful forger). For example, the evidence in Malone-Lee's scheme [15] is an element k_2 which can be generated by the receiver as well as the sender.

Our construction, which will be described in detail in the next section, is different from the traditional idea. The generation of evidence d makes use of the identity-based technique [7]. If one takes the receiver's private key as a master key of the public key generator (PKG), then d can be regarded as a private key

---

[1] Since the proofs are long and can be readily derived from existing proofs of those schemes, we omit them from this paper.

of identity ID whose value is determined by the current signcryptext σ. The judge decrypts σ by making use of d, and then checks whether it matches the value of the given message M. Informally, since d can only be used to decrypt σ rather than other signcryptexts, the exposure of d does not pose risks to confidentiality. Furthermore only the receiver, who is the only one holding the master key, can generate d. Therefore, the unforgeability of non-repudiation evidence is also ensured.

4   The Proposed Signcryption Scheme with NINR

4.1   Construction

Our signcryption scheme with NINR follows the six algorithm approach we defined in Section 3.1. We first describe the SetupPub algorithm, and then list other algorithms in Table 1 and Table 2.

- ***SetupPub***(1^η) by Trusted Party:
  On input a security parameter 1^η, a trusted party runs the following steps:

  1. Set up $\{\mathbb{G}, \mathbb{G}_T, e, g\}$, where $\mathbb{G}$ and $\mathbb{G}_T$ are groups of prime order p, $g \in \mathbb{G}$ is a generator, and $e : \mathbb{G} \times \mathbb{G} \to \mathbb{G}_T$ is a bilinear map.
  2. Set up $\{g_1, g_2, g_3, u_0, U\}$: Choose random elements g_1, g_2, g_3, u_0 from $\mathbb{G}$, and a random n-length vector $U = (u_1, ..., u_n) \in \mathbb{G}^n$. For each i $(1 \le i \le n)$, u_i is a random element in $\mathbb{G}$.
  3. Set up two collision-resistant hash functions H_1 and H_2, where $H_1 : \mathbb{G}_T \times \mathbb{G} \times \mathbb{G} \to \mathbb{Z}_p$ and $H_2 : \mathbb{G} \to \{0,1\}^n$.

  The system's public parameter is: $Pub = \{\mathbb{G}, \mathbb{G}_T, e, g, g_1, g_2, g_3, u_0, U, H_1, H_2\}$.

For consistency, one can verify that

$$\sigma_0/e(\sigma_1, g_1^{\alpha_R}) = M \cdot e(g_1, g_R)^t/e(g^t, g_1^{\alpha_R}) = M.$$

For completeness, we have

$$
\begin{aligned}
\frac{\sigma_0 \cdot e(\sigma_2, d_2)}{e(\sigma_1, d_1) \cdot e(d_3, g_S)} &= \frac{M \cdot e(g_1, g_R)^t \cdot e(g_2^{\alpha_S}(u_0 \prod_{i=1}^n u_i^{c_i})^t, g^r)}{e(g^t, g_1^{\alpha_R} \cdot (u_0 \prod_{i=1}^n u_i^{c_i})^r) \cdot e(g_2^r, g_S)} \\
&= \frac{M \cdot e(g_1, g_R)^t \cdot e(g_2^{\alpha_S}, g^r) \cdot e(u_0 \prod_{i=1}^n u_i^{c_i}, g)^{t \cdot r}}{e(g_1, g_R)^t \cdot e(g, u_0 \prod_{i=1}^n u_i^{c_i})^{t \cdot r} \cdot e(g_2^r, g_S)} \\
&= M.
\end{aligned}
$$

4.2   Security Proofs

Now we will prove that the above signcryption scheme with NINR is strong SCNINR secure.

Table 1. KeyGen& Signcryption & Unsigncryption Algorithms

KeyGen(Pub, ID_P) by User P:
1. randomly chooses $\alpha_P \in \mathbb{Z}_p$,
2. compute $g_P \leftarrow g^{\alpha_P}$,
3. let the private key be $SK_P \leftarrow \{\alpha_P\}$,
4. let the public key be $PK_P \leftarrow \{g_P\}$.

Signcryption(SK_S, PK_R, M) by Sender S:
To signcrypt $M \in \mathbb{G}_T$ to be communicated to receiver R, sender S runs:
1. choose random elements $t, s \in \mathbb{Z}_p$,
2. compute $\sigma_0 \leftarrow M \cdot e(g_1, g_R)^t$,
3. compute $\sigma_1 \leftarrow g^t$,
4. compute $\theta \leftarrow H_1(\sigma_0, \sigma_1, g_S)$,
5. compute $z \leftarrow g^\theta g_3^{\ s}$,
6. compute $C \leftarrow H_2(z)$, write as $(c_1...c_n) \in \{0, 1\}^n$,
7. compute $\sigma_2 \leftarrow g_2^{\alpha_S} (u_0 \prod_{i=1}^{n} u_i^{c_i})^t$,
8. set $\sigma_3 \leftarrow s$,
9. let the signcryptext be $\sigma \leftarrow (\sigma_0, \sigma_1, \sigma_2, \sigma_3)$.

Unsigncryption(SK_R, PK_S, σ) by Receiver R:
To unsigncrypt σ from sender S, receiver R runs:
1. compute $\theta \leftarrow H_1(\sigma_0, \sigma_1, g_S)$,
2. compute $z \leftarrow g^\theta g_3^{\sigma_3}$,
3. compute $C \leftarrow H_2(z)$, and write it as $(c_1...c_n) \in \{0, 1\}^n$,
4. if $e(\sigma_2, g) \neq e(g_2, g_S) \cdot e(\sigma_1, u_0 \prod_{i=1}^{n} u_i^{c_i})$, return $\perp$.
5. otherwise compute and return $M \leftarrow \sigma_0 / e(\sigma_1, g_1^{\alpha_R})$.

Proof of Confidentiality

Theorem 1. *The signcryption scheme is $(t, q_s, q_u, q_n, \epsilon_{H_1} + \epsilon_{H_2} + \epsilon_{Dlog} + (q_u + q_n)/p + \epsilon_{dbdh})$ IND-SCNINR-CCA secure, under the (t, ϵ_{dbdh}) DBDH assumption, the (t, ϵ_{Dlog}) Discrete Logarithm assumption in $\mathbb{G}$, and the assumption that the hash functions H_1 and H_2 are (t, ϵ_{H_1}) and (t, ϵ_{H_2}) collision resistent respectively.*

Proof of Theorem 1: We are going to use the game technique [19] to prove this theorem. Throughout this proof, we will list six games, from Game 0 to Game 5. All the games are executed between an adversary and a simulator. Game 0 is the IND-SCNINR-CCA game defined above, and other games will be quite similar to Game 0 in their overall structure, and will only differ from Game 0 in terms of how the simulator works. The key point for the proof is that we want to make sure that for each i $(1 \leq i \leq 5)$, either $Pr[\gamma = \gamma'$ in game $i] = Pr[\gamma = \gamma'$ in game $i-1]$ or $|Pr[\gamma = \gamma'$ in game $i] - Pr[\gamma = \gamma'$ in game $i - 1]| \leq Pr[F_i]$ where $Pr[F_i]$ is a negligible value.

In order to analyze the value of $|Pr[\gamma = \gamma'$ in game $i] - Pr[\gamma = \gamma'$ in game $i - 1]|$, we need the following lemma whose proof can be found in [19]:

Table 2. NR-Evidence-Gen & JG-Verification Algorithms

NR-Evidence-Gen(SK_R, PK_S, σ) by Receiver R:
To compute non-repudiation evidence d, receiver R runs:
1. steps 1-4 of Unsigncryption in Table 1,
2. choose a random $r \in \mathbb{Z}_p$,
3. compute $d_1 \leftarrow g_1^{\alpha_R}(u_0 \prod_{i=1}^{n} u_i^{c_i})^r$,
4. compute $d_2 \leftarrow g^r$,
5. compute $d_3 \leftarrow g_2^r$,
6. return $d \leftarrow (d_1, d_2, d_3)$.

JG-Verification$(\sigma, M, d, PK_S, PK_R)$ by Judge:
To verify whether $M = Unsigncryption(SK_R, PK_S, \sigma)$, the judge runs:
1. steps 1-4 of Unsigncryption in Table 1,
2. if $e(d_2, g_2) \neq e(g, d_3)$, return $\perp$,
3. else if $e(d_1, g) \neq e(g_1, g_R) \cdot e(u_0 \prod_{i=1}^{n} u_i^{c_i}, d_2)$, return $\perp$,
4. else if $M \neq \frac{\sigma_0 \cdot e(\sigma_2, d_2)}{e(\sigma_1, d_1) \cdot e(d_3, g_S)}$, return $\perp$,
5. otherwise return $\top$.

Lemma 1. *Let S_1, S_2 and F be events defined on some probability spaces. Suppose that the event $S_1 \wedge \neg F$ occurs if and only if $S_2 \wedge \neg F$ occurs. Then*

$$| Pr[S_1] - Pr[S_2] | \leq Pr[F].$$

We are now ready to describe the six games.

- **Game 0:** This game is the usual game used to define IND-SCNINR-CCA security. Therefore, the advantage for adversary $\mathcal{A}$ in winning the IND-SCNINR-CCA game is

$$\epsilon = |Pr[\gamma = \gamma' \text{ in game } 0] - 1/2|. \tag{1}$$

- **Game 1:** Game 1 is the same as Game 0, except that the simulator keeps a list of data $(\sigma_0, \sigma_1, \sigma_3, \theta, z, C, g_S, g_R)$ for all unsigncryption and non-repudiation oracles, and he also keeps the data of $(\sigma_0^*, \sigma_1^*, \sigma_3^*, \theta^*, z^*, C^*, y_{S^*}, y_{R^*})$ produced in the challenge oracle.

  At the end of the step "oracles after challenge", the simulator checks the whole list to find out whether the following three cases happen:

  - Case (1) $(\sigma_0, \sigma_1, g_S) \neq (\sigma_0^*, \sigma_1^*, g_{S^*})$, $\theta = \theta^*$;
  - Case (2) $\theta \neq \theta^*$, $z = z^*$;
  - Case (3) $z \neq z^*$, $C = C^*$.

If any one of the three cases happens, it aborts.

Analysis: For Case (1) and Case (3), we can find a collision in H_1 and H_2 respectively. For Case (2), we can compute $\log g_3 \leftarrow \frac{\theta - \theta^*}{\sigma_3^* - \sigma_3}$. According to the previous security definition of H_1, H_2 and D-Log assumption, the possibility for Case (1) to be true is ϵ_{H_1}, Case (2) is ϵ_{Dlog}, and Case (3) is ϵ_{H_2}. Then,

$$Pr[new\ abort\ in\ game\ 1] = \epsilon_{H_1} + \epsilon_{H_2} + \epsilon_{Dlog}. \qquad (2)$$

Without this new abort, simulators in Game 0 and Game 1 run in the same manner. Therefore, according to Lemma 1, we have

$$|Pr[\gamma = \gamma'\ in\ game\ 1] - Pr[\gamma = \gamma'\ in\ game\ 0]| \leq Pr[new\ abort\ in\ game\ 1]. (3)$$

Now in Game 1, if the simulator does not abort, then for all unsigncryption and non-repudiation oracles, $C \neq C^*$. This conclusion will be useful for analysis in the latter games. We analyze it from the following four cases:

1. If $(\sigma_0, \sigma_1, y_S) \neq (\sigma_0^*, \sigma_1^*, y_{S^*})$, and since all the above three cases for abort do not happen, then we get $C \neq C^*$.
2. Else if $(\sigma_0, \sigma_1, y_S) = (\sigma_0^*, \sigma_1^* \cdot y_{S^*})$ and $\sigma_3 \neq \sigma_3^*$, then $z \neq z^*$. Since case (3) does not happen, we get $C \neq C^*$.
3. Else if $(\sigma_0, \sigma_1, \sigma_3) = (\sigma_0^*, \sigma_1^*, \sigma_3^*)$, and $g_S = g_{S^*}$, according to the verification equation $e(\sigma_2, g) = e(g_2, g_S) \cdot e(\sigma_1, u_0 \prod_{i=1}^n u_i^{c_i})$, we get that $\sigma_2 = \sigma_2^*$ when verification passed. Therefore, in this case $\sigma = \sigma^*$, which is not allowed according to the attack game.
4. Else if $(\sigma_0, \sigma_1, \sigma_3) = (\sigma_0^*, \sigma_1^*, \sigma_3^*)$, and $g_S \neq g_{S^*}$, then $\theta \neq \theta^*$. Case (2) and case (3) do not happen to cause an abort, therefore, $C^* \neq C$.

- **Game 2:** Game 2 is mostly the same as Game 1, with the following three changes:
  1. In setup system step, generate $\{g_2, g_3, u_0, U\}$ as follows:
     - Choose random elements $x, y \in \mathbb{Z}_p$, and compute $g_2 \leftarrow g^x$, $g_3 \leftarrow g^y$.
     - To generate U, choose random elements $k_1, ..., k_n \in \mathbb{Z}_p$, and from $i = 1$ to n compute $u_i \leftarrow g_1^{k_i}$.
     - To generate u_0, choose random elements $\alpha, \lambda \in \mathbb{Z}_p$, compute $z^* \leftarrow g^\alpha$, $C^* \leftarrow H_2(z^*)$, write C^* as $(c_1^*, ..., c_n^*) \in \{0,1\}^n$. Compute $\tau^* \leftarrow \sum_{i=1}^n k_i c_i^*$, then $u_0 \leftarrow g_1^{-\tau^*} g^\lambda$.
  2. In the challenge step, the simulator generates σ_0^*, σ_1^* according to the signcryption algorithm, but computes σ_2^*, σ_3^* as follows:

$$\sigma_2^* \leftarrow g_{S^*}^x \cdot \sigma_1^{*\lambda}, \quad \sigma_3^* \leftarrow \frac{\alpha - H_1(\sigma_0^*, \sigma_1^*, g_{S^*})}{y}.$$

  3. For all unsigncryption and non-repudiation oracles, if $\sum_{i=1}^n k_i c_i = \tau^*$, then the simulator aborts.

  Analysis: We now analyze the above three changes one by one.
  1. For changes in 1, it is easy to see that $U \in \mathbb{G}^n$, $u_0 \in \mathbb{G}$, $g_2 \in \mathbb{G}$ and $g_3 \in \mathbb{G}$ are still random vector and elements. Therefore, these changes are only notational changes.

2. For changes in 2, if we take $s \leftarrow \frac{\alpha - H_1(\sigma_0^*, \sigma_1^*, g_{S^*})}{y}$, which is also a random element in $\mathbb{Z}_p$, then it is easy to verify that $\sigma_2^* = g_2^{\alpha s^*}(u_0 \prod_{i=1}^n u_i^{c_i^*})^t, \sigma_3^* = s$, which is a valid setting.

3. For changes in 3, recall the conclusion in Game 1 that, if not abort, for all unsigncryption and non-repudiation $C \neq C^*$. And $(k_1, ..., k_n) \in \mathbb{Z}_p^n$ are independent elements chosen randomly by the simulator (independent of the adversary), and for the complexity of discrete logarithm assumption, the value of $(k_1, ..., k_n)$ are computationally hidden from the value of $(u_1, .., u_n)$. Therefore, the value of $(k_1, ..., k_n)$ and independent of the adversary's view. For each unsigncryption oracle and non-repudiation oracle, we have $Pr[\sum_{i=1}^n k_i c_i = \tau^*] = 1/p$.

Finally, we have

$$Pr[new \ abort \ in \ game \ 2] = (q_u + q_n)/p. \tag{4}$$

Without this new abort, the simulator provides the same environment as in Game 1. According to Lemma 1, we have

$$|Pr[\gamma = \gamma' \ in \ game \ 2] - Pr[\gamma = \gamma' \ in \ game \ 1]| \leq Pr[new \ abort \ in \ game \ 2]. \tag{5}$$

Now in Game 2, if not abort, then for all unsigncryption and non-repudiation oracles, $\sum_{i=1}^n k_i c_i \neq \tau^*$.

- **Game 3:** Game 3 is similar to Game 2, except that in both oracles before challenge step and oracles after challenge step, the simulator computes answers for oracles as follows:

  - For each signcryption oracle: Compute $g_2^{\alpha_B} \leftarrow g_B^x$, and signcrypt the message according to the Signcryption algorithm.
  - For each non-repudiation oracle: First, run steps 1-4 in unsigncryption algorithm. If $\sum_{i=1}^n k_i c_i = \tau^*$, then the simulator aborts, otherwise it computes $d \leftarrow (d_1, d_2, d_3)$ as follows:

$$(d_1 \leftarrow g_B^{\frac{-\lambda}{\sum_{i=1}^n k_i c_i - \tau^*}}, d_2 \leftarrow g_B^{\frac{-1}{\sum_{i=1}^n k_i c_i - \tau^*}}, d_3 \leftarrow d_2^x).$$

  - For each unsigncryption oracle: The simulator first runs the non-repudiation oracle to get d, and then decrypt the signcryptext as follows:

$$M \leftarrow \frac{\sigma_0 \cdot e(\sigma_2, d_2)}{e(\sigma_1, d_1)e(d_3, g_S)}.$$

Analysis: It is easy to verify that

$$d_1 = g_1^{\alpha_B}(u_0 \prod u_i^{c_i})^r, d_2 = g^r, d_3 = g_2^r, \ where \ r \leftarrow \frac{-\alpha_B}{\sum_{i=1}^n k_i c_i - \tau^*}.$$

Recall that in Game 2, if $\sum_{i=1}^{n} k_i c_i = \tau^*$, then the simulator also aborts. Therefore, all the changes in the game are just notational. We have:

$$Pr[\gamma = \gamma' \ in \ game \ 3] = Pr[\gamma = \gamma' \ in \ game \ 2]. \tag{6}$$

Now in Game 3, if not abort, the simulator runs the attack game perfectly without the knowledge of α_B.

– **Game 4:** Game 4 is mostly the same as Game 3, except that the simulator tries to embed $BDH = \{g, g^a, g^b, g^c, T \leftarrow e(g,g)^{abc}\}$ (a, b, c are random elements in $\mathbb{Z}_p$) into the simulation by taking the following different steps:
  1. In Setup system step, the simulator sets $g_1 \leftarrow g^a$, $g_B \leftarrow g^b$.
  2. In Challenge step, the simulator computes σ_0^*, σ_1^* as follows:

$$\sigma_0^* \leftarrow e(g,g)^{abc} \cdot M_\gamma, \sigma_1^* \leftarrow g^c.$$

Analysis: If we take $t \leftarrow c$, then we have $\sigma_0^* = e(g_1, g_B)^t \cdot M, \sigma_1^* = g^t$. Since a, b, c are random elements in $\mathbb{Z}_p$, then $g_1 \in \mathbb{G}$, $g_B \in \mathbb{G}$ and $t \in \mathbb{Z}_p$ are also random elements. Therefore, the changes in Game 4 are only notational. Then, we have:

$$Pr[\gamma = \gamma' \ in \ game \ 4] = Pr[\gamma = \gamma' \ in \ game \ 3] \tag{7}$$

Now in Game 4, if not abort, the simulator runs the attack game perfectly with the values of $\{g^a, g^b, g^c, e(g,g)^{abc}\}$, but without the knowledge of (a, b, c).

– **Game 5:** Game 5 represents a slightly modified version of Game 4. Specifically, in this game instead of BDH, the simulator embeds $Random = \{g, g^a, g^b, g^c, T \leftarrow e(g,g)^k\}$ (k is randomly chosen from $\mathbb{Z}_p$) into the simulation by computing $\sigma_0^* \leftarrow e(g,g)^k \cdot M$ in the Challenge step.

Analysis: If the adversary distinguishes the difference between Game 4 and Game 5, then he also distinguishes the two cases of T. From the definition of DBDH assumption, we have:

$$|Pr[\gamma = \gamma' \ in \ game \ 5] - Pr[\gamma = \gamma' \ in \ game \ 4]| \leq \epsilon_{dbdh} \tag{8}$$

For the random and independent choice of T, the adversary's output γ' in this game is independent of the hidden bit γ. We have

$$Pr[\gamma = \gamma' \ in \ game \ 5|\overline{abort}] = 1/2 \tag{9}$$

Now in Game 5, the simulator aborts with the same probability as in Game 4. If not abort, it simulates Game 5 perfectly with the value of $\{g^a, g^b, b^c, e(g,g)^k\}$, but without the knowledge of (a, b, c, k). According to previous analysis, we can reduce that the simulator aborts in Game 5 with probability $\epsilon_{H_1} + \epsilon_{H_2} + \epsilon_{Dlog} + (q_u + q_n)/p$, which can be regard as a constant when the times of unsigncryption and non-repudiation oracles are fixed. Therefore, we have

$$Pr[\gamma = \gamma' \ in \ game \ 5] = Pr[\gamma = \gamma' \ in \ game \ 5|\overline{abort}] \qquad (10)$$

Combing all the above formulas in this proof, we get our conclusion that

$$|Pr[\gamma = \gamma' \ in \ game \ 0] - 1/2| \leq \epsilon_{H_1} + \epsilon_{H_2} + \epsilon_{Dlog} + (q_u + q_n)/p + \epsilon_{dbdh}. \qquad \square$$

Proof of Unforgeability

Theorem 2. *The signcryption scheme is $(t, q_s, q_u, q_n, \epsilon)$ SEU-SCNINR-CMA secure, assuming that the Waters signature scheme in [25] is $(t, q_s, \epsilon/4)$ existential unforgeable, H_1 is $(t, \epsilon/4)$ collision resistant, H_2 is $(t, \epsilon/4)$ collision resistant and the Discrete Logarithm assumption in $\mathbb{G}$ holds for $(t, \epsilon/4)$.*

Proof of Theorem 2: In the SEU-SCNINR-CMA game, the adversary $\mathcal{A}$'s goal is to forge a valid signcryptext $\sigma^* = (\sigma_0^*, \sigma_1^*, \sigma_2^*, \sigma_3^*)$ where $\sigma^* \neq \sigma^{(i)}$. Throughout this proof, the variables with superscript $^{(i)}$ denote the variables computed in the i-th signcryption oracle. And the variables with superscript * denote the variables computed in the Challenge stage. According to the result of $\mathcal{A}$'s forgery, we divide it into four types as follows:

- Type I: $C^* \neq C^{(i)}$ (for all i form 1 to q_s),
- Type II: $C^* = C^{(i)}$ and $z^* \neq z^{(i)}$ for some $i \in \{1, ..., q_s\}$,
- Type III: $C^* = C^{(i)}$, $z^* = z^{(i)}$ and $\sigma_3^* = \sigma_3^{(i)}$ for some $i \in \{1, ..., q_s\}$,
- Type IV: $C^* = C^{(i)}$, $z^* = z^{(i)}$ and $\sigma_3^* \neq \sigma_3^{(i)}$ for some $i \in \{1, ..., q_s\}$.

We will show that a successful type I forgery will lead to a successful attack on the Waters signature scheme, a successful type II forgery will lead to a break for the collision-resistant hash function H_2, a successful type III forgery will lead to a break of the collision-resistant hash function H_1, and a successful type IV forgery will lead to a solution to the Discrete Logarithm assumption in $\mathbb{G}$.

Before this attack, the simulator $\mathcal{A}'$ flips a random coin to guess which kind of forgery $\mathcal{A}$ will output, then sets up the public parameter and performs appropriately, and all our simulations are perfect.

- **Type I forgery:** We first briefly review the Waters signature scheme [25]. Given a public parameter $Pub_s \leftarrow \{e, \mathbb{G}, \mathbb{G}_T, u_0, U, g, g_2\}$, $\{\alpha_B, g_B \leftarrow g^{\alpha_B}\}$ are computed as private/public key pair of user B (α_B is randomly chosen from $\mathbb{Z}_p$), the signature σ_s on message $C = (c_1, ..., c_n) \in \{0, 1\}^n$ is: $(\sigma_{s_0}, \sigma_{s_1}) \leftarrow (g_2^{\alpha_B}(u_0 \prod_{i=1}^{n} u_i^{c_i})^t, g^t)$. The Waters signature scheme is said to be $(t, q_s, \epsilon/4)$ existential unforgeable (EUF), if given user B's public key g_B, and has access to q_s times signature oracles, the adversary $\mathcal{A}'$ can forge a valid signature on a new message C^* with probability at most $\epsilon/4$.

We let $\mathcal{A}'$ be the simulator of the SEU-SCNINR-CMA game as well as an attacker of existential unforgeability (EUF) game of Waters scheme. $\mathcal{A}'$ will simulate the SEU-SCNINR-CMA game with the knowledge he gets from the EUF game. Next, we show how $\mathcal{A}'$ deals with the simulation as follows:

- In the Setup system step: $\mathcal{A}'$ first gets the public parameter and user B's public key PK_B from the EUF game. Then $\mathcal{A}'$ chooses random $x, y \in \mathbb{Z}_p$, computes $g_1 \leftarrow g^x$, $g_3 \leftarrow g^y$. Finally, $\mathcal{A}'$ runs the SetupPub algorithm to get the other elements of public parameter Pub, and returns Pub and PK_B to $\mathcal{A}$.
- In the Oracles step: $\mathcal{A}'$ is able to answer all the unsigncryption and non-repudiation oracles easily, since $\mathcal{A}'$ can computes $g_1^{\alpha_B} \leftarrow g_B^x$. For signcryption oracles, $\mathcal{A}'$ answers it with the help of signature oracle in EUF game. When $\mathcal{A}$ asks for a signcryption oracle on $(M, PK_S = PK_B, PK_R)$, $\mathcal{A}'$ chooses a random $\alpha \in \mathbb{Z}_p$, computes $C = H_2(g^\alpha)$, and then gets $\sigma_s = (\sigma_{s_0}, \sigma_{s_1})$ on C from the signature oracle. Finally, $\mathcal{A}'$ computes $\sigma_0 = e(\sigma_{s_1}, g_R)^x \cdot M$, $\sigma_1 \leftarrow \sigma_{s_1}$, $\sigma_2 \leftarrow \sigma_{s_0}$, $\sigma_3 \leftarrow (\alpha - H_1(\sigma_0, \sigma_1, g_B))/y$, returns $\sigma = \{\sigma_0, \sigma_1, \sigma_2, \sigma_3\}$ to $\mathcal{A}$.
- In the Forge step: If $\mathcal{A}$ outputs a successful type I forgery, $\sigma^* = (\sigma_0^*, \sigma_1^*, \sigma_2^*, \sigma_3^*)$. Then $\mathcal{A}'$ can also generate a successful forgery $\sigma_s^* \leftarrow \{\sigma_2^*, \sigma_1^*\}$ on a new message $C^* \leftarrow H_2(g^{H_1(\sigma_0^*, \sigma_1^*, g_B)} g_3^{\sigma_3^*})$.

Now we can see that if $\mathcal{A}$ (adversary in SEU-SCNINR-CMA game) finally makes a successful forgery, then $\mathcal{A}'$ (as an attacker of EUF game) also makes a valid forgery for the Waters scheme.

- **Type II forgery:** $\mathcal{A}$ is a type II adversary for the signcryption scheme, $\mathcal{A}'$ is the simulator. Besides, $\mathcal{A}'$ is aimed to find a collision for H_2.

  In this case, $\mathcal{A}'$ simulates the game as a normal challenger in the definition. Finally, if $\mathcal{A}$ outputs a successful type II forgery that $C^* = C^{(i)}$ and $z^* \neq z^{(i)}$ for some $i \in \{1, ..., q_s\}$, then $\mathcal{A}'$ finds a collision for hash function H_2.

- **Type III forgery:** $\mathcal{A}$ is a type III adversary for the signcryption scheme, $\mathcal{A}'$ is the simulator. Besides, $\mathcal{A}'$ is aimed to find a collision for H_1.

  In this case, $\mathcal{A}'$ simulates the game as a normal challenger in the definition. If $\mathcal{A}$ outputs a successful type III forgery that $C^* = C^{(i)}$, $z^* = z^{(i)}$ and $\sigma_3^* = \sigma_3^{(i)}$ for some $i \in \{1, ..., q_s\}$, then it implies that $\theta^{(i)} = \theta^*$. There are two cases follows:

  1. $(\sigma_0^{(i)}, \sigma_1^{(i)}) = (\sigma_0^*, \sigma_1^*)$. According to the check equation $e(\sigma_2, g) = e(g_2, g_S) \cdot e(\sigma_1, u_0 \prod_{i=1}^n u_i^{c_i})$ in the unsigncryption algorithm, we get that if $(\sigma_0^{(i)}, \sigma_1^{(i)}, \sigma_3^{(i)}) = (\sigma_0^*, \sigma_1^*, \sigma_3^*)$, then $\sigma_2^{(i)} = \sigma_2^*$. It is an impossible case, because it contradicts with the requirement of the attack game that $\sigma^{(i)} \neq \sigma^*$.
  2. $(\sigma_0^{(i)}, \sigma_1^{(i)}) \neq (\sigma_0^*, \sigma_1^*)$. Then $\mathcal{A}'$ finds a collision in H_1.

– **Type IV forgery:** $\mathcal{A}$ is a type IV adversary for the signcryption scheme, $\mathcal{B}'$ is the simulator. Besides, $\mathcal{A}'$ is given a random element $g_3' \in \mathbb{G}$, and is aimed to compute $y \in \mathbb{Z}_p$ where $g_3' = g^y$.

$\mathcal{A}'$ simulates the game as a normal challenger in the definition except that in the Setup system step, he sets $g_3 \leftarrow g_3'$. Finally, if $\mathcal{A}$ outputs a successful type IV forgery that $C^* = C^{(i)}$, $z^* = z^{(i)}$ and $\sigma_3^* \neq \sigma_3^{(i)}$ for some $i \in \{1, ..., q\}$, then $\mathcal{A}'$ can computes $y \leftarrow (\theta^* - \theta^{(i)})/(\sigma_3^{(i)} - \sigma_3^*)$.   □

Proof of Soundness of Non-repudiation

Theorem 3. *The signcryption scheme has perfect soundness of non-repudiation.*

Proof of Theorem 3. In this game, the adversary $\mathcal{A}$ is given the system's public parameter Pub, and he generates a challenge user B's public/privete key pair (PK_B, SK_B). $\mathcal{A}$ is given access to a signcryption oracle. In this oracle, $\mathcal{A}$ outputs a pair of sender/receiver public key (PK_S, PK_B) and a message M, then gets $\sigma \leftarrow Signcryption(SK_S, PK_B, M)$. If the check equation $e(\sigma_2, g) = e(g_2, g_S) \cdot e(\sigma_1, u_0 \prod_{i=1}^{n} u_i^{c_i})$ holds, then the signcryptext σ must be formed as $\sigma = (e(g_1, g_R)^t \cdot M, g^t, g_2^{\alpha_S}(u_0 \prod_{i=1}^{n} u_i^{c_i})^t, s)$ for some $t \in \mathbb{Z}_p$.

Finally, $\mathcal{A}$ outputs a message M' and a non-repudiation evidence d'. If the check equations $e(d_2', g_2) = e(g, d_3')$ and $e(d_1', g) = e(g_1, g_R) \cdot e(u_0 \prod_{i=1}^{n} u_i^{c_i}, d_2')$ both hold, then the non-repudiation evidence d' must be formed as $d' \leftarrow (g_1^{\alpha_R} \cdot (u_0 \prod_{i=1}^{n} u_i^{c_i})^{r'}, g^{r'}, g_2^{r'})$ for some $r' \in \mathbb{Z}_p$. Hence we have

$$M' = \frac{\sigma_0 \cdot e(\sigma_2, d_2')}{e(\sigma_1, d_1')e(d_3', g_S)} = M.$$

It contradicts the hypothesis that $M \neq M'$. Therefore, $\mathcal{A}$ has probability 0 in wining this game. In other words, our proposed scheme satisfies perfect soundness of non-repudiation.   □

Proof of Unforgeability of Non-repudiation Evidence

Theorem 4. *The signcryption scheme is $(t, q_s, q_u, q_n, \epsilon)$ EUF-NR-evidence - SCNINR-CMA secure, assuming that the Waters signature scheme in [25] is $(t, q_u + q_n, \epsilon/4)$ existential unforgeable, H_1 is $(t, \epsilon/4)$ collision resistant, H_2 is $(t, \epsilon/4)$ collision resistant and the Discrete Logarithm assumption in $\mathbb{G}$ holds for $(t, \epsilon/4)$.*

Proof of Theorem 4. The proof for this theorem is very similar to that for unforgeability. In what follows we highlight key differences between them.

In the EUF-NR-evidence-SCNINR-CMA game, the adversary $\mathcal{A}$'s goal is to forge a valid non-repudiation evidence d^* on σ^* and M^*. According to the result of $\mathcal{A}$'s forgery, we divide it into four types as follows:

- Type I: $C^* \neq C^{(i)}$ (for all i form 1 to $q_u + q_n$),
- Type II: $C^* = C^{(i)}$ and $z^* \neq z^{(i)}$ for some $i \in \{1, ..., q_u + q_n\}$,
- Type III: $C^* = C^{(i)}$, $z^* = z^{(i)}$ and $\sigma_3^* = \sigma_3^{(i)}$ for some $i \in \{1, ..., q_u + q_n\}$,
- Type IV: $C^* = C^{(i)}$, $z^* = z^{(i)}$ and $\sigma_3^* \neq \sigma_3^{(i)}$ for some $i \in \{1, ..., q_u + q_n\}$.

Note that in this proof, the variables with superscript $^{(i)}$ denote the variables computed in the i-th unsigncryption oracle (when $i \leq q_u$) or in the $(i - q_u)$-th non-repudiation oracle (when $q_u < i \leq q_u + q_n$). And the variables with superscript * denote the variables computed in the Challenge stage.

At the beginning of the attack, the simulator $\mathcal{A}'$ firstly flips a random coin to guess which kind of forgery $\mathcal{A}$ will output, then sets up a public parameter and performs appropriately. It turns out that all our simulations are perfect.

Analysis of Type II, III and IV is the same as in the proof of Theorem 2. Therefore, we only analyze Type I forgery and omit analysis for other types here.

- **Type I forgery:** We let $\mathcal{A}'$ be the simulator of the EUF-NR-evidence-SCNINR-CMA game as well as an attacker of existential unforgeablility (EUF) game of Waters scheme. We note that the Waters signature used in this proof has one notational difference from what we have used in the proof of Theorem 2, that is, g_1 is used to replace g_2. Thus, the Waters signature σ_s on message $C = (c_1, ..., c_n) \in \{0, 1\}^n$ is: $(\sigma_{s_0}, \sigma_{s_1}) \leftarrow (g_1^{\alpha_B} (u_0 \prod_{i=1}^{n} u_i^{c_i})^t, g^t)$. $\mathcal{A}'$ will simulate the EUF-non-repudiation evidence-SCNINR-CMA game with the knowledge he gets from the EUF game. Next, we show how $\mathcal{A}'$ simulates the game as follows:

  - In the Setup system step: $\mathcal{A}'$ first gets the public parameter and user B's public key PK_B from the EUF game. Then $\mathcal{A}'$ chooses random $x \in \mathbb{Z}_p$, computes $g_2 \leftarrow g^x$. Finally, $\mathcal{A}'$ runs the SetupPub algorithm in signcryption scheme to get the other elements in public parameter Pub, and returns Pub and PK_B to $\mathcal{A}$.
  - In the Orales step: $\mathcal{A}'$ is able to answer the all the signcryption oracles easily, since $\mathcal{A}'$ can computes $g_2^{\alpha_B} \leftarrow g_B^x$. For non-repudiation oracles, $\mathcal{A}'$ will answer them with the help of signature oracles in EUF game. When $\mathcal{A}$ asks for a non-repudiation oracle on (σ, PK_S, PK_B), $\mathcal{A}'$ computes C according to the unsigncryption algorithm, and gets $\sigma_s = (\sigma_{s_0}, \sigma_{s_1})$ on C from the signature oracle. Finally, $\mathcal{A}'$ computes $d \leftarrow (\sigma_{s_0}, \sigma_{s_1}, \sigma_{s_1}^x)$. And for each unsigncryption oracle, $\mathcal{A}'$ first runs the non-repudiation oracle to get d, then decrypts $M \leftarrow \frac{\sigma_0 \cdot e(\sigma_2, d_2)}{e(\sigma_1, d_1) e(d_3, g_S)}$.
  - In the Forge step: If $\mathcal{A}$ outputs a successful forgery d^* on (σ^*, M^*) with sender/receiver public keys (PK_{S^*}, PK_B), then $\mathcal{A}'$ can also generate a successful forgery $\sigma_s^* \leftarrow \{d_1^*, d_2^*\}$ for the Waters signature on a new message $C^* \leftarrow H_2(g^{H_1(\sigma_0^*, \sigma_1^*, g_S^*)} g_3^{\sigma_3^*})$.

Now we can see that $\mathcal{A}'$ (as an attacker) will finally make a valid forgery for Waters signature scheme, if $\mathcal{A}$ (the adversary in EUF-non-repudiation-evidence-SCNINR-CMA game) makes a successful forgery. □

5   Discussions

5.1   Efficiency Comparison

Our proposed signcryption scheme is based on the signature scheme of Boneh, Shen and Waters[8] (for short, we call it BSW signature). In order to give a better intuition on the comparison of efficiency, we review the BSW signature as follows:

- SetupPub: $Pub_{bsw} = \{\mathbb{G}, \mathbb{G}_T, e, g, g_2, g_3, u_0, U, H_2\}$. Most of the elements in Pub_{bsw} are generated the same way as SetupPub in in Table 1, except that $H_1 : \{0,1\}^* \to Z_p$.
- KeyGen: The same as KeyGen in Table 1.
- Sign: To sign on $M \in SP_{\mathcal{M}}$, the signer runs almost the same as Signcryption in Table 1, except that there is no σ_0 in the signature and $\theta \leftarrow H_1(\sigma_1, M)$. The signature is $\sigma_{bsw} \leftarrow (\sigma_1, \sigma_2, \sigma_3)$.
- Verify: To verify a signature σ_{bsw} from a signer S, the verifier runs almost the same as Unsigncryption in Table 1, except that it computes $\theta \leftarrow H_1(\sigma_1, M)$ and there is no need to compute M in the last step. If all the check passed, it returns $\top$.

First, we compare our proposed signcryption scheme with the BSW signature scheme on computational cost. From the above description, it is clear the additional cost in signcryption is to compute σ_0 ($\sigma_0 \leftarrow M \cdot e(g_1, g_R)^t$) and the additional cost in unsigncryption is to compute M ($M \leftarrow \sigma_0/e(\sigma_1, g_1^{\alpha_R})$). Therefore, our signcryptext requires one additional exponentiation in $\mathbb{G}_T$ in signcryption and one additional bilinear computation in unsigncryption, when pre-computation (which will be claimed latter) is applied.

Second, we compare the communication overhead with the BSW signature. In usual communication, the BSW scheme needs to send $(M, \sigma_1, \sigma_2, \sigma_3, ID_S)$, our scheme needs to send $(\sigma_0, \sigma_1, \sigma_2, \sigma_3, ID_S, ID_R)$. When $|M| \approx |\mathbb{G}_T|$, there is nearly no expansion in terms of communication overload (we assume the user ID be a very short string compared with other elements in communication).

Third, we claim that our scheme takes advantage of the the compositional method (either sign-then-encrypt or encrypt-then-sign). For consistency of comparison, we fix the underlying signature scheme as BSW scheme. Since the cost for the compositional method is $1 + 1 = 2$ (that means $Total\text{-}Cost = Cost_{signature} + Cost_{encryption}$), we only has to compare our additional cost with the encryption scheme. For example, we choose the encryption scheme in [7]. The cost for computation cost (if pre-computation applied) is approximately 4 exponentiation in encryption and one bilinear computation in decryption. And the ciphertext size is $2|\mathbb{G}| + |\mathbb{G}_T|$. Clearly, the cost for the encryption scheme is larger than our additional cost.

5.2   Improve Efficiency of the Proposed Scheme

Increase Online Computation Speed. In our scheme, the online computation efficiency can be improved if pre-computation applied. For example, a sender S can compute $g_2^{\alpha_S}$ and a receiver can compute $g_1^{\alpha_R}$ immediately after the computation of public/private key pair. Then it can be stored for latter use. And when a sender S communicates with a receiver R the first time, the sender S can store the value of $e(g_1, g_R)$, then he does not need to repeatedly compute it in latter communication. Similarly, when a receiver R received a signcryptext from S the first time, he can also store the value of $e(g_2, g_S)$. The judge can also store the value of $e(g_1, g_R)$ and $e(g_2, g_S)$ after the first time of solving computation.

This method costs a little more space for storage, but greatly improves the online computation efficiency. According to an approximate estimation, the online computation time can reduce 56.5% in Signcryption, 25.5% in Unsigncryption, 26% in NR-Evidence-Gen, and 17.3% in JG-verification[2].

Considering that in practise, the cost for storage is cheaper than online computation, the above per-computation method does work on improving the whole efficiency in most cases, except the following two cases. 1. One user communicates with another user once. 2. One judge just deal with repudiation problems between two specific users once.

Reduce the Signcryptext Size. In our original scheme, the signcryptext size is $\sigma \in \mathbb{G}_T \times \mathbb{G}^2 \times \mathbb{Z}_p$. To get a shorter signcryptext, we can replace the symmetric bilinear map with an asymmetric bilinear map [7]: $e : \mathbb{G}_1 \times \mathbb{G}_2 \to \mathbb{G}_T$, and there is an efficiently computable homomorphism $\varphi : \mathbb{G}_2 \to \mathbb{G}_1$. Consider the case where h is a generator of $\mathbb{G}_2$, and $g \leftarrow \varphi(h)$ is a generator of $\mathbb{G}_1$. Then we can get a shorter signcryptext $\sigma \in \mathbb{G}_T \times \mathbb{G}_1^2 \times \mathbb{Z}_p$. The size of the representation of elements in $\mathbb{G}_1$ is $1/k$ of that of $\mathbb{G}_2$, where k is the embedding degree [13]. This method results in lower computation speed, but it leads to a more compact signcryptext and a boarder range of choices of elliptic curve implementations. More details about bilinear maps used in cryptography can be found in [13].

The changes of bilinear maps result in a lot of changes in the scheme, which are shown in detail in Table 3 and Table 4.

The security of this modified scheme is quite similar to the original scheme, except with some small changes corresponding to the change of bilinear maps (from symmetric ones to asymmetric ones).

5.3   Applications of Signcryption with NINR

Signcryption with NINR is suitable for those applications where we assume there will be repudiation disputes between the sender and the receiver. For example, emails, ATM networks, and cryptographic protocols that aims to transport, exchange or establish keys etc.

We take the above mentioned "key" related cryptographic protocols as an example. In such scenarios, since the "key" is a very sensitive message, we normally

---

[2] We assume for simplicity that a single computation of exponential computation cost one unit of time, a bilinear computation takes 6 units of time, a multi-exponential computation takes 1.5 units of time, and an n-time multiply computation costs one unit of time.

Table 3. SetupPub& KeyGen& Signcryption& Unsigncryption

SetupPub(1^η) by Trusted Party:
1. generate $(\mathbb{G}_1, \mathbb{G}_2, \mathbb{G}_T, e, g, h)$ as described above,
2. choose random $h_1, h_2, w_0 \in \mathbb{G}_2$ and a random vector $W \in \mathbb{G}_2^n$,
3. compute the images of elements and vector in step 2 by φ to get $g_1, g_2, u_0 \in \mathbb{G}_1$ and $U \in \mathbb{G}_1^n$.
4. choose a random element $g_3 \in \mathbb{G}_1$,
5. set collision-resistant hash functions $H_1 : \mathbb{G}_T \times \mathbb{G}_1 \times \mathbb{G}_1 \to \mathbb{Z}_p$, $H_2 : \mathbb{G}_1 \to \{0,1\}^n$.
6. $Pub = \{\mathbb{G}_1, \mathbb{G}_2, \mathbb{G}_T, e, g, h, g_1, g_2, g_3, h_1, h_2, u_0, w_0, U, W, H_1, H_2\}$

KeyGen(Pub, ID_P) by User P:
1. private key for user P is a random $\alpha_P \in \mathbb{Z}_p$,
2. public key for user P is $h_P \leftarrow h^{\alpha_P}$.

Signcryption(SK_S, PK_R, M) by Sender S:
To signcrypt $M \in \mathbb{G}_T$ to be communicated to receiver R, sender S runs:
1. steps 1 and 3 of Signcryption in Table 1.
2. compute $\sigma_0 \leftarrow e(g_1, h_R)^t \cdot M$,
3. steps 4-9 of Signcryption in Table 1.

Unsigncryption(SK_R, PK_S, σ) by Receiver R:
To unsigncrypt σ from sender S, receiver R runs:
1. steps 1 and 3 of Unsigncryption Table 1.
2. if $e(\sigma_2, h) \neq e(g_2, h_S)e(\sigma_1, w_0 \Pi_{i=1}^n w_i^{c_i})$, return $\perp$,
3. compute $M \leftarrow \sigma_0 / e(\sigma_1, h_1^{\alpha_R})$.

Table 4. NR-Evidence-Gen & JG-Verification

NR-Evidence-Gen$(\sigma, SK_R, PK_S)$by Receiver R:
To compute non-repudiation evidence d, receiver R runs:
1. steps 1-2 of Unsigncryption in Table 3,
2. choose a random $r \in \mathbb{Z}_p$,
3. compute $d_1 \leftarrow h_1^{\alpha_R}(w_0 \prod w_i^{c_i})^r$,
4. steps 4-6 of NR-Evidence-Gen in Table 2.

JG-Verification$(\sigma, M, d, PK_S, PK_R)$ by Judge:
To verify whether $M = Unsigncryption(SK_R, PK_S, \sigma)$, the judge runs:
1. steps 1-2 in Unsigncryption in Table 3,
2. if $e(g_2, d_2) \neq e(d_3, h)$, return $\perp$,
3. else if $e(g, d_1) \neq e(g_1, h_R) \cdot e(u_0 \prod u_i^{c_i}, d_2)$, return $\perp$,
4. else if $M \neq \frac{\sigma_0 \cdot e(\sigma_2, d_2)}{e(\sigma_1, d_1) \cdot e(d_3, h_S)}$, return $\perp$,
5. otherwise return $\top$.

have the following basic security requirements. From one aspect, the user who generated the "key" (or part of the "key"), should never deny on it, and from the other aspect, the user who exposes the fact that the sender translates such a "key" by a well-formed evidence should also responsible for his act. Fortunately, if we apply signcryption scheme with NINR to construct the cryptographic protocols, soundness of non-repudiation ensures that the non-repudiation evidence d correctly reveals the relationship of a signcryptext σ and a message M, and at the same time, unforgeability of non-repudiation evidence guarantees that the receiver has to be responsible for exposing this relationship if he offered a well-formed evidence.

6   Conclusion

In this work, we propose a model for signcryption with NINR. Compared with the model of Malone-Lee, our model focuses more on the security of NINR by considering two more security requirements. Soundness of non-repudiation makes sure that the property of NINR really works. And unforgeability of evidence data offers a strong requirement for some particular scenarios. Besides, we also come up with a concrete scheme, which is the first signcryption scheme with NINR that can be proved secure without random oracles.

Our scheme should be considered to be a first step in constructing provably secure signcryption with NINR without random oracles. There is still a lot of work that needs to be done. One interesting future research direction relates to efficiency. Our construction makes use of bilinear maps which may take more computational time than that can be afforded in some light applications where low power computing devices dominate. As efficiency is the most important motivation for signcryption, deigning more efficient signcryption schemes with NINR (e.g. avoid using bilinear computations) will be very valuable.

References

1. An, J., Dodis, Y., Rabin, T.: On the Security of Joint Signature and Encryption. In: Knudsen, L.R. (ed.) EUROCRYPT 2002. LNCS, vol. 2332, pp. 83–107. Springer, Heidelberg (2002)
2. Boneh, D., Boyen, X.: Short signatures without random oracles. In: Cachin, C., Camenisch, J. (eds.) EUROCRYPT 2004. LNCS, vol. 3027, pp. 56–73. Springer, Heidelberg (2004)
3. Bao, F., Deng, R.H.: A signcryption scheme with signature directly verifiable by public key. In: Imai, H., Zheng, Y. (eds.) PKC 1998. LNCS, vol. 1431, pp. 55–59. Springer, Heidelberg (1998)
4. Boneh, D., Franklin, M.: Identity-based encryption from the weil pairing. SIAM Journal on Computing 32(3), 586–615 (2003)
5. Baek, J., Steinfeld, R., Zheng, Y.: Formal Proofs for the Security of Signcryption. In: Naccache, D., Paillier, P. (eds.) PKC 2002. LNCS, vol. 2274, pp. 80–98. Springer, Heidelberg (2002)

6. Bellare, M., Rogaway, P.: Random oracle are practical: A paradigm for designing efficient protocols. In: ACM-CCS 1993, pp. 62–73. ACM press, Fairfax (1993)
7. Boyen, X., Mei, Q., Waters, B.: Direct Chosen Ciphertext Security from Identity-Based Techniques. In: Atluri, V., Meadows, C., Juels, A. (eds.) ACM-CCS 2005, pp. 320–329. ACM press, Alexandria (2005)
8. Boneh, D., Shen, E., Waters, B.: Strongly Unforgeable Signatures Based on Computational Difie-Hellman. In: Yung, M., Dodis, Y., Kiayias, A., Malkin, T. (eds.) PKC 2006. LNCS, vol. 3958, pp. 229–240. Springer, Heidelberg (2006)
9. Chow, S.S.M., Yiu, S.M., Hui, L.C.K., Chow, K.P.: Efficient forward and provably secure ID-based signcryption scheme with public verifiability and public ciphertext authenticity. In: Lim, J.I., Lee, D.H. (eds.) ICISC 2003. LNCS, vol. 2971, pp. 352–369. Springer, Heidelberg (2004)
10. Cramer, R., Shoup, V.: A Practical Public Key Cryptosystem Provably Secure against Adaptive Chosen Ciphertext Attack. In: Krawczyk, H. (ed.) CRYPTO 1998. LNCS, vol. 1462, pp. 13–25. Springer, Heidelberg (1998)
11. Damgard, I., Holfheins, D., Kiltz, E., Thorbek, R.: Public-Key with Non-interactive Opening. In: Malkin, T. (ed.) CT-RSA 2008. LNCS, vol. 4964, pp. 239–255. Springer, Heidelberg (2008)
12. Galindo, D., Libert, B., Fischlin, M., Fuchsbauer, G., Lehmann, A., Manulis, M., Schroder, D.: Public-Key Encryption with Non-Interactive Opening: New Constructions and Stronger Definitions. In: Bernstein, D.J., Lange, T. (eds.) AFRICACRYPT 2010. LNCS, vol. 6055, pp. 333–350. Springer, Heidelberg (2010)
13. Galbraith, S.D., Paterson, K.G., Smart, N.P.: Pairings for Cryptographers, Cryptology ePrint Archive: Report 2006/165, http://eprint.iacr.org/2006/165
14. Malone-Lee, J.: A general Construction for Simutaneous Signing and Encrypting. In: Smart, N.P. (ed.) Cryptography and Coding 2005. LNCS, vol. 3796, pp. 116–135. Springer, Heidelberg (2005)
15. Malone-Lee, J.: Signcryption with Non-interactive Non-repudiation. J. Designs, Codes and Cryptography 37(1), 81–109 (2005)
16. Li, F., Shirase, M., Takagi, T.: Efficient Signcryption Key Encapsulation without Random Oracles. In: Yung, M., Liu, P., Lin, D. (eds.) Inscrypt 2008. LNCS, vol. 5487, pp. 47–59. Springer, Heidelberg (2009)
17. Libert, B., Quisquater, J.J.: Efficient signcryption with key privacy from gap Diffie-Hellman groups. In: Bao, F., Deng, R.H., Zhou, J. (eds.) PKC 2004. LNCS, vol. 2947, pp. 187–200. Springer, Heidelberg (2004)
18. Libert, B., Quisquater, J.J.: Improved Signcryption from q-Diffie-Hellman Problems. In: Blundo, C., Cimato, S. (eds.) SCN 2004. LNCS, vol. 3352, pp. 220–234. Springer, Heidelberg (2005)
19. Shoup, V.: Sequences of games: a tool for taming complexity in security proofs. Cryptology ePrint Archive, Report 2004/332 (2004)
20. Shin, J.B., Lee, K., Shim, K.: New DSA-verifiable signcryption schemes. In: Lee, P.J., Lim, C.H. (eds.) ICISC 2002. LNCS, vol. 2587, pp. 35–47. Springer, Heidelberg (2003)
21. Tan, C.H.: Security Analysis of Signcryption Scheme from q-Diffie-Hellman Problems. J. IEICE Transactions E89-A(1), 206–208 (2006)
22. Tan, C.H.: Insider-secure Hybrid Signcryption Scheme Without Random Oracles. In: ARES 2007, pp. 1148–1154. IEEE Press, Vienna (2007)
23. Tan, C.H.: Insider-secure Signcryption KEM/Tag-KEM Schemes without Random Oracles. In: ARES 2008, pp. 1275–1281. IEEE Press, Barcelona (2008)
24. Toorani, M., Shirazi, A.A.B.: An Elliptic Curve-Based Signcryption Scheme with Forward Secrecy. J. Applied Sciences 9(6), 1025–1035 (2009)

25. Waters, B.: Efficient identity based encryption without random oracles. In: Cramer, R. (ed.) EUROCRYPT 2005. LNCS, vol. 3494, pp. 114–127. Springer, Heidelberg (2005)

26. Zheng, Y.: Digital signcryption or how to achieve cost (signature&encryption)≪ cost(signature)+cost (encryption). In: Kaliski Jr., B.S. (ed.) CRYPTO 1997. LNCS, vol. 1294, pp. 165–179. Springer, Heidelberg (1997)

Appendix: A More Efficient Construction in the Random Oracle Model

A.1 The Construction

If random oracle model is allowed, we can construct a modified scheme which is more efficient from all aspects. The public parameter can be reduced from $\mathcal{O}(\log p)$ to $\mathcal{O}(1)$, the size of signcryptext can be reduced from $\mathbb{G}_T \times \mathbb{G}^2 \times \mathbb{Z}_p$ to $\mathbb{G}_T \times \mathbb{G}^2$, and the computational efficiency can also be improved. In this paper, our main goal is to generate signcryption with NINR without random oracles, but we stress that this modified scheme is also meaningful. Since even in the random oracle model, there are no existing signcryption schemes with NINR that fulfilling all the four security requirements of our model.

The main difference is that in the modified scheme $u_0 u_1^\theta$ is used to replace $u_0 \prod_{i=1}^n u_i^{c_i}$ in the original scheme. The construction is described in Table A-1 and Table A-2, and all the security theorems and proofs for this scheme will be provided in the next subsection.

A.2 Security Proofs

We are going to provide security theorems and proofs for the modified signcryption scheme with NINR in the random oracle model. The difference between the standard model and the random oracle model is that, in the random oracle model, the attacker has access to additional hash oracles in the oracles stage. In this proof, we assume that in each attack game, the attacker can ask for at most q_h time hash oracles on H_1.

Theorem A. 1. *The modified signcryption scheme is* $(t, q_h, q_s, q_u, q_n, \epsilon)$ *IND-SCNINR-CCA secure, assuming that the* (t, ϵ) *DBDH assumption holds, and hash function* H_1 *is a random oracle.*

Proof of Theorem A. 1: We will prove that if $\mathcal{A}$ has advantage ϵ that wins the attack game, then the simulator $\mathcal{A}'$ can solve the DBDH problem with the same advantage ϵ. Initially $\mathcal{A}'$ is given input a tuple (g^a, g^b, g^c, T), T is either g^{abc} or a random element in $\mathbb{G}$.

- In the Setup system stage, $\mathcal{A}'$ sets $g_1 \leftarrow g^a$, the challenge user B's public key $g_B \leftarrow g^b$. Choose random elements $k_1, k_2, \theta^*, \tau \in Z_p$, and compute $u_0 \leftarrow g_1^{-\theta^* \cdot k_1} g^{k_2}$, $u_1 \leftarrow g_1^{k_1}$, $g_2 \leftarrow g^\tau$.

Table A-1. SetupPub& KeyGen& Signcryption& Unsigncryption

$\textbf{\textit{SetupPub}}(1^\eta)$ by Trusted Party: $Pub = \{\mathbb{G}, \mathbb{G}_T, e, g, g_1, g_2, g_3, u_0, u_1, H_1\}$ is generated the same way as in SetupPub in Table 1. But here we take H_1 as a random oracle.
$\textbf{\textit{KeyGen}}(Pub, ID_P)$ by User P: The same as KeyGen in Table 1.
$\textbf{\textit{Signcryption}}(SK_S, PK_R, M)$ by Sender S: To signcrypt $M \in \mathbb{G}_T$ to be communicated to receiver R, sender S runs: 1. steps 1-4 of Signcryption in Table 1, 2. compute $\sigma_2 \leftarrow g_2^{\alpha_S}(u_0 u_1^\theta)^t$, 3. the signcryptext is $\sigma \leftarrow (\sigma_0, \sigma_1, \sigma_2)$.
$\textbf{\textit{Unsigncryption}}(SK_R, PK_S, \sigma)$ by Receiver R: To unsigncrypt σ from sender S, receiver R runs: 1. compute $\theta \leftarrow H_1(\sigma_0, \sigma_1, g_S)$, 2. if $e(\sigma_2, g) \neq e(g_2, g_S) \cdot e(\sigma_1, u_0 u_1^\theta)$, return $\perp$, 3. otherwise compute $M \leftarrow \sigma_0/e(\sigma_1, g_1^{\alpha_R})$.

Table A-2. NR-Evidence-Gen & JG-Verification

$\textbf{\textit{NR-Evidence-Gen}}(\sigma, SK_R, PK_S)$ by Receiver R: To compute non-repudiation evidence d, receiver R runs: 1. steps 1-2 of Unsigncryption in Table A-1, 2. choose a random $r \in \mathbb{Z}_p$, 3. compute $d_1 \leftarrow g_1^{\alpha_R} \cdot (u_0 u_1^\theta)^r$, $d_2 \leftarrow g^r$, $d_3 \leftarrow g_2^r$, 4. return $d \leftarrow (d_1, d_2, d_3)$.
$\textbf{\textit{JG-Verification}}(\sigma, M, d, PK_S, PK_R)$ by Judge: To verify whether $M = Unsigncryption(SK_R, PK_S, \sigma)$, the judge runs: 1. steps 1-2 of Unsigncryption in Table A-1, 2. if $e(d_2, g_2) \neq e(g, d_3)$, return $\perp$, 3. else if $e(d_1, g) \neq e(g_1, g_R) \cdot e(u_0 u_1^\theta, d_2)$, return $\perp$, 4. else if $M \neq \frac{\sigma_0 \cdot e(\sigma_2, d_2)}{e(\sigma_1, d_1) e(d_3, g_S)}$, return $\perp$, 5. otherwise return $\top$.

– In the Oracles before challenge stage,
  1. For each hash oracle on $(\sigma_0, \sigma_1, g_S)$, the simulator keeps a list for the input and output for hash oracles (which is initially empty). If the input has already been asked, check the list to find the output, else it returns a random element θ that $\theta \neq \theta^*$, and add $\{(\sigma_0, \sigma_1, g_S), \theta\}$ to the list.
  2. For each signcryption oracle on M with $(PK_S \leftarrow PK_B, PK_R)$, the simulator first computes $g_2^{\alpha_B} \leftarrow g_B^\tau$, then it can compute a signcryptext according to the Signcryption algorithm.
  3. For each non-repudiation oracle on σ with $(PK_S, PK_R = PK_B)$, the simulator first runs step 1 of the NR-Evidence-Gen algorithm. If it does not abort, the simulator chooses a random element $r' \in Z_p$, then computes $d_1 \leftarrow g_1^{k_1(\theta - \theta^*)r'} g_B^{\frac{k_2}{k_1(\theta^* - \theta)}} g^{k_2 r'}$, $d_2 \leftarrow g_B^{\frac{1}{k_1(\theta^* - \theta)}} g^{r'}$, $d_3 \leftarrow d_2^\tau$. Taking $r \leftarrow \frac{b}{k_1(\theta^* - \theta)} + r'$, then $d_1 \leftarrow g_1^{\alpha_B}(u_0 u_1^\theta)^r$, $d_2 \leftarrow g^r$, $d_3 \leftarrow g_2^r$.
  4. For each unsigncryption oracle on σ with $(PK_S, PK_R = PK_B)$, the simulator first runs the the non-repudiation oracle to get d, then computes $M \leftarrow \frac{\sigma_0 \cdot e(\sigma_2, d_2)}{e(\sigma_1, d_1) e(d_3, g_S)}$.
– In the challenge stage, $\mathcal{A}$ outputs (M_0, M_1) with $(PK_{S^*}, PK_{R^*} = PK_B)$, the simulator computes $\sigma_0^* \leftarrow T \cdot M_\gamma$ (γ is a random bit), $\sigma_1^* \leftarrow g^c$, $\sigma_2^* \leftarrow g_{S^*}^\tau$. Finally, it returns $\sigma^* = (\sigma_0^*, \sigma_1^*, \sigma_2^*)$ and then add $\{(\sigma_0^*, \sigma_1^*, g_S), \theta^*\}$ to the hash list.
– In the oracles after challenge stage, the simulator operates similar as in the oracle before challenge stage.
– In the Guess stage, $\mathcal{A}$ outputs a guess bit γ'. If $\gamma = \gamma'$, the simulator outputs a bit 1, or outputs a bit 0 for the DBDH assumption.

If the input tuple is sampled in experiment 0, where $T = e(g, g)^{abc}$, then $|Pr[\gamma = \gamma'$ in experiment $0] - 1/2| = \epsilon$. Else if the input tuple is sampled from in experiment 1 where $T = e(g, g)^k$, then $Pr[\gamma = \gamma'$ in experiment $1] = 1/2$. Thus we have
$|Pr[\mathcal{A}' = 1$ in experiment $0] - Pr[\mathcal{A}' = 1$ in experiment $1]| = |(1/2 \pm \epsilon) - 1/2| = \epsilon$. Therefore, if the adversary $\mathcal{A}$ has advantage ϵ in wining the attack game, then the simulator $\mathcal{A}'$ also has advantage ϵ in solving the DBDH assumption. $\qquad \square$

Theorem A. 2. *The signcryption scheme is* $(t, q_h, q_s, q_u, q_n, \epsilon)$ *SEU-SCNINR-CMA secure, assuming the CDH assumption in* $\mathbb{G}$ *holds for* $(t, \epsilon/q_h)$*, and hash function* H_1 *is a random oracle.*

Proof of Theorem A. 2: We will prove that if $\mathcal{A}$ has advantage ϵ that wins the attack game, then the simulator $\mathcal{A}'$ can solve the CDH problem with advantage at least ϵ/q_h. For CDH assumption, $\mathcal{A}'$ is given input (g^a, g^b), and aims to compute g^{ab}.

– In the Setup system stage, $\mathcal{A}'$ sets $g_2 \leftarrow g^a$, the challenge user B's public key $g_B \leftarrow g^b$. Choose random elements $k_1, k_2, \theta^*, \tau \in Z_p$, and compute $u_0 \leftarrow g_2^{-\theta^* k_1} g^{k_2}$, $u_1 \leftarrow g_2^{k_1}$, $g_1 \leftarrow g^\tau$.

- In the Oracles stage,

  1. For each hash oracle on $(\sigma_0, \sigma_1, g_S)$, the simulator keeps a list for the input and output for hash oracles (which is initially empty). If the input has already been asked, check the list to find the output. Else it returns $\theta \leftarrow \theta^*$ with probability $1/q_h$, and returns a random element θ that $\theta \neq \theta^*$ with probability $1 - 1/q_h$, and add $\{(\sigma_0, \sigma_1, g_S), \theta\}$ to the list.

  2. For each signcryption oracle on M with $(PK_S = PK_B, PK_R)$, the simulator first chooses random elements $t', \theta \in Z_p$, and computes $\sigma_0 \leftarrow e(g_B^{\frac{\tau}{k_1(\theta^* - \theta)}} g_1^{t'}, g_R) \cdot M$, $\sigma_1 \leftarrow g_B^{\frac{1}{k_1(\theta^* - \theta)}} g^{t'}$, $\sigma_2 \leftarrow g_2^{k_1(\theta - \theta^*)t'} g_B^{\frac{k_2}{k_1(\theta^* - \theta)}} g^{k_2 t'}$. Taking $t \leftarrow \frac{b}{k_1(\theta^* - \theta)} + t'$, then $\sigma_0 \leftarrow e(g_1, g_R)^t \cdot M, \sigma_1 \leftarrow g^t, \sigma_2 \leftarrow g_2^{\alpha_S}(u_0 u_1^{\theta})^t$. Finally, the simulator add $\{(\sigma_0, \sigma_1), \theta\}$ the the hash list.

  3. For each non-repudiation oracle on σ with $(PK_S, PK_R = PK_B)$, the simulator first computes the $g_1^{\alpha_B} \leftarrow g_B^{\tau}$, then it can compute an answer according to the NR-Evidence-Gen algorithm.

  4. For each unsigncryption oracle on σ with $(PK_S, PK_R = PK_B)$, the simulator first runs the the non-repudiation oracle to get d, then computes $M \leftarrow \frac{\sigma_0 \cdot e(\sigma_2, d_2)}{e(\sigma_1, d_1) e(d_3, g_S)}$.

- In the forge stage, if $\mathcal{A}$ outputs a signcryptext $\sigma^* \leftarrow (\sigma_0^*, \sigma_1^*, \sigma_2^*)$ with $(PK_{S^*} = PK_B, PK_{R^*})$, the simulator checks the hash list with input $(\sigma_0^*, \sigma_1^*, g_B)$. If it is not on the input list, then sets the output as θ^*.

If the signcryptext is a valid one, and the output of hash oracle for $(\sigma_0^*, \sigma_1^*, g_B)$ is θ^*, then the simulator can solve the CDH assumption by computing $g^{ab} \leftarrow \sigma_2^*/\sigma_1^{*k_2}$. Now we can see the probability that $\{(\sigma_0^*, \sigma_1^*, g_B), \theta^*\}$ is on the hash list is at least $1/q_h$. Therefore, if $\mathcal{A}$ has advantage ϵ in winning the attack game, then the simulator can solves the CDH assumption with advantage at least ϵ/q_h. $\qquad\square$

Theorem A. 3. *The modified scheme has perfect soundness of non-repudiation.*

Proof of Theorem A. 3: In this game, the adversary $\mathcal{A}$ is given the system's public parameter Pub, and he generates a challenge user B's public/privete key pair (PK_B, SK_B). And $\mathcal{A}$ is given access to a signcryption oracle. In this oracle, $\mathcal{A}$ outputs a pair of sender/receiver public key $(PK_S, PK_R = PK_B)$ and a message M, then gets $\sigma \leftarrow Signcryption(SK_S, PK_B, M)$. If the check equation $e(\sigma_2, g) = e(g_2, g_S) \cdot e(\sigma_1, u_0 u_1^{\theta})$ holds, then the signcryptext σ must be formed as $\sigma = (e(g_1, g_R)^t \cdot M, g^t, g_2^{\alpha_S}(u_0 u_1^{\theta})^t)$ for some $t \in \mathbb{Z}_p$.

Finally, $\mathcal{A}$ outputs a message M' and an non-repudiation evidence d'. If the check equations $e(d_2', g_2) = e(g, d_3')$ and $e(d_1', g) = e(g_1, g_R) \cdot e(u_0 u_1^{\theta}, d_2')$ both hold, then the non-repudiation evidence d' must be formed as follows: $d' \leftarrow (g_1^{\alpha_R} \cdot (u_0 u_1^{\theta})^{r'}, g^{r'}, g_2^{r'})$ for some $r' \in \mathbb{Z}_p$.

Hence we have

$$M' = \frac{\sigma_0 \cdot e(\sigma_2, d_2')}{e(\sigma_1, d_1') e(d_3', g_S)} = M.$$

It contradicts the hypothesis that $M \neq M'$. Therefore, $\mathcal{A}$ has probability 0 in wining this game. In other words, this signcryption scheme satisfies perfect soundness of non-repudiation.   □

Theorem A. 4. *The modified scheme is* $(t, q_h, q_s, q_u, q_n, \epsilon)$ *EUF-NR-evidence-SCNINR-CMA secure, assuming that CDH assumption in* $\mathbb{G}$ *holds for* $(t, \epsilon/q_h)$, *and hash function* H_1 *is a random oracle.*

Proof of Theorem A. 4: We will prove that if $\mathcal{A}$ has advantage ϵ that wins the attack game, then the simulator $\mathcal{A}'$ can solve the CDH assumption with advantage at least ϵ/q_h. Initially $\mathcal{A}'$ is given input (g^a, g^b).

- In the Setup system stage, $\mathcal{A}'$ sets public parameter as the simulator in the proof of Theorem A.1.
- In the oracles stage, $\mathcal{A}'$ operates similarly as the the simulator in stage of oracles before challenge in the proof of Theorem A.1, except that $\mathcal{A}'$ answers the hash oracles in a different way. For each hash oracle on $(\sigma_0, \sigma_1, g_S)$, it returns $\theta \leftarrow \theta^*$ with probability $1/q_h$, and returns a random element θ that $\theta \neq \theta^*$ with probability $1 - 1/q_h$,
- In the forge stage, $\mathcal{A}$ outputs $(d^*, \sigma^*, M^*, PK_{S^*}, PK_{R^*})$ with $PK_{R^*} = PK_B$. The simulator checks the hash list, if $(\sigma_0^*, \sigma_1^*, g_{S^*})$ is not on the hash list as input, then adds $\{(\sigma_0^*, \sigma_1^*, g_S), \theta^*\}$ to the list.

If d^* is a valid one, and $\{(\sigma_0^*, \sigma_1^*, g_{S^*}), \theta^*\}$ is on the hash list, then the simulator can solve the CDH assumption by computing $g^{ab} \leftarrow \sigma_2^*/\sigma_1^{*k_2}$. Now we can see the probability that $\{(\sigma_0^*, \sigma_1^*), \theta^*\}$ is on the hash list is at least $1/q_h$. Therefore, if $\mathcal{A}$ has advantage ϵ in winning the attack game, then the simulator can solves the CDH assumption with advantage at least ϵ/q_h.   □

Block-Level Added Redundancy Explicit Authentication for Parallelized Encryption and Integrity Checking of Processor-Memory Transactions

Reouven Elbaz[1], Lionel Torres[2], Gilles Sassatelli[2], Pierre Guillemin[3], Michel Bardouillet[3], and Albert Martinez[3]

[1] Intel Corporation, SeCoE, Security Center of Excellence,
2111 N.E. 25th Avenue, Hillsboro, OR 97124, USA
Reouven.Elbaz@intel.com
[2] University of Montpellier, LIRMM, CNRS, 161 rue Ada, 34392 Montpellier, France
{Lionel.Torres,Gilles.Sassatelli}@lirmm.fr
[3] STMicroelectronics, AST, Advanced System Technology, Rousset, France
{Pierre.Guillemin,Michel.Bardouillet,Albert.Martinez}@st.com

Abstract. The bus between the System on Chip (SoC) and the external memory is one of the weakest points of computer systems: an adversary can easily probe this bus in order to read private data (data confidentiality concern) or to inject data (data integrity concern). The conventional way to protect data against such attacks and to ensure data confidentiality and integrity is to implement two dedicated engines: one performing data encryption and another data authentication. This approach, while secure, prevents parallelizability of the underlying computations. In this paper, we introduce the concept of Block-Level Added Redundancy Explicit Authentication (BL-AREA) and we describe a Parallelized Encryption and Integrity Checking Engine (PE-ICE) based on this concept. BL-AREA and PE-ICE have been designed to provide an effective solution to ensure both security services while allowing for full parallelization on processor read and write operations and optimizing the hardware resources. Compared to standard encryption which ensures only confidentiality, we show that PE-ICE additionally guarantees code and data integrity for less than 4% of run-time performance overhead.

Keywords: Data Integrity and Confidentiality, Computer Security, Hardware Attacks, Encryption, Authentication, Memory.

1 Introduction

PDAs, mobile phones, MP3 players, set-top boxes, digital video equipments are widespread nowadays. The range of services provided by every single embedded system tends to widen rapidly and applications like on-line banking transactions, web browsing, email, application / game download are usual on mobile devices. As a consequence, the amount of sensitive information such as private data, e.g., bank information, passwords, email, photo, or intellectual property, e.g., software, digital

M.L. Gavrilova et al. (Eds.): Trans. on Comput. Sci. X, LNCS 6340, pp. 231–260, 2010.

multimedia content, contained or transiting in those devices rapidly increases. The issue is that today's embedded systems cannot be considered as trustworthy hosts [1] since the owner, or anyone else who succeeds in getting access, is a potential adversary. Thus, one of the challenges for the high-technology industry in the development of pervasive computing relies on the development of trusted computing and secured storage solutions.

The attacks conducted on embedded systems [2] challenge several security services such as data confidentiality, data integrity and system availability. Data confidentiality ensures that data stored in or transiting through embedded systems are only read by authorized parties while data integrity guarantees that those data are not tampered with, deleted or altered by malicious entities. Availability refers to the requirement of ensuring user access to the device without unexpected delay or obstacle.

Several projects (e.g., Trustzone [3]) and consortiums (e.g., the Trusting Computing Group [4] TCG) shows the increasing importance of security in the industry. However, all these efforts do not consider hardware-based (physical) attacks. More specifically, they work under the assumption that the communication channels between the processor chip and the other components can be trusted despite the fact that data exchanges are often done in clear. The well known cracking of the Xbox gaming console shows that designing computer systems with such an assumption leads to simple physical attacks. In [5], the hacker Andrew Huang explained his approach to break the Xbox security features and demonstrated that one of the weakest points of computing systems are buses because they offer a low-cost spot for attacks.

In this work we focus on physical non-invasive attacks (i.e., such attacks do not necessitate any modifications of the processor chip) called board level attacks. These attacks are conducted on buses between the System on Chip and off-chip volatile memory or directly in the memory – typically Random Access Memory (RAM). The objectives of the adversary can be the unauthorized use or the illegal distribution of intellectual properties, to corrupt private data retrieved on buses or directly in memory, or to take control of the underlying system. Our goal is to ensure i) the confidentiality of the off-chip memory content during storage or execution to prevent the leakage of any sensitive information ii) and the integrity of data stored in these memories to preclude the execution or processing of intentionally altered data.

Smartcards offer a countermeasure against such attacks by putting all processing and storage elements in a single chip. Another common solution is secure co-processors which encapsulate the components handling sensitive computations and data in a tamper-resistant and tamper-responsive package, such as the IBM 4578 [6]. However, these solutions are not suited for handheld embedded systems because the latter requires an expensive and large package to provide a high performance system while the former does not allow storing a large amount of code and data and does not offer a high computing power.

A trade-off between the above mentioned countermeasures is to limit the trust boundaries to the SoC and to embed memory protection apparatus on-chip. This concept was introduced by Best with bus-encryption microprocessor [43, 44] in 1979: data are encrypted before being stored off-chip and are only decrypted once back on-chip. However, encryption only ensures data confidentiality and does not provide tamper-detection mechanisms to guarantee data integrity. Later on, several research works [9, 10, 11, 12] considered this additional issue to offer a private and authenticated tamper resistant environment to software execution. They achieved this task by providing both security services – data confidentiality and integrity – separately (generic composition schemes). The shortcoming of such an approach is the serialization of the underlying cryptographic computations on write or on read operations, introducing non-parallelizable latencies on off-chip memory accesses. Moreover, the hardware resources needed are not optimized since the implementation of a dedicated cryptographic engine for each security service is required.

In the present work, the goal is to prevent board level attacks involving bus probing and memory tampering. To do so, the proposed hardware mechanisms must ensure the confidentiality and the integrity of the off-chip memory content while considering the constraints relative to the processor context – particularly random access of variable data size – to optimize hardware resources, memory access latencies and the memory bandwidth at runtime.

In order to reach the above mentioned objectives, we explore the concept of Added Redundancy Explicit Authentication (AREA [37]) at the block level during block encryption to ensure data integrity[1] in addition to confidentiality. We call this technique Block-Level Added Redundancy Explicit Authentication (BL-AREA). We also describe the hardware mechanism PE-ICE – for Parallelized Encryption and Integrity Checking Engine – implementing the concept of Block-Level AREA on an ARM-AHB bus. PE-ICE performs the encryption and the integrity checking of the external memory content with the following advantages:

i)   Full parallelization of the encryption and integrity checking process on off-chip write and read operations allowing latency optimization.

ii)   Hardware optimization: Use/Implementation of a single encryption algorithm to provide both security services: data confidentiality and integrity.

iii)   Optimization of Read-Modify-Write operations by optimizing narrow block encryption.

The rest of the paper is organized as follow. Section 2 presents our threat model. Section 3 describes the existing techniques providing both data confidentiality and integrity (including authenticated encryption modes) and the related hardware mechanisms designed for memory encryption and authentication. Section 4 presents the Block-Level AREA technique. Section 5 describes PE-ICE (Parallelized Encryption and Integrity Checking Engine), the engine implementing the Block-Level AREA technique in the context of a System-on-Chip for memory encryption and authentication. Section 6 provides a security analysis of the proposed mechanisms. Section 7 evaluates a SoC implementation of PE-ICE; we first describe the engine architecture and provide the experimental results. In this section, PE-ICE is compared to a memory encryption only engine and then to a memory encryption and integrity checking engine based on a generic composition scheme. Finally Section 8 concludes this work.

---

[1] In this work we consider precise authentication only, i.e., memory blocks are authenticated before being sent to the processor pipeline or in cache memory.

2 Threat and Trust Model

The device to protect is supposedly exposed to a hostile environment where physical attacks are feasible. The main assumption in our trust model is that the processor chip is considered as resistant to physical attacks. As highlighted in [5] by Andrew Huang who hacked the Xbox, an ASIC die is too expensive and time-consuming to cut compared to connect a custom device to buses. Therefore, the SoC is considered as a trusted area and on-chip registers and memories are trusted. Software attacks are not considered and we assume the presence of a trusted OS kernel. Moreover, the cryptographic engines used are considered resistant to attacks, called Side-Channel Attacks (SCA), that exploit the information leaked by their physical implementation (e.g., power consumption [45]).

We focus mainly on board-level attacks involving Processor-Memory (PM) bus probing or memory tampering. Such attacks allow the observation of the memory contents and the injection of arbitrary data on the PM bus or directly into the memory chip. We are particularly concerned by "Man in the middle" attacks. The corresponding protocol implementing such attacks is divided into two parts:

i) First the attacker monitors the PM communications and intercepts the data on the bus (passive attacks). Another possibility is to directly read data in memory. This first step raises the issue of data confidentiality.

ii) Then the adversary may insert chosen data on the PM bus (active attack) and thus he/she challenges data integrity. The objective of the attacker could be to take control of the system by injecting malicious code. There are three classes of active attacks defined with respect to the attacker's choice for the inserted data:

• *Spoofing attacks*: the adversary exchanges a memory block with an arbitrary fake one. The attacker mainly alters program behavior but cannot foresee the results of his attack if data are encrypted.

• *Splicing or relocation attacks*: the attacker replaces a memory block at address A with a block from address B, where A≠B. Such an attack may be viewed as a *spatial permutation* of memory blocks. When data are ciphered, the benefit of using an existing memory block as a fake block is the knowledge of its behavior if this one had been previously observed.

• *Replay attacks*: a memory block located at a given address is recorded and inserted at the same address at a later point in time; by doing so, the current block's value is replaced by an older one. Such an attack may be viewed as a *temporal permutation* of memory blocks at a specific address location.

In [13], a detailed description of those attacks is proposed. Markus Kuhn shows in [38] how he successfully broke the encryption scheme implemented in the DS5002FP Microcontroller by using such active attacks on encrypted code.

3 Memory Encryption and Authentication: Existing Techniques and Related Works

In this section, we present the existing techniques providing *both* data confidentiality and integrity. Then, we highlight the main sources of performance degradation introduced at runtime when encryption and integrity checking are implemented. Finally, we describe the related works proposed in our field of study.

3.1 Encryption and Authentication Techniques

In the following, the underlying block cipher processes b-bit blocks under k-bit keys. E_K and D_K are respectively the encryption and decryption functions under the key K. The plaintext message to encrypt P is divided into m b-bit plaintext blocks p_i with ($1 \leq i \leq m$). Similarly, C the ciphertext (C = E_K(P)) is divided into m n-bit ciphertext blocks c_i with ($1 \leq i \leq m$).

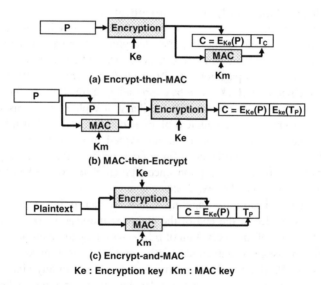

Fig. 1. The Generic Composition Schemes (a) Encrypt-then-MAC (b) MAC-then-Encrypt (c) Encrypt-and-MAC

The Conventional Way: The Generic Composition

The conventional way to provide both data confidentiality and integrity is to pair a data authentication technique and an encryption mode, and therefore to perform two passes on data. A first pass is dedicated to encryption and a second one is done to compute a tag with a MAC (Message Authentication Code) algorithm. The three possible schemes defined in [39] are depicted in Figure 1:

- *Encrypt-then-MAC* (Fig.1a) encrypts the plaintext P into a ciphertext C, and then appends to C a tag T computed with a MAC algorithm over C.

- *MAC-then-Encrypt* (Fig.1b) calculates a tag over the plaintext P, appends the resulting tag to P and then encrypts them together.
- *Encrypt-and-MAC* (Fig.1c) encrypts the plaintext P to get a ciphertext C and appends to C a tag T computed over P.

The main drawback of such techniques is that both cryptographic processing (encryption and MAC computation) are non-parallelizable on either read or write operations or on both. On write operations, for the Encrypt-then-MAC scheme, the tag computation starts only at the end of the encryption process while for the MAC-then-Encrypt, encryption only terminates after the completion of the tag calculation. On read operations, for the Encrypt-and-MAC and the MAC-then-Encrypt schemes, the tag reference computation begins only when the decryption process is completed.

In [39], Bellare and al. proved that the most secure way to pair an authentication and an encryption mode is to use the Encrypt-then-MAC scheme and to enroll a different key for each computation.

AREA: Added Redundancy Explicit Authentication
The principle of AREA [37] schemes is to insert redundancy into the plaintext message before encryption and to check it after decryption. Such a scheme is constructed with cipher modes with infinite error propagation on encryption and on decryption (infinite two-way error propagation). A cipher mode has infinite error propagation on encryption if a ciphertext block c_i can be expressed as a function of all previous plaintext blocks p_0 to p_i of the message P. Similarly, a cipher mode has infinite error propagation on decryption if a plaintext block p_i can be expressed as a function of all previous ciphertext blocks c_0 to c_i in the encrypted message C. For instance, CBC (Ciphered Block Chaining [40]) has infinite error propagation on encryption but has limited error propagation on decryption since a given plaintext block can be expressed as a function of only two ciphertext blocks.

In order to authenticate a message in addition to encrypt it, a value p_{m+1} – the redundancy – is appended at the end of the plaintext message before encryption. This way, c_{m+1} – the result of the encryption of p_{m+1} – will depend on all plaintext blocks p_i composing the message to authenticate. p_{m+1} and c_{m+1} are sent along with the encrypted message. On decryption, the corruption of one bit in any ciphertext block c_i will impact the decryption of c_{m+1} since it depends on all previous ciphertext blocks. The recipient can detect a malicious modification by comparing the result of the decryption of c_{m+1} with p_{m+1}.

AREA schemes seem really efficient since it is the only existing technique performing only one pass over the data on encryption and decryption to provide both data confidentiality and integrity. However, the infinite error propagation is usually achieved by chaining encryption (e.g. CBC, PCBC[41], and PCFB[42]) and decryption (e.g. PCBC, PCFB) operations. A chaining mode implies that blocks belonging to the same message are processed sequentially (i.e., a given block in a message must wait for the previous block to be processed before being itself cryptographically processed) and, therefore, prevents processing all blocks in a message in parallel.

Authenticated Encryption Modes

As shown in [39] and [41], providing both data confidentiality and authentication with schemes based on generic composition or on AREA could be a risky task. Hence, an important effort led by the cryptographic research community through the NIST's modes-of-operation [35] activities was deployed to define Authenticated Encryption (AE) modes. It aimed at providing a secure way to ensure data confidentiality and integrity. However, those encryption modes are based on AREA (PCFB) or on a generic composition schemes (GCM, CCM, OCB and IAPM) and thus suffer from the same drawbacks. Moreover, some modes (e.g., GCM) require specific hardware, in addition to the cipher, to perform signatures.

3.2 Sources of Performance Degradation at Runtime

As highlighted in section 3.1, the sequential processing of encryption (or decryption) and tag computation can be a source of run-time performance overhead. Other sources of run-time performance overhead in embedded systems, when memory encryption and authentication is implemented, are:

•   The intrinsic latencies of cryptographic functions (e.g., AES) involved in encryption and tag computation,
•   The memory bandwidth pollution generated by the loading of meta-data such as tags and by the size of the atomic block loaded for decryption or for integrity checking. Such a block is called *chunk* in the following.

However, the processing of data by the security engines implies specific operations which represent another source of degradation. Whatever the size of the chunk, a performance overhead is to be expected on:

1) *Read operations of data smaller than a chunk*: such operations occur mainly for non-cacheable data and require:

> i) loading the whole matching chunk from external memory with its tag
> ii) deciphering it and check its integrity
> iii) forwarding the requested data to the CPU.

In addition to the latencies introduced by the security mechanisms, such a processing pollutes the memory bandwidth by loading not relevant data.

2) *Write operations of data smaller than a chunk* require:

> i) loading the matching chunk with its tag from off-chip
> ii) deciphering it and check its integrity
> iii) modifying the corresponding sequence in the chunk
> iv) re-ciphering it and re-compute its tag
> v) writing it back into memory with its new tag.

This chain of operations is referred in the following as Read Modify Writes (RMW). The additional performance slowdown implied by such an operation is mainly due to the generation of a read/decryption/checking process triggered by *narrow block encryption*. Therefore, to reduce the run-time performance overhead introduced by RMW, the chunk size should be ideally defined as small as possible without affecting security.

3.3 Related Work

In this section we focus on works that aim at providing both memory encryption and authentication.

AEGIS [10, 11], XOM [9], SP [12] architectures aim at providing memory authentication and encryption in the context of the design of trusted processor architecture. Those three projects, therefore, include countermeasures against board level attacks. The proposed architectures implement a generic composition scheme (Encrypt-then-MAC) and, hence, all suffer from the drawback highlighted above: no parallelization and not optimized in term of hardware resources.

In AEGIS, XOM and SP the computation of tags is done over the data block and address (addressed-MAC), this way providing a countermeasure against spoofing and splicing attacks. This ensures the authentication of Read Only (RO)[2] data, but Read Write (RW) data are still sensitive to replay. XOM [19] failed in preventing replay attacks since it treats RW data as RO. Storing hash of RW data block on-chip is a countermeasure against replay but is expensive in term of on-chip memory overhead. Tree techniques (Merkle Tree [16, 19], Parallelizable Authentication Tree (PAT) [17], Tamper-Evident Counter Tree (TEC-Tree) [21]) have been proposed as a technique to reduce this on-chip memory overhead to only one hash. Gassend and al. [19] implemented the hash tree techniques combined with tree nodes caching to efficiently thwart replay attacks and several work have been proposed to improve performance of tree-based authentication scheme [14, 15, 18]. However, in this paper we focus on the authentication and encryption technique requiring a single access to memory. Indeed, tree schemes require recursive calls to the authentication primitive and multiple accesses to metadata stored off-chip. These calls and off-chip memory accesses are extremely expensive for some applications like low cost embedded systems that do not include prefetching engines, large caches, or out-of-order execution mechanisms that could hide tree overhead. For more details on those techniques, refer to [13, 20].

Vaslin and al. [7, 8] proposed a solution, dedicated to embedded systems, which encrypts data using One Time Pad (OTP) encryption and authenticates data by storing a CRC checksum of the plaintext blocks on the trusted on-chip area. The solution is effective in term of performance but this improvement comes at the cost of security since CRCs are not collision resistant.

4 The Block-Level AREA Technique

The proposed technique, called Block-Level AREA (BL-AREA) relies on the diffusion property identified by Shannon [34] for block ciphers. Theoretically a block cipher must be indistinguishable from a random permutation with equiprobable outputs. In other words, the redundancy in the statistics of the plaintext block p has to be dissipated in the statistics of the ciphertext block c. Once a block encryption is

---

[2] RO data are not modified at runtime by the application they belong to. RO data are further described later.

performed, the resulting position and value of each bit in c are a function of all bits of the corresponding p, thus providing the property of infinite error propagation at the block level.

In the proposed technique, we leverage the diffusion property of block ciphers to add the integrity checking capability to this type of encryption. To do so, p is composed of two fields: an l_p-bit field P_L – hereafter called the payload – and a t-bit field T – hereafter called the tag – such as $b^3 = t + l_p$ ($p = P_L\|T$). Considering the diffusion property presented above, after block encryption it is impossible to identify P_L and T within the ciphertext block $c = E_K(p)$. Moreover, if a c' is derived by flipping a single bit in c, there is a large probability that the last t-bit of the plaintext $p' = D_K(c')$ will be different from the value of T in p; this probability depends on the tag size t. The number of possible plaintext blocks with the same last t-bit is equal to 2^{b-t}; hence the probability these last t-bit match the value of T after decryption of a tampered c is $1/2^t$ ($= 2^{b-t}/2^t$).

We call this authentication technique *Block-Level AREA*: the redundancy is added in each plaintext block before encryption and checked for each ciphertext block after decryption. The diffusion property of block ciphers provides the two-way infinite error propagation of the original AREA technique at the block level. As opposed to regular AREA schemes, BL-AREA does not require any chaining of cryptographic operations, and hence, can process the blocks belonging to the same message in parallel. BL-AREA is similar to ECB (Electronic Code Book) mode in the sense that it encrypts blocks one at a time without any chaining feedback. However, BL-AREA does not suffer from the security flaw of the ECB mode: multiple encryption of the same plaintext never produces to the same ciphertext. This property is obtained by inserting a nonce in every plaintext blocks, making each plaintext block different from each others and ensuring that the encryption of the same payload twice produces two different ciphertext blocks.

5 System-on-Chip Architecture of the Parallelized Encryption and Integrity Checking Engine (PE-ICE)

In this section we describe the architecture of the engine, PE-ICE (Parallelized Encryption and Integrity Checking Engine), implementing the Block-Level AREA technique.

5.1 Architecture Overview

PE-ICE authenticates and encrypts data on off-chip memory operations. It is located on-chip between the last level of cache memory and the memory controller. As depicted in Figure 2, the main building block for PE-ICE is a block cipher. On write operations (Fig. 2a), a payload P_L – data to be written off-chip – is concatenated with a tag T to produce each plaintext block p to be processed by the block cipher. After encryption, the resulting ciphered block c is written in the external memory.

---

[3] As defined earlier, b is the size, in bits, of a block processed by a block cipher.

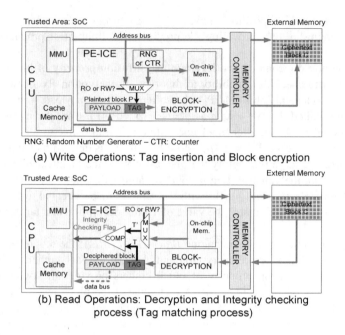

Fig. 2. PE-ICE: Encryption and Integrity checking (a) Write operations (b) Read operations

On read operations (Fig. 2b) c is loaded and decrypted. The tag T issued from the resulting plaintext block is compared to the tag re-generated on-chip, called the tag reference, T'. If T does not match T', it means – as explained in section 4 – that at least one bit of c has been modified during transmission on the bus or in the off-chip memory (spoofing attack). In such a case, PE-ICE raises an integrity checking flag to prevent further processing. Thus the block encryption provides data confidentiality and the Block-level AREA technique allows for data authentication using the same block cipher engine and by performing a single pass on data.

The general overview of PE-ICE presented above assumes that we are able to re-generate a tag reference on read operations upon integrity checking. In the next sub-section, we describe the tag generation and its composition and how it is re-generated to perform the authentication process.

5.2   The Tag Generation

PE-ICE being on the SoC, the SoC should hold the tag value T of each ciphered block stored off-chip or be able to regenerate it on read operations to achieve the integrity checking process described above. The challenge is to reach this objective by storing as little tag information as possible on the SoC to optimize the on-chip memory usage. The composition of the tag is different for each kind of data, RO (Read Only) and RW (Read Write), and depends on the properties of the respective data types.

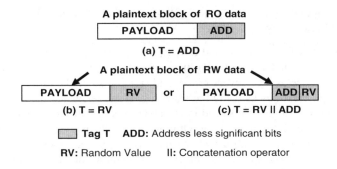

Fig. 3. Plaintext blocks and tag composition before encryption

Tag for Read Only (RO) Data

We assume that RO data are only written once in main memory when the application is loaded and are not modified at runtime. Hence, such payloads are only sensitive to spoofing and splicing attacks. Therefore, a payload P_L of RO data can be associated with a fixed tag (i.e., the tag is never changed during the lifetime of the payload in memory). This tag can be public because an adversary would need the secret encryption key to create an accepted ciphertext block $c=E_K(P_L\|T)$. The secret key, being stored in an on-chip register, where storage is trusted, is out-of reach for adversaries. Also, an adversary should not be able to choose the reference tag T' or to influence its generation. Hence, PE-ICE uses the address of the ciphered block as a tag (Fig.2a and 3a). If an attacker performs a splicing attack, the address used by the processor to fetch a block and by PE-ICE to generate the reference tag T' will not match the last t-bit (T) of the plaintext issued from decryption of the fake ciphered block (Fig.2b).

RO data are constants and code sections in an executable (e.g., .rodata and .txt in ELF executables). As specified in the threat model we assume a trusted OS kernel. Hence, we trust the kernel to correctly store these data in separated memory pages with adequate access rights (i.e., pages of code must not be writable in user mode). Also, the trusted OS is responsible for securely swapping in and out pages of RO data (i.e.; during the lifetime of the secure application in memory, a page of RO data must be loaded every time it is brought in at the same address). Finally, the trusted OS is responsible for differentiating two instances of the same application (e.g., by generating a new encryption key every time a secure application is loaded). *If the trusted OS does not meet such requirements[4]*, the designer should consider *all* data as RW and use the tag generation process described next.

Tag for Read Write (RW) Data

RW data are modified at runtime and are consequently sensitive to replay attacks. Using only the address of the data block as tag does not prevent such an attack. Indeed, on read operations the processor would not be able to verify that the data read at a given address is the most recent one or a stale data previously stored at this address.

---

[4] These requirements can be difficult to meet for complex embedded systems running several applications and, in these cases, data should be all considered as RW. However, they can be met in microcontroller applications.

For this reason the tag T must be changed on every off-chip store operation; this can be achieved in two different ways:

1) T is a NONCE, a Number used ONCE, for a given encryption key, which can be generated with a counter (T = CTR) incremented on each write operation (Fig. 2a). The use of a nonce as tag prevent replay and splicing since the processor never produces two ciphertext blocks using the same tag. However, when the counter reaches its limit we must change the encryption key and re-encrypt the corresponding memory region for T to remain a true nonce. Otherwise, an adversary can perform what we call a *periodic replay/splicing attack*: he records a ciphered block c in memory and predicts when c can be replayed or relocated by counting the number of store operations performed by the processor. Each time the number of store is a multiple of the period[5] of the counter, a periodic replay/splicing of c succeeds at the address targeted by the processor.

2) Re-encryption requirement can be inconvenient and frequent particularly when the size of the counter is chosen small. To avoid re-encryption, we propose an alternative solution where T is generated with a random value generator assumed embedded on-chip (T = RV; Fig. 2a and Fig. 3b). Using a random value provides unpredictability and thus prevents the periodic replay/splicing attack to be successful: the tag value is unpredictable, so an adversary is unable to know when two encrypted blocks have the same tag and thus when to perform a periodic replay/splicing. However, since the same random value can occur several times, this implies that replay and splicing attacks may succeed. With random values, the security lies on the difficulty for an adversary to find two ciphered blocks processed by PE-ICE (at the same address for a replay and at different address for a splicing) with the same tag. The probability of success is the same for replay and splicing attacks and is defined in section 4. This point is further developed in section 6 that presents our security analysis.

Regardless of the tag composition, the SoC must be able to retrieve the correct random or counter values – called in the following the reference random values RV' or reference counter values CTR' – to generate the reference tag T' during the integrity checking process. The set of RV' and of CTR' must be tamper-proof, otherwise the attacker could carry out a replay attack by replaying a data with the corresponding stale RV' or CTR'. In order to solve this issue the random values or counter values generated on write operations are stored on-chip (Fig. 2a) in a dedicated memory. This way, these values are tamper-proof since the SoC is considered as trusted and can be easily retrieved on read operations (Fig. 2b).

The size of RV or CTR fixes a trade-off between the strength of the countermeasure against replay and the on-chip memory overhead. An alternative tag configuration of the tag is proposed for RW data in which the least significant bits of the address addressing each ciphered block are concatenated with an RV or a CTR (T=RV‖ADD - Fig. 3c - or T=CTR‖ADD). Such a configuration decreases the strength against replay (by decreasing the size of the value which changes on each off-chip store operation) but maintains a countermeasure against splicing while reducing the on-chip memory cost.

---

[5] The period of a counter is defined by the number of distinct value it generates (e.g. for a ctr-bit counter the period is of 2^{ctr}).

For sake of clarity, in the following PE-ICE is described only for tag composed of random values (fig.3b and c). For a description of PE-ICE using counter values and the security implications of such a choice, refer to [20].

Parallelizability. Tags are either generated from the address, from a counter or from a random generator. In any cases, *on write operations*, the tag generation can be triggered at the same time as the processor request. Therefore the tag generation process can be parallelized with loading the payload through the on-chip bus (e.g., loading 128-bit of data through the 32-bit AHB bus takes four bus cycles). Another solution is for PE-ICE to include a small buffer to store counter or random values generated in advance. *On read operations*, the tag generation latency is always hidden by the off-chip memory access latency:

i) when the reference tag is composed of the address of the block: the reference tag is already known before the read memory block arrives on-chip and hence, before the decryption process starts,

ii) when the reference tag is a counter value or a random number: it is contained in an on-chip memory and it is, therefore, known before the end of the decryption process.

The tag generation (for BL-AREA encryption) and re-generation (for BL-AREA decryption and authentication) processes are, therefore, parallelizable with the cryptographic operations required by BL-AREA or have their latency hidden by processor operations.

5.3 Physical Address vs. Virtual Address Space Protection

The tag composition presented in the previous section makes use of the block address without specifying if this address is the physical or the virtual address. In this section we discuss the pros and cons of using the physical or the virtual address as part of the tag T.

The main advantage of using the virtual address in tags is that the application can be loaded in memory already encrypted. However, the use of the virtual address requires some deep processor core modifications. As mentioned above, PE-ICE is localized between the cache memory and the memory controller; hence, for physically-addressed cache memory it would be necessary to also store the virtual address to be able to write-back dirty cache blocks in main memory. Such a modification would require an additional on-chip memory overhead. Also, for shared libraries or data, the fact that several virtual addresses map to the same physical address complicates [23] or prevents [24] their protection. In previous works [24], this point remains an open question. Considering this non negligible architectural obstacle, we choose to use the physical address to generate tags at the cost of having to encrypt pages of code at load-time and to trust the OS in protecting RO pages swapped in and out (if the designer ever decides to consider some data as RO).

5.4 Address Computation

PE-ICE shifts the physical addressing by inserting tags between payloads. This shift must be transparent for the CPU, hence, PE-ICE handles the address translation. In the following t_b and l_{pb} denotes respectively the size, in bytes, of the tag and of the payload contained in a chunk. Moreover, we consider that PE-ICE protects the whole physical memory space. Hence, to retrieve an address A_P of a PE-ICE chunk from the address A_{CPU} provided by the CPU, PE-ICE first computes the position P of a payload in the address space seen by the CPU:

$$P = \frac{A_{CPU}}{l_{pb}}$$

Then, A_P can be computed as follows:

$$A_P = A_{CPU} + P \times t_b$$

Hence, l_{pb} and t_b must be a power of 2 to allow a simple computation of P and A_P in hardware.

6 Security Analysis

6.1 Active Attacks

The security of PE-ICE against the three active attacks (spoofing, splicing and replay) described in the threat model and carried out on a chunk is quantified in Table 1 depending on four parameters:

- t, the bit-width of the tag,
- a, the number of address bits in the tag,
- r, the bit width of the random value RV,
- and b, the ciphered block length (in bytes).

Spoofing attacks
Our threat model considers that an adversary can only access off-chip data, and hence, encrypted data. Therefore, in order to spoof data, the adversary would need to know how to create ciphertexts or how to manipulate existing ciphertexts to make them pass the authentication process. Since we consider the underlying block encryption algorithm as secure, an adversary cannot deduce the effect of ciphertext bit manipulations in the resulting plaintext (e.g., tag bits). As mentioned in Section 4, attacks consisting in the insertion of random ciphertext or the tampering with certain ciphertext bits succeed with probability $1/2^t$.

Replay and Splicing attacks
The outputs of the random number generator implemented to produce RVs are assumed equiprobable; therefore the probability of success of a replay is equal to $1/2^t$ and is the same for a splicing attack when $t = r$ (Fig. 3b). When the address is used in the tag ($t=a+r$ – Fig. 3c), the physical address space protected against splicing attacks is determined by a and b; this address pace is equal to (2^a x b) bytes and is called in the following a *splicing-free-segment*. However, a might have a size which could be insufficient to cover the whole address space; hence a different key must be attributed to encrypt every splicing-free-segment contained in the physical address space. The

key is thus said *splicing-free-segment-dependent*. This way an adversary which swaps two memory blocks with the same address bits in the tag from a splicing-free-segment to another will be detected. Such a requirement for the key only applies to RO data since the tag for RW data already includes a countermeasure against replay which protects against this attack. As a consequence, considering that the keys used to encrypt the RO memory section are *splicing-free-segment-dependent*, an adversary cannot perform a splicing attack on such a memory section. Thus, we consider that it is impossible to perform a splicing attack on a chunk of RO data while for RW data a splicing attack carried out on a chunk from a splicing-free-segment to another has $1/2^r$ chance to succeed and 0 inside a splicing-free-segment.

6.2   Confidentiality and Passive Attacks

Considering our threat model (SoC trusted), the adversary might only perform two passive attacks to challenge data confidentiality: ciphertext-only attacks – the eavesdropper tries to deduce the secret key or the plaintext by observing the ciphertext – and known plaintext attacks – the adversary additionally knows a part of the plaintext (e.g., the address of the block used for the tag generation). Therefore, the choice of the block cipher algorithm is essential and must be secure against these two kinds of attacks. However, this is the minimum requirement for a block encryption algorithm, and in the following the block cipher implemented in PE-ICE fulfills this necessary condition.

Table 1. Security limitations of PE-ICE with regard to the defined active attacks – Probability of success

Attack		RO data	RW data	
			$t = a + r$	$t = r$
Spoofing attack		$1/2^t$	$1/2^t$	$1/2^t$
Splicing attack	Inside a Splicing-free-segment	0	0	$1/2^t$
	Outside a Splicing-free-segment	0	$1/2^r$	
Replay attack		N/A	$1/2^r$	$1/2^t$

7   Experimental Results

In the following, a *PE-ICE configuration* is defined as an implementation of PE-ICE with a given block cipher. A PE-ICE configuration is denoted PE-ICE-*bw* where *bw* is the bit width of the block processed by the underlying block cipher.

In this section, we first define PE-ICE-160, the PE-ICE configuration using the Rijndael [26] block cipher processing 160-bit blocks. Then, performance of several PE-ICE configurations at runtime are evaluated and compared. Finally, PE-ICE configurations are compared to a generic composition scheme.

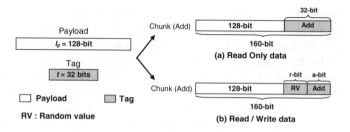

Fig. 4. Layout of a PE-ICE-160 chunk before encryption

7.1 PE-ICE-160 – A PE-ICE Configuration

The Rijndael algorithm is the block cipher who won the NIST contest for a new block encryption standard. The related standard is called AES [25] (Advanced Encryption Standard). AES processes 128-bit blocks and enrolls 128, 192 or 256-bit key. However, the original Rijndael [26] block cipher supports any key and block sizes that is a multiple of 32, between 128 and 256. This leads to several possible configurations for PE-ICE based on this block cipher. We studied three of them PE-ICE-128, PE-ICE-160 and PE-ICE-192, which use the Rinjdael algorithm processing respectively 128-bit (AES), 160-bit (Rijn-160) and 192-bit (Rijn-192) blocks. For sake of clarity, we only describe PE-ICE-160 configuration in this paper; for a description of the other configurations, refer to [20].

Layout of a chunk
For PE-ICE-160 we choose $l_{pb} = 16$ and $t_b = 4$. The composition of the resulting PE-ICE-160 chunk is depicted in Fig. 4 (where a may be 0).

Security Analysis for PE-ICE-160
The security limitations of PE-ICE-160 are directly deduced from Table 1 (i.e. we fixed the parameter t as defined for PE-ICE-160, $t = 32$). For RO data, the 32-bit address of each ciphered block is used as tag (Fig. 4a). Hence, a splicing-free-segment is of the size of an addressing space of 4GB. Thus only one encryption key dedicated to RO data is required per application.

For RW data, the strength of the proposed countermeasure against replay and splicing attacks depends on the designer's choice of the values of r and a. For example, if $a = 24$ and $r = 8$, a splicing-free-segment is 256 MB long (224 x 16B); thus a replay attack has a $1/2^8$ chance to succeed, while an adversary carrying out a splicing attack has a $1/2^8$ chance to succeed from a splicing-free-segment to another and 0 within a splicing-free-segment. When $t = r = 32$, for both replay and splicing attacks, the chance to succeed is of $1/2^{32}$.

When r is chosen small to save on-chip memory, a simple technique enabling to improve the strength against splicing and replay is to foresee in PE-ICE a counter which memorizes the number of detected intrusions. When this counter reaches a threshold value determined by the designer or by the software programmer, the

Table 2. Security limitations of PE-ICE-160

Attack		RO data	RW data	
			$t = a + r$	$t = r$
Spoofing attack		$1/2^{32}$	$1/2^{32}$	$1/2^{32}$
Splicing attack	Inside a Splicing-free-segment	0	0	$1/2^{32}$
	Outside a Splicing-free-segment	N/A	$1/2^r$	
Replay attack		N/A	$1/2^r$	$1/2^{32}$

external memory space dedicated to RW data is zeroized and a new key is generated This will most probably result in a reset. This implementation countermeasure can also be implemented to prevent brute force spoofing attack where the adversary inject random chunks until finding one passing the integrity checking process.

For both kinds of data the tag is at least 32-bit long, hence an adversary has a $1/2^{32}$ chance to succeed with a spoofing attack. Table 2 summarizes the security limitations of PE-ICE-160 evaluated in likelihood of success.

Memory Requirement
The amount of memory required by PE-ICE comes from the tag storage for off-chip memory and from the storage of the reference random values for on-chip memory. The off-chip memory overhead is defined by the ratio R_{OF} between the tag and the payload bit widths ($R_{OF} = t/l_p$). For PE-ICE-160 the off-chip memory overhead is 25%. The on-chip memory overhead is defined by the ratio R_{ON} between the bit-length of a random value used to protect a RW chunk against replay and the corresponding protected payload bit-length ($R_{OF} = r/l_p$). For PE-ICE-160 the on-chip memory overhead for r equals to 8 or 32 is respectively 6.25% or 25%.

Latencies
In this section, we present the additional latencies introduced on off-chip memory accesses by PE-ICE-160 and AES-ECB encryption/decryption. The underlying CPU considered in this study is the ARM9E for which the optimum frequency (0.18μm CMOS process) is around 200MHz with a 32-bit AMBA AHB bus running at 100MHz [27].

Our implementation of the AES algorithm is non-pipelined and takes 11 cycles to encrypt one 128-bit block of plaintext in ECB (1 cycle per round plus 1 cycle to buffer the result). The AES implementation (0.18μm CMOS) presented in [28] shows that such latency is valid until 330 MHz. Hence, in the following we consider a realistic case for the ratio $R_{E/B}$ between the AES frequency (F_{AES}) and the bus frequency (F_{AHB}): $R_{E/B}=2$, $F_{AHB}=F_{AES}/2$. When $R_{E/B}=2$ the intrinsic latency of the AES encryption seen on the AHB bus is of 6 cycles. The difference between all Rijndael versions lies in the number of rounds required to output a ciphertext block (or a plaintext

Table 3. Additional latencies introduced by PE-ICE-160 and by AES-ECB on an AHB bus for operations requested by an ARM9E core

Payload size - Operations	AES-ECB	PE-ICE-160	
	Latencies (AHB cycles)	Latencies (AHB cycles)	Overhead vs. AES-ECB
8 to 32-bit Write	28	30	7%
8 to 32-bit Read	10	11	10%
4-word Write	10	11	10%
4-word Read	10	11	10%
8-word Write	10	12	20%
8-word Read	10	12	20%
16-word Write	10	14	40%
16-word Read	10	14	40%

block). This number of rounds Nr is defined in [26] and is equal to: $Nr = max(Nk; Nb) + 6$; where Nk is the number of 32-bit words in the key and Nb the number of 32-bit words in the block processed. For Rijn-160 - processing 160-bit block and enrolling a 128-bit key - Nr is equal to 11. Hence the intrinsic latency of Rijn-160 seen on the AHB bus is of 6 cycles.

PE-ICE has been implemented in VHDL to be compliant with the AHB bus. Table 3 sums up the additional latencies[6] (expressed in bus cycles and obtained by simulation) introduced by PE-ICE-160 and by the AES-ECB encryption. The overhead of PE-ICE compared to AES-ECB encryption gives the cost of achieving data authentication in addition to data encryption. On average this cost is of 22%. This latency overhead is mainly due to the increase of the intrinsic latency of the underlying block cipher (i.e., Rijn-160 instead of AES). Also, we can observe that the latencies for PE-ICE-160 increase along with the number of read/write words while the latencies for AES-ECB do not. This is due to the extra cycles required to process the tag: the AHB interface needs to load 32-bit of tag for each 4-word of payload to read or write.

Silicon Area Overhead

The hardware resources for PE-ICE-160 and for the AES-ECB engine reported in this section are those required to match the processor bandwidth. The hardware resources are first evaluated in number N of Rijn-160 or AES cores. All versions of Rijndael, including AES, implement the same operations (i.e., AddRoundKey, SubBytes, Mix-Columns and ShiftRows [26]), therefore a core refers to the implementation of these four operations. The main difference in term of silicon area between an AES and a Rijn-160 comes from the different data path width (i.e., 128-bit for AES and 160-bit for Rijn-160). We consider this difference when we evaluate the hardware resources in number of gates.

---

[6] Rijndael algorithm requires a decryption key which is computed from the encryption key. We make the realistic assumption that this decryption key is computed once and then stored in a dedicated register on-chip.

The processor can read or write a 32-bit data per AHB bus cycle. Thus, considering that a plaintext (or ciphertext) block is collected in 4 bus cycles and that the AES intrinsic latency seen on the AHB bus (6 cycles), the AES-ECB engine must implement two AES cores to reach the optimum throughput of 32-bit per cycle.

For PE-ICE-160, on write operations, 4 cycles are required to collect a plaintext block on the 32-bit AHB bus and 5 cycles to output a ciphertext block to the memory controller whereas on read operations, 5 cycles are required to collect a ciphertext block and 4 to output a plaintext block. The maximum throughput is theoretically higher on write operations than on read operations. However, the available bandwidth between PE-ICE and the memory controller limits the throughput on write operations; hence on both read and write operations a ciphered text block is processed only every 5 cycles. Considering the intrinsic latencies of the Rijn-160 (6 cycles), to reach the optimum throughput N has to be of two, as for the AES-ECB engine.

For an atomic bus transfer the same key is shared by all AES cores, hence only one key expander core is needed for PE-ICE-160 and for the AES-ECB engine. By considering the figures provided by Ocean Logic [29] an AES encryption/decryption core with 11 cycles of latency takes 24 Kgates and the corresponding key expander core 32 Kgates in the 0.18µ technology. This means that considering the chosen ratio $R_{E/B} = 2$, the hardware cost of the AES-ECB is of 80 Kgates. The data path width of Rijn-160 being 25% larger than AES, the hardware cost of PE-ICE-160 is of 100 Kgates.

At low hardware cost and low latency overhead, we showed that PE-ICE: i) strengthens AES-ECB encryption – the tag inserted before encryption prevents an adversary from detecting when the same data is transferred twice by monitoring bus transactions – ii) provides data authentication in addition to data confidentiality.

7.2 Performance Evaluation

Simulation Framework

In order to evaluate the performance at runtime of the studied PE-ICE configurations the SoC designer tool set [33] is used. This toolset provided by ARM consists in two separate applications: SoCDesigner - used to integrate custom components modeled in SystemC (CABA, Cycle Accurate Bit Accurate) into complex SoC platforms - and SoCExplorer - a cycle accurate simulator allowing to run benchmarks and to profile the platforms defined with SoCDesigner.

In the following we refer to the Base platform to denote the SoC platform which does not include hardware mechanisms for data security (encryption and integrity checking engine). To define the Base latencies we use the figures provided in the datasheet of an AHB compliant memory controller, the PL172[30]. We choose the lower read (9 cycles) and write (1 cycle) latencies assuming the following parameters for the underlying SDRAM memory: Precharge latency = 2, Activate latency = 2 and CAS latency = 2. This way, ideal memory accesses are defined and PE-ICE is pushed in the worst simulation case. In this section several PE-ICE configurations are evaluated: PE-ICE-128, PE-ICE-160, PE-ICE-192[7] and AES-ECB using respectively AES, Rijn-160 and Rijn-192, and are compared to an AES-ECB engine. One simulation platform per security engine has been designed in SoCDesigner. These platforms are referred in the following as PE-ICE-128, PE-ICE-160, PE-ICE-192 and AES-ECB. The architectural parameters defining the simulation frameworks are summarized in Table 4.

Table 4. Architectural parameters used for simulation

Processor Core	ARM9E
Processor-memory bus width	32-bit
AHB Clock ratio (FCPU / FAHB)	2
Cache line size	256-bit
Cache policy	Write-back
RE/B (FAES / FAHB)	2
Base off-chip Read latency (AHB bus cycles)	9
Base off-chip Write latency (AHB bus cycles)	1

Results

Eight benchmarks [32] designed for embedded systems were used in this evaluation. The simulation results for the Base platform serve as reference and are shown in IPC (Instruction Per Cycles) in Fig.5 for two different sizes of data cache and instruction cache (4KB and 128KB). Fig.6 gives this cache miss rate for each benchmark and for both sizes of the data cache. Note that considering the low Base latencies and the fact that all applications are entirely protected, the worst case results are presented in this section. Indeed, all data processed during software execution do not require to be necessarily encrypted and integrity checked.

In order to illustrate the impact of the studied hardware mechanisms for data security we show in Fig.7 the simulation results of the platforms emulating the AES-ECB engine, PE- ICE-128, PE-ICE-160 and PE-ICE-192, in IPC normalized to the Base platform performance. The AES-ECB engine performance clearly highlights that the overhead is mainly due to encryption; it is 50% in the worst case (CJPEG – 4KB) and, 31.5% and 14.3% on average respectively for 4KB and 128KB data cache. Increasing the data cache size decreases the overhead of the security engines by reducing the number of off-chip memory accesses, except for the DES benchmark for which the data cache miss rate remains almost the same.

This quite important performance cost can be drastically reduced by using a wider processor-memory bus (e.g. 64-bit) or by running the encryption algorithm at its maximum frequency. Moreover, we did not explore how to take advantage of the waiting time in the write buffer and of the Base write latency. The latencies introduced by the different security engines could be partially hidden on write operations by starting the encryption before storing data in the write buffer or at least at the same time as the memory access request.

---

[7] For a complete description of these PE-ICE configuration, refer to [20].

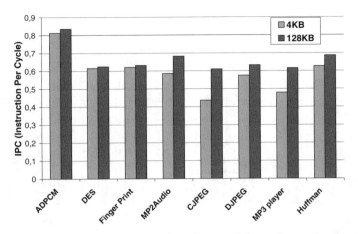

Fig. 5. Simulation Results for the Base Platform for two different data cache sizes (4KB and 128KB)

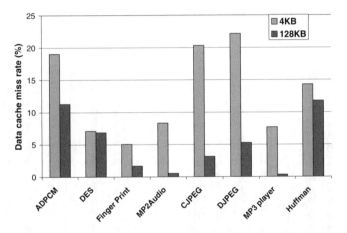

Fig. 6. Data cache miss rate for two different data cache sizes (4KB and 128KB)

Nevertheless the interesting point is the low overhead implied by PE-ICE compared to the AES engine. We evaluate the performance slowdown of the integrity checking mechanisms proposed by PE-ICE when compared to AES encryption alone by normalizing the IPCs of the PE-ICE platforms to the AES-ECB engine performance (Fig.8). The best results are obtained with PE-ICE-128 since on average the degradation is 1.9% and 1.1% respectively for a data cache size of 4KB and of 128KB and in the worst case it is 4.1% (DES – 4KB). However PE-ICE-160 results are close since on average it implies a performance slowdown of 3.3% for a data cache of 4KB and of only 1.7% for a data cache of 128KB.

We evaluated the implementation of PE-ICE with several block ciphers and we showed that it provides data integrity in addition to data confidentiality with a low hardware cost and a negligible runtime performance overhead when compared to standard encryption. In the next section we further highlight the advantage of PE-ICE through comparison with a generic composition scheme.

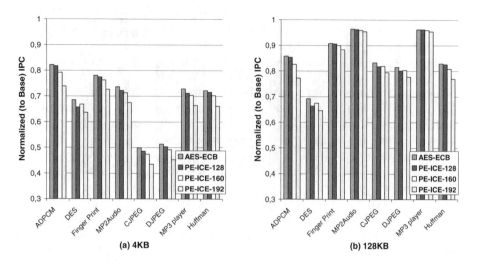

Fig. 7. Run-time overhead of AES-ECB encryption and of PE-ICE configurations for two data cache sizes (4KB - 128KB)

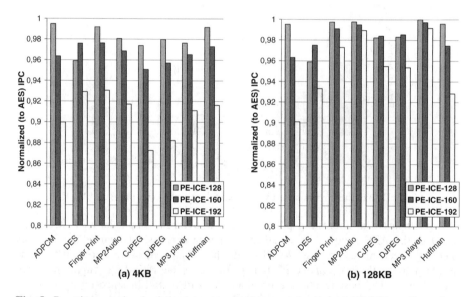

Fig. 8. Run-time overhead of the integrity checking mechanism of PE-ICE configurations compared to AES-ECB encryption alone for two data cache sizes (4KB and 128KB)

7.3   Comparison with a Generic Composition Scheme

In this section a comparison of PE-ICE with a generic composition scheme implemented in the Encrypt-then-Mac fashion is proposed. We first describe the generic composition scheme, referred to as GC, and then we compare it to PE-ICE-160.

Description and Evaluation of the Generic Composition Scheme

Description of GC. GC is the association of an AES encryption with a CBC-MAC [40] algorithm in the Encrypt-then-MAC fashion. Encrypt-then-MAC is chosen because it is the most secured conventional method to pair an authenticated mode and an encryption mode as proved in [39]. As for PE-ICE the encryption mode is ECB in order to perform a fair comparison between GC and PE-ICE concerning the integrity checking overhead. We consider ECB encryption secure in GC even though the same block encrypted twice always yields to the same ciphertext block, which is not the case for PE-ICE. The tag required for the integrity checking process is computed over a chunk with the CBC-MAC algorithm. The underlying block cipher E_k for our CBC-MAC implementation is AES. The Encrypt-then-MAC construction is implemented, hence the tag is computed over the ciphered chunk composed of *m* AES blocks (C_1, C_2, ..., C_m) by using a different key than the one required for the encryption [39]. A 128-bit vector N is additionally enrolled in the CBC-MAC computation to thwart replay and splicing attacks. N is composed of the 32-bit chunk address concatenated with an *r*-bit vector RV and padded with zeroes to be 128-bit. The address serves to thwart splicing attacks by making N different for each ciphered chunk stored off-chip. For RW data, RV is the countermeasure against replay attacks, it is an *r*-bit random value generated on-chip, with its reference RV' stored also on-chip. Thus it can be retrieved for integrity checking on read operations while making it secret and tamper-proof from an adversary point of view. For RO data RV is padded with zeroes. In the literature [12, 37] the chunk size is defined by the cache line length. However, this choice for the CBC-MAC is inefficient for big cache blocks in terms of latency due to the chaining nature of such a MAC algorithm. Thus, the tag is computed over a chunk *M* composed of two ciphered blocks – *M* = (*N*, C_1, C_2) – independently of the size of the cache line. This tag is then truncated to 32-bit to decrease the memory bandwidth pollution generated by its transmission on the bus and to optimize the off-chip memory overhead. The resulting CBC-MAC implemented is depicted Fig 9.

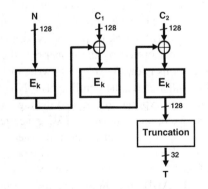

Fig. 9. CBC-MAC implemented in the proposed Generic Composition scheme

Table 5. Additional latencies introduced by GC on an AHB bus for the operations requested by an ARM9E

Payload size - Operations	GC (AES + CBC-MAC)	
	Latencies (AHB cycles)	Overhead vs. AES-ECB
8 to 32-bit Write	38	+36%
8 to 32-bit Read	15	+50%
128-bit Write	20	+100%
128-bit Read	15	+50%
256-bit Write	14	+40%
256-bit Read	15	+50%
512-bit Write	14	+40%
512-bit Read	15	+50%

Security analysis. In the following, the defined CBC-MAC implementation is evaluated relatively to the three attacks exposed in the threat model (spoofing, splicing and replay) and carried out on a chunk. CBC-MAC is based on block cipher encryption; therefore its outputs are equiprobable from an adversary's standpoint. Concerning spoofing and splicing attacks, the chance to succeed for an attacker depends on the size of the tag and is equal to $1/2^{32}$. The strength of the countermeasure against replay depends on r: the chance for replay to succeed is equal to $1/2^r$. The latter probability is limited by the size of the tag, meaning that there is no sense in choosing $r > 32$.

Memory overhead. The off-chip memory overhead of GC is of 12.5% since it requires to store 32-bit of tag for 256-bit of payload. The on-chip memory overhead depends on the size of RV and is defined by the ratio between r and the protected payload.

Latencies. In this section we consider an implementation of GC on the AHB bus to evaluate the latencies introduced on read and write operations. On read operations the encryption of N is parallelized with the memory access latency, hence the CBC-MAC latency seen on the AHB bus is only due to two consecutives AES encryptions plus 1 cycle of buffering, resulting in 11 cycles (for $R_{E/B} = 2$) with 4 additional cycles to collect the first block. The integrity checking process is parallelizable with decryption process since they are both performed on the ciphertext, therefore the resulting latency for GC on read operations is of 15 cycles. On write operations, the CBC-MAC has the same latency (11 cycles) since the enrollment of N is hidden by the AES encryption. However, the data encryption process and the tag computation latencies are only partially parallelized. Moreover, the CBC-MAC generates a RMW write on the tag for the 8 to 32-bit and 128-bit write operations; this means that the chunk and the corresponding tag are loaded and checked, to be recomputed by enrolling the new 128-bit value in the CBC-MAC computation. Table 5 sums up the additional latencies introduced by GC on the AHB bus. On average the overhead of GC compared to AES encryption alone is of 52% for $R_{E/B} = 2$.

Hardware cost. On read operations the decryption and integrity checking processes are parallelized; thus despite the fact that they are both based on the AES algorithm, the AES- ECB engine and the CBC-MAC scheme of GC cannot share hardware. As shown in section 7.1, the AES-ECB encryption requires two AES encryption/decryption cores when $R_{E/B} = 2$. Considering the intrinsic latency of the CBC-MAC (11 cycles) algorithm three AES cores are required to reach the maximum throughput of 32-bit/cycle. However, only the encryption process is involved in the CBC-MAC computation, therefore the hardware cost can be optimized by using an AES core implementing the encryption process only. The silicon area consumed by such a core is estimated at 16 Kgates by Ocean Logic [29] in the 0.18µ technology. Moreover, the AES-ECB encryption and the CBC-MAC computation require separated key expansion cores since they enroll two different keys. The resulting hardware cost for GC is of 160 Kgates when $R_{E/B} = 2$.

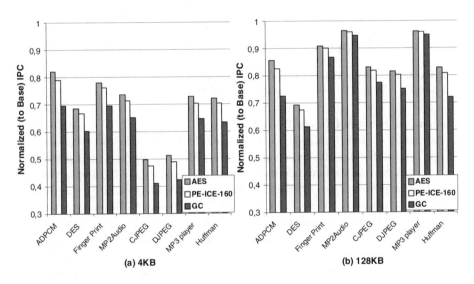

Fig. 10. Runtime overhead of GC, of the AES-ECB engine and of PE-ICE-160 for two data cache sizes (4KB and 128KB)

Runtime performance. A simulation platform has been designed for GC in SoC Designer with the latencies given in Table 5 added to the Base ones. The simulation framework is the same as the one described in section 7.2. GC has also been evaluated for two data cache sizes: 4 KB and 128 KB. Similarly to PE-ICE configurations the overhead of GC compared to the Base performance is mainly due to the encryption as shown in Fig.10. Nevertheless the additional performance slowdown of the integrity checking mechanisms of GC (CBC-MAC) is non negligible (Fig.10) when compared to the AES-ECB engine since it is of 18% in the worst case scenario (DJPEG – 4KB), and of 13.7% and 7.8% respectively in average for a data cache of 4 KB and of 128 KB.

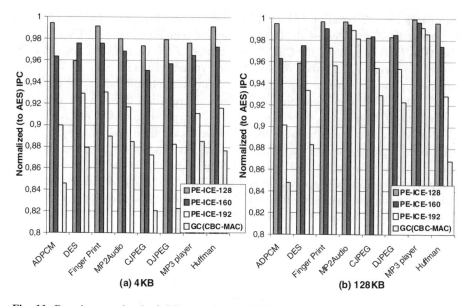

Fig. 11. Run-time overhead of GC and of several PE-ICE configurations (PE-ICE-128, PE-ICE-160, PE-ICE-192) for two data cache sizes (4KB and 128KB)

Comparison between GC and PE-ICE

To compare GC and PE-ICE-160, we evaluate their respective cost to ensure data integrity in addition to data confidentiality. The AES-ECB engine is used as the reference cost to provide data confidentiality since PE-ICE-160 and GC implement both the ECB encryption mode. Table 6 shows the overhead implied by the integrity checking mechanisms in PE-ICE-160 and in GC in terms of hardware area, latencies and run-time performance hit. PE-ICE-160 requires 25% additional silicon area to achieve the integrity checking process while GC implies an overhead of 100%. In term of latencies the overhead of GC reaches up to 52% on average while for PE-ICE-160 it remains always under 22% on average. The additional performance slowdown when compared to the AES-ECB encryption is roughly four times lower for PE-ICE-160 than for GC. In term of security, PE-ICE-160 has the same security limitations as GC regarding the defined active attacks when $r = 32$. Moreover, PE-ICE-160 increases the robustness of the ECB mode by introducing a random value – for RW data – or a nonce – for RO data. Hence for RO data a same plaintext block encrypted twice never produces the same ciphertext block while for RW data there is a little probability that the same plaintext block ciphered twice leads to the same ciphertext block. This is not ensured by GC. The main advantage of GC is the memory consumption since for the same value of r, GC implies an on-chip and off-chip memory overhead twice smaller than PE-ICE-160. Indeed, to maintain a strong security level with a fine granularity of integrity checking (to optimize narrow block encryption and RMW) PE-ICE requires having a dedicated tag to each processed ciphered block.

Table 6. Summary of the Cost of the Integrity Checking Mechanisms of GC and PE-ICE compared to AES-ECB

		GC (AES-ECB + CBC-MAC)	PE-ICE-160
Hardware cost		160 Kgates ⇔ +100%	100 Kgates ⇔25%
Latencies		+52%	+22%
Run-time slowdown	DC=4KB	+13.7%	+3.3%
	DC=128KB	+7.8%	+1.7%
Off-chip memory		+12.5%	+25%
On-chip memory		r/256	r/128

8 Conclusion

We introduced in this paper the concept of Added Redundancy Explicit Authentication at the Block Level (BL-AREA). Existing authenticated encryption schemes either require chaining cryptographic operations (i.e., one pass on data but each block is sequentially processed – AREA) or process blocks first for encryption/decryption and then for authentication (i.e., two passes on data, one for encryption and one for authentication – generic composition). As opposed to these techniques, BL-AREA performs a single pass on data and cryptographically processes blocks independently and, thereby, enables parallelization. In this sense, BL-AREA is similar to ECB encryption mode. However, BL-AREA ensures authentication in addition to confidentiality and it does not suffer from the security weakness of ECB (i.e., the same payload is never encrypted twice to the same ciphertext). BL-AREA also improves the performance upon RMW operations triggered upon narrow block encryption.

We described and evaluated an engine, PE-ICE, based on the concept of BL-AREA to highlight its relevance and efficiency in ensuring data integrity in addition to data confidentiality in the context of processor-memory transaction. PE-ICE provides integrity checking in addition to encryption for a low hardware overhead and for a low run-time performance hit (less than 4%). We also showed that PE-ICE is more efficient at run-time and in terms of hardware than a generic composition scheme. Compared to PE-ICE, a generic composition scheme can require 100% of additional hardware and almost 14% of run-time performance overhead to provide integrity checking in addition to encryption.

Therefore, implementing PE-ICE in commercial devices to provide memory encryption and integrity checking is a more realistic solution than generic composition schemes using block encryption. Future works include comparing BL-AREA to generic composition scheme using counter mode encryption. We are also exploring how to adapt the concept of BL-AREA to stream ciphers [46].

References

1. Kocher, P., Lee, R.B., McGraw, G., Raghunathan, A., Ravi, S.: Security as a New Dimension in Embedded System Design. In: Proceedings of the Design Automation Conference (DAC), pp. 753–760 (June 2004)
2. Ravi, S., Raghunathan, A., Chakradhar, S.: Tamper Resistance Mechanisms for Secure Embedded Systems. In: IEEE Intl. Conf. on VLSI Design (January 2004)
3. Alves, T., Felton, D.: Trustzone: Integrated hardware and software security, ARM white paper (July 2004)
4. Trusted Computing Group. TCG Specification Architecture Overview Revision 1.2 (April 2004), https://www.trustedcomputinggroup.org/groups/ TCG_1_0_Architecture_Overview.pdf
5. Huang, A.: Keeping secrets in hardware the microsoft xbox case study. MIT AI Memo (2002)
6. Smith, S.W., Weingart, S.H.: Building a High-Performance, Programmable Secure Coprocessor. Computer Networks (Special Issue on Computer Network Security) 31, 831–860 (1999)
7. Vaslin, R., Gogniat, G., Diguet, J.P., Wanderley Netto, E., Tessier, R., Burleson, W.P.: A security approach for off-chip memory in embedded microprocessor systems. Microprocessors and Microsystems - Embedded Hardware Design, 37–45 (2009)
8. Vaslin, R., Gogniat, G., Diguet, J.P., Tessier, R., Burleson, W.: High-efficiency protection solution for off-chip memory in embedded systems. In: ERSA 2007, pp. 117–123 (2007)
9. Lie, D., Thekkath, C., Mitchell, M., Lincoln, P., Boneh, D., Mitchell, J., Horowitz, M.: Architectural Support for Copy and Tamper Resistant Software. In: Proceedings of the 9th Int'l Conference on Architectural Support for Programming Languages and Operating Systems (ASPLOS-IX), pp. 168–177 (November 2000)
10. Suh, G.E., Clarke, D., Gassend, B., van Dijk, M., Devadas, S.: AEGIS: Architecture for Tamper-Evident and Tamper-Resistant Processing. In: Proceedings of the 17th Int'l Conference on Supercomputing (June 2003)
11. Suh, G.E.: AEGIS: A Single-Chip Secure Processor, PhD thesis, Massachusetts Institute of Technology (September 2005)
12. Lee, R.B., Kwan, P.C.S., McGregor, J.P., Dwoskin, J., Wang, Z.: Architecture for Protecting Critical Secrets in Microprocessors. In: Proceedings of the 32nd International Symposium on Computer Architecture (ISCA 2005), pp. 2–13 (June 2005)
13. Elbaz, R., Champagne, D., Gebotys, C.H., Lee, R.B., Potlapally, N.R., Torres, L.: Hardware Mechanisms for Memory Authentication: A Survey of Existing Techniques and Engines. Transactions on Computational Science 4, 1–22 (2009)
14. Yan, C., Rogers, B., Englender, D., Solihin, Y., Prvulovic, M.: Improving Cost, Performance, and Security of Memory Encryption and Authentication. In: Proc. of the International Symposium on Computer Architecture (2006)
15. Rogers, B., Chhabra, S., Solihin, Y., Prvulovic, M.: Using Address Independent Seed Encryption and Bonsai Merkle Trees to Make Secure Processors OS– and Performance–Friendly. In: Proc. of the 40th IEEE/ACM Symposium on Microarchitecture, MICRO (2007)
16. Merkle, R.C.: Protocols for Public Key Cryptography. In: IEEE Symp. on Security and Privacy, pp. 122–134 (1980)
17. Hall, W.E., Jutla, C.S.: Parallelizable authentication trees. In: Preneel, B., Tavares, S. (eds.) SAC 2005. LNCS, vol. 3897, pp. 95–109. Springer, Heidelberg (2006)

18. Duc, G., Keryell, R.: CryptoPage: An Efficient Secure Architecture with Memory Encryption, Integrity and Information Leakage Protection. In: ACSAC 2006, pp. 483–492 (2006)

19. Gassend, B., Suh, G.E., Clarke, D., van Dijk, M., Devadas, S.: Caches and Merkle Trees for Efficient Memory Integrity Verification. In: Proceedings of Ninth International Symposium on High Performance Computer Architecture (February 2003)

20. Elbaz, R.: Hardware Mechanisms for Secured Processor Memory Transactions in Embedded Systems, PhD Thesis, University of Montpellier -LIRMM (2006)

21. Elbaz, R., Champagne, D., Lee, R.B., Torres, L., Sassatelli, G., Guillemin, P.: TEC-Tree: A Low Cost and Parallelizable Tree for Efficient Defense against Memory Replay Attacks. In: Paillier, P., Verbauwhede, I. (eds.) CHES 2007. LNCS, vol. 4727, pp. 289–302. Springer, Heidelberg (2007)

22. Lie, D., Thekkath, C., Horowitz, M.: Implementing an Untrusted Operating System on Trusted Hardware. In: Proc. of the 19th ACM Symposium on Operating Systems Principles (October 2003)

23. Lie, D.: Architectural Support for Copy and Tamper-Resistant Software, Ph.D Thesis, Stanford University (December 2003)

24. Yang, J., Gao, L., Zhang, Y.: Improving Memory Encryption Performance in Secure Processors. IEEE Transactions on Computers 54(5), 630–640 (2005)

25. National Institute of Science and Technology (NIST), FIPS PUB 197: Advanced Encryption Standard (AES) (November 2001)

26. Daemen, J., Rijmen, V.: AES Proposal: Rijndael (March 1999),
    http://csrc.nist.gov/CryptoToolkit/aes/rijndael/
    Rijndael-ammended.pdf

27. http://www.arm.com/pdfs/ARM9E_flyer_063_4.pdf

28. Hodjat, A., Hwang, D., Lai, B.C., Tiri, K., Verbauwhede, I.: A 3.84 gbits/s AES crypto coprocessor with modes of operation in a 0.18-μm CMOS technology. In: ACM Great Lakes Symposium on VLSI 2005, pp. 60–63 (2005)

29. http://www.arm.com/products/DevTools/MaxSim.html

30. ARM PrimeCell MultiPort Memory Controller PL172 - Technical Reference Manual,
    http://www.nalanda.nitc.ac.in/industry/appnotes/arm/soc/
    DDI0215B_MPMC_PL172.pdf

31. Elbaz, R., Torres, L., Sassatelli, G., Guillemin, P., Bardouillet, M., Martinez, A.: A parallelized way to provide data encryption and integrity checking on a processor-memory bus. In: DAC 2006, pp. 506–509 (2006)

32. The Embedded Microprocessor Benchmark Consortium (EEMBC),
    http://www.eembc.org/

33. http://www.arm.com/products/DevTools/MaxSim.html

34. Shannon, C.: Communication theory of secrecy systems. Bell System Technical Journal 28 (1949)

35. C S R C (Computer Security Resource Center) - Modes of Operation at,
    http://csrc.nist.gov/CryptoToolkit/modes/proposedmodes/

36. http://www.gaisler.com/

37. Fruhwirth, C.: New Methods in Hard Disk Encryption. In: Institute for Computer Languages, Theory and Logic Group, Vienna University of Technology (2005)

38. Kuhn, M.G.: Cipher Instruction Search Attack on the Bus-Encryption Security Microcontroller DS5002FP. IEEE Trans. Comput. 47, 1153–1157 (1998)

39. Bellare, M., Namprempre, C.: Authenticated Encryption: Relations among Notions and Analysis of the Generic Construction Paradigm. In: Okamoto, T. (ed.) ASIACRYPT 2000. LNCS, vol. 1976, pp. 531–545. Springer, Heidelberg (2000)

40. Menezes, A.J., van Oorschot, P.C., Vanstone, S.A.: Handbook of Applied Cryptography. CRC Press, Boca Raton (1996)
41. Mitchell, C.J.: Cryptanalysis of Two Variants of PCBC Mode When Used for Message Integrity. In: Boyd, C., González Nieto, J.M. (eds.) ACISP 2005. LNCS, vol. 3574, pp. 560–571. Springer, Heidelberg (2005)
42. Hellström, H.: Propagating Cipher Feedback (2001),
    http://csrc.nist.gov/CryptoToolkit/modes/proposedmodes/pcfb/pcfb-spec.pdf
43. Best, R.M.: Microprocessor for Executing Enciphered programs, U.S. Patent No. 4 168 396, September 18 (1979)
44. Best, R.M.: Crypto Microprocessor for Executing Enciphered Programs, U.S. Patent No. 4 278 837, July 14 (1981)
45. Kocher, P.C., Jaffe, J., Jun, B.: Differential Power Analysis. In: Wiener, M. (ed.) CRYPTO 1999. LNCS, vol. 1666, pp. 388–397. Springer, Heidelberg (1999)
46. Elbaz, R., Daemen, J., Bertoni, G.: Data parallelized encryption and integrity checking method and device. Patent pending

A Weakest Precondition Approach to Robustness[*]

Musard Balliu[1] and Isabella Mastroeni[2]

[1] School of Computer Science and Communication, Royal Institute of Technology,
Stockholm, Sweden
musard@kth.se

[2] Dipartimento di Informatica, Università di Verona, Strada Le Grazie 15, I-37134,
Verona, Italy
isabella.mastroeni@univr.it

Abstract. With the increasing complexity of information management computer systems, security becomes a real concern. E-government, web-based financial transactions or military and health care information systems are only a few examples where large amount of information can reside on different hosts distributed worldwide. It is clear that any disclosure or corruption of confidential information in these contexts can result fatal. Information flow controls constitute an appealing and promising technology to protect both data confidentiality and data integrity. The certification of the security degree of a program that runs in untrusted environments still remains an open problem in the area of language-based security. Robustness asserts that an active attacker, who can modify program code in some fixed points (*holes*), is unable to disclose more private information than a passive attacker, who merely observes unclassified data. In this paper, we extend a method recently proposed for checking declassified non-interference in presence of passive attackers only, in order to check robustness by means of weakest precondition semantics. In particular, this semantics simulates the kind of analysis that can be performed by an attacker, i.e., from public output towards private input. The choice of semantics allows us to distinguish between different attacks models and to characterize the security of applications in different scenarios.

Our results are sound to address confidentiality and integrity of software running in untrusted environments where different actors can distrust one another. For instance, a web server can be attacked by a third party in order to steal a session cookie or hijack clients to a fake web page.

Keywords: program semantics, non-interference, robustness, declassification, active attackers, abstract interpretation, security.

1 Introduction

Security is an enabling technology, hence security means power. So to cite some examples, the correct functionality and coordination of large scale organizations, e-government, web services in general relies on confidentiality and integrity of data

---

[*] We would like to thank Mads Dam and anonymous referees for insightful suggestions and comments.

M.L. Gavrilova et al. (Eds.): Trans. on Comput. Sci. X, LNCS 6340, pp. 261–297, 2010.

exchanged between different agents. Nowadays, distributed and service oriented architectures are the first business alternative to the old fashioned client-server architectures. According to OWASP (Open Web Application Security Project) [1], the most critical security risks are due to application level attacks as injections flaws or XSS (Cross Site Scripting). Moreover, current and future trends in software engineering prognosticate mobile code technology (multi application smart cards, software for embedded systems), extensibility and platform independence. It is worth noting that all these features, almost unavoidable, become real opportunities for the attackers to exploit system bugs in order to disclose and/or corrupt valuable information. For instance, in such a context, it is easier to distribute worms or viruses that run everywhere or to embed malicious code to exploit vulnerabilities in a web server.

In many scenarios, different agents, each having their own security policy and probably not trusting each other, have to cooperate for a certain goal, for example electing the winner in an online auction. It can happen that the host used for computation violates security by either leaking information itself or causing other hosts to leak information [27,5]. In a cryptographic context, secure multi-party computation (MPC) [25] consists of computing a function between different agents, each knowing a secret they don't want to reveal to the other participating agents. It is very common that an adversary is part of such a systems by taking the control of some hosts and trying to reveal private data of the other participating hosts. As a result, it is both useful and necessary to address problems on confidential information disclosed by an adversary that can control and observe part of the system, to characterize the possible harm in case some condition is verified or to state conditions when the whole system is robust to some extent. Application level enforcement that combines programming languages and static analysis seems a promising remedy to such a problem [26,5]

Secure information flow concerns the problem of disclosing private information to an untrusted observer. This problem is indeed actual each time a program, manipulating both sensitive and public information, is executed in an untrusted environment. In this case, security is usually enforced by means of *non-interference* policies [13], stating that private information must not affect the observable public information. In the non-interference context, variables have a confidentiality level, usually public/low and private/high, and variations of the private input has not to affect the public output. In this case, we are considering attackers that can only observe the I/O behavior of programs and that, from these observations, can make some kind of *reverse engineering* in order to derive private information from the observation of public data.

Our starting idea is that of finding the program vulnerabilities by simulating the possible reasonings that an attacker can perform on programs. Indeed, we can think that the attacker can use the output observation in order to derive, *backward*, some (even partial) private input information. This is the idea of the *backward analysis* recently proposed in [3] for declassified non-interference, where declassification is modeled by means of abstract domains [8]. The ingredients of this method are: the initial declassification policy modeled as an abstraction of private input domain and the weakest liberal precondition semantics of programs [12,11], characterizing the backward analysis (i.e., from outputs to inputs) and the simulation of the attacker observational activity. The certification process consists in considering a possible output (public) observation and computing the weakest liberal precondition semantics of the program starting from this observation. By definition, the *weakest* precondition semantics provides the *greatest* set of possible input states leading to the given output observation. In other words, it characterizes the greatest collection of input states, and in particular of private inputs, that an attacker can identify starting from the given observation. In this way, the attacker can restrict the range of private inputs inside this collection, which corresponds to a partial release of private information. Moreover, we can note that, the fact that we compute the *weakest* precondition for the given observation, provides a characterisation of the *maximal* information released by the observation, in the lattice of abstract interpretations. Namely, starting from the results provided by the analysis, we construct an abstract domain, representing the private abstract property released, which is the most concrete one released by the program [3].

Our aim is to use these ideas also in presence of *active attackers*, namely attackers that can both observe and modify program semantics. We consider the model of active attackers proposed in [20] which can transform program semantics simply by inserting malicious code in some fixed program points (*holes*), known by the programmer. We can show that, also in presence of this kind of attackers, the weakest precondition semantics computation can be exploited for characterising the information disclosed, and therefore for revealing program vulnerabilities. This characterisation can be interpreted from two opposite points of view: the attacker and the program administrator. The attacker can be any malicious adversary trying to disclose confidential information about the system; the administrator wants to know whether the system releases private information due to particular inputs.

An important security property concerning active attackers, and related to the information disclosed, is *robustness* [26]. It "measures" the security degree of programs wrt active attackers by certifying that active attackers cannot disclose more information than what a passive attacker (a simple observer) can do.

We propose to use the weakest precondition-based analysis in order to certify also robustness of programs. The first idea we consider is to compute the maximal information disclosed both for passive attackers [3] and for active attackers, and then compare the results in the lattice of abstract interpretations for certifying robustness: if there exists at least one active attacker disclosing more than the passive one, the program fails to be robust. The problem of this technique is that it requires a program analysis for each attack, this means that it becomes unfeasible when dealing with an infinite number of possible active attacks. In order to overcome this problem, we need an analysis independent of the code of the particular active attack. For this reason, we exploit the weakest precondition computation in order to provide a *sufficient condition* that guarantees robustness independently of the attack. In particular we provide a condition that has to hold before each hole, for preventing the attacker to be successful. We initially study this condition for I/O attackers, i.e., attackers that can only observe the I/O program behavior, and afterwards we extend it to attackers able to observe also intermediate states, i.e., trace semantics of programs. Finally, we note that, in some restricted contexts, for example where the activity of the attackers is limited by the environment, the standard notion of robustness may become too strong. For dealing with these situations we introduce a weakening of robustness, i.e., *relative robustness*, where we restrict the set of active attackers that we are checking for robustness.

There are various interesting applications where our approach is successful to capture confidential information flaws. Here we select two cases concerning API (Application Programming Interface) security and XSS attacks and apply the weakest precondition analysis to check robustness. The first case enforces the security of an API used to verify the password inserted in an ATM cash machine. The adversary is able to reveal the entire password by tampering with low integrity data prior to call API function [4]. The second example concerns a web attacks using Javascript. As we will see, a naive control of code integrity can reveal the session cookie to the adversary [23,6]. Our robustness analysis by weakest precondition semantics is sufficient to prevent attacks in both examples.

Roadmap. The rest of the paper is organized as follows. In Section 2 we give a general overview of abstract interpretation, which constitutes the underlying framework that we use to compare the information disclosed. In Section 3 we present the target security background that we address in our approach. In particular we recall notions of non-interference, robustness, declassification, decentralized label model and decentralized robustness. In Section 4 we compute (qualitatively) the maximal private information disclosed by active attackers. In particular, Section 4.1 introduces the problem of computing the maximal release by active attackers for I/O (denotational) semantics. Section 4.2 extends the analysis for attacks observing program traces. In Section 5 we discuss conditions to enforce robustness, which constitutes our main contribution. Section 5.1 presents a static analysis approach based on weakest preconditions to enforce robustness for I/O semantics; Section 5.3 extends these results for trace semantics; In Section 5.4 we compare our method with type-based methods. Section 6 introduces relative robustness which deals with restricted classes of attacks; in Section 6.1 we interpret decentralized robustness in our approach. In Section 7 we use the current approach in the context of real applications and explain how it captures the security properties we are interested in. Sect. 8 we present the most relevant related works. We conclude with Section 9 by discussing the current state of art and devising new directions for future work. This is an extended and revised version of [2].

2   Abstract Interpretation: An Informal Introduction

We use the standard framework of abstract interpretation [8,9] for modeling properties. For example, instead of computing on integers we might compute on more abstract properties, such as the sign $\{+, -, 0\}$ or parity $\{\mathsf{even}, \mathsf{odd}\}$. Consider the program $\mathrm{sum}(x, y) = x + y$, then it is abstractly interpreted as sum^*: $\mathrm{sum}^*(+, +) = +$, $\mathrm{sum}^*(-, -) = -$, but $\mathrm{sum}^*(+, -) = $ *"I don't know"* since we are not able to determine the sign of the sum of a negative number with a positive one (modeled by the fact that the result can be any value). Analogously, $\mathrm{sum}^*(\mathsf{even}, \mathsf{even}) = \mathsf{even}$,

$\text{sum}^*(\text{odd}, \text{odd}) = \text{even}$ and $\text{sum}^*(\text{even}, \text{odd}) = \text{odd}$. More formally, given a concrete domain C we choose to describe abstractions of C as upper closure operators. An *upper closure operator* (uco for short) $\rho : C \to C$ on a poset C is monotone, idempotent, and extensive: $\forall x \in C. \ x \leq_C \rho(x)$. The upper closure operator is the function that maps the concrete values with their abstract properties, namely with the best possible approximation of the concrete value in the abstract domain. For example, the operator $Sign : \wp(\mathbb{Z}) \to \wp(\mathbb{Z})$, on the powerset of integers, associates each set of integers S with its sign: $Sign(\varnothing) = \text{"none"}$, $Sign(S) = +$ if $\forall n \in S.x > 0$, $Sign(0) = 0$, $Sign(S) = -$ if $\forall n \in S. \ n < 0$ and $Sign(S) = \text{"I don't know"}$ otherwise. The used property names *"none"*, $+,0,-$ and *"I don't know"* are the names of the following sets in $\wp(\mathbb{Z})$: $\varnothing$, $\{ n \in \mathbb{Z} \mid n > 0 \}$, $\{0\}$, $\{ n \in \mathbb{Z} \mid n < 0 \}$ and $\mathbb{Z}$. Namely the abstract elements, in general, correspond to the set of values with the property they represent. Analogously, we can define an operator $Par : \wp(\mathbb{Z}) \to \wp(\mathbb{Z})$ associating each set of integers with its parity. $Par(\varnothing) = \text{"none"} = \varnothing$, $Par(S) = \text{even} = \{ n \in \mathbb{Z} \mid n \text{ is even} \}$ if $\forall n \in S. \ n$ is even, $Par(S) = \text{odd} = \{ n \in \mathbb{Z} \mid n \text{ is odd} \}$ if $\forall n \in S. \ n$ is odd and $Par(S) = \text{"I don't know"} = \mathbb{Z}$ otherwise. Formally, closure operators ρ are uniquely determined by the set of their fix-points $\rho(C)$, for instance $Sign = \{\mathbb{Z}, > 0, < 0, 0, \varnothing\}$. Abstract domains on the complete lattice $\langle C, \leq, \vee, \wedge, \top, \bot \rangle$ form a complete lattice, formally denoted $\langle uco(C), \sqsubseteq, \sqcup, \sqcap, \lambda x. \ \top, \lambda x. \ x \rangle$, where $\rho \sqsubseteq \eta$ means that ρ is more concrete than η, namely it is more precise, $\sqcap_i \rho_i$ is the greatest lower bound taking the most abstract domain containing all the ρ_i, $\sqcup_i \rho_i$ is the least upper bound taking the most concrete domain contained in all the ρ_i, $\lambda x. \ \top$ is the most abstract domain unable to distinguish concrete elements, the identity on C, $\lambda x. \ x$, is the most concrete abstract domain, the concrete domain itself.

3   Security Background

Information flow models of confidentiality, also called non-interference [13], are widely studied in literature [21]. Generally they consider the denotational semantics of a program P, denoted $\llbracket P \rrbracket$ and all program variables, in addition to their base type (int, float etc.), have a security type that varies between private (H) and public (L). In this paper we consider only terminating computations. Hence, there are basically two ways the program can release private information by the observation of the public outputs: due to an explicit flow corresponding to a direct assignment of a private variable to a public variable and due to an implicit flow corresponding to control structures of the program, such as the conditional **if** or the **while** loop [21].

3.1   Non-interference and Declassification

A program satisfies *standard non-interference* if for all the variations of private input data there is no variation of public output data. More formally, given a set of program states Σ, namely a set of functions mapping variables to values $\mathbb{V}$, we represent a state as a tuple $(\vec{h}, \vec{l})$ where the first component denotes the value of private variables and the second component denotes the value of public variables. Let P be a program, then P satisfies non-interference if

$$\forall l \in \mathbb{V}^L, \forall h_1, h_2 \in \mathbb{V}^H. \llbracket P \rrbracket (h_1, l)^L = \llbracket P \rrbracket (h_2, l)^L$$

where $v \in \mathbb{V}^{\mathbb{T}}$, $\mathbb{T} \in \{H, L\}$, denotes the fact that v is a possible value of a variable with security type $\mathbb{T}$ and $(h, l)^L = l$. Declassified non-interference considers a property on private inputs which can be observed [7,3]. Consider a predicate ϕ on $\mathbb{V}^H$, a program P satisfies *declassified* non-interference if

$$\forall l \in \mathbb{V}^L, \forall h_1, h_2 \in \mathbb{V}^H.$$
$$\phi(h_1) = \phi(h_2) \Rightarrow [\![P]\!](h_1, l)^L = [\![P]\!](h_2, l)^L$$

3.2 Robust Declassification

In language-based settings, active attackers are known for their ability to control, i.e., observe and modify, part of the information used by the program.

Security levels form a lattice whose ordering specifies the relation between different security levels. Each program variable has two security types that model, respectively, the confidentiality level and the integrity level. In our context, all the variables have only two security levels; L stands for *low, public, modifiable* and H stands for *high, private, unmodifiable*. Moreover, we assume, for each variable x, the existence of two functions, $\mathcal{C}(x)$ (confidentiality level) which shows whether the variable x is observable or not and $\mathcal{I}(x)$ (integrity level) which shows whether the variable x is modifiable or not. Definitively, each variable can have four possible security types, i.e., LL, LH, HL, HH. For example, if the variable x has type LL then x can be both *observed* and *modified* by the attacker, if the variable x has type HL then x can be *modified* by the attacker, but it cannot be *observed*, and so on.

The programs are written according to the syntax of a simple *while* language. In order to allow semantic transformations during the computation, we consider another construct, called *hole* and denoted by [•], which models the program locations where a potential attacker can insert some code [20].

$$c ::= \mathbf{skip} \mid x := e \mid c_1; c_2 \mid \mathbf{if}\ e\ \mathbf{then}\ c_1\ \mathbf{else}\ c_2 \mid$$
$$\mathbf{while}\ e\ \mathbf{do}\ c \mid [\bullet]$$

where $e ::= v \in \mathbb{V} \mid x \mid e_1\ \mathrm{op}\ e_2$. The low integrity code inserted in holes models the untrusted code assumed under the control of the attacker. Hence, let $P[\vec{\bullet}]$ denote a program with holes and $\vec{a}$ (vector of fixed attacks for each program hole) an attack, $P[\vec{a}]$ denotes the program under control of the given attack. A *fair attack* is a program respecting the following syntax [20]:

$$a ::= \mathbf{skip} \mid x := e \mid a_1; a_2 \mid \mathbf{if}\ e\ \mathbf{then}\ a_1\ \mathbf{else}\ a_2 \mid$$
$$\mathbf{while}\ e\ \mathbf{do}\ a$$

where all variables in e and x have security type LL. It is worth noting that fair attackers can use in their attacks only the variables that are both observable and modifiable.

An important notion when dealing with active attackers is *robustness* [26]. Informally, a program is said to be *robust* when no active attacker, who actively controls the code in the holes, can disclose more information about private inputs than what can be disclosed by a passive attacker, who merely observes the programs I/O. Note that, by using this attacker definition it becomes possible to translate robustness into a language-based setting. Indeed, robust declassification holds if for all attacks $\vec{a}$ whenever program $P[\vec{a}]$ cannot distinguish program behavior on some memories, any other attacker code $\vec{a}'$ cannot distinguish program behavior on these memories [20]. Thus, we can formally recall the notion of *robustness*, for terminating programs, in presence of active fair attackers [20].

$$\forall h_1, h_2 \in \mathbb{V}^{\mathrm{H}}, \forall l \in \mathbb{V}^{\mathrm{L}}, \forall \vec{a}, \vec{a}' \text{ active fair attack :}$$
$$\llbracket P[\vec{a}] \rrbracket (h_1, l)^{\mathrm{L}} = \llbracket P[\vec{a}] \rrbracket (h_2, l)^{\mathrm{L}} \Rightarrow \llbracket P[\vec{a}'] \rrbracket (h_1, l)^{\mathrm{L}} = \llbracket P[\vec{a}'] \rrbracket (h_2, l)^{\mathrm{L}}$$

Namely, a program is robust if any active (fair) attacker can disclose at most the same information (property of private inputs) as a passive attacker can disclose. A passive attacker is an attacker able only to observe program execution, which in this context corresponds to the active attacker $\vec{a} = \overrightarrow{\mathbf{skip}}$.

3.3 Weakest Liberal Precondition Semantics

In this section we briefly present the *weakest liberal precondition* semantics (*Wlp* for short), which constitutes our basic instrument for performing static analysis. In particular, given a program c and a predicate P, $Wlp(c, P)$ corresponds to the greatest set of input states σ such that if (c, σ) terminates in a final state σ', then σ' satisfies the predicate P [15,14]. In our case, these predicates correspond to quantifier-free first order formulas which are transformed by the *Wlp* semantics. Below, we present the rules of the semantics.

- $Wlp(\mathbf{skip}, \Phi) = \Phi$
- $Wlp(x := e, \Phi) = \Phi[e/x]$
- $Wlp(c_1; c_2, \Phi) = Wlp(c_1, Wlp(c_2, \Phi))$
- $Wlp(\mathbf{if}\ e\ \mathbf{then}\ c_1\ \mathbf{else}\ c_2, \Phi) = (e \wedge Wlp(c_1, \Phi)) \vee (\neg e \wedge Wlp(c_2, \Phi))$
- $Wlp(\mathbf{while}\ e\ \mathbf{do}\ c, \Phi) = \bigvee_{i=0}^{n} Wlp_i(\mathbf{while}\ e\ \mathbf{do}\ c, \Phi)$
  where given $(C \overset{\text{def}}{=} \mathbf{while}\ B\ \mathbf{do}\ C_1)$

$$\begin{cases} Wlp_0(C, \Phi) \overset{\text{def}}{=} \neg B \wedge \Phi \\ Wlp_{i+1}(C, \Phi) \overset{\text{def}}{=} Wlp(\mathbf{if}\ B\ \mathbf{then}\ C_1\ \mathbf{else}\ \mathbf{skip}, Wlp_i(C, \Phi)) \end{cases}$$

Almost all the above rules are easy to read. For instance, the weakest precondition of the conditional, given a postcondition Φ, corresponds to the disjunction of conjunctions of *Wlp* of each branch and the boolean condition of the guard. It is also worth noting that the *Wlp* of the loop requires the computation of some invariant formula. There exists techniques for doing that [16], but in this paper we don't consider them explicitly. The automatic generation of such invariants would be an interesting future direction we plan to explore more in details. Unlike weakest precondition semantics, *Wlp* defines a partial verification condition, namely only if the program does terminate the post-condition Φ should hold. In any case, for the purposes of this paper, we will be interested only in terminating programs, so we can establish the weakest liberal precondition in a finite number of iterations.

3.4 Certifying Declassification

In this section, we introduce a technique recently proposed for certifying declassification policies [3,18] in presence of passive attackers only, i.e., attackers that can only observe program execution. The method performs a backward analysis, computing the weakest precondition semantics starting from output observation, in order to derive the maximal information that an attacker can disclose from a given observation. We use abstract interpretation for modeling the declassified properties.

Certifying declassification. In [3,18] the authors present a method to compute the maximal private input information disclosed by passive attackers. They consider only terminating computations, which means that the logical language does not have expressiveness limits [24]. Their method has two main characteristics: it is a static analysis, and it performs a backward analysis from the observed outputs towards the inputs to protect. The first aspect is important since we would like to certify programs without executing them, the latter is important because non-interference aims to protect the system private *input* while attackers can observe public *outputs*. Both these characteristics are embedded in the weakest liberal precondition semantics of programs. Starting from a given observed output *Wlp* semantics computes, by definition, the *greatest* set of input states leading to the given observation. From this characterisation we can derive in particular the private input information released by observing output public variables. This corresponds exactly to the maximal private information disclosed by the program semantics. In this way, we are statically simulating the kind of analysis an attacker can perform in order to obtain initial values of (or initial relations among) private information. We can model this information by a first order predicate; the set of program states disclosed by the *Wlp* semantics are the ones which satisfy this predicate. In order to be as general as possible, we consider the public observations parametric on some symbolic value represented by some logical variable. We denote by $\vec{l} = \vec{n}$ the parametric value of each low confidentiality program variable. For instance, the formula $(l = n)$ means that the program variable l has the symbolic value n. Generally, the public output observation corresponds to a first order formula that is the conjunction of all low confidentiality variables, i.e., variables with security types LL or LH.

$$\Phi_0 \stackrel{\text{def}}{=} \{l_1 = n_1 \wedge l_2 = n_2 \wedge \cdots \wedge l_k = n_k\} = \bigwedge_{i=1}^{k} (l_i = n_i)$$

where $\forall l_i . \mathcal{C}(l_i) = \text{L}$. Without loss of generality, we can assume this formula to be in a disjoint normal form, namely a disjunction of conjunctions. We call *free variables* of a logical formula Φ and denote $\mathcal{FV}(\Phi)$ the set of program variables occurring in Φ, where Φ is a quantifier-free. Moreover, we assume to eliminate all possible redundancies and all subformulas that can be subsumed by others in the same formula. For instance, let $(l > 1 \wedge l > 0)$ be a logical formula. We can simply write $(l > 1)$ because this subsumes the fact that $l > 0$. From now on we'll suppose to have each logical formula in this form called *normal form*.

For instance, consider the program P with h_1, h_2 : HH and l : LL.

$$P \stackrel{\text{def}}{=} \textbf{if } (h_1 = h_2) \textbf{ then } l := 0; \textbf{ else } l := 1;$$

$Wlp(P, l = n) = \{(h_1 = h_2 \wedge n = 0) \vee (h_1 \neq h_2 \wedge n = 1)\}.$

If we observe $l = 0$ in public output, all we can say about private inputs h_1, h_2 is $h_1 = h_2$. Otherwise, if we observe $l = 1$, we can conclude that $h_1 \neq h_2$.

In [3,18] this technique is formally justified by considering an abstract domain completeness-based [8] model of declassified non-interference. Here we avoid the formal details, and we simply show where and how we use abstract interpretation. Note that, usually Wlp semantics is applied to specific output states in order to derive the greatest set of input states leading to the output one. Here, the technique starts from the state $\vec{l} = \vec{n}$, which is indeed an *abstract state*, namely the state where the private variables can have any value, while the public variables $\vec{l}$ have the specific symbolic value $\vec{n}$. This corresponds to the abstraction $\mathcal{H} \in uco(\wp(\mathbb{V}))$ [3] modeling the fact that the attacker cannot observe private data. Formally, it associates with a generic output state $\langle h, l \rangle$ the abstract state $\langle \mathbb{V}^{\text{H}}, l \rangle = \{ \langle h', l \rangle \mid h' \in \mathbb{V}^{\text{H}} \}$. As far as the input characterisation is concerned, we know that an abstract property is described by the set of all the concrete values satisfying the property. Hence, if the Wlp semantics characterises a set of inputs, and in particular of private inputs, then this set can be uniquely modeled as an abstract domain, i.e., the abstract property released. Consider, for instance, the trivial program fragment P above. According to the output value observed, $l = 0$ or $l = 1$, we have respectively the set of input states $\{\langle h_1, h_2, l \rangle \mid h_1 = h_2\}$ or $\{\langle h_1, h_2, l \rangle \mid h_1 \neq h_2\}$. This characterisation can be uniquely modeled by the abstract domain[1]

$$\phi = \{\top, \{\langle h_1, h_2, l \rangle \mid h_1 = h_2\}, \{\langle h_1, h_2, l \rangle \mid h_1 \neq h_2\}, \varnothing\}$$

Hence, if we declassify ϕ, the program is secure since the information released corresponds to what is declassified. While if, as in standard non-interference, nothing is declassified, modeled by the declassification policy $\phi' = \lambda x. \top$[2], then $\phi \sqsubseteq \phi'$, namely the policy is violated since the information released is more (concrete) than what is declassified.

3.5 Decentralized Label Model and Decentralized Robustness

Decentralized label model was proposed as a fine-grained model to enforce end-to-end security for systems with mutual distrust and decentralized authority that want to share data with each other [19]. Basically, every agent in the system defines and controls his own security policy and states which data, under his ownership, could be visible (declassified) to other agents in the system. The system itself must ensure that security policies are not circumvented and satisfy security concerns of all agents. More precisely, decentralized label model consists of two basic flavors: *principals*, whose security should be ensured in the model and *labels*, which constitute the means to enforce security policies. Principals can be users, processes, groups, roles possibly related by an *acts-for*

---

[1] The elements $\top$ and $\varnothing$ are necessary for obtaining an abstract domain.

[2] Since $\forall x, y$ we have $\phi'(x) = \phi'(y)$, declassified non-interference with ϕ' corresponds to standard non-interference.

relation which allows delegation of authority between them. For instance, if principal P *acts-for* principal Q, formally $P \succeq Q$, it means that P has all privileges of Q. On the other hand, labels are data annotations that express the security policy the owner sets on his data. In particular, if some data are annotated by label *owner: reader*, the policy on that data defines the owner and the set of principals that can read such data. Security labels form a security lattice where the higher an element is in the lattice, the more restrictive are the security concerns of the data it labels. Moreover, the decentralized label model supports a declassification mechanism and allows to express policies regarding both confidentiality and integrity. The model is used to perform static analysis based on type systems to enforce information flow policies.

Decentralized robustness is an approach to enforce the security condition of robustness in the decentralized label model [5]. In particular, the fact that each principal does not trust the others means that each principal may be a potential attacker. Hence, robustness is analyzed relatively to two principals: one fixes the point of view of the analysis, the other is the potential attacker. In particular, the former *fixes* which data it believes the latter can read and/or write. More formally, decentralized robustness is defined wrt a pair of principals p and q, with power $\langle R_{p \to q}, W_{p \leftarrow q} \rangle$, where $R_{p \to q}$ allows to characterise the data p believes that q can read, while $W_{p \leftarrow q}$ allows to characterise the data p believes that q can modify. A system is robust wrt all the attackers if it is robust with respect to all the pairs p, q of principals. In [5], the authors use type systems to enforce robustness against all attackers in a simple while language with holes and explicits declassification. Basically, it allows holes to occur in low confidentiality contexts and prevents attackers to influence both (explicit) declassification decision and data to be declassified as explained in [20]. Once we fix the point of view of the attacker, a safe hole insertion relation defines the admissible holes for the attacker in question together with variables he can modify and/or observe in the program.

4   Maximal Release by Active Attackers

The notion of robustness defined in Sect. 3 implicitly concerns the confidential information released by the program. Indeed, if we are able to measure the maximal release (the most concrete private property observable) in presence of active attacks, then we can compare it with the private information disclosed by passive attackers and conclude about program robustness. Thus, in this section we compute (when possible) the maximal private information disclosed by an active attacker.

The active attack model we use here is more powerful than the one defined in Sect. 3.2, i.e., fair attacks. In addition, our attackers can manipulate (use and modify) variables of security type HL, i.e., variables that the attacker cannot observe but can use. Indeed, HL is the type of those variables whose name is *visible*, i.e., usable by the attacker in his code, but whose value is not observable. Thus, in the following active attacks are programs (without holes) such that, for all the variables x occurring in the attacks code, $\mathcal{I}(x) = L$. We call them *unfair attacks*. *Unfair attacks* are more general than fair attacks because they can modify variables of security type LL and HL. For instance, suppose that a system user wants to change his password, he accesses a variable (the password) he can write but not read (blind writing), i.e., of type HL. Now we want to compute the maximal information release in presence of unfair attacks.

4.1 Observing Input-Output

It is clear that, in order to certify the security degree of a program, also in presence of active attackers, it is important to compute which is the maximal private information released. Such information can help the programmer to understand what happens in the worst case, namely when an active attacker inserts the most harmful unfair code. Moreover, if we compute the most concrete property of private input data released by program semantics for all active attacks, we can compare it with the private information disclosed by a passive attacker and conclude about program robustness. In this section, we consider denotational semantics, namely input/output semantics. Hence, the set of program points where the attacker can observe low confidentiality data corresponds to program inputs and program outputs. Note that, the active attacker can insert code (fair or unfair) in fixed points, therefore he can change program semantics and consequently the property of confidential information released can be different in presence of different active attacks. Moreover, the number of possible unfair attacks may be infinite, thus, it becomes hard to compute the private information disclosed by all of them. The real problem is that it is impossible to characterise the maximal information released to attackers that modify program semantics, because different attacks obtain different private properties which may be incomparable if there are infinitely many such attacks.

This problem is overcome when we consider a finite number of attackers, for instance a finite class of attacks for which we want to certify our program. In this case, we can compute the maximal information disclosed by each attacker and, afterwards, we can consider the *greatest lower bound* (in the lattice of abstract domains) characterising the maximal information released for the fixed class of attackers. Let us introduce an example to illustrate the problem.

Example 1. Consider the program $P ::= l := h; [\bullet];$ with variables h : HH, l : LL and k : HL. We can have the following attacks:

- $Wlp(l := h; [skip], \{l = n\}) = \{h = n\}$
- $Wlp(l := h; [l := k], \{l = n\}) = \{k = n\}$
- $Wlp(l := h; [l := l + k], \{l = n\}) = \{h + k = n\}$

For all cases the attacker discloses different information about confidential data. In particular, in the first case the attacker obtains the exact value of variable h, in the second he obtains the exact value of variable k and in the third case he obtains a relation (the sum) between h and k. Note that if all possible active attacks were only those considered above, we can compute the greatest lower bound (*glb* for short) of private information disclosed by all of them. In this case *glb* corresponds to the identity value of confidential variables h and k.

However, as shown in the previous example, we can compute the private information disclosed by an attacker who fixes his attack and check if that particular attack compromises program robustness. To this end, we just have to use the method introduced in [3] and verify that the method described in Sect. 3.4 holds for the transformed program.

In the previous example, we have seen that, even though we have a finite number of attackers, we have to compute a *Wlp* analysis for each active attacker. In the following, we suggest a method for computing only one analysis dealing with a (possible infinite) set of active attackers. We follow the idea proposed in [3], where, in order to avoid an analysis for each possible output observation, the authors compute the analysis parametrically on the symbolic output observation $l = n$. In particular, note that an attacker, being an imperative program, corresponds to a function manipulating low integrity variables, i.e., LL and HL variables.

Hence, we propose a *Wlp* computation parametric on the possible expressions $f(\vec{l})$ assigned by the active attacker to low integrity variables $\vec{l}$, which we call *attack schemas* (in line with program schemas [10]). In other words, the attacker can assign to all low integrity variables an expression which can possibly depend on all other low integrity variables. For instance, given a program where the only low integrity variables are l and k, all possible unfair attacks concern the variables l and k, namely $l := f(l, k)$ and $k = g(l, k)$, where f, g are expressions that can contain variables l, k free.

The confidential information released by such parametric computations can be exploited by both the programmer and the attacker. Indeed, looking at the final formula which can contain f as parameter, the former can detect vulnerabilities about the confidential information released by the program, while the latter can exploit such vulnerabilities to build the most harmful attack in order to disclose as much as possible about private input data. Let us introduce an example that shows the above technique.

Example 2. Consider the program in Ex. 1. The only low integrity variables are l : LL and k : HL. According to the method described above we have to substitute possible unfair attacks in $[\bullet]$ with attack schema $\langle l, k \rangle := \langle f(l, k), g(l, k) \rangle$. The initial formula is $\Phi_0 = \{l = n\}$ because l is the only program variable s.t. $\mathcal{C}(l) = $ L. Thus, the *Wlp* calculation yields the following formula:

$$\{f(h, k) = n\}$$
$$l := h;$$
$$\{f(l, k) = n\}$$
$$[\langle l, k \rangle := \langle f(l, k), g(l, k) \rangle;]$$
$$\{l = n\}$$

Note that the final formula ($f(h, k) = n$) contains information about high confidentiality variables h and k. Thus, fixing the unfair attacks as we did in the previous example, we obtain information about symbolic value of h, k or any relation between them.

It is worth pointing out that attack schemas capture pretty well the idea of classes of attacks which have a *similar* semantic effect (up to stuttering) on confidential information disclosed by an active attacker. We conjecture a close relationship between attack schemas and program schemas [10] and postpone their investigation as part of our future work.

4.2 Observing Program Traces

So far we have tried to compute the maximal private information disclosed by an active attacker which tampers with low integrity data in predefined program points (holes) and observes public input and public output of target program. In particular, the attacker could not observe low confidentiality data in any intermediate program point (random traces or holes). This condition is unrealistic in a mutual distrust scenario, where the attacker can control a compromised machine. Indeed, nothing prevents it to analyze low confidentiality data in points he is tampering code with and reveal secrets even though the overall computation has not terminated yet. This man-in-the-middle kind of attack requires to extend the analysis and consider intermediate program points as possible channels of information leakage. In many practical applications, it is common to have scenarios where a bunch of threads are running concurrently together with a malicious thread which reads the content of shared variables and dumps them in output each time the thread is scheduled to run.

In [18] the authors notice that the semantic model constitutes an important dimension for program security, the *where* dimension [22], which influences both the observation policy and the declassification policy. It seems obvious that an attacker who observes low confidentiality variables in intermediate program points is able to disclose more information than an attacker that observes only input/output. In this section, we aim to characterise the maximal information released by a program in presence of unfair attacks. In general, we can fix the set of program points where the attacker can observe low confidentiality variables (say $\mathbb{O}$) and we can denote by $\mathbb{H}$ the set of program points where there is a hole, namely where the attacker can insert malicious code. Moreover, we assume that the attacker can observe the low confidentiality variables for all program points in $\mathbb{H}$, namely $\mathbb{H} \subseteq \mathbb{O}$. In order to compute the maximal release of confidential information, an attacker can combine, at each observation point, the public information he can observe at that point together with the information he can derive by computing *Wlp* from the output to that observation point [18]. For instance, with trace semantics, an attacker can observe low confidentiality data for all intermediate program point. Let us introduce an example that presents this technique for passive attackers.

Example 3. Consider the program P with variables l_1, l_2 : LL and h_1, h_2 : HH.

$$P ::= \begin{bmatrix} h_1 := h_2; h_2 := h_2 \bmod 2; \\ l_1 := h_2; h_2 := h_1; l_2 := h_2; l_2 := l_1; \end{bmatrix}$$

We want to compute the private information disclosed by an attacker that observes program traces. As for standard non-interference, here we want to protect private inputs h_1 and h_2. In order to make only one iteration on the program even when dealing with traces, the idea is to combine the *Wlp* semantics computed at each observable point of execution, together with the observation of public data made at the particular observation point. We denote in square brackets the value observed in that program point. The *Wlp* calculation yields the following result.

$$\{h_2 \bmod 2 = m \land h_2 = n \land l_2 = p \land l_1 = q\}$$
$$h_1 := h_2;$$
$$\{h_2 \bmod 2 = m \land h_1 = n \land l_2 = p \land l_1 = q\}$$
$$h_2 := h_2 \bmod 2;$$
$$\{h_2 = m \land h_1 = n \land l_2 = p \land [l_1 = q]\}$$
$$l_1 := h_2;$$
$$\{l_1 = m \land h_1 = n \land l_2 = p\}$$
$$h_2 := h_1;$$
$$\{l_1 = m \land h_2 = n \land [l_2 = p]\}$$
$$l_2 := h_2;$$
$$\{l_1 = m \land [l_2 = n]\}$$
$$l_2 := l_1;$$
$$\{l_1 = l_2 = m\}$$

For instance the information observed by the assignment $l_2 := l_1$ is the combination of *Wlp* calculation ($l_1 = m$) and attackers observation at that point ($[l_2 = n]$). The attacker is able to deduce the exact value of h_2. It is worth noting that this attacker is more powerful than the one who merely observes the input-output behavior; in fact, the latter can only distinguish the parity of variable h_2. This is made clear by the fact that the value of h_2's parity (m) is the value derived by the output, while the value of h_2 (n) is a value observed *during* the computation.

We would like to compute the maximal private information release in presence of unfair attacks. Here the problem is similar to the one described in the previous section. Unfair attacks, by definition, manipulate (modify and use) both variables of type LL and HL. Even though the attacker can observe low confidentiality variables in presence of holes, he cannot observe the variables of type HL. Hence, different unfair attacks cause different information releases, as it happens for attackers observing only the I/O, and in general there can be an infinite number of these attacks. However, if we fix the unfair attack we can use the method described above and compute the maximal release for that particular attack.

Things change when we consider only fair attacks, i.e., manipulating only LL variables. The following proposition shows that we can generalise all possible fair attacks to constant assignments $\vec{l} := \vec{c}$ to variables of type LL.

Proposition 1. *Let $P[\bullet]$ be a program with holes and $\mathbb{H} \subseteq \mathbb{O}$. Then, all fair attacks can be written as $\vec{l} := \vec{n}$, where l : LL.*

Proof. In general, all fair attacks have the form $\vec{l} := f(\vec{l})$. Moreover, $\mathbb{H} \subseteq \mathbb{O}$ so the attacker can observe at least the program points where there is a hole. Thus, all the formal parameters of expression $f(\vec{l})$ are known. We conclude that $\vec{l} := \vec{n}$.

Now we are able to measure the maximal private information disclosed by an active attacker. Indeed, we can use the approach of Ex. 3 and whenever we have a program hole, we substitute it by the assignment $\vec{l} := \vec{c}$, parametric on symbolic constant values $\vec{c}$. The following example shows this method.

Example 4. Consider the program P with variables h : HH and l : LL. $\mathbb{O}$ is set of all program points.

$$P ::= l := 0; [\bullet]; \text{ if } (h > 0) \text{ then skip else } l := 0;$$

In presence of passive attackers P does not release any information about private variable h. Indeed, the output value of variable l is always 0. An active attacker who observes each program point and injects fair attacks, discloses the following private information:

$$\{((h > 0 \wedge c = m) \vee (h \leq 0 \wedge m = 0)) \wedge c = n \wedge p = 0\}$$
$$l := 0;$$
$$\{((h > 0 \wedge c = m) \vee (h \leq 0 \wedge m = 0)) \wedge c = n \wedge [l = p]\}$$
$$[l := c;]$$
$$\{((h > 0 \wedge l = m) \vee (h \leq 0 \wedge m = 0)) \wedge [l = n]\}$$
$$\text{if } (h > 0) \text{ then skip else } l := 0;$$
$$\{l = m\}$$

Thus, an active attacker is able to disclose whether the variable h is positive or not. Hence, this is the maximal private information disclosed by an attacker who observes program traces and injects fair code in the holes.

5 Enforcing Robustness

In this section, we want to understand, by static program analysis, when an active attacker that transforms program semantics is not able to disclose *more* private information than a passive attacker, who merely observes public data. The idea is to consider *Wlp* semantics in order to find sufficient conditions which guarantee program robustness. Here we introduce a method to enforce programs which are robust in presence of active attackers.

We know [3] that declassified non-interference is a completeness problem in abstract interpretation theory and there exists systematic methods to enforce this notion. Let $P[\bullet]$ be a program with holes and Φ a first order formula that models the declassification policy. In order to check robustness for this program, we must check the corresponding completeness problem for each possible attack a, as introduced in Sect. 3.4 where $P[\vec{a}]$ is program P under the attack $\vec{a}$. We want to characterise those situations where the semantic transformation induced by the active attack does not generate incompleteness. If there exists at least one attack a such that the program releases more confidential information than the one released by the policy, then the program is deemed not robust.

The following example shows the ability of active attackers to disclose more confidential information wrt passive attackers.

Example 5. Consider the program P with h : HH, l : LL.

$$P ::= l := 0; [\bullet] \text{ if } (h > 0) \text{ then } (l := 1) \text{ else } (l := l + 1);$$

Suppose the declassification policy is $\top$, i.e., nothing has to be released. In presence of a passive attacker (the hole substituted by **skip**) program P satisfies the security policy, namely non-interference, because public output is always 1. *Wlp* semantics formalizes this fact.

$$\{(h > 0 \wedge n = 1) \vee (h \leq 0 \wedge n = 1)\} = \{n = 1\}$$
$$l := 0;$$
$$\{(h > 0 \wedge n = 1) \vee (h \leq 0 \wedge n = l + 1)\}$$
$$\textbf{if } (h > 0) \textbf{ then } (l := 1) \textbf{ else } (l := l + 1);$$
$$\{l = n\}$$

Now suppose that an active attacker inserts the code $l := 1$. In this case *Wlp* semantics shows that the attacker is able to distinguish positive values of private variable h from non positive ones. Using the *Wlp* calculation parametric on public output $\{l = n\}$ we have the following result.

$$\{(h > 0 \wedge n = 1) \vee (h \leq 0 \wedge n = 2)\}$$
$$l := 0;$$
$$\{(h > 0 \wedge n = 1) \vee (h \leq 0 \wedge n = 2)\}$$
$$[l := 1;]$$
$$\{(h > 0 \wedge n = 1) \vee (h \leq 0 \wedge n = l + 1)\}$$

The final formula shows that the adversary is able to distinguish values of h greater than 0 from values less or equal than 0 by observing, respectively, the values 1 or 2 of public output l. We can conclude that program P is not robust and the active attackers are effectively more powerful than passive ones.

If we had a method to compute the maximal private information release in presence of unfair attacks, then we could conclude about program robustness by comparing it with the information disclosed by a passive attacker. Unfortunately, in the previous section, we have seen that it is not possible to compute the maximal information released for all possible attacks, which can possibly be infinite. Hence, our aim is to look for methods enforcing robust programs without computing the maximal information released.

5.1   Robustness by *Wlp*

In this section we first distinguish between active attacks of different power and, afterwards, we present the proof of our approach to certify robust programs. The proof is organised as follows: it starts with a lemma that applies to sequential programs with one hole only, then we give a a theorem that generalizes the lemma to sequential programs with more holes and conclude with another theorem that applies the robustness condition to all terminating while programs.

Let us make some considerations about logical formulas and the set of program states they manipulate. The free variables of the output observation formula Φ_0 correspond to the set of low confidentiality variables LL and LH, namely

$$\mathcal{FV}(\Phi_0) = \{x \in \mathit{Var}(\Phi_0) | \mathcal{C}(x) = \mathtt{L}\}.$$

If a low confidentiality variable does not occur free at some program point, it means that such variable was previously, wrt backward analysis of *Wlp* semantics, substituted by an expression that does not contain that variable. This means that, it can have any value in that point. From the viewpoint of information flow, even if the variable contains some confidential information in that point this is useless for the analysis, because the variable is going to be subsequently overwritten and therefore this information can never be disclosed through public outputs.

Our aim is to generalise the most powerful active attacks and study their impact on program robustness. As a first approach one can try to represent all possible active attacks by a constant assignment to low integrity variables. Hence, the attacker observes only the input/output value of low confidentiality variables, i.e., LL and LH variables. The following example shows that this is not sufficient enough and there exist more powerful attacks that disclose more private information and break robustness.

Example 6. Consider the program P with variables l : LL, k : LL, h : HH and declassification policy that releases nothing about private variables.

$$P ::= \begin{bmatrix} k := h; [\bullet]; \\ \textbf{if } (l = 0) & \textbf{then } (l := 0; k := 0) \\ & \textbf{else } (l := 1; k := 1); \end{bmatrix}$$

First notice that P does not release private information in presence of a passive attacker who merely observes the I/O variation of public data. Indeed, the assignment of h to k is subsequently overwritten by constants 0 or 1 and depends exclusively on the variation of public input l. If it was possible to represent all active attacks by constant assignments we can see that P would be robust. In fact, if the attacker assigns constants c_1 and c_2, respectively, to variables l and k, *Wlp* calculation deems the program robust.

$$\{(c_1 = 0 \wedge m = 0 \wedge n = 0) \vee (c_1 \neq 0 \wedge m = 1 \wedge n = 1)\}$$
$$k := h;$$
$$[l := c_1; k := c_2;]$$
$$\{(l = 0 \wedge m = 0 \wedge n = 0) \vee (l \neq 0 \wedge m = 1 \wedge n = 1)\}$$
$$\textbf{if } (l = 0) \textbf{ then } (l := 0; k := 0) \textbf{ else } (l := 1; k := 1);$$
$$\{l = m \wedge k = n\}$$

The final formula shows that such program satisfies non-interference. But if we assign to low integrity variables an expression depending on other low integrity variables, then we obtain more powerful attacks, which make P not robust. For instance, the assignment $a ::= l := k;$ makes the attacker distinguish the zeroness of private variable h.

$$\{(h = 0 \wedge m = 0 \wedge n = 0) \vee (h \neq 0 \wedge m = 1 \wedge n = 1)\}$$
$$k := h;$$
$$\{(k = 0 \wedge m = 0 \wedge n = 0) \vee (k \neq 0 \wedge m = 1 \wedge n = 1)\}$$
$$[l := k;]$$
$$\{(l = 0 \wedge m = 0 \wedge n = 0) \vee (l \neq 0 \wedge m = 1 \wedge n = 1)\}$$

Definitely, program P is not robust and therefore we cannot reduce active attacks to a constant assignment to low integrity variables.

In general, an active attack is a piece of code that concerns low integrity variables, i.e., a function manipulating low integrity variables. If we assign to low integrity variables a constant value then we erase the high confidentiality information that this variables might have accumulated before reaching that point or we are not considering the possibility of assigning to that variable another one which contains some private information that possibly may be lost subsequently as shown in Ex. 6.

We can use the ideas discussed so far to present a *sufficient* condition ensuring program robustness. Remember that we represent formally the observable public output as a first order formula, Φ_0, that corresponds to the conjunction of program variables x such that $\mathcal{C}(x) = \mathsf{L}$, parametric on the observed public outputs n_i, namely

$$\Phi_0 = \bigwedge_{i=1}^{k} (l_i = n_i) \text{ and } \forall i. \mathcal{C}(l_i) = \mathsf{L}.$$

In particular, we first describe how to characterise the sufficient condition when the holes are not nested in control structures. This is obtained in two steps, the lemma shows the result for programs with only one hole, while the first theorem extends the result to programs with an arbitrary number of holes. Afterwards, we show how to exploit this result in order to characterise the sufficient condition to robustness also when holes are nested in control structures.

In the following, we denote by $\bullet_i$ the i-th hole in P and by P_i the portion of code in P after the hole $\bullet_i$ where all the following holes ($\bullet_j$, with $j \in \mathbb{H}$, $j > i$) are substituted with **skip**. Then $\Phi_i = Wlp(P_i, \Phi_0)$ is the formula corresponding to the execution of the subprogram P_i.

Lemma 1. *Let* $P = P_2; [\bullet]; P_1$ *be a program* (P_1 *without holes, possibly empty). Let* $\Phi = Wlp(P_1, \Phi_0)$. *Then* P *is robust wrt unfair attacks if* $\forall v \in \mathcal{FV}(\Phi). \mathcal{I}(v) = \mathsf{H}$.

Proof. We prove this theorem by induction on the attack's structure and on the length of its derivation. In particular, we prove that for any attack a, $Wlp(a, \Phi) = \Phi$, namely the formula Φ does not change, hence from the semantic point of view, the attack behaves like **skip**, namely like a passive attacker. Note that, here we consider unfair attacks, hence it can use both LL and HL variables.

- a ::= **skip**: The initial formula Φ does not change, namely $Wlp(\mathbf{skip}, \Phi) = \Phi$, and the attacker acts as a passive one.
- a ::= l := e: By definition of active attack we have $\mathcal{I}(l) = \mathsf{L}$ and by hypothesis variable l does not occur free in Φ. Applying the Wlp definition for assignment, we have $Wlp(l := e, \Phi) = \Phi[e/l] = \Phi$.
- $a ::= c_1; c_2$: By inductive hypothesis we have $Wlp(c_1, \Phi) = Wlp(c_2, \Phi) = \Phi$ as attacks of minor length. The Wlp definition for sequential composition states that $Wlp(c_1; c_2, \Phi) = Wlp(c_1, Wlp(c_2, \Phi)) = \Phi$
- $a := \mathbf{if}\ B\ \mathbf{then}\ c_1\ \mathbf{else}\ c_2$: By inductive hypothesis (applied to an attack of minor length) we have $Wlp(c_1, \Phi) = Wlp(c_2, \Phi) = \Phi$. Applying the definition of Wlp for the conditional construct $Wlp(\mathbf{if}\ B\ \mathbf{then}\ c_1\ \mathbf{else}\ c_2, \Phi) = (B \wedge Wlp(c_1, \Phi)) \vee (\neg B \wedge Wlp(c_2, \Phi)) = (B \wedge \Phi) \vee (\neg B \wedge \Phi) = \Phi$.

– $a ::= $ **while** B **do** c: By hypothesis we consider terminating computations, so the **while** loop halts in a finite number of iterations. Applying the inductive hypothesis to command c we have $Wlp(c, \Phi) = \Phi$, so every iteration the formula does not change. Moreover, if the guard is *false* the formula remains unchanged too. Applying Wlp rule for the **while** loop and the inductive hypothesis we have:
$Wlp(\textbf{while } B \textbf{ do } c, \Phi) = (\neg B \wedge \Phi) \vee (B \wedge \Phi) \vee \cdots \vee (B \wedge \Phi) \vee (B \wedge \Phi) = \Phi$

Theorem 1. *Let $P[\bullet]$ be a program. Then we say that P is robust wrt unfair attacks if* $\forall i \in \mathbb{H}. \forall v \in \mathcal{FV}(\Phi_i). \mathcal{I}(v) = \mathbb{H}.$

Proof. Suppose P has n holes:

$$P \equiv P'_{n+1}; [\bullet_n]; P'_n \ldots P'_2; [\bullet_1]; P'_1$$

Let us define the following programs from $1 \leq i \leq n + 1$

$$P_i \overset{\text{def}}{=} \begin{cases} P'_1 & \text{if } i = 1 \\ P'_i P_{i-1} & \text{otherwise} \end{cases}$$

Namely P_i is the portion of code in P after the hole $\bullet_i$ where all the following holes ($\bullet_j$, with $j \in \mathbb{H}$, $j > i$) are substituted with **skip**. We prove by induction on n that $\forall 1 \leq i \leq n. P'_{i+1}; [\bullet_i]; P'_i; [\bullet_{i-1}]; \ldots; [\bullet_1]; P'_1$ is robust wrt unfair attacks. By proving this fact, we prove the thesis since when $i = n$ we obtain exactly P.

BASE: Consider the first hole from the end of the program P, i.e., $P'_2; [\bullet_1]; P'_1$. Then by Lemma 1 we have that $P'_2; [\bullet_1]; P'_1$ is robust, being P'_1 without holes by construction. This implies that any active attacker can disclose the same information as the passive (**skip**) attacker can do, hence $\bullet_1$ can be substituted with **skip**, namely $P'_2[\bullet_1]P'_1$ can be substituted by P_2 in P without changing the robustness property of P.

INDUCTIVE STEP: Suppose, by inductive hypothesis, that $P'_i; [\bullet_{i-1}]; P'_{i-1}; \ldots; P'_2; [\bullet_1]; P'_1$ is robust. This means that, exactly as we noticed in the base of the induction, the holes are useless for an attacker, therefore we can substitute all the $\bullet_j$ with **skip** obtaining a program (from the robustness point of view) equivalent to P_i. Hence, $P'_{i+1}; [\bullet_i]; P'_i; [\bullet_{i-1}]; \ldots; [\bullet_1]; P'_1 \equiv P'_{i+1}; [\bullet_i]; P_i$, and robustness of this last program holds by Lemma 1, being P_i without holes by construction.

In this way we prove that $P \equiv P'_{n+1}; [\bullet_n]; P_n$ is robust.

In other words, the fact that a low integrity variable is not free in the formula means that the information in the corresponding program point cannot be exploited for revealing confidential properties. In this case we can say that a generic active attacker is not stronger than a passive one. Before showing what happens for control structures, let us introduce an example that illustrates Th. 1.

Example 7. Let us check robustness of program P with variables l : LL, h : HH and k : HL.

$$P ::= \begin{bmatrix} l := h + l; [\bullet]; l := 1; k := h; \\ \textbf{while } (h > 0) \textbf{ do } (l := l - 1; l := h); \end{bmatrix}$$

Analysing P from the hole $[\bullet]$ to the end we have:

$$\{(h \leq 0 \wedge n = 1) \vee (h > 0 \wedge n = 0)\}$$
$$l := 1; k := h;$$
$$\{(h \leq 0 \wedge l = n) \vee (h > 0 \wedge n = 0)\}$$
$$\textbf{while } (h > 0) \textbf{ do } (l := l - 1; l := h);$$
$$\{l = n\}$$

The formula $\Phi = (h \leq 0 \wedge n = 1) \vee (h > 0 \wedge n = 0)$ satisfies the conditions of Th. 1. We can conclude the program P is robust. Intuitively, even though the value of private input h flows to public variable l ($l := l + h$), such relation is immediately canceled when we assign the constant 1 ($l := 1$) after the hole.

The following example shows that Th. 1 is just a sufficient condition, namely there exists a robust program that violates the preconditions. This is because Th. 1 corresponds to a local condition for robustness, but one must analyze the entire program in order to have a global vision about the confidential information revealed.

Example 8. Consider the program

$$P ::= \begin{bmatrix} l := h; l := 1; [\bullet]; \\ \textbf{while } (h = 0) \textbf{ do } (h := 1; l := 0); \end{bmatrix}$$

where $h :$ HH and $l :$ LL. The precondition of the **while** is:

$$\textit{Wlp} (\textbf{while } (h = 0) \textbf{ do } (h := 1; l := 0), \{l = n\}) =$$
$$\{(h = 0 \wedge n = 0) \vee (h \neq 0 \wedge l = n)\}$$

This formula does not satisfy the conditions of Th. 1, since it contains a free occurrence of a low integrity variable, namely $l = n$. However, we can see that program P is robust. No modification of the public variable l contains information about the private variable h because the guard of the **while** loop depends exclusively on private variables. Every terminating attack modifies the subformula $\{l = a\}$ and influences the final value of the observed public output. Moreover, the private information obtained by the assignment $l := h$ is canceled by the successive assignment $l := 1$. So the only confidential information released by P concerns the zeroness of h, the same as a passive attacker. This means that P is robust and Th. 1 is a sufficient and not necessary condition for robustness.

Let us show, now, how Theorem 1 applies to programs where the hole occurs in the branch of a conditional or in a loop. As the following theorem shows, in such cases we need to apply recursively Theorem 1 to the formula corresponding to each branch. It is worth noting that the loop can be unfolded a finite number of times until we reach the invariant formula (see the *Wlp* rule for **while** in section 3.3), as the computations we are dealing with are all terminating ones.

Theorem 2. *Let $P_c[\vec{\bullet}] \equiv \textbf{if } B \textbf{ then } P_1[\vec{\bullet}] \textbf{ else } P_2[\vec{\bullet}]$ and $P_w[\vec{\bullet}] \equiv \textbf{while } B \textbf{ do } P[\vec{\bullet}]$ be a program with holes and a first order formula Φ. Then,*

- *$P_c[\vec{\bullet}]$ is robust wrt unfair attacks iff $P_1[\vec{\bullet}]$ and $P_2[\vec{\bullet}]$ are robust wrt unfair attacks and post-condition Φ.*

– $P_w[\vec{\bullet}]$ is robust wrt unfair attacks iff $P[\vec{\bullet}]$ is robust wrt unfair attacks and post-conditions $\text{Wlp}_i(P_w[\vec{\bullet}], \Phi)$

Proof. We do induction on the structure of $P_1[\vec{\bullet}]$; the other case is symmetric. If $P_1[\vec{\bullet}]$ straight line program with holes (as in the hypothesis of Theorem 1), we apply the theorem to check robustness. Otherwise, $P_1[\vec{\bullet}]$ is a conditional and it trivially holds from the induction hypothesis.

In the case of a loop we need to apply the recursive computation as described in section 3.3. If $P[\vec{\bullet}]$ is a straight line program we apply theorem 1 as before and check at each step of *Wlp* computation whether low integrity variables occur in the formula when we reach the hole. Note that the occurrence of the loop guard B in the formula makes sure that the active attacker never influences the variables of B. In this way, we are sure that if the condition is verified the formula remains unchanged for all active attacks. Otherwise, if $P[\vec{\bullet}]$ is a loop or a conditional we apply the induction hypothesis and we are done.

The result above shows how to treat situations where the construct $[\bullet]$ may be placed in an arbitrary depth inside an **if** conditional or a **while** loop. The following example describes this situation.

Example 9. Consider the program P

$$P ::= \left[\begin{array}{l} k := h \bmod 3; \\ \textbf{if } (h \bmod 2 = 0) \textbf{ then}[\bullet]; l := 0; k := l; \\ \qquad\qquad\qquad\quad \textbf{else } l := 1; \end{array} \right.$$

where h : HH, l : LL and k : LL. Applying the weakest liberal precondition rules to the initial formula $\{l = m \wedge k = n\}$ we have:

$$\left\{ \begin{array}{c} (h \bmod 2 = 0 \wedge m = 0 \wedge n = 0) \vee \\ (h \bmod 2 \neq 0 \wedge m = 1 \wedge k = n) \end{array} \right\}$$
$$\textbf{if } (h \bmod 2 = 0) \textbf{ then } [\bullet]; l := 0; k := l; \textbf{ else } l := 1;$$
$$\{l = m \wedge k = n\}$$

The subformula corresponding to the **then** branch (which contains the hole $[\bullet]$) satisfies the conditions of Th.1, therefore P is robust. Every possible attack in this point manipulates the variables l, k which will immediately be substituted by constant 0 and will lose all private information they have accumulated so far.

Note that the invariant enforced by the theorems is the fact that the first order formula determined by the active attack remains inalterate compared to the formula determined by the passive attack. In particular, Theorem 1 proves our security condition, while Theorem 2 model the fact that such condition should be applied recursively in case of conditionals and loops. In the next section we present and algorithmic approach that puts all the pieces together.

5.2   An Algorithmic Approach to Robustness

In this section we present our approach algorithmically in order to make clear how the above theorems apply to terminating while programs. In particular, $Robust(P[\vec{\bullet}], \Phi, \mathcal{S})$

is the main procedure that takes in input a program with holes $P[\bullet]$, a first order formula Φ and a set of low integrity variables S and if it returns a formula, the program is robust and such formula corresponds to the private information disclosed to both passive and active attackers, otherwise (if it returns false) we don't know whether the program is robust or not. The procedure $Check(\Phi, S)$ corresponds to our security condition, namely, it returns true if no low integrity variables in S occur in Φ as well. Moreover, we assume that we have a procedure that transforms a first order formula in the normal form in order to reduce the false alarms in our analysis. The algorithm runs recursively over the syntactical structure of while programs (with holes) and applies, at each step, the rules of Wlp semantics, as described in section 3.3. The procedure $Compute(\textbf{while } B \textbf{ do } c, \Phi, S)$ checks whether the formula remains unchanged for the while loop. In particular, this corresponds to the unfolding of the loop, with a finite number of conditionals. In particular, it applies a finite number of times the security condition of Theorem 2.

$$Robust(P[\vec{\bullet}], \Phi, S) :$$

$$
\begin{array}{l}
\textbf{case}(P[\vec{\bullet}]) : \\[1em]
\begin{array}{ll}
[\bullet] : & Check(\Phi, S) \\
\textbf{skip} : & \Phi \\
x := e : & \Phi[e/x] \\
P_1[\bullet]; P_2[\bullet] : & \Phi' := Robust(P_2[\bullet], \Phi, S) \\
& Robust(P_1[\bullet], \Phi', S) \\
\textbf{if } B \textbf{ then } P_1[\vec{\bullet}] \textbf{ else } P_2[\vec{\bullet}] : & (B \wedge Robust(P_1[\vec{\bullet}], \Phi, S)) \vee \\
& (\neg B \wedge Robust(P_2[\vec{\bullet}], \Phi, S)) \\
\textbf{while } B \textbf{ do } P_1[\vec{\bullet}] : & Compute(\textbf{while } B \textbf{ do } P_1[\vec{\bullet}], \Phi, S)
\end{array}
\end{array}
$$

$$
Check(\Phi, S) : \left[
\begin{array}{lll}
\text{Normalize the formula } \Phi & & \\
\textbf{if } \mathcal{FV}(\Phi) \cap S = \emptyset & & \text{return true} \\
\text{otherwise} & & \text{return false}
\end{array}
\right.
$$

$$
Compute(\textbf{while } B \textbf{ do } c, \Phi, S) : \left[
\begin{array}{l}
\Phi_{i+1} := \neg B \wedge \Phi \\
result := \Phi_{i+1} \\
\textbf{do} \\
\quad \Phi_i := \Phi_{i+1} \\
\quad \Phi_{i+1} := Robust(\textbf{if } B \textbf{ then } c \textbf{ else skip}, \Phi_i, S) \\
\quad result \vee := \Phi_{i+1} \\
\textbf{while } \Phi_i \neq \Phi_{i+1}
\end{array}
\right.
$$

5.3   Robustness on Program Traces

In this section, we want to find local conditions guaranteeing robustness also in presence of active attackers which observe trace semantics instead of I/O semantics. In other words, we want to characterise the analogous of Th. 1 when dealing with trace semantics. Note that, in this case, the problem becomes really different because the attacker is still able to modify low integrity variables, but he can also *observe* low confidentiality variables in the holes. In this case, the problem is that the attacker can assign variables of type HL to variables of type LL, observe the corresponding trace and disclose immediately the value of HL variables. Hence, it is necessary to analyse the global program behavior in order to check robustness for all possible unfair attacks. On the other hand, if we consider fair attacks, i.e., attacks that manipulate only LL variables, the attackers capability to observe program points where the hole occurs allows us to reduce all the possible attacks to constant assignments to variables of type LL.

By using the method introduced in [18], illustrated for active attackers in Sect. 4.2, we are able to state a sufficient condition of robustness in presence of fair attacks for trace semantics. The idea is that an attacker can combine the public information he can observe at a program point together with the information he can derive by computing the *Wlp* from the output to that observation point. Moreover, he can manipulate program semantics by inserting fair code in the holes. If the formula corresponding to *Wlp* semantics of the subprogram before reaching the hole does not contain free any variables of type LL then we can conclude that the program is robust. The following example shows the robustness condition similar to Th. 1.

Example 10. Consider the program P with variables l : LH, k : LL and h_1, h_2, h_3 : HH:

$$P ::= k := h_1 + h_2; [\bullet]; k := h_3 \bmod 2; l := h_3; l := k;$$

A passive attacker who observes each program point discloses the following private information.

$$\{h_3 \bmod 2 = m \wedge h_3 = n \wedge l = p \wedge h_1 + h_2 = q\}$$
$$k := h_1 + h_2;$$
$$[skip;]$$
$$\{h_3 \bmod 2 = m \wedge h_3 = n \wedge l = p \wedge [k = q]\}$$
$$k := h_3 \bmod 2;$$
$$\{k = m \wedge h_3 = n \wedge [l = p]\}$$
$$l := h_3;$$
$$\{k = m \wedge [l = n]\}$$
$$l := k;$$
$$\{l = k = m\}$$

Hence, a passive attacker reveals the symbolic value of variable h_3 and the sum of variables h_1 and h_2. In what follows we notice that no fair attack (in our case manipulating k) can do better, because the subformula corresponding to the information disclosed by the attacker does not contain free the variable k : LL. Thus, no constant assignment influences the private information released. Indeed, if we compute the information disclosed in presence of a fair attack the final formula is the same.

$$\{h_3 \bmod 2 = m \wedge h_3 = n \wedge l = p \wedge h_1 + h_2 = r\}$$
$$k := h_1 + h_2;$$
$$\{h_3 \bmod 2 = m \wedge h_3 = n \wedge l = p \wedge q = d_1 \wedge [k = r]\}$$
$$[k := d_1;]$$
$$\{h_3 \bmod 2 = m \wedge h_3 = n \wedge l = p \wedge [k = q]\}$$

Note that, it is useless to consider the observed value of LL variable before the hole because the attacker knows exactly what fair attack he is going to inject in.

Now we can introduce a sufficient condition for robustness for trace semantics. Basically, the idea is to propose an extension of Th. 1 to traces. We have first to note that in Th. 1 we deal with unfair attackers, which can use also variables of type HL. In the trace semantics context this may be a problem whenever attackers can observe low confidentiality data in at least one point where they can inject their code, i.e., if $\mathbb{H} \cap \mathbb{O} \neq \varnothing$. In particular what may happen is that the attacker can use variables of type HL and observe the result at the same time, possibly disclosing the value of these variables. This clearly means that the program is trivially not robust as shown in the following example.

Example 11. Consider the program

$$P := l := k \ mod \ 2; [\bullet]; \ \textbf{if} \ (h = 0) \ \textbf{then} \ l := 0 \ \textbf{else} \ l := 1;$$

where $l : $ LL, $k : $ HL and $h : $ HH. We want to check robustness in presence of unfair attacks who observe each program point. First, we notice that a passive attacker discloses the zeroness of variable h and the parity of variable k. Now let us compute the information released in the hole.

$$\{(h = 0 \wedge n = 0) \vee (h \neq 0 \wedge n = 1)\}$$
$$\textbf{if} \ (h = 0) \ \textbf{then} \ l := 0 \ \textbf{else} \ l := 1;$$
$$\{l = n\}$$

This formula satisfies the conditions of Prop. 2: no low integrity variables occur free in it. But, if we attack this program with the unfair attack (e.g., $l := k$), we can see that the program releases the exact symbolic value of the private variable k.

$$\left\{ \begin{array}{c} ((h = 0 \wedge n = 0) \vee (h \neq 0 \wedge n = 1)) \wedge \\ k = p \wedge k \ mod \ 2 = q \end{array} \right\}$$
$$l := k \ mod \ 2;$$
$$\{((h = 0 \wedge n = 0) \vee (h \neq 0 \wedge n = 1)) \wedge k = p \wedge [l = q]\}$$
$$[l := k;]$$
$$\{((h = 0 \wedge n = 0) \vee (h \neq 0 \wedge n = 1)) \wedge [l = p]\}$$

We can conclude that program P is not robust (wrt unfair attacks) even though the conditions of Th. 1 are satisfied.

At this point we can provide, in the following proposition, the robustness sufficient condition that has to hold for traces, depending on the relation between hole points $\mathbb{H}$ and observable points $\mathbb{O}$. In particular, if we consider attackers that observe low confidentiality data in at least one hole point, i.e., $\mathbb{H} \cap \mathbb{O} \neq \varnothing$, then we can prove robustness only wrt fair attacks, otherwise we can consider general unfair attackers. In fact, when $\mathbb{H} \cap \mathbb{O} = \varnothing$ the attackers cannot combine their capabilities of observing low confidentiality variables and of modifying low integrity variables, making possible to guarantee robustness.

Proposition 2. *Consider $P[\bar{\bullet}]$ and $\Phi_i = Wlp(P_i, \Phi_0)$ (where P_i is obtained as in Th. 1). Then we have that:*

1. *If* $\mathbb{H} \cap \mathbb{O} \neq \varnothing$ *then P is robust wrt fair attacks if* $\forall i \in \mathbb{H}. \forall v \in \mathcal{FV}(\varPhi_i).\mathcal{I}(v) = \mathtt{H}.$
2. *If* $\mathbb{H} \cap \mathbb{O} = \varnothing$ *then P is robust wrt* **unfair** *attacks if* $\forall i \in \mathbb{H}. \forall v \in \mathcal{FV}(\varPhi_i).\mathcal{I}(v) = \mathtt{H}.$

Proof. Consider the program P. First of all note that the difference between observing I/O semantics and trace semantics consists simply on the fact that the attacker can enrich the *Wlp* analysis with the observation that it can perform during the computation. Hence, we can define an enriched weakest precondition semantic function: $Wlp'(c, \phi) \stackrel{\text{def}}{=} Wlp(c, \phi \wedge \phi')$, where $\phi' = true$ if the corresponding program point is not in $\mathbb{O}$, ϕ' is the observable property otherwise. At this point, by using Wlp' instead of *Wlp* we can apply Th. 1 with the following restrictions:

1. If $\mathbb{H} \cap \mathbb{O} \neq \varnothing$ then the attacker can use variables of type HL and observe the result at the same time, disclosing the HL variables and violating robustness. In particular, if the program has $l : \mathtt{LL}$ and $k : \mathtt{HL}$, then the attacker can always insert the code $l := k$, and by observing the result can directly know the value of k violating confidentiality and, obviously, robustness. This is not a problem for fair attackers, since these attackers cannot use variables of type HL.
2. If $\mathbb{H} \cap \mathbb{O} = \varnothing$ then the unfair attacker cannot observe the result of the added code and therefore robustness can again hold, at least when the sufficient condition of Th. 1 is satisfied.

5.4 *Wlp* vs. Security Type System

In [20] the authors define the notion of robustness in presence of active attackers and enforce it by using a security type system. The active attacker can replace the holes by fair attacks which manipulate variables of security type LL. The key result of the article states that typable programs satisfy robust declassification. Thus, it is important, when dealing with robustness, for the holes not to be placed into high confidentiality contexts. In particular they introduce a security environment and a program counter pc in order to trace the security contexts and avoid implicit flows. The following typing rule considers cases where the construct $[\bullet]$ is admissible.

$$\frac{\mathcal{C}(\mathrm{pc}) \in L_C}{\varGamma, \mathrm{pc} \vdash \bullet}$$

Let A be the attacker code, then $L_C \stackrel{\text{def}}{=} \{l | \mathcal{C}(l) \sqsubseteq \mathcal{C}(A)\}$, namely L_C is the set of variables whose confidentiality level is not greater than attackers confidentiality level. Hence, an active attacker that manipulates this variables does not obtain further confidential information. The type system is highly imprecise with respect to standard non-interference since it rules out all programs containing low assignments under high guards or any sub-command with an explicit assignment from high to low. Basically, the type system admits programs that *associate* low with low, high with high and do not use high expressions on guards of conditionals or loops. This corresponds to a trace-based characterization of non-interference where the attacker can observe the content of low variables in each program point. Now if we ignore the explicit declassification (*declassify(e)*) and consider only programs with holes, the typing rule for the hole requires them to occur in low confidentiality security context, namely program is robust if there is no interaction between high and low, neither explicit nor implicit and this is quite restrictive. Getting back to explicit declassification, the rule requires it occurs in low confidentiality and high integrity program context, namely the guard of a conditional or a loop is allowed to evaluate only on variables of security type LH if we want to embed declassification. Moreover, only high integrity variables can be declassified, i.e., declassification from variables of security type HH to variables of security type LH is allowed. Putting all together, the type system approach deems robust programs that never branch on a secret value (unless each branch assigns only to high) and admit explicit flow (from high to low) in certain program points because of declassification.

Our approach, in particular Th. 2, captures exactly those situations where the hole occurs in some confidentiality context (possibly high) and, nevertheless, the fair attack does not succeed, namely where there are no low integrity variables in the corresponding first order formula. If our condition holds, we are more precise to capture the main goal of robustness, i.e., an active attacker does not disclose more private information than a passive one, as we perform a flow sensitive analysis. Indeed, if the target program has some intended global interference (the *what* dimension in [22]), the type system is unable to model it (as it considers the *where* dimension in [22]), while our approach characterizes robustness with respect to a program and a global declassification policy. Moreover, our method deals with more powerful active attacks, the unfair attacks, which can manipulate code that contains variables with security type LL and HL. However, both these approaches study program robustness as a local condition and therefore cannot provide a precise characterisation of robustness: Th. 2 provides only a sufficient condition and the type system is not complete. Anyway, we can say that, when it can be applied, namely when the hypotheses of the theorems hold, then our semantic-based method is more precise, in the sense that it generates less *false alarms*, than the type-based one. For instance, let us consider the program $P ::= [\bullet];$ **if** $h > 0$ **then** $l := 0$ **else** $l := 0$ where h : HH and l : LL. Our method certifies this program as robust since, there are no low integrity variables in the formula corresponding to the *Wlp* semantics of the control statement **if**. If we try to type check this program by using the rules in [20] we notice that the environment before hole is a high confidentiality one. Thus, this program is deemed not robust.

We have, anyway, to note that our approach, if compared with the type-based one, loses effectiveness in order to keep precision, i.e., in order to reduce false alarms. Indeed, in the future, in order to make our certification approach systematic we will surely have to weaken the semantic precision.

6   Relative Robustness

So far, we have given only sufficient conditions to enforce robust programs. The problem is that an active attacker transforms program semantics and these transformations can be infinitely many or of infinitely many kinds. This may be an issue, first of all because it becomes hard to compute the private information released by all the active attacks (as underlined in Sect. 4), but also because, in some restricted contexts, standard robustness can be too strong a requirement.

Indeed, we can consider a restricted class of active attacks and check robustness wrt to these attacks. Namely, we aim to check whether the program, in presence of these attacks, does not release more private information than a passive attacker. Thus, we define a relaxed notion of robustness, called *relative robustness*.

Definition 1. *Let* $P[\bullet]$ *be a program and* $\mathcal{A}$ *a set of attacks. The program is said relatively robust iff for all* $\vec{a} \in \mathcal{A}$, *then* $P[\vec{a}]$ *does not release more confidential information than* $P[\overrightarrow{skip}]$.

Recall that we model the information disclosed by the attacker by first order formulas, which we interpret by means of abstract domains in the lattice of abstract interpretations as explained in section 3.4. In particular, if the attacker a_1 discloses more private information than attacker a_2, it means that the abstract domain corresponding to the private property revealed to a_1 is contained in the abstract domain corresponding to the private property realeed to a_2.

In order to check relative robustness we can compute the confidential information released for all possible attacks, compute the greatest lower bound of all information and compare it with the confidential information released by a passive attacker. Moreover, given a program and a set of attacks we can statically certify the security degree of the program with respect to that particular finite class of active attacks. This corresponds to the *glb* of private information released by all these attacks. Hence, a programmer who wants to certify program robustness in presence of a fixed class of attacks, have to declassify at least the *glb* of private information disclosed by all attacks.

Consider Ex. 1. We noticed that different active attackers can disclose different kind of private information, for this reason the program P is not robust. Now, consider a restriction of the possible active attacks, for example we restrict to fair attacks only. This implies that the attacker can use only variable l and derive information exclusively about private variable h. In particular, P already releases in l the exact value of h and consequently no attack involving variable l can disclose more private information. Thus, we can conclude that program P satisfies *relative robustness* with respect to the class of fair attacks.

We can extend Th. 1 in order to cope with relative robustness. In particular, we recall that this theorem provides a sufficient condition to robustness requiring that the formulas before each hole do not contain *any* low integrity variable. We weaken this sufficient condition by requiring that the formulas before each hole do not contain *only* the variables modifiable and usable by the attackers in $\mathcal{A}$. It is worth noting that both Prop. 3 and Prop. 4 are easily extended to programs with more holes occuring at different depths, exactly the same way as we derived Th. 1 from Lemma 1 and Th. 2 from Th. 1. Next proposition is a rewriting of Lemma 1 for relative robustness.

Proposition 3. *Let* $P = P_2; [\bullet]; P_1$ *be a program (where* P_1 *is without holes). Let* $\Phi = Wlp(P_1, \Phi_0)$. P *is relatively robust wrt unfair attacks in* $\mathcal{A}$ *if* $\forall a \in \mathcal{A}. Var(a) \cap \mathcal{FV}(\Phi) = \varnothing$.

Proof. Note that the variables used by the active attacker do not occur free in Φ as the intersection is empty (by hypothesis). By Lemma 1 program P is robust.

It is worth noting that we can use this result also for deriving the class of *harmless* active attackers starting from the semantics of the program. Indeed, we can certify that a program is relatively robust wrt all the active attackers that involve low integrity variables not occurring free in the formulas corresponding to the private information disclosed before reaching each hole.

6.1   Relative vs. Decentralized Robustness

In this section, we claim that, from certain viewpoints, relative robustness is a more general notion than decentralized robustness. The reasons are the same as the ones discussed in 5.4. In a nutshell, we can observe that, once the pair of principals is fixed, also the data security levels are fixed, namely we know which are the variables readable and/or modifiable by the attacker q from the point of view of a principal p. We can denote by $\mathcal{C}_{p \to q}$ the confidentiality levels and by $\mathcal{I}_{p \leftarrow q}$ the integrity levels characterised so far. For instance, for each variable x, $\mathcal{I}_{p \leftarrow q}(x) = L$ if p believes that q can modify x, $\mathcal{I}_{p \leftarrow q}(x) = H$ otherwise. In particular, given a program and a security policy in DLM fashion, we compute the set of readers and writers for each pair of principals p, q, as in [5], and check robustness for each pair by using Proposition 3. Hence, we have the following generalisation of relative robustness in DLM.

Proposition 4. *Let* $P = P_2; [\bullet]; P_1$ *be a program (where P_1 is without holes). Let* $\Phi = \text{Wlp}(P_1, \Phi_0)$. *P satisfies decentralized robustness wrt principals p, q if we have that* $\{ x \mid \mathcal{I}_{p \leftarrow q}(x) = L \} \cap \mathcal{FV}(\Phi) = \varnothing$.

Proof. Given a pair of principals (p, q) we compute the set of *readers* and *writers* as for decentralized robustness. Consequently, we have a static labeling of program data with respect to confidentiality and integrity. At this point we apply Lemma 1 as the hypothesis of proposition guarantees that no low integrity variable occurring free in Φ is used by the active attack. Since this holds for all possible pairs of principals, the claim is true.

This characterization suits perfectly to client-side web languages such as Javascript as it allows to prevent injection attacks or dynamically loaded third-party code. In particular, suppose we have a web page that accepts advertising adds from different sources, with different security concerns and wonder if it leaks private information to a malicious attacker. Moreover, we can assume that the web page has different trust relations with domains providing adds and this is specified in the security policy. Given this information, one can analyze the DOM (Document Object Model) tree and classify each attribute in sensitive and insensitive with respect to a possible attacker [17]. The *session cookie* might be an attribute to protect wrt all attackers, while the *history object* might be public to some trusted domains and private to others. At this point we can apply weakest precondition analysis to web server from the point it discloses information on any public channel such as the output web page or the reply information sent as response to a client request. The holes correspond to program points where the server receives adds from different clients and embeds them in its code. Analyzing the formula corresponding to the sensitive information disclosed before parsing and embedding such adds, namely using the *eval()* operation in Javascript, we can identify harmless low integrity variables and certify security modulo (relative to) programs manipulating this variables.

Example 12. Consider the following Javascript-like code (modified version of the example in [6]). Lines 3-6 correspond to an add received from a third party to be displayed on the web page. Moreover, the web site contains a simple function *login()* which authenticates users by verifying *username* and *password* inserted in a form. The function runs when the user clicks on a button, lines 7-16. Function *initSettings* corresponds to the output channel of the web page as it identifies the server used to authenticate the user, i.e., to send username and password.

```
1.   <script type="javascript">
             // 2: initialization of the output server
2.   initSettings("mysite.com/login.php", 1.0);
             // 3-4-5: definition of the add
3.   <div id="AdNode">
4.      <script src="adserver.com/display.js">
5.   </div>
6.   eval(src)

7.   var login = function() {
8.      var pwd = document.nodes.PasswordTextBox.value;
9.      var user = document.nodes.UsernameTextBox.value;
11.     var params = "u=" + user + "&p=" + pwd;
             //12: sends the parameters (params) to baseUrl
12.     post(document.settings.baseUrl, params);}
14.  </script>
             //15-16:login interface
15.  <text id="UsernameTextBox"> <text id="PasswordTextBox">
16.  <button id="ButtonLogin" onclick="login()">
```

Now, suppose the add code corresponds to the hole and the public output is the final web page together with the result (*out* : LL) of *post* in line 12. Since formal parameters of function *initSettings* (defining variable *baseUrl* : LL) have low integrity, a malicious add could overwrite the parameters and redirect the high confidentiality part of the output of *post* (login and password, i.e., *user, pwd*: HH) to the attacker. Let us see how our approach allows to identify such security flaws. First, we compute the weakest precondition of function login and obtain the following formula:

$$[\bullet]$$
$$\{baseUrl + user + pwd = a\}$$
$$var\ pwd = document.nodes.PasswordTextBox.value;$$
$$var\ user = document.nodes.UsernameTextBox.value;$$
$$var\ params = "u = " + user + "\&p = " + pwd;$$
$$\{baseUrl + params = a\}$$
$$post(document.settings.baseUrl, params)$$
$$\{out = a\}$$

Observing the final formula we can state that private information concerning username and password is related to the low integrity variable *baseUrl* and therefore the program does not satisfy confidentiality. Moreover, the program is not even robust since low integrity variable *baseUrl* is free before the "hole". In particular, a malicious add could hijack such information to a malicious website and obtain username and password. However, we can deem this program robust relative to fair attacks which do not manipulate the low integrity variable *baseUrl*. In decentralized robustness, this corresponds to say that the program is robust wrt all the pairs (p, q) such that p does not believes that q can write the low integrity variable *baseUrl*.

7   Applications

In this section we present two applications where our approach captures soundly the possible security violations. The first example considers a secure API function widely used to perform PIN checking in a bank and is retrieved from [4]. The attacker is able to play with low integrity variables and reveal the real PIN by analyzing the implicit flow released by the API. The second example concerns a web application where third party code is allowed to be embedded in. Cross Site Scripting attacks (XSS) are name of the game in such contexts. In particular [23], the attacker tries to steal a session cookie and hijack the user to an evil website. In both examples our analysis is sufficient to capture the possible security violations.

7.1   Secure API Attack

This example concerns the use of secure API to authenticate and authorize a user to access an ATM cash machine. The user inserts the credit card and the PIN code at the machine. The PIN code gets encrypted and travels along the network until it reaches the issuing bank. At this point, a verifying API is executed in order to check the equality of the real user PIN and the trial PIN inserted at the cash machine. The verifying API, called PIN_V, is the one exploited by the attacker to disclose the real PIN.

The real PIN is derived through the PIN derivation key *pdk* and public data *offset, vdata, dectab*, while the trial PIN comes encrypted by key k. Of course, the two keys, *pdk* and k are pre-loaded in the Hardware Security Modules (HSM) of the bank server and never travel the network. Here is the description of the API, PIN_V.

```
PIN_V(EPB, len, offset, vdata,dectab) {
    x1 := enc_pdk(vdata);
    x2 := left(len, x1);
    x3 := decimalize(dectab, x2);
    x4 := sum_mod10(x3, offset);
    x5 := dec_k(len, EPB);
    if(x4 == x5) then return ("PIN correct");
                else return ("PIN wrong");
}
```

where:

- *len* is the length of real PIN obtained by the encryption of the validation data *vdata* (a kind of user profile) with the PIN derivation key *pdk* (x1), taking the *len* hexadecimal digits (x2), decimalising through *dectab* (x3), and digit-wise summing modulo 10 the offset (x4).

- EPB (Encrypted PIN Block) is the ciphertext containing the trial password encrypted with the key k. The trial PIN is recovered by decrypting EPB with key k.

The above snippet of code is insecure and there is a very nice attack used to disclose the exact PIN code just by modifying low integrity variables *offset* and *dectab* (of type LL) and observing low confidentiality output, namely by observing the I/O behavior of API method [4].

Example 13. Let $len = 4$, $offset = 4732$, $x1 = A47295FDE32A48B1$ and $dectab = 9753108642543210$ which is a substitution function encoding the mapping $0 \rightarrow 9, 1 \rightarrow 7, \cdots, F \rightarrow 0$. Moreover, let $EPB = enc_k(9897)$, where 9897 is the correct PIN. With these parameters PIN_V returns *PIN correct*.

Indeed, consider $x2 = left(4, A47295FDE32A48B1) = A472$, and consider $x3 = decimalize(dectab, A472) = 5165$ and $x4 = sum\_mod10(5165, 4732) = 9897$ which is the same as the trial PIN.

Now the attacker first chooses $dectab1 = 9753\underline{11}8642543\underline{211}$ where the two 0's have been replaced by 1's. In this way the intruder discovers whether or not 0 appears in x3. Invoking the API with *dectab1* we obtain the same intermediate and final values, as $decimalize(dectab1, A472) = decimalize(dectab, A472) = 5165$. This means that 0 does not appear in x3.

The attacker proceeds by replacing the 1 of *dectab* by 2.

If $dectab2 = 9753208642543220$ he obtains that $decimalize(dectab2, A472) = 5265 \neq decimalize(dectab, A472) = 5165$, reflecting the presence of in the original value of x3. Then, $x4 = sum\_mod10(5265, 4732) = 9997$ instead of 9897 returning *PIN wrong*.

Now, the attacker knows that digit 1, occurs in x3 for sure. In order to discover its position and its multiplicity, he varies the *offset* so to *compensate* for the modification of *dectab*. In particular, the attacker decrements each *offset* digit by 1 until it finds the one that makes the API return *PIN correct*. For this particular instance the possible variations of the *offset* are: $\underline{3}732, 4\underline{6}32, 47\underline{2}2, 473\underline{1}$ and the one that succeeds is the *offset* 4632. So, the attacker revealed that the second digit of $x3$ is 1. Given that the offset is public, he derives the second digit of user PIN as $1 + 7mod10$, where 7 is the second digit of the initial *offset*. Iterating this procedure the attacker discloses the entire value of PIN.

In the following computation we show weakest precondition approach captures the security flaws in API.

Let us observe the final formula corresponding to the weakest precondition of the API. Clearly, we can first note that the program does not satisfy confidentiality since the public output (the answer to the comparison between the real and the trial password) depends clearly on the high confidentiality variable containing the real password. From the viewpoint of robustness we can note that our sufficient condition is not satisfied since there are low integrity variables, i.e., *dectab* and *offset*, which are free before the hole (supposed to be in the input of the API, namely in the communication phase). Indeed, exactly those are the variables used by the attacker for disclosing the PIN.

$$
\left\{
\begin{array}{c}
(sum\_mod10(decimalize(dectab, left(len, enc_p\, dk(vdata))), offset) = dec_k(len, EPB) \\
\wedge a = 1) \vee \\
(sum\_mod10(decimalize(dectab, left(len, enc_p\, dk(vdata))), offset) \neq dec_k(len, EPB) \\
\wedge a = 0)
\end{array}
\right\}
$$
$$ x1 := enc_p\, dk(vdata); $$
$$
\left\{
\begin{array}{c}
(sum_m\, od10(decimalize(dectab, left(len, x1)), offset) = dec_k(len, EPB) \wedge a = 1) \vee \\
(sum_m\, od10(decimalize(dectab, left(len, x1)), offset) \neq dec_k(len, EPB) \wedge a = 0)
\end{array}
\right\}
$$
$$ x2 := left(len, x1); $$
$$
\left\{
\begin{array}{c}
(sum\_mod10(decimalize(dectab, x2), offset) = dec_k(len, EPB) \wedge a = 1) \vee \\
(sum\_mod10(decimalize(dectab, x2), offset) \neq dec_k(len, EPB) \wedge a = 0)
\end{array}
\right\}
$$
$$ x3 := decimalize(dectab, x2); $$
$$
\left\{
\begin{array}{c}
(sum\_mod10(x3, offset) = dec_k(len, EPB) \wedge a = 1) \vee \\
(sum\_mod10(x3, offset) \neq dec_k(len, EPB) \wedge a = 0)
\end{array}
\right\}
$$
$$ x4 := sum\_mod10(x3, offset); $$
$$ \{(x_4 = dec_k(len, EPB) \wedge a = 1) \vee (x_4 \neq dec_k(len, EPB) \wedge a = 0)\} $$
$$ x5 := dec_k(len, EPB); $$
$$ \{(x_4 = x_5 \wedge a = 1) \vee (x_4 \neq x_5 \wedge a = 0)\} $$
$$ if\ (x_4 == x_5)\ then\ (return\ 1)\ else\ (return\ 0) $$
$$ \{l = a\} $$

The authors [4] fix this problem by using a MAC (Message Authentication Code) security primitive. In particular, MACs are used to guarantee the integrity of information received from an untrusted source, namely any modification of data before calling the API is prevented by MAC. Semantically, this means that the variables *dectab* and *offset* can be modified only by authorised agents. In our approach, this can be modelled by assigning the security level LH to *dectab* and *offset*, i.e., by considering them as high integrity. In this way, we are done, because our weakest precondition approach yields a formula containing free only high integrity variables. Hence the robustness condition is satisfied.

7.2   Cross Site Scripting Attack

Javascript is a very flexible dynamic object-based scripting language running in almost all modern web browsers. The language allows to transfer, parse and run code sent over the network between different web-based applications. While very useful and user-friendly, such flexibility comes at a great price as the underlying applications become vulnerable to code injection attacks. These attacks circumvent the security enforcement mechanism of Javascript, namely *the same-origin* policy which prevents a document or script loaded from one origin from getting or setting properties of a document from another origin [17]. Indeed, when the browser receives a compromised web page, it is executed in the context of the website hosting it, therefore, the same-origin policy deems the operation secure. Afterwards, the malicious code can establish a connection to the attacker server and transfer sensitive information such as cookie sessions for instance. The following example shows that language-based security techniques can be used to prevent this kind of attacks.

Suppose a user visits a untrusted web site in order to download a picture, where an attacker has inserted his own malicious Javascript code (Fig. 1), and execute it on the clients browser [23].

In the following we described a simplified version. The Javascript code snippet in Fig. 1 can be used by the attacker to send users cookie[3] to a web server under the attackers control.

```
var cookie = document.cookie;
          /*initialisation of the cookie by the server*/
var dut;
if (dut == undefined) {dut = "";}
while(i<cookie.length) {
    switch(cookie[i]) {
        case 'a': dut += 'a'; break;
        case 'b': dut += 'b'; break;
        ...
    }
}
          /* dut contains now copy of cookie*/
document.images[0].src =  "http://badsite/cookie?" + dut;
          /* when the user click on the image dut is sent
             to the web server under the attackers control*/
```

Fig. 1. Code creating a XSS vulnerability

One can easily see that the variable *dut* contains a copy of users cookie. This attack circumvents same-origin policy in client browser as it is correctly received after a request to some server where the attacker injected the malicious code. Now lets apply our analysis to the above Javascript snippet. In particular, suppose that variable *cookie* has security type HL and variable *dut* has security type LL. Moreover, imagine we emulate the switch-case operator by a chain of if-then-else constructs and *cookie.length* has security type LL .

$$[\bullet]$$
$$\{cookie + dut = res\}$$
$$while(i < cookie.length)\{$$
$$switch(cookie[i])\{$$
$$case'a' : dut+ =' a'; break;$$
$$case'b' : dut+ =' b'; break;$$
$$...\}\}$$
$$\{dut = res\}$$

---

[3] A cookie is a text string stored by a user's web browser. A cookie consists of one or more name-value pairs containing bits of information, sent as an HTTP header by a web server to a web browser (client) and then sent back unchanged by the browser each time it accesses that server. It can be used, for example, for authentication.

By observing the final formula we can notice that confidentiality is violated since there is a (implicit) flow of information from private variable *cookie* towards the public variable *dut*. However, this is the sensitive information disclosed by a passive attacker when *dut* is initialised in the code to the empty string. Nevertheless, *dut* is free before the hole, i.e., where the attacker can insert other malicious code, therefore the (active) attacker can exploit *dut* for disclosing other user confidential information. Suppose, for instance, the attacker to be interested in the *history* object (with security type HL) together with its attributes[4]. In this case, an active attack could loop over the elements of the *history* object and pass through variable *dut* all the web pages the client has had access to. Consider for example the injection of the code in Fig. 2.

```
<script language="JavaScript">
var dut = "";
for (i=0; i<history.length; i++){
    dut = dut + history.previous;
}
</script>
```

Fig. 2. Malicious code exploiting XSS vulnerability

Hence, in this case the program violates the robustness condition since the attacker can exploit the low integrity variable *dut*, which occurs free in the formula before the hole, in order to disclose more confidential information. Moreover we have shown that the attacker can exploit this vulnerability by inserting the code in Fig. 2 just before the malicious code (Fig. 1) in the untrusted web page, getting both *history* and *cookie* through the variable *dut*.

It is worth noting that our approach provides a theoretical model for the existing techniques used in practice for protecting code from XSS attacks [23].

8   Related Work

Prior work on robustness, in the language-based setting, has been addressed in [26,20]. In these papers the authors give a trace-based definition of robustness and enforce it with a flow-insensitive type system. They consider a simple while language, as we do in the this paper, but, in addition they consider an additional construct for declassifying the security of variables in fixed program points (the *where* dimension in [22]). Therefore, a program is robust is an active attacker is unable to manipulate program semantics and declassify more information than a passive attacker does. The security type system enforces both non-interference and robustness so a program is ruled out if neither of the two security properties holds. On the other hand, our semantic approach is different as we model global declassification policies (the *what* dimension in [22]). Moreover, we capture a cleaner characterization of robustness, namely the active attacker does

---

[4] The history object allows to navigate through the history of websites that a browser has visited.

not disclose more private information than a passive one, even though the program under passive attacker does not satisfy non-interference. Other differences between two approaches are shown in section 5.4.

The idea of considering the weakest liberal precondition semantics for static certification of program security is borrowed from [18]. The authors define declassified non interference as a completeness problem in abstract interpretation and the semantic function corresponds to the *Wlp* semantics. However this paper considers only passive attackers and moreover the idea of computing *Wlp* wrt first order formulas is novel in our approach.

Decentralized robustness [5] expresses robustness in the context of the decentralized label model and enforces it statically by a type system. In this paper we showed that the approach can be characterized by our notion of relative robustness. Section 6.1 compares the two approaches.

Language-based techniques for security are more and more being applied to client-side web languages such as Javascript to prevent different attacks [6,23]. Basically, they combine static and dynamic analysis to enforce information flow properties such as non interference. However, our idea of interpreting robustness for Javascript, to the best of our knowledge, is novel and could nicely fit in as a good security model for such language. In particular, the security type HL can model the code injected by an attacker, which knows a certain variable exists (password for instance), but doesn't know its value.

9   Conclusions

In this paper, we addressed an important notion in language-based security called robustness [26,20]. In general a program can run in any distributed environment in presence of untrusted components. This fact is modeled by fixed program points called *holes*, namely program points where the attacker can insert untrusted code. At this point, the program is robust if an active attacker cannot disclose more private information than a passive one. We noted that an active attacker can transform program semantics and control private information released by the program. Moreover, different active attacks can release different properties of private data. Hence, the total number of attacks may be infinite so it is impossible to find the most harmful attack for a given program. Here we characterised a sufficient condition that enforces robustness for unfair attacks (using LL and HL variables). Moreover, we have considered robustness in two different semantic models, I/O and trace semantics. Then we introduced the notion of *relative robustness* which is a relaxation of robustness dealing with a restricted class of attacks. Finally, we conclude with two real application: the analysis of the API for PIN verification and the analysis of code vulnerable to XSS attacks.

The analysis we performed in this paper results very interesting from both theoretical and practical point of view. On the one hand the semantic condition of robustness addresses the issue of systematic transformations of program code that preserve interesting extensional properties, robustness for instance. Indeed abstract interpretation is a possible framework to play with in order to guarantee such properties. On the other hand, we saw that our approach is a good remedy to the lack of precise static analysis approaches in real application domains concerning security.

However, this is just the beginning and there is much more work to do. First, we need to implement the algorithm for static certification of robust programs. Hence, given a program we need to effectively compute when it happens to be robust. It would be important to characterize classes of attacks that induce the same semantic transformation, namely disclose the same property of private inputs. In this way, we can hope for finding a finite number of such attack classes. Second, our work can be generalised to deal with abstract active attackers. Namely, as it happens for abstract non-interference, one can consider attackers modifying *properties* of low integrity data. Third, we plan to extend our approach to different attacker models such as concurrent attackers or attackers able to erase parts of program code. Off we go.

References

1. http://www.owasp.org
2. Balliu, M., Mastroeni, I.: A weakest precondition approach to active attacks analysis. In: PLAS, pp. 59–71 (2009)
3. Banerjee, A., Giacobazzi, R., Mastroeni, I.: What you lose is what you leak: Information leakage in declassification policies. In: Proc. of the 23th Internat. Symp. on Mathematical Foundations of Programming Semantics MFPS 2007. Electronic Notes in Theoretical Computer Science, vol. 1514. Elsevier, Amsterdam (2007)
4. Centenaro, M., Focardi, R., Luccio, F.L., Steel, G.: Type-based analysis of pin processing apis. In: Backes, M., Ning, P. (eds.) ESORICS 2009. LNCS, vol. 5789, pp. 53–68. Springer, Heidelberg (2009)
5. Chong, S., Myers, A.C.: Decentralized robustness. In: Proc. the IEEE Computer Security Foundations Workshop (CSFW-19), Washington, DC, USA, pp. 242–256. IEEE Computer Society, Los Alamitos (2006)
6. Chugh, R., Meister, J.A., Jhala, R., Lerner, S.: Staged information flow for javascript. In: PLDI, pp. 50–62 (2009)
7. Cohen, E.S.: Information transmission in sequential programs. In: DeMillo, et al. (eds.) Foundations of Secure Computation, pp. 297–335. Academic Press, New York (1978)
8. Cousot, P., Cousot, R.: Abstract interpretation: A unified lattice model for static analysis of programs by construction or approximation of fixpoints. In: Proc. of Conf. Record of the 4th ACM Symp. on Principles of Programming Languages POPL 1977, pp. 238–252. ACM Press, New York (1977)
9. Cousot, P., Cousot, R.: Systematic design of program analysis frameworks. In: Proc. of Conf. Record of the 6th ACM Symp. on Principles of Programming Languages POPL 1979, pp. 269–282. ACM Press, New York (1979)
10. Danicic, S., Harman, M., Hierons, R., Howroyd, J., Laurence, M.: Applications of linear program schematology in dependence analysis. In: PLID (2004)
11. Dijkstra, E.W.: A discipline of programming. Series in automatic computation. Prentice Hall, Englewood Cliffs (1976)
12. Dijkstra, E.W.: Guarded commands, nondeterminism and formal derivation of programs. Comm. of The ACM 18(8), 453–457 (1975)
13. Goguen, J.A., Meseguer, J.: Security policies and security models. In: Proc. IEEE Symp. on Security and Privacy, pp. 11–20. IEEE Comp. Soc. Press, Los Alamitos (1982)
14. Gries, D.: The Science of Programming. Springer, Heidelberg (1981)
15. Hehner, E.C.R.: The Logic of Programming. In: Hoare, C.A.R. (ed.) Series in Computer Science. Prentice Hall, Englewood Cliffs (1984)

16. Rustan, K., Leino, M.: Efficient weakest preconditions. Inf. Process. Lett. 93(6), 281–288 (2005)
17. Ingo Lutkebohle. Same origin policy for javascript
18. Mastroeni, I., Banerjee, A.: Modelling declassification policies using abstract domain completeness. Technical Report RR 61/2008, Department of Computer Science, University of Verona (May 2008)
19. Myers, A.C., Liskov, B.: Protecting privacy using the decentralized label model. ACM Trans. Softw. Eng. Methodol. 9(4), 410–442 (2000)
20. Myers, A.C., Sabelfeld, A., Zdancewic, S.: Enforcing robust declassification. In: Proc. IEEE Symp. on Security and Privacy, pp. 21–34. IEEE Comp. Soc. Press, Los Alamitos (2004)
21. Sabelfeld, A., Myers, A.C.: Language-based information-flow security. IEEE J. on Selected Areas in Communications 21(1), 5–19 (2003)
22. Sabelfeld, A., Sands, D.: Declassification: Dimensions and principles. J. of Computer Security (2007)
23. Vogt, P., Nentwich, F., Jovanovic, N., Kirda, E., Krügel, C., Vigna, G.: Cross site scripting prevention with dynamic data tainting and static analysis. In: NDSS (2007)
24. Winskel, G.: The formal semantics of programming languages: an introduction. MIT Press, Cambridge (1993)
25. Yao, A.C.-C.: Protocols for secure computations (extended abstract). In: FOCS, pp. 160–164 (1982)
26. Zdancewic, S., Myers, A.C.: Robust declassification. In: Proc. of the IEEE Computer Security Foundations Workshop, pp. 15–23. IEEE Comp. Soc. Press, Los Alamitos (2001)
27. Zdancewic, S., Zheng, L., Nystrom, N., Myers, A.C.: Untrusted hosts and confidentiality: Secure program partitioning. In: SOSP, pp. 1–14 (2001)

PET SNAKE: A Special Purpose Architecture to Implement an Algebraic Attack in Hardware

Willi Geiselmann[1], Kenneth Matheis[2], and Rainer Steinwandt[2]

[1] Institut für Kryptographie und Sicherheit, Fakultät für Informatik,
Universität Karlsruhe (TH), Am Fasanengarten 5, 76128 Karlsruhe, Germany
geiselma@ira.uka.de

[2] Department of Mathematical Sciences, Florida Atlantic University,
777 Glades Road, Boca Raton, FL 33431
{rsteinwa,kmatheis}@fau.edu

Abstract. In [23] Raddum and Semaev propose a technique to solve systems of polynomial equations over $\mathbb{F}_2$ as occurring in algebraic attacks on block ciphers. This approach is known as *MRHS*, and we present a special purpose architecture to implement MRHS in a dedicated hardware device. Our preliminary performance analysis of this **P**arallel **E**limination **T**echnique **S**upporting **N**ice **A**lgebraic **K**ey **E**limination shows that the use of ASICs seems to enable significant performance gains over a software implementation of MRHS. The main parts of the proposed architecture are scalable, the limiting factor being mainly the available bandwidth for interchip communication. Our focus is on a design choice that can be implemented within the limits of available fab technology. The proposed design can be expected to offer a running time improvement in the order of several magnitudes over a software implementation.

We do not make any claims about the practical feasibility of an attack against AES-128 with our design, as we do not see the necessary theoretical tools to be available: deriving reliable running time estimates for an algebraic attack with MRHS when being applied to a full-round version of AES-128 is still an open problem.

Keywords: block cipher, algebraic attack, cryptanalytic hardware, MRHS.

1 Introduction

Algebraic attacks have become an important cryptanalytic tool, and the security of major cryptographic algorithms relies on the infeasibility of solving certain systems of polynomial equations. Popular approaches for dealing with such systems of equations are based on the use of Gröbner basis techniques and SAT-solvers—prominent examples including Buchmann et al.'s discussion of AES-128 [8] and Courtois et al.'s discussion of KeeLoq [10]. Adding to the toolbox of algebraic cryptanalysis, in [23] Raddum and Semaev propose a technique known as *MRHS* (**M**ultiple **R**ight **H**and **S**ides) to handle polynomial systems of equations over $\mathbb{F}_2$. This algorithm is particulary well-suited for describing systems of equations

M.L. Gavrilova et al. (Eds.): Trans. on Comput. Sci. X, LNCS 6340, pp. 298–328, 2010.

for an algebraic key recovery attack against common block ciphers such as AES or DES.

A full running time analysis of MRHS is to the best of our knowledge not available, but the observed performance in software seems quite favorable, and in comparison to algebraic attacks involving the computation of a Gröbner basis, the required amount of memory seems easier to predict. Given arbitrarily large amounts of memory, MRHS should in principle be able to solve large systems of equations, but this is obviously not practical. Consequently, the hardware architecture we propose builds on an adaption of MRHS where the amount of memory is fixed. The specific design choices made are motivated by the limits of currently available fab technology, and the scalability of major components should facilitate the construction of small prototypes with technology that is available at moderate cost.

Our contribution. We propose an ASIC design for implementing MRHS, which according to our analysis enables significant performance gains compared to an MRHS implementation in software. Owing to the modular design and scalability, we think the proposed architecture to be of considerable interest when trying to mount algebraic attacks on relevant block ciphers. Building on a 45 nm manufacturing process, already a moderately sized network of chips of standard size seems capable of coping with rather non-trivial systems of equations. Our architecture is certainly far from optimal, and we hope that the promising results obtained so far stimulate further research along this line. Certain components of the architecture, specifically those for row reduction and multiplication of matrices over $\mathbb{F}_2$, might be of independent interest.

Related work. A first (unpublished) proposal for using dedicated hardware to implement MRHS has been developed by Semaev in 2007, and, after modifications, recently been published in [25,26]. The architecture described below has been developed independently and uses a very different approach. The use of special hardware for attacking a specific symmetric cipher has been proposed in [3]. In addition, numerous special purpose architectures for cryptanalytic purposes have been devised and discussed in the research literature—some prominent examples being TWINKLE [27,18], TWIRL [28] and their successors [12,16] for factoring integers, or Deep Crack [11] and COPACOBANA [17] for attacking DES. As linear algebra over $\mathbb{F}_2$ plays an essential role in MRHS, it comes to no surprise that our design benefits from available work related to the Number Field Sieve: For the row reduction over $\mathbb{F}_2$ we modify the linear algebra design SMITH of Bogdanov et al. [5,6] to enable a more efficient handling of sparse matrices as occurring in the context of MRHS. (Note that SMITH has enjoyed previous success in [3].) The resulting JONES (**J**ustifiable **O**ptimization **N**eatly **E**nhancing **S**MITH) device might be of independent interest for other applications involving sparse matrices over $\mathbb{F}_2$.

The overall data flow in our architecture is remotely reminiscent of the systolic linear algebra design in [14], a main difference being the emphasis on a two-dimensional data flow. Two-dimensional data flows are well-known from special purpose designs for the Number Field Sieve, like [2,19,15], but the organization of the data flow in the new design is quite different and explains the choice of the acronym PET SNAKE for our architecture.

Structure of the paper. We start with a brief discussion of MRHS where we detail the variant of the algorithm underlying our proposal. Section 3 gives a description of the overall architecture we use. The overall architecture uses several identical copies of a *main processing unit* whose various components are explained in Section 4. Further details on the individual components can be found in [13]. Finally,Sections 5–7 analyze the expected performance of the complete device, comparing it with a software implementation of MRHS.

2   Preliminaries: Multiple Right Hand Sides (MRHS)

For a detailed discussion of MRHS, we refer to Raddum and Semaev's work [23]. Here we restrict to an informal review of those aspects of the MRHS technique which are needed to explain the proposed hardware architecture. In particular, we do not discuss how to set up an MRHS system of linear equations to mount an algebraic attack on a block cipher like AES-128 [20] and refer to [23, Section 6] for more details on this (cf. also [21] and [24, Chapter 5]). In our software experiments we worked with a reduced round version of PRESENT [4]. The derivation of the pertinent MRHS system is fairly standard—we do not claim any relevant originality for this, and omit the somewhat tedious details.

2.1   Basic Terminology

For our purposes, all matrices and vectors are assumed to have entries from $\mathbb{F}_2$, and it is helpful to fix some terminology:

Let $x := (x_1, \ldots, x_y)^{\mathrm{t}}$ be a column vector consisting of y Boolean variables, A a $k \times y$ matrix of rank k, and $b_1, b_2, \ldots, b_s$ column vectors of length k. An equation

$$Ax = b_1, b_2, \ldots, b_s \tag{1}$$

is called an *MRHS system of linear equations* with *right hand sides* $b_1, b_2, \ldots, b_s$. A *solution* to (1) is a vector in $\mathbb{F}_2^y$ satisfying one of the particular linear equation systems $Ax = b_i$. The set of *all solutions to* (1) is the union of solutions to the individual linear systems $Ax = b_i$ ($i = 1, \ldots, s$). In an effort to manipulate the data contained in the above column vectors b_i, we write them side-by-side to form a matrix L and rewrite Equation (1) as $Ax = [L]$. The brackets around L emphasize that we are not working with a regular equation of matrices, and instead of the term *MRHS system of linear equations* the term *symbol* is often used.

Given a system of symbols

$$S_1 : A_1 x = [L_1]$$

$$\vdots \tag{2}$$

$$S_n : A_n x = [L_n]$$

by a *solution to such a system* we mean a vector in $\mathbb{F}_2^y$ satisfying all of the underlying n MRHS systems of linear equations (where $x = (x_1, \ldots, x_y)^t$). The goal of the algorithm discussed next, and consequently of the PET SNAKE design below, is to find all solutions of (2).

2.2   Solving a System of Symbols

There are three main steps, to which we refer as *agreeing*, *gluing*, and *equation extraction*. The proposed PET SNAKE architecture exploits similarities between these algorithmic building blocks for reusing hardware components—therewith reducing the area complexity of the design.

Agreeing of Symbols. The basic approach is to remove some of the columns b in a right hand side L_i, if no one solution of $A_i x = b$ can be a solution to the System (2). The mechanism by which this is achieved is pairwise *agreeing* of symbols. Namely, let $S_i : A_i x = [L_i]$ and $S_j : A_j x = [L_j]$ be two symbols. Then S_i and S_j *agree* if for every $b \in L_i$, there exists a $b' \in L_j$ such that the linear system

$$\begin{pmatrix} A_i \\ A_j \end{pmatrix} x = \begin{pmatrix} b \\ b' \end{pmatrix} \tag{3}$$

is consistent, and, vice versa, for each $b' \in L_j$ there exists a $b \in L_i$ such that (3) is consistent.

When S_i and S_j do not agree, one removes those columns b from L_i for which the linear system $A_i x = b$ is inconsistent with $A_j x = [L_j]$. Dually, those columns b' from L_j are removed, for which $A_j x = b'$ is inconsistent with $A_i x = [L_i]$. Different strategies can be used for this approach, and for the design of PET SNAKE we follow the technique in Figure 1 (see [23, Section 3]) and realize it with a specialized hardware architecture.

---

1. Produce a nonsingular transform matrix $U = U_{ij}$ of size $t \times t$ such that the product UA is a matrix with zeroes in its last $r = r_{ij}$ rows and of rank $t - r$. If $r = 0$, the symbols agree.
2. If $r > 0$, then compute the matrices UT_{ij} and UT_{ji}. Let Pr_{ij} denote the set of of UT_{ij}-column projections to the last r coordinates. If $Pr_{ij} = Pr_{ji}$, the symbols agree.
3. If $Pr_{ij} \neq Pr_{ji}$, first remove all columns from L_i whose UT_{ij}-associated column is such that its last-r-coordinate projection is not found in Pr_{ji}. Name the resulting matrix L'_i. Then similarly remove columns from L_j and name the resulting matrix L'_j. The symbols $A_i x = [L'_i]$ and $A_j x = [L'_j]$ agree.

Fig. 1. Agreeing two symbols $A_i x = [L_i]$ and $A_j x = [L_j]$, where $L_\eta \in \mathbb{F}_2^{k_\eta \times s_\eta}$. Here $A := \begin{pmatrix} A_i \\ A_j \end{pmatrix}$ is the vertical concatenation of A_i and A_j, i.e., A has $t := k_i + k_j$ rows. Similarly $T_{ij} := \begin{pmatrix} L_i \\ 0 \end{pmatrix}$ and $T_{ji} := \begin{pmatrix} 0 \\ L_j \end{pmatrix}$ have t rows each.

It is important to note that if two symbols S_h and S_i agree, but S_i and S_j disagree, columns may be deleted in one or both of L_i and L_j. After this happens, it is possible for S_h to disagree with either of the modified symbols, and so S_h will have to be *re-agreed* with them. During that agreement, columns from L_h may have to be deleted, and so on. In this manner, a chain reaction of column deletions may occur. Hence, in order to ensure that a system of symbols gets to a pairwise-agreed state, in PET SNAKE we perform the *Agreeing1 Algorithm* in Figure 2 (see [23, Section 3.1]).

While the symbols in a System (2) do not pairwise agree,

1. find S_i and S_j which do not agree
2. agree S_i and S_j with the agreeing procedure in Figure 1.

Fig. 2. Agreeing1 Algorithm

Gluing of Symbols. After a system of symbols is in a pairwise-agreed state, we may choose to glue some symbols. The *gluing* of two symbols $S_i : A_i x = [L_i]$ and $S_j : A_j x = [L_j]$ is a new symbol $Bx = [L]$ whose set of solutions is the set of common solutions to $A_i x = [L_i]$ and $A_j x = [L_j]$. Once this new symbol is formed, it is inserted into the system and the two symbols S_i and S_j which formed it are no longer necessary and hence removed from the system. Obtaining the matrix B is easy: with the notation in Figure 1, B is just the submatrix of UA in its last $t - r$ nonzero rows. The matrix L has $t - r$ rows and the columns are formed by adding one column from UT_{ij} to one column from UT_{ji}. More specifically, we add a column from UT_{ij} and one from UT_{ji}, if they have the same projection to the last r coordinates. Reducing the sum to its first $t - r$ coordinates yields a column of L, and forming all such matching pairs yields the complete matrix L. Gluing two matrices L_i, L_j of width s_i and s_j may result in an L with as many as $s_i \cdot s_j$ columns. Consequently, we may not be able to afford to actually compute certain glues, and instead restrict to gluing only pairs of symbols where the number of columns in the resulting symbol does not exceed a certain *threshold*.

Once several pairs of symbols have been glued, the resulting system will usually not be in a pairwise-agreed state, so the Agreeing1 Algorithm in Figure 2 can be run again, initiating another round of agreeing and gluing. The eventual goal of successive agreements and gluings is to obtain a system of symbols consisting only of a single symbol.

Equation Extraction. From a given Symbol $S : Ax = [L]$, where $L \in \mathbb{F}_2^{k \times s}$, we can try to extract *URHS (Unique Right Hand Side) equations*: choosing an appropriate nonsingular transformation matrix V of size $k \times k$, the product VL is upper triangular with zeroes in its last r rows. Denoting by Pr the matrix formed by the VA-column projections to the last r coordinates, we obtain the r linear equations $Pr \cdot x = 0$. Next to these homogeneous equations, it may be possible to extract a nonhomogeneous linear equation: from the upper triangular matrix VL we can read off if the all-one-vector $(1, \ldots, 1)$ is in the span of the rows of L. If this is the case, we obtain the nonhomogeneous linear equation $(zA)x = 1$, where z is a row vector of length k such that $zL = (1, \ldots, 1)$. The resulting r or $r+1$ URHS equations can be combined into a *gather symbol* which then can be added to the system of symbols under consideration.

Guessing Variables. Owing to the chosen threshold, it may happen that a system is in a pairwise-agreed state, no URHS equation can be computed and no pair of symbols can be glued anymore. In such a situation, one is forced to guess a value of a variable. Before a guess is committed, the system of symbols—to which we will refer as *state*—is stored. Then the guess is performed by constructing a new symbol whose A part is one row of all zeroes except for a single 1 in the position of the guessed variable, and whose L part is a single value, either 0 or 1, depending on the value of the guess. Such a symbol is inserted into the system, and then pairwise agreeing, computation of URHS equations, and gluing continue as normal. If after some steps the state, again, does not allow any URHS equation to be extracted or pair of symbols to be glued, the state is again saved and another guess is committed.

Of course it is possible that in this process a guess for a variable is incorrect. This discovery manifests in the following manner: during the agreement of two symbols, all right hand sides of at least one of the symbols get removed. When this happens, the state must be rolled back to a previous state, and a different guess must be made. The practice of guessing variables, then, follows something akin to a depth-first search.

2.3   Implementation Choices

Fundamental design parameters for the PET SNAKE architecture have been chosen in such a way that it is possible to host a complete system of symbols as needed for a key recovery attack on a modern block cipher like AES-128. For AES-128 specifically, the pertinent system of symbols involves 1,600 variables, and the initial system requires only 320 symbols. (As comparison, for PRESENT, which has 31 rounds, the initial system consists of more than 500 symbols, and also the number of variables is higher than for AES-128). In general, handling systems with no more than 2^{12} symbols still seems within the reach of PET SNAKE, and up to 2047 variables can be handled. For gluing symbols, we chose our threshold to be 2^{20} right hand sides. This seems a nice balance between the upper limits of software implementations and the upper limits of current hardware storage abilities. In light of the multiplicative nature of the growth of right hand sides during gluing, giving one or two more powers of 2 to the threshold does not seem to readily contribute to a significantly reduced running time.

In the described form, PET SNAKE has a storage capacity of 4.792 TB (not including the 'active' DRAMs in the traffic control chips), or enough to store

18,000 full-size symbols. This number was chosen based on the following observations: the symbol count for AES-128 will drop to 180 before threshold takes over, and it is possible we may have to guess up to 100 key variables before we find the key; hence up to 100 states may need to be stored along the way. Very rarely will a state actually be comprised of nothing but full-size (that is, 257 MB) symbols, so it will almost always be possible to store more than 100 states; 400 or more states are not unlikely.

3   Overall Architecture

A complete PET SNAKE architecture consists of a several interconnected boards with each board hosting several *Main Processing Units* (MPUs). Each MPU is comprised of a small group of chips wired in a particular way, and there are $p \times p$ such MPUs placed in a grid across the individual boards, where $p = 2^\lambda$ is a power of 2. Subsequently we use $\lambda = 5$, yielding a total of $2^5 \cdot 2^5 = 1024$ MPUs, but the proposed architecture scales within reasonable limits; depending on the resources available, other parameter values, like $p^2 = 2^8$ might be an interesting option.

Each MPU can communicate with its north, south, east, and west neighbor MPUs (with no wraparound). For directing the action of the p^2 MPUs, a single *Master Control Processor* (MCP) is used. The MCP will make most of the decisions regarding which symbols to send where, which symbols to glue, and when to guess a variable.[1] The MCP, which sits in a north corner, has *agents* which sit at the north end of the board, one per column. Each agent has a southbound bus that connects to each MPU in that column via 'hops' between MPUs, so each off-chip part of the bus is short. Each agent communicates to the MCP horizontally via 'hops' between agents. Figure 3 gives a schematic view of the overall architecture.

3.1   Initialization

The initial system of n symbols is derived from a particular known (plaintext, ciphertext)-pair, and a solution to the system of symbols yields a secret key for the attacked symmetric cipher that is consistent with the particular (plaintext, ciphertext)-pair. The symbols are loaded onto the p^2 MPUs as evenly as possible. Let g be the number of symbols stored in each MPU—should the symbol count not be evenly divisible by the number of MPUs, we imagine empty symbols to fill in the gaps. Now imagine labelling each symbol in each MPU with a number in $\{1, \ldots, g\}$. We call all symbols labelled with the same number a *snake*. Hence we have g snakes. If at this point $g = 1$, we halve the number of MPUs to use, redistribute the symbols to this half, and try again; we continue this process until $g = 2$. The collection of MPUs now occupied with symbols is called the *active area* for this computation. Any inactive MPUs will be taken advantage

---

[1] By replacing the MCP, the overall algorithm can be changed, e. g., to accomodate a different MRHS variant.

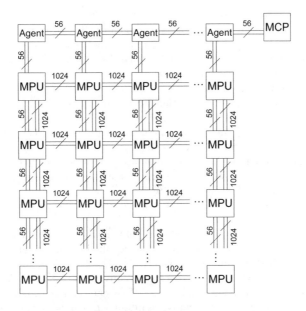

Fig. 3. Overall architecture of PET SNAKE

of with parallelism, discussed later. The MCP determines a Hamiltonian cycle through all MPUs, i.e., a path through all the MPUs such that one can move from one MPU to one of its neighbors in a closed circuit, without visiting the same MPU twice. The MCP will do the same for smaller groups of MPUs: $p \times \frac{p}{2}$, $\frac{p}{2} \times \frac{p}{2}$, $\frac{p}{2} \times \frac{p}{4}$, etc.—all the way down to 2×1. This data can be hardwired into the MCP, and we may assume that the MCP knows a path for each possible size active area.

3.2 Processing of Symbols

During a computation, it may happen that the symbol count n drops below the number of MPUs used to process them. If this happens, we move the symbols so that only half of the MPUs will be occupied with symbols. (This guarantees $g = 2$.) The active area is then halved. Any inactive MPUs will be taken advantage of with parallelism. Hence, at all points in the process, if g is not a power of 2, it will proceed as if g were the next highest power of 2 for board divisibility purposes. The overall algorithm run by PET SNAKE is summarized in Figure 4.

Before going into details of the overall algorithm, we want to reiterate that, to the best of our knowledge, the existing theoretical analysis of MRHS does not allow a precise prediction of how often the individual steps in Figure 4 are to be performed. This problem is not specific to PET SNAKE and arises for software implementations as well. For the subsequent analysis this means that we focus on judging PET SNAKE's performance *relative* to a software implementation.

Absolute running times obviously depend on the particular block cipher/system of symbols, but even for a specific block cipher like AES-128 we do not see how to

---

1. Enter the agreement phase:
   - Each symb. is agreed to each other symb. until all symbs. are pairwise-agreed.
   - If, in the agreement phase, we get a symbol whose L-matrix got all its columns deleted, then the system is inconsistent, so go to (6).
2. Enter the equation propagation phase:
   - Equations are generated from each symbol, and then are row reduced, and then are row reduced against the current eq. set, forming the new eq. set.
   - If an inconsistency is found, go to (6).
   - If the new eq. set is of max rank, we terminate as a key has been found.
   - If there is no new information in the new equation set, go to (5).
3. Make the new gather symbol from the new eq. set and agree it to all symbols.
   - If we get a symbol whose L-matrix got all its columns deleted, then the system is inconsistent, so go to (6).
4. Glue the gather symbol to all symbols in the system, and go back to (1).
5. Enter the glue phase:
   - If no two symbols can be glued such that the result's L matrix has no more than 2^{20} columns, save the state (that is, all the symbols and the equation set) in the MPUs and then go to (7).
   - If necessary, move symbols so that any given pair of symbols to be glued appear in the same MPU. Different MPUs can be used for different pairs.
   - Pairwise glue the symbols whose resultant's L matrix has no more than 2^{20} columns. Delete the symbols which contributed to each glue.
   - If necessary, move symbols among the MPUs so that they have the same number of symbols. If there are less symbols than MPUs, move the symbols so that they only occupy half the MPUs. This halves the active area.
   - If one symb. remains, terminate as keys have been found. Else go to (1).
6. If a guess of a variable has not yet been made, terminate with failure as the original system has no solutions. Else, roll back the symbols to a good state.
7. Make a new guess of the variables:
   - The head MPU loads the equation set into its row reducer and introduces a row corresponding to the guess.
   - If the new guess is inconsistent with the current equation set, roll back the equation set and go to (7). Otherwise, go to (3).

Fig. 4. Overall algorithm run by PET SNAKE

extrapolate reliable running time estimates for the full-round version from experimental results with reduced round versions.

3.3   PET SNAKE's Agreement Phase

The majority of activity on the board will be during the agreement phase. This is broken down into k stages, where $k = \lceil \log_g n \rceil$.

First Stage. In the first stage, the entire active area is used. All but one snake (i. e., snakes 1 through $g - 1$) stay put on the MPUs. On each MPU, the symbol in the *motile snake* (i. e., snake g) is agreed to every other symbol on that MPU. When the last such agreement is taking place, the MPU sends the motile snake's updated symbol (that is, with deletions incorporated) to the next

MPU in the active area's path. Since this is happening simultaneously for all MPUs in the active area, each MPU gets the next symbol in the motile snake. This continues q times, where q is the number of MPUs in the active area. If a deletion has occurred somewhere in this process, the MCP records the affected symbol's number, but otherwise continues normally.

Now, snake g will be fixed, and snake $g - 1$ will move. The only difference here is that symbols from snake $g - 1$ will not need to be agreed with those from snake g since that agreement has already been performed. After q times, snakes g and $g - 1$ will be fixed, but snake $g - 2$ will move. And so on. If a deletion has occurred for any of the g snakes, the MCP moves the affected symbols into larger-numbered snakes (e. g., g, $g - 1$) and moves unaffected symbols into smaller-numbered snakes. Often this is just a renumbering inside an MPU, so no movement happens in these cases. Then the first stage is repeated again, noting that if all the symbols in a lower-numbered snake have no deletions in the previous run, it is not required to become motile. If a deletion occurs, the MCP repeats the process of moving affected symbols and starting the stage again.

Second Stage. At this point, all snakes are agreed to all other snakes, but the symbols within each snake still need to be addressed. The active area is split up into g *stage areas*, each with q/g MPUs. For each $1 \leq j \leq g$, symbols from snake j move to stage area j. After this move is complete, we relabel each symbol in each MPU so that different snakes are formed, but the snakes only move in their given stage area. Hence, each snake is $1/g$ the size it used to be. Now, the same process is performed as in the first stage, but with smaller snakes and smaller paths.

If a deletion has been recorded in this stage, the stage is allowed to complete, but not recur nor go into the next stage. Then the affected symbols (from *all* stage areas) are grouped together into one (or possibly more) q-sized snakes with large snake numbers, they are moved into appropriate positions, and the first stage is entered again.

Subsequent Stages. If the second stage records no deletions, we continue this process of dividing the snakes and the stage areas by g until the stage area is one MPU. (Deletions found in any subsequent stage are handled the same way as described in the second stage.) At the last stage, the g symbols comprise g snakes of size 1 each, and so they are simply agreed to each other inside that MPU.

Time Estimate. The initial load's symbols will most likely have A parts whose 1s are in different positions, so any particular pair of symbols will likely be already agreed, so no deletions will occur. After the first glue, it is still likely no deletions will occur. After the second glue, however, things get less predictable, but by this point the symbol count will drop by a factor of 4. (In the case of AES-128, the threshold will take hold before the second glue, so we can only expect the symbol count to halve before guesses must be performed.) After these initial turns, deletion prediction becomes much less obvious, and it is certainly possible to go through many agreement phases before considering a glue. Handling deletions is needed in both software and hardware implementations, and it seems fair to consider PET SNAKE's efficiency in handling deletions as being at least comparable to that of a software implementation (see Section 6.2 and [13, Appendix A]). To get a handle on a time estimate for PET SNAKE's agreement phase we consider only the case that no deletions will occur.

We note that per stage there are $g(g-1)/2$ agreements per MPU, and this happens q times in the first stage, q/g in the second, and so forth, up to 1 in the last. Since $g = n/q$, adding up the costs we have

$$\sum_{i=0}^{k-1} \frac{g(g-1)}{2} \cdot \frac{q}{g^i} = \frac{g(g-1)}{2} \cdot \frac{n}{g} \cdot \left(\frac{1 - \frac{1}{g^k}}{1 - \frac{1}{g}} \right) = \frac{(g-1)n}{2} \cdot \left(\frac{\frac{n-1}{n}}{\frac{g-1}{g}} \right) = \frac{g(n-1)}{2}$$

total agreements. Since we try to arrange things so that g is 2 as often as possible, this translates into $n - 1$ agreements in these cases.

What is not included so far is the time of moving symbols between stages. Let the active area have dimensions $q_1 \times q_2 = q$ where $q_1 \leq q_2$, and suppose g is 2. After the first stage, a symbol moves along the longer dimension, but halfway so that it can find its new position. Another symbol from that position must get to where the first started, so they both must use those directions. This will introduce a factor two slowdown in all movement calculations. Hence, after the first stage it takes $2 \cdot \left(\frac{q_2}{2} \right)$ moves to get the symbols into their new positions, and the stage area then has dimensions $q_1 \times \frac{q_2}{2}$. We alternate which dimension we travel on in each stage, so the next stage cost is $2 \left(\frac{q_1}{2} \right)$. Then $2 \cdot \left(\frac{q_2}{4} \right)$, then $2 \cdot \left(\frac{q_1}{4} \right)$, and so on. Presuming k is even, this gives a time estimate of

$$(q_1 + q_2) \cdot \sum_{i=0}^{\frac{k}{2}-1} \frac{1}{2^i} = (q_1 + q_2) \cdot \left(\frac{1 - \left(\frac{1}{2}\right)^{k/2}}{1 - \frac{1}{2}} \right) = 2 \cdot (q_1 + q_2) \cdot \frac{2^{k/2} - 1}{2^{k/2}}$$

$$< 2 \cdot (q_1 + q_2)$$

total moves for the whole agreement phase.

The situation for $g = 4$ is not as easy, since symbols have to move to different quadrants of the active area $q_1 \times q_2$. We observe that it must be the case that $q_1 = q_2$, since the only time we might have $g > 2$ is in the beginning, when we have the full board at our disposal.

Hence, we perform a sort of rotation, where each quadrant of symbols (one symbol per MPU per move) moves to the next clockwise (or counterclockwise) quadrant simultaneously. This is possible since all four directional buses of each MPU can be used simultaneously, and no directional bus needs to be used more than once at a time. After the first stage, in the first rotation the symbols whose target locations are in the diagonal quadrant move $\frac{q_1}{2}$ in one direction. In the second rotation, these same symbols move $\frac{q_1}{2}$ in the appropriate perpendicular direction to get to their target location. In the third rotation, symbols whose target quadrant are clockwise of them will move $\frac{q_1}{2}$ in that direction. The fourth rotation is similar to the third, but for counterclockwise-bound symbols. Thus, we have $4 \cdot \left(\frac{q_1}{2}\right) = 2 \cdot q_1$ moves for this stage. Subsequent stages are similar but the distance is half of the previous distance. Thus we have

$$\sum_{i=0}^{k-1} 2 \cdot \left(\frac{q_1}{2^i}\right) = 2 \cdot q_1 \cdot 2 \cdot \left(\frac{2^k - 1}{2^k}\right) < 4q_1$$

total moves for the whole agreement phase.

3.4   PET SNAKE's Equation Propagation Phase

During agreement, it is recorded whether a symbol had columns deleted. PET SNAKE will extract equations from such symbols using each MPU simultaneously and gather them all (together with the current equation set) into a *gather symbol*, which is then agreed and glued to every symbol. The propagation phase consists of either one or two extraction stages (depending on if g is 2 or 4, respectively) followed by the resolution stage, followed by the propagation stage.

Extraction Stages. In the first extraction stage, equations from all symbols in snake 1 are extracted simultaneously and stored in each MPU. Then equations from all symbols in snake 2 are extracted simultaneously. All equations that have been extracted are then *mass row reduced* down to at most 2047 equations. To illustrate this process, first, imagine a label number from 0 through $q - 1$ for each MPU in the path. (Label 0 is given to the *head* MPU, which sits in the upper left corner of its active area. Label 1 is given to the next MPU in the Hamiltonian cycle. And so on. For ease of discussion, we also define the notation $x \equiv_m y$ to mean that m divides $x - y$, or alternately, x is congruent to y modulo m.)

Mass row reduction is then accomplished by the following process: each MPU row reduces the equations from its symbols in snakes 1 and 2. Then the MPUs with labels $\equiv_2 1$ send their results to the MPU with label 1 less. Now those MPUs with labels $\equiv_2 0$ have up to 4094 equations, and each row reduces its set. This results in no more than 2047 equations. Then the MPUs with labels $\equiv_4 2$ send their resulting equations to the MPU with label 2 less. Another row reduction takes place. Then the MPUs with labels $\equiv_8 4$ send their resulting equations to the MPU with label 4 less. And so on, until equations get to the head MPU and are row reduced. These results are then stored.

If there is a second extraction stage, equations from symbols in snakes 3 and 4 are extracted and mass row reduced to at most 2047 more equations (which will also lie in the head MPU); these are then row reduced with the previous group of equations. The result is a group of at most 2047 equations called the *gather equations*.

Resolution Stage. The head MPU will then retrieve from storage the current *equation set*—which corresponds to the symbol S_0 in [24, Section 3]. (In the beginning, the equation set consists of no equations.) Then this is row reduced with the gather equations and the result is checked for consistency. If an inconsistency is found, this is signaled to the MCP; the MCP will then deem the current guess incorrect and move on to a new guess. If no inconsistency is found, the result is checked for maximal rank (i.e. number of nontrivial rows equal to n). If it has maximal rank, the MCP is alerted that a solution has been found. Otherwise, the result is stored as the new equation set. This is checked to see if there is a new equation that was not in the old equation set via a row count. If there is no new information, the glue phase begins; else, the propagation stage begins.

Propagation Stage. The head MPU creates the gather symbol and sends it to its east neighbor, and after that is done, it sends it to its south neighbor. The east neighbor will store it and then send it to its east neighbor, and then its south neighbor. And so on for all MPUs in the top row of the active area. An MPU that received the symbol from its north neighbor merely stores it and sends it to its south neighbor. Once all MPUs receive the gather symbol, it is agreed to every symbol in the MPU, with the results of the agreements propagated to the next MPU in the Hamiltonian cycle. As with normal agreement, if every column of a symbol's L part gets deleted, the MPU signals the MCP that an inconsistency is found. Otherwise, after all agreements are complete, each MPU glues the gather symbol to each symbol it has.

Time Estimate. Since there are g symbols in an MPU and each MPU extracts simultaneously, we pay the time cost of an extraction g times. There are $\frac{q}{2}$ mass row reductions, each comprising $\log_2 q + 1$ row reductions and $1 + 2 + 4 + \cdots + \frac{q}{2} = q - 1$ moves of at most 2047 equations. (Moving one such equation set is much faster than moving a symbol, since an equation is expressed in 2048 bits.) In the case of two extraction stages, we row reduce an additional time. Propagating the gather symbol takes $q_1 + q_2$ moves, and finally since each MPU agrees, and then glues, simultaneously, we pay the agreement time of two symbols g times and the glue time g times.

3.5   PET SNAKE's Glue Phase

Since the MCP knows which pairs of symbols will glue to produce a symbol with 2^{20} or less columns, it merely directs moves to get these pairs into MPUs, and then the MPUs glue them in parallel. The number of moves needed is not completely predictable, but we observe the following: in the early stages of the algorithm, a given symbol can be glued to almost every other symbol, so in particular each MPU won't have to move any symbols at all before gluing. In the later stages of the algorithm, very few glues are called for (often only one or two), so symbols can be moved directly to where they need to go. Since the active area is $q_1 \times q_2$ MPUs, this constitutes at most $q_1 + q_2 - 2$ moves.

Whatever the case, we can always elect to move symbols in the following manner: for each pair of symbols to be glued, label one member as a first component and the other as a second component. Symbols that are not to be glued remain unlabelled. If $g = 2$ and there are two first components in an MPU, relabel one as a second component and relabel its mate as a first. Do this again if the new labelling causes another double. And so on. Note this process cannot result in an infinite loop. Perform a similar process for MPUs with two second components. If $g = 4$ and there are three or more first components (or three or more second components) in an MPU, perform a similar relabelling process.

Now, we move symbols along the snake in a two-stroke process. In the first stroke, we move an out-of-place second component (or failing that, an unlabelled symbol) from MPU 0 to MPU 1, from MPU 2 to MPU 3, and so forth. In the second stroke, we move an out-of-place second component (or failing that, an unlabelled symbol) from MPU 1 to MPU 2, from MPU 3 to MPU 4, and so forth. Observe that an MPU keeps a second component if it also has the associated first component. This results in $q - 1$ moves if $g = 2$, or $2(q - 1)$ moves if $g = 4$. The glue time, is in general higher than an agreement time. With $g = 2$, we only pay the glue time once, since each MPU will be gluing all gluable pairs in parallel with none waiting to be glued. With $g = 4$, we pay the glue time at most twice; in general, the glue time is paid at most $g/2$ times.

3.6   Parallelism

Once the active area becomes half the original board (or less), and a guess is required, the MCP considers performing a parallel computation on the inactive area. The MCP will make a guess for a key variable in one area, and make the opposite guess for the same key variable in the other. Then both areas will be considered active areas, but their computations will be completely separated.

4   Main Processing Unit

The MPU is a collection of seven chips comprising five functional units, each with its own responsibilities and behavior. We discuss each functional unit in turn: the traffic controller, the row reducer, the multiplier, the hash table, and the adder. Each functional unit is connected to a 2048-bit-wide bus called the *MPU bus*.

4.1   MPU Data Flow

We describe the sequence of events that will occur inside each MPU when it is agreeing, when it is extracting equations and when it is gluing. The particular details of each component are discussed in that component's section below. Figure 5 gives an overview of how most of the components are interconnected. (The traffic controller sits on the north end of the MPU bus, directing traffic between it and other traffic controllers of other MPUs.)

The high level order of operations during an agreement between two symbols S_i and S_j is as given in Figure 6, and the—somewhat similar—procedure for gluing two symbols S_i and S_j is described in Figure 7.

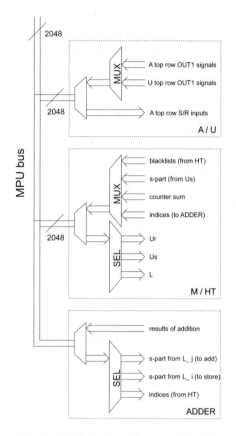

Fig. 5. MPU Busing Diagram (High Level)

Finally, Figures 9 and 8 list the high level order of operations for extracting equations from a symbol and for a mass row reduction respectively. Subsequently we discuss the individual components of an MPU, but for the sake of readability postpone low-level details and area estimates to the appendix of [13].

4.2 Traffic Controller

The traffic controller is a collection of four chips responsible for receiving symbol data from neighbor MPUs, storing it, and pushing it across the MPU bus if need be. After the results of various computations from other functional units are complete, the traffic controller will store or forward to a neighbor MPU those results, depending on what is currently being done. This is the only functional unit that is connected to other MPUs and the MCP, as well as the MPU bus. Details on the architecture of the traffic controller and how it operates are given in [13, Appendix A].

1. A_i is sent across the MPU bus and the row reducer picks it up.
2. A_j is sent across the MPU bus and the row reducer picks it up.
3. The row reducer calculates both B and U.
4. The row reducer determines if r is 0. If $r = 0$, terminate with agreement signal. Otherwise,
5. The row reducer sends the left $\text{cols}(L_i)$ part of U across the MPU bus to the multiplier.
6. For each column c of L_i:
   - c is sent across the MPU bus and the multiplier picks it up.
   - The multiplier sends its r-part to the hash table.
   - The hash table stores an indicator that that r-part has been created.
7. The row reducer sends the right $\text{cols}(L_j)$ part of U across the MPU bus to the multiplier.
8. For each column d of L_j:
   - d is sent across the MPU bus and the multiplier picks it up.
   - The multiplier sends its r-part to the hash table.
   - If the r-part had been formed by L_i, the hash table stores an indicator for this.
   - If not, the hash table reports the column index of d across the MPU bus to be deleted.
9. For each entry in the hash table's buffer DRAM, if the entry is not found in the table itself, the column index is reported across the MPU bus to be deleted.
10. If no deletions have been recorded, the hash table sends the value of its glue counter across the MPU bus to the traffic controller.

Fig. 6. High level order of operations during an agreement

4.3   Row Reducer

The row reducer is comprised of a chip named A/U, which is connected to the MPU bus. Each part of its name will refer to a separate processing area inside this chip. The row reducer has four responsibilities: compute a row-reduced version of A (i.e., the vertical concatenation of A_i and A_j when they are received), compute the matrix U such that UA yields the row-reduced matrix that will appear in the A part, compute the matrix V such that VL is row reduced, and determine which rows of VA correspond to URHS equations. During a glue, the data stored in the A part will be sent back across the MPU bus. (This corresponds to B in the MRHS gluing algorithm.) During agreeing and gluing, the data stored in the U part will be sent across the MPU bus to the multiplier. During equation extraction, the data stored in both parts will be sent to the multiplier. Details on the architecture of A and U and how it operates are given in [13, Appendix B]. The JONES element used in A and U builds on ideas from SMITH [5,6] and may be of independent interest.

4.4   Multiplier

The multiplier occupies one part of a chip named M/HT. If the MPU is agreeing two symbols, the multiplier receives data from A/U and stores it in a processing

1. A_i is sent across the MPU bus and the row reducer picks it up.
2. A_j is sent across the MPU bus and the row reducer picks it up.
3. The row reducer calculates both B and U, determines if r is 0, and sends B across the MPU bus to be stored.
4. The row reducer sends the left $\text{cols}(L_i)$ part of U across the MPU bus to the multiplier.
5. For each column c of L_i:
   - c is sent across the MPU bus and the multiplier picks it up.
   - The multiplier sends its s-part to the adder for storage.
   - If $r \neq 0$, the multiplier sends its r-part to the hash table, and the hash table stores the L_i column index that gave rise to the r-part.
6. The hash table re-examines its DRAM buffer, possibly sending pairs of data across the MPU bus to the adder.
7. The row reducer sends the right $\text{cols}(L_j)$ part of U across the MPU bus to the multiplier.
8. For each column d of L_j:
   - d is sent across the MPU bus and the multiplier picks it up.
   - The multiplier sends its s-part s to the adder for adding.
   - If $r \neq 0$, the multiplier sends its r-part to the hash table.
   - If $r \neq 0$, the hash table sends all indices from L_i that match the r-part across the MPU bus to the adder. For each such index i,
     • The s-part at index i is looked up in the adder.
     • The s-part is retrieved, added to s, and sent across the MPU bus.
   - If $r = 0$, the adder runs through all its contents. For each such index i,
     • The s-part at index i is looked up in the adder.
     • The s-part is retrieved, added to s, and sent across the MPU bus.

Fig. 7. High level order of operations during gluing

area called Ur. If the MPU is gluing two symbols, the multiplier will also receive additional data from A/U and store it in a separate processing area called Us. It then receives the L-part of a symbol one column at a time, and multiplies it with the contents in Ur and (if gluing) Us. Once this multiplication is complete for the received L-column, the multiplier will send the result from Ur (called an *r-part*) to the hashtable. If gluing, it will also send the result from Us (called an *s-part*) to the adder across the MPU bus. If extracting equations, it will receive data from traffic control or A/U, store it in Us, receive more data from A/U, and send results back to A/U. Details on the architecture and working of the multiplier are discussed in [13, Appendix C]. Similarly like the row reducer, this architecture might be of independent interest.

4.5 Hash Table

The hash table is used in both the agreeing and gluing phase, and it is designed to process one write query per clock cycle—similarly, for look-ups, one look-up query per clock cycle can be coped with. Elements to be stored or looked up in the hash table are r-parts with a (zero padded) size of $r_{max} = 135$ bit, and the

For each MPU in the Hamiltonian cycle:
1. Equations are extracted from symbol 1 and reside in the row reducer's A part.
2. The row reducer sends each row of its A part across the MPU bus. The adder picks them up and stores them in its SRAM.
3. Equations are extracted from symbol 2 and reside in the row reducer's A part.
4. The adder sends the previous equations in its SRAM across the MPU bus and the row reducer's A part picks them up (rotating its currently-stored equations).
5. The row reducer reduces its contents.
6. If there is a second extraction stage:
   - The resulting equations (call them E) are sent from the row reducer's A part across the MPU bus. The adder picks them up and stores them in its SRAM.
   - Extraction is performed on the symbols in snakes 3 and 4 and row reduced, similarly as was done in steps 1–5.
   - The adder retrieves E from its SRAM and sends these rows across the MPU bus. The row reducer's A part picks them up (rotating its currently-stored equations).
   - The row reducer reduces its contents.
   End For.

   Define $\mathbb{W} = \{0, 1, 2, 3, \ldots\}$. Set $i \leftarrow 2$. While $i \leq q$:
1. Each MPU with label in $\{i/2 + ki \mid k \in \mathbb{W}\}$ sends its equations to the MPU with label $i/2$ less.
2. Each receiving MPU sends this data across its MPU bus to its row reducer, rotating the current contents downward.
3. The combined contents are row reduced.
4. $i \leftarrow i \times 2$.
   End While.

Fig. 8. High level order of operations during a mass row reduction

hash table is designed to store up to 2^{20} such r-parts. Details on the architecture and the inner working of the hash table are discussed in [13, Appendix D].

Remark 1. Having no more than 2^{20} columns, identifying each column with a 135 bit hash value seems a safe choice: taking the hash values for being uniformly distributed, the probability that no collision occurs is $\geq \prod_{i=0}^{2^{20}-1}(1 - \frac{i}{2^{135}}) \geq 1 - 2^{-90}$.

4.6   Adder

The adder is comprised of its own chip, which is largely a memory storage device. The adder is only used during gluing and equation extraction. During a glue, while the columns of L_i are being processed, M/HT will send out s-parts across the MPU bus. These will be picked up by the adder and stored in a collection of 256 DRAMs. Later, for each column in L_j that is being processed, the adder first acquires an s-part and stores it in a separate row of flip-flops called the *adding register*. Then the hash table will send across the MPU bus either a series of indices in L_i that match to that particular L_j column (i. e., whose Pr_{ij} columns

1. The row reducer is reset. (Note that this produces the identity matrix in U.)
2. Starting with the first group of 2^{11} columns of L, for each such group of L:
   - The A part of the row reducer is reset but the U part is preserved.
   - The group of 2^{11} columns of L is sent across the MPU bus and Us of the multiplier picks it up.
   - For each row of the row reducer's current U:
     • The row reducer sends the left 2^{11} bits of the next row of its current U across the MPU bus and the multiplier's L bus picks it up.
     • The multiplier sends the resulting row across the MPU bus and the row reducer picks it up.
   - The row reducer reduces its contents, modifying the current U.
   > Now U contains the matrix we are interested in. We multiply it to all of L:
3. The A part of the row reducer is reset but the U part is preserved.
4. Starting with the first group of 2^{11} columns of L, for each such group of L:
   - The group of 2^{11} columns of L is sent across the MPU bus and Us of the multiplier picks it up.
   - For each row of the row reducer's U:
     • The row reducer sends the left 2^{11} bits of the next row of U across the MPU bus and the multiplier's L bus picks it up.
     • The multiplier sends the resulting row across the MPU bus to A.
   - The row reducer performs zero and one detection on its current A part.
   > At this point, the row reducer's A part knows which rows will correspond to equations. We just need to multiply U to the symbol's A part:
5. The row reducer's A part is reset, preserving its detection flip-flops, and the U part is preserved.
6. The rows of the symbol's A part are sent across the MPU bus to Us.
7. The multiplier sends the columns of A across the MPU bus to the row reducer.
   > At this point, the A part of the row reducer holds A^T.
8. The row reducer sends the columns of A across the MPU bus and Us of the multiplier picks them up.
9. The A part of the row reducer is reset but the U part is preserved.
10. For each row of the row reducer's U:
    - The row reducer sends the left 2^{11} bits of the next row of U across the MPU bus and the multiplier's L bus picks it up.
    - The multiplier sends the resulting row across the MPU bus to A.
11. The row reducer rotates through its A part, setting the 2048th bit of each row according to its detection flip-flops.

Fig. 9. High level order of operations of extracting equations from a symbol

are the same), or a popularity number of the resulting r-part. In the first case, the adder will look up the indices in its DRAM collection. In the second case, it will use the popularity number to find indices in its own table, and look those up in its DRAM collection. The resulting s-parts are then added to the adding register, and the sum is sent back across the MPU bus. During equation extraction, the adder will store groups of equations temporarily to be row reduced later. More details on the architecture and the internal working of the adder are given in [13, Appendix E].

5   Performance Analysis I: Total Chip Area and Cost

With the area estimates in [13, Appendix A–E], the size of the five functional units per MPU can be summarized as shown in Table 1.

Table 1. Size of individual MPU components

Component	Traffic Controller	Row Reducer	Multiplier	Hash Table	Adder
Area in cm^2	4× 3.9	3.8	0.43	0.41	1.1

Thus, the total chip area of the (seven) chips comprising one MPU computes to $\underbrace{4 \cdot 3.9}_{\text{4 chips}} + \underbrace{3.8}_{\text{1 chip}} + \underbrace{0.43 + 0.41}_{\text{1 chip}} + \underbrace{1.1}_{\text{1 chip}} = 21.34 < 22$ cm^2.

For a PET SNAKE architecture with $p^2 = 2^5 \times 2^5$ MPUs, this results into a total chip area of about 2.25 m^2. To enable the necessary wiring, cooling etc. for actually placing the chips (along with the MCP and its agents) some more space will be required. Obviously this is a non-trivial size requirement, but it is important to note that none of the involved chips is larger than 3.9 cm^2, and the resulting device is designed to host a system of symbols as needed to attack a modern block cipher like AES-128. As far as cooling goes, the most critical part of our design appears to be the row reducer, specifically the A/U chip. We estimate this chip to have about 2/3 of the number of transistors of an Intel® Xeon® X7460, the latter being clocked at more than 2.5 times the rate of what we anticipate for PET SNAKE [9]. Further, high switching activity of A/U is expected to occur only over short time periods, followed by a longer time where most of the chip is inactive. Overall, we do not expect cooling to pose a major obstacle.

One MPU uses some 22 cm^2 of silicon. If we assume a 30 cm wafer to cost \$5000, the pure silicon for one MPU calculates to about \$160. If we apply a factor 4 for the full design, including the board and some safety margin, one MPU is about the price of one PC. Therefore we compare the performance of one MPU with one PC. The next section gives a simplified model to analyze the running time in a software implementation on a PC, and in Section 6.5 we present measurements when working with 4 rounds of PRESENT.

6   Performance Analysis II: PET SNAKE versus Software

To measure the time cost of an MPU versus software, the MPU's time is measured in clock cycles. For PET SNAKE we assume a 1 GHz clocking rate: with each component of our architecture having a gate depth of four or less, we believe such a clocking rate not to be implausible. Software's time is given in number of processor *steps*. Factors which relate to the software moving data in and out of memory, cache, and so forth can be captured via a constant α (i. e., each step takes α clocks on average), so a step count serves as a sort of best case scenario for software.

Suppose we are agreeing two symbols S_i and S_j. Let A_i have dimensions $w_i \times y$, A_j have dimensions $w_j \times y$, L_i have dimensions $w_i \times c_i$, and L_j have dimensions $w_j \times c_j$. Note that y then is the number of variables in the cryptosystem. Let β be the number of bits of a value that the processor can perform arithmetic on at once; in modern machines, $\beta \in \{32, 64\}$.

6.1   Linear Algebra

Let A be the vertical join of A_i and A_j. Then A has size $(w_i + w_j) \times y$. We suppose that each row will rarely have more than one 1 in A; this is usually true in the middle and later stages of a run. Let γ be the chance a second 1 exists in a column of A provided a 1 exists already in that column. Note that γ will change from symbol to symbol, but $0 \leq \gamma \leq 1$.

Hardware. JONES has two advantages over software: if a zero column exists, we dispense with it in one step, and if an add is to be performed, this also takes one step. Further, the modifications to U are done in parallel to A.

Let h be the number of columns of A that have more than one 1. Then we have that $\gamma = \frac{h}{w_i + w_j - h}$, and so $h = \frac{\gamma}{1+\gamma}(w_i + w_j)$. Thus, the number of columns of A that have exactly one 1 are $w_i - h + w_j - h$, which yields $\frac{1-\gamma}{1+\gamma}(w_i + w_j)$. Label this value t. Adding h and t gives the total number of populated columns of A. So, if we let z be the number of columns of A which are all zero, then $y - z = h + t = \frac{1}{1+\gamma}(w_i + w_j)$.

Now, since the matrices A_i and A_j are already row-reduced prior to this process, we have some reasonable expectations on where to find a 1 if it exists in a column at all; that is, if it is not near the main diagonal of A_i, it is near the main diagonal of A_j. It could happen that $h = 0$ and we are extremely unlucky with 1 placement, in which case JONES will take $y + \frac{1}{2}(w_i + w_j)^2$ clocks.

This will almost never happen, however. If there are two ones in the leftmost column of A, one of them will be near or at the top. If there is only one 1, it will either be at or near the top, or it will be roughly halfway down. If there are none, we just shiftover without further examining the column. So, for the h columns, we won't have to shift the rows of A up, and for about $\frac{1}{2}t$ columns, we still won't. For the other $\frac{1}{2}t$ columns, we can expect to perform shiftups equal to about half of the unlocked rows.

After an add, another locked row is created, so the number of unlocked rows is lessened. Further, we can expect at least two such adds to be performed between times we have to shiftup half of the unlocked rows. Hence, the first time we encounter such a column we shiftup $\frac{1}{2}(w_i + w_j)$ rows, but the next time we encounter such a column we will shiftup $\frac{1}{2}(w_i + w_j - 2) = \frac{1}{2}(w_i + w_j) - 1$ rows. Hence, we have a truncated triangular sum of shiftups to count. Since the number of unlocked rows starts at $w_i + w_j$, we expect a total shiftup count of

$$\frac{1}{2}(\frac{1}{2}(w_i + w_j))^2 - \frac{1}{2}\left[\frac{1}{2}(w_i + w_j) - \frac{1}{2}t\right]^2, \text{ which yields } \frac{1}{8}\left(1 - \frac{4\gamma^2}{(\gamma+1)^2}\right)(w_i + w_j)$$

shiftups. Hence, our total clock count is $y + \frac{1}{8}\left(1 - \frac{4\gamma^2}{(\gamma+1)^2}\right)(w_i + w_j) = y + \frac{1}{8}\frac{(1-\gamma)(1+3\gamma)}{(1+\gamma)^2}(w_i + w_j)$.

Software. Different choices for the algorithm can be made, and here we consider a situation where Gauß elimination is used to perform the row reduction. For the matrix sizes at hand, this seems a plausible option. Then software must examine $w_i + w_j$ elements in the first column. It first must find a 1, and if successful, it scans the rest of the column looking to add a row. If it finds such a row (i. e., with a 1 in this column), it performs an add of the two rows which takes y/β steps.

It then proceeds to the next column, examining the bottommost $w_i + w_j - 1$ elements, and addition of rows costs $(y-1)/\beta$ steps. And so on. We note that any additions that are performed in A are also performed in the U that is being built, and U has dimensions $(w_i + w_j) \times (w_i + w_j)$, though we do not explicitly count them.

If $y \geq w_i + w_j$, then in total there are $\frac{1}{2}(w_i + w_j)^2$ locations to visit, with a truncated triangular sum of addition steps in A equal to $\frac{\gamma}{\beta}\left[\frac{1}{2}y^2 - \frac{1}{2}(y - (w_i + w_j))^2\right] = \frac{\gamma}{\beta}(w_i + w_j)(y - \frac{1}{2}(w_i + w_j))$. In these cases we expect γ to be closer to 0 than to 1, and so hardware offers at least a factor 4 improvement in clocks over steps.

If $y \leq w_i + w_j$, then we have a truncated triangular sum of locations to visit equal to $\frac{1}{2}(w_i + w_j)^2 - \frac{1}{2}(w_i + w_j - y)^2 = y(w_i + w_j - \frac{1}{2}y)$. The addition steps total $\frac{\gamma}{\beta}\frac{1}{2}y^2$. In these cases we expect γ to be closer to 1 than to 0, and we expect few, if any, zero columns. Hence we use $y = \frac{1}{1+\gamma}(w_i + w_j)$, and putting just the locations expression over the clocks expression, we have a factor improvement equal to

$$\frac{\frac{1}{1+\gamma}(w_i + w_j)\left((w_i + w_j) - \frac{1}{2}\frac{1}{1+\gamma}(w_i + w_j)\right)}{\frac{1}{1+\gamma}(w_i + w_j) + \frac{1}{8}\frac{(1-\gamma)(1+3\gamma)}{(1+\gamma)^2}(w_i + w_j)^2} = \frac{\frac{1+2\gamma}{2+2\gamma}(w_i + w_j)}{\frac{1}{8}\frac{(1-\gamma)(1+3\gamma)}{1+\gamma}(w_i + w_j) + 1}$$

As γ increases towards 1, this expression will tend towards a factor $\frac{3}{4}(w_i + w_j)$ improvement (i. e. JONES takes linear time). This does not come as a surprise, for when γ gets closer to 1, there is less and less need to perform shiftups to find 1s.

6.2   Matrix Multiplication and Recording Deletions

Hardware. Once `Ur` and `Us` are loaded, their multiplications to L_i occur in parallel; similarly for L_j. Because of the pipeline structure of the multiplier, all the columns of UT_{ij} (similarly, UT_{ji}) are computed at a rate of one clock per column, plus a few clocks of latency in the beginning. The hash table then picks up the resulting r-parts and processes them at a rate of one clock per r-part, and it is also structured in a pipeline fashion.

Hence, processing L_i takes c_i clocks, plus a few clocks of latency. Then, processing L_j also takes c_j clocks, plus a few clocks of latency. Since the MPU bus must be used to report a deletion, it will take one clock per deletion, up to a maximum of c_j clocks to report all of L_j's deletions. Finally, L_i is processed again from the hash table's DRAM buffer, and those entries are looked up (for deletions) at the same rate. Since the hash table can report a deletion at the same time as looking up the next value, we count c_i clocks to report any deletions for L_i.

Since the traffic controller can record a deletion in a pipeline fashion and send a column at the same time, no additional overhead is counted for this. Finally, because of the 'just in time' nature of symbol transmission, it takes no additional time for a deletion to actually take hold in a symbol.

Thus, two symbols will have their deletions processed in $2c_i + 2c_j$ clocks, plus some small latency. (At the very end of an agreement phase, an additional c_i clocks will also be spent for one symbol. This is a one-time latency cost.)

Software. Using a Method of Four Russians (cf. [1]) approach in software is certainly helpful in constructing Pr_{ij}. The T-storage matrix is set up on each pass. Arranging the data the same way the hardware handles it, this T matrix has 2^k rows of r entries each, where k is the storage constant (typically $k = 8$, but can be increased), and $r = \text{rows}(A) - \text{rank}(A)$. It is built in $2^k \frac{r}{\beta}$ steps. Then, for (the given k bits of) each L_i column, the appropriate entry in the T matrix is read off and stored (taking $\frac{r}{\beta}$ steps), waiting to be added later. This continues for the entire pass. Hence, a pass takes $2^k \frac{r}{\beta} + c_i \frac{r}{\beta}$ steps. Afterwards, a new T matrix will need to be built. Since there are $\frac{w_i}{k}$ passes, all passes total comprise $\frac{w_i}{k}(2^k + c_i)\frac{r}{\beta}$ steps.

After all passes are complete, the subresults are added together to produce the final result of the multiplication. We can use $\log \frac{w_i}{k}$ additions of matrices, each addition taking $c_i \frac{r}{\beta}$ steps. This gives a total step count of

$$\frac{w_i}{k}(2^k + c_i)\frac{r}{\beta} + c_i\frac{r}{\beta}\log\frac{w_i}{k} = \frac{r}{\beta}\left(\frac{w_i}{k}2^k + c_i(\frac{w_i}{k} + \log\frac{w_i}{k})\right)$$

to construct Pr_{ij}. A similar expression will result when constructing Pr_{ji}.

One could try to optimize by increasing k to 16 or so, but $k = 32$ is troublesome as the 2^k term starts to dominate.

The situation gets worse for software; it still has to search through the data to find matching r-parts. Sorting Pr_{ij} will take at least $c_i \log c_i$ steps and as many as $\frac{r}{\beta}c_i \log c_i$, should many r-parts become popular. Similar expressions result when sorting Pr_{ji}. Finally, a bilinear search taking $\frac{r}{\beta}(c_i + c_j)$ more steps must be performed to find matching r-parts. Once the mismatches are found, columns have to be deleted from L_i and L_j; this takes $\frac{r}{\beta}(c_i + c_j)$ steps. Hence, total sorting and searching for both matrices takes $\frac{r}{\beta}(c_i(2 + \log c_i) + c_j(2 + \log c_j))$ steps.

In total, we have

$$\frac{r}{\beta}\left(\frac{w_i + w_j}{k}2^k + c_i(\frac{w_i}{k} + 2 + \log c_i\frac{w_i}{k}) + c_j(\frac{w_j}{k} + 2 + \log c_j\frac{w_j}{k})\right)$$

steps to agree the symbols S_i and S_j.

The MPU has a very clear and obvious advantage. Aside from the additional terms the software induces in its step count, it is important to stress that the hardware does not rely on the values of r, w_i, or w_j at all. Hence, large r (whose maximum value is 2^{11}) will dramatically slow down the software, but the hardware will be unaffected. Since r will steadily increase over the entire run, hardware's advantage will grow over time.

6.3   Gluing

Both hardware and software must pay the linear algebra times and the multiplication times as described earlier. From there the situation changes slightly. At this point we know that we may only construct a symbol whose L-part has no more than 2^{20} columns, so we label the number of such columns d.

Hardware. During the matrix multiplication of L_i, r-parts are being stored in the hash table at the same time, so we do not count this cost again. However, s-parts are being sent to the adder at the same time, so the adder's DRAM collection is filled for free.

Afterwards, the hash table will go through a preprocessing of its c_i entries. It may happen that these values hit the SRAM of the adder entirely too quickly, at which point we must pay upwards of an 8-clock penalty per such index. In the worst case this takes $8c_i$ clocks in total, but is expected to average to more like $2c_i$ over the course of an entire run.

Then, L_j is processed. We get an s-part in one clock (after some latency), and at the same time, its r-part is examined for matches in the hash table. If the hash table has the matching indices, it simply sends them, one per clock. If the adder has them, the adder uses its SRAM to produce them to the s-lookup chain. Since the SRAM produces values 128 bits at a time (that is, 6 indices per 8 clocks), the penalty of multiple fast read requests is mitigated.

Hence, we have worst case behavior of $8c_i + \frac{8}{6}d$ and best case behavior of $c_i + d$ clocks to finish all additions.

Software. It is plain that the software will suffer tremendously if it has to re-match r-parts to find corresponding s-parts to add, so we give it a fighting chance by allowing it to store the matching indices during agreement. (This gets expensive in memory with a state of several hundred symbols, but can nonetheless be theorized.)

Then it merely performs lookups of its storage data. Since there are d pairs of s-parts to be added, software takes $\frac{r}{\beta}d$ steps to finish all additions. Again, as r steadily increases over a run, software becomes vastly inferior to hardware, which does not rely on the value of r.

6.4   Equation Extraction

We begin by analyzing the time taken by extracting equations from a particular symbol with A of dimensions $w \times y$ and L of dimensions $w \times c$. We suppose A has the same bias of data as described in Section 6.1, but L is not guaranteed to have any bias of data. We calculate supposing that L's 0s and 1s are uniformly distributed.

Hardware. We follow Figure 9. In step 1, the row reducer is reset, taking 4096 clocks to bring U back to the identity matrix. Then we have $\lceil c/2^{11} \rceil$ groups of columns of L to process to find U such that UL is row reduced. For each of these groups, we first send the 2^{11} columns to Us, taking 2^{11} clocks, followed by sending the top 2^{11} rows of the row reducer's U part, each producing a row that the A part must store. Each row takes two clocks (one to read, one to write, as data must go back and forth across the MPU bus). So, to get a temporary result of a multiplication in A, we require 2^{12} clocks. To rotate U back into position, we require another 2^{11} clocks.

Then A gets row reduced, modifying the current U. Because L's bits are uniformly distributed, UL's bits will be also, and JONES will behave at least as well as SMITH under these conditions. Since it has been reported that SMITH will take $2k$ time for such a $k \times k$ matrix [6], JONES will take at most 2^{13} cycles to row reduce A. In total, step 2 takes $\lceil c/2^{11} \rceil (2^{11} + 2^{12} + 2^{11} + 2^{13})$ clocks, which is at most $c/2^{11} \times 8(2^{11}) = 8c$ clocks.

Step 3 takes at most 2^{12} clocks, since we just need to reset A. In step 4, we again have $\lceil c/2^{11} \rceil$ groups of columns of L to process. For each group, we first send it to Us taking 2^{11} clocks. Then the multiplication happens once more, taking 2^{12} clocks, with the temporary result in A. Then zero and one detection commence, requiring A to cyclically shift upwards completely, taking 2^{12} clocks. In the first 2^{11} of these, the ZD column is populated, and the OD row gets set to the sum of all rows in A. Then in the second 2^{11} clocks, the OD row cyclically shifts left, setting the OD flag. Hence, step 4 takes $\lceil c/2^{11} \rceil (2^{11} + 2^{12} + 2^{12})$, which is at most $5c$ clocks.

Step 5 is similar to step 3, taking 2^{12} clocks. Step 6 takes w clocks to populate Us. Step 7 takes at most 2^{12} clocks (one to multiply, one to send) to send the columns of A back to A. Step 8 takes 2^{11} clocks to repopulate Us. Step 9 is similar to step 5, taking 2^{12} clocks. Step 10 will require 2^{12} clocks (one to send, one to receive the multiplication, for each row in U). Step 11 will require 2^{12} clocks to set the 2048th element according to its detection flip-flops, followed by another 2^{12} clocks to put the (potentially) nonhomogeneous equation at the top.

Hence, to extract the equations from a symbol, PET SNAKE uses at most $2^{12} + 2^{11} + 8c + 2^{12} + 5c + 2^{12} + w + 2^{12} + 2^{11} + 2^{12} + 2^{12} + 2^{12} + 2^{12} = 18(2^{11}) + 13c + w \leq 13,670,400$ clocks.

Software. We once again consider Gauß elimination for the row reduction. In almost all cases $w \ll c$, and since each entry of L is equally likely to have a 0 or a 1, we note it will take one or two steps to find a pivot row for row i. However, once a pivot row is found, it will have to be added to about half the remaining rows, and each such addition will take $\frac{c-i}{\beta}$ steps. Hence, the step count is

$$\sum_{i=1}^{w} \frac{w-i}{2} \frac{c-i}{\beta} = \frac{w}{4\beta} \left[cw - \frac{1}{3}w^2 - c + \frac{1}{3} \right]$$

which is easily dominated by the $\frac{cw^2}{4\beta}$ term. As the run continues, w approaches y, and c almost always remains at 2^{20}. Taking an average value of w to be 2^{10} and $\beta = 32$, this term becomes 2^{33}.

Once L is row reduced, we must take the corresponding U (of size $w \times w$) and multiply it to A. The cost for this is negligible, though, using the Method of Four Russians again. Each T matrix costs $2^k \frac{y}{\beta}$ to set up, reading off the correct row costs $\frac{y}{\beta}$ steps, so each pass takes $\frac{y}{\beta}(2^k + w)$ steps. There are $\frac{w}{k}$ passes, giving a step count of $\frac{wy}{k\beta}(2^k + w)$ to construct all $\frac{w}{k}$ matrices to be added. We can structure things to take $\log \frac{w}{k}$ additions, each addition costing $\frac{wy}{\beta}$ steps, for a total of

$$\frac{wy}{\beta}\left(\frac{1}{k}(2^k + w) + \log \frac{w}{k}\right)$$

steps for the entire multiplication. However, using the same values as above (with $y = 2^{11}$ and $k = 8$), this reduces to approximately 2^{23} steps.

We see that the cost in software is about a factor of 1000 in steps over clocks for the equation extraction in the common case.

Assigning the final 0/1 column to construct the equations is trivial in both settings. Software provides no benefit over hardware when bringing all the equations together to be row reduced, so we do not perform an analysis of this. Finally, reducing with the current equation set to determine consistency is also trivial in both settings.

6.5   Software Measurement

It should be noted that, in the above derivations, the linear algebra is almost always dominated by matrix multiplication and recording deletions, both in hardware and in software.

In order to get a handle on performance metrics, four rounds of PRESENT were cryptanalyzed in software ($k = 8$, $y = 308$) using MRHS with the above options, and this entire session's timing values were recorded. The platform was an Intel E2180 processor, $\beta = 32$, on a single core of 2 GHz, with 2 GByte of RAM. Out of the nearly 10,000 agreements that took place, the vast majority took less than two seconds. We removed these from consideration since fractions of seconds were not measured. Many calculations were made on the remaining 350 or so agreements using the above step count formulas, some results of which are illustrated in Table 2. We see no problem using just these ~350 values since in a full cryptosystem operated on by PET SNAKE, there will commonly be high w_i, w_j, r, c_i, and c_j values, and these data points are more reflective of this scenario. It should be noted that we calculated steps using $\gamma = 0.5$; varying γ in either direction does not adversely affect our overall results.

An average of the ~350 time improvement factors gives an average improvement of 2,281 for four rounds of PRESENT. As noted above, as r gets larger, we suspect PET SNAKE will only improve from there.

Table 2. Some measured values of software performance ($k = 8$, $\beta = 32$, $\gamma = 0.5$, $y = 308$)

w_1	c_1	w_2	c_2	r	time (s)	total steps	pent clocks	α	PET SNAKE clocks	PET SNAKE time (s)	improv.
208	32768	236	524144	192	4	185372686.4	$8 \cdot 10^9$	43.16	1127822	0.001127822	3547
211	98304	236	196796	192	2	94214489.28	$4 \cdot 10^9$	42.46	604383.625	0.000604384	3309
211	98304	236	524144	192	4	205688510.1	$8 \cdot 10^9$	38.90	1259079.625	0.00125908	3177
229	121856	236	196796	192	2	103100923.9	$4 \cdot 10^9$	38.80	652627.625	0.000652628	3065
213	14336	237	196796	190	2	68614875.44	$4 \cdot 10^9$	58.30	436634.5	0.000436635	4580
207	32768	229	248832	190	3	89847645.61	$6 \cdot 10^9$	66.78	576709.1111	0.000576709	5202
207	32768	229	248832	190	2	89847645.61	$4 \cdot 10^9$	44.52	576709.1111	0.000576709	3468
212	16384	229	248832	189	2	85166930.02	$4 \cdot 10^9$	46.97	544245.625	0.000544246	3675
217	16384	229	248832	189	2	85273467.77	$4 \cdot 10^9$	46.91	544553.6111	0.000544554	3673
212	16384	229	497664	189	3	168450194.4	$6 \cdot 10^9$	35.62	1041909.625	0.00104191	2879
212	16384	229	786432	189	5	266482279.2	$10 \cdot 10^9$	37.53	1619445.625	0.001619446	3087
213	28672	236	524144	189	3	184351734.1	$6 \cdot 10^9$	32.55	1119940.069	0.00111994	2679
213	57344	229	497664	189	6	180808589.4	$12 \cdot 10^9$	66.37	1123890.944	0.001123891	5339
213	57344	229	497664	189	3	180808589.4	$6 \cdot 10^9$	33.18	1123890.944	0.001123891	2669
210	98304	229	248832	189	2	110163469.2	$4 \cdot 10^9$	36.31	707963.4028	0.000707963	2825
210	98304	229	497664	189	3	193446733.7	$6 \cdot 10^9$	31.02	1205627.403	0.001205627	2488
212	12288	229	248832	187	2	83962706.02	$4 \cdot 10^9$	47.64	536053.625	0.000536053	3731
212	12288	229	497664	187	3	167245970.4	$6 \cdot 10^9$	35.88	1033717.625	0.001033718	2902
212	12288	229	786432	187	5	265278055.2	$10 \cdot 10^9$	37.67	1611253.625	0.001611254	3103
213	57344	229	497664	185	6	180808589.4	$6 \cdot 10^9$	33.18	1123890.944	0.001123891	2669
213	57344	229	786432	185	5	278840674.1	$10 \cdot 10^9$	35.86	1701426.944	0.001701427	2939
213	16384	236	524144	184	3	180691970.9	$6 \cdot 10^9$	33.20	1095364.069	0.001095364	2739
134	1048576	147	131072	102	5	202949079.1	$10 \cdot 10^9$	49.27	2365087.403	0.002365087	2114
125	4096	141	450816	101	5	78081960.56	$4 \cdot 10^9$	51.23	915045.6111	0.000915046	2186
125	4096	137	1048576	101	4	185889011.7	$8 \cdot 10^9$	43.04	2110418.944	0.002110419	1895
122	8192	137	1048576	101	4	186478052	$8 \cdot 10^9$	42.90	2118502.403	0.002118502	1888
129	16384	137	524288	101	2	93036403.87	$4 \cdot 10^9$	42.99	1086565.611	0.001086566	1841
129	65536	140	450816	101	3	87773276.82	$6 \cdot 10^9$	68.36	1038037.069	0.001038037	2890
129	65536	137	1048576	101	6	195580582.3	$12 \cdot 10^9$	61.36	2233445.611	0.002233446	2686
135	1048576	152	131072	101	5	202950785.3	$10 \cdot 10^9$	49.27	2365324.069	0.002365324	2114
134	1048576	139	1048576	101	7	366057846.9	$14 \cdot 10^9$	38.25	4199787.625	0.004199788	1667

To get a better feeling for just how much more favorable PET SNAKE will be, we see that an average of the $\sim$350 α data points gives $\alpha = 66.068$, where α is the metric of steps per processor clock. Some things are not included in the step count, such as loop counter variables incrementing, allocation space instructions, and low-level memory management.

Once we have a good handle on the α that a given processor exhibits, we can predict software behavior for larger systems. For example, if PET SNAKE runs an MRHS attack on AES-128 or more rounds of PRESENT, it won't be uncommon for $y > 1500$, $w_i > 1024$, and $r > 1024$. Modeling such systems in software directly is problematic owing to the lack of sufficient on-board memory at the time of this writing, but we can predict step counts for software under these conditions. Table 3 gives the relevant predictions fixing $\alpha = 66.068$. In the later stages of a given attack of a full cipher of something like AES-128, we'll see symbol sizes listed in this table. The relative improvement of PET SNAKE is now even clearer, touching a six-digit improvement.

Finally, it is worth noting that other software methods may be used to multiply large matrices; it is certainly possible that some of them may be more efficient than the Method of Four Russians, and so the improvement factor may be reduced. However, PET SNAKE's time is still unaffected by these large symbols, processing each pair in less than half of a hundredth of a second. We feel that such absolute speed is too compelling to be dismissed.

Table 3. Some projected values of software performance ($k = 8$, $\beta = 32$, $\gamma = 0.5$, $y = 308$, $\alpha = 66.068$)

w_1	c_1	w_2	c_2	r	time (s)	total steps	pentium clks	PS clocks	PS time (s)	improv.
1000	1048576	1000	1048576	500	170.7644	5169289689	$3.41529 \cdot 10^{11}$	4474081	0.004474082	38167
750	1048576	750	1048576	300	84.95722	2571779869	$1.69914 \cdot 10^{11}$	4352054	0.004352054	19521
500	1048576	1000	1048576	200	59.44129	1799375263	$1.18883 \cdot 10^{11}$	4352304	0.004194304	14171
500	1048576	1000	1048576	400	110.3584	3340712542	$2.20717 \cdot 10^{11}$	4352304	0.004194304	26311
500	1048576	1000	1048576	600	161.2756	4882049821	$3.22551 \cdot 10^{11}$	4352304	0.004194304	38451
500	1048576	1000	1048576	800	212.1927	6423387100	$4.24386 \cdot 10^{11}$	4352304	0.004194304	50590
1500	1048576	1500	1048576	1000	482.5320	14606952758	$9.65064 \cdot 10^{11}$	4821304	0.004194304	115044

7   Performance Analysis III: Parallelization

Guessing Variables. PET SNAKE will, in its depth-first search of keys, eventually guess enough keys so that either the system is found to be inconsistent or the key is correct. This number of keys we refer to as δ. So that it may make appropriate use of parallelism, PET SNAKE will eventually guess enough keys discovering δ, and then make note of its available storage. Then the MCP will be able to determine how high in the guess tree it can fork a new guess into another area of the board, while having the ability to store the states required for a sub-branch of this new guess as well as for the original branch. The idea here is that PET SNAKE will use all of its MPUs to finish off a branch of a guess tree as quickly as possible. If more MPUs become available, more guesses can potentially be forked.

Should the MCP determine that storage will run out, it will delete some states higher in the guess tree. Any such state which needs to be recovered later can always be recalculated based on the next-highest state in the guess tree, and the remaining key guess symbols to affect the deleted state's guess. It is true that these (possibly several) guesses will need to be re-performed in one series of agrees and glues, increasing the overall running time, but PET SNAKE at least has recovery options should storage requirements vary wildly across parallel branches of the guess tree. For this reason, PET SNAKE will never delete the highest state in the guess tree, that is, the state which was arrived at before any guesses were committed.

Using Multiple PCs. To cope with a cipher like AES-128, the only plausible option seems to use a cluster of PCs, but here the communication cost between these PCs will add another significant factor to the overall running time of the algorithm. Connecting networked PCs in the same way as PET SNAKE connects its MPUs will introduce additional time spent: suppose that a grid of PCs is connected so each can talk to its neighbor in each cardinal direction using gigabit Ethernet, and suppose that this network actually communicates perfectly (i. e., 1 gigabit/sec). PET SNAKE's connections are 1024 wires clocked at 1 GHz, so it can transmit 1000 gigabit/sec between MPUs. This makes the PC network 1000 times as slow. With the observation that a PC agrees $\gg$1000 times slower than an MPU, the PCs could also implement a 'just in time' delivery method to reduce agreement communication times. However, when symbols need to be moved between agreement stages or to prepare for a glue, we see that the movement time for a PC is a little over 2.15 sec per symbol per hop (over 4.5 minutes per agreement phase, assuming no deletions), whereas for PET SNAKE it is 0.00215 sec per symbol per hop. Hence, a faster network between PCs will need to be established, which in turn adds to the cost of such a solution.

Finally, for multiple PCs to provide the same storage as PET SNAKE, a single PC has to store 4680 MB, not including active memory of at least 325 MB. This is slightly larger than 4 GB per PC, and so more expensive motherboards that can provide larger memory will need to be acquired. (Slower storage solutions like hard drives can be used instead, but given their notorious relative slowness, the times for loading and storing would start to dominate an overall time estimate, and this would make finding a key infeasible.)

8   Conclusion

In this paper we propose a dedicated hardware design to implement an algebraic attack, based on MRHS, against block ciphers. We think that our analysis gives ample evidence that PET SNAKE is an architecture of significant cryptanalytic interest. The overall running time of MRHS is dominated by the time spent to agree symbols, and basing on our experiments with four rounds of PRESENT, a speed-up by a factor of $\gg 2000$ of PET SNAKE over our (reasonably optimized) software implementation is plausible. Actually, when looking at full round versions of AES-128, we expect symbols to be involved in the computation, where the performance advantage of PET SNAKE becomes more drastic. As documented in Section 6.5, here expected improvement factors in agreeing timings might well be in the range of 5 digit factors. Thus, even more conservative PET SNAKE clocking rates than 1 GHz still can be expected to realize several magnitudes of improvement over software.

Lacking the theory for a reliable running time estimate of an MRHS-based algebraic attack, we cannot give a reliable estimate on the absolute running time of our design when being applied to a modern block cipher like AES-128. Notwithstanding this, the above discussion gives ample evidence that the practical feasibility of (MRHS-based) algebraic attacks can be improved significantly through the use of a dedicated hardware design: substantial performance improvements over software implementations can be achieved, and owing to the scalability of PET SNAKE, exploring small prototypes seems a plausible next step in research along this line. Some of the building blocks of PET SNAKE, like the JONES design for the linear algebra part, might be of independent interest.

References

1. Arlazarov, V.L., Dinic, E.A., Kronrod, M.A., Faradzev, I.A.: On economic construction of the transitive closure of a directed graph. Sov. Math. Dokl. 11, 1209–1210 (1975); Original in Russian in Dokl. Akad. Nauk. SSSR 194, 477–488 (1970)

2. Bernstein, D.J.: Circuits for Integer Factorization: a Proposal (2001), At the time of writing available electronically at, http://cr.yp.to/papers/nfscircuit.pdf
3. Bogdanov, A., Eisenbarth, T., Rupp, A.: A Hardware-Assisted Realtime Attack on A5/2 Without Precomputations. In: Paillier, P., Verbauwhede, I. (eds.) CHES 2007. LNCS, vol. 4727, pp. 394–412. Springer, Heidelberg (2007)
4. Bogdanov, A., Knudsen, L.R., Leander, G., Paar, C., Poschmann, A., Robshaw, M.J.B., Seurin, Y., Vikkelsoe, C.: PRESENT: An Ultra-Lightweight Block Cipher. In: Paillier, P., Verbauwhede, I. (eds.) CHES 2007. LNCS, vol. 4727, pp. 450–466. Springer, Heidelberg (2007)
5. Bogdanov, A., Mertens, M.C., Paar, C., Pelzl, J., Rupp, A.: A Parallel Hardware Architecture for fast Gaussian Elimination over GF(2). In: IEEE Symp. on Field-Programmable Custom Computing Machines — FCCM 2006, Napa, CA, USA (2006)
6. Bogdanov, A., Mertens, M.C., Paar, C., Pelzl, J., Rupp, A.: SMITH - A Parallel Hardware Architecture for fast Gaussian Elimination over GF(2). In: 2nd Workshop on Special-purpose Hardware for Attacking Cryptographic Systems – SHARCS 2006 (2006), http://www.crypto.ruhr-uni-bochum.de/imperia/md/content/texte/publications/conferences/sharcs2006_matrix.pdf
7. Bosma, W., Cannon, J.J., Playoust, C.: The Magma Algebra System I: The User Language. Journal of Symbolic Computation 24, 235–265 (1997)
8. Buchmann, J., Pyshkin, A., Weinmann, R.-P.: A Zero-Dimensional Gröbner Basis for AES-128. In: Robshaw, M.J.B. (ed.) FSE 2006. LNCS, vol. 4047, pp. 78–88. Springer, Heidelberg (2006)
9. Intel Corporation. Intel® Xeon® Processor X7460 (16M Cache, 2.66 GHz, 1066 MHz FSB), http://ark.intel.com/Product.aspx?id=36947
10. Courtois, N.T., Bard, G.V., Wagner, D.: Algebraic and Slide Attacks on KeeLoq. In: Nyberg, K. (ed.) FSE 2008. LNCS, vol. 5086, pp. 97–115. Springer, Heidelberg (2008)
11. Electronic Frontier Foundation. Cracking DES: Secrets of Encryption Research, Wiretap Politics & Chip Design. OReilly & Associates, Sebastopol (July 1998)
12. Franke, J., Kleinjung, T., Paar, C., Pelzl, J., Priplata, C., Stahlke, C.: SHARK: A Realizable Special Hardware Sieving Device for Factoring 1024-Bit Integers. In: Rao, J.R., Sunar, B. (eds.) CHES 2005. LNCS, vol. 3659, pp. 119–130. Springer, Heidelberg (2005)
13. Geiselmann, W., Matheis, K., Steinwandt, R.: PET SNAKE: A Special Purpose Architecture to Implement an Algebraic Attack in Hardware. Cryptology ePrint Archive: Report 2009/222 (2010), http://eprint.iacr.org/2009/222
14. Geiselmann, W., Shamir, A., Steinwandt, R., Tromer, E.: Scalable Hardware for Sparse Systems of Linear Equations, with Applications to Integer Factorization. In: Rao, J.R., Sunar, B. (eds.) CHES 2005. LNCS, vol. 3659, pp. 131–146. Springer, Heidelberg (2005)
15. Geiselmann, W., Steinwandt, R.: Yet Another Sieving Device. In: Okamoto, T. (ed.) CT-RSA 2004. LNCS, vol. 2964, pp. 278–291. Springer, Heidelberg (2004)
16. Geiselmann, W., Steinwandt, R.: Non-wafer-Scale Sieving Hardware for the NFS: Another Attempt to Cope with 1024-bit. In: Naor, M. (ed.) EUROCRYPT 2007. LNCS, vol. 4515, pp. 466–481. Springer, Heidelberg (2007)
17. Güneysu, T., Kasper, T., Novotný, M., Paar, C., Rupp, A.: Cryptanalysis with COPACOBANA. IEEE Transactions on Computers 75(11), 1498–1513 (2008)
18. Lenstra, A.K., Shamir, A.: Analysis and Optimization of the TWINKLE Factoring Device. In: Preneel, B. (ed.) EUROCRYPT 2000. LNCS, vol. 1807, pp. 35–52. Springer, Heidelberg (2000)

19. Lenstra, A.K., Shamir, A., Tomlinson, J., Tromer, E.: Analysis of Bernstein's Factorization Circuit. In: Zheng, Y. (ed.) ASIACRYPT 2002. LNCS, vol. 2501, pp. 1–26. Springer, Heidelberg (2002)
20. National Institute of Standards and Technology. Federal Information Processing Standards Publication 197. Specification for the ADVANCED ENCRYPTION STANDARD (AES) (November 2001)
21. Raddum, H.: MRHS Equation Systems. In: Adams, C., Miri, A., Wiener, M. (eds.) SAC 2007. LNCS, vol. 4876, pp. 232–245. Springer, Heidelberg (2007)
22. Raddum, H., Semaev, I.: Solving MRHS linear equations. Cryptology ePrint Archive, Report 2007/285 (2007), http://eprint.iacr.org/2007/285
23. Raddum, H., Semaev, I.: Solving Multiple Right Hand Sides linear equations. Designs, Codes and Cryptography 49, 147–160 (2008); Preprint available in [22]
24. Schoonen, A.C.C.: Multiple right-hand side equation. Master's thesis, Eindhoven University of Technology, Department of Mathematics and Computer Science (May 2008), http://alexandria.tue.nl/extra1/afstversl/wsk-i/schoonen2008.pdf
25. Semaev, I.: Sparse Boolean equations and circuit lattices. Presentation at Int. Workshop on Coding and Cryptography WCC 2009, Ullensvang (Norway) (May 2009)
26. Semaev, I.: Sparse Boolean equations and circuit lattices. Cryptology ePrint Archive, Report 2009/252 (2009), http://eprint.iacr.org/2009/252
27. Shamir, A.: Factoring Large Numbers with the TWINKLE Device. In: Koç, Ç.K., Paar, C. (eds.) CHES 1999. LNCS, vol. 1717, pp. 2–12. Springer, Heidelberg (1999)
28. Shamir, A., Tromer, E.: Factoring Large Numbers with the TWIRL Device. In: Boneh, D. (ed.) CRYPTO 2003. LNCS, vol. 2729, pp. 1–26. Springer, Heidelberg (2003)

Green Secure Processors: Towards Power-Efficient Secure Processor Design

Siddhartha Chhabra and Yan Solihin

Dept. of Electrical and Computer Engineering, North Carolina State University
Raleigh, USA
{schhabr,solihin}@ncsu.edu

Abstract. With the increasing wealth of digital information stored on computer systems today, security issues have become increasingly important. In addition to attacks targeting the software stack of a system, hardware attacks have become equally likely. Researchers have proposed *Secure Processor Architectures* which utilize hardware mechanisms for memory encryption and integrity verification to protect the confidentiality and integrity of data and computation, even from sophisticated hardware attacks. While there have been many works addressing performance and other system level issues in secure processor design, power issues have largely been ignored. In this paper, we first analyze the sources of power (energy) increase in different secure processor architectures. We then present a power analysis of various secure processor architectures in terms of their increase in power consumption over a base system with no protection and then provide recommendations for designs that offer the best balance between performance and power without compromising security. We extend our study to the embedded domain as well. We also outline the design of a novel hybrid cryptographic engine that can be used to minimize the power consumption for a secure processor. We believe that if secure processors are to be adopted in future systems (general purpose or embedded), it is critically important that power issues are considered in addition to performance and other system level issues. To the best of our knowledge, this is the first work to examine the power implications of providing hardware mechanisms for security.

Keywords: Power Analysis, Secure Processor Architectures, Memory Encryption, Memory Authentication, Embedded Systems Security.

1 Introduction

Many applications handle security sensitive data like consumer credit card numbers, bank account numbers, personal information etc. With the increasing wealth of digital information stored on computer systems today, attackers have increased motivation to attack systems for financial gains. Traditionally, attackers have exploited vulnerabilities in application code and Operating System (OS) to mount software attacks resulting in the application leaking sensitive data.

M.L. Gavrilova et al. (Eds.): Trans. on Comput. Sci. X, LNCS 6340, pp. 329–351, 2010.

However, with the computation becoming increasingly mobile and mobile devices being prone to theft or loss, attackers can get physical access to the system to launch *physical* or *hardware* attacks. Hardware attacks are made possible as most computer systems communicate data in its plaintext form between the processor chip and off-chip devices such as the main memory. This presents the attackers with a situation where they can place a bus analyzer that snoops data communicated between the processor chip and other chips [1]. In addition, data is also stored in its plaintext form in the main memory which allows an attacker having physical access to the system to dump the memory contents and scan it, possibly gaining a lot of valuable information such as passwords [2]. Although physical attacks may be more difficult to perform than software-based attacks, they are very powerful as they can bypass all software security solutions that might be deployed on the system. The recent proliferation of modchips in gaming systems has shown that given sufficient financial payoffs, hardware attacks are realistic threats.

Recognizing these threats, researchers have proposed secure processor architectures [3–17]. Secure processors assume that all off chip devices are vulnerable and the processor chip itself provides a natural security boundary. Secure processor architectures deploy hardware mechanisms to protect the *privacy* and *integrity* of application code and data. **Memory encryption** protects the privacy of data by encrypting data and code as it moves off the processor chip and decrypting it back once it is reloaded. Memory encryption provides protection against *passive* attacks, where an adversary tries to silently observe application data. **Memory authentication** protects the integrity of code and data by associating and verifying a Message Authentication Code (MAC) with each data block as it moves on and off the processor chip. Memory authentication provides protection against active attacks where the attacker tries to modify data in off-chip structures to change application behavior, potentially resulting in leaking sensitive information.

Secure processor research thus far has primarily focussed on reducing the performance and storage overheads of providing hardware mechanisms for security or on resolving system-level issues like lack of support for inter-process communication, virtual memory etc. Unfortunately power issues have largely been ignored for secure processor architectures. Figure 1 shows the power density increase for contemporary processors over the last 40 years.

The trend clearly indicates the need to consider power as one of the key design considerations. The hardware security mechanisms not only result in performance and storage overheads, but also increase the overall power consumption and based on the actual mechanisms used, this increase in power can be very significant(Section 2). There has been prior work in designing low power security cryptographic algorithms [18, 19], however, power issues have not been considered at the architecture level. If secure processors are to be adopted in future systems, it is critically important that power issues are considered in addition to performance and system-level issues. To the best of our knowledge, this is the first work to explore power implications of secure processor architectures.

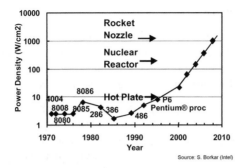

Fig. 1. Power Density Increase in Processors

Contributions: In this paper we analyze the power implications of using secure processor architectures. Overall, we make the following contributions:

- We analyze the sources of power consumption in various secure processor designs.
- We present a power analysis of various secure processor architectures in terms of their increase in power consumption over a base system with no protection and provide recommendations for designs that offer the best balance between performance and power without compromising security.
- We extend our study to the embedded domain and show that some design decisions offering the best power-performance balance in the general purpose domain do not necessarily apply to the embedded domain.
- We explore a novel *hybrid* cryptographic engine that combines multiple encryption mechanisms designed with the primary goal to minimize power overheads without compromising performance or security.

The rest of the paper is organized as follows. Section 2 presents the sources of power overhead in secure processor designs. Section 3 describes our experimental setup. Section 4 presents a power evaluation of currently proposed secure processor architectures. Section 5 presents a parallel evaluation for the embedded domain. Section 6 presents a discussion on our novel cryptographic engine and we conclude in Section 7.

2 Power Overheads in Secure Processors

Secure processors employ hardware mechanisms for memory encryption and authentication for protecting the privacy and integrity of data. Each mechanism contributes to increasing the overall power consumption of the processor. In this section, we first present the currently proposed mechanisms for memory encryption and authentication and then discuss the factors associated with each mechanism that contribute to power overheads in a secure processor architecture.

2.1   Memory Encryption

Memory encryption mechanisms are used to protect the privacy of data by encrypting and decrypting the data block as it moves on and off the processor chip. Direct encryption and counter-mode encryption form the most widely used forms of encryption for current proposals on secure processor architectures.

Direct Encryption: In direct encryption, as a cache block is evicted off the processor chip, an on-chip cryptographic engine encrypts it before storing it in the main memory [5]. When the block is reloaded from main memory, the cryptographic engine decrypts it before supplying it to the processor. Based on its operation, direct encryption results in the following power overheads:

Static power: Direct encryption in effect increases the latency of fetching a block from the main memory. The decryption of the block lies directly in the processor's critical path and this results in increased static power consumption for other processor structures that might be idle due to the decryption latency.

Counter Mode Encryption: Recently proposed memory encryption mechanisms have utilized *counter-mode encryption* [7, 9–15] due to its ability to hide cryptographic delays on the critical path of memory accesses. This is done by decoupling the cryptographic work from the actual data. In counter-mode encryption, a per-block *seed* is encrypted to generate a cryptographic *pad*, which is then XORed with the memory block to encrypt or decrypt it (Figure 2). However, the choice of seed is critical for both performance and security. The security of counter-mode encryption is contingent on the uniqueness of the pads which are XORed with blocks to encrypt/decrypt them. This essentially means that the seeds used to generate the pads must be unique. Prior works use the block address (virtual or physical) as a component of the seed to ensure *spatial* uniqueness when the blocks are stored in memory. In addition, a per-block counter incremented on every writeback of the block to main memory is also included as a component of the seed to ensure *temporal* uniqueness. From a performance point of view, the seed components must be known at cache miss time to overlap the pad generation (cryptographic) latency with the memory fetch latency. The block address is known at cache miss time and in order to have the block counter available too, an on-chip *counter cache* is used to cache the per-block counters. If the counter is found in the cache, the pad generation latency can be overlapped with the memory fetch latency. Based on its operation, counter-mode encryption results in the following power overheads:

Static power: While a counter cache hit will hide the cryptographic latency of generating the pad, a miss will result in a separate memory request issued to fetch the counter. Only when the counter is fetched can the cryptographic operation start. Thus a counter cache miss can increase the idle time of processor structures, thereby increasing their static power consumption.

Counter Cache: On each cache miss, the counter cache needs to be consulted to find the per-block counter. The addition of the cache contributes to both dynamic and static power consumption of the processor.

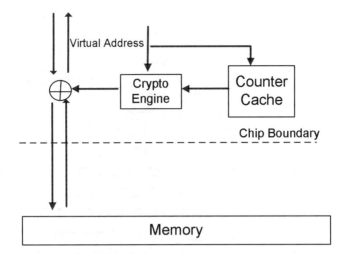

Fig. 2. Counter-mode Encryption

2.2 Memory Authentication

Memory authentication is used to protect the integrity of data. One of the early mechanisms for memory authentication [5] used a Message Authentication Code (MAC) associated with each block which is computed and verified as a block moves on and off the processor chip. However, per-block MAC based authentication is vulnerable to replay attacks, where an attacker can record an old data block with its MAC and replay it as the current value to the processor. Due to its security limitations, *Merkle tree* authentication was proposed and represents the family of memory authentication mechanisms used by current proposals.

Merkle tree Authentication: In Merkle tree memory integrity verification, a tree of MACs is computed over the memory. The root of this tree is stored securely in an on-chip register and never goes off the processor chip. On loading a block, its integrity is verified by checking its chain of MAC values up to the root MAC (Figure 3). Since the root of the authentication tree stores information about all the blocks in memory and never goes off the processor chip, an attacker cannot modify or replay any value without detection.

In the standard Merkle tree mechanism, a tree of MACs is built over the *entire* main memory. However, a recent work showed that if counter-mode encryption is used, it is not necessary to build the Merkle tree over the entire main memory. A tree of MACs built only over the per-block counters in main memory along with a per-block MAC can provide the same level of security as a standard Merkle tree, and at the same time result in a much smaller and shallower tree(Figure 4). This tree formation was called Bonsai Merkle Trees (BMTs) and it was shown that they can significantly reduce the overheads of memory authentication mechanism [20].

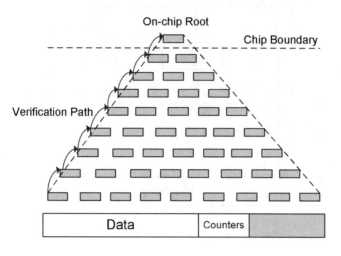

Fig. 3. Standard Merkle Tree Integrity Verification

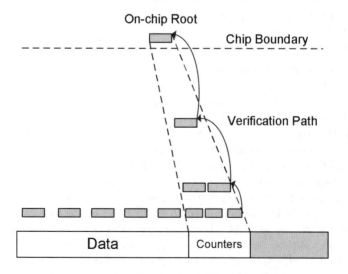

Fig. 4. Bonsai Merkle Tree Integrity Verification

Based on its operation, Merkle tree authentication has the following power overheads:

Static Power: Authentication can be *imprecise*, where the processor is allowed to continue execution and retire the instruction loading the data. However, if *precise* authentication is used, the instruction cannot retire until the authentication is completed. Once again, this can result in a significant increase in the static power consumption depending on the number of MACs that need to be fetched and verified to establish the integrity of the block.

Dynamic Power: As an optimization, the MAC values can be cached and on verification of the first block found in the cache, the block can be considered to be verified for integrity as the MAC block found in the cache can be assumed to form the root of a small Merkle tree which is guaranteed to be secure as it is on-chip. These additional cache accesses result in an increase in the power consumption of caches and the processor as a whole.

2.3   Other Power Sources

There are other sources that contribute to the power consumption of a system equipped with hardware mechanisms for security. We describe the sources here, however, the results presented in the following sections do not account for these power sources and hence present a lower bound on the power overheads of secure processors.

Cryptographic engine power consumption: The on-chip cryptographic engine is responsible for all the cryptographic work required for memory encryption and authentication and forms another major source of additional power consumption in secure processor architectures.

Increased power consumption of other structures: Cryptographic metadata (counters and MACS) needs to be fetched on the processor chip for decrypting or verifying the block. This results in increased work for off-chip structures like the memory bus, memory controller, memory etc., thereby, contributing to a further increase in the power consumption of the system as a whole.

3   Experimental Setup

3.1   Machine Models

We use SESC [21], an open source execution driven simulator, to model the secure processor architectures evaluated in this paper. We use Wattch [22] power models for our power evaluations. For uniprocessor evaluations, we model a 3-issue, out-of-order processor with split L1 data and instruction caches. Both caches have 16KB size, 2-way set associativity, and 2-cycle hit latency. The L2 is a unified 1MB, 8-way set associative, cache with 10-cycle hit latency. All caches have 64-byte block size and use LRU replacement. We assume 2GB main memory with 490-cycle round-trip latency. The cryptographic engine used is a 16-stage pipelines, 128-bit AES [23] engine with 80-cycle latency [24]. The counter cache used for counter-mode encryption is a 32KB, 16-way set associative cache. The default MAC size is 128-bits. The process parameters for the simulated architecture are 5GHz clock and 70nm feature size. Note that we assume a very optimistic latency of 80-cycles for the cryptographic engine to account for technological advances. Hence, the figures presented in this paper represent a lower bound and the energy overheads on a real system are likely to be even higher.

For the CMP evaluation, we model a two-core CMP where each core has private L1 data and instruction caches. The l2 cache and all lower levels of the memory hierarchy are shared by both cores. To better match current CMP configurations, we have increased the L2 cache size to 2MB. All other system parameters are the same as the uniprocessor case.

The simulated embedded processor is modeled after ARM's cortex A-8 processor [25] with the cryptographic parameters kept the same as the modeled general purpose processor.

3.2 Benchmarks

We use all C/C++ SPEC2K benchmarks [26] for our general purpose system evaluations. We use the reference input set for each benchmark and simulate it for 1 billion instructions after skipping 5 billion instructions. The figures show the individual results for benchmarks having an L2 miss rate of more than 20%, however, the average is calculated across all 21 benchmarks.

For our CMP evaluations, we have created 21 pairs of benchmarks using SPEC2K benchmarks. Each pair consists of two SPEC2K benchmarks which are spawned as two separate threads on each of the two cores of the modeled CMP system. To capture different memory behaviors, we classify the benchmarks into two categories: those that have an L2 miss rate of of more than 20%, when run alone, and those that have an L2 miss rate of less than 20%, when run alone. We select benchmarks from each group and combine them so all memory behaviors are represented. In the first group of benchmark pairs, the benchmarks in a pair are both taken from low miss rate category: *perlbmk_twolf* and *twolf_vpr*. In the second group of benchmark pairs, one benchmark is taken from the low miss rate category while the other is taken from the hiss miss rate category: *apsi_bzip2, gzip_applu, gzip_apsi, perlbmk_art, swim_gzip, swim_twolf, vpr_applu, vpr_art, applu_gzip,* and *swim_perlbmk*. The last group of benchmark pairs is the one where both benchmarks are taken from the high mate rate category: *apsi_art, art_mcf, art_swim, mcf_art, mcf_swim, swim_art, swim_mcf, equake_apsi,* and *mcf_apsi*. For each simulation, we use the reference input set and simulate for 1 billion instructions after skipping 5 billion instructions. The instructions are skipped only on the first benchmark in the benchmark pair and the simulation ends when the combined number of instructions simulated reaches 1 billion.

For our embedded domain evaluations, we use nine benchmarks from the MiBench [27] embedded benchmark suite (We excluded the benchmarks that had a compilation error in our simulation framework). The benchmarks have been picked from the four categories: Automotive and industrial control(*basicmath, bitcount, qsort, susan*), Network (*dijkstra, patricia*), Security (*rijndael, sha*), and telecommunications (*fft*). Each benchmark is simulated to completion.

4   Recommendations for Energy Efficient Secure Processor Design

In this section, we present a power evaluation of the currently proposed secure processor architectures and provide recommendations towards energy- efficient secure processor design. All figures plot the overall energy consumption of the discussed architecture, unless otherwise stated. We first present our study for general purpose processor architectures and then present a parallel discussion for embedded systems domain.

4.1   General Purpose Secure Processors

We first present the energy overheads for the most commonly used memory encryption and authentication mechanisms: Counter-mode encryption and standard Merkle trees. Figure 5 shows the energy overheads for SPEC2K benchmarks.

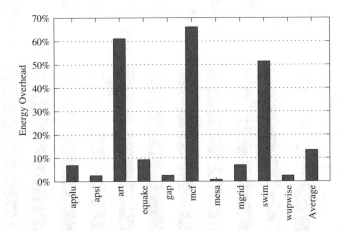

Fig. 5. Energy Overhead of Counter-mode Encryption with Standard Merkle Trees

It can be seen from the figure that secure processor mechanisms result in an average overhead of 13.42% across SPEC2K benchmarks. For memory intensive applications like art, mcf, and swim, the overheads are in excess of 50% with mcf resulting in as much as 67% overhead over a system with no protection. These overheads are extremely high considering the fact that the power increase from one processor generation to another, accompanied by a significant performance improvement due to increased clock speeds, is roughly around 10%. For example, Pentium III, running at 500MHz, consumes 7.8% additional power compared to a Pentium II, running at 233MHz.

Observation: Secure processor mechanisms add non-trivial power overheads, making power even more important in the context of secure processor design.

In order to better understand the overheads and possible avenues for power (energy) reduction techniques, we provide a breakdown of the overheads. Figure 6(a) shows the breakdown of power overheads into encryption and integrity verification components and Figure 6(b) shows the breakdown of the increase in energy consumption into the increase in pipeline energy vs increase in energy dissipated by caches (including the counter cache used for encryption).

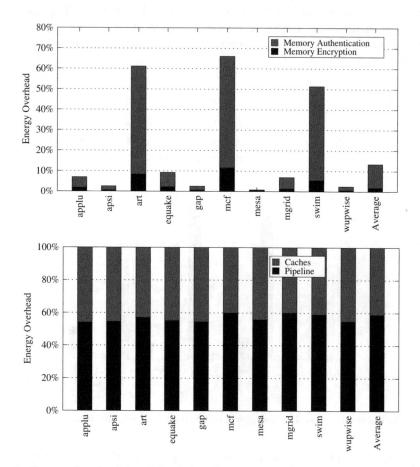

Fig. 6. Energy Overhead breakdown for Counter-mode Encryption with Standard Merkle Trees

As can be seen from Figure 6(a), the memory authentication mechanism is the primary contributor to the overall energy overheads (nearly 78% overhead comes from the authentication mechanism). Figure 6(b) shows that the overall increase in the energy consumption comes in a near equal proportion from both the pipeline (58%) and on-chip caches (42%). The increase in pipeline energy is mainly the static component, as the processor pipeline does not carry out any of the cryptographic operations to decrypt or verify the integrity of a block, however, the pipeline structures can be idle for a longer duration due to the security mechanisms, thereby dissipating energy (leakage) and contributing to the overall energy increase. The increase in cache energy is mainly the dynamic component coming from increased switching due to data cache accesses to fetch MACs associated with a block to verify its integrity and the additional energy required for the counter cache operation.

Observation: It is important to design power-efficient memory encryption and authentication mechanisms, but a power-efficient authentication mechanism will result in greater savings than a power-efficient encryption mechanism. Mechanisms that reduce the overall delay associated with decryption and integrity verification will help reduce the increase in pipeline energy and mechanisms that reduce cache accesses for security will reduce the cache energy consumption.

As we discussed earlier, Bonsai Merkle trees were proposed to reduce the performance overheads associated with memory authentication mechanisms. BMT integrity verification affords the same security as a standard Merkle tree but requires the tree of MACs to be built only over the per-block counters used for encrypting/decrypting blocks along with a MAC associated with each data block. This results in a much shallower and smaller tree of MACs. The smaller and shallower the tree, the smaller will be the number of accesses to the cache to fetch MACs to verify the integrity of a block. Hence, intuitively, BMTs used with counter mode encryption should reduce the overall energy consumption of the processor. Figure 7 shows the energy overheads of using BMTs with counter-mode encryption.

Using BMTs as the integrity verification mechanism reduces the overall energy overheads from 13.42% on an average to 2.42%. In addition, the maximum overheads suffered by memory intensive benchmarks are reduced from 67% to 14%. Another interesting observation that we make is, of the 2.42% overheads, only

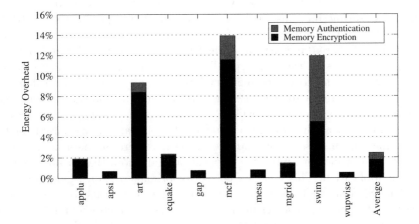

Fig. 7. Energy Overhead of Counter-mode Encryption with Bonsai Merkle Trees

0.67% comes from the memory integrity verification mechanism. Hence, using BMTs significantly reduces the overall energy overheads of the secure processor. In addition to reducing the energy overheads, BMTs significantly also reduce the performance overheads of the memory integrity verification mechanism. Figure 8 compares the Energy-Delay product (EDP) for a secure processor using standard Merkle tree vs one using BMTs normalized to the EDP of a system with no protection. As can be seen from the figure BMT integrity verification mechanism has a normalized EDP of 1.04, while standard Merkle Tree integrity verification has a normalized EDP of 1.32. In essence, BMTs are very effective in reducing the overall performance as well as energy overheads of a secure processor with an EDP within 4% of a system with no protection.

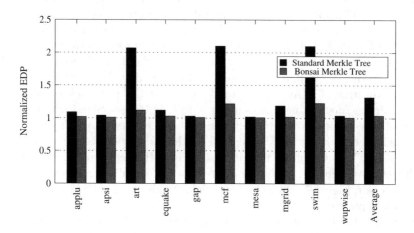

Fig. 8. Normalized Energy-Delay Product (EDP) for Standard vs Bonsai Merkle tree

We further strengthen this observation by showing the energy overheads of secure processor mechanisms on the simulated CMP system. Existing CMP designs [28–30] are typically organized with private L1 caches per core and some combination of shared and private lower-level caches, such as L2 and possibly L3 caches. All cores on the chip typically share a single, common memory bus and off-chip main memory. The memory integrity and verification mechanisms discussed above, can be applied to such CMP architectures in the same manner as a uniprocessor system. For our CMP evaluations, the number of instructions executed for each application in a benchmark pair can change based on the security mechanisms used. For example, using hardware mechanisms for security will make a memory intensive application stall more than a non-memory intensive application. This can be due to two primary reasons. One, for every block fetched from main memory, a cryptographic pad needs to be generated to decrypt it. This can also result in extra misses (to fetch counters), thereby contenting with the demand fetches for memory bandwidth, further slowing the application down. Secondly, the authentication mechanisms fetch MACs for each block fetched from memory to verify the integrity of the block. These MACs are placed in the last level cache and contend for space with application data, which can further increase the miss rate of the application. As in our simulation infrastructure, the total number of instructions is kept constant, these increased stalls for memory intensive application results in the other application making more progress compared to the base case. Hence, instead of plotting energy numbers directly, we calculate the (*Energy Per Instruction (EPI)* for each individual benchmark and calculate the average EPI for the system as the average of the EPIs of the individual benchmarks. Figure 9 shows the average EPI overhead for using standard Merkle tree with counter-mode encryption.

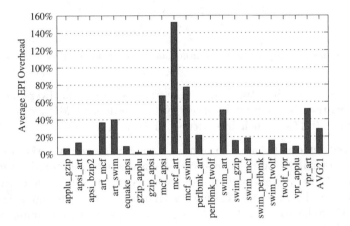

Fig. 9. Average EPI Overhead of Counter-mode Encryption with Standard Merkle Trees

As can be seen from the figure, majority of the pairs suffer from a high average EPI overhead, with the simulated benchmark pairs suffering an average EPI overhead of 29.8% on an average. For memory intensive benchmark pairs, the overheads can be as high as 152% (*mcf_art*). Hence, the energy overheads of using standard Merkle tree with counter-mode encryption are significantly higher for CMPs that for the uniprocessor case. CMPs are likely to be used in server platforms where Energy (Power) consumption is even more important. A recent article [31] pointed out that power could cost more than the servers themselves. Hence, if hardware mechanisms for security are to be adopted for server platforms, it is even more important that their overheads in terms of power are brought down significantly.

Figure 10 shows the average EPI overhead for using BMTs with counter-mode encryption.

As can be seen from the figure, BMTs are even more effective, compared to the uniprocessor case, in reducing energy overheads of CMP systems with the simulated benchmark pair suffering an average EPI overhead of 2.9% on an average with the worst case average EPI overhead declining steeply to 11.8%

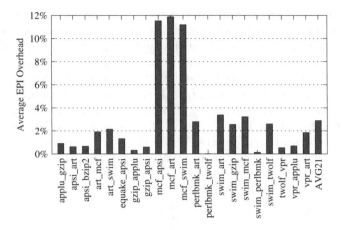

Fig. 10. Average EPI Overhead of Counter-mode Encryption with Bonsai Merkle Trees

(compared to 152% with Standard Merkle trees). Hence, if hardware mechanisms for security are to be adopted for server systems utilizing CMPs, it is imperative that they use BMTs as their integrity verification mechanism.

Recommendation: In order to minimize the energy consumption of a secure processor, Bonsai Merkle trees must be used as the memory integrity verification mechanism. BMTs are not only important to reduce the performance overheads, they achieve the best power-performance balance without compromising security.

Now that we have established BMTs as the preferred memory integrity verification mechanism for general purpose processors, we next look at the two most prominently used memory encryption mechanisms, direct and counter mode encryption, and analyze them in greater detail to see if we can achieve further power savings. Figure 11 shows the power overheads of using counter-mode and direct encryption alone, without using a memory authentication mechanism. We observe that counter-mode encryption, even with better latency hiding capabilities suffers 2× higher energy overheads than direct mode encryption. In particular, for memory intensive benchmarks counter-mode encryption results in even higher overheads (*mcf: 12% vs 4%, art: 8% vs 2% and swim: 5.5% vs 2.2%*).

In addition to counter-mode encryption having 2× higher energy overheads compared to direct encryption, counter-mode encryption requires the memory authentication mechanism for its security. More specifically, the security of counter mode encryption is contingent on the counters being fresh (unmodified and not replayed). This necessitates an authentication mechanism to be in place for the security of the encryption mechanism. Direct encryption, on the other hand, has no such limitation, it can be used independently of the authentication mechanism. There can be environments which do not have authentication requirements (i.e. active attacks are not possible) but only privacy needs to be guaranteed. For such environments using counter-mode encryption will result in unnecessary overheads, both from the encryption mechanism and the authentication mechanism needed to ensure its security.

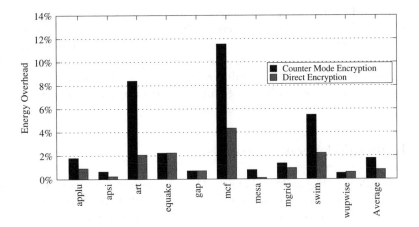

Fig. 11. Energy overhead for Direct vs Counter-mode Encryption

The above discussion would suggest using direct encryption in energy constrained environments instead of counter-mode encryption. However, direct encryption as discussed previously lies directly in the critical path of memory fetches and results in non-trivial performance overheads. Figure 12 shows the EDP for counter-mode encryption vs direct encryption. As shown in the figure, despite having lower energy overheads, direct encryption has a higher normalize EDP of 1.12 vs 1.02 compared to counter-mode encryption. Hence, neither counter-mode nor direct encryption offers the best balance in power and performance. This observation is the basis of our design for hybrid cryptographic engine discussed in Section 6.

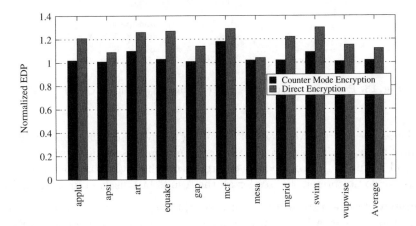

Fig. 12. Normalized Energy-Delay Product (EDP) for Counter-mode vs Direct Encryption

Recommendation: Use direct encryption for power-constrained environments, where power forms the first design constraint ahead of performance. Direct encryption not only has lower power overheads compared to counter-mode encryption, but also does not need the authentication mechanism for its security, thereby, further reducing the overall power overheads. For environments, where performance and power both are of equal importance, a hybrid cryptographic engine (described in Section 6) should be used.

5   Embedded Secure Processors

Embedded devices like mobile phones, PDAs etc. represent a category of devices increasingly used for computation and storage, but they also represent the category of devices that can easily be stolen or lost. This gives the attackers an increased opportunity to get physical access to the system and conduct hardware attacks to extract sensitive information off the system. Hence, hardware mechanisms for security assume even more importance for embedded devices. However, a majority of embedded systems are battery powered and naturally power constrained. In addition, the recent years have seen a significant growth in the computation requirements of embedded devices but the battery capacity has not scaled with the computation needs. Figure 13 shows this trend.

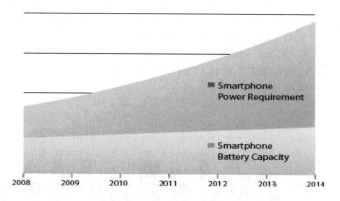

Fig. 13. Power Requirement vs Battery Capacity (Source: Quicklogic [32])

Hence, the energy overheads of providing hardware mechanisms for security assume a greater importance for such systems. In this section, we present our parallel evaluation for embedded environments, however, due to space limitations, we do not present figures for all the results but discuss our main findings.

Memory Authentication: As with general purpose systems, if counter-mode encryption is used with standard merkle tree, it results in much higher overheads $(4.57\times)$ compared to counter-mode encryption with BMTs. Figure 14 presents these results. Since, applications running on embedded systems are typically much smaller and much less memory intensive, the absolute energy overheads for provide hardware security mechanisms are much lower than for a general purpose processor. However, at the same time, embedded systems present environments where any energy overheads can pose showstopper issues causing, for example, degradation of battery life etc. Hence, even with small absolute values, it is critically important to minimize these overheads for embedded environments.

Recommendation: Even for embedded systems, BMTs must be used for memory integrity verification, similar to general purpose systems.

Memory Encryption: In terms of encryption mechanism, direct mode encryption in addition to saving energy (similar to general purpose processors), also does not result in any significant performance overheads for applications running on embedded processors. Figure 15 show the EDP for all the benchmarks simulated, normalized to a base system with no protection. As can be seen from the figure, direct encryption closely follows counter-mode encryption, with a worst case degradation of 2% in normalized EDP.

This is primarily due to the fact that embedded benchmarks are not memory intensive and hence suffer very few cache misses. Since encryption overheads are exposed only when blocks are loaded from memory, the low cache miss rate of embedded benchmarks ensures that direct encryption does not result in any significant performance overheads. We observe EDP for direct mode encryption and counter-mode encryption to be within 0.05% for all the embedded benchmarks we simulated.

Recommendation: For embedded systems, the application characteristics make direct encryption as the chosen mode for encryption, offering the best power-performance balance.

6 Power-Efficient Hybrid Cryptographic Engine

In this section, we describe the outline for a power-efficient cryptographic engine design. The design outlined here is based on the observation that direct encryption consumes less power when compared to counter-mode encryption. Also, in addition, direct encryption can avoid the overheads of a memory authentication mechanism for environments which do not need authentication. Counter-mode encryption on the other hand necessitates a memory authentication mechanism for its own security. Without an authentication mechanism that defends against replay attacks, the block counters used by counter-mode encryption to generate seeds (pads) can be replayed, resulting in pad reuse, thereby, breaking the security of counter-mode encryption. However, despite its power benefits, direct encryption can result in significant performance overheads, particularly for memory intensive applications. However, for applications that are compute intensive and do not miss much in the cache, direct encryption can result in potential power savings. Achieving the best power-performance balance necessitates alternating between the two modes of encryption. For memory-intensive applications (or phases), counter-mode encryption along with the authentication mechanism

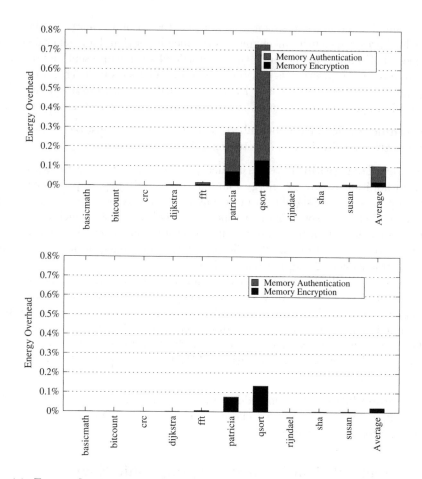

Fig. 14. Energy Overhead breakdown for Counter-mode Encryption with Standard Merkle Trees(a), and Bonsai Merkle Trees (b)

should be used. For compute-intensive applications (or phases), direct encryption can be used in isolation, if the environment does not need authentication.

Challenges: Designing such a *hybrid cryptographic engine* poses interesting challenges. One, in order to switch between the two encryption modes, on-chip circuitry is needed to establish whether an application (or phase) is memory intensive or not. To this end, one could envisage designing a miss rate monitoring system which keeps track of the number of cache accesses and cache misses, to calculate a running miss rate for the system. However, we observed that the miss rate does not directly correlate to energy overheads, for example, the correlation coefficient for miss rate and the energy overheads of counter-mode encryption is rather low at 0.43, which implies that miss rate cannot directly be used as an indicator to switch the encryption mode for the hybrid cryptographic engine. We observe that Misses-per-Instruction (MPI) correlates extremely well with

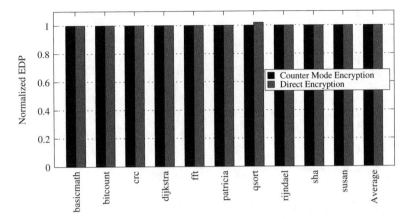

Fig. 15. Normalized Energy-Delay Product (EDP) for Counter-mode vs Direct Encryption

the energy overheads, with the correlation coefficient between MPI and counter-mode encryption energy overheads being 0.984. Hence, MPI can serve as a good input to the hybrid cryptographic engine. To this end, we introduce a low cost and reliable MPI Monitoring System (MMS). Our MMS requires two counters to keep track of the number of retired instructions, and cache misses[1]. Each counter is 4 bytes in size. Therefore, our MMS requires a total storage overhead of 8 bytes. The hybrid cryptographic engine uses direct encryption by default due to its lower energy overheads. However, to keep the performance overheads low as well, MMS keeps track of the MPI and when the MPI exceeds a certain threshold, X, it switches the cryptographic engine to use counter-mode encryption. The value of X, can be decided based on the characterization of the workloads that are expected to run on the system. The value of X also depends on the primary goal (minimum power overheads or minimum performance overheads) of the system. Figure 16 plots the MPI and the energy overheads of counter-mode encryption and direct encryption for the SPEC2000 benchmark suit. If for example, the *security energy budget* for the system is fixed at 4%, then fixing the MPI at 0.07 would ensure that the energy overheads are always lower than 4% as the engine would always use direct encryption which suffers less than 4% overheads for all the benchmarks. A similar (but more involved) analysis can be done to fix the value of X, if performance is to be factored in as well in the overall goals of the system.

As another challenge, the main memory will now store blocks that have been encrypted using either counter-mode or direct encryption. When a block is loaded from the main memory, it is necessary to identify the mechanism used for its encryption, so it can be decrypted correctly. To this end, we propose tagging

---

[1] Note that these counters might already be available as hardware performance counters, thereby eliminating the need for maintaining additional counters.

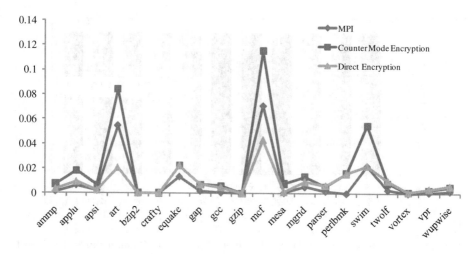

Fig. 16. Determining the value of X

the main memory blocks with a single bit, the *counter-mode encrypted bit*. This bit is set when a block is evicted off the processor chip and the cryptographic engine used counter-mode encryption to encrypt it. Our hybrid cryptographic design is show in Figure 17.

Qualitative Analysis of Hybrid Cryptographic Engine: The hybrid cryptographic engine outlined will add complexity in terms of extra on-chip circuitry to switch between the two cryptographic modes of encryption. However, the additional circuitry needed to switch between the two modes can be as simple as division circuitry to calculate the current MPI of the system (MMS), using the two 4-byte counters that we introduced, which is then fed to a comparator to determine the mode of encryption to be used. The core of the cryptographic engine, however, needs no modifications. Lets assume that AES is used as the encryption algorithm. For a secure processor substrate using direct encryption, the on-chip cryptographic hardware will consist of an AES engine to which the data blocks are fed for encryption/decryption as they move off and on the processor chip. On the other hand, for a secure processor substrate using counter-mode encryption, the on-chip cryptographic hardware will still consist of an AES engine. However, in this case, instead of feeding the data block directly, the seed associated with the data block is fed to the AES engine to generate a cryptographic pad which is then XORed with the data block to encrypt/decrypt it. Hence, the proposed hybrid cryptographic engine, using both direct and counter-mode encryption, does not add any additional cryptographic hardware. The simple MMS circuit introduced will determine whether to feed the seed associated with the block to generate a cryptographic pad (for counter-mode encryption) or to feed the data block directly (for direct encryption).

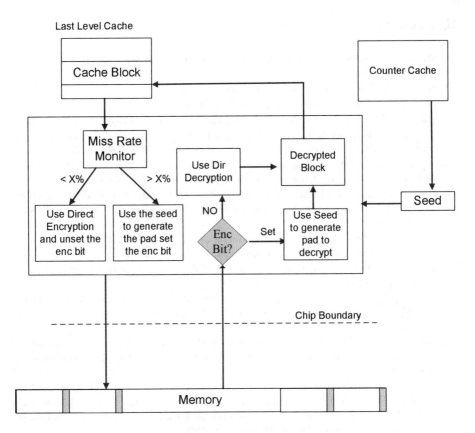

Fig. 17. Power-Efficient Hybrid Cryptographic Engine

We believe that our hybrid cryptographic engine will reap the power benefits of using direct encryption and at the same time ensure that applications do not suffer any major performance penalties by switching to counter-mode encryption, when need be. A quantitative evaluation of the proposed cryptographic engine is left as future work.

7   Conclusion

Secure processor architectures have been proposed to defend against hardware attacks. While previous works have concentrated on resolving the performance, storage and system-level issues of secure processor architectures, power issues have largely been ignored. In this paper, we evaluated the sources of power in currently proposed secure processor mechanisms. We analyzed the power overheads of various hardware security mechanisms for general purpose as well as embedded systems. Finally, we outlined the design of a hybrid cryptographic engine that has been designed with the primary goal of minimizing power overheads, but at the same time ensuring an insignificant loss in performance.

References

1. Huang, A.: Hacking the Xbox: An Introduction to Reverse Engineering. No Starch Press, San Francisco (2003)
2. Kumar, A.: Discovering Passwords in Memory (2004),
   http://www.infosec-writers.com/text_resources/
3. Gassend, B., Suh, G., Clarke, D., Dijk, M., Devadas, S.: Caches and Hash Trees for Efficient Memory Integrity Verification. In: Proc. of the 9th International Symposium on High Performance Computer Architecture, HPCA-9 (2003)
4. Gilmont, T., Legat, J.D., Quisquater, J.J.: Enhancing the Security in the Memory Management Unit. In: Proc. of the 25th EuroMicro Conference (1999)
5. Lie, D., Mitchell, J., Thekkath, C., Horowitz, M.: Specifying and Verifying Hardware for Tamper-Resistant Software. In: IEEE Symposium on Security and Privacy (2003)
6. Lie, D., Thekkath, C., Mitchell, M., Lincoln, P., Boneh, D., MItchell, J., Horowitz, M.: Architectural Support for Copy and Tamper Resistant Software. In: Proc. of the 9th International Conference on Architectural Support for Programming Languages and Operating Systems (2000)
7. Rogers, B., Solihin, Y., Prvulovic, M.: Efficient data protection for distributed shared memory multiprocessors. In: International Conference on Parallel Architectures and Compilation Techniques (2006)
8. Shi, W., Lee, H.H.: Authentication Control Point and Its Implications for Secure Processor Design. In: Proc. of the 39th Annual International Symposium on Microarchitecture (2006)
9. Shi, W., Lee, H.H., Ghosh, M., Lu, C.: Architectural Support for High Speed Protection of Memory Integrity and Confidentiality in Multiprocessor Systems. In: Proceedings of the International Conference on Parallel Architectures and Compilation Techniques, pp. 123–134 (September 2004)
10. Shi, W., Lee, H.H., Ghosh, M., Lu, C., Boldyreva, A.: High Efficiency Counter Mode Security Architecture via Prediction and Precomputation. In: Proceedings of the 32nd International Symposium on Computer Architecture (June 2005)
11. Shi, W., Lee, H.H., Lu, C., Ghosh, M.: Towards the Issues in Architectural Support for Protection of Software Execution. In: Proceedings of the Workshop on Architectureal Support for Security and Anti-virus, pp. 1–10 (October 2004)
12. Suh, G., Clarke, D., Gassend, B., van Dijk, M., Devadas, S.: Efficient Memory Integrity Verification and Encryption for Secure Processor. In: Proc. of the 36th Annual International Symposium on Microarchitecture (2003)
13. Yan, C., Rogers, B., Englender, D., Solihin, Y., Prvulovic, M.: Improving cost, performance, and security of memory encryption and authentication. In: Proc. of the International Symposium on Computer Architecture (2006)
14. Yang, J., Zhang, Y., Gao, L.: Fast Secure Processor for Inhibiting Software Piracy and Tampering. In: Proc. of the 36th Annual International Symposium on Microarchitecture (2003)
15. Zhang, Y., Gao, L., Yang, J., Zhang, X., Gupta, R.: SENSS: Security Enhancement to Symmetric Shared Memory Multiprocessors. In: International Symposium on High-Performance Computer Architecture (February 2005)
16. Chhabra, S., Rogers, B., Solihin, Y., Prvulovic, M.: Making secure processors os- and performance-friendly. ACM Transactions on Architecture and Code Optimization 5(4), 1–35 (2009)

17. Chhabra, S., Rogers, B., Solihin, Y.: SHIELDSTRAP: Making Secure Processors Truly Secure. In: ICCD (2009)
18. NIST: Cryptographic hash algorithm competition (2008), http://csrc.nist.gov/groups/ST/hash/sha-3/index.html
19. Stajano, F., Anderson, R.: The resurrecting duckling: Security issues for ubiquitous computing (supplement to computer magazine). Computer 35, 22–26 (2002)
20. Rogers, B., Chhabra, S., Solihin, Y., Prvulovic, M.: Using Address Independent Seed Encryption and Bonsai Merkle Trees to Make Secure Processors OS- and Performance-Friendly. In: Proc. of the 36th Annual International Symposium on Microarchitecture (2007)
21. Renau, J., et al.: SESC (2004), http://sesc.sourceforge.net
22. Brooks, D., Tiwari, V., Martonosi, M.: Wattch: a framework for architectural-level power analysis and optimizations. In: Proceedings of the 27th Annual International Symposium on Computer Architecture, ISCA 2000, pp. 83–94. ACM, New York (2000)
23. FIPS Publication 197: Specification for the Advanced Encryption Standard (AES). National Institute of Standards and Technology, Federal Information Processing Standards (2001)
24. Kgil, T., Falk, L., Mudge, T.: ChipLock: Support for Secure Microarchitectures. In: Proceedings of the Workshop on Architectural Support for Security and Anti-Virus (WASSA) (October 2004)
25. http://infocenter.arm.com/help/index.jsp?topic=/com.arm.doc.ddi0344c/index.html
26. Standard Performance Evaluation Corporation (2004), http://www.spec.org
27. http://www.eecs.umich.edu/mibench/ (2001)
28. Barroso, L.A., Gharachorloo, K., McNamara, R., Nowatzyk, A., Qadeer, S., Sano, B., Smith, S., Stets, R., Verghese, B.: Piranha: A scalable architecture based on single-chip multiprocessing. In: Proc. of the 27th International Symposium on Computer Architecture, pp. 282–293. ACM, New York (2000)
29. Mowry, T.C., Lam, M.S., Gupta, A.: Design and Evaluation of a Compiler Algorithm for Prefetching. In: 5th Intl. Conf. on Architectural Support for Programming Languages and Operating Systems (1992)
30. Sinharoy, B., Kalla, R.N., Tendler, J.M., Eickemeyer, R.J., Joyner, J.B.: Power5 system microarchitecture. IBM Journal of Research and Development 49(4/5), 505–521 (2005)
31. CNET: Power could cost more than servers, Google warns, http://news.cnet.com/Power-could-cost-more-than-servers,-Google-warns/2100-1010_3-5988090.html
32. Quicklogic: Display Power Optimizer (2008), http://www.quicklogic.com/display-power-optimizer-dpo-overview/

A New Peer-to-Peer Micropayment Protocol Based on Transferable Debt Token[*]

Sung-Ming Yen, Kuo-Zhe Chiou, Je Zhang, and Po-Han Lee

Laboratory of Cryptography and Information Security (LCIS),
Dept. of Computer Science and Information Engineering,
National Central University, Chung-Li, Taiwan 320, R.O.C.
{yensm,kzchiou,975202056,975202082}@csie.ncu.edu.tw

Abstract. A peer-to-peer (P2P) micropayment can support practical applications that typical micropayment protocols being difficult to achieve, and has received attention recently. However, existing P2P micropayment schemes, e.g., PPay and OFPPay, may suffer from either computational overhead of frequent digital signature signing and verification, or maintenance overhead of the holder path of P2P micropayment coins. In order to overcome the aforementioned disadvantages, we propose a new P2P micropayment scheme based on the idea of transferable debt token.

Keywords: Electronic payment, Micropayment, Peer-to-peer micropayment, Transferable coin.

1 Introduction

In recent years, peer-to-peer (P2P) network has become a popular medium to share the peers' resource for information spread and collection [16]. A major problem of P2P network is free-riding [1] which makes a peer enjoy much more than contribute information and resource to the network. One possible solution [3] against the free-riding problem is to employ P2P micropayment to encourage peers to balance what they take from with what they contribute to the system.

In a typical micropayment scheme, such as Millicent [2,7] and PayWord [8,9], some users serve just as a vendor and the others only play the role of a buyer. A buyer pays coins of small denominations (e.g., ten cents or one dollar) to a vendor for purchasing, and finally the vendor will deposit the coins to the broker, instead of spending them directly. The overhead of frequent withdrawal and deposit of a large amount of coins, each of an extremely small denomination, makes the application of typical micropayment schemes for P2P environment be impractical. P2P micropayment schemes [4,12,14] were therefore proposed to reflect the new requirement. A typical P2P micropayment scheme assumes that transactions occur frequently and the peers are often online. Most importantly,

---

[*] This study is conducted under the "Wireless Broadband Communications Technology and Application Project" of the Institute for Information Industry which is subsidized by the Ministry of Economy Affairs of the Republic of China.

M.L. Gavrilova et al. (Eds.): Trans. on Comput. Sci. X, LNCS 6340, pp. 352–363, 2010.

each peer can play both the roles of a vendor as well as a buyer, and a token (or coin) can be used repeatedly in many transactions. The aforementioned P2P micropayment schemes tried to reduce the overhead of the broker, while any transaction fraud such as double-spending should be detected and misbehaving peers should be identified.

The PPay scheme [14] is a pioneering work of P2P micropayment in which the concept of floating and self-managed currency is proposed to reduce the broker's involvement. The coin owner has to record and maintain all the transaction information of each coin instead. However, if the coin owner is offline, the broker needs to take over the payment procedure.

Motivated by the work of [14], various P2P micropayment schemes have been proposed. Zou *et al.* presented a P2P micropayment scheme, namely CPay [15], in which the coins can only be withdrawn by specified peers who equip with enough bandwidth and computational capability. In other words, these peers with good resource will be selected by the broker to distribute and manage the coins.

The WhoPay scheme [13] is constructed based on the PPay scheme and group signatures to achieve anonymity property such that the identity of each peer (except the coin owner) can be concealed even if the coin is deposited. However, the coin owner in the WhoPay suffers from high computational cost and storage space requirement due to group signatures.

Unlike the PPay scheme, Liu *et al.* [5,6] proposed different approaches to manage the transaction records. In [6], the coin withdrawer needs to prepare all the transaction records in advance and to distribute them to a specified peer group. Due to this design, the withdrawers need not to participate in each transaction but they suffer from high computational cost because of the heavy load of preparing the transaction records. In contrast to [6], the transaction records (called the *holderpath*) of the scheme in [5] (namely the OFPPay scheme in this paper) are managed by each peer. When a transaction is issued, the holderpath along with the coin will be transferred from the current coin holder to the next peer and it will be updated with a new signature on new transaction information signed by the new coin holder. The broker eventually receives the holderpath when the coin is deposited. In case of coin fraud, the broker can identify the malicious peers by verifying the holderpath.

The WAT scheme [10] and the i-WAT scheme [11] present a different idea to construct a P2P micropayment which allows each peer to create his own token and to become the token owner. When an owner purchases service from another peer, the token will be transferred to that peer (called the token holder). Clearly, the major problem of these two schemes is security risk due to the lack of central authority, such as a broker or a judge, to manage the currency.

The contributions of this paper. PPay and OFPPay are two representative P2P micropayment schemes. In the PPay scheme, some peers might have limited storage space and this will discourage those peers to be a coin owner due to the storage overhead. A peer in the OFPPay scheme who involved in a later transaction suffers from a heavy computational overhead to verify a longer holderpath. Cryptanalysis on the above two schemes will be provided in this paper. The PPay scheme is vulnerable to a replay attack by which a malicious peer can cheat other peers by replaying the assigned coin. Two or more malicious peers of the OFPPay scheme can conspire and disable the broker to identify the dishonest peers. Possible countermeasure and improvement have also been proposed in this paper.

A new P2P micropayment scheme is proposed in this paper by exploiting an idea of debt token. This debt token based P2P micropayment scheme is secure against double spending and can overcome the aforementioned disadvantages. A token owner only needs to involve in the first transaction and, unlike OFPPay, the computational cost of signature verification is constant.

The rest of this paper is organized as follows. Section 2 reviews the PPay scheme and then points out a replay attack as well as an improved PPay scheme. Section 3 reviews the OFPPay scheme and shows a collusion attack followed by a possible countermeasure. Subsequently, Section 4 proposes a new P2P micropayment scheme and provides the security analysis and performance comparison. Finally, Section 5 concludes the paper.

2   Attack on the PPay Scheme

2.1   Review of the PPay Scheme

The PPay scheme [14] allows a coin to be transferred from one peer to another one without the involvement of the centralized broker B. In PPay, the peer U withdraws coins from the broker, and at the same time becomes the owner and the holder of the coins. The peer U can pay a coin to another peer, say P_1, and P_1 now becomes the current holder of the coin while U is still the owner. If P_1 wants to trade with another peer P_2, he can transfer the coin via U. After the transaction, the current holder of the coin will be P_2 and U remains to be the owner. The peer P_2 can further transfer the coin to others until certain holder deposits the coin. The following provides the details of PPay.

To proceed a transaction, the peer U purchases a coin C from the broker in advance and the coin C is formed as follows

$$C = Sig_B(U, sn)$$

where sn is a unique sequence number. $Sig_B(U, sn)$ is a signature on message U and sn signed by the broker with the private key SK_B. Note that the signature indicates that the owner of this coin is U. If U wants to pay another peer P_1, the coin C will be sent to P_1 via the following format:

$$A_{U,P_1} = Sig_U(P_1, C, seq_1)$$

where seq_1 is a sequence number maintained by U. The sequence number is increased each time when the coin is transferred. This signature serves as a proof that P_1 is the current holder of the coin.

If P_1 wants to pay this coin to the peer P_2, and then P_1 has to issue the following reassignment request to the coin owner U

$$R_{U,P_1,P_2} = Sig_{P_1}(P_2, A_{U,P_1}).$$

The coin owner U will store this request in case of any potential dispute and sends P_1 as well as P_2 a new format of the coin as

$$A_{U,P_2} = Sig_U(P_2, C, seq_2).$$

This new format of the coin reveals that the current holder is P_2. Each subsequent coin holder P_i follows the above procedure for transactions. Finally, a certain coin holder P_n can deposit the coin to the broker by providing $A_{U,P_n} = Sig_U(P_n, C, seq_n)$.

If U is offline, the current holder of the coin can issue another coin that he holds from another owner, or the broker must involve the transaction on behalf of U to perform a similar process. Once U is online, the broker sends him the record of the transaction for some further processing. After all, the owner of the coin is required to be online and has to record each transaction which consists of two signatures, the coin itself and the request signature. Therefore, in PPay a double spending by a misbehaving peer can be easily detected and traced.

2.2 A Replay Attack on PPay

Without loss of generality, suppose that U is the owner of the coin C and P_1 is a malicious peer. We assume that the malicious peer is able to wiretap or to intercept communication of a specific peer to whom transactions have ever been made. After P_1 has completed a transaction with another peer P_2, both of them will receive a newly assigned coin $A_{U,P_2} = Sig_U(P_2, C, seq_2)$ from the owner U. The attacker P_1 starts wiretapping P_2 until P_2 spends A_{U,P_2} somewhere, and then P_1 can make another transaction with P_2 by intercepting the communication between P_2 and U, impersonating U, and replaying the old assigned coin A_{U,P_2}. According to the design of PPay, P_2 does not store any coin information after spending a coin, he will accept the validity of A_{U,P_2}.

Therefore, P_1 can spend the coin twice successfully while U will refuse P_2 to spend it because seq_2 is invalid. The double spending committed by P_1 will not be detected since P_1 only sends the reassignment request to U once and P_2 cannot prove that P_1 had traded with him twice.

2.3 A Countermeasure against the Attack on PPay

The primary reason to enable the above replay attack is that the victim P_2 cannot check the freshness of the coin. A simple solution against the attack is to include a time stamp to the new formated coin, but this requires a well developed time synchronization service. An alternative solution is designed in the following based on the technique of challenge-response and a redirected information flow of the PPay.

When P_1 pays a coin to P_2, P_1 sends the reassignment request $R_{U,P_1,P_2} = Sig_{P_1}(P_2, A_{U,P_1})$ to P_2 instead of U. After verifying the validity of R_{U,P_1,P_2}, P_2 forwards the request as well as a random number r (called a nonce) to U. If the reassignment request is correct, U records $\{R_{U,P_1,P_2}, r\}$ and responds P_2 a new formated coin as

$$A_{U,P_2} = Sig_U(P_2, C, seq_2, r).$$

The freshness of A_{U,P_2} can be verified by P_2 due to the usage of a nonce r. The improved PPay is therefore secure against the proposed replay attack while the signature size is slightly enlarged because of involvement of the nonce r.

3   Weakness of the OFPPay Scheme

3.1   Review of the OFPPay Protocol

Y. Liu [5] proposed two peer-to-peer micropayment schemes. The first one is the basic construction (OFPPay) which imports a concept of holderpath to manage the transferable token. In consideration of the fair exchange, the extension of the basic construction is proposed. In order to introduce the proposed attacks and our attack does not concern the issue of fair exchange, this section only introduces the basic construction as follows.

To purchases a token $Token$ from the broker, the peer P_0 sends the following digital note, $DigitalNote$, to the broker

$$DigitalNote = \{SN, GID, BID, value, IssueDate, Expiration\},$$

where SN is an unique serial number, GID is the peer-to-peer group identifier, BID is the broker's identity, $value$ indicates the amount of money, $IssueDate$ denotes the issuing date, and $Expiration$ is the expiration date. The broker deducts $value$ from P_0's account and returns his signature $BrokerStamp = Sig_B(DigitalNote)$ to P_0. Then, P_0 generates the token $Token$ and a initial holderpath $holderpath_0$ which are formed as

$$Token = \{DigitalNote, BrokerStamp\},$$

$$holderpath_0 = Sig_{P_0}(DigitalNote).$$

Without loss of generality, support that the current holder of the token is P_i who wants to pay it to another peer, P_{i+1}, the following payment protocol will be performed.

1. $P_i \rightarrow P_{i+1} : P_i, DigitalNote, holderpath_i,$
2. $P_{i+1} \rightarrow P_i : Sig_{P_{i+1}}(P_i, DigitalNote),$
3. $P_i \rightarrow P_{i+1} : BrokerStamp, Sig_{P_i}(DigitalNote, P_i, P_{i+1}),$
4. $P_{i+1} : holderpath_{i+1} = Sig_{P_{i+1}}(holderpath_i, P_i)$

After the payment, P_{i+1} becomes the current holder of the token $Token$.

Any holder can deposit the token $Token$ to the broker by sending it and the corresponding holderpath. If the verification on the holderpath and the token is valid, the broker credits money to the holder's account.

In case of double spending, the broker will receive two different holderpaths with the same $Token$. By verifying these two holderpaths, the broker can identify the malicious peer.

3.2   The Collusion Attack on OFPPay

This section points out the OFPPay scheme is vulneratle to the proposed collusion attack. If two malicious peers are conspired, they can re-generate a new holderpath and spend tokens illegitimately.

Assume that the two malicious peers are P_1 and P_2. U is the token owner and his initial holderpath is

$$holderpath_U = Sig_U(DigitalNote).$$

When P_1 is the current holder of the token, he sends $BrokerStamp$ and $holderpath_{P_1}\}$ to P_2, and then P_2 can create a new initial holderpath formed as

$$holderpath_{P_2} = Sig_{P_2}(DigitalNote).$$

Note that the $DigitalNote$ in $holderpath_U$ is the same as that in $holderpath_{P_2}$. Therefore, P_1 can pay the token to other peers with $holderpath_{P_1}$ while P_2 can spend the same token with $holderpath_{P_2}$ to other peers. This result leads to that the broker can not identify who the correct withdrawer is.

3.3   A Countermeasure against the Attack on OFPPay

Because the forged initial holderpath is generated after the real initial holderpath, one of trivial solutions is to attach time stamp to the initial holderpath so that the broker can identify the real withdrawer by checking time stamp. However, this solution must ask the time in the scheme to be synchronized.

Another solution is to bind the identity of the coin withdrawer to $DigitalNote$ so that the broker can easily identify who is the owner of the coin by verifying $BrokerStamp$.

4   The Proposed Peer-to-Peer Micropayment Based on Transferable Debt Token

In the real life, Alice might want to buy a drink but she does not have money. So, Alice borrows money from her friend Bob and promises she will redeem her debt later. But before Alice redeems her debt, a similar story occurs again and this time Charles borrows money from Alice. To simplify matters, Alice may ask Charles to return the money back to Bob on behalf of her.

Motivated by the above scenario, we present a new concept of transferable debt token and use it to construct a new peer-to-peer micropayment scheme. A debt token indicates that the holder of the token is responsible for redeeming the debt. Initially, the debt token is ceated by a peer, called debt token owner. When another peer purchase from him, he issues the token to the peer, and then the token will be transferred across peers for payment. Finally, the peer who is the last token holder has to pay back the money to the owner.

The proposed idea is different from the typical transferable token. A transferable token used in the P2P micropayment schemes usually presents an e-coin or a commitment, the last token holder therefore can deposit it for money. However, the proposed transferable debt token in which *debt token* is emphasized that the token itself is a debt. The peer who is the last debt token holder has to redeem this debt. The result is that both kinds of token are of different purposes.

4.1   Protocol Description

The proposed scheme contains peers denoted by P_i and a broker denoted by B, and three procedures including Registration, Payment, and Redeeming. Each peer P has his own public key pair (pk_P, sk_P) and the broker, who is trustworthy in our scheme, has the public key pair (pk_B, sk_B) as well. A function $Sig_E(m)$ indicates a signature on message m under the party E's private key sk_E.

Registration: Registration procedure requires that each peer has to register his personal information (e.g., his name, address, and phone number) and an account at the broker and deposit fixed amount of money in his account in advance. Once the broker finds that the peer has any misconduct, he can deduct the money from the peer's account. Because of this strategy, the loss of the bank can be reduced.

Payment: Suppose that a peer P_0 serves as a vendor, he creates a debt token $DToken_{P_0}$ formed as

$$DToken_{P_0} = Sig_{P_0}\{ID_{P_0}, sn, Expiration\},$$

where ID_{P_0} is the identity of P_0, $Expiration$ is the expiration date of the token, and sn is a sequence number selected by P_0. This token indicates that P_0 is the owner and the token should be redeemed before $Expiration$. For different transactions, P_0 selects different sn to issue debt tokens and at the same time he is the owner as well as the holder of the debt token.

To generally describe the proposed payment protocol, we assume that the peer P_i is the current holder of the debt token, and another peer P_{i+1} purchases services from P_i. They do the following payment procedure.

1. $P_i \to P_{i+1} : ID_{P_i}, DToken_{P_0}$,
2. $P_{i+1} \to P_i : Com_{P_{i+1}} = Sig_{P_{i+1}}(DToken_{P_0}, ID_{P_i}, TimeStamp)$,

where $TimeStamp$ denotes the time stamp of the commitment. After verifying the commitment $Com_{P_{i+1}}$, P_i provides his services to P_{i+1} and P_{i+1} becomes the current holder of the debt token.

Redeeming: Let P_n be the last holder of the debt token $DToken_{P_0}$ and P_n has to redeem $DToken_{P_0}$ to the broker. He sends a redeeming request Red_{P_n} which is constructed as follows:

$$Red_{P_n} = Sig_{P_n}\{DToken_{P_0}, Info\},$$

where $Info$ is the necessary information of the redeeming request (e.g., redeeming time). The broker verifies Red_{P_n} and $DToken_{P_0}$ by using P_n's public key pk_{P_n} and P_0's public key pk_{P_0}, respectively. If the verification is valid, the broker credits money from P_n's account to P_0's, and then returns a redeeming proof $RPrf_{P_n} = Sig_B(\text{"}P_n \text{ has redeemed"}, DToken_{P_0})$ to P_n. Finally, the broker sends a notice to P_0.

If the debt token is overdue and no peer redeems it, the debt token owner asks the broker to identify the last holder of the debt token by providing $DToken_{P_0}$ and Com_{P_1}. The broker will ask each peer Pi, who was the debt token holder, to prove that he is not the last token holder by providing $Com_{P_{i+1}}$. Once a certain peer cannot give any commitment, he will be identified as a dishonest peer and punished by the broker.

Note that the broker should store the redeeming request until it is expired. If the broker receives two redeeming requests with the same debt token (their sn are the same), the broker should refuses the second request because one debt token should be only issued for one transaction by the token owner.

4.2   Security Analysis

In the typical P2P micropayment schemes, double-spending is one of the most concerned security issues [5,14]. This section therefore shows that the proposed scheme is secure against double spending. Moreover, this section also states that the proposed scheme can identify the malicious peers who do not redeem their debt even if there is a conspirator.

Claim 1. The peer who spends the same debt token twice in two different payments will not gain any additional advantage. Therefore, double-spending is unprofitable in our scheme.

In the proposed scheme, the debt token floats from the vendor peer to the buyer peer, the double-spending therefore denotes that a vendor peer transfers the same debt token to other buyer peers in two different payments.

Recall that, in the proposed scheme, the last debt token holder has to redeem it to the token owner. If a certain token holder transfers the same debt token twice, he has to provide two services to buyer peers but the money will be credited to the token owner. On the other hand, if the token owner issues the same token twice, the broker will refuse the second redeeming request.

If the redeeming procedure is changed to that the broker will process all of received redeeming requests, the double spender still obtains nothing. If the owner transfers the token twice, he also has to provide his services twice. Moreover, no vender peers (except the owner of the token) will cause double-spending because he has to provide more services without getting additional advantages.

Therefore, the double-spending is unprofitable in the proposed scheme.

Claim 2. If the peer who is the last holder of the debt token does not redeem the token, the broker can identify him, even if there exists a conspirator to help the peer to avoid redeeming.

In the proposed scheme, when the debt token is expired but no one redeems it, the token owner will ask the broker to trace the malicious peer. Each peer who was the token holder ever has to provide the commitment to prove that he is not the last token holder. Otherwise, he will be punished by the broker.

Assume that the transferred path of a debt token is $\{P_1, P_2, P_3\}$, and P_3 is the current token holder. When a new payment is made between P_1 and P_3, P_1 becomes the current holder again. If no one redeems the token, P_1 may try to cheat the broker that he is not the last token holder by sending the commitment Com_{P_2} again after P_3 shows Com_{P_1} to the broker. Since each commitment contains $TimeStamp$, the broker can know Com_{P_2} is generated before Com_{P_1} and identifies P_1 as a cheater.

4.3   Performance Analysis

PPay and OFPPay are two representative peer-to-peer micropayment schemes. Because the other literatures mentioned in this paper concern other additional issues, their schemes are more complicated than PPay and OFPPay. Moreover, the performance of the proposed improvement in Section 2 and Section 3 are almost the same as their original schemes, respectively. Therefore, this section will only present the efficiency comparison of PPay, OFPPay, and our scheme (called Ours in the following). The following comparison is made under the assumption that only one coin (or token) is issued by its owner, and it is transferred through n peers (called holders).

Computational cost analysis: Table 1 is the performance comparison of PPay, OFPPay, and Ours under the assumption that no fraud occurs. The symbols s and v indicate the computational cost of signature generation and signature verification, respectively. The discussion of the computational cost of the broker, the token owner, and the token holder in the three schemes is given as follows. First and foremost, the second column in Table 1 presents the computational cost of the broker. In the PPay scheme, the computational cost of the broker is $s + 2v$ because of one signature generation operation of withdrawal and two signature verification operations of deposit. Similarly, the cost of the broker in the OFPPay scheme and Ours are $s + (n + 2)v$ and $2v$, respectively.

For evaluating the computational cost of the token owner, we treat the withdrawer of OFPPay as the token owner and show the result in the third column. The last column states the computational cost of *each* holder. The length of holderpath in the OFPPay scheme is increased each time the token is transferred, therefore, the cost of each holder is $((n+1)(n+2)v)/2n$ for verifying the holderpath on average. To sum up, the above comparison result shows that the proposed scheme is more efficient than PPay and OFPPay.

Table 1. Computational cost comparison of the three P2P micropayment schemes

Comput. cost	Broker	Owner	Holder
PPay	$s+2v$	$n(s+v)$	$s+3v$
OFPPay	$s+(n+2)v$	$2s+2v$	$3(s+v)+((n+1)(n+2)v)/2n$
Ours	$2v$	$s+v$	$s+v$

Storage requirement: To have a fair comparison of storage requirement among the three schemes, we assume that a standard digital signature will be used in all the schemes and $|S|$ denotes the size of a signature. In the PPay scheme, a coin owner has to store the coin as well as all related transaction information each of which consists of two signatures, a reassignment request signature and an assignment signature. The information maintained by the coin owner will eventually be provided to the broker, and therefore both the owner and the broker in PPay require a storage space of size $(2n+1)|S|$. On the other hand, all other peers have nothing to store. In the OFPPay scheme, the last coin holder has to store *BrokerStamp* and also a holderpath, and totally a storage space of size $(n+2)|S|$ is necessary. All other peers including the coin owner need not to store anything. In the proposed scheme, it is obvious that the storage requirement for the broker, the coin owner, and each holder is only $|S|$. In both the PPay and the OFPPay schemes, storage overhead of the broker is increased linearly in the number of transactions. The proposed scheme however can decrease the heavy burden of the broker.

Cost of tracing malicious peers: In case of coin fraud, the broker is in charge of tracing the malicious peers. In the PPay scheme, the broker has to verify all the transaction information to determine who the cheater is. In the OFPPay scheme, the broker identifies the cheater by verifying the holderpath which is composed of a list of signatures. In the proposed scheme, each peer once holding the fraud debt token will be requested by the broker to provide a commitment to prove that he is not the last holder. Communication overhead of performing tracing malicious peers would be slightly larger than in the other two schemes. However, tracing coin fraud is of a rare case in all the schemes and will not be a real burden of the proposed scheme. In case a certain peer has left the system and just acting as the last token holder, the loss of the system is small since we consider a micropayment scenario.

5 Conclusions

This paper points out that both the PPay and the OFPPay peer-to-peer micropayment schemes are vulnerable to double spending by presenting a replay attack and a collusion attack against them, respectively. Possible countermeasure and improvement have also been proposed in this paper.

Moreover, a new peer-to-peer micropayment scheme is proposed by exploiting an idea of transferable debt token. Security analysis shows that the proposed scheme is secure against double spending. In addition, performance analysis explains that the proposed scheme is superior to the PPay scheme and the OFPPay scheme.

Acknowledgment

We would like to thank all the anonymous referees for their useful comments and suggestions.

References

1. Adar, E., Huberman, B.A.: Free riding on Gnutella. First Monday 5(10) (2000)
2. Glassmann, S., Manasse, M., Abadi, M., Gauthier, P., Sobalvarro, P.: The Millicent protocol for inexpensive electronic commerce. In: Proc. of 4th International World Wide Web Conference, pp. 603–618 (1995)
3. Golle, P., Leyton-Brown, K., Ilya, M.: Incentives for sharing in peer-to-peer networks. In: Proc. of the 3rd ACM Conference on Electronic Commerce, pp. 264–267 (2001)
4. Horne, B., Pinkas, B., Sander, T.: Escrow services and incentives in peer-to-peer networks. In: Proc. of the 3rd ACM Conference on Electronic Commerce, pp. 85–94 (2001)
5. Liu, Y.: An optimistic fair peer-to-peer payment system. In: Proc. of IEEE International Conference on Management Science and Engineering 2007, ICMSE 2007, pp. 228–233 (2007)
6. Liu, Y., Fu, J., Zhang, H.: An optimistic fair protocol for p2p chained transaction. In: Grumbach, S., Sui, L., Vianu, V. (eds.) ASIAN 2005. LNCS, vol. 3818, pp. 136–145. Springer, Heidelberg (2005)
7. Manasse, M.: The Millicent protocols for electronic commerce. In: Proc. of 1st USENIX Workshop on Electronic Commerce, New York, pp. 11–12 (1995)
8. Micali, S., Rivest, R.L.: Micropayments revisited. In: Preneel, B. (ed.) CT-RSA 2002. LNCS, vol. 2271, pp. 149–163. Springer, Heidelberg (2002)
9. Rivest, R.L., Shamir, A.: PayWord and MicroMint: Two simple micropayment schemes. In: Lomas, M. (ed.) Security Protocols 1996. LNCS, vol. 1189, pp. 69–87. Springer, Heidelberg (1997); (Also in CryptoBytes. Pressed by RSA Laboratories, vol.2(1), pp. 7–11 (1996))
10. Saito, K.: Peer-to-peer money: Free currency over the Internet. In: Chung, C.-W., Kim, C.-k., Kim, W., Ling, T.-W., Song, K.-H. (eds.) HSI 2003. LNCS, vol. 2713, pp. 404–414. Springer, Heidelberg (2003)

11. Saito, K., Morino, E., Murai, J.: Fair trading of information: A proposal for the economics of peer-to-peer systems. In: Proc. of the First International Conference on Availability, Reliability and Security, ARES 2006, pp. 764–771 (2006)

12. Steinmetz, R., Wehrle, K. (eds.): Peer-to-Peer Systems and Applications. LNCS, vol. 3485. Springer, Heidelberg (2005)

13. Wei, K., Chen, Y.-F., Smith, A.J., Vo, B.: WhoPay: A scalable and anonymous payment system for peer-to-peer environments. In: Proc. of the 26th IEEE International Conference on Distributed Computing Systems, ICDCS 2006, pp. 13–22 (2006)

14. Yang, B., Garcia-Molina, H.: PPay: Micropayments for peer-to-peer systems. In: Proc. of 10th ACM Conference on Computer and Communications Security, pp. 300–310 (2003)

15. Zou, J., Si, T., Huang, L., Dai, Y.: A new micro-payment protocol based on p2p networks. In: Proc. of the 2005 IEEE International Conference on E-Business Engineering, ICEBE 2005, pp. 449–455 (2005)

16. KaZaA website, http://www.kazaa.com

Author Index

Printing: Mercedes-Druck, Berlin
Binding: Stein+Lehmann, Berlin